'An awesome achievement' Iain Finlayson, *The Times*, Books of the Year

'A wonderfully rich read, packed with illumination and insight into an artistically rich civilization at once brilliant and savage, a raw tangled mix of the rational and the mystical, "Eastern" and European'
Lisa Jardine, *Observer*

'Splendid . . . a gripping panorama of Russian art and life'
George Walden, *Independent*

'A rivetingly compendious rumination on how painting, poetry, plays and music reflect Russia's perennial tug-of-war between peasant and aristocratic cultures'
Michael Church, *Evening Standard*, Books of the Year

'Remarkable . . . I know of no parallel to compare with the tapestry that this Professor of History has been able to weave . . . Professor Figes has achieved the impossible with a portrait that is hugely entertaining and, astonishingly, actually gives the reader that "smell of Russian earth" . . . he has painted the vast Russian landscape in terms of its cultural roots, its absurdities, its genius, its humanity as well as its cruelty. A formidable achievement' Geoffrey Goodman, *Tribune*

'Richly informative and marvellously entertaining. It is full of sparkling vignettes and sharp, sometimes funny, often moving pen portraits . . . Figes gives an incomparable insight into the nature of the beast'
Piers Brendon, *Oldie*, Books of the Year

ABOUT THE AUTHOR

Orlando Figes is Professor of History at Birkbeck College, University of London. He was born in London in 1959 and studied History at Cambridge. Before moving to Birkbeck he was a University Lecturer in History and Fellow of Trinity College, Cambridge. He is the author of *Peasant Russia*, *Civil War* and *A People's Tragedy*, which in 1997 was the winner of the Wolfson History Prize, the WH Smith Literary Award, the Longman/*History Today* Book of the Year Award, the NCR Book Award and the *Los Angeles Times* Book Prize.

Orlando Figes

NATASHA'S DANCE

A Cultural History of Russia

PENGUIN BOOKS

PENGUIN BOOKS

Published by the Penguin Group
Penguin Books Ltd, 80 Strand, London WC2R 0RL, England
Penguin Putnam Inc., 375 Hudson Street, New York, New York 10014, USA
Penguin Books Australia Ltd, 250 Camberwell Road, Camberwell, Victoria 3124, Australia
Penguin Books Canada Ltd, 10 Alcorn Avenue, Toronto, Ontario, Canada M4V 3B2
Penguin Books India (P) Ltd, 11, Community Centre, Panchsheel Park, New Delhi – 110 017, India
Penguin Books (NZ) Ltd, Cnr Rosedale and Airborne Roads, Albany, Auckland, New Zealand
Penguin Books (South Africa) (Pty) Ltd, 24 Sturdee Avenue, Rosebank 2196, South Africa

Penguin Books Ltd, Registered Offices: 80 Strand, London WC2R 0RL, England

www.penguin.com

First published by Allen Lane The Penguin Press 2002
Published in Penguin Books 2003
1

Copyright © Orlando Figes, 2002
All rights reserved

The moral right of the author has been asserted

Typeset by Rowland Phototypesetting Ltd, Bury St Edmunds, Suffolk
Printed in England by Clays Ltd, St Ives plc

For Lydia and Alice

Contents

List of Illustrations and Photographic Acknowledgements

Every effort has been made to contact all copyright holders. The publishers will be happy to make good in future editions any errors or omissions brought to their attention.

INSIDE COVER

Ivan Bilibin: set design for *Grad Kitezh*, 1928. Ashmolean Museum, Oxford

CHAPTER OPENERS

1. Benjamin Paterssen: *Vue de la grande parade au Palais de l'Empereur Alexandre 1er à St Petersburg*, c. 1803. Ashmolean Museum, Oxford
2. Adolphe Ladurnier: *View of the White Hall in the Winter Palace, St Petersburg*, 1838. State Hermitage Museum, St Petersburg/Petrushka, Moscow
3. St Basil's Cathedral, Red Square, Moscow, during the late nineteenth century (photo: David King Collection, London)
4. A typical one-street village in central Russia, c. 1910. Photograph by Netta Peacock. Victoria & Albert Museum Picture Library, London
5. Natalia Goncharova: backdrop design for *The Firebird* (1926) Victoria & Albert Museum Picture Library, London
6. Scythian figures: late nineteenth-century archaeological engraving

TEXT ILLUSTRATIONS

12. Vladimir Shervud: Russian Museum, Red Square, Moscow. Photograph, early 1900s (photo: Alexander Meledin Collection/Mary Evans Picture Library, London)

13. Ilia Repin: sketches for *The Volga Barge Haulers*, 1870. National Gallery, Prague

14. Tolstoy's estate at Yasnaya Polyana. Late-nineteenth-century photograph

15. Elena Polenova: 'Cat and Owl' carved door, Abramtsevo workshop, early 1890s. Courtesy Izobrazitel'noe Iskusstvo, Moscow

16. Church at Abramtsevo. Designed by Viktor Vasnetsov, 1881–2. Photograph copyright © William C. Brumfield

17. *Gusli* player. Reproduced from Chloe Oblensky, *The Russian Empire: A Portrait in Photographs* (London: Jonathan Cape, 1979)

18. Nikolai Roerich: costumes for the Adolescents in the first production of *The Rite of Spring*, Paris, 1913 (photo: Lebrecht Collection, London)

19. Stravinsky transcribes a folk song sung by a peasant *gusli* player on the porch of the Stravinsky house at Ustilug, 1909 (photo: Fondation Théodore Strawinsky/Lebrecht Collection, London)

20. Hermits at a monastery in northern Russia (photo: Popperfoto, Northampton)

21. Group of Komi people in typical clothing. Photograph, *c.* 1912, by S. I. Sergel. Reproduced from L. N. Molotova, *Folk Art of the Russian Federation from the Ethnographical Museum of the Peoples of the U.S.S.R.* (Leningrad: Khudozhnik RSFSR, 1981)

22. Vasily Kandinsky: sketches of buildings in the Komi region. From the Vologda Diary, 1889. Centre Pompidou, Musée National d'Art Moderne, Paris. (Copyright © Photo CNAC/MNAM Dist. RMN) © ADAGP, Paris and DACS, London 2002

23. Masked Buriat shaman with drum, drumstick and horse-sticks. Photograph by Toumanoff, early 1900s

24. Watercolour copy of a lost self-portrait with Circassian sword and cloak by Mikhail Lermontov, 1837 (photo: Novosti, London)

25. Vladimir Stasov: study of the Russian letter 'B' from a fourteenth-century manuscript of Novgorod. Reproduced in Stasov, *Russkii naroodnyi ornament*, 1872) (photo copyright © British Library, London [ref. 7743])

26. Vladimir Stasov: title page of Rimsky-Korsakov's opera score *Sadko*, 1897. Photograph copyright © British Library, London [ref. G.1073.a]

27. Akhmatova and Punin in the courtyard of the Fountain House, 1927. Copyright © Museum of Anna Akhmatova in the Fountain House, St Petersburg

28. Liubov Popova: stage design for Meyerhold's 1922 production of the *Magnanimous Cuckold*. Tretyakov Gallery Moscow (photo: Bridgeman Art Library, London)

29. Alexander Rodchenko: 'To Her and Me', illustration from Mayakovsky's *Pro eto*, 1923. Private collection. © DACS 2002

30. 'The Russian house inside the Italian cathedral'. Final shot from Andrei Tarkovsky's *Nostalgia*, 1983 (photo: Ronald Grant Archive, London)

31. Sergei Efron and Marina Tsvetaeva, 1911. Courtesy Viktoria Schweitzer

COLOUR PLATE SECTION 1

1. Nikolai Argunov: *Portrait of Praskovya Sheremeteva*, 1802. Copyright © 2002, State Museum of Ceramics and XVIII Century Estate, Kuskovo/Petrushka, Moscow

2. Vasily Tropinin: *Portrait of Pushkin*, 1827. Pushkin Museum, Moscow (photo: AKG London)

3. Alexei Venetsianov: *Morning of the Lady of the Manor*, 1823. Copyright © 2002, State Russian Museum, St Petersburg/Petrushka, Moscow

4. Alexei Venetsianov: *In the Ploughed Field: Spring*, 1827. State Tretyakov Gallery, Moscow (photo: Bridgeman Art Library, London)

5. Vasily Perov: *Hunters at Rest*, 1871. State Tretyakov Gallery, Moscow (photo: Bridgeman Art Library, London)

6. Interior of the Terem Palace, the Kremlin, Moscow, restored by Fedor Solntsev (photo: Novosti, London)

7. Vasily Surikov: *The Boyar's Wife Morozova*, 1884. State Tretyakov Gallery, Moscow (photo: Scala, Florence)

COLOUR PLATE SECTION 2

Galerie im Lenbachhaus, Munich © ADAGP, Paris and DACS, London 2002

21. Vasily Kandinsky: *Oval No. 2*, 1925. Centre Pompidou, Musée National d'Art Moderne, CCI, Paris. (Copyright © Photo CNAC/MNAM Dist. RMN) © ADAGP, Paris and DACS, London 2002

22. Shaman bird head-dress, cedar wood, first half of nineteenth century. From the collection of Peter the Great Museum of Anthropology and Ethnography (Kunstkamera), Russian Academy of Sciences, St Petersburg

23. Isaak Levitan: *Vladimirka*, 1892. State Tretyakov Gallery, Moscow (photo: Scala, Florence)

24. Vasily Vereshchagin: *Surprise Attack*, 1871 (photo: Christie's Images, London)

25. Kuzma Petrov-Vodkin: *Bathing the Red Horse*, 1912. State Tretyakov Gallery, Moscow (photo: Scala, Florence)

26. Kazimir Malevich: *Red Cavalry*, 1930. State Russian Museum, St Petersburg (photo: Scala, Florence)

27. Natan Altman: *Portrait of Anna Akhmatova*, 1914. Copyright © 2002, State Russian Museum, St Petersburg/Petrushka, Moscow © DACS 2002

Notes on the Maps and Text

MAPS

Place names indicated in the maps are those used in Russia before 1917. Soviet names are given in the text where appropriate. Since 1991, most Russian cities have reverted to their pre-revolutionary names.

RUSSIAN NAMES

Russian names are spelled in this book according to the standard (Library of Congress) system of transliteration, but common English spellings of well-known Russian names (Tolstoy and Tchaikovsky, or the Tsar Peter, for example) are retained. To aid pronounciation some Russian names (Vasily, for example) are slightly changed (in this case, from Vasilii).

DATES

From 1700 until 1918 Russia adhered to the Julian calendar, which ran thirteen days behind the Gregorian calendar in use in western Europe. Dates in this book are given according to the Julian calendar until February 1918, when Soviet Russia switched to the Gregorian calendar.

USE OF METRIC

All measurements of distance, weight and area are given in the metric system.

NOTES

Literary works cited in this book are, wherever possible, from an English-language translation available in bookshops.

Maps

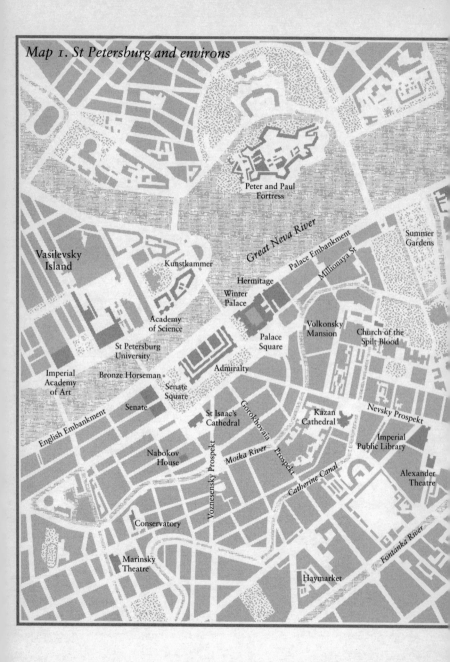

Map 1. St Petersburg and environs

Peter and Paul Fortress

Great Neva River

Summer Gardens

Vasilevsky Island

Kunstkammer

Palace Embankment

Millionaya St

Hermitage

Winter Palace

Volkonsky Mansion

Church of the Spilt Blood

Academy of Science

Palace Square

St Petersburg University

Admiralty

Imperial Academy of Art

Bronze Horseman

Senate Square

Kazan Cathedral

Nevsky Prospekt

Senate

St Isaac's Cathedral

Gorokhovaia Prospekt

Imperial Public Library

English Embankment

Nabokov House

Voznesensky Prospekt

Moika River

Catherine Canal

Alexander Theatre

Conservatory

Fontanka River

Marinsky Theatre

Haymarket

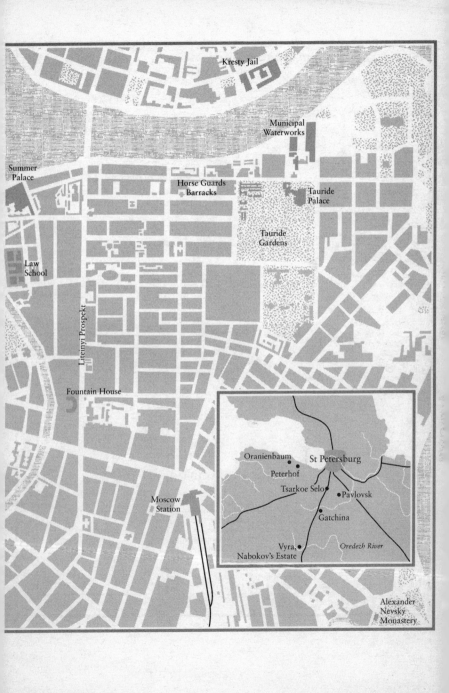

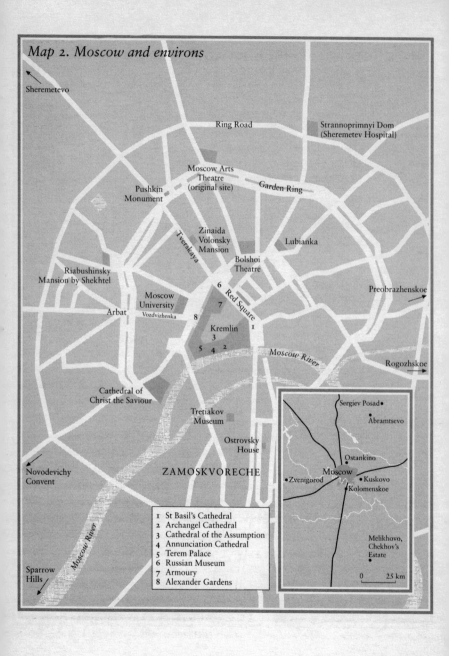

Map 2. Moscow and environs

Sheremetevo

Ring Road

Strannoprimnyi Dom
(Sheremetev Hospital)

Moscow Arts
Theatre
(original site)

Garden Ring

Pushkin
Monument

Zinaida
Volonsky
Mansion

Lubianka

Tverskaya

Bolshoi
Theatre

Riabushinsky
Mansion by Shekhtel

Moscow
University

6

Red Square

Preobrazhenskoe

Arbat

Vozdvizhenka

7

8

Kremlin
3

1

5   4   2

Moscow River

Rogozhskoe

Cathedral of
Christ the Saviour

Tretiakov
Museum

Ostrovsky
House

ZAMOSKVORECHE

Novodevichy
Convent

Moscow River

Sparrow
Hills

1 St Basil's Cathedral
2 Archangel Cathedral
3 Cathedral of the Assumption
4 Annunciation Cathedral
5 Terem Palace
6 Russian Museum
7 Armoury
8 Alexander Gardens

Sergiev Posad
Abramtsevo

Ostankino

Moscow

Zvenigorod

Kuskovo

Kolomenskoe

Melikhovo,
Chekhov's
Estate

0   25 km

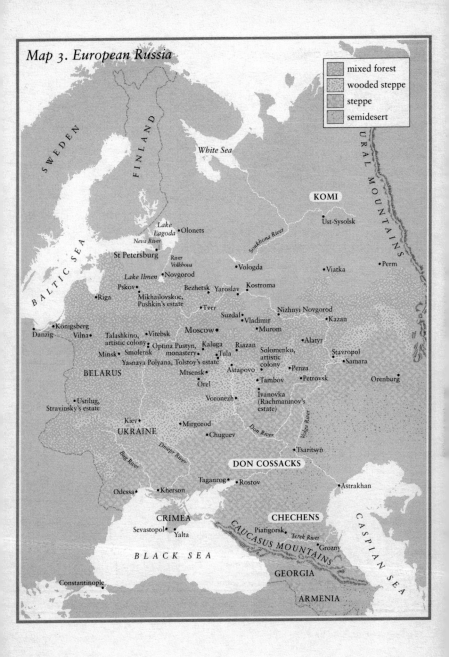

Map 3. European Russia

Legend:
- mixed forest
- wooded steppe
- steppe
- semidesert

SWEDEN

FINLAND

White Sea

KOMI

URAL MOUNTAINS

Lake Lagoda • Olonets

Neva River

BALTIC SEA

St Petersburg

River Volkhova

Sookhona River

Ust-Sysolsk

• Vologda

• Viatka

• Perm

Lake Ilmen • Novgorod

Pskov •

Riga •

Bezhetsk • Yaroslav • Kostroma

Mikhailovskoe, Pushkin's estate

• Tver

• Suzdal • Vladimir

Nizhnyi Novgorod

• Kazan

Königsberg •

Danzig • Vilna •

Talashkino, artistic colony •

• Vitebsk

Moscow •

• Murom

• Alatyr

Minsk •

Smolensk •

Optina Pustyn, monastery

• Kaluga

• Tula

Riazan •

Solomenko, artistic colony

Stavropol •

• Samara

Yasnaya Polyana, Tolstoy's estate

• Penza

• Petrovsk

BELARUS

Mtsensk •

• Astapovo

• Orel

• Tambov

Ivanovka (Rachmaninov's estate)

Orenburg •

Ustilug, Stravinsky's estate •

Voronezh •

Volga River

Kiev •

• Mirgorod

UKRAINE

• Chuguev

Don River

Dnepr River

Bug River

• Tsaritsyn

DON COSSACKS

Odessa •

• Kherson

Taganrog • • Rostov

• Astrakhan

CRIMEA

CHECHENS

Sevastopol • • Yalta

Piatigorsk • Grozny

Terek River

CASPIAN SEA

BLACK SEA

CAUCASUS MOUNTAINS

GEORGIA

Constantinople •

ARMENIA

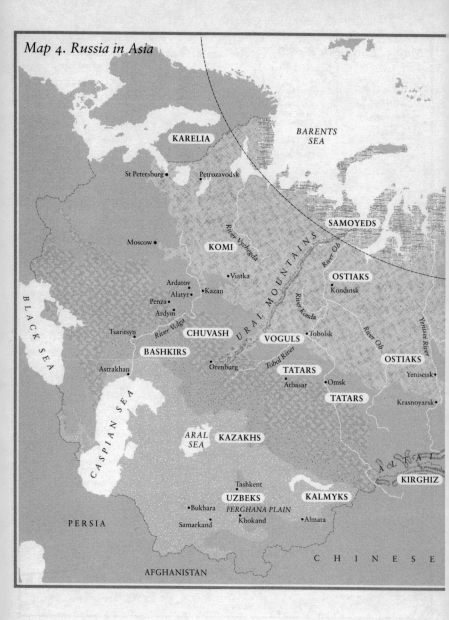

Map 4. Russia in Asia

KARELIA

BARENTS
SEA

St Petersburg •   • Petrozavodsk

SAMOYEDS

Moscow •   KOMI

River Vychegda

URAL MOUNTAINS

River Ob

OSTIAKS

• Viatka

Ardatov   Kondinsk •
Alatyr   • Kazan
Penza •
Ardym

River Konda

Tsaritsyn   River Volga   CHUVASH   VOGULS   • Tobolsk   River Ob   Yenisei River

BASHKIRS   OSTIAKS

Astrakhan •   • Orenburg   Tobol River   TATARS   Yeniseisk •

BLACK SEA

Atbasar •   • Omsk   Krasnoyarsk •

TATARS

CASPIAN SEA

ARAL
SEA   KAZAKHS

ALTAI

KIRGHIZ

Tashkent •
UZBEKS   KALMYKS
• Bukhara   FERGHANA PLAIN
Samarkand   Khokand •   • Almata

PERSIA

C H I N E S E

AFGHANISTAN

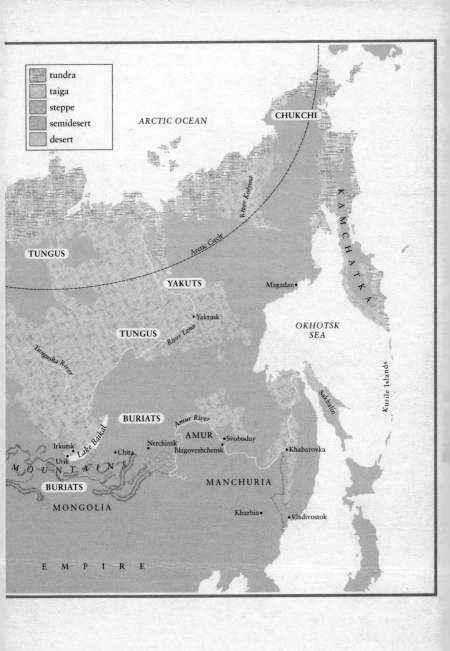

INTRODUCTION

In Tolstoy's *War and Peace* there is a famous and rather lovely scene where Natasha Rostov and her brother Nikolai are invited by their 'Uncle' (as Natasha calls him) to his simple wooden cabin at the end of a day's hunting in the woods. There the noble-hearted and eccentric 'Uncle' lives, a retired army officer, with his housekeeper Anisya, a stout and handsome serf from his estate, who, as it becomes clear from the old man's tender glances, is his unofficial 'wife'. Anisya brings in a tray loaded with homemade Russian specialities: pickled mushrooms, rye-cakes made with buttermilk, preserves with honey, sparkling mead, herb-brandy and different kinds of vodka. After they have eaten, the strains of a *balalaika* become audible from the hunting servants' room. It is not the sort of music that a countess should have liked, a simple country ballad, but seeing how his niece is moved by it, 'Uncle' calls for his guitar, blows the dust off it, and with a wink at Anisya, he begins to play, with the precise and accelerating rhythm of a Russian dance, the well-known love song, 'Came a maiden down the street'. Though Natasha has never before heard the folk song, it stirs some unknown feeling in her heart. 'Uncle' sings as the peasants do, with the conviction that the meaning of the song lies in the words and that the tune, which exists only to emphasize the words, 'comes of itself'. It seems to Natasha that this direct way of singing gives the air the simple charm of birdsong. 'Uncle' calls on her to join in the folk dance.

'Now then, niece!' he exclaimed, waving to Natasha the hand that had just struck a chord.

Natasha threw off the shawl from her shoulders, ran forward to face

'Uncle', and setting her arms akimbo, also made a motion with her shoulders and struck an attitude.

Where, how, and when had this young countess, educated by an *émigrée* French governess, imbibed from the Russian air she breathed that spirit, and obtained that manner which the *pas de châle* would, one would have supposed, long ago have effaced? But the spirit and the movements were those inimitable and unteachable Russian ones that 'Uncle' had expected of her. As soon as she had struck her pose and smiled triumphantly, proudly, and with sly merriment, the fear that had at first seized Nikolai and the others that she might not do the right thing was at an end, and they were all already admiring her.

She did the right thing with such precision, such complete precision, that Anisya Fyodorovna, who had at once handed her the handkerchief she needed for the dance, had tears in her eyes, though she laughed as she watched this slim, graceful countess, reared in silks and velvets and so different from herself, who yet was able to understand all that was in Anisya and in Anisya's father and mother and aunt, and in every Russian man and woman.[1]

What enabled Natasha to pick up so instinctively the rhythms of the dance? How could she step so easily into this village culture from which, by social class and education, she was so far removed? Are we to suppose, as Tolstoy asks us to in this romantic scene, that a nation such as Russia may be held together by the unseen threads of a native sensibility? The question takes us to the centre of this book. It calls itself a cultural history. But the elements of culture which the reader will find here are not just great creative works like *War and Peace* but artefacts as well, from the folk embroidery of Natasha's shawl to the musical conventions of the peasant song. And they are summoned, not as monuments to art, but as impressions of the national consciousness, which mingle with politics and ideology, social customs and beliefs, folklore and religion, habits and conventions, and all the other mental bric-à-brac that constitute a culture and a way of life. It is not my argument that art can serve the purpose of a window on to life. Natasha's dancing scene cannot be approached as a literal record of experience, though memoirs of this period show that there were indeed noblewomen who picked up village dances in this way.[2] But art can be looked at as a record of belief – in this case, the writer's yearning for a broad community with the Russian peasantry which Tolstoy shared with the 'men of 1812', the liberal noblemen and patriots who dominate the public scenes of *War and Peace*.

Russia invites the cultural historian to probe below the surface of artistic appearance. For the past two hundred years the arts in Russia have served as an arena for political, philosophical and religious debate in the absence of a parliament or a free press. As Tolstoy wrote in 'A Few Words on *War and Peace*' (1868), the great artistic prose works of the Russian tradition were not novels in the European sense.[3] They were huge poetic structures for symbolic contemplation, not unlike icons, laboratories in which to test ideas; and, like a science or religion, they were animated by the search for truth. The overarching subject of all these works was Russia – its character, its history, its customs and conventions, its spiritual essence and its destiny. In a way that was extraordinary, if not unique to Russia, the country's artistic energy was almost wholly given to the quest to grasp the idea of its nationality. Nowhere has the artist been more burdened with the task of moral leadership and national prophecy, nor more feared and persecuted by the state. Alienated from official Russia by their politics, and from peasant Russia by their education, Russia's artists took it upon themselves to create a national community of values and ideas through literature and art. What did it mean to be a Russian? What was Russia's place and mission in the world? And where was the true Russia? In Europe or in Asia? St Petersburg or Moscow? The Tsar's empire or the muddy one-street village where Natasha's 'Uncle' lived? These were the 'accursed questions' that occupied the mind of every serious writer, literary critic and historian, painter and composer, theologian and philosopher in the golden age of Russian culture from Pushkin to Pasternak. They are the questions that lie beneath the surface of the art within this book. The works discussed here represent a history of ideas and attitudes – concepts of the nation through which Russia tried to understand itself. If we look carefully, they may become a window on to a nation's inner life.

Natasha's dance is one such opening. At its heart is an encounter between two entirely different worlds: the European culture of the upper classes and the Russian culture of the peasantry. The war of 1812 was the first moment when the two moved together in a national formation. Stirred by the patriotic spirit of the serfs, the aristocracy of Natasha's generation began to break free from the foreign conventions of their society and search for a sense of nationhood based on 'Russian' principles. They switched from speaking French to their native tongue; they Russified their customs and their dress, their eating habits and their taste in interior design; they went out to the countryside to learn folklore, peasant dance and music, with the aim of fashioning a national style in all their arts to reach out to and educate the common man; and, like Natasha's 'Uncle' (or indeed her brother at the end of *War and Peace*), some of them renounced the court culture of St Petersburg and tried to live a simpler (more 'Russian') way of life alongside the peasantry on their estates.

The complex interaction between these two worlds had a crucial influence on the national consciousness and on all the arts in the nineteenth century. That interaction is a major feature of this book. But the story which it tells is not meant to suggest that a single 'national' culture was the consequence. Russia was too complex, too socially divided, too politically diverse, too ill-defined geographically, and perhaps too big, for a single culture to be passed off as the national heritage. It is rather my intention to rejoice in the sheer diversity of Russia's cultural forms. What makes the Tolstoy passage so illuminating is the way in which it brings so many different people to the dance: Natasha and her brother, to whom this strange but enchanting village world is suddenly revealed; their 'Uncle', who lives in this world but is not a part of it; Anisya, who is a villager yet who also lives with 'Uncle' at the margins of Natasha's world; and the hunting servants and the other household serfs, who watch, no doubt with curious amusement (and perhaps with other feelings, too), as the beautiful countess performs their dance. My aim is to explore Russian culture in the same way Tolstoy presents Natasha's dance: as a series of encounters or creative social acts which were performed and understood in many different ways.

To view a culture in this refracted way is to challenge the idea of a pure, organic or essential core. There was no 'authentic' Russian peasant dance of the sort imagined by Tolstoy and, like the melody to which Natasha dances, most of Russia's 'folk songs' had in fact come from the towns.[4] Other elements of the village culture Tolstoy pictured may have come to Russia from the Asiatic steppe – elements that had been imported by the Mongol horsemen who ruled Russia from the thirteenth century to the fifteenth century and then mostly settled down in Russia as tradesmen, pastoralists and agriculturalists. Natasha's shawl was almost certainly a Persian one; and, although Russian peasant shawls were coming into fashion after 1812, their ornamental motifs were probably derived from oriental shawls. The *balalaika* was descended from the *dombra*, a similar guitar of Central Asian origin (it is still widely used in Kazakh music), which came to Russia in the sixteenth century.[5] The Russian peasant dance tradition was itself derived from oriental forms, in the view of some folklorists in the nineteenth century. The Russians danced in lines or circles rather than in pairs, and the rhythmic movements were performed by the hands and shoulders as well as by the feet, with great importance being placed in female dancing on subtle doll-like gestures and the stillness of the head. Nothing could have been more different from the waltz Natasha danced with Prince Andrei at her first ball, and to mimic all these movements must have felt as strange to her as it no doubt appeared to her peasant audience. But if there is no ancient Russian culture to be excavated from this village scene, if much of any culture is imported from abroad, then there is a sense in which Natasha's dance is an emblem of the view to be taken in this book: there is no *quintessential* national culture, only mythic images of it, like Natasha's version of the peasant dance.

It is not my aim to 'deconstruct' these myths; nor do I wish to claim, in the jargon used by academic cultural historians these days, that Russia's nationhood was no more than an intellectual 'construction'. There was a Russia that was real enough – a Russia that existed before 'Russia' or 'European Russia', or any other myths of the national identity. There was the historical Russia of ancient Muscovy, which had been very different from the West, before Peter the Great forced it to conform to European ways in the eighteenth century. During Tolstoy's lifetime, this old Russia was still animated by the traditions of the Church, by the customs of the merchants and many of the gentry on the land, and by the empire's 60 million peasants, scattered in half a million remote villages across the forests and the steppe, whose way of life remained little changed for centuries. It is the heartbeat of this

Russia which reverberates in Natasha's dancing scene. And it was surely not so fanciful for Tolstoy to imagine that there was a common sense which linked the young countess to every Russian woman and every Russian man. For, as this book will seek to demonstrate, there is a Russian temperament, a set of native customs and beliefs, something visceral, emotional, instinctive, passed on down the generations, which has helped to shape the personality and bind together the community. This elusive temperament has proved more lasting and more meaningful than any Russian state: it gave the people the spirit to survive the darkest moments of their history, and united those who fled from Soviet Russia after 1917. It is not my aim to deny this national consciousness, but rather to suggest that the apprehension of it was enshrined in myth. Forced to become Europeans, the educated classes had become so alienated from the old Russia, they had so long forgotten how to speak and act in a Russian way, that when, in Tolstoy's age, they struggled to define themselves as 'Russians' once again, they were obliged to reinvent that nation through historical and artistic myths. They rediscovered their own 'Russianness' through literature and art, just as Natasha found her 'Russianness' through the rituals of the dance. Hence the purpose of this book is not simply to debunk these myths. It is rather to explore, and to set out to explain, the extraordinary power these myths had in shaping the Russian national consciousness.

The major cultural movements of the nineteenth century were all organized around these fictive images of Russia's nationhood: the Slavophiles, with their attendant myth of the 'Russian soul', of a natural Christianity among the peasantry, and their cult of Muscovy as the bearer of a truly 'Russian' way of life which they idealized and set out to promote as an alternative to the European culture adopted by the educated élites since the eighteenth century; the Westernizers, with their rival cult of St Petersburg, that 'window on to the West', with its classical ensembles built on marshland reclaimed from the sea – a symbol of their own progressive Enlightenment ambition to redraw Russia on a European grid; the Populists, who were not far from Tolstoy, with their notion of the peasant as a natural socialist whose village institutions would provide a model for the new society; and the Scythians, who saw Russia as an 'elemental' culture from the Asiatic steppe which, in the revolution yet to come, would sweep away the dead weight of European civilization and establish a new culture where man and nature, art and life, were one. These myths were more than just 'constructions' of a national identity. They all played a crucial role in shaping the ideas and allegiances of Russia's politics, as well as in developing the notion of the self, from the most elevated forms of personal and national identity to the most quotidian matters of dress or food, or the type of language one used. The Slavophiles illustrate the point. Their idea of 'Russia' as a patriarchal family of homegrown Christian principles was the organizing kernel of a new political community in the middle decades of the nineteenth century which drew its members from the old provincial gentry, the Moscow merchants and intelligentsia, the priesthood and certain sections of the state bureaucracy. The mythic notion of Russia's nationhood which brought these groups together had a lasting hold on the political imagination. As a political movement, it influenced the government's position on free trade and foreign policy, and gentry attitudes towards the state and peasantry. As a broad cultural movement the Slavophiles adopted a certain style of speech and dress, distinct codes of social interaction and behaviour, a style of architecture and interior design, their own approach to literature and art. It was all bast shoes and homespun coats and beards, cabbage soup and *kvas*, folk-like wooden houses and brightly coloured churches with onion domes.

In the Western imagination these cultural forms have all too often been perceived as 'authentically Russian'. Yet that perception is a myth as well: the myth of exotic Russia. It is an image first exported by the Ballets Russes, with their own exoticized versions of Natasha's dance, and then shaped by foreign writers such as Rilke, Thomas Mann and Virginia Woolf, who held up Dostoevsky as the greatest novelist and peddled their own versions of the 'Russian soul'. If there is one myth which needs to be dispelled, it is this view of Russia as exotic and elsewhere. Russians have long complained that the Western public does not understand their culture, that Westerners see Russia from afar and do not want to know its inner subtleties, as they do with the cultures of their own domain. Though based partly on resentment and wounded national pride, the complaint is not unjustified. We are inclined to consign Russia's artists, writers and composers to the cultural ghetto of a 'national school' and to judge them, not as individuals, but by how far they conform to this stereotype. We expect the Russians to be 'Russian' – their art easily distinguished by its use of folk motifs, by onion domes, the sound of bells, and full of 'Russian soul'. Nothing has done more to obscure a proper understanding of Russia and its central place in European culture between 1812 and 1917. The great cultural figures of the Russian tradition (Karamzin, Pushkin, Glinka, Gogol, Tolstoy, Turgenev, Dostoevsky, Chekhov, Repin, Tchaikovsky and Rimsky-Korsakov, Diaghilev, Stravinsky, Prokofiev, Shostakovich, Chagall and Kandinsky, Mandelstam, Akhmatova, Nabokov, Pasternak, Meyerhold and Eisenstein) were not simply 'Russians', they were Europeans too, and the two identities were intertwined and mutually dependent in a variety of ways. However hard they might have tried, it was impossible for Russians such as these to suppress either part of their identity.

For European Russians, there were two very different modes of personal behaviour. In the salons and the ballrooms of St Petersburg, at court or in the theatre, they were very *comme il faut*: they performed their European manners almost like actors on a public stage. Yet on another and perhaps unconscious plane and in the less formal spheres of private life, native Russian habits of behaviour prevailed. Natasha's visit to her 'Uncle's' house describes one such switch: the way she is expected to behave at home, in the Rostov palace, or at the ball where she is presented to the Emperor, is a world apart from this village scene where her expressive nature is allowed free rein. It is evidently her gregarious enjoyment of such a relaxed social setting that communicates itself in her dance. This same sense of relaxation, of becoming 'more oneself' in a Russian milieu, was shared by many Russians of Natasha's class, including her own 'Uncle', it would seem. The simple recreations of the country house or *dacha* – hunting in the woods, visiting the bath house or what Nabokov called the 'very Russian sport of *hodit' po gribï* (looking for mushrooms)'[6] – were more than the retrieval of a rural idyll: they were an expression of one's Russianness. To interpret habits such as these is one of this book's aims. Using art and fiction, diaries and letters, memoirs and prescriptive literature, it seeks to apprehend the structures of the Russian national identity. 'Identity' these days is a fashionable term.

But it is not very meaningful unless one can show how it manifests itself in social interaction and behaviour. A culture is made up not simply of works of art, or literary discourses, but of unwritten codes, signs and symbols, rituals and gestures, and common attitudes that fix the public meaning of these works and organize the inner life of a society. So the reader will find here that works of literature, like *War and Peace*, are intercut with episodes from daily life (childhood, marriage, religious life, responses to the landscape, food and drinking habits, attitudes to death) where the outlines of this national consciousness may be discerned. These are the episodes where we may find, in life, the unseen threads of a common Russian sensibility, such as Tolstoy had imagined in his celebrated dancing scene.

A few words are in order on the structure of the book. It is an interpretation of a culture, not a comprehensive history, so readers should beware that some great cultural figures will perhaps get less than their full pages' worth. My approach is thematic. Each chapter explores a separate strand of the Russian cultural identity. The chapters progress from the eighteenth century to the twentieth century, but the rules of strict chronology are broken in the interest of thematic coherence. There are two brief moments (the closing sections of chapters 3 and 4) where the barrier of 1917 is crossed. As on the other few occasions where periods of history, political events or cultural institutions are handled out of sequence, I have provided some explanation for readers who lack detailed knowledge of Russian history. (Those needing more may consult the Table of Chronology.) My story finishes in the Brezhnev era. The cultural tradition which it charts reached the end of a natural cycle then, and what has come afterwards may well be the start of something new. Finally, there are themes and variations that reappear throughout the book, leitmotifs and lineages like the cultural history of St Petersburg and the family narratives of the two great noble dynasties, the Volkonskys and the Sheremetevs. The meaning of these twists and turns will be perceived by the reader only at the end.

1

overleaf:
Benjamin Paterssen: Vue de la grande parade au Palais
de L'Empereur Alexandre 1er à St Petersburg, c.*1803*

EUROPEAN
RUSSIA

1

On a misty spring morning in 1703 a dozen Russian horsemen rode across the bleak and barren marshlands where the Neva river runs into the Baltic sea. They were looking for a site to build a fort against the Swedes, then at war with Russia, and the owners of these long-abandoned swamps. But the vision of the wide and bending river flowing to the sea was full of hope and promise to the Tsar of land-locked Russia, riding at the head of his scouting troops. As they approached the coast he dismounted from his horse. With his bayonet he cut two strips of peat and arranged them in a cross on the marshy ground. Then Peter said: 'Here shall be a town.'[1]

Few places could have been less suitable for the metropolis of Europe's largest state. The network of small islands in the Neva's boggy delta were overgrown with trees. Swept by thick mists from melting snow in spring and overblown by winds that often caused the rivers to rise above the land, it was not a place for human habitation, and even the few fishermen who ventured there in summer did not stay for long. Wolves and bears were its only residents.[2] A thousand years ago the area was underneath the sea. There was a channel flowing from the Baltic sea to lake Ladoga, with islands where the Pulkovo and Pargolovo heights are found today. Even in the reign of Catherine the Great, during the late eighteenth century, Tsarskoe Selo, where she built her Summer Palace on the hills of Pulkovo, was still known by the locals as Sarskoe Selo. The name came from the Finnish word for an island, *saari*.

When Peter's soldiers dug into the ground they found water a metre or so below. The northern island, where the land was slightly higher, was the only place to lay firm foundations. In four months of furious activity, in which at least half the workforce died, 20,000 conscripts built the Peter and Paul Fortress, digging out the land with their bare hands, dragging logs and stones or carting them by back, and carrying the earth in the folds of their clothes.[3] The sheer scale and tempo of construction was astonishing. Within a few years the estuary became an energetic building site and, once Russia's control of the coast had been secured with victories over Sweden in 1709–10, the city took on a new shape with every passing day. A quarter of a million serfs and soldiers from as far afield as the Caucasus and Siberia worked around the clock to clear forests, dig canals, lay down roads and erect palaces.[4] Carpenters and stonemasons (forbidden by decree to work elsewhere) flooded into the new capital. Hauliers, ice-breakers, sled-drivers, boatsmen and labourers arrived in search of work, sleeping in the wooden shacks that crowded into every empty space. To start with, everything was done in a rough and ready fashion with primitive hand tools: axes predominated over saws, and simple carts were made from unstripped trunks with tiny birch-log wheels. Such was the demand for stone materials that every boat and vehicle arriving in the town was obliged to bring a set tonnage of rock. But new industries soon sprang up to manufacture brick, glass, mica and tarpaulin, while the shipyards added constantly to the busy traffic on the city's waterways, with sailing boats and barges loaded down with stone, and millions of logs floated down the river every year.

Like the magic city of a Russian fairy tale, St Petersburg grew up with such fantastic speed, and everything about it was so brilliant and new, that it soon became a place enshrined in myth. When Peter declared, 'Here shall be a town', his words echoed the divine command, 'Let there be light.' And, as he said these words, legend has it that an eagle dipped in flight over Peter's head and settled on top of two birch trees that were tied together to form an arch. Eighteenth-century panegyrists elevated Peter to the status of a god: he was Titan, Neptune and Mars rolled into one. They compared 'Petropolis' to ancient Rome. It was a link that Peter also made by adopting the title of 'Imperator' and by casting his own image on the new rouble coin, with laurel wreath and armour, in emulation of Caesar. The famous opening lines of Pushkin's epic poem *The Bronze Horseman* (1833) (which every Russian schoolchild knows by heart) crystallized the myth of Petersburg's creation by a providential man:

> On a shore by the desolate waves
> He stood, with lofty thoughts,
> And gazed into the distance . . .[5]

Thanks to Pushkin's lines, the legend made its way into folklore. The city that was named after Peter's patron saint, and has been renamed three times since as politics have changed, is still called simply 'Peter' by its residents.*

In the popular imagination the miraculous emergence of the city from the sea assigned to it a legendary status from the start. The Russians said that Peter made his city in the sky and then lowered it, like a giant model, to the ground. It was the only way they could explain the creation of a city built on sand. The notion of a capital without foundations in the soil was the basis of the myth of Petersburg which inspired so much Russian literature and art. In this mythology, Petersburg was an unreal city, a supernatural realm of fantasies and ghosts, an alien kingdom of the apocalypse. It was home to the lonely haunted figures who inhabit Gogol's *Tales of Petersburg* (1835); to fantasists and murderers like Raskolnikov in Dostoevsky's novel *Crime and Punishment* (1866). The vision of an all-destroying flood became a constant theme in the city's tales of doom, from Pushkin's *Bronze Horseman* to Bely's *Petersburg* (1913–14). But that prophecy was based on fact: for the city had been built above the ground. Colossal quantities of rubble had been laid down to lift the streets beyond the water's reach. Frequent flooding in the city's early years necessitated repairs and reinforcements that raised them higher still. When, in 1754, building work began on the present Winter Palace, the fourth upon that site, the ground on which its foundations were laid was three metres higher than fifty years before.

A city built on water with imported stone, Petersburg defied the natural order. The famous granite of its river banks came from Finland and Karelia; the marble of its palaces from Italy, the Urals and the Middle East; gabbro and porphyry were brought in from Sweden; dolerite and slate from lake Onega; sandstone from Poland and Germany; travertine from Italy; and tiles from the Low Countries and Lübeck. Only limestone was quarried locally.[6] The achievement of transporting such quantities of stone has been surpassed only by the building of the pyramids. The huge granite rock for the pedestal of

---

* The name in Russian is pronounced 'Pyotr' – so 'Peter' (from the original Dutch spelling and pronunciation of 'Sankt Piter Burkh') suggests a certain foreignness which, as the poet Joseph Brodsky pointed out, somehow sounds correct for such a non-Russian town (see Joseph Brodsky, 'A Guide to a Renamed City', in *Less Than One: Selected Essays* (London, 1986), p. 71).

1. *Shifting the huge granite rock for the pedestal of* The Bronze Horseman.
Engraving after a drawing by A. P. Davydov, 1782

Falconet's equestrian statue of Peter the Great was twelve metres high and nearly thirty metres in circumference. Weighing in at some 660,000 kilograms, it took a thousand men over eighteen months to move it, first by a series of pulleys and then on a specially constructed barge, the thirteen kilometres from the forest clearing where it had been found to the capital.[7] Pushkin's *Bronze Horseman* turned the inert monument into an emblem of Russia's destiny. The thirty-six colossal granite columns of St Isaac's Cathedral were cut out of the ground with sledgehammers and chisels, and then hauled by hand over thirty kilometres to barges on the gulf of Finland, from where they were shipped to St Petersburg and mounted by huge cranes built out of wood.[8] The heaviest rocks were shifted during the winter, when snow made hauling easier, although this meant waiting for the thaw in spring before they could be shipped. But even then the job required an army of several thousand men with 200-horse sleigh teams.[9]

Petersburg did not grow up like other towns. Neither commerce nor geopolitics can account for its development. Rather it was built as a work of art. As the French writer Madame de Staël said on her visit to the city in 1812, 'here everything has been created for visual perception'. Sometimes it appeared that the city was assembled as a giant *mise-en-scène* – its buildings and its people serving as no more than theatrical props. European visitors to Petersburg, accustomed to the *mélange* of architectural styles in their own cities, were particularly struck by the strange unnatural beauty of its ensembles and often compared them to something from the stage. 'At each step I was amazed by the combination of architecture and stage decoration', wrote the travel writer the Marquis de Custine in the 1830s. 'Peter the Great and his successors looked upon their capital as a theatre.'[10] In a sense St Petersburg was just a grander version of that later stage production, the 'Potemkin villages': cardboard cut-out classic structures rigged up overnight along the Dniepr river banks to delight Catherine the Great as she sailed past.

Petersburg was conceived as a composition of natural elements – water, stone and sky. This conception was reflected in the city panoramas of the eighteenth century, which set out to emphasize the artistic harmony of all these elements.[11] Having always loved the sea, Peter was attracted by the broad, fast-flowing river Neva and the open sky as a backdrop for his tableau. Amsterdam (which he had visited) and Venice (which he only knew from books and paintings) were early inspirations for the layout of the palace-lined canals and embankments. But Peter was eclectic in his architectural tastes and borrowed what he liked from Europe's capitals. The austere classical baroque style of Petersburg's churches, which set them apart from Moscow's brightly coloured onion domes, was a mixture of St Paul's cathedral in London, St Peter's in Rome, and the single-spired churches of Riga, in what is now Latvia. From his European travels in the 1690s Peter brought back architects and engineers, craftsmen and artists, furniture designers and landscape gardeners.* Scots, Germans, French, Italians – they all settled in large numbers in St Petersburg in the eighteenth century. No expense was spared for Peter's 'paradise'. Even at the height of the war with Sweden in the 1710s he meddled constantly in details of the plans. To make the Summer Gardens 'better than Versailles' he ordered peonies and citrus trees from Persia, ornamental fish from the Middle

---

* The main architects of Petersburg in Peter the Great's reign were Domenico Trezzini (from Italy), Jean Leblond (from France) and Georg Mattarnovy (from Germany).

East, even singing birds from India, although few survived the Russian frost.[12] Peter issued decrees for the palaces to have regular façades in accordance with his own approved designs, for uniform roof lines and prescribed iron railings on their balconies and walls on the 'embankment side'. To beautify the city Peter even had its abattoir rebuilt in the rococo style.[13]

'There reigns in this capital a kind of bastard architecture', wrote Count Algarotti in the middle of the eighteenth century. 'It steals from the Italian, the French and the Dutch.'[14] By the nineteenth century, the view of Petersburg as an artificial copy of the Western style had become commonplace. Alexander Herzen, the nineteenth-century writer and philosopher, once said that Petersburg 'differs from all other European towns by being like them all'.[15] Yet, despite its obvious borrowings, the city had its own distinctive character, a product of its open setting between sea and sky, the grandeur of its scale, and the unity of its architectural ensembles, which lent the city a unique artistic harmony. The artist Alexander Benois, an influential figure in the Diaghilev circle who made a cult of eighteenth-century Petersburg, captured this harmonious conception. 'If it is beautiful', he wrote in 1902, 'then it is so as a whole, or rather in huge chunks.'[16] Whereas older European cities had been built over several centuries, ending up at best as collections of beautiful buildings in diverse period styles, Petersburg was completed within fifty years and according to a single set of principles. Nowhere else, moreover, were these principles afforded so much space. Architects in Amsterdam and Rome were cramped for room in which to slot their buildings. But in Petersburg they were able to expand their classical ideals. The straight line and the square were given space to breathe in expansive panoramas. With water everywhere, architects could build mansions low and wide, using their reflections in the rivers and canals to balance their proportions, producing an effect that is unquestionably beautiful and grandiose. Water added lightness to the heavy baroque style, and movement to the buildings set along its edge. The Winter Palace is a supreme example. Despite its immense size (1,050 rooms, 1,886 doors, 1,945 windows, 117 staircases) it almost feels as if it is floating on the embankment of the river; the syncopated rhythm of the white columns along its blue façade creates a sense of motion as it reflects the Neva flowing by.

The key to this architectural unity was the planning of the city as a series of ensembles linked by a harmonious network of avenues and squares, canals and parks, set against the river and the sky. The first real plan dates from the establishment of a Commission for the Orderly Development of St Petersburg in 1737, twelve years after Peter's death. At its centre was the idea of the city fanning out in three radials from the Admiralty, just as Rome did from the Piazza del Popolo. The golden spire of the Admiralty thus became the symbolic and topographical centre of the city, visible from the end of the three long avenues (Nevsky, Gorokhovaia and Voznesensky) that converge on it. From the 1760s, with the establishment of a Commission for the Masonry Construction of St Petersburg, the planning of the city as a series of ensembles became more pronounced. Strict rules were imposed to ensure the use of stone and uniform façades for the palaces constructed on the fashionable Nevsky Prospekt. These rules underlined the artistic conception of the avenue as a straight unbroken line stretching as far as the eye could see. It was reflected in the harmonious panoramas by the artist M. I. Makhaev commissioned by the Empress Elizabeth to mark the fiftieth anniversary of the founding of the city in 1753. But visual harmony was not the only purpose of such regimentation: the zonal planning of the capital was a form of social ordering as well. The aristocratic residential areas around the Winter Palace and the Summer Gardens were clearly demarcated by a series of canals and avenues from the zone of clerks and traders near the Haymarket (Dostoevsky's Petersburg) or the workers' suburbs further out. The bridges over the Neva, as readers who have seen Eisenstein's film *October* (1928) know, could be lifted to prevent the workers coming into the central areas.

St Petersburg was more than a city. It was a vast, almost utopian, project of cultural engineering to reconstruct the Russian as a European man. In *Notes from Underground* (1864) Dostoevsky called it 'the most abstract and intentional city in the whole round world'.[17] Every aspect of its Petrine culture was intended as a negation of 'medieval' (seventeenth-century) Muscovy. As Peter conceived it, to become a citizen of Petersburg was to leave behind the 'dark' and 'backward' customs of the Russian past in Moscow and to enter, as a European Russian, the modern Western world of progress and enlightenment.

Muscovy was a religious civilization. It was rooted in the spiritual traditions of the Eastern Church which went back to Byzantium. In some ways it resembled the medieval culture of central Europe, to which it was related by religion, language, custom and much else besides. But historically and culturally it remained isolated from Europe. Its western territories were no more than a toehold on the European continent: the Baltic lands were not captured by the Russian empire until the 1720s, the western Ukraine and the lion's share of Poland not until the end of the eighteenth century. Unlike central Europe Muscovy had little exposure to the influence of the Renaissance or the Reformation. It took no part in the maritime discoveries or the scientific revolutions of the early modern era. It had no great cities in the European sense, no princely or episcopal courts to patronize the arts, no real burgher or middle class, and no universities or public schools apart from the monastery academies.

The dominance of the Church hindered the development in Muscovy of the secular art forms that had taken shape in Europe since the Renaissance. Instead, the icon was the focal point of Muscovy's religious way of life. It was an artefact of daily ritual as much as it was a creative work of art. Icons were encountered everywhere – not just in homes and churches but in shops and offices or in wayside shrines. There was next to nothing to connect the icon to the European tradition of secular painting that had its origins in the Renaissance. True, in the late seventeenth century Russian icon-painters such as Simon Ushakov had started to abandon the austere Byzantine style of medieval icon-painting for the classical techniques and sensuality of the Western baroque style. Yet visitors from Europe were invariably shocked by the primitive condition of Russia's visual arts. 'Flat and ugly', observed Samuel Collins, English physician to the Russian court, of the Kremlin's icons in the 1660s; 'if you saw their images, you would take them for no better than gilded gingerbread'.[18] The first secular portraits (*parsuny*) date from as late as the 1650s. However, they still retain a flat iconic style. Tsar Alexei, who reigned from 1645 to 1676, is the first Russian ruler for whom we have anything remotely resembling a reliable likeness. Other types of painting (still life, landscape, allegory, genre) were entirely absent from the Russian repertoire until Peter's reign, or even later still.

The development of other secular forms of art was equally impeded by the Russian Church. Instrumental music (as opposed to sacred singing) was regarded as a sin and was ruthlessly persecuted by the ecclesiastical authorities. However, there was a rich folk tradition of minstrels and musicians, or *skomorokhi* (featured by Stravinsky in *Petrushka*), who wandered through the villages with tambourines and *gusli* (a type of zither), avoiding the agents of the Church. Literature as well was held back by the omnipresent Church. There were no printed news sheets or journals, no printed plays or poetry, although there was a lively industry of folk tales and verse published in the form of illustrated prints (*lubki*) as cheap printing techniques became available towards the end of the seventeenth century. When Peter came to the throne in 1682 no more than three books of a non-religious nature had been published by the Moscow press since its establishment in the 1560s.[19]

Peter hated Muscovy. He despised its archaic culture and parochial-ism, its superstitious fear and resentment of the West. Witch hunts were common and foreign heretics were burned in public on Red Square – the last, a Protestant, in 1689, when Peter was aged seventeen. As a young man, Peter spent a great deal of his time in the special 'German' suburb where, under pressure from the Church, Moscow's foreigners were forced to live. He dressed in Western clothes, shaved his beard and, unlike the Orthodox, he ate meat during Lent. The young Tsar travelled through northern Europe to learn for himself the new technologies which Russia would need to launch itself as a continental military power. In Holland he worked as a shipbuilder. In London he went to the observatory, the arsenal, the Royal Mint and the Royal Society. In Königsberg he studied artillery. From his travels he picked up what he needed to turn Russia into a modern European state: a navy modelled on the Dutch and the English ones; military schools that were copies of the Swedish and the Prussian; legal systems borrowed from the Germans; and a Table of (civil service) Ranks adapted from the Danes. He commissioned battle scenes and portraits to publicize the prestige of his state; and he purchased sculptures and decorative paintings for his European palaces in Petersburg.

Everything in the new capital was intended to compel the Russians to adopt a more European way of life. Peter told his nobles where to live, how to build their houses, how to move around the town, where to stand in church, how many servants to keep, how to eat at banquets, how to dress and cut their hair, how to conduct themselves at court, and how to converse in polite society. Nothing in his dragooned capital was left to chance. This obsessive regulation gave St Petersburg the image of a hostile and oppressive place. Here were the roots of the nineteenth-century myth of the 'unreal city' – alien and threatening to the Russian way of life – which was to play a central role in Russian literature and art. 'In Petersburg', wrote Benois, 'there is that same Roman spirit, a hard and absolute spirit of order, a spirit of formally perfect life, unbearable for the general Russian slovenliness, but unquestionably not without charm.' Benois compared the city to a 'sergeant with a stick' – it had a 'machine-like character' – whereas the Russians were like a 'dishevelled old woman'.[20] The nineteenth-century image of the Imperial city was defined by the notion of its regimentation. De Custine remarked that Petersburg was more like 'the general staff of an army than the capital of a nation'.[21] And Herzen said that its uniformity reminded him of a 'military barracks'.[22] This was a city of inhuman proportions, a city ordered by the abstract symmetry of its architectural shapes rather than by the lives of its inhabitants. Indeed, the very purpose of these shapes was to regiment the Russians, like soldiers, into line.

Yet underneath the surface of this European dream world the old Russia still showed through. Badgered by the Tsar to build classical façades, many of the nobles allowed animals to roam in the courtyards of their palaces in Petersburg, just as they did in their Moscow yards, so that Peter had to issue numerous decrees forbidding cows and pigs from wandering on to his fine European avenues.[23] But even the Nevsky, the most European of his avenues, was undone by a 'Russian' crookedness. Designed as a formal 'prospekt' running in a straight line from the Admiralty, at one end, to the Alexander Nevsky monastery, three kilometres away at the other, it was built by separate crews from either end. But they failed to keep the line and when it was completed in 1715 there was a distinct kink where the two teams met.[24]

2

The Sheremetev palace on the Fontanka river is a legendary symbol of the Petersburg tradition. The people of that city call it 'Fountain House'. The poet Anna Akhmatova, who lived there, on and off, in an annexe flat from 1926 to 1952, thought of it as a precious inner space which she co-inhabited with the spirits of the great artistic figures of the past. Pushkin, Krylov, Tiutchev and Zhukovsky – they had all been there.

> I don't have special claims
> On this illustrious house,
> But it happens that almost my whole life
> I have lived under the celebrated roof
> Of the Fountain Palace . . . As a pauper
> I arrived and as a pauper I will leave . . .[25]

The history of the palace is a microcosm of the Petrine plan to set down Western culture on Russian soil. It was built on a plot of marshland granted in 1712 by the Tsar to Boris Sheremetev, the Field Marshal of Peter's army at the battle of Poltava. At that time the site was on the edge of Petersburg and its forests gave the palace a rural character. Peter's gift was one of several to distinguished servitors. They were ordered to construct European-style palaces with regular façades on the Fontanka side as part of the Tsar's plan to develop Petersburg. Legend has it that the land was empty in 1712. But Akhmatova believed that a Swedish farmstead had been there, since she distinguished oak trees from pre-Petrine times.[26]

By the beginning of the eighteenth century the Sheremetev family was already well established as a hugely wealthy clan with close connections to the court. Distantly related to the Romanovs, the Sheremetevs had been rewarded with enormous tracts of land for their loyal service to the ruling house as military commanders and diplomats. Boris Sheremetev was a long-standing ally of Peter's. In 1697 he had travelled with the Tsar on his first trip to Europe, where he remained as Russian ambassador to Poland, Italy and Austria. A veteran of the wars against the Swedes, in 1705 he became Russia's first appointed count (*graf*) – a title Peter imported from Europe as part of his campaign to Westernize the Russian aristocracy. Boris was the last of the old *boyars*, the leading noblemen of Muscovy whose wealth and power derived from the favour of the Tsar (they had all but disappeared by the end of Peter's reign as newly titled nobles superseded them). Russia did not have a gentry in the Western sense – an independent class of landowners that could act as a counterbalance to the power of the Tsar. From the sixteenth century the state had swept away the quasi-feudal rights of the local princes and turned all nobles (*dvoriane*) into servants of the court (*dvor*). Muscovy was conceived as a patrimonial state, owned by the Tsar as his personal fiefdom, and the noble was legally defined as the Tsar's 'slave'.* For his services the nobleman was given land and serfs, but not as outright or allodial property, as in the West, and only on condition that he served the Tsar. The slightest suspicion of disloyalty could lead to demotion and the loss of his estates.

Before the eighteenth century Russia had no grand noble palaces. Most of the Tsar's servitors lived in wooden houses, not much bigger than peasant huts, with simple furniture and clay or wooden pots. According to Adam Olearius, the Duke of Holstein's envoy to Muscovy during the 1630s, few Russian noblemen had feather beds; instead, 'they lie on benches covered with cushions, straw, mats, or clothes; in winter they sleep on flat-topped stoves . . . [lying] with their servants . . . the chickens and the pigs'.[27] The nobleman seldom visited his various estates. Despatched from one place to another in the Tsar's vast empire, he had neither the time nor the inclination to put down roots in one locality. He looked upon his estates as a source of revenue, to be readily exchanged or sold. The beautiful estate of Yasnaya Polyana, near Tula, for example, exchanged hands over twenty times during the seventeenth and early eighteenth centuries. It was lost in games of cards and drinking bouts, sold to different people at the same time, loaned and bartered, mortgaged and remortgaged, until after

---

* Even as late as the nineteenth century noblemen of every rank, including counts and barons, were required to sign off their letters to the Tsar with the formulaic phrase 'Your Humble Slave'.

2. Seventeenth-century Muscovite costumes. Engraving, 1669

years of legal wrangling to settle all the questions of its ownership, it was bought by the Volkonsky family in the 1760s and eventually passed down through his mother to the novelist Tolstoy.[28] Because of this constant state of flux there was little real investment by the nobles in the land, no general movement to develop estates or erect palaces, and none of what took place in Western Europe from medieval times: the gradual concentration of a family domain in one locality, with property passed down from one generation to the next, and ties built up with the community.

The cultural advancement of the Muscovite *boyars* was well behind that of the European nobles in the seventeenth century. Olearius considered them 'among the barbarians ... [with] crude opinions about the elevated natural sciences and arts'.[29] Dr Collins complained that 'they know not how to eat peas and carrots boiled but, like swine, eat them shells and all'.[30] This backwardness was in part the result of the Mongol occupation of Russia from about 1230 to the middle of the fifteenth century. The Tatars left a profound trace on *boyar* customs and habits. For over three hundred years, the period of the Renaissance in the West, Russia was cut off from European civilization. The country which emerged from the Mongol period was far more inward-looking than it had been at the start of the thirteenth century, when Kievan Rus', the loose confederation of principalities which constituted the first Russian state, had been intimately linked with Byzantium. The old princely families were undermined and made more servile to the state of Muscovy, whose economic and military power provided the key to Russia's liberation from the Mongol khans. The Russian nobleman of the Muscovite era (*c.* 1550–1700) was not a landed lord in the European sense. He was a servant of the Crown. In his material culture there was little to distinguish him from the common folk. He dressed like the merchant in the semi-oriental *kaftan* and fur coat. He ruled his family, like the merchant and the peasant, via the patriarchal customs of the *Domostroi* – the sixteenth-century manual that instructed Russians how to discipline their households with the Bible and the birch. The manners of the Russian nobleman were proverbially boorish. Even magnates such as Boris Sheremetev could behave at times like drunken louts. During Tsar Peter's trip to England his entourage resided at the villa of the diarist John Evelyn at Sayes Court, Kent. The damage which they caused in their three-month stay was so extensive – lawns dug up, curtains torn, furniture destroyed, and family portraits used for target practice by the visitors – that Evelyn was obliged to present the Russian court with a large bill.[31] The majority of the nobility could not read and many of them could not even add up simple sums.[32] Little travelled or exposed to Europeans, who were forced to settle in a special suburb in Moscow, the nobleman mistrusted new or foreign ways. His life was regulated by the archaic rituals of the Church – its calendar arranged to count the years from the notional creation of the world (with the birth of Adam) in 5509 BC.*

With Peter's reformation of society, the nobleman became the agency, and his palace the arena, of Russia's introduction to European

---

* Peter the Great introduced the Western system of counting years in 1700. However, Russia continued to adhere to the Julian calendar – thirteen days behind the Gregorian calendar in use in the rest of Europe – until 1918. In terms of time, Imperial Russia always lagged behind the West.

ways. His palace was much more than a noble residence, and his estate was far more than a noble pleasure ground or economic entity: it became its locality's centre of civilization.

Peter laid the basis of the modern absolutist (European) state when he turned all the nobles into servants of the Crown. The old *boyar* class had enjoyed certain rights and privileges that stemmed from its guardianship of the land and serfs – there had been a Boyars' Council, or Duma, that had approved the Tsar's decrees, until it was replaced by the Senate in 1711. But Peter's new aristocracy was defined entirely by its position in the civil and military service, and its rights and privileges were set accordingly. Peter established a Table of Ranks that ordered the nobles according to their office (rather than their birth) and allowed commoners to be given noble status for their service to the state. This almost military ordering of the nobles had a deep and lasting effect on their way of life. As readers of Gogol will know, the Russian nobleman was obsessed by rank. Every rank (and there were fourteen in Peter's Table) had its own uniform. The progression from white to black trousers, the switch from a red to a blue ribbon, from silver to gold thread, or the simple addition of a stripe, were ritual events of immense significance in the nobleman's well-ordered life. Every rank had its own noble title and mode of address: 'Your High Excellency' for the top two ranks; 'Your Excellency' for those in ranks three and four; and so on down the scale. There was a strict and elaborate code of etiquette which set out how nobles of each rank should address the other ranks, or those older or younger than themselves. A senior nobleman writing to a younger nobleman could sign off his letter with simply his surname; but the younger nobleman, in his reply, was expected to add his title and rank to his surname, and failure to do so was considered an offence which could end in scandal and a duel.[33] Etiquette further demanded that a nobleman in the civil service should pay his respects at a superior civil servant's household on the namedays and the birthdays of his family, as well as on all religious holidays. At balls and public functions in St Petersburg it was considered a grave error if a young man remained seated while his elders stood. Hence at the theatre junior officers would remain standing in the slips in case a senior officer entered during the performance. Every officer was said to be on duty at all times. G. A. Rimsky-

Korsakov (a distant forebear of the composer) was kicked out of the Guards in 1810 because at a dinner following a ball he loosened the top button of his uniform.[34] Rank also carried considerable material privileges. Horses at post stations were allocated strictly according to the status of the travellers. At banquets food was served first to the higher-ranking guests, seated with the hosts at the top end of the Russian P(П)-shaped table, followed by the lower ranking at the bottom end. If the top end wanted second helpings, the bottom ends would not be served at all. Prince Potemkin once invited a minor nobleman to a banquet at his palace, where the guest was seated at the bottom end. Afterwards he asked him how he had enjoyed the meal. 'Very much, Your Excellency,' the guest replied. 'I saw everything.'[35]

The Sheremetevs rose very quickly to the top of this new social hierarchy. When Boris Sheremetev died in 1719, the Tsar told his widow that he would be 'like a father' to his children. Pyotr Sheremetev, his sole surviving son, was brought up at the court, where he became one of the few selected companions to the heir to the throne (Peter II).[36] After a teenage career in the Guards, Sheremetev became a chamberlain to the Empress Anna, and then to the Empress Elizabeth. Under Catherine the Great, he became a senator and was the first elected Marshal of the Nobility. Unlike other court favourites, who rose and fell with the change of sovereign, Sheremetev remained in office for six consecutive reigns. His family connections, the protection he enjoyed from the influential courtier Prince Trubetskoi, and his links with Catherine's diplomatic adviser Count Nikitza Panin, prevented him from being made a victim to the whim of any sovereign. He was one of Russia's first noblemen to be independent in the European sense.

The fantastic wealth of the Sheremetev clan had a lot to do with this new confidence. With land in excess of 800,000 hectares and more than 200,000 'census serfs' (which meant perhaps a million actual serfs), by the time of Pyotr's death in 1788, the Sheremetevs were, by some considerable distance, the biggest landowning family in the world. In monetary terms, with an annual income of around 630,000 roubles (£63,000) in the 1790s, they were just as powerful, and considerably richer than, the greatest English lords, the Dukes of Bedford and Devonshire, Earl Shelburne and the Marquess of Rockingham, all of whom had annual incomes of approximately £50,000.[37] Like most noble fortunes, the Sheremetevs' was derived in the main from enormous Imperial grants of land and serfs in reward for their service to the state. The richest dynasties of the aristocracy had all stood near the summit of the Tsarist state during its great territorial expansion between the sixteenth and the eighteenth centuries and had consequently been rewarded with lavish endowments of fertile land in the south of Russia and Ukraine. These were the Sheremetevs and the Stroganovs, the Demidovs and Davydovs, the Vorontsovs and Yusupovs. Like a growing number of magnates in the eighteenth century, the Sheremetevs also made a killing out of trade. In that century the Russian economy grew at a fantastic rate, and as the owners of vast tracts of forest land, paper mills and factories, shops and other urban properties, the Sheremetevs earned huge profits from this growth. By the end of the eighteenth century the Sheremetevs were almost twice as rich as any other Russian noble family, excluding the Romanovs. This extraordinary wealth was in part explained by the fact that, unlike the majority of Russian dynasties, which divided their inheritance between all the sons and sometimes even daughters, the Sheremetevs passed the lion's share of their wealth to the first male heir. Marriage, too, was a crucial factor in the Sheremetevs' rise to the top of the wealth league – in particular the brilliant marriage in 1743 between Pyotr Sheremetev and Varvara Cherkasskaya, the heiress of another hugely wealthy clan, through whom the Sheremetevs acquired the beautiful estate of Ostankino on the outskirts of Moscow. With the immense fortune that was spent on it in the second half of the eighteenth century by their son Nikolai Petrovich, the first great impresario of the Russian theatre, Ostankino became the jewel in the Sheremetev crown.

The Sheremetevs spent vast sums of money on their palaces – often much more than they earned, so that by the middle of the nineteenth century they had amassed debts of several million roubles.[38] Extravagant spending was a peculiar weakness of the Russian aristocracy. It derived in part from foolishness, and in part from the habits of a class whose riches had arrived through little effort and at fantastic speed. Much of this wealth was in the form of Imperial grants designed to create a superb court that would compare with Versailles or Potsdam.

To succeed in this court-centred culture the nobleman required a fabulous lifestyle. The possession of an opulent palace, with imported works of art and furniture, lavish balls and banquets in the European style, became a vital attribute of rank and status that was likely to win favour and promotion at court.

A large part of the Sheremetevs' budget went on their enormous household staffs. The family retained a huge army in livery. At the Fountain House alone there were 340 servants, enough to place a chamberlain at every door; and in all their houses combined the Sheremetevs employed well in excess of a thousand staff.[39] Such vast retinues were the luxury of a country with so many serfs. Even the grandest of the English households had tiny servant numbers by comparison: the Devonshires at Chatsworth, in the 1840s, had a live-in staff of just eighteen.[40] Foreigners were always struck by the large number of servants in Russian palaces. Even Count Ségur, the French ambassador, expressed astonishment that a private residence might have 500 staff.[41] Owning lots of servants was a peculiar weakness of the Russian aristocracy – and perhaps a reason for their ultimate demise. Even middling gentry households in the provinces would retain large staffs beyond their means. Dmitry Sverbeyev, a minor civil servant from the Moscow region, recalled that in the 1800s his father kept an English carriage with 6 Danish horses, 4 coachmen, 2 postilions and 2 liveried footmen, solely for the purpose of his short annual journey to Moscow. On the family estate there were 2 chefs, a valet and an assistant, a butler and 4 doormen, a personal hairdresser and 2 tailors, half a dozen maids, 5 laundrywomen, 8 gardeners, 16 kitchen and various other staff.[42] In the Selivanov household, a middling gentry family in Riazan province, the domestic regime in the 1810s continued to be set by the culture of the court, where their ancestor had once served in the 1740s. They retained an enormous staff – with eighty footmen dressed in dark green uniforms, powdered wigs and special shoes made from plaited horse-tail hair, who were required to walk backwards out of rooms.[43]

In the Sheremetev household clothes were another source of huge extravagance. Nikolai Petrovich, like his father, was a dedicated follower of continental fashions and he spent the equivalent of several thousand pounds a year on imported fabrics for his clothes. An inventory of his wardrobe in 1806 reveals that he possessed no less than thirty-seven different types of court uniform, all sewn with gold thread and all in the dark green or dark brown cashmere or tricot colours that were fashionable at that time. There were 10 sets of single-breasted tails and 18 double-breasted; 54 frock coats; 2 white fur coats, one made of polar bear, the other of white wolf; 6 brown fur coats; 17 woollen jackets; 119 pairs of trousers (53 white, 48 black); 14 silk nightgowns; 2 dominoes made of pink taffeta for masquerades; two Venetian outfits of black taffeta lined with blue and black satin; 39 French silk *kaftans* embroidered in gold and silver thread; 8 velvet *kaftans* (one in lilac with yellow spots); 63 waistcoats; 42 neck scarves; 82 pairs of gloves; 23 tricorn hats; 9 pairs of boots; and over 60 pairs of shoes.[44]

Entertaining was a costly business, too. The Sheremetev household was itself a minor court. The two main Moscow houses – Ostankino and the Kuskovo estate – were famous for their lavish entertainments, with concerts, operas, fireworks and balls for several thousand guests. There was no limit to the Sheremetevs' hospitality. At the Fountain House, where the Russian noble custom of opening one's doors at mealtimes was observed with unstinting generosity, there were often fifty lunch and dinner guests. The writer Ivan Krylov, who dined there frequently, recalled that there was one guest who had eaten there for years without anybody ever knowing who he was. The phrase 'on the Sheremetev account' entered into the language meaning 'free of charge'.[45]

Nearly everything in the Sheremetev household was imported from Europe. Even basic items found abundantly in Russia (oak wood, paper, grain, mushrooms, cheese and butter) were preferable, though more expensive, if from abroad. Information about Peter Sheremetev's foreign purchases between 1770 and 1788 has been preserved in the archives. He bought from foreign merchants in St Petersburg, or through agents especially commissioned to import goods for him. Clothes, jewels and fabrics came directly from Paris, usually from the tailor to Versailles; wines came from Bordeaux. Chocolate, tobacco, groceries, coffee, sweets and dairy products came from Amsterdam; beer, dogs and carriages from England. Here is one of Sheremetev's shopping lists:

kaftan of downy material

camisole sewn with gold and pearls

kaftan and trousers made of silk in puce plus yellow camisole

kaftan made of red cotton with blue on both sides

blue silk camisole sewn with gold

kaftan and trousers in fabric with camisole in raspberry silk sewn
with gold and silver

kaftan and trousers in chocolate colour with green velour camisole

black velvet frock coat

tails in black velvet with speckles

tails with 24 silver buttons

2 pique camisoles sewn with gold and silver

7 *arshins** of French silk for camisoles

24 pairs of lace cuffs for nightshirts

12 *arshins* of black material for trousers and 3 *arshins* of black velvet

various ribbons

150 pounds of superior tobacco

60 pounds of ordinary tobacco

36 tins of pomade

6 dozen bottles of capillary syrup

golden snuffbox

2 barrels of lentils

2 pounds of vanilla

60 pounds of truffles in oil

200 pounds of Italian macaroni

240 pounds of parmesan

150 bottles of anchovies

12 pounds of coffee from Martinique

24 pounds of black pepper

20 pounds of white pepper

6 pounds of cardamom

80 pounds of raisins

160 pounds of currants

12 bottles of English dry mustard

various kinds of ham and bacon, sausages

* One *arshin* is 71 centimetres.

moulds for blancmange
600 bottles of white burgundy
600 bottles of red burgundy
200 bottles of sparkling champagne
100 bottles of non-sparkling champagne
100 bottles of pink champagne.[46]

If Boris Sheremetev was the last of the old *boyars*, his son Pyotr was perhaps the first, and certainly the grandest, of Russia's European gentlemen. Nothing demonstrated more clearly that a nobleman had made the transition from Muscovite *boyar* to Russian aristocrat than the construction of a palace in the European style. Under its grand roof the palace brought together all the European arts. With its salon and its ballroom, it was like a theatre for members of the aristocracy to play out their airs and graces and European ways. But it was not just a building or a social space. The palace was conceived as a civilizing force. It was an oasis of European culture in the desert of the Russian peasant soil, and its architecture, its paintings and its books, its serf orchestras and operas, its landscaped parks and model farms, were meant to serve as a means of public enlightenment. In this sense the palace was a reflection of Petersburg itself.

Fountain House, like Russia, was originally made of wood, a single-storey *dacha* hurriedly erected by Boris Sheremetev in his final years. Pyotr rebuilt and enlarged the house in stone during the 1740s – the beginning of the craze for palace building in St Petersburg, after the Empress Elizabeth had ordered the construction of her own great Imperial residences there: the Summer Palace on the Fontanka river (1741–4), the Great Palace at Tsarskoe Selo (1749–52), and the Winter Palace (1754–62) which we know today. All these baroque master-pieces were built by the Italian architect Bartolomeo Rastrelli, who had come to Russia at the age of sixteen. Rastrelli perfected the synthesis of the Italian and Russian baroque styles which is so charac-teristic of St Petersburg. That essential style – distinguished from its European counterparts by the vastness of its scale, the exuberance of its forms and the boldness of its colours – was stamped on the Fountain House, which may have been designed by Rastrelli himself; certainly the building work was overseen by Rastrelli's main assistant at

Tsarskoe Selo, Savva Chevakinsky, a minor nobleman from Tver who had graduated from the Naval School to become Russia's first architect of note. The classical façade was ornately decorated with lion masks and martial emblems trumpeting the glories of the Sheremetev clan, and this theme was continued on the iron railings and the gates. Behind the palace were extensive gardens, reminiscent of those at Tsarskoe Selo, with paths lined by marble statues from Italy, an English grotto, a Chinese pavilion, and, with a more playful touch, fountains to reflect the house's name.[47]

Inside, the house was a typical collection of European sculpture, bas-relief, furniture and décor, reflecting a taste for expensive luxury. Wallpaper (from France) was just coming into fashion and was used, it seems, for the first time in Russia at the Fountain House.[48] Pyotr Sheremetev was a follower of fashion who had the house redecorated almost every year. On the upper floor was a grand reception hall, used for balls and concerts, with a parquet floor and a high painted ceiling, lined on one side by full-length windows that looked on to the water and, on the other, by enormous mirrors with gold-leaf candelabras whose wondrous effect was to flood the room with extraordinary light. There was a chapel with valuable icons in a special wing; a parade gallery on the upper floor; a museum of curiosities; a library of nearly 20,000 books, most of them in French; a gallery of family and royal portraits painted by serf artists; and a collection of European paintings, which the Sheremetevs purchased by the score. The galleries contained works by Raphael, Van Dyck, Correggio, Veronese, Vernet and Rembrandt. Today they are found in the Hermitage of the Winter Palace.[49]

Not content with one palace, the Sheremetevs built two more, even more expensive ones, at Kuskovo and at Ostankino, on the western outskirts of Moscow. The Kuskovo estate, to the south of Moscow, though it had a relatively simple wooden house which gave the place a rural feel, was extraordinarily ambitious in its conception. In front of the house there was a man-made lake, large enough to stage mock sea battles watched by up to 50,000 guests; a hermitage that housed several hundred paintings; pavilions and grottoes; an open amphitheatre for the summer season; and a larger inside theatre (the most advanced in Russia when it was constructed in the 1780s) with a seating capacity of 150 people and a stage deep enough for the scene

Photograph by William C. Brumfield

3. *The Sheremetev theatre at Ostankino. View from the stage. The parterre is covered by the floor, which was used for balls*

changes of French grand opera.[50] Nikolai Petrovich, who took the Sheremetev opera to its highest levels, had the theatre rebuilt at Ostankino after the auditorium at Kuskovo burnt down in 1789. The Ostankino theatre was even larger than the Kuskovo one, with a seating capacity of 260 people. Its technical facilities were much more sophisticated than those at Kuskovo; it had a specially designed contraption that could transform the theatre into a ballroom by covering the parterre with a floor.

3

The civilization of the aristocracy was based upon the craftsmanship of millions of serfs. What Russia lacked in technology, it more than made up for in a limitless supply of cheap labour. Many of the things that make the tourist gasp at the splendour and the beauty of the Winter Palace – the endless parquet flooring and abundance of gold leaf, the ornate carpentry and bas-relief, the needlework with thread finer than a human hair, the miniature boxes with their scenes from fairy tales set in precious stones, or the intricate mosaics in malachite – are the fruits of many years of unacknowledged labour by unknown serf artists.

Serfs were essential to the Sheremetev palaces and their arts. From the 200,000 census serfs the Sheremetevs owned, several hundred were selected every year and trained as artists, architects and sculptors, furniture makers, decorative painters, gilders, engravers, horticulturalists, theatrical technicians, actors, singers and musicians. Many of these serfs were sent abroad or assigned to the court to learn their craft. But where skill was lacking, much could be achieved through sheer numbers. At Kuskovo there was a horn band in which, to save time on the training of players, each musician was taught to play just one note. The number of players depended on the number of different notes in a tune; their sole skill lay in playing their note at the appropriate moment.[51]

The Argunov family had a vital role in the development of the Russian arts. All the Argunovs were Sheremetev serfs. The architect and sculptor Fedor Argunov designed and built the main reception rooms at Fountain House. His brother Ivan Argunov studied painting with Georg Grot at the Imperial court and quickly established his reputation as one of the country's leading portrait painters. In 1759 he painted the portrait of the future Empress Catherine the Great – a rare honour for a Russian artist at a time when the court looked to Europe for its portrait painters. Pavel Argunov, Ivan's eldest son, was an architect who worked with Quarenghi at Ostankino and Fountain House. Yakov Argunov, Ivan's youngest son, was well known for his 1812 portrait of the Emperor Alexander. But the most important of the three Argunov brothers was the second, Nikolai, who was indisputably one of Russia's finest painters of the nineteenth century.[52]

The position of the creative serf was complicated and ambiguous. There were artists who were greatly valued and rewarded by their lords. Prized chefs and singers were the highest paid in the Sheremetev world. In the 1790s Nikolai Petrovich paid his chef an annual salary of 850 roubles (four times the amount paid to the best chefs in English houses), and his best opera singer 1,500 roubles. But other serf artists were extremely poorly paid: Ivan Argunov, who was placed in charge of all artistic matters at the Fountain House, received a mere 40 roubles a year.[53] Serf artists had a higher status than the other household staff. They lived in better housing, received better food, and they were allowed to work sometimes as freelance artists on commissions from the court, the Church, or other noble families. Yet, like any serf, they were the property of their master and they could be punished just like any other serf. Such servitude was a dreadful obstacle to those artists who strived for independence. As the artistic manager of the Fountain House, Ivan Argunov was responsible for supervising the frequent changes to the palace's interior design, for organizing masquerades and costume balls, for painting sets for theatrical productions, for firework displays, as well as countless menial household tasks. His own artistic projects were constantly abandoned so that he could perform some minor duty on his master's summons and, if he failed in this, the count would have him fined or even flogged. Ivan died a serf. But his children would be freed. According to the will of Nikolai Petrovich, twenty-two domestic serfs, including Nikolai and Yakov Argunov, received their liberty in 1809. Nine years later Nikolai Argunov was elected to the Imperial Academy of Arts, the first Russian artist of serf origin to be honoured by the state.[54]

One of Argunov's most memorable portraits represents another former Sheremetev serf: Countess Praskovya Sheremeteva. Argunov painted her in a red shawl with a sparkling miniature of her husband, Count Nikolai Petrovich Sheremetev, suspended from her neck (plate 1). At the time of this portrait (in 1802) the marriage of the count to his former serf, the prima donna of his opera, was concealed from the public and the court. It would remain so until her death. In this prescient and moving portrait Argunov conveyed their tragedy. It is an extraordinary story that tells us a great deal about the obstacles confronting the creative serf and about the mores of society.

Praskovya was born to a family of serfs on the Sheremetev estate at Yukhotsk in Yaroslav province. Her father and grandfather were both blacksmiths, so the family had been given the name of Kuznetsov ('blacksmith'), although Ivan, her father, was known by all the serfs as 'the hunchback'. In the mid-1770s Ivan became the chief blacksmith at Kuskovo, where the family was given its own wooden house with a large allotment at the back. He sent his first two sons to train as tailors, while the third became a musician in the Sheremetev orchestra. Praskovya was already noted for her beauty and her voice, and Pyotr Sheremetev had her trained for the opera. Praskovya learned Italian and French, both of which she spoke and wrote with fluency. She was trained to sing and act and dance by the finest teachers in the land. In 1779, at the age of eleven, she first appeared on stage as the servant girl in the Russian première of André Grétry's comic opera *L'Amitié à l'épreuve* and, within a year, she had been given her first leading role as Belinda in Antonio Sacchini's *La Colonie*.[55] From that point on she nearly always sang the leading female role. Praskovya possessed a fine soprano voice, distinguished by its range and clarity. The rise of the Sheremetev opera to pre-eminence in Russia in the last two decades of the eighteenth century was intimately linked with her popularity. She was Russia's first real superstar.

The story of Praskovya's romance with the count could have come straight out of a comic opera. The eighteenth-century stage was filled with servant girls who had fallen for young and dashing noblemen. Praskovya herself had sung the part of the young serf girl in *Anyuta*, a hugely popular opera in which the humble background of the charming heroine prevents her marrying the prince. Nikolai Petrovich was not handsome or dashing, it is true. Nearly twenty years Praskovya's senior, he was rather short and stout and suffered from poor health, which brought on melancholia and hypochondria.[56] But he was a romantic, with fine artistic sensibilities, and he shared a love of music with Praskovya. Having watched her grow up as a girl on the estate, then blossom as a singer in his opera, he recognized her spiritual qualities as much as her physical beauty. Eventually he fell in love with her. 'I felt the most tender and passionate feelings for her,' he wrote in 1809,

but I examined my heart to know whether it was seeking pleasures of the flesh or other pleasures to sweeten the mind and soul apart from beauty. Seeing it sought bodily and spiritual pleasures rather than friendship, I observed the qualities of the subject of my love for a long time, and found a virtuous mind, sincerity, love of mankind, constancy and fidelity. I found an attachment to the holy faith and a sincere respect for God. These qualities charmed me more than her beauty, for they are stronger than all external delights and they are extremely rare.[57]

Not that it started out that way. The young count was fond of hunting and of chasing girls; and until his father died in 1788, when he took up the running of the family estates, Nikolai Petrovich spent most of his time in these sensual pursuits. The young squire often claimed his 'rights' over the serf girls. During the day, while they were at work, he would go round the rooms of the girls on the estates and drop a handkerchief through the window of his chosen one. That night he would visit her and, before he left, would ask her to return his handkerchief. One summer evening in 1784 Praskovya was driving her father's two cows down to the stream when some dogs began to chase her. The count, who was riding home after a day's hunting, called the dogs away and approached Praskovya. He had heard that her father was intending to marry her off to a local forester. She was sixteen years of age – relatively old for a serf girl to marry. The count asked her if this was so and, when she replied that it was, he said he would forbid any such marriage. 'You weren't born for this! Today you are a peasant but tomorrow you will become a lady!' The count then turned and rode away.[58]

It is not exactly clear when the count and Praskovya became *de facto* 'man and wife'. To begin with, she was only one of several divas given special treatment by her master. He named his favourite singers and dancers after jewels – 'The Emerald' (Kovaleva), 'The Garnet' (Shlykova) and 'The Pearl' (Praskovya) – and showered them with expensive gifts and bonuses. These 'girls of my house', as Sheremetev called them in his letters to his accountant, were in constant attendance on the count. They accompanied him on trips to St Petersburg during the winter and returned with him to Kuskovo during the summer.[59] Everything suggests that they were the count's harem – not least the fact that just before his marriage to Praskovya he had the rest of them married off and gave them all dowries.[60]

Serf harems were extremely fashionable in the eighteenth and the early nineteenth centuries. Among Russian noblemen the possession of a large harem was ironically seen as a mark of European manners and civilization. Some harems, like Sheremetev's, were sustained by gifts and patronage; but others were maintained by the squire's total power over his own serfs. Sergei Aksakov, in his *Family Chronicle* (1856), tells the story of a distant relative who established a harem among his female serfs: anyone who tried to oppose it, including his own wife, was physically beaten or locked up.[61] Examples of such behaviour abound in the memoir literature of the nineteenth century.[62] The most detailed and interesting such memoir was written by Ianuarius Neverov, whose father was steward on the estate of an octogenarian nobleman called Pyotr Koshkarov. Twelve to fifteen of his prettiest young serf girls were strictly segregated in a special female quarter of his house and placed under the control of the main housekeeper, Koshkarov's former mistress Natalia Ivanovna, who had given birth to seven of his sons. Within the harem was the master's room. When he went to bed he was joined by all his girls, who said their prayers with him and placed their mattresses around his bed. One of the girls would undress the master and help him into bed and read them all a fairy tale. Then they would be left together for the night. In the morning Koshkarov would dress and say his prayers, drink a cup of tea and smoke his pipe, and then he would begin 'the punishments'. Disobedient girls, or the ones it simply pleased him to punish, would be birched or slapped across the face; others would be made to crawl along the floor. Such sadistic violence was partly sexual 'play' for Koshkarov. But it also served to discipline and terrorize. One girl, accused of secret liaisons with a male servant, was locked for a whole month in the stocks. Then, before the whole serf community, the girl and her lover were flogged by several men until each collapsed from exhaustion and the two poor wretches were left as bloody heaps upon the floor. Yet alongside such brutality Koshkarov took great care to educate and improve his girls. All of them could read and write, some of them in French; one taught Neverov to learn by heart Pushkin's *Fountain of Bakhchisarai*. They were dressed in European clothes, given special places in church, and when they were replaced in the harem by younger girls they were married to the master's hunting serfs, the élite of his male servants, and given dowries.[63]

By the beginning of the 1790s Praskovya had become Sheremetev's unofficial wife. It was no longer just the pleasures of the flesh that attracted him to her but, as he said, the beauty of her mind and soul as well. For the next ten years the count would remain torn between his love for her and his own high position in society. He felt that it was morally wrong not to marry Praskovya but his aristocratic pride would not allow him to do so. Marriages to serfs were extremely rare in the status-obsessed culture of the eighteenth-century Russian aristocracy – although they would become relatively common in the nineteenth century – and unthinkable for a nobleman as rich and grand as him. It was not even clear, if he married Praskovya, whether he would have a legitimate heir.

The count's dilemma was one faced by noblemen in numerous comic operas. Nikolai Petrovich was a man susceptible to the cult of sentimentalism that swept over Russia in the last two decades of the eighteenth century. Many of the works which he produced were variations on the conflict between social convention and natural senti-ment. One was a production of Voltaire's *Nanine* (1749), in which the hero, Count Olban, in love with his poor ward, is forced to choose between his own romantic feelings and the customs of his class that rule against marriage to the humble girl. In the end he chooses love. The parallels in his own life were so obvious that Nikolai Petrovich gave the role of Nanine to Anna Izumudrova, even though Praskovya was his leading actress at this time.[64] In the theatre the public sympa-thized with the unequal lovers and applauded the basic Enlightenment ideal that informed such works: that all people are equal. But it did not take the same view in real life.

Praskovya's secret relationship with the count placed her in an almost impossible position. For the first few years of their liaison she remained his serf and lived among the other serfs at Kuskovo. But the truth could not be concealed from her fellow serfs, who became resentful of her privileged position and called her spiteful names. Her own family tried to take advantage of the situation and cursed her when she failed to make their petty requests to the count. The count, meanwhile, was entertaining thoughts of leaving her. He would tell her of his duties to his family, of how he had to marry someone equal in status, while she would try to conceal her torment, listening silently and bursting into tears only after he had gone. To protect Praskovya and himself from malicious gossip, the count built a special house, a simple wooden *dacha*, near the main mansion so that he could visit her in privacy. He forbade her to see anyone, or to go anywhere except to the theatre or to church: all she could do to while away the days was play the harpsichord or do needlework. But this could not prevent the gossip of the serfs from spreading to the public in Moscow: visitors would come to snoop around her house and sometimes even taunt the 'peasant bride'.[65] For the count this was reason good enough to abandon Kuskovo. Sometime during 1794-5 he moved to the new palace at Ostankino, where he could accommodate Praskovya in more luxurious and secluded apartments.

Yet even at Ostankino Prasvovya's situation remained extremely difficult. Resented by the serfs, she was also shunned by society. It was only through her strength of character that she managed to retain her dignity. It is symbolic that her greatest roles were always those of tragic heroines. Her most celebrated performance was as Eliane in *Les Mariages Samnites*, put on for the visit by the newly crowned Emperor Paul to Ostankino in April 1797.[66] The plot of Grétry's opera could have been the story of Praskovya's life. In the Samnite tribe there is a law forbidding girls to show their feelings for a man. Eliane breaks the law and declares her love to the warrior Parmenon, who will not and cannot marry her. The Samnite chief condemns and bans her from the tribe, whereupon she disguises herself as a soldier and joins his army in its battle against the Romans. During the battle an unknown soldier saves the life of the Samnite chief. After the victorious Samnite army returns home, the chief orders that this unknown man be found. The soldier is revealed as Eliane. Her heroic virtues finally win over Parmenon, who, in defiance of the tribe's conventions, declares his love for her. It turned out to be Praskovya's final role.

Shortly before *Les Mariages* Nikolai Petrovich had been summoned to the court by the Emperor Paul. The count was an old friend of the Emperor. The Sheremetev household on Millionaia Street, where he had grown up, was a stone's throw away from the Winter Palace and in his childhood the count used to visit Paul, who was three years his junior and very fond of him. In 1782 he had travelled incognito with the future Emperor and his wife abroad. Sheremetev was one of the few grandees to get along with Paul, whose outbursts of rage and disciplinarian attitudes had alienated most of the nobility. On his assumption of the throne in 1796 Paul appointed Sheremetev Senior Chamberlain, the chief administrator of the court. The count had little inclination towards court service – he was drawn to Moscow and the arts – but he had no choice. He moved back to Petersburg and

Fountain House. It was at this stage that the first signs of Praskovya's illness became clear. The symptoms were unmistakable: it was tuberculosis. Her singing career was now at an end and she was confined to the Fountain House, where a secret set of rooms, entirely segregated from the reception and official areas, was specially constructed for her use.

Praskovya's confinement to the Fountain House was not just the result of her illness. Rumours of the serf girl living in the palace had caused a scandal in society. Not that people of good taste talked of it – but everybody knew. When he first arrived in Petersburg, it was naturally assumed that the count would take a wife. 'Judging by the rumours,' his friend Prince Shcherbatov wrote to him, 'the city here has married you a dozen times, so I think we will see you with a countess, which I am extremely glad about.'[67] So when this most eligible of men was found to have wasted himself on a peasant girl, the disappointment of the aristocracy was compounded by a sense of anger and betrayal. It seemed almost treasonable that the count should be living with a serf as man and wife – especially considering the fact (which had since attained a legendary status) that he had once turned down an offer by the Empress Catherine the Great to arrange a marriage between him and her granddaughter, the Grand Duchess Alexandra Pavlovna. The count was isolated by society. The Sheremetevs disowned him and descended into squabbles about what would happen to the legacy. The vast reception rooms of the Fountain House were devoid of guests – and the only people who remained as friends were loyal childhood comrades such as Prince Shcherbatov or artists, like the poet Derzhavin and the architect Quarenghi, who rose above the snobbish prejudices of society. The Emperor Paul also was in this category. Several times he arrived incognito at the back entrance of Fountain House – either to visit the count when he was sick or to hear Praskovya sing. In February 1797 she gave a recital in the concert hall of Fountain House attended by the Emperor and a few close friends. Paul was enchanted by Praskovya and presented her with his own personal diamond ring, which she wore for her portrait by Argunov.[68]

The moral support of the Emperor must have been a factor in the count's decision to flout social conventions and to take Praskovya as his legal wife. Nikolai Petrovich had always believed that the Sheremetev family was different from other aristocratic clans, a little bit above the social norm, and this arrogance undoubtedly provoked some of the hostile views held about him in society.[69] In 1801 the count gave Praskovya her liberty and then at last, on 6 November, he married her in a secret ceremony at the small village church of Povarskaya on the outskirts of Moscow. Prince Shcherbatov and a few close friends and servants were the only witnesses. The wedding was kept so discreet that the marriage certificate remained buried in the local parish archives until 1905.[70]

One year later Praskovya gave birth to a son, Dmitry, who was christened, like his father, in the private chapel of the Fountain House. But she was weakened by the birth and, already suffering from advanced tuberculosis, she died after three weeks of painful suffering. Six years later, still struck down by grief, the count recalled her death in his testimony to his son:

The easy pregnancy of your mother heralded a happy resolution; she brought you into the world without pain, and I was overjoyed, seeing her good health did not falter after giving birth to you. But you must know, dearest son, that barely did I feel this joy, barely had I covered your tender infant face with my first father's kisses when severe illness struck your mother, and then her death turned the sweet feelings of my heart into bitter grief. I sent urgent prayers to God about saving her life, summoned expert doctors to bring back her health, but the first doctor inhumanely refused to help, despite my repeated requests, and then the illness worsened; others applied all their efforts, all the knowledge of their art, but could not help her. My groans and sobbing almost took me to the grave as well.[71]

At this moment, the most desperate time in his life, the count was abandoned by the whole of Petersburg society. In preparation for the funeral he publicized the news of Praskovya's death and, in accordance with the Orthodox ritual, gave the times for visitors to pay their last respects before her open coffin at Fountain House.[72] Few people came – so few, in fact, that the time for viewing the coffin was reduced from the customary three days to just five hours. The same small group of mourners – small enough for them all to be listed by name – were at the funeral and accompanied the coffin from the Fountain House to the Alexander Nevsky monastery, where it was buried next to the grave of the count's father. Present were close friends of Praskovya, mainly serf performers from the opera; some domestic servants from the Fountain House who had been her only form of social contact in the final years; several of the count's illegitimate offspring from previous serf lovers; one or two church clerks; Praskovya's confessor; the architect Giacomo Quarenghi; and a couple of the Count's aristocratic friends. There was no one from the court (Paul had been murdered in 1801); no one from the ancient noble families; and perhaps most shockingly of all, no one from the Sheremetev family.[73] Six years later it was still a source of bitterness and sorrow to the count.

I thought I had friends who loved me, respected me and shared my pleasures, but when my wife's death put me in an almost desperate state I found few people to comfort me and share my sorrow. I experienced cruelty. When her body was taken to be buried, few of those who called themselves my friends displayed any sensitivity to the sad event or performed the Christian duty of accompanying her coffin.[74]

Lost in grief, the count resigned from the court, turned his back on society and, retreating to the country, devoted his final years to religious study and charitable works in commemoration of his wife. It is tempting to conclude that there was an element of remorse and even guilt in this charity – perhaps an attempt to make amends to the enserfed ranks of people from which Praskovya came. He liberated dozens of his favourite domestic serfs, spent vast sums on building village schools and hospitals, set up trusts for the care of orphans, endowed monasteries to give the peasants food when the harvest failed, and reduced the payments levied from the serfs on his estates.[75] But by far his most ambitious project was the alms house which he founded in Praskovya's memory on the outskirts of Moscow – the Strannoprimnyi Dom, which at that time, in 1803, was by some way the largest public hospital in the Empire, with sixteen male and sixteen female wards. 'My wife's death,' he wrote, 'has shocked me to the point that the only way I know to calm my suffering spirit is to devote myself to fulfilling her behest of caring for the poor man and the sick.'[76]

For years the grief-stricken count would leave the Fountain House and walk incognito through the streets of Petersburg distributing money to the poor.[77] He died in 1809, the richest nobleman in the whole of Russia, and no doubt the loneliest as well. In his testimony to his son he came close to rejecting root and branch the civilization embodied in his own life's work. 'My taste and passion for rare things,' he wrote,

was a form of vanity, like my desire to charm and surprise people's feelings with things they had never seen or heard . . . I came to realize that the brilliance of such work could only satisfy for a short time and vanished instantly in the eyes of my contemporaries. It did not leave the remotest impression on the soul. What is all this splendour for?[78]

On Praskovya's death the count wrote to the new Emperor, Alexander I, to inform him of his marriage and appealed to him (successfully) to recognize the rights of Dmitry as his sole legitimate heir.[79] He claimed that his wife had only been the ward of the blacksmith Kuznetsov and that she was really the daughter of an ancient Polish noble family called the Kovalevskys, from the western provinces.[80] The fiction was in part to distinguish Dmitry's claim from that of all the older sons he had begotten with various serf women (there were six in all, as far as one can tell from the many claims).[81] But it was also uncannily like the denouement of a comic opera – it was in fact the ending of *Anyuta* – where the servant girl in love with the nobleman is finally allowed to marry him, at which point it is revealed that she is, after all, of noble origins and had only been adopted by her humble parents as an orphaned little girl. The count, it seems, was attempting to tie up the ends of his own life as if it was a work of art.

Praskovya was blessed with a rare intelligence and strength of character. She was the finest singer in the Russia of her day, literate and conversant with several languages. Yet until a year before her death she remained a serf. What were her feelings? How did she respond to the prejudice she met? How did she reconcile her deep religious faith, her acceptance of the sin of sexual relations outside marriage, with her feelings for the count? It is very seldom that one gets the chance to hear the confession of a serf. But in 1863 a document was found among the papers of the recently deceased Tatyana Shlykova, the opera singer (Sheremetev's 'Garnet') and Praskovya's lifelong friend, who had raised Dmitry, as if her own son, at the Fountain House after 1803. The document, in Praskovya's own neat hand, was written in the form of a 'prayer' to God, clearly in the knowledge that she was about to die. It was handed by Praskovya to her friend before her death with instructions not to let the count see it. The language of the prayer is disjointed and obscure, its mood delirious with guilt and repentance, but the intense cry for salvation is unmistakable:

... O merciful Lord, the source of all goodness and endless charity, I confess to you my sins and place before your eyes all my sinful and unlawful deeds. I have sinned, my Lord, and my illness, all these scabs upon my body, is a heavy punishment. I bear a heavy labour and my naked body is defiled. My body is defiled by sinful bonds and thoughts. I am bad. I am proud. I am ugly and lascivious. A devil is inside my body. Cry, my angel, my soul has died. It is in a coffin, lying unconscious and oppressed by bitterness, because, my Lord, my base and unlawful deeds have killed my soul. But compared with my sins the power of my Lord is very great, greater than the sand in all the seas, and from the depths of my despair I beg you, Lord Almighty, do not reject me. I am begging for your blessing. I am praying for your mercy. Punish me, my Lord, but please don't let me die.[82]

4

The musical life of eighteenth-century Russia was dominated by the court and by small private theatres such as Sheremetev's. Public theatres, which were long-established in the towns of western Europe, did not really feature in the cultural life of Russia until the 1780s. The aristocracy preferred their own society and they rarely attended the public theatres, which catered mainly to the clerks and traders of the towns with vaudevilles and comic operas. 'In our day,' one Princess Yankova recalled, 'it was considered more refined to go [to the theatre] by the personal invitation of the host, and not to one where anyone could go in exchange for money. And who indeed among our intimate friends did not possess his own private theatre?'[83]

There were serf theatres on 173 estates, and serf orchestras on 300 estates, between the late eighteenth and the early nineteenth centuries.[84] Besides the Sheremetevs, the Goncharovs, the Saltykovs, the Orlovs and Shepelevs, the Tolstoys and Nashchokins all had large serf troupes and separate theatre buildings that could be compared with the court theatres of Catherine the Great (the Hermitage Theatre in the Winter Palace and the Chinese Theatre at Tsarskoe Selo) from which they took their cue. Catherine set the pattern for the theatre in Russia. She herself wrote plays and comic operas; she began the fashion for the high French style in the Russian theatre; and it was she who first advanced the Enlightenment idea of the theatre as a school of public manners and sensibilities. The serf theatre played a central role on the noble estate during Catherine's reign.

In 1762, Peter III liberated the nobility from compulsory service to the state. Catherine the Great, Peter's wife, wanted her nobility to resemble a European one. It was a turning point in the cultural history of the aristocracy. Relieved of their stately duties, many noblemen retired to the country and developed their estates. The decades following the emancipation of the nobility were the golden age of the pleasure palace, with galleries for art, exquisite parks and gardens, orchestras and theatres appearing for the first time in the Russian countryside. The estate became much more than just an economic unit or living space. It became an island of European culture on Russian peasant soil.

The Sheremetev serf troupe was the most important theatre of its kind, and it played a major role in the development of the Russian opera. It was ranked on a level with the court theatre in Petersburg and was considered far superior to the leading company in Moscow, whose theatre was located on the site of the Bolshoi Theatre today. The Moscow theatre's English director, Michael Meddox, complained that Kuskovo, which did not charge admission, had deprived his theatre of an audience.[85] Pyotr Sheremetev had established the serf troupe at Kuskovo in the 1760s. He was not an artistic man, but the theatre was a fashionable addition to his grand estate and it enabled him to entertain the court. In 1775 the Empress Catherine attended a performance of the French opera in the open-air theatre at Kuskovo. This encouraged Sheremetev to build a proper theatre, large enough to stage the foreign operas so beloved by the Empress, between 1777 and 1787. He left its direction to his son, Count Nikolai Petrovich, who was well acquainted with the French and Italian opera from his European travels in the early 1770s. Nikolai trained his serf performers in the disciplined techniques of the Paris Opéra. Peasants were selected at an early age from his various estates and trained as musicians for the theatre orchestra or as singers for the troupe. There was also a German who taught the violin, a French singing teacher, a language instructor in Italian and French, a Russian choir master, and several foreign ballet masters, most of them from the court. The Sheremetev theatre was the first in Russia to stage ballets on their own, rather than as part of an opera, as was common in the eighteenth century. Under the direction of Nikolai Petrovich it produced over twenty French and Russian ballets, many of them receiving their first performance in Russia, long before they were put on at court.[86] The Russian ballet was born at Kuskovo.

So, too, was the Russian opera. The Sheremetev theatre began the practice of performing operas in Russian, which stimulated the composition of native works. The earliest, *Anyuta* (premièred at Tsarskoe Selo in 1772), was produced at Kuskovo in 1781; and *Misfortune from a Carriage* by Vasily Pashkevich, with a libretto by Kniazhnin (first put on at the Hermitage Theatre in 1779) was seen at Kuskovo within a year.* Before the final quarter of the eighteenth century, opera was imported from abroad. Italians made the running early on. Giovanni Ristori's *Calandro* was performed by a group of Italian singers from the Dresden court in 1731. The Empress Anna, enchanted by this 'exotic and irrational entertainment', recruited Francesco Araia's Venetian company to entertain her court in Petersburg, which staged *La Forza dell'amore* in the Winter Palace on the Empress's birthday in 1736. Starting with Araia, Italians occupied the post of *maestro di capella* at the Imperial court, with just two exceptions, until the nineteenth century. Consequently, the first Russian composers were strongly influenced by the Italian style. Maxim Berezovsky, Dmitry Bortnyansky and Yevstignei Fomin were all taught by the Italians of St Petersburg, and then sent to study in Italy itself.

---

* Stepan Degterov, the composer of *Minin and Pozharsky* (1811), was a former Sheremetev serf.

Berezovsky was Mozart's fellow student in the composition school of Padre Martini.*

The love affair between Petersburg and Venice was continued by Glinka, Tchaikovsky and Stravinsky. It was ironically a Venetian, Catterino Cavos, who pioneered the Russian national opera. Cavos came to Petersburg in 1798 and immediately fell in love with the city, which reminded him of his native town. In 1803 the Emperor Alexander took control of the public theatres and placed Cavos in charge of the Bolshoi Kamenny, until then the only public opera house and exclusively reserved for Italian opera. Cavos built the Bolshoi Kamenny into a stronghold of Russian opera. He wrote works such as *Ilya Bogatyr* (1807) on heroic national themes with librettos in Russian, and his music was strongly influenced by Russian and Ukrainian folk songs. Much of Glinka's operatic music, which the nationalists would champion as the foundation of the Russian tradition, was in fact anticipated by Cavos. The 'national character' of Russian music was thus first developed by a foreigner.†

The French were also instrumental in the development of a distinctive Russian musical style. Catherine the Great had invited a French opera troupe to the Petersburg court as one of her first acts on the assumption of the throne in 1762. During her reign the court opera was among the best in Europe. It staged the première of several major works, including Giovanni Paisiello's *Il barbiere di Siviglia* (1782). The French comic opera, with its rustic village setting and its reliance on folk dialect and music, was a major influence on early Russian operas and *Singspiels* like *Anyuta* (similar to Favart's *Annette et*

---

* Berezovsky was elected to the Accademia Philharmonica in Bologna. He returned to Russia in 1775 and, two years later, committed suicide. Tarkovsky's film *Nostalgia* (1983) is a commentary on exile as told through the story of Berezovsky's life. It tells of a Russian émigré in Italy engaged in research on his *doppelgänger* and fellow countryman, an ill-fated eighteenth-century Russian composer.

† This was not the end of the Cavos connection with the Russian opera. Catterino's son, the architect Alberto Cavos, redesigned the Bolshoi Theatre in Moscow after it was burned down in 1853. He also built the Marinsky Theatre in St Petersburg. His daughter, Camille Cavos, married the court architect and portrait painter Nikolai Benois, whose family had fled to St Petersburg from the French Revolution in the 1790s, and their son, Alexander Benois, established the Ballets Russes with Sergei Diaghilev.

Lubin), *St Petersburg Bazaar* and *The Miller Magician* (based on Rousseau's *Le devin du village*). These operas were the staple of the Sheremetev repertoire: huge numbers of them were performed at Kuskovo and Ostankino. With their comic peasant characters and their stylized motifs from folk song, they gave voice to an emerging Russian national consciousness.

One of the earliest Russian operas was specially commissioned by the Sheremetevs for the open-air theatre at Kuskovo in 1781. *Green with Jealousy, or The Boatman from Kuskovo* was a panegyric to the Sheremetev palace and its park, which served as a backdrop to the opera on the stage.[87] The production was a perfect illustration of the way in which the palace had itself become a kind of theatre for the acting out of Russian noble life, a huge stage set for the display of wealth and European ways.

The design and the décor of the palace and its park contained much theatricality. The high stone archway into the estate marked the entrance into another world. The landscaped gardens and the manor house were laid out, like the props upon a stage, to create a certain emotion or theatrical effect. Features such as sculptured 'peasants' or 'cattle' in the woods, or temples, lakes and grottoes in the English park, intensified this sense of being in a place of make-believe.[88] Kuskovo was full of dramatic artifice. The main house was made of wood that was carved to look like stone. In the park Fedor Argunov's extraordinary grotto pavilion was full of playfulness: its internal walls were lined with artificial shells and sea creatures; and (in a reference to the house in Petersburg) its baroque cupola was constructed in the form of a fountain.

In its everyday routines and public entertainments the palace was a kind of theatre, too. The daily ceremonies of the nobleman – the rituals connected with his morning prayer, his breakfast, lunch and dinner, his dressing and undressing, his office work and hunting, his washing and his bed – were performed from a detailed script that needed to be learned by the master and a huge supporting cast of domestic serfs. Then there were certain social functions which served as an arena for the ritualized performance of cultivated ways, the salon or the ball where the nobles demonstrated their European manners and good taste. Women put on wigs and beauty spots. They were conscious of the need to take a leading role – dancing, singing at the piano, playing the coquette. Dandies turned their social lives into performance art: every mannered pose was carefully rehearsed. They prepared themselves, like Eugene Onegin, as actors going out before an audience.

> At least three hours he peruses
> His figure in the looking-glass.[89]

Etiquette demanded that they hold themselves and act in the directed form: the way they walked and stood, the way they entered or left a room, the way they sat and held their hands, the way they smiled or nodded their heads – every pose and gesture was carefully scripted. Hence in the ballroom and reception hall the walls were lined with mirrors for the beau monde to observe their performance.

The aristocracy of eighteenth-century Russia was aware of acting out its life as if upon a stage. The Russian nobleman was not born a 'European' and European manners were not natural to him. He had to learn such manners, as he learned a foreign language, in a ritualized form by conscious imitation of the West. Peter the Great began it all – reinventing himself and his aristocracy in the European mould. The first thing he did on his return from Europe, in 1698, was to order all the *boyars* to give up their *kaftans* for Western codes of dress. In a symbolic rupture with the past, he forbade them to wear beards, traditionally seen as a sign of holiness, and himself took the shears to reluctant courtiers.* Peter commanded his nobles to entertain after the European fashion: with his head of police he personally supervised the lists of guests at balls to be thrown by his selected hosts. The aristocracy was to learn to speak in French, to converse politely and to dance the minuet. Women, who had been confined to private quarters in the semi-Asiatic world of Muscovy, were to squeeze their bodies into corsets and grace society.

These new social manners were expounded in a manual of etiquette,

---

* In the Orthodox belief the beard was a mark of God and Christ (both were depicted wearing beards) and a mark of manhood (animals had whiskers). Because of Peter's prohibition, wearing beards became a sign of 'Russianness' and of resistance to his reforms.

The Honourable Mirror to Youth, which Peter had adapted and embellished from the German original. It advised its readers, among other things, not to 'spit their food', nor to 'use a knife to clean their teeth', nor 'blow their nose like a trumpet'.[90] To perform these manners required a conscious mode of action very different from the unselfconscious or 'natural' behaviour of the Russian; at such moments the Russian was supposed to be aware of acting differently from the way he would behave as a Russian. Books of etiquette like *The Honourable Mirror* advised the Russian nobleman to imagine himself in the company of foreigners while, at the same time, remaining conscious of himself as a Russian. The point was not to become a European, but rather to act as one. Like an actor with an eye to his own image on the stage, the nobleman was told to observe his own behaviour from a Russian point of view. It was the only way to judge its foreignness.[91]

The diaries and memoirs of the aristocracy are filled with descriptions of how young nobles were instructed to act in society. 'The point was not to be but to appear,'[92] recalled one memoirist. In this society, external appearances were everything and success was dependent on a subtle code of manners displayed only by those of breeding. Fashionable dress, good comportment, modesty and mildness, refined conversation and the capacity to dance with elegance – these were the qualities of being '*comme il faut*'. Tolstoy boiled them down to first-class French; long, well-kept and polished nails; and 'a constant expression of elegant and contemptuous ennui'.[93] Polished nails and a cultivated air of boredom were also the defining features of the fop, according to Pushkin (this was how the poet was depicted in the famous portrait by Orest Kiprensky which appears to have been painted in the Fountain House).

The European Russian had a split identity. His mind was a state divided into two. On one level he was conscious of acting out his life according to prescribed European conventions; yet on another plane his inner life was swayed by Russian customs and sensibilities. The distinction was not absolute, of course: there could be conscious forms of 'Russianness', as the Slavophiles would prove, just as it was possible for European habits to be so ingrained that they appeared and felt 'natural'. But generally speaking, the European Russian was a 'European' on the public stage and a 'Russian' in those moments of his private life when, without even thinking, he did things in a way that only Russians did. This was the legacy from his ancestors which no European influence could totally erase. It enabled a countess like Natasha to dance the Russian dance. In every Russian aristocrat, however European he may have become, there was a discreet and instinctive empathy with the customs and beliefs, the habits and the rhythms of Russian peasant life. How, indeed, could it not be so when the nobleman was born in the countryside, when he spent his childhood in the company of serfs, and lived most of his life on the estate – a tiny island of European culture in a vast Russian peasant sea?

The layout of the palace was a map of this divide in the nobleman's emotional geography. There were the grand reception rooms, always cold and draughty, where formal European manners were the norm; and then there were the private rooms, the bedrooms and the boudoirs, the study and the parlour, the chapel and the icon room, and the corridors that ran through to the servants' quarters, where a more informal, 'Russian' way of life was to be found. Sometimes this divide was consciously maintained. Count Sheremetev rearranged the rooms at the Fountain House so that all his public life was conducted on its left, or embankment, side, while the right side and the rooms that faced on to the garden at the rear were sealed off for his secret life. These private rooms were entirely different in their feel and style, with warm-coloured fabrics, wallpaper, carpets and Russian stoves, compared to the cold and stoveless public rooms with their parquet floors and marble mirrored walls.[94] It was as if the count was attempting to create an intimate, domestic and more 'Russian' space in which to relax with Praskovya.

In 1837 the Winter Palace in St Petersburg was gutted by a fire so immense it could be seen from villages some eighty kilometres away. It began in a wooden basement room and soon spread to the upper floors, which all had wooden walls and cavities behind the stone façades. The symbolism of the fire did not go unnoticed in a city built on myths of apocalypse: the old Russia was wreaking its revenge. Every palace had a 'wooden Russia' underneath its grand reception rooms. From the brilliant white ballroom in the Fountain House you could exit through a concealed mirror door and descend by a staircase to the servants' quarters and another world. Here were kitchens where the open fires raged all day, a storehouse in the yard where peasant

4. *Gérard de la Barthe:* A Cure Bath in Moscow, *1790*

carts delivered farm produce, a carriage house, a smithy, workshops, stables, cow sheds, an aviary, a large greenhouse, a laundry and a wooden *banya* or bath house.[95]

Going to the *banya* was an old Russian custom. From medieval times it was popularly seen as a national institution, and not to bathe in one at least three times a week was practically taken as a proof of foreign origins. Every noble household had its own steam house. In towns and villages there was invariably a communal bath, where men and women sat steaming themselves, beating one another, according to the custom, with young birch leaf whips, and cooling themselves down by rolling around together in the snow. Because of its reputation as a place for sex and wild behaviour, Peter the Great attempted to stamp out the *banya* as a relic of medieval Rus' and encouraged the building of Western bathrooms in the palaces and mansions of St Petersburg. But, despite heavy taxes on it, noblemen continued to prefer the Russian bath and, by the end of the eighteenth century, nearly every palace in St Petersburg had one.[96]

The *banya* was believed to have special healing powers – it was called the 'people's first doctor' (vodka was the second, raw garlic the third). There were all sorts of magical beliefs associated with it in folklore.[97] To go to the *banya* was to give both your body and your soul a good cleaning, and it was the custom to perform this purge as a part of important rituals. The *banya* was a place for giving birth: it was warm and clean and private, and in a series of bathing rituals that lasted forty days, it purified the mother from the bleeding of the birth which, according to the Church and the popular belief that held to the idea of Christ's bloodless birth, symbolized the fallen state of womanhood.[98] The *banya*'s role in prenuptial rites was also to ensure the woman's purity: the bride was washed in the *banya* by her maids on the eve of her wedding. It was a custom in some places for the bride and groom to go to the bath house before their wedding night. These were not just peasant rituals. They were shared by the provincial nobility and even by the court in the final decades of the seventeenth century. According to the customs of the 1670s Tsar Alexei's bride was washed in the *banya* on the day before her wedding, while a choir chanted sacred songs outside, after which she received the blessing of a priest.[99] This intermingling of pagan bathing rites with Christian rituals was equally pronounced at Epiphany and Shrovetide ('Clean Monday'), when ablution and devotion were the order of the day. On these holy days it was customary for the Russian family, of whatever social class, to clean the house, washing all the floors, clearing out the cupboards, purging the establishment of any rotten or unholy foods, and then, when this was done, to visit the bath house and clean the body, too.

In the palace, the salon upstairs belonged to an entirely different, European world. Every major palace had its own salon, which served as the venue for concerts and masked balls, banquets, soirées, and sometimes even readings by the greatest Russian poets of the age. Like all palaces, the Fountain House was designed for the salon's rituals. There was a wide sweeping driveway for the grand arrival by coach-and-four; a public vestibule for divesting cloaks and furs; a 'parade' staircase and large reception rooms for the guests to advertise their tasteful dress and etiquette. Women were the stars of this society. Every salon revolved around the beauty, charm and wit of a particular hostess – such as Anna Scherer in Tolstoy's *War and Peace*, or Tatiana in Pushkin's *Eugene Onegin*. Having been excluded from the public domain under Muscovy, women took up leading roles in the European culture of the eighteenth century. For the first time in the history of the Russian state there was even a succession of female sovereigns. Women became educated and accomplished in the European arts. By the end of the eighteenth century the educated noblewoman had become the norm in high society – so much so that the uneducated noblewoman became a common subject of satire. Recalling his experience as the French ambassador in Petersburg during the 1780s, Count Ségur believed that Russian noblewomen 'had outstripped the men in this progressive march towards improvement: you already saw a number of elegant women and girls, remarkable for their graces, speaking seven or eight languages with fluency, playing several instruments, and familiar with the most celebrated romance writers and poets of France, Italy and England'. The men, by comparison, had nothing much to say.[100]

Women set the manners of the salon: the kissing of the hand, the balletic genuflections and the feminized apparel of the fop were all reflections of their influence. The art of salon conversation was distinctly feminine. It meant relaxed and witty conversation which skipped imperceptibly from one topic to another, making even the most trivial thing a subject of enchanting fascination. It was also *de rigueur* not to talk for long on serious, 'masculine' topics such as politics or philosophy, as Pushkin underlined in *Eugene Onegin*:

> The conversation sparkled bright;
> The hostess kept the banter light
> And quite devoid of affectations;
> Good reasoned talk was also heard,
> But not a trite or vulgar word,
> No lasting truths or dissertations –
> And no one's ears were shocked a bit
> By all the flow of lively wit.[101]

Pushkin said that the point of salon conversation was to flirt (he once claimed that the point of life was to 'make oneself attractive to women'). Pushkin's friends testified that his conversation was just as memorable as his poetry, while his brother Lev maintained that his real genius was for flirting with women.[102]

The readership of literature in Pushkin's age was by and large female. In *Eugene Onegin* we first meet the heroine Tatiana with a French book in her hands. Russian literary language, which developed at this time, was consciously designed by poets such as Pushkin to reflect the female taste and style of the salon. Russia barely had a national literature until Pushkin appeared on the literary scene (hence his god-like status in that society). 'In Russia', wrote Madame de Staël in the early 1800s, 'literature consists of a few gentlemen.'[103] By the 1830s, when Russia had a growing and vibrant literature, the persistence of attitudes like this had become a source of literary satire by patriotic writers such as Pushkin. In his story *The Queen of Spades* (1834), the old countess, a lady from the reign of Catherine the Great, is astonished when her grandson, whom she has requested to bring her a new novel, asks if she would like a Russian one. 'Are there any Russian novels?' the old lady asks.[104] Yet at the time when de Staël was writing the absence of a major literary canon was a source of great embarrassment to literate Russians. In 1802 the poet and historian Nikolai Karamzin compiled a 'Pantheon of Russian Writers', beginning with the ancient bard Bojan and ending in the present day: it stretched to only twenty names. The literary high points of the eighteenth century – the satires of Prince Antioch Kantemir, the odes of Vasily Trediakovsky and Alexander Sumarokov, the poetry of Lomonosov and Derzhavin, the tragedies of Yakov Kniazhnin and the comedies of Denis Fonvizin – hardly amounted to a vibrant national literature. All their works were derived from genres in the neoclassical tradition. Some were little more than translations of European works with Russian names assigned to the characters and the action transferred to Russia. Vladimir Lukin, Catherine's court playwright, Russified a large number of French plays. So did Fonvizin in the 1760s. In the last three-quarters of the eighteenth century some 500 works of literature were published in Russia. But only seven were of Russian origin.[105]

The absence of a national literature was to haunt Russia's young intelligentsia in the early decades of the nineteenth century. Karamzin explained it by the absence of those institutions (literary societies, journals, newspapers) that helped constitute European society.[106] The Russian reading public was extremely small – a minuscule proportion of the total population in the eighteenth century – and publishing was dominated by the Church and the court. It was very difficult, if not impossible, for a writer to survive from his writings. Most Russian writers in the eighteenth century were obliged, as noblemen, to serve as state officials, and those like the fabulist Ivan Krylov who turned their backs on the civil service and tried to make a living from their own writings nearly always ended up extremely poor. Krylov was obliged to become a children's tutor in the houses of the rich. He worked for some time at the Fountain House.[107]

But the biggest impediment to the development of a national literature was the undeveloped state of the literary language. In France or England the writer wrote largely as people spoke; but in Russia there was a huge divide between the written and the spoken forms of the language. The written language of the eighteenth century was a clumsy combination of archaic Church Slavonic, a bureaucratic jargon known as Chancery, and Latinisms imported by the Poles. There was no set grammar or orthography, and no clear definition of many abstract words. It was a bookish and obscure language, far removed from the spoken idiom of high society (which was basically French) and the plain speech of the Russian peasantry.

Such was the challenge that confronted Russia's poets at the beginning of the nineteenth century: to create a literary language that was rooted in the spoken language of society. The essential problem was that there were no terms in Russian for the sort of thoughts and feelings that constitute the writer's lexicon. Basic literary concepts, most of them to do with the private world of the individual, had never been developed in the Russian tongue: 'gesture', 'sympathy', 'privacy', 'impulsion' and 'imagination' – none could be expressed without the use of French.[108] Moreover, since virtually the whole material culture of society had been imported from the West, there were, as Pushkin commented, no Russian words for basic things:

> But *pantaloons*, *gilet*, and *frock* –
> These words are hardly Russian stock.[109]

Hence Russian writers were obliged to adapt or borrow words from the French to express the sentiments and represent the world of their readers in high society. Karamzin and his literary disciples (including the young Pushkin) aimed to 'write as people speak' – meaning how the people of taste and culture spoke, and in particular the 'cultivated woman' of polite society, who was, they realized, their 'principal reader'.[110] This 'salon style' derived a certain lightness and refinement from its Gallicized syntax and phraseology. But its excessive use of French loan words and neologisms also made it clumsy and verbose. And in its way it was just as far removed from the plain speech of the people as the Church Slavonic of the eighteenth century. This was the language of social pretension that Tolstoy satirized in the opening passages of *War and Peace*:

Anna Pavlovna had had a cough for some days. She was, as she said, suffering from *la grippe*; *grippe* being then a new word in St Petersburg, used only by the *élite*.[111]

Yet this salon style was a necessary stage in the evolution of the literary language. Until Russia had a wider reading public and more writers who were willing to use plain speech as their literary idiom, there would be no alternative. Even in the early nineteenth century, when poets such as Pushkin tried to break away from the foreign hold on the language by inventing Russian words, they needed to explain these to their salon audience. Hence in his story 'The Peasant Girl', Pushkin had to clarify the meaning of the Russian word '*samobytnost*'' by adding in parenthesis its French equivalent, '*individualité*'.[112]

5

In November 1779 the Hermitage court theatre in St Petersburg staged the première of Kniazhnin's comic opera *Misfortune from a Carriage*. It was an ironic venue for this hilarious satire on the slavish imitation of foreign ways. The sumptuous theatre, recently constructed by the Italian Quarenghi in the Winter Palace, was the home of the French opera, the most prestigious of the foreign companies. Its élite public was impeccably turned out in the latest French clothes and hairstyles. Here was precisely the sort of Gallomania that Kniazhnin's opera blamed for the moral corruption of society. The opera tells the story of a pair of peasant lovers, Lukian and Anyuta, who are prevented from getting married by their master's jealous bailiff, Klimenty, who desires Anyuta for himself. As serfs, the pair belong to a foolish noble couple called the Firiulins (the 'Ninnies') whose only aim in life is to ape the newest fashions in Paris. The Firiulins decide that they must have a new coach that is all the rage. To raise the cash they instruct Klimenty to sell some of their serfs into military service. Klimenty picks Lukian. It is only when the lovers plead with their owners in the sentimental language of the Gallicized salon that Lukian is finally released. Until then, the Firiulins had regarded them as simply Russian serfs, and hence, they assumed, entirely unaffected by such emotions as love. But everything is put into a different perspective once Lukian and Anyuta speak in French clichés.[113]

Kniazhnin's satire was one of several to equate the foreign pretensions of Petersburg with the moral ruin of society. The Petersburg dandy, with his fashionable clothes, his ostentatious manners and effeminate French speech, had become an anti-model of the 'Russian man'. He was the butt of comedies, from the character of Medor in Kantemir's satire *A Poor Lesson* (1729) to Fonvizin's Ivan in *The Brigadier* (1769). These comedies contained the ingredients of a national consciousness based on the antithesis of foreign and native. The decadent and artificial manners of the fop were contrasted with the simple, natural virtues of the peasantry; the material seductions of the European city with the spiritual values of the Russian countryside. Not only did the young dandy speak a foreign language to his Russian elders (whose inability to understand his Gallicisms was a source of comic misunderstanding), he also lived by a foreign moral code that threatened Russia's patriarchal traditions. In Kheraskov's comedy *The Detester*, which ran in Petersburg during the same year as *Misfortune from a Carriage*, the dandy figure Stovid advises a friend, who is unable to persuade a young girl to go out with him against her parents' wishes, to 'convince her that in Paris a child's love for her parents is considered philistine'. The impressionable girl is won over by this argument, and Stovid then relates how he heard her tell her father: '"Stay away! In France fathers do not keep the company of their children, and only merchants let their hands be kissed by their daughters." And then she spat at him.'[114]

At the heart of all these satires was the notion of the West as a negation of Russian principles. The moral lesson was simple: through their slavish imitation of Western principles, the aristocrats had lost all sense of their own nationality. Striving to make themselves at home with foreigners, they had become foreigners at home.

The nobleman who worships France – and thus despises Russia – was a stock character in all these comedies. 'Why was I born a Russian?' laments Diulezh in Sumarokov's *The Monsters* (1750). 'O Nature! Are you not ashamed to have given me a Russian father?' Such was his contempt for his fellow countrymen that in a sequel to the play, Diulezh even challenges an acquaintance to a duel because he had dared to call him a 'fellow Russian and a brother'.[115] Fonvizin's Ivan, in *The Brigadier*, considers France his 'spiritual homeland' for the simple reason that he was once taught by a French coachman. Returning from a trip to France, Ivan proclaims that 'anyone who has ever been in Paris has the right not to count himself a Russian any more'.[116]

This literary type continued as a mainstay of the nineteenth-century stage. Alexander Griboedov's Chatsky in *Woe from Wit* (1822–4) becomes so immersed in European culture on his travels that he cannot bear to live in Moscow on his return. He departs again for Paris, claiming there is no longer any place for him in Russian life. Chatsky was a proto-type of those 'superfluous men' who inhabit nineteenth-century Russian literature: Pushkin's *Eugene Onegin*, Lermontov's Pechorin (the *Hero of Our Times* (1840)), Turgenev's *Rudin* (1856); the root of all their troubles a sense of alienation from their native land.

There were many Chatskys in real life. Dostoevsky encountered some of them in the Russian émigré communities of Germany and France in the 1870s:

[T]here have been all sorts of people [who have emigrated] but the vast majority, if not all of them, have more or less hated Russia, some of them on moral grounds, on the conviction that 'in Russia there's nothing to do for such decent and intelligent people as they', others simply hating her without any convictions – naturally, one might say, physically: for her climate, her fields, her forests, her ways, her liberated peasants, her Russian history: in short, hating her for absolutely everything.[117]

But it was not just the émigrés – or the almost permanent encampment of wealthy Russians in the spa and sea resorts of Germany and France – who became divorced from their native land. The whole idea of a European education was to make the Russian feel as much at home in Paris as in Petersburg. This education made for a certain cosmopolitanism, which was one of Russia's most enduring cultural strengths. It gave the educated classes a sense that they belonged to a broader European civilization, and this was the key to the supreme achievements of their national culture in the nineteenth century. Pushkin, Tolstoy, Turgenev, Tchaikovsky, Diaghilev and Stravinsky – they all combined their Russianness with a European cultural identity. Writing from the summit of the 1870s, Tolstoy evoked the almost magic charm of this European world as seen through the eyes of Levin as he falls in love with the Shcherbatsky household in *Anna Karenina* (1873–6):

Strange as it may seem, Levin was in love with the whole family – especially the feminine half of it. He could not remember his mother, and his only sister was older than himself, so that in the Shcherbatskys' house he encountered for the first time the home life of a cultured, honourable family of the old aristocracy, of which he had been deprived by the death of his own father and mother. All the members of the family, in particular the feminine half, appeared to him as though wrapped in some mysterious, poetic veil, and he not only saw no defects in them but imagined behind that poetic veil the loftiest sentiments and every possible perfection. Why the three young ladies had to speak French one day and English the next; why they had, at definite times and each in her turn, to practise the piano (the sound of which reached their brothers' room upstairs, where the boys were studying); why those masters of French literature, music, drawing, and dancing came to the house; why at certain hours the three young ladies accompanied by Mademoiselle Linon were driven in a barouche to the Tverskoy boulevard wearing satin pelisses – long for Dolly, shorter for Natalie, and so short for Kitty that her shapely little legs in the tightly pulled-up red stockings were quite exposed; why they had to walk up and down the Tverskoy boulevard accompanied by a footman with a gold cockade in his hat – all this and much more that happened in their mysterious world he did not understand; but he knew that everything was perfect, and he was in love with the mystery of it all.[118]

Yet this sense of being part of Europe also made for divided souls. 'We Russians have two fatherlands: Russia and Europe,' Dostoevsky wrote. Alexander Herzen was a typical example of this Westernized élite. After meeting him in Paris Dostoevsky said that he did not emigrate – he was born an emigrant. The nineteenth-century writer Mikhail Saltykov-Shchedrin explained this condition of internal exile well. 'In Russia,' he recalled of the 1840s, 'we existed only in a factual sense, or as it was said then, we had a "mode of life". We went to the office, we wrote letters to our relatives, we dined in restaurants, we conversed with each other and so on. But spiritually we were all inhabitants of France.'[119] For these European Russians, then, 'Europe' was not just a place. It was a region of the mind which they inhabited through their education, their language, their religion and their general attitudes.

They were so immersed in foreign languages that many found it challenging to speak or write their own. Princess Dashkova, a vocal advocate of Russian culture and the only female president ever of the Russian Academy of Sciences, had the finest European education. 'We were instructed in four different languages, and spoke French fluently,' she wrote in her memoirs, 'but my Russian was extremely poor.'[120] Count Karl Nesselrode, a Baltic German and Russia's foreign minister from 1815 to 1856, could not write or even speak the language of the country he was meant to represent. French was the language of high society, and in high-born families the language of all personal relationships as well. The Volkonskys, for example, a family whose fortunes we shall follow in this book, spoke mainly French among themselves. Mademoiselle Callame, a French governess in the Volkonsky household, recalled that in nearly fifty years of service she never heard the Volkonskys speak a word of Russian, except to give orders to the domestic staff. This was true even of Maria (née Raevskaya), the wife of Prince Sergei Volkonsky, Tsar Alexander's favourite aide-de-camp in 1812. Despite the fact that she had been brought up in the Ukrainian provinces, where noble families were more inclined to speak their native Russian tongue, Maria could not write in Russian properly. Her letters to her husband were in French. Her spoken Russian, which she had picked up from the servants, was very primitive and full of peasant slang. It was a common paradox that the most refined and cultured Russians could speak only the peasant form of Russian which they had learnt from the servants as children.[121] Here was the European culture of Tolstoy's *War and Peace* – a culture in which Russians 'spoke in that refined French in which our grandfathers not only spoke but thought'.[122] They conversed in their native Russian as if they were Frenchmen who had only been in Russia for a year.

This neglect of the Russian language was most pronounced and persistent in the highest echelons of the aristocracy, which had always been the most Europeanized (and in more than a few cases of foreign origin). In some families children were forbidden to speak Russian except on Sundays and religious holidays. During her entire education Princess Ekaterina Golitsyn had only seven lessons in her native tongue. Her mother was contemptuous of Russian literature and thought Gogol was 'for the coachmen'. The Golitsyn children had a French governess and, if she ever caught them speaking Russian, she would punish them by tying a red cloth in the shape of a devil's tongue around their necks.[123] Anna Lelong had a similar experience at the Girls' Gymnasium, the best school for noble daughters in Moscow. Those girls caught speaking Russian were made to wear a red tin bell all day and stand like dunces, stripped of their white aprons, in the corner of the class; they were forced to remain standing even during meals, and received their food last.[124] Other children were even more severely punished if they spoke Russian – sometimes even locked in a room.[125] The attitude seems to have been that Russian, like the Devil, should be beaten out of noble children from an early age, and that even the most childish feelings had to be expressed in a foreign tongue. Hence that tiny yet revealing episode in the Oblonsky drawing-room in *Anna Karenina*, when Dolly's little daughter comes into the room where her mother is in conversation with Levin:

'You are very, very absurd!' Dolly repeated, tenderly looking into his face. 'Very well, then, let it be as though we had not spoken a word about it. What is it, Tanya?' she said in French to the little girl who had come in.

'Where's my spade, Mama?'

'I am speaking French, and you must answer in French.'

The little girl tried to, but she could not remember the French for spade; her mother prompted her, and then told her in French where to look. All this made a disagreeable impression on Levin.

Everything in Dolly's house and children struck him now as by no means so charming as before.

'Why does she talk French with the children?' he thought. 'It's so affected and unnatural. And the children sense it. Learning French and unlearning sincerity,' he thought to himself, unaware that Dolly had reasoned over and over again in the same fashion and yet had decided that, even at the cost of some loss of sincerity, the children must be taught French in that way.[126]

Such attitudes continued to be found in high-born families throughout the nineteenth century, and they shaped the education of some of Russia's most creative minds. As a boy in the 1820s, Tolstoy was instructed by the kind of German tutor he portrayed so memorably in *Childhood* (1852). His aunt taught him French. But apart from a few of Pushkin's poems, Tolstoy had no contact with Russian literature before he went to school at the age of nine. Turgenev was taught by French and German tutors, but he only learned to read and write in Russian thanks to the efforts of his father's serf valet. He saw his first Russian book at the age of eight, after breaking into a locked room that contained his father's Russian library. Even at the turn of the twentieth century there were Russian noblemen who barely spoke the language of their fellow countrymen. Vladimir Nabokov described his 'Uncle Ruka', an eccentric diplomat, as talking in a

fastidious combination of French, English and Italian, all of which he spoke with vastly more ease than he did his native tongue. When he resorted to Russian, it was invariably to misuse or garble some extremely idiomatic or even folksy expression, as when he would say at table with a sudden sigh: '*Je suis triste et seul comme une bylinka v pole* (as lonesome as a "grass blade in the field").'[127]

Uncle Ruka died in Paris at the end of 1916, the last of the old-world Russian aristocracy.

The Orthodox religion was equally remote from the consciousness of the Westernized élites. For religion played but a minor role in the upbringing of the aristocracy. Noble families, immersed in the secular culture of the French Enlightenment, thought little of the need to educate their children in the Russian faith, although by force of habit and conformity they continued to baptize them in the state religion and observed its rituals. The Voltairean attitudes that ruled in many noble households brought a greater sense of religious tolerance – which was just as well since, with all their foreign tutors and their peasant serfs, the palace could be home to several different faiths. Orthodoxy, in so far as it was practised mainly in the servants' quarters, came at the bottom of the social pile – below the Protestantism of the German tutors and the Catholicism of the French. This pecking order was reinforced by the fact that there was no Russian Bible – only a Psalter and a Book of Hours – until the 1870s. Herzen read the New Testament in German and went to church in Moscow with his Lutheran mother. But it was only when he was fifteen (and then only because it was an entry requirement for Moscow University) that his father hired a Russian priest to instruct him in the Orthodox religion. Tolstoy received no formal religious education as a child, while Turgenev's mother was openly contemptuous of Orthodoxy, which she saw as the religion of the common people, and instead of the usual prayers at meals substituted a daily reading from a French translation of Thomas à Kempis. This tendency to patronize Orthodoxy as a 'peasant faith' was commonplace among the aristocracy. Herzen told the story of a dinner-party host who, when asked if he was serving Lenten dishes out of personal conviction, replied that it was 'simply and solely for the sake of the servants'.[128]

Set against this domination by Europe, satires such as Kniazhnin's and Kheraskov's began to define the Russian character in terms which were distinct from the values of the West. These writers set up the antithesis between foreign artifice and native truth, European reason and the Russian heart or 'soul', that would form the basis of the national narrative in the nineteenth century. At the heart of this discourse was the old romantic ideal of the native soil – of a pure 'organic' Russia uncorrupted by civilization. St Petersburg was all deceit and vanity, a narcissistic dandy constantly observing its own reflection in the Neva river. The real Russia was in the provinces, a place without pretensions or alien conventions, where simple 'Russian' virtues were preserved.

For some this was a question of the contrast between Moscow and St Petersburg. The roots of the Slavophile movement go back to the late eighteenth century and the defence of the old gentry culture of Moscow and its provinces against the Europeanizing Petrine state. The landed gentry, it was said, were closer to the customs and religion of the people than Peter's courtiers and career bureaucrats. The writer Mikhail Shcherbatov was the most vocal spokesman of the old nobility. In his *Journey to the Land of Ophir* (1784) he portrays a northern country ruled by the king Perega from his newly founded city of Peregrab. Like St Petersburg, the intended object of Shcherbatov's satire, Peregrab is cosmopolitan and sophisticated but it is alien to the national traditions of Ophir, whose people still adhere to the moral virtues of Kvamo (read: Moscow), their former capital. At last the people of Peregrab rise up, the city falls and Ophir is returned to Kvamo's simple way of life. Such idyllic views of the unspoilt past were commonplace in Rousseau's age. Even Karamzin, a Westernist who was certainly not nostalgic for the old nobility, idealized the 'virtuous and simple life of our ancestors', when 'the Russians were real Russians', in his story *Natalia* (1792).

For others, Russia's virtues were preserved in the traditions of the countryside. Fonvizin found them in the Christian principles of the 'old thinker' Starodum, the homespun village mystic in his satire *The Minor* (1782). 'Have a heart, have a soul, and you'll always be a man,' advises Starodum. 'Everything else is fashion.'[129] The idea of a truly Russian self that had been concealed and suppressed by the alien conventions of Petersburg society became commonplace. It had its origins in the sentimental cult of rural innocence – a cult epitomized by Karamzin's tearful tale of *Poor Liza* (1792). Karamzin tells the story of a simple flower girl who is deceived in love by a dandy from St Petersburg and kills herself by drowning in a lake. The tale contained all the elements of this vision of a new community: the myth of the wholesome Russian village from which Liza is ejected by her poverty; the corruption of the city with its foreign ways; the tragic and true-hearted Russian heroine; and the universal ideal of marriage based on love.

Poets like Pyotr Viazemsky idealized the village as a haven of natural simplicity:

> Here there are no chains,
> Here there is no tyranny of vanity.[130]

Writers like Nikolai Novikov pointed to the village as the place where native customs had survived. The Russian was at home, he behaved more like himself, when he lived close to the land.[131] For Nikolai Lvov, poet, engineer, architect, folklorist, the main Russian trait was spontaneity.

> In foreign lands all goes to a plan,
> Words are weighed, steps measured.
> But among us Russians there is fiery life,
> Our speech is thunder and sparks fly.[132]

Lvov contrasted the convention-ridden life of the European Russians with the spontaneous behaviour and creativity of the Russian peasantry. He called on Russia's poets to liberate themselves from the constraints of the classical canon and find inspiration from the free rhythms of folk song and verse.

Central to this cult of simple peasant life was the notion of its moral purity. The radical satirist Alexander Radishchev was the first to argue that the nation's highest virtues were contained in the culture of its humblest folk. His proof for this was teeth. In his *Journey from St Petersburg to Moscow* (1790) Radishchev recalls an encounter with a group of village women dressed up in their traditional costumes for a holiday – their broad smiles 'revealing rows of teeth whiter than the purest ivory'. The ladies of the aristocracy, who all had rotten teeth, would 'be driven mad by teeth like these':

Come hither, my dear Moscow and Petersburg ladies, look at their teeth and learn from them how they keep them white. They have no dentists. They do not scrape their teeth with brushes and powders every day. Stand mouth to mouth with any one of them you choose: not one of them will infect your lungs with her breath. While yours, yes yours may infect them with the germ – of a disease . . . I am afraid to say what disease.[133]

6

In eighteenth-century panoramas of St Petersburg the open sky and space connect the city with a broader universe. Straight lines stretch to the distant horizon, beyond which, we are asked to imagine, lies the rest of Europe within easy reach. The projection of Russia into Europe had always been the *raison d'être* of St Petersburg. It was not simply Peter's 'window on to Europe' – as Pushkin once described the capital – but an open doorway through which Europe entered Russia and the Russians made their entry to the world.

For Russia's educated élites Europe was more than a tourist destination. It was a cultural ideal, the spiritual source of their civilization, and to travel to it was to make a pilgrimage. Peter the Great was the model of the Russian traveller to the West in search of self-improvement and enlightenment. For the next two hundred years Russians followed Peter's journey to the West. The sons of the Petersburg nobility went to universities in Paris, Göttingen and Leipzig. The 'Göttingen soul' assigned by Pushkin to Lensky, the fashionable student in *Eugene Onegin*, became a sort of emblem of the European outlook shared by generations of Russian noblemen:

> Vladimir Lensky, just returning
> From Göttingen with soulful yearning,
> Was in his prime – a handsome youth
> And poet filled with Kantian truth.
> From misty Germany our squire
> Had carried back the fruits of art:
> A freedom-loving, noble heart,
> A spirit strange but full of fire,
> An always bold, impassioned speech,
> And raven locks of shoulder reach.[134]

All the pioneers of Russia's arts learned their crafts abroad: Trediakovsky, the country's first real poet, was sent by Peter to study at the University of Paris; Andrei Matveev and Mikhail Avramov, its first secular painters, were sent to France and Holland; and, as we have seen, Berezovsky, Fomin and Bortnyansky learned their music in Italy. Mikhail Lomonosov, the nation's first outstanding scholar and scientist, studied chemistry at Marburg, before returning to help found Moscow University, which today bears his name. Pushkin once quipped that the polymath '*was* our first university'.[135]

The Grand Tour was a vital rite of passage for the aristocracy. The emancipation of the nobles from obligatory state service in 1762 had unleashed Russia's more ambitious and curious gentry on the world. They arrived in droves in Paris, Amsterdam and Vienna. But England was their favourite destination. It was the homeland of a prosperous and independent landed gentry, which the Russian nobles aspired to become. Their Anglomania was sometimes so extreme that it bordered on the denial of their own identity. 'Why was I not born an Englishwoman?' lamented Princess Dashkova, a frequent visitor to and admirer of England, who had sung its praises in her celebrated *Journey of a Russian Noblewoman* (1775).[136] Russians flocked to the sceptred isle to educate themselves in the latest fashions and the designs of its fine houses, to acquire new techniques of estate management and landscape gardening, and to buy *objets d'art*, carriages and wigs and all the other necessary accoutrements of a civilized lifestyle.

The travel literature that accompanied this traffic played a vital role in shaping Russia's self-perception *vis-à-vis* the West. Karamzin's *Letters of a Russian Traveller* (1791–1801), the most influential of this genre, educated a whole generation in the values and ideas of European life. Karamzin left St Petersburg in May 1789. Then, travelling first through Poland, Germany and Switzerland, he entered revolutionary France in the following spring before returning via London to the Russian capital. Karamzin provided his readers with a panorama of the ideal European world. He described its monuments, its theatres and museums, celebrated writers and philosophers. His 'Europe' was a mythic realm which later travellers, whose first encounter with Europe had been through reading his work, would look for but never really find. The historian Mikhail Pogodin took the *Letters* with him when he went to Paris in 1839. Even the poet Mayakovsky responded to that city, in 1925, through the sentimental prism of Karamzin's work.[137] The *Letters* taught the Russians how to act and feel as cultivated Europeans. In his letters Karamzin portrayed himself as perfectly at ease, and accepted as an equal, in Europe's intellectual circles. He described relaxed conversations with Kant and Herder. He showed himself approaching Europe's cultural monuments, not as some barbaric Scythian, but as an urbane and cultivated man who was already familiar with them from books and paintings. The overall effect was to present Europe as something close to Russia, a civilization of which it was a part.

Yet Karamzin also managed to express the insecurity which all the Russians felt in their European self-identity. Everywhere he went he was constantly reminded of Russia's backward image in the European mind. On the road to Königsberg two Germans were 'amazed to learn that a Russian could speak foreign languages'. In Leipzig the professors talked about the Russians as 'barbarians' and could not believe that they had any writers of their own. The French were even worse, combining a condescension towards the Russians as students of their culture with contempt for them as 'monkeys who know only how to imitate'.[138] At times such remarks provoked Karamzin to exaggerated claims for Russia's achievements. As he travelled around Europe, however, he came to the conclusion that its people had a way of thinking that was different from his own. Even after a century of reform, it seemed to him that perhaps the Russians had been Europeanized in no more than a superficial way. They had adopted Western manners and conventions. But European values and sensibilities had yet to penetrate their mental world.[139]

Karamzin's doubts were shared by many educated Russians as they struggled to define their 'Europeanness'. In 1836 the philosopher Chaadaev was declared a lunatic for writing in despair that, while the Russians might be able to imitate the West, they were unable to internalize its essential moral values and ideas. Yet, as Herzen pointed out, Chaadaev had only said what every thinking Russian had felt for many years. These complex feelings of insecurity, of envy and resentment, towards Europe, still define the Russian national consciousness.

Five years before Karamzin set off on his travels, the writer and civil servant Denis Fonvizin had travelled with his wife through Germany and Italy. It was not their first trip to Europe. In 1777–8 they had toured the spas of Germany and France looking for a cure for Fonvizin's migraines. On this occasion it was a stroke, which paralysed his arm and made him slur his speech, that compelled the writer to go abroad. Fonvizin took notes and wrote letters home with his observations on foreign life and the character of various nationalities. These *Travel Letters* were the first attempt by a Russian writer to define Russia's spiritual traditions as different from, and indeed superior to, those of the West.

Fonvizin did not set out as a nationalist. Fluent in several languages, he cut the figure of a St Petersburg cosmopolitan, with his fashionable dress and powdered wig. He was renowned for the sharpness of his tongue and his clever wit, which he put to good effect in his many satires against Gallomania. But if he was repelled by the trivialities and false conventions of high society, this had less to do with xenophobia than with his own feelings of social alienation and superiority. The truth was that Fonvizin was a bit of a misanthrope. Whether in Paris or St Petersburg, he nursed a contempt for the whole beau monde – a world in which he moved as a senior bureaucrat in the Foreign Ministry. In his early letters from abroad Fonvizin depicted all the nations as the same. 'I have seen,' he wrote from France in 1778, 'that in any land there is much more bad than good, that people are people everywhere, that intelligence is rare and idiots abound in every country, and that, in a word, our country is no worse than any other.' This stance of cultural relativism rested on the idea of enlightenment as the basis of an international community. 'Worthwhile people,' Fonvizin concluded, 'form a single nation among themselves, regardless of the country they come from.'[140] In the course of his second trip, however, Fonvizin developed a more jaundiced view of Europe. He denounced its achievements in no uncertain terms. France, the symbol of 'the West', was Fonvizin's main target, perhaps in part because he was not received in the salons of its capital.[141] Paris was 'a city of moral decadence', of 'lies and hypocrisy', which could only corrupt the young Russian who came to it in search of that crucial '*comme il faut*'. It was a city of material greed, where 'money is the God'; a city of vanity and external appearances, where 'superficial manners and conventions count for everything' and 'friendship, honesty and spiritual values have no significance'. The French made a great deal of their 'liberty' but the actual condition of the ordinary Frenchman was one of slavery – for 'a poor man cannot feed himself except by slave labour, so that "liberty" is just an empty name'. The French philosophers were fraudulent because they did not practise what they preached. In sum, he concluded, Europe was a long way from the ideal the Russians imagined it to be, and it was time to acknowledge that 'life with us is better':

If any of my youthful countrymen with good sense should become indignant over the abuses and confusions prevalent in Russia and in his heart begin to feel estranged from her, then there is no better method of converting him to the love he should feel for his Fatherland than to send him to France as quickly as possible.[142]

The terms Fonvizin used to characterize Europe appeared with extraordinary regularity in subsequent Russian travel writing. 'Corrupt' and 'decadent', 'false' and 'superficial', 'materialist' and 'egotistical' – such was the Russian lexicon for Europe right up to the time of Herzen's *Letters from France and Italy* (1847–52) and Dostoevsky's *Winter Notes on Summer Impressions* (1862), a travel sketch which echoed Fonvizin's. In this tradition the journey was merely an excuse for a philosophical discourse on the cultural relationship between Europe and Russia. The constant repetition of these epithets signalled the emergence of an ideology – a distinctive view of Russia in the mirror of the West. The idea that the West was morally corrupt was echoed by virtually every Russian writer from Pushkin to the Slavophiles. Herzen and Dostoevsky placed it at the heart of their messianic visions of Russia's destiny to save the fallen West. The idea that the French were false and shallow became commonplace. For Karamzin, Paris was a capital of 'superficial splendour and enchantment'; for Gogol it had 'only a surface glitter that concealed an abyss of fraud and greed'.[143] Viazemsky portrayed France as a 'land of deception and falsity'. The censor and littérateur Alexander Nikitenko wrote of the French: 'They seem to have been born with a love of theatre and a bent to create it – they were created for showmanship. Emotions, principles, honour, revolution are all treated as play, as games.'[144] Dostoevsky agreed that the French had a unique talent for 'simulating emotions and feelings for nature'.[145] Even Turgenev, an ardent Westernizer, described them in *A Nest of Gentlefolk* (1859) as civilized and charming yet without any spiritual depth or intellectual seriousness. The persistence of these cultural stereotypes illustrates the mythical proportions of 'Europe' in the Russian consciousness. This imaginary 'Europe' had more to do with the needs of defining 'Russia' than with the West itself. The idea of 'Russia' could not exist without 'the West' (just as 'the West' could not exist without 'the Orient'). 'We needed Europe as an ideal, a reproach, an example,' Herzen wrote. 'If she were not these things we would have to invent her.'[146]

The Russians were uncertain about their place in Europe (they still are), and that ambivalence is a vital key to their cultural history and identity. Living on the margins of the continent, they have never been quite sure if their destiny is there. Are they of the West or of the East? Peter made his people face the West and imitate its ways. From that moment on the nation's progress was meant to be measured by a foreign principle; all its moral and aesthetic norms, its tastes and social manners, were defined by it. The educated classes looked at Russia through European eyes, denouncing their own history as 'barbarous' and 'dark'. They sought Europe's approval and wanted to be recognized as equals by it. For this reason they took a certain pride in Peter's achievements. His Imperial state, greater and more mighty than any other European empire, promised to lead Russia to modernity. But at the same time they were painfully aware that Russia was not 'Europe' – it constantly fell short of that mythical ideal – and perhaps could never become part of it. Within Europe, the Russians lived with an inferiority complex. 'Our attitude to Europe and the Europeans,' Herzen wrote in the 1850s, 'is still that of provincials towards the dwellers in a capital: we are servile and apologetic, take every difference for a defect, blush for our peculiarities and try to hide them.'[147] Yet rejection by the West could equally engender feelings of resentment and superiority to it. If Russia could not become a part of 'Europe', it should take more pride in being 'different'. In this nationalist mythology the 'Russian soul' was awarded a higher moral value than the material achievements of the West. It had a Christian mission to save the world.

Russia's idealization of Europe was profoundly shaken by the French Revolution of 1789. The Jacobin reign of terror undermined Russia's belief in Europe as a force of progress and enlightenment. 'The "Age of Enlightenment"'! I do not recognize you in blood and flames,' Karamzin wrote with bitterness in 1795.[148] It seemed to him, as to many of his outlook, that a wave of murder and destruction would 'lay waste to Europe', destroying the 'centre of all art and science and the precious treasures of the human mind'.[149] Perhaps history was a futile cycle, not a path of progress after all, in which 'truth and error, virtue and vice, are constantly repeated'? Was it possible that 'the human species had advanced so far, only to be compelled to fall back again into the depths of barbarism, like Sisyphus' stone'?[150]

Karamzin's anguish was widely shared by the European Russians of his age. Brought up to believe that only good things came from France, his compatriots could now see only bad. Their worst fears appeared to be confirmed by the horror stories which they heard from the émigrés who had fled Paris for St Petersburg. The Russian government broke off relations with revolutionary France. Politically the once Francophile nobility became Francophobes, as 'the French' became a byword for inconstancy and godlessness, especially in Moscow and the provinces, where Russian political customs and attitudes had always mixed with foreign convention. In Petersburg, where the aristocracy was totally immersed in French culture, the reaction against France was more gradual and complicated – there were many liberal noblemen and patriots (like Pierre Bezukhov in *War and Peace*) who retained their pro-French and Napoleonic views even after Russia went to war with France in 1805. But even in the capital there was a conscious effort by the aristocracy to liberate themselves from the intellectual empire of the French. The use of Gallicisms became frowned upon in the salons of St Petersburg. Russian noblemen gave up Cliquot and Lafite for *kvas* and vodka, *haute cuisine* for cabbage soup.

In this search for a new life on 'Russian principles' the Enlightenment ideal of a universal culture was finally abandoned for the national way. 'Let us Russians be Russians, not copies of the French', wrote Princess

Dashkova; 'let us remain patriots and retain the character of our ancestors'.[151] Karamzin, too, renounced 'humanity' for 'nationality'. Before the French Revolution he had held the view that 'the main thing is to be, not Slavs, but men. What is good for Man, cannot be bad for the Russians; all that Englishmen or Germans have invented for the benefit of mankind belongs to me as well, because I am a man'.[152] But by 1802 Karamzin was calling on his fellow writers to embrace the Russian language and 'become themselves':

Our language is capable not only of lofty eloquence, of sonorous descriptive poetry, but also of tender simplicity, of sounds of feeling and sensibility. It is richer in harmonies than French; it lends itself better to effusions of the soul ... Man and nation may begin with imitation but in time they must become themselves to have the right to say: 'I exist morally!'[153]

Here was the rallying cry of a new nationalism that flourished in the era of 1812.

2

overleaf:
Adolphe Ladurnier: View of the White Hall in the Winter Palace,
St Petersburg, *1838*

CHILDREN
OF 1812

1

At the height of Napoleon's invasion of Russia, in August 1812, Prince Sergei Volkonsky was delivering a report to the Emperor Alexander in St Petersburg. Alexander asked the young aide-de-camp about the morale of the troops. 'Your Majesty!' the prince replied. 'From the Supreme Commander to the ordinary soldier, every man is prepared to lay down his life in the patriotic cause.' The Emperor asked the same about the common people's mood, and again Volkonsky was full of confidence. 'You should be proud of them. For every single peasant is a patriot.' But when that question turned to the aristocracy, the prince remained silent. Prompted by the Emperor, Volkonsky at last said: 'Your Majesty! I am ashamed to belong to that class. There have been only words.'[1] It was the defining moment of Volkonsky's life – a life that tells the story of his country and his class in an era of national self-discovery.

There were many officers who lost their pride in class but found their countrymen in the ranks of 1812. For princes like Volkonsky it must have been a shock to discover that the peasants were the nation's patriots: as noblemen they had been brought up to revere the aristocracy as the 'true sons of the fatherland'. Yet for some, like Volkonsky, this revelation was a sign of hope as well – the hope that in its serfs the nation had its future citizens. These liberal noblemen would stand up for 'the nation' and the 'people's cause', in what would become known as the Decembrist uprising on 14 December 1825.* Their alliance with the peasant soldiers on the battlefields of 1812 had shaped their democratic attitudes. As one Decembrist later wrote, 'we were the children of 1812'.[2]

Sergei Volkonsky was born in 1788 into one of Russia's oldest noble families. The Volkonskys were descended from a fourteenth-century prince, Mikhail Chernigovsky, who had attained glory (and was later made a saint) for his part in Moscow's war of liberation against the Mongol hordes, and had been rewarded with a chunk of land on the

* They shall be referred to here as the Decembrists, even though they did not gain that name until after 1825.

Volkona river, to the south of Moscow, from which the dynasty derived its name.[3] As Moscow's empire grew, the Volkonskys rose in status as military commanders and governors in the service of its Grand Dukes and Tsars. By the 1800s the Volkonskys had become, if not the richest of the ancient noble clans, then certainly the closest to the Emperor Alexander and his family. Sergei's mother, Princess Alexandra, was the Mistress of the Robes to the Dowager Empress, the widow of the murdered Emperor Paul, and as such the first non-royal lady of the Empire. She lived for the most part in the private apartments of the Imperial family at the Winter Palace and, in the summer, at Tsarskoe Selo (where the schoolboy poet Pushkin once caused a scandal by jumping on this cold and forbidding woman whom he had mistaken for her pretty French companion Josephine). Sergei's uncle, General Paul Volkonsky, was a close companion of the Emperor Alexander and, under his successor Nicholas I, was appointed Minister of the Court, in effect the head of the royal household, a post he held for over twenty years. His brother Nikita was married to a woman, Zinaida Volkonsky, who became a maid of honour at Alexander's court and (perhaps less honourably) the Emperor's mistress. His sister Sophia was on first name terms with all the major European sovereigns. At the Volkonsky house in Petersburg – a handsome mansion on the Moika river where Pushkin rented rooms on the lower floor – there was a china service that had been presented to her by the King of England, George IV. 'That was not the present of a king,' Sophia liked to say, 'but the gift of a man to a woman.'[4] She was married to the Emperor's closest friend, Prince Pyotr Mikhailovich Volkonsky, who rose to become his general chief-of-staff.

Sergei himself had practically grown up as an extended member of the Imperial family. He was educated at the Abbot Nicola's on the Fontanka, an institute established by the émigrés from France and patronized by the most fashionable families of Petersburg. From there he graduated to the Corps des Pages, the most élite of the military schools, from which, naturally, he joined the Guards. At the battle of Eylau in 1807 the young cornet was wounded by a bullet in his side. Thanks to his mother's lobbying, he was transferred to the Imperial staff in St Petersburg, where he joined a select group of glamorous young men – the aides-de-camp to the Emperor. The Tsar was fond of the serious young man with charming manners and softly spoken views, even though his idol-worship of Napoleon – a cult shared at that time by many noblemen (like Pierre Bezukhov at the start of *War and Peace*) – was frowned upon at court. He called him 'Monsieur Serge', to distinguish him from his three brothers (who were also aides-de-camp) and the other Volkonskys in his entourage.[5] The prince dined with the Emperor every day. He was one of the few who were permitted to enter the Emperor's private apartments unannounced. The Grand Duke Nicholas – later to become Tsar Nicholas I – who was nine years younger than Sergei, would, as a boy, ask the aide-de-camp to position his toy soldiers in the formation of Napoleon's armies at Austerlitz.[6] Two decades later he sent his playmate to Siberia.

In 1808 Volkonsky returned to the army in the field and, in the course of the next four years, he took part in over fifty battles, rising by the age of twenty-four to the rank of major-general. Napoleon's invasion shook the Prince from the pro-French views he had held in common with much of the Petersburg élite. It stirred in him a new sense of 'the nation' that was based upon the virtues of the common folk. The patriotic spirit of the ordinary people in 1812 – the heroism of the soldiers, the burning-down of Moscow to save it from the French, and the peasant partisans who forced the Grande Armée to hurry back to Europe through the snow – all these were the signs, it seemed to him, of a national reawakening. 'Russia has been honoured by its peasant soldiers,' he wrote to his brother from the body-littered battlefield of Borodino on 26 August 1812. 'They may be only serfs, but these men have fought like citizens for their motherland.'[7]

He was not alone in entertaining democratic thoughts. Volkonsky's friend (and fellow Decembrist), the poet Fedor Glinka, was equally impressed by the patriotic spirit of the common folk. In his *Letters of a Russian Officer* (1815) he compared the serfs (who were 'ready to defend their motherland with scythes') with the aristocracy (who 'ran off to their estates' as the French approached Moscow).[8] Many officers came to recognize the peasant's moral worth. 'Every day,' wrote one, 'I meet peasant soldiers who are just as good and rational as any nobleman. These simple men have not yet been corrupted by the absurd conventions of our society, and they have their own moral ideas which are just as good.'[9] Here, it seemed, was the spiritual potential for a national liberation and spiritual rebirth. 'If only we could find a common language with these men', wrote one of the future Decembrists, 'they would quickly understand the rights and duties of a citizen.'[10]

Nothing in the background of these officers had prepared them for the shock of this discovery. As noblemen they had been brought up to regard their fathers' serfs as little more than human beasts devoid of higher virtues and sensibilities. But in the war they were suddenly thrown into the peasants' world: they lived in their villages, they shared their food and fears with the common soldiers, and at times, when they were wounded or lost without supplies, they depended on those soldiers' know-how to survive. As their respect for the common people grew, they adopted a more humanitarian approach to the men under their command. 'We rejected the harsh discipline of the old system,' recalled Volkonsky, 'and tried through friendship with our men to win their love and trust.'[11] Some set up field schools to teach the soldiers how to read. Others brought them into discussion circles where they talked about the abolition of serfdom and social justice for the peasantry. A number of future Decembrists drew up 'army constitutions' and other proposals to better the conditions of the soldiers in the ranks. These documents, which were based on a close study of the soldier's way of life, may be seen as embryonic versions of the ethnographic works which so preoccupied the Slavophile and democratic intelligentsia in the 1830s and 1840s. Volkonsky, for example, wrote a detailed set of 'Notes on the Life of the Cossacks in Our Battalions', in which he proposed a series of progressive measures (such as loans from the state bank, communal stores of grain and the establishment of public schools) to improve the lot of the poorer Cossacks and lessen their dependence on the richer ones.[12]

After the war these democratic officers returned to their estates with a new sense of commitment to their serfs. Many, like Volkonsky, paid for the upkeep of the soldiers' orphaned sons on their estates, or, like him, gave money for the education of those serfs who had shown their potential in the ranks of 1812.[13] Between 1818 and 1821 Count Mikhail Orlov and Vladimir Raevsky, both members of the Union of Welfare out of which the Decembrist conspiracy would evolve, established schools for soldiers in which they disseminated radical ideas of political reform. The benevolence of some of these former officers was extraordinary. Pavel Semenov dedicated himself to the welfare of his serfs with the fervour of a man who owed his life to them. At the battle of Borodino, a bullet hit the icon which he had been given by his soldiers and had worn around his neck. Semenov organized a clinic for his serfs, and turned his palace into a sanctuary for war widows and their families. He died from cholera in 1830 – an illness he contracted from the peasants in his house.[14]

For some officers it was not enough to identify themselves with the common people's cause: they wanted to take on the identity of common men themselves. They Russified their dress and behaviour in an effort to move closer to the soldiers in the ranks. They used Russian words in their military speech. They smoked the same tobacco as their men; and in contravention of the Petrine ban, they grew beards. To some extent such democratization was necessary. Denis Davydov, the cele-brated leader of the Cossack partisans, had found it very hard to raise recruits in the villages: the peasants saw his glittering Hussar uniform as alien and 'French'. Davydov was forced, as he noted in his diary, to 'conclude a peace with the villagers' before he could even speak to them. 'I learned that in a people's war it is not enough to speak the common tongue: one must also step down to the people's level in one's manners and one's dress. I began to wear a peasant's *kaftan*, I grew a beard, and instead of the Order of St Anne, I wore the image of St Nicholas.'[15] But the adoption of these peasant ways was more than just a strategy of quick-thinking officers. It was a declaration of their nationality.

Volkonsky took command of a partisan brigade and pursued Napo-leon's troops as far as Paris during 1813–14. The next year, with 20,000 roubles in his chest, a carriage and three servants provided by his mother, he travelled to Vienna for the Peace Congress. He then returned to Paris, where he moved in the circles of the political reformers Chateaubriand and Benjamin Constant, and went on to London, where he saw the principles of constitutional monarchy in operation as he watched the House of Commons discuss the lunacy of George III. Volkonsky had planned to go to the United States – 'a country that had captured the imagination of all Russian youth because of its independence and democracy' – but the resumption of the war with Napoleon's escape from Elba obliged him to return to Petersburg.[16] None the less, like those of many Decembrists, Volkonsky's views had been deeply influenced by his brief encounter with the West. It confirmed his conviction in the personal dignity of every human being – an essential credo of the Decembrists which lay at the foundation of their opposition to the autocratic system and serfdom. It formed his belief in meritocracy – a view strengthened by his conversations with Napoleon's officers, who impressed him with their free thought and confidence. How many Neys and Davouts had been stifled by the rigid caste system of the Russian army? Europe made him think of Russia's backwardness, of its lack of basic rights or public life, and helped him focus his attention on the need to follow Europe's liberal principles.

The young officers who came back from Europe were virtually unrecognizable to their parents. The Russia they returned to in 1815 was much the same as the Russia they had left. But they had greatly changed. Society was shocked by their 'rude peasant manners'.[17] And no doubt there was something of a pose – the swagger of the veteran – in these army ways. But they differed from their elders in far more than their manners and dress. They also differed from them in their artistic tastes and interests, their politics and general attitudes: they turned their backs on the frivolous diversions of the ballroom (though not their own revelry) and immersed themselves in serious pursuits. As one explained: 'We had taken part in the greatest events of history, and it was unbearable to return to the vacuous existence of St Petersburg, to listen to the idle chatter of old men about the so-called virtues of the past. We had advanced a hundred years.'[18] As Pushkin wrote in his verse 'To Chaadaev' in 1821:

> The fashionable circle is no longer in fashion.
> You know, my dear, we're all free men now.
> We keep away from society; don't mingle with the ladies.
> We've left them at the mercy of old men,
> The dear old boys of the eighteenth century.[19]

Dancing, in particular, was regarded as a waste of time. The men of 1812 wore their swords at formal balls to signal their refusal to take part. The salon was rejected as a form of artifice. Young men retreated to their studies and, like Pierre in *War and Peace*, went in search of the intellectual key to a simpler and more truthful existence. Together, the Decembrists formed a veritable 'university'. Between them they had an encyclopaedic range of expertise, from folklore, history and archaeology to mathematics and the natural sciences, and they published many learned works, as well as poetry and literature, in the leading journals of their day.

The alienation felt by these young men from their parents' generation and society was common to all 'children of 1812', poets and philosophers as well as officers. It left a profound imprint on the cultural life of Russia in the nineteenth century. The 'men of the last century' were defined by the service ethic of the Petrine state. They set great store by rank and hierarchy, order and conformity to rational rules. Alexander Herzen – who was actually born in 1812 – recalled how his father disapproved of all emotional display. 'My father disliked every sort of *abandon*, every sort of frankness; all this he called familiarity, just as he called every feeling sentimentality.'[20] But the children who grew up in Herzen's age were all impulsiveness and familiarity. They rebelled against the old disciplinarianism, blaming it for 'Russia's slave mentality', and they looked instead to advance their principles through literature and art.[21] Many withdrew from the military or civil service with the aim of leading a more honest life. As Chatsky put it, in Griboedov's drama *Woe from Wit*, 'I'd love to serve, but I am sickened by servility.'

It is hard to overstate the extent to which the Russian cultural renaissance of the nineteenth century entailed a revolt against the service ethic of the eighteenth century. In the established view, rank quite literally defined the nobleman: unlike all other languages, the word in Russian for an official (*chinovnik*) derived from that for rank (*chin*). To be a nobleman was to take one's place in the service of the state, either as a civil servant or as an officer; and to leave that service, even to become a poet or an artist, was regarded as a fall from grace. 'Service now in Russia is the same as life', wrote one official in the 1810s: 'we leave our offices as if we are going to our graves.'[22] It was inconceivable for a nobleman to be an artist or a poet, except in his spare time after office work, or as a gentleman enthusiast on his estate. Even the great eighteenth-century poet Gavril Derzhavin combined his writing with a military career, followed by appointments as a senator and provincial governor, before ending up as Minister of Justice in 1802–3.

During the early nineteenth century, as the market for books and painting grew, it became possible, if not easy, for the independent writer or artist to survive. Pushkin was one of the first noblemen to shun the service and take up writing as a 'trade'; his decision was seen as derogation or breaking of ranks. The writer N. I. Grech' was accused of bringing shame upon his noble family when he left the civil service to become a literary critic in the 1810s.[23] Music too was thought unsuitable as a profession for the nobleman. Rimsky-Korsakov was pushed into the naval service by his parents, who looked upon his music 'as a prank'.[24] Musorgsky was sent to the Cadet School in Petersburg and was then enrolled in the Preobrazhensky Guards. Tchaikovsky went to the School of Jurisprudence where his family expected him to graduate to the civil service and not forget but put away his childish passion for music. For the nobleman to become an artist, then, was to reject the traditions of his class. He had, in effect, to reinvent himself as an 'intelligent' – a member of the intelligentsia – whose duty was defined as service to 'the nation' rather than to the state.

Only two of the great nineteenth-century Russian writers (Goncharov and Saltykov-Shchedrin) ever held high rank in the government service, although nearly all of them were noblemen. Goncharov was a censor. But Saltykov-Shchedrin was a tireless critic of the government, and as a vice-governor and a writer he always took the side of the 'little man'. It was axiomatic to this literary tradition that the writer should stand up for human values against the service ethic based on rank. Thus in Gogol's 'The Diary of a Madman' (1835), the literary lunatic, a humble councillor, ridicules a senior official: 'And what if he is a gentleman of the court? It's only a kind of distinction conferred on you, not something that you can see, or touch with your hands. A court chamberlain doesn't have a third eye in the middle of his forehead.' Similarly, in Chekhov's story 'Abolished!' (1891) we are meant to laugh at the retired major (Izhits) who is thrown into confusion by the abolition of his former rank: 'God knows who I am,' the old major says. 'They abolished all the majors a year ago!'[25]

Unwilling to conform to their fathers' rules and bored by the routines of the civil service, the young men of Pushkin's generation sought release in poetry, philosophy and drunken revelry. As Silvio remarks in Pushkin's *Tales of Belkin* (1831), wild behaviour 'was the fashion in our day'.[26] Carousing was perceived as a sign of freedom, an assertion of the individual spirit against the regimentation of the army and bureaucracy. Volkonsky and his fellow officers demonstrated their independence from the deferential customs of high society by mocking those who followed the Emperor and his family on their Sunday promenades around St Petersburg.[27] Another officer, the Decembrist Mikhail Lunin, was well known for his displays of the free will. On one occasion he turned his brilliant wit against a general who had forbidden his officers to 'offend propriety' by bathing in the sea at Peterhof, a fashionable resort on the Gulf of Finland near St Petersburg where there was a garrison. One hot afternoon Lunin waited for the general to approach. He leapt into the water fully clothed, and stood at attention and saluted him. The bewildered general asked what this was all about. 'I am swimming,' Lunin said, 'and so as not to disobey Your Excellency's order, I am swimming in a manner not to offend propriety.'[28]

The young men of the Decembrist circles spent much time in revelry. Some, like the serious Volkonsky, disapproved. But others, like Pushkin and his friends of the Green Lamp, a loose symposium of libertines and poets, saw the fight for freedom as a carnival. They found liberty in a mode of life and art that dispensed with the stifling conventions of society.[29] When they were playing cards or drinking and debating with their friends, they were able to relax and express themselves, 'as Russians', in the easy language of the street. This was the idiom of much of Pushkin's verse – a style that fused the language of politics and philosophical thought with the vocabulary of intimate emotion and the crude colloquialisms of the whorehouse and the inn.

Friendship was the saving grace of these wild orgies, according to Pushkin:

> For one can live in friendship
> With verses and with cards, with Plato and with wine,
> And hide beneath the gentle cover of our playful pranks
> A noble heart and mind.[30]

Volkonsky said the same of his fellow officers. They happily transgressed the public code of decency, but in their dealings with each other they kept themselves in moral check through the 'bonds of comradeship'.[31] There was a cult of brotherhood in the Decembrist camp. It evolved into the cult of the collective which would become so important to the political life of the Russian intelligentsia. The spirit was first forged in the regiment – a natural 'family' of patriots. Nikolai Rostov in *War and Peace* discovers this community on his return from leave. Suddenly he

felt for the first time how close was the bond that united him to Denisov and the whole regiment. On approaching [the camp] Rostov felt as he had done when approaching his home in Moscow. When he saw the first hussar with the unbuttoned uniform of his regiment, when he recognized red-haired Dementyev and saw the picket ropes of the roan horses, when Lavrushka gleefully shouted to his master, 'The Count has come!' and Denisov, who had been asleep on his bed, ran all dishevelled out of the mud hut to embrace him, and the officers collected round to greet the new arrival, Rostov experienced the same feeling as when his mother, his father, and his sister had embraced him, and tears of joy choked him so that he could not speak. The regiment was also a home, and as unalterably dear and precious as his parents' house.[32]

Through such bonds young officers began to break away from the rigid hierarchies of the service state. They felt themselves to belong to a new community – a 'nation', if you will – of patriotic virtue and fraternity where the noble and the peasant lived in harmony. The nineteenth-century quest for Russian nationhood began in the ranks of 1812.

This outlook was shared by all the cultural figures in the orbit of the Decembrists: not just by those in its leading ranks, but by those, more numerous, who sympathized with the Decembrists without actively engaging in plans for a rebellion ('Decembrists without December'). Most of the poets among them (Gnedich, Vostokov, Merzliakov, Odoevsky and Ryleev, though less so Pushkin) were preoccupied with civic themes. Renouncing the aesthetics and the frivolous concerns of Karamzin's salon style, they wrote epic verses in a suitably spartan style. Many of them compared the soldiers' bravery in the recent wars to the heroic deeds of ancient Greece and Rome.

Some monumentalized the peasants' daily toil; they raised it to the
status of patriotic sacrifice. The duty of the poet, as they saw it, was
to be a citizen, to dedicate himself to the national cause. Like all the
men of 1812, they saw their work as part of a democratic mission to
learn about and educate the common people so as to unite society on
Russian principles. They rejected the Enlightenment idea that 'all the
nations should become the same' and, in the words of one critic, called
on 'all our writers to reflect the character of the Russian folk'.[33]

Pushkin holds a special place in that enterprise. He was too young
– just thirteen in 1812 – to fight against the French, but as a schoolboy
at the *lycée* he watched the Guards from the garrison at Tsarskoe Selo
march off to war. The memory remained with him throughout his life:

> You'll recollect: the wars soon swept us by,
> We bade farewell to all our elder brothers,
> And went back to our desks with all the others,
> In envy of all those who had gone to die
> Without us . . .[34]

Though Pushkin, unlike them, had never been to Europe, he breathed
the European air. As a boy he had immersed himself in the French
books of his father's library. His first verse (written at the age of eight)
was composed in French. Later he discovered Byron's poetry. This
European heritage was strengthened by the years he spent between
1812 and 1817 at the *lycée* at Tsarskoe Selo – a school modelled on
the Napoleonic *lycées* that drew heavily on the curriculum of the
English public schools, stressing the humanities: classical and modern
languages, literature, philosophy and history. The cult of friendship
was strong at the *lycée*. The friendships he formed there strengthened
Pushkin's sense of European Russia as a spiritual sphere:

> My friends, our union is wondrous!
> Like a soul, it will last for eternity –
> Undivided, spontaneous and joyous,
> Blessed by the muse of fraternity.
> Whatever partings destiny may bring,
> Whatever fortunes fate may have in hand,

We are still the same: the world to us an alien thing,
And Tsarskoe Selo our Fatherland.[35]

Yet, for all his Western inclinations, Pushkin was a poet with a Russian
voice. Neglected by his parents, he was practically brought up by his
peasant nurse, whose tales and songs became a lifelong inspiration for
his verse. He loved folk tales and he often went to country fairs to pick
up peasant stories and turns of phrase which he then incorporated in
his poetry. Like the officers of 1812, he felt that the landowner's
obligation as the guardian of his serfs was more important than his
duty to the state.[36]

He felt this obligation as a writer, too, and looked to shape a written
language that could speak to everyone. The Decembrists made this a
central part of their philosophy. They called for laws to be written in
a language 'that every citizen can understand'.[37] They attempted to
create a Russian lexicon of politics to replace imported words. Glinka
called for a history of the war of 1812 to be written in a language that
was 'plain and clear and comprehensible by people of all classes,
because people of all classes took part in the liberation of our motherland'.[38] The creation of a national language seemed to the veterans of
1812 a means of fostering the spirit of the battlefield and of forging a
new nation with the common man. 'To know our people', wrote the
Decembrist poet Alexander Bestuzhev, 'one has to live with them and
talk with them in their language, one has to eat with them and celebrate
with them on their feast days, go bear-hunting with them in the woods,
or travel to the market on a peasant cart.'[39] Pushkin's verse was the
first to make this link. It spoke to the widest readership, to the literate
peasant and the prince, in a common Russian tongue. It was Pushkin's
achievement to complete the creation of this national language through
his verse, and to use it with extraordinary grace.

2

Volkonsky returned to Russia in 1815 and took up the command of
the Azov regiment in the Ukraine. Like all the Decembrists, he was
deeply disillusioned by the reactionary turn taken by the Emperor

Alexander, on whom he had pinned his liberal hopes. In the first years of his reign (1801–12) Alexander had passed a series of political reforms: censorship was immediately relaxed; the Senate was promoted to the supreme judicial and administrative institution in the Empire – an important counterbalance to the personal power of the sovereign; a more modern system of government began to take shape with the establishment of eight new ministries and an upper legislative chamber (the State Council) modelled on Napoleon's Conseil d'Etat. There were even some preliminary measures to encourage noblemen to emancipate their serfs. To the liberal officers, Alexander seemed like one of them: a man of progressive and enlightened views.

The Emperor appointed his adviser Mikhail Speransky to draw up plans for a constitution that was largely based on the Code Napoléon. Had Speransky got his way, Russia would have moved toward becoming a constitutional monarchy governed by a law-based bureaucratic state. But Alexander hesitated to implement his minister's proposals and, once Russia went to war with France, they were condemned by the conservative nobility, which mistrusted them because they were 'French'. Speransky fell from power – to be replaced by General Arakcheev, the Minister of War, as the outstanding influence on Alexander's reign in its second half, from 1812 to 1825. The harsh regime of Arakcheev's military settlements, where serf soldiers were dragooned into farming and other labour duties for the state, enraged the men of 1812, whose liberal sympathies had been born of respect for the soldiers in the ranks. When the Emperor, against their opposition, persevered with the military camps and put down the peasants' resistance with a brutal massacre, the Decembrists were enraged. 'The forcible imposition of the so-called military colonies was received with amazement and hostility', recalled Baron Vladimir Steigel. 'Does history show anything similar to this sudden seizure of entire villages, this taking over of the houses of peaceful cultivators, this expropriation of everything which they and their forefathers earned and their involuntary transformation into soldiers?'[40] These officers had marched to Paris in the hope that Russia would become a modern European state. They had dreamed of a constitution where every Russian peasant would enjoy the rights of a citizen. But they came back disappointed men – to a Russia where the peasant was still treated as a slave. As

Volkonsky wrote, to return to Russia after Paris and London 'felt like going back to a prehistoric past'.[41]

The prince fell into the circle of Mikhail Orlov, an old school friend and fellow officer from 1812, who was well connected to the main Decembrist leaders in the south. At this stage the Decembrist movement was a small and secret circle of conspirators. It began in 1816, when six young Guards officers formed what they initially called the Union of Salvation, a clandestine organization committed to the establishment of a constitutional monarchy and a national parliament. From the start the officers were divided over how to bring this end about: some wanted to wait for the Tsar to die, whereupon they would refuse to swear their oath of allegiance to the next Tsar unless he put his name to their reforms (they would not break the oath they had already sworn to the present Tsar); but Alexander was not even forty years of age and some hotheads like Mikhail Lunin favoured the idea of regicide. In 1818 the society broke up – its more moderate members immediately regrouping as the Union of Welfare, with a rather vague programme of educational and philanthropic activities but no clear plan of action for revolt, although Count Orlov, a leading member of the Union, organized a brave petition to the Tsar calling for the abolition of serfdom. Pushkin, who had friends in the Decembrist camp, characterized their conspiracy as no more than a game in these immortal (but, in Tsarist times, unpublishable) lines intended for his novel *Eugene Onegin*, whose action was set in 1819:

> 'Twas all mere idle chatter
> 'Twixt Château-Lafite and Veuve Cliquot.
> Friendly disputes, epigrams
> Penetrating none too deep.
> This science of sedition
> Was just the fruit of boredom, of idleness,
> The pranks of grown-up naughty boys.[42]

Without a plan for insurrection, the Union concentrated on developing its loose network of cells in Petersburg and Moscow, Kiev, Kishinev and other provincial garrison towns like Tulchin, the headquarters of the Second Army, where Volkonsky was an active member. Volkonsky had entered Orlov's conspiracy through the Masonic Lodge in Kiev – a common means of entry into the Decembrist movement – where he also met the young Decembrist leader, Colonel Pavel Ivanovich Pestel.

Like Volkonsky, Pestel was the son of a provincial governor in western Siberia (their fathers were good friends).[43] He had fought with distinction at Borodino, had marched to Paris, and had returned to Russia with his head full of European learning and ideals. Pushkin, who met Pestel in 1821, said that he was 'one of the most original minds I have ever met'.[44] Pestel was the most radical of the Decembrist leaders. Charismatic and domineering, he was clearly influenced by the Jacobins. In his manifesto *Russian Truth* he called for the Tsar's overthrow, the establishment of a revolutionary republic (by means of a temporary dictatorship if necessary), and the abolition of serfdom. He envisaged a nation state ruling in the interests of the Great Russians. The other national groups – the Finns, the Georgians, the Ukrainians, and so on – would be forced to dissolve their differences and 'become Russian'. Only the Jews were beyond assimilation and, Pestel thought, should be expelled from Russia. Such attitudes were commonplace among the Decembrists as they struggled in their minds to reform the Russian Empire on the model of the European nation states. Even Volkonsky, a man of relatively enlightened views, referred to the Jews as 'little yids'.[45]

By 1825 Pestel had emerged as the chief organizer of an insurrection against the Tsar. He had a small but committed band of followers in the Southern Society, which had replaced the Union of Salvation in the south, and an ill-conceived plan to arrest the Tsar during his inspection of the troops near Kiev in 1826, and then march on Moscow and, with the help of his allies in the Northern Society in St Petersburg, seize power. Pestel brought Volkonsky into his conspiracy, placing him in charge of co-ordinating links with the Northern Society and with the Polish nationalists, who agreed to join the movement in exchange for independence should they succeed. The Northern Society was dominated by two men: Nikita Muraviev, a young Guards officer in 1812, who had built up good connections at the court; and the poet Ryleev, who attracted officers and liberal bureaucrats to his 'Russian lunches', where cabbage soup and rye bread were served up in preference to European dishes, vodka toasts were drunk to Russia's liberation from the foreign-dominated court, and revolutionary songs were sung. The Northern Society's political demands were more moderate than those of Pestel's group – a constitutional monarchy with a parliament and civil liberties. Volkonsky shuttled between Petersburg and Kiev, mustering support for Pestel's planned revolt. 'I have never been so happy as I was at that time', he later wrote. 'I took pride in the knowledge that I was doing something for the people – I was liberating them from tyranny.'[46] Although he was in love with, and then married to, Maria Raevsky, he saw very little of his beautiful young bride.

Maria was the daughter of General Raevsky, a famous hero of 1812 who had even been praised by Napoleon. Born in 1805, Maria met Volkonsky when she was seventeen; she had extraordinary grace and beauty for her years. Pushkin called her the 'daughter of the Ganges' on account of her dark hair and colouring. The poet was a friend of the Raevskys and had travelled with the general and his family to the Crimea and the Caucasus. According to some sources, Pushkin fell in love with Maria. He often fell in love with beautiful young girls – but this time perhaps it was serious, judging by the appearance of Maria in his poetry. At least two of Pushkin's heroines – Princess Maria in *The Fountain of Bakhchisarai* (1822) and the young Circassian girl in *The Prisoner of the Caucasus* (1820–21) – may have been inspired by her. It is perhaps significant that both are tales of unrequited love. The memory of Maria playing in the waves in the Crimea may have inspired him to write in *Eugene Onegin*:

> How I envied the waves –
> Those rushing tides in tumult tumbling
> To fall about her feet like slaves!
> I longed to join the waves in pressing
> Upon those feet these lips . . . caressing.[47]

Volkonsky was given the task of recruiting Pushkin to the conspiracy. Pushkin belonged to the broad cultural circles of the Decembrists and had many friends in the conspiracy (he later claimed that, had it not been for a hare that crossed his path and made him superstitious about travelling, he might well have gone to Petersburg to join his friends on Senate Square). As it was, he had been banished to his estate at Mikhailovskoe, near Pskov, because his poetry had inspired them:

There will rise, believe me, comrade
A star of captivating bliss, when
Russia wakes up from her sleep
And when our names will both be written
On the ruins of despotism.[48]

It seems, however, that Volkonsky was afraid of exposing the great poet to the risks involved – so he did not carry out this promise to Pestel. In any case, as Volkonsky no doubt knew, Pushkin was so famous for his indiscretion, and so well connected at court, that he would have been a liability.[49] Rumours of an uprising were already circulating around St Petersburg, so, in all likelihood, the Emperor Alexander knew about the Decembrists' plans. Volkonsky certainly thought so. During an inspection of his regiment, the Emperor gently warned him: 'Pay more attention to your troops and a little less to my government, which, I am sorry to say, my dear prince, is none of your business.'[50]

The insurrection had been scheduled for the late summer of 1826. But these plans were hastily brought forward by the Emperor's sudden death and the succession crisis caused by the refusal of the Grand Duke Constantine to accept the throne in December 1825. Pestel resolved to seize the moment for revolt, and with Volkonsky he travelled up from Kiev to St Petersburg for noisy arguments with the Northern society about the means and timing of the uprising. The problem was how to muster the support of the ordinary troops, who showed no inclination towards either regicide or armed revolt. The conspirators had only the vaguest notion of how to go about this task. They thought of the uprising as a military putsch, carried out by order from above; as its commanding officers, they based their strategy on the idea that they could somehow call upon their old alliance with the soldiers. They rejected the initiatives of some fifty junior officers, sons of humble clerks and small landowners, whose organization, the United Slavs, had called upon the senior leaders to agitate for an uprising among the soldiers and the peasantry. 'Our soldiers are good and simple', explained one of the Decembrist leaders. 'They don't think much and should serve merely as instruments in attaining our goals.'[51] Volkonsky shared this attitude. 'I am convinced that I will carry my brigade', he wrote to a friend on the eve of the revolt, 'for the simple reason that I have my soldiers' trust and love. Once the uprising commences they will follow my command.'[52]

In the end, the Decembrist leaders carried with them only some 3,000 troops in Petersburg – far less than the hoped-for 20,000 men, but still enough perhaps to bring about a change of government if well organized and resolute. But that they were not. On 14 December, in garrisons throughout the capital, soldiers were assembled for the ceremony of swearing an oath of allegiance to the new Tsar, Nicholas I. The 3,000 mutineers refused to swear their oath and, with flags unfurled and drums beating, marched to Senate Square, where they thronged in front of the *Bronze Horseman* and called for 'Constantine and a Constitution'. Two days earlier, Nicholas had decided to take the crown when Constantine had made it clear that he would not. Constantine had a large following among the soldiers, and when the Decembrist leaders heard the news, they sent out leaflets misinforming them that Nicholas had usurped the throne, and calling on them to 'fight for their liberty and human dignity'. Most of the soldiers who appeared on Senate Square had no idea what a 'constitution' was (some thought it was the wife of Constantine). They displayed no inclination to capture the Senate or the Winter Palace, as envisaged in the hasty plans of the conspirators. For five hours the soldiers stood in freezing temperatures, until Nicholas, assuming the command of his loyal troops, ordered them to commence firing against the mutineers. Sixty soldiers were shot down; the rest ran away.

Within hours the ringleaders of the insurrection had all been arrested and imprisoned in the Peter and Paul Fortress (the police had known who they were all along). The conspirators might still have had some chance of success in the south, where it was possible to combine with the Poles in a march on Kiev, and where the main revolutionary forces (something in the region of 60,000 troops) were massed in garrisons. But the officers who had previously declared their support for an uprising were now so shocked by the events in Petersburg that they dared not act. Volkonsky found only one officer who was prepared to join him in the call for a revolt, and in the end, the few hundred troops who marched on Kiev on 3 January were easily dispersed by the government's artillery.[53] Volkonsky was arrested two days later, while on his way to Petersburg to see Maria one last time. The police had an arrest warrant signed in person by the Tsar.

Five hundred Decembrists were arrested and interrogated, but most of them were released in the next few weeks, once they had provided evidence for the prosecution of the main leaders. At their trial, the first show trial in Russian history, 121 conspirators were found guilty of treason, stripped of their noble titles and sent as convict labourers to Siberia. Pestel and Ryleev were hanged with three others in a grotesque scene in the courtyard of the Fortress, even though officially the death penalty had been abolished in Russia. When the five were strung up on the gallows and the floor traps were released, three of the condemned proved too heavy for their ropes and, still alive, fell down into the ditch. 'What a wretched country!' cried out one of them. 'They don't even know how to hang properly.'[54]

Of all the Decembrists, none was closer to the court than Volkonsky. His mother, the Princess Alexandra, could be found in the Winter Palace, smiling in attendance on the Dowager Empress, at the same time as he sat, just across the Neva river in the Peter and Paul Fortress, a prisoner detained at His Majesty's pleasure. Nicholas was harsh on Volkonsky. Perhaps he felt betrayed by the man he had once played with as a boy. Thanks to the intervention of his mother, Volkonsky was spared the death sentence handed down to the other leaders. But twenty years of penal labour followed by a lifetime of compulsory settlement in Siberia was a draconian enough punishment. The prince was stripped of his noble title and all his medals from the battlefields of the wars against France. He lost control of all his lands and serfs. Henceforth his children would officially belong to the category of 'state peasants'.[55]

Count Alexander Benckendorff, the Chief of Police who sent him into exile, was an old school friend of Volkonsky. The two men had been fellow officers in 1812. Nothing better illustrates the nature of the Petersburg nobility, a small society of clans in which everybody knew each other, and most families were related in some way.* Hence the shame the Volkonskys felt on Sergei's disgrace. None the less, it is

---

* In 1859 Volkonsky's son Misha would marry the granddaughter of Count Benckendorff. One of his cousins would marry Benckendorff's daughter (S. M. Volkonskii, *O dekabristakh: po semeinum vospominaniiam*, p. 114).

hard to comprehend their attempt to erase his memory. Sergei's elder brother, Nikolai Repnin, disowned him altogether, and in the long years Volkonsky spent in Siberia he never sent him a single letter. A typical courtier, Nikolai was worried that the Tsar might not forgive him if he wrote to an exile (as if the Tsar was incapable of understanding the feelings of a brother). Such small-minded attitudes were symptomatic of an aristocracy which had been brought up to defer all values to the court. Sergei's mother, too, put her loyalty to the Tsar before her own feelings for her son. She attended the coronation of Nicholas I and received the diamond brooch of the Order of St Catherine on the same day as Sergei, with heavy chains around his feet, began the long journey to Siberia. An old-fashioned lady of the court, Princess Alexandra had always been a stickler for 'correct behaviour'. The next day she retired to her bed and stayed there, crying inconsolably. 'I only hope,' she would tell her visitors, 'that there will be no other monsters in the family.'[56] She did not write to her son for several years. Sergei was profoundly wounded by his mother's rejection: it contributed to his own rejection of the mores and the values of the aristocracy. In his mother's view, Sergei's civil death was a literal death as well. '*Il n'ya plus de Serge*,' the old princess would tell her courtly friends. 'These words', Sergei wrote in one of his last letters in 1865, 'haunted me throughout my life in exile. They were not just meant to satisfy her conscience but to justify her own betrayal of me.'[57]

Maria's family was just as unforgiving. They blamed her for her marriage and attempted to persuade her to use her right to petition for its annulment. They had reason to suppose that she might do so. Maria had a newborn son to think about and it was far from clear whether she would be allowed to take him with her if she followed Sergei to Siberia. Besides, she did not appear to be entirely happy in the marriage. During the past year – only the first year of their marriage – she had hardly seen her husband, who was absent in the south and preoccupied with the conspiracy, and she had complained to her family that she found the situation 'quite unbearable'.[58] Yet Maria chose to share her husband's fate. She gave up everything and followed Sergei to Siberia. Warned by the Tsar that she would have to leave her son behind, Maria wrote to him: 'My son is happy but my husband is unhappy and he needs me more.'[59]

It is hard to say exactly what was in Maria's mind. When she made her choice she did not realize that she would be stripped of the right to return to Russia if she followed Sergei – she was told only when she reached Irkutsk, on the border between Russia and the penal region of Siberia – so it is possible that she was expecting to return to Petersburg. That indeed was what her father thought. But would she have turned back if she had known?

Maria acted out of her sense of duty as a wife. Sergei appealed to this when he wrote to her from the Peter and Paul Fortress on the eve of his departure for Siberia. 'You yourself must decide what to do. I am placing you in a cruel situation, but *chère amie*, I cannot bear the sentence of eternal separation from my lawful wife.'[60] Such a sense of duty was ingrained in Maria by her noble upbringing. Romantic love, though by no means uncommon, was not a high priority in the conjugal relations of the early nineteenth-century Russian aristocracy. And nor does it seem to have played a major role in Maria's decision. In this sense she was very different from Alexandra Muraviev, the wife of the Decembrist Nikita Muraviev, who came from a rather less aristocratic background than Maria Volkonsky. It was romantic love that compelled Alexandra to give up everything for a life of penal exile in Siberia – she even claimed that it was her 'sin' to 'love my Nikitishchina more than I love God'.[61] Maria's conduct, by contrast, was conditioned by the cultural norms of a society in which it was not unusual for a noblewoman to follow her husband to Siberia. Convoys of prisoners were frequently accompanied by carts carrying their wives and children into voluntary exile.[62] There was a custom, moreover, for the families of officers to go along with them on military campaigns. Wives would speak about 'our regiment' or 'our brigade' and, in the words of one contemporary, 'they were always ready to share in all the dangers of their husbands, and lay down their lives'.[63] Maria's father, General Raevsky, took his wife and children on his main campaigns – until his young son was injured when a bullet pierced his breeches as he gathered berries near the battlefield.[64]

It has also been suggested that Maria was responding to the literary cult of heroic sacrifice.[65] She had read Ryleev's poem 'Natalia Dolgorukaya' (1821–3), which may indeed have served as the moral inspiration for her own behaviour. The poem was based on the true story of a young princess, the favourite daughter of Field Marshal Boris Sheremetev, who had followed her husband, Prince Ivan Dolgoruky, to Siberia when he was banished there by the Empress Anna in 1730.*

> I have forgotten my native city,
> Wealth, honours, and family name
> To share with him Siberia's cold
> And endure the inconstancy of fate.[66]

Maria's doting father was convinced that the reason she followed Sergei to Siberia was not because she was 'a wife in love' but because she was 'in love with the idea of herself as a heroine'.[67] The old general never stopped suffering over his beloved daughter's voluntary exile – he blamed Sergei for it – and this led to a tragic break in their relationship. Maria felt her father's disapproval in his infrequent letters to Siberia. No longer able to suppress her anguish, she wrote to him (in the last letter he received before his death) in 1829:

I know that you have ceased to love me for some time, though I know not what I have done to merit your displeasure. To suffer is my lot in this world – but to make others suffer is more than I can bear . . . How can I be happy for a moment if the blessing which you give me in your letters is not given also to Sergei?[68]

On Christmas Eve Maria said farewell to her son and family and left for Moscow on the first leg of her journey to Siberia. In the old capital she stopped at the house of her sister-in-law Princess Zinaida Volkonsky, a famous beauty and close friend of the late Emperor Alexander, called by Pushkin the 'Tsarina of the arts'. Zinaida was the hostess of a dazzling literary salon where, unusually for that time, no French verses were declaimed. Pushkin and Zhukovsky, Viazemsky and Delvig, Baratynsky, Tiutchev, the Kireevsky brothers and the Polish poet Mickiewicz were all *habitués*. On the eve of Maria's departure there was a special evening where Pushkin read. He was later to compose a 'Message to Siberia' (1827):

---

* Allowed to return to St Petersburg in the 1730s, Natalia Dolgorukaya became the first woman in Russian history to write her memoirs.

In deep Siberian mines retain
A proud and patient resignation;
Your grievous toil is not in vain
Nor yet your thought's high aspiration.
Grief's constant sister, hope, is nigh,
Shines out in dungeons black and dreary
To cheer the weak, revive the weary;
The hour will come for which you sigh,

When love and friendship reaching through
Will penetrate the bars of anguish,
The convict warrens where you languish,
As my free voice now reaches you.

Each hateful manacle and chain
Will fall; your dungeons break asunder;
Outside waits freedom's joyous wonder
As comrades give you swords again.[69]

One year after Maria had arrived in Siberia, her baby boy Nikolenka died. Maria never ceased to grieve for him. At the end of her long life, after thirty years of penal exile, when someone asked her how she felt about Russia, she gave this reply: 'The only homeland that I know is the patch of grass where my son lies in the ground.'[70]

3

Maria took eight weeks to travel to Nerchinsk, the penal colony on the Russian–Chinese border where her exiled husband, Sergei Volkonsky, was a convict labourer in the silver mines. It was about 6,000 kilometres across the snow-bound steppe by open carriage from Moscow to Irkutsk, at that time the last outpost of Russian civilization in Asia, and from there a hazardous adventure by cart and sledge around the icy mountain paths of Lake Baikal. At Irkutsk the governor had tried to dissuade Maria from continuing with her journey, warning her that, if she did so, she would be deprived of all her rights by a special order of the Tsar for all the wives of the Decembrists. By entering the penal zone beyond Irkutsk, the Princess would herself become a prisoner. She would lose direct control of her property, her right to keep a maid or any other serfs, and even on the death of her husband, she would never be allowed to return to the Russia she had left. This was the import of the document she had signed to join her husband in Nerchinsk. But any doubts she might have had about her sacrifice were immediately dispelled on her first visit to his prison cell.

At first I could not make out anything, it was so dark. They opened a small door on the left and I entered my husband's tiny cell. Sergei rushed towards me: I was frightened by the clanking of his chains. I had not known that he was manacled. No words can ever describe what I felt when I saw the immensity of his suffering. The vision of his shackles so enraged and overwhelmed my soul that at once I fell down to the floor and kissed his chains and feet.[71]

Nerchinsk was a bleak, ramshackle settlement of wooden huts built around the stockades of the prison camp. Maria rented a small hut from one of the local Mongolian settlers. 'It was so narrow,' she recalled, 'that when I lay down on my mattress on the floor my head touched the wall and my feet were squashed against the door.'[72] She shared this residence with Katya Trubetskoi, another young princess who had followed her Decembrist husband to Siberia. They survived on the small income the authorities allowed them from their dispossessed estates. For the first time in their lives they were forced to do the chores that had always been performed for them by the huge domestic staff in their palaces. They learned to clean clothes, bake bread, grow vegetables and to cook their food on the wood stove. They soon forgot their taste for French cuisine and began to live 'like Russians, eating pickled cabbage and black bread'.[73] Maria's strength of character – reinforced by the routines of the culture she had left behind was the key to her survival in Siberia. She scrupulously observed all the saints' days and the birthdays of the relatives in Russia who had long forgotten hers. She always made a point of dressing properly, in a fur hat and a veil, even on her journeys to the peasant market in Nerchinsk. She played the French clavichord she had carefully packed up and carted all the way across the frozen Asian steppes, no doubt at enormous inconvenience. She kept up her English by translating books and journals sent out in the post; and every day she took dictation from the prisoners, who as 'politicals' were strictly barred from writing letters in the camp. They called Maria their 'window on to the world'.[74]

Siberia brought the exiles together. It showed them how to live truly by the principles of communality and self-sufficiency which they had so admired in the peasantry. In Chita, where they moved in 1828, the dozen prisoners and their families formed themselves into an *artel*, a collective team of labourers, and divided up the tasks between themselves. Some built the log huts in which their wives and children were to live, later to be joined by the prisoners themselves. Others took up trades like carpentry, or making shoes and clothes. Volkonsky was the gardener-in-chief. They called this community their 'prison family' and in their imaginations it came close to re-creating the egalitarian simplicity of the peasant commune.[75] Here was that spirit of togetherness which the men of 1812 had first encountered in the regiment.

Family relations became closer, too. Gone were the servants who had taken over child care for the noble family of the eighteenth century. The Siberian exiles brought up their own children and taught them all they knew. 'I was your wet nurse,' Maria told her children, 'your nanny and, in part, your tutor, too.'[76] Misha, a new son, was born in 1832; Elena ('Nellinka'), a daughter, in 1834. The following year the Volkonskys were resettled in the village of Urik, thirty kilometres outside Irkutsk, where they had a wooden house and a plot of land, just like all the other villagers. Misha and Elena grew up with the local peasant children. They learned to play their games – hunting for birds' nests, fishing for brown trout, setting rabbit traps and catching butterflies. 'Nellinka is growing up a true Siberian', Maria wrote to her friend Katya Trubetskoi.

She talks only in the local dialect and there is no way of stopping her doing so. As for Misha, I have to allow him to go camping in the woods with the wild boys from the village. He loves adventure; he wept uncontrollably the other day because he had slept through an alarm caused by the appearance of a wolf on our doorstep. My children are growing up *à la Rousseau*, like two little savages, and there is very little I can do about it except to insist that they talk French with us when at home . . . But I must say that this existence suits their health.[77]

The boy's father took a different view. Full of pride, he told a friend that Misha had grown up a 'true Russian in feeling'.[78]

For the adults, too, exile meant a simpler and more 'Russian' way of life. Some of the Decembrist exiles settled in the countryside and married local girls. Others took up Russian customs and pastimes, in particular hunting in the game-rich forests of Siberia.[79] And all of them were forced, for the first time in their lives, to become fluent in their native tongue. For Maria and Sergei, accustomed as they were to speak and think in French, this was one of the hardest aspects of their new existence. On their first encounter in that Nerchinsk prison cell they were forced to speak in Russian (so that the guards could understand), but they did not know the words for all the complex emotions they were feeling at that moment, so their conversation was somewhat artificial and extremely limited. Maria set about the study of her native language from a copy of the Scriptures in the camp. Sergei's Russian, which he had written as an officer, became more vernacular. His letters from Urik are littered with Siberian colloquialisms and misspellings of elementary words ('if', 'doubt', 'May' and 'January').[80]

Sergei, like his son, was 'going native'. With every passing year he became more peasant-like. He dressed like a peasant, grew his beard, rarely washed, and began to spend most of his time working in the fields or talking with the peasants at the local market town. In 1844 the Volkonskys were allowed to settle in Irkutsk. Maria was immediately accepted into the official circles of the new governor, Muraviev-Amursky, who made no secret of his sympathy for the Decembrist exiles and looked upon them as an intellectual force for the development of Siberia. Maria welcomed this opportunity to become integrated in society again. She set up several schools, a foundling hospital and a theatre. She hosted the town's main salon in their house, where the governor himself was a frequent visitor. Sergei was seldom there. He found the 'aristocratic atmosphere' of Maria's household disagreeable and preferred to remain at his farm in Urik, coming into Irkutsk just for market days. But after twenty years of seeing his wife suffer in Siberia, he was not about to stand in her way.

5. *The 'peasant prince': Sergei Volkonsky in Irkutsk.*
Daguerreotype, 1845

The 'peasant prince', for his part, was widely viewed as an eccentric. N. A. Belogolovy, who grew up in Irkutsk in the 1840s, recalls how people were shocked 'to see the prince on market days sitting on the seat of a peasant cart piled high with flour bags and engaged in a lively conversation with a crowd of peasants whilst they shared a grey bread roll'.[81] The couple had constant petty arguments. Maria's brother, A. N. Raevsky, who had been entrusted with the management of her estates, used the rents to pay his gambling debts. Sergei accused Maria of siding with her brother, who had the support of the Raevskys, and in the end he made legal provisions to separate his own estates from hers so as to secure his children's legacy.[82] From the annual income which they received from their land back in Russia (approximately 4,300 roubles) Sergei assigned 3,300 roubles to Maria (enough for her to live comfortably in Irkutsk), leaving just 1,000 roubles for himself to manage on his little farm.[83] Increasingly estranged, Sergei and Maria began to live separately (in his letters to his son, Sergei later called it a 'divorce')[84] – although at the time only the 'prison family' was aware of their arrangements.* Maria had a love affair with the handsome and charismatic Decembrist exile Alessandro Poggio, the son of an Italian nobleman who had come to Russia in the 1770s. In Irkutsk Poggio was a daily visitor to Maria's house, and, although he was a friend of Sergei, he was seen there much too often in her husband's absence for the gossip not to spread. It was rumoured that Poggio was the father of Misha and Elena – a suggestion which still bothered Sergei in 1864, the year before his death, when he wrote his final letter to his 'dear friend' Poggio.[85] Eventually, to keep up the appearance of a married life, Sergei built a wooden cabin in the courtyard of Maria's house, where he slept and cooked his meals and received his peasant friends. Belogolovy recalls a rare appearance in Maria's drawing room. 'His face was smeared with tar, his long unkempt beard had bits of straw, and he smelled of the cattle yard . . . Yet he still spoke perfect French, pronouncing all his "r's" like a true Frenchman.'[86]

The urge to lead a simple peasant life was shared by many noblemen (Volkonsky's distant cousin, Leo Tolstoy, comes to mind). This very 'Russian' quest for a 'Life of Truth' was more profound than the romantic search for a 'spontaneous' or 'organic' existence which motivated cultural movements elsewhere in Europe. At its heart was a religious vision of the 'Russian soul' that encouraged national prophets – from the Slavophiles in the 1830s to the Populists in the 1870s – to

---

* Their marital problems were later covered up by the Raevsky and Volkonsky families by excising whole chunks of their correspondence from their family archives, and this was continued in the publications of the Soviet period, when the Decembrists were heroized. None the less, traces of their separation are still to be found in the archives.

worship at the altar of the peasantry. The Slavophiles believed in the moral superiority of the Russian peasant commune over modern Western ways and argued for a return to these principles. The Populists were convinced that the egalitarian customs of the commune could serve as a model for the socialist and democratic reorganization of society; they turned to the peasants in the hope of finding allies for their revolutionary cause. For all these intellectuals, Russia was revealed, as a messianic truth, in the customs and beliefs of its peasantry. To enter into Russia, and to be redeemed by it, entailed a renunciation of the sinful world into which these children of the gentry had been born. Volkonsky, in this sense, was the first in a long line of Russian noblemen who found their nation, and their salvation, in the peasantry, and his moral quest was rooted in the lessons he had drawn from 1812. He turned his back on what he saw as the false relations of the old class-based society and looked with idealistic expectations towards a new society of equal men. 'I trust no one with society connections', he wrote to Ivan Pushchin, his old Decembrist friend, in 1841. 'There is more honesty and integrity of feeling in the peasants of Siberia.'[87]

Like all the Decembrist exiles, Volkonsky saw Siberia as a land of democratic hope. Here, it seemed to them, was a young and childlike Russia, primordial and raw, rich in natural resources. It was a frontier land (an 'America') whose pioneering farmers were not crushed by serfdom or the state (for there were few serf owners in Siberia), so that they had retained an independent spirit and resourcefulness, a natural sense of justice and equality, from which the old Russia might renew itself. The youthful energy of its unbridled peasants contained Russia's democratic potential. Hence the Decembrists immersed themselves in the study of Siberian folklore and history; they set up village schools or, like Maria, taught the peasants in their homes; and, like Sergei, they took up peasant crafts or worked the land themselves. The Prince found comfort and a sense of purpose in his peasant toil. It was a release from the endlessness of captive time. 'Manual labour is such a healthy thing', Volkonsky wrote to Pushchin. 'And it is a joy when it feeds one's family and is of benefit to other people too.'[88]

But Volkonsky was more than a farmer; he was an agricultural institute. He imported textbooks and new types of seed from European Russia (Maria's letters home were filled with lists of gardening needs) and he spread the fruits of his science to the peasants, who came to him for advice from miles around.[89] The peasants, it would seem, had a genuine respect for 'our prince', as they called Volkonsky. They liked his frankness and his openness with them, the ease with which he spoke in their local idiom. It made them less inhibited than they normally were with noblemen.[90]

This extraordinary ability to enter into the world of the common people requires comment. Tolstoy, after all, never really managed it, even though he tried for nearly fifty years. Perhaps Volkonsky's success is explained by his long experience of addressing the peasant soldiers in his regiments. Or perhaps, once the conventions of his European culture were stripped away, he could draw on the Russian customs he had grown up with. His transformation was not unlike the one that takes place in Natasha in the scene in *War and Peace* when she suddenly discovers in her 'Uncle's' forest cabin that the spirit of the peasant dance is in her blood.

4

As readers of *War and Peace* will know, the war of 1812 was a vital watershed in the culture of the Russian aristocracy. It was a war of national liberation from the intellectual empire of the French – a moment when noblemen like the Rostovs and the Bolkonskys struggled to break free from the foreign conventions of their society and began new lives on Russian principles. This was no straightforward metamorphosis (and it happened much more slowly than in Tolstoy's novel, where the nobles rediscover their forgotten national ways almost overnight). Though anti-French voices had grown to quite a chorus in the first decade of the nineteenth century, the aristocracy was still immersed in the culture of the country against which they were at war. The salons of St Petersburg were filled with young admirers of Bonaparte, such as Pierre Bezukhov in *War and Peace*. The most fashionable set was that of Counts Rumiantsev and Caulaincourt, the French ambassador in Petersburg, the circle in which Tolstoy's Hélène moved. 'How can we fight the French?' asks Count Rostopchin, the Governor of Moscow, in *War and Peace*. 'Can we arm ourselves against our teachers and divinities? Look at our youths! Look at our ladies! The French are our Gods. Paris is our Kingdom of Heaven.'[91] Yet even in these circles there was horror at Napoleon's invasion, and their reaction against all things French formed the basis of a Russian renaissance in life and art.

In the patriotic climate of 1812 the use of French was frowned upon in the salons of St Petersburg – and in the streets it was even dangerous. Tolstoy's novel captures perfectly the spirit of that time when nobles, who had been brought up to speak and think in French, struggled to converse in their native tongue. In one set it was agreed to ban the use of French and impose a forfeit on those who made a slip. The only trouble was that no one knew the Russian word for 'forfeit' – there was none – so people had to call out *'forfaiture'*. This linguistic nationalism was by no means new. Admiral Shishkov, sometime Minister of Public Education, had placed the defence of the Russian language at the heart of his campaign against the French as early as 1803. He was involved in a long dispute with the Karamzinians, in which he attacked the French expressions of their salon style and wanted literary Russian to return to its archaic Church Slavonic roots.* For Shishkov the influence of French was to blame for the decline of the Orthodox religion and the old patriarchal moral code: the Russian way of life was being undermined by a cultural invasion from the West.

Shishkov's stock began to rocket after 1812. Renowned as a card player, he was a frequent guest in the fashionable houses of St Petersburg, and between rounds of *vingt-et-un* he would preach the virtues of the Russian tongue. Among his hosts, he took on the status of a 'national sage' and (perhaps in part because they owed him gambling debts) they paid him to tutor their sons.[92] It became a fashion

---

* These disputes over language involved a broader conflict about 'Russia' and what it should be – a follower of Europe or a unique culture of its own. They looked forward to the arguments between the Slavophiles and the Westerners. The Slavophiles did not emerge as a distinct grouping for another thirty years, but the term 'Slavophile' was first used in the 1800s to describe those, like Shishkov, who favoured Church Slavonic as the 'national' idiom (see Iu. Lotman and B. Uspenskii, 'Spory o iazyke v nachale XIX v. kak fakt russkoi kul'tury', in *Trudy po russkoi i slavianskoi filologii*, 24, *Uchenye zapiski tartuskogo gosudarstvennogo universiteta*, vyp. 39 (Tartu, 1975), pp. 210–11).

for the sons of noblemen to learn to read and write their native tongue. Dmitry Sheremetev, the orphaned son of Nikolai Petrovich and Praskovya, spent three years on Russian grammar and even rhetoric as a teenager in the 1810s – as much time as he spent on learning French.[93] For lack of Russian texts, children learned to read from the Scriptures – indeed, like Pushkin, they were often taught to read by the church clerk or a local priest.[94] Girls were less likely to be taught the Russian script than boys. Unlike their brothers, who were destined to become army officers or landowners, they would not have much business with the merchants or the serfs and hence little need to read or write their native tongue. But in the provinces there was a growing trend for women as well as men to learn Russian. Tolstoy's mother, Maria Volkonsky, had a fine command of literary Russian, even writing poems in her native tongue.[95] Without this growing Russian readership the literary renaissance of the nineteenth century would have been inconceivable. Previously the educated classes in Russia had read mainly foreign literature.

In the eighteenth century the use of French and Russian had demarcated two entirely separate spheres: French the sphere of thought and sentiment, Russian the sphere of daily life. There was one form of language (French or Gallicized 'salon' Russian) for literature and another (the plain speech of the peasantry, which was not that far apart from the spoken idiom of the merchants and the clergy) for daily life. There were strict conventions on the use of languages. For example, a nobleman was supposed to write to the Tsar in Russian, and it would have seemed audacious if he wrote to him in French; but he always spoke to the Tsar in French, as he spoke to other noblemen. On the other hand, a woman was supposed to write in French, not just in her correspondence with the sovereign but with all officials, because this was the language of polite society; it would have been deemed a gross indecency if she had used Russian expressions.[96] In private correspondence, however, there were few set rules, and by the end of the eighteenth century the aristocracy had become so bilingual that they slipped quite easily and imperceptibly from Russian into French and back again. Letters of a page or so could switch a dozen times, sometimes even in the middle of a sentence, without prompting by a theme.

Tolstoy played on these differences in *War and Peace* to highlight the social and cultural nuances involved in Russian French. For example, the fact that Andrei Bolkonsky speaks Russian with a French accent places him in the élite pro-French section of the Petersburg aristocracy. Or that Andrei's friend, the diplomat Bilibin, speaks by preference in French and says 'only those words in Russian on which he wished to put a contemptuous emphasis' indicates that Bilibin was a well-known cultural stereotype that readers would easily recognize: the Russian who would rather he were French. But perhaps the best example is Hélène – the princess who prefers to speak in French about her extramarital affairs because 'in Russian she always felt that her case did not sound clear, and French suited it better'.[97] In this passage Tolstoy is deliberately echoing the old distinction between French as the language of deceit and Russian as the language of sincerity. His use of dialogue has a similarly nationalist dimension. It is no coincidence that the novel's most idealized characters speak exclusively in Russian (Princess Maria and the peasant Karataev) or (like Natasha) speak French only with mistakes.

Of course, no novel is a direct window on to life and, however much it might approach that realist ideal in *War and Peace*, we cannot take these observations as an accurate reflection of reality. To read the correspondence of the Volkonskys – of course not forgetting that they became the Bolkonskys of *War and Peace* – is to find a far more complex situation than that presented by Tolstoy. Sergei Volkonsky wrote in French but inserted Russian phrases when he mentioned daily life on the estate; or he wrote in Russian when he aimed to underline a vital point and emphasize his own sincerity. By inclination, particularly after 1812, he wrote mostly in Russian; and he was obliged to in his letters from Siberia after 1825 (for his censors only read Russian). But there were occasions when he wrote in French (even after 1825): for example, when he wrote in the subjunctive mode or used formal phrases and *politesses*; or in passages where, in contravention of the rules, he wanted to express his views on politics in a language the censors would not understand. Sometimes he used French to explain a concept for which there was no Russian word – '*diligence*', '*duplicité*' and '*discrétion*'.[98]

In its customs and its daily habits the aristocracy was struggling to become more 'Russian', too. The men of 1812 gave up feasts of *haute cuisine* for spartan Russian lunches, as they strived to simplify and Russianize their opulent lifestyle. Noblemen took peasant 'wives' with growing frequency and openness (what was good for a Sheremetev was also good for them) and there were even cases of noblewomen living with or marrying serfs.[99] Even Arakcheev, the Minister of War who became so detested for his brutal regime in the army, kept an unofficial peasant wife by whom he had two sons who were educated in the Corps des Pages.[100] Native crafts were suddenly in vogue. Russian china with scenes from rural life was increasingly preferred to the classical designs of imported eighteenth-century porcelain. Karelian birch and other Russian woods, especially in the more rustic stylings of serf craftsmen, began to compete with the fine imported furniture of the classical palace, and even to displace it in those private living spaces where the nobleman relaxed. Count Alexander Osterman-Tolstoy, a military hero of 1812, was the owner of a magnificent mansion on the English Embankment in St Petersburg. The reception rooms had marble walls and mirrors with sumptuous decorations in the French Empire style, but after 1812 he had his bedroom lined with rough wooden logs to give it the appearance of a peasant hut.[101]

Recreations were going Russian, too. At balls in Petersburg, where European dances had always reigned supreme, it became the fashion to perform the *pliaska* and other Russian dances after 1812. Countess Orlova was renowned for these peasant dances, which she studied and performed at Moscow balls.[102] But there were other noblewomen who, like Natasha Rostov, had somehow taken in the spirit of the dance, as if they had breathed it 'from the Russian air'. Princess Elena Golitsyn danced her first *pliaska* several decades later at a ball in Novgorod. 'Nobody had taught me how to dance the *pliaska*. It was simply that I was a "Russian girl". I had grown up in the country, and when I heard the refrain of our village song, "The Maid Went to Fetch the Water", I could not stop myself from the opening hand movements of the dance.'[103]

Rural recreations were another indication of this newfound Russian-ness. It was at this time that the *dacha* first emerged as a national institution, although the country or suburban summer house did not become a mass phenomenon until the final decades of the nineteenth century (Chekhov's *Cherry Orchard* was famously cut down for *dacha* building land). The high aristocracy of Petersburg was renting *dachas* in the eighteenth century. Pavlovsk and Peterhof were their preferred resorts, where they could escape the city's heat and take in the fresh air of the pinewood forests or the sea. The Tsars had elaborate summer palaces with immense pleasure gardens in both of these resorts. During the early nineteenth century the *dacha* fashion spread to the minor gentry, who built more modest houses in the countryside.

In contrast to the formal classicism of the urban palace, the *dacha* was constructed in a simple Russian style. It was usually a double-storeyed wooden building with a mezzanine verandah that ran all round the house with ornate window and door-frame carvings seen more commonly on peasant huts, although some of the grander *dachas* might incongruously add a Roman arch and columns to the front. The *dacha* was a place for Russian relaxations and pursuits: picking mushrooms in the woods, making jams, drinking tea from the *samovar*, fishing, hunting, visiting the bath house, or spending the whole day, like Goncharov's Oblomov, in an oriental *khalat*. A month in the country allowed the nobleman to throw off the pressures of the court and official life, to become more himself in a Russian milieu. It was common to dispense with formal uniforms and to dress in casual Russian clothes. Simple Russian food took the place of *haute cuisine*, and some dishes, such as summer soup with *kvas* (*okroshka*), fish in aspic and pickled mushrooms, tea with jam, or cherry brandy, became practically synonymous with the *dacha* way of life.[104]

Of all the countryside pursuits, hunting was the one that came the closest to a national institution, in the sense that it united nobleman and serf as fellow sportsmen and fellow countrymen. The early nineteenth century was the heyday of the hunt – a fact that was connected to the gentry's rediscovery of 'the good life on the estate' after 1812. There were noblemen who gave up their careers in the civil service and retired to the country for a life of sport. The Rostovs' 'Uncle' in *War and Peace* was typical:

'Why don't you enter the service, Uncle?'

  'I did once, but gave it up. I am not fit for it . . . I can't make head or tail of it. That's for you – I haven't brains enough. Now hunting is another matter . . .'[105]

There were two kinds of hunting in Russia – the formal chase with hounds, which was very grand, and the simple type of hunting by a man on foot with a solitary hound and a serf companion, as immortalized in Turgenev's *Sketches from a Hunter's Album* (1852). The formal chase was conducted in the manner of a military campaign, sometimes lasting several weeks, with hundreds of riders, huge packs of dogs and a vast retinue of hunting serfs camping out on the estates of the nobility. Lev Izmailov, Marshal of the Riazan Nobility, took 3,000 hunters and 2,000 hounds on his 'campaigns'.[106] Baron Mengden kept an élite caste of hunting serfs with their own scarlet livery and special Arab horses for the hunt. When they left, with the baron at their head, they took several hundred carts with hay and oats, a hospital on wheels for wounded dogs, a mobile kitchen and so many servants that the baron's house was emptied, leaving his wife and daughters with only a bartender and a boy.[107] This type of hunting was dependent on the gentry's ownership of vast serf armies and virtually all the land – conditions which persisted until the emancipation of the serfs in 1861. Like the English hunt, it was serious and stuffy, rigidly observing the social hierarchy, with the hunting serfs, if not running with the hounds, then clearly in a subservient role.

By contrast, Turgenev's type of hunting was relatively egalitarian – and it was so in a distinctly Russian way. When the nobleman went hunting with his serf companion he left behind the civilization of his palace and entered the world of the peasantry. Squire and serf were brought together by this type of sport. They dressed much the same; they shared their food and drink when they stopped along the way; they slept side by side in peasant huts and barns; and, as described in Turgenev's *Sketches*, they talked about their lives in a spirit of companionship that often made them close and lasting friends.[108] There was much more to this than the usual 'male bonding' around sport. As far as the squire was concerned, the hunt on foot was a rural odyssey, an encounter with an undiscovered peasant land; it was almost incidental how many birds or beasts were shot. In the final lyrical episode of the *Sketches*, where the narrator sums up all the joys of hunting, there is barely mention of the sport itself. What emerges from this perfect piece of writing is the hunter's intense love of the Russian countryside and its changing beauty through the different seasons of the year:

And a summer morning in July! Has anyone save a hunter ever experienced the delight of wandering through bushes at dawn? Your feet leave green imprints in grass that is heavy and white with dew. You push aside wet bushes – the warm scent accumulated in the night almost smothers you; the air is impregnated with the fresh bitter-sweet fragrance of wormwood, the honeyed scent of buckwheat and clover; far off an oak forest rises like a wall, shining purple in the sunshine; the air is still fresh, but the coming heat can already be felt. Your head becomes slightly dizzy from such an excess of sweet scents. And there's no end to the bushes. Away in the distance ripening rye glows yellow and there are narrow strips of rust-red buckwheat. Then there's the sound of a cart; a peasant drives by at walking pace, leaving his horse in the shade before the sun gets hot. You greet him, pass on, and after a while the metallic rasping of a scythe can be heard behind you. The sun is rising higher and higher, and the grass quickly dries out. It's already hot. First one hour, then another passes. The sky darkens at the edges and the motionless air is aflame with the prickly heat.[109]

Russian forms of dress became the height of fashion after 1812. At balls and receptions in St Petersburg, and from the 1830s at the court as well, society ladies began to appear in national costume, complete with the *sarafan* tunic and *kokoshnik* head-dress of old Muscovy. The Russian peasant shawl was hugely popular with noblewomen in the 1810s. There had been a fashion for oriental shawls in Europe during the last decades of the eighteenth century which the Russians had copied by importing their own shawls from India. But after 1812 it was Russian peasant shawls that became the rage, and serf workshops emerged as major centres of the fashion industry.[110] The Russian gown (*kapot*), traditionally worn by peasant and provincial merchant wives, entered *haute couture* slightly earlier, in the 1780s, when Catherine the Great took to wearing one, but it too was widely worn from about 1812. The *kaftan* and *khalat* (a splendid sort of housecoat or dressing gown in which one could lounge about at home and receive guests) came back into fashion among noblemen. The *podyovka*, a short *kaftan* traditionally worn by the peasantry, was added to the wardrobe of the nobleman as well. To wear such clothes was not just to relax and be oneself at home; it was, in the words of one memoirist, 'to make a conscious statement of one's Russianness'.[111] When, in 1827,

Tropinin painted Pushkin wearing a *khalat* (plate 22), he was portraying him as a gentleman who was perfectly at ease with the customs of his land.

A fashion for the 'natural' look took hold of noblewomen in the 1820s. The new ideal of beauty focused on a vision of the purity of the female figures of antiquity and the Russian peasantry. Fidel Bruni's portrait of Zinaida Volkonsky (1810) illustrates this style. Indeed, according to society rumour, it was precisely her simplicity of dress that had attracted the amorous attentions of the Emperor,[112] who was himself susceptible to all of Nature's charms.* Women took to wearing cotton clothes. They dressed their hair in a simple style and rejected heavy make-up for the pale complexion favoured by this cult of unadorned Nature.[113] The turn toward Nature and simplicity was widespread throughout Europe from the final decades of the eighteenth century. Women had been throwing out their powdered wigs and renouncing heavy scents like musk for light rose waters that allowed the natural fragrance of clean flesh to filter through. There it had developed under the influence of Rousseau and Romantic ideas about the virtues of Nature. But in Russia the fashion for the natural had an extra, national dimension. It was linked to the idea that one had to strip away the external layers of cultural convention to reveal the Russian personality. Pushkin's Tatiana in *Eugene Onegin* was the literary incarnation of this natural Russianness – so much so that the simple style of dress worn by noblewomen became known as the 'Onegin'.[114] Readers saw Tatiana as a 'Russian heroine' whose true self was revealed in the memories of her simple childhood in the countryside:

> 'To me, Onegin, all these splendours,
> This weary tinselled life of mine,

---

* The Emperor Alexander began taking a daily promenade along the Palace Embankment and the Nevsky Prospekt as far as the Anichkov bridge. It was, in the words of the memoirist Vigel, a 'conscious striving by the Tsar for simplicity in daily life' (F. F. Vigel', *Zapiski*, chast' 2 (Moscow, 1892), p. 32). Before 1800, no self-respecting nobleman would go anywhere in Petersburg except by carriage, and (as Kniazhnin's comic opera testified) vast personal fortunes would be spent on the largest carriages imported from Europe. But, under Alexander's influence, it became the fashion in St Petersburg to '*faire le tour impérial*'.

This homage that the great world tenders,
My stylish house where princes dine –
Are empty . . . I'd as soon be trading
This tattered life of masquerading,
This world of glitter, fumes, and noise,
For just my books, the simple joys
Of our old home, its walks and flowers,
For all those haunts that I once knew . . .
Where first, Onegin, I saw you;
For that small churchyard's shaded bowers,
Where over my poor nanny now
There stands a cross beneath a bough.'[115]

Pushkin's masterpiece is, among many other things, a subtle exploration of the complex Russian-European consciousness that typified the aristocracy in the age of 1812. The literary critic Vissarion Belinsky said that *Eugene Onegin* was an encyclopaedia of Russian life, and Pushkin himself, in its final stanzas, developed the idea of the novel as life's book. In no other work can one see so clearly the visceral influence of cultural convention on the Russian sense of self. In many ways, indeed, the novel's central subject is the complex interplay between life and art. The syncretic nature of Tatiana's character is an emblem of the cultural world in which she lives. At one moment she is reading a romantic novel; at another listening to her nanny's superstitions and folk tales. She is torn between the gravitational fields of Europe and Russia. Her very name, Tatiana, as Pushkin underlines in a footnote, comes from the ancient Greek, yet in Russia it is 'used only among the common people'.[116] In the affairs of the heart, as well, Tatiana is subject to the different cultural norms of European Russia and the peasant countryside. As a rather young and impressionable girl from the provinces, she inhabits the imaginary world of the romantic novel and understands her feelings in these terms. She duly falls in love with the Byronic figure of Eugene and, like one of her fictional heroines, she writes to declare her love to him. Yet when the lovesick Tatiana asks her nanny if she has ever been in love, she becomes exposed to the influence of a very different culture where romantic love is a foreign luxury and obedience is a woman's main virtue. The peasant nurse tells Tatiana how she was married off at the age of just thirteen to an even younger boy whom she had never seen before:

> I got so scared . . . my tears kept falling;
> And weeping, they undid my plait,
> Then sang me to the churchyard gate.[117]

This encounter between the two cultures represents Tatiana's own predicament: whether to pursue her own romantic dreams or sacrifice herself in the traditional 'Russian' way (the way chosen by Maria Volkonsky when she gave up everything to follow her Decembrist husband to Siberia). Onegin rejects Tatiana – he sees her as a naive country girl – and then, after killing his friend Lensky in a duel, he disappears for several years. Meanwhile Tatiana is married to a man she does not really love, as far as one can tell, a military hero from the wars of 1812 who is 'well received' at court. Tatiana rises to become a celebrated hostess in St Petersburg. Onegin now returns and falls in love with her. Years of wandering through his native land have somehow changed the former dandy of St Petersburg, and finally he sees her natural beauty, her 'lack of mannerisms or any borrowed tricks'. But Tatiana remains faithful to her marriage vows. She has come, it seems, to embrace her 'Russian principles' – to see through the illusions of romantic love. Looking through the books in Onegin's library, she understands at last the fictive dimension of his personality:

> A Muscovite in Harold's cloak,
> Compendium of affectation,
> A lexicon of words in vogue . . .
> Mere parody and just a rogue?[118]

Yet even here, when Tatiana tells Onegin,

> I love you (why should I dissemble?);
> But I am now another's wife,
> And I'll be faithful all my life[119]

we see in her the dense weave of cultural influences. These lines are adapted from a song well known among the Russian folk. Thought in Pushkin's time to have been written by Peter the Great, it was translated into French by Pushkin's own uncle. Tatiana could have read it in an old issue of *Mercure de France*. But she could also have heard it from her peasant nurse.[120] It is a perfect illustration of the complex intersections between European and native Russian culture during Pushkin's age.

Pushkin himself was a connoisseur of Russian songs and tales. Chulkov's *ABC of Russian Superstitions* (1780–83) and Levshin's *Russian Tales* (1788) were well-thumbed texts on Pushkin's shelves. He had been brought up on the peasant tales and superstitions of his beloved nanny, Arina Rodionovna, who became the model for Tatiana's nurse. 'Mama' Rodionovna was a talented narrator, elaborating and enriching many standard tales, judging by the transcripts of her stories that Pushkin later made.[121] During his years of exile in the south in 1820–24 he became a serious explorer of the folk traditions, those of the Cossacks in particular, and then, when exiled to his family estate at Mikhailovskoe in 1824–6, he carried on collecting songs and tales. Pushkin used these as the basis of *Ruslan and Liudmila* (1820), his first major poem, which some critics panned as mere 'peasant verse', and for his stylized 'fairy tales' like *Tsar Sultan* which he composed in his final years. Yet he had no hesitation in mixing Russian stories with European sources, such as the fables of La Fontaine or the fairy tales of the Grimm brothers. For *The Golden Cockerel* (1834) he even borrowed from the *Legend of the Arabian Astrologer* which he had come across in the 1832 French translation of *The Legends of the Alhambra* by Washington Irving. As far as Pushkin was concerned, Russia was a part of Western and world culture, and it did not make his 'folk tales' any less authentic if he combined all these sources in literary re-creations of the Russian style. How ironic, then, that Soviet nationalists regarded Pushkin's stories as direct expressions of the Russian folk.*

---

* Akhmatova was denounced by the Soviet literary authorities for suggesting, quite correctly, that some of Pushkin's sources for his 'Russian tales' were taken from *The Thousand and One Nights*.

By Pushkin's death, in 1837, the literary use of folk tales had become commonplace, almost a condition of literary success. More than any other Western canon, Russian literature was rooted in the oral narrative traditions, to which it owed much of its extraordinary strength and originality. Pushkin, Lermontov, Ostrovsky, Nekrasov, Tolstoy, Leskov and Saltykov-Shchedrin – all to some degree could be thought of as folklorists, all certainly used folklore in many of their works. But none captured the essential spirit of the folk tale better than Nikolai Gogol.

Gogol was in fact a Ukrainian, and, were it not for the success of Pushkin, who was his mentor and gave him the true plots of his major works, *The Government Inspector* (1836) and *Dead Souls* (1835–52), he might have written in the peasant dialect of his native Mirgorod, where Gogol's father was well known (though unpublishable under Tsarist laws) as a writer in Ukrainian. During his childhood Gogol fell in love with the earthy idiom of the local peasantry. He loved their songs and dances, their terrifying tales and comic stories, from which his own fantastic tales of Petersburg would later take their cue. He first rose to fame as 'Rudy [i.e. redhead] Panko, Beekeeper', the pseudonymous author of a bestselling collection of stories, *Evenings on a Farm near Dikanka* (1831–2), which fed the growing craze for Ukrainian folk tales. Aladin's *Kochubei*, Somov's *Haïdamaki* and Kulzhinsky's *Cossack Hat* had all been great successes in the Russian capital. But Gogol was nothing if not ambitious and, in 1828, when barely out of school, he came to Petersburg in the hope of making his own literary name. Working during the day as a humble clerk (of the sort that filled his stories), he wrote at night in his lonely attic room. He badgered his mother and sister to send him details of Ukrainian songs and proverbs, and even bits of costume which he wanted them to buy from the local peasants and send to him in a trunk. Readers were delighted with the 'authenticity' of *Evenings on a Farm*. Some critics thought that the stories had been spoilt by a 'coarse' and 'improper' folk language. But the language of the stories was their principal success. It echoed perfectly the musical sonorities of peasant speech – one of the reasons why the stories were adapted by Musorgsky for the unfinished *Sorochintsy Fair* (1874–) and for *St John's Night on Bald Mountain* (1867), and by Rimsky-Korsakov for *May Night* (1879) – and it could be understood by Everyman. During the proof stage of *Evenings on a Farm* Gogol paid a visit to the typesetters. 'The strangest thing occurred', he explained to Pushkin. 'As soon as I opened the door and the printers noticed me, they began to laugh and turned away from me. I was somewhat taken aback and asked for an explanation. The printer explained: "The items that you sent are very amusing and they have greatly amused the typesetters." '[122]

More and more, common speech entered literature, as writers like Gogol began to assimilate the spoken idiom to their written form. Literary language thus broke free from the confines of the salon and flew out, as it were, into the street, taking on the sounds of colloquial Russian and ceasing in the process to depend on French loan words for ordinary things. Lermontov's civic poetry was filled with the rhythms and expressions of the folk, as recorded by himself from peasant speech. His epic *Song of the Merchant Kalashnikov* (1837) imitates the style of the *bylina*; while his brilliantly patriotic *Borodino* (1837) (written to commemorate the twenty-fifth anniversary of the defeat of Napoleon's army) re-creates the spirit of the battlefield by having it described from the peasant soldiers' point of view:

> For three long days we fired at random,
> We knew that we had not unmanned them,
> And neither meant to yield.
> Each soldier thought it should be ended:
> For had we fought or just pretended?
> And then it was that night descended
> Upon that fateful field.[123]

Russian music also found its national voice through the assimilation of folk song. The first *Collection of Russian Folk Songs* was assembled by Nikolai Lvov and annotated by Ivan Prach in 1790. The distinctive features of the peasant chant – the shifting tones and uneven rhythms that would become such a feature of the Russian musical style from Musorgsky to Stravinsky – were altered to conform to Western musical formulas so that the songs could be performed with conventional keyboard accompaniment (Russia's piano-owning classes needed their folk music to be 'pleasing to the ear').[124] The Lvov–Prach collection was an instant hit, and it quickly went through several editions. Throughout the nineteenth century it was plundered by composers in search of 'authentic' folk material, so that nearly all the folk tunes in the Russian repertory, from Glinka to Rimsky-Korsakov, were derived from Lvov–Prach. Western composers also turned to it for exotic Russian colour and *thèmes russes*. Beethoven used two songs from the Lvov collection in the 'Razumovsky' string quartets (opus 59), commissioned in 1805 by the Russian ambassador in Vienna, Count Razumovsky, at the height of the Russo-Austrian alliance against Napoleon. One of the songs was the famous 'Slava' ('Glory') chorus – later used by Musorgsky in the coronation scene of *Boris Godunov* – which Beethoven used as the subject for the *Thème Russe*: Allegro in the opus 59 number 1 quartet. It was originally a *sviatochnaya*, a folk song sung by Russian girls to accompany their divination games at the New Year. Trinkets would be dropped into a dish of water and drawn out one by one as the maidens sang their song. The simple tune became a great national chorus in the war of 1812 – the Tsar's name being substituted for the divine powers in the 'Glory' choruses; in later versions, the names of officers were added, too.[125]

The Imperial recruitment of this peasant theme was equally pronounced in Glinka's opera *A Life for the Tsar* (1836). Its climactic version of the same 'Glory' chorus practically became a second national anthem in the nineteenth century.* Mikhail Glinka was exposed to Russian music from an early age. His grandfather had been in charge of music at the local church of Novospasskoe – in a region of Smolensk that was famous for the strident sound of its church bells – and his uncle had a serf orchestra that was renowned for performing Russian songs. In 1812 the Glinka home was overrun and pillaged by French troops as they advanced towards Moscow. Though he was only eight at the time, it must have stirred the patriotic feelings of the future composer of *A Life*, whose plot was suggested by the peasant partisans. The opera tells the story of Ivan Susanin, a peasant from the estate of Mikhail Romanov, the founder of the Romanov dynasty, in Kostroma. According to legend, in the winter of 1612 Susanin had saved Mikhail's

---

* After 1917 there were suggestions that the 'Glory' chorus should become the national anthem.

life by misdirecting the Polish troops who had invaded Russia in its 'Time of Troubles' (1605–13) and had come to Kostroma to murder Mikhail on the eve of his assumption of the throne. Susanin lost his life, but a dynasty was saved. The obvious parallels between Susanin's sacrifice and the peasant soldiers' in 1812 stimulated a romantic interest in the Susanin myth. Ryleev wrote a famous ballad about him and Mikhail Zagoskin two bestselling novels, set respectively in 1612 and 1812.

Glinka said that his opera was conceived as a battle between Polish and Russian music. The Poles were heard in the polonaise and the mazurka, the Russians in his own adaptations of folk and urban songs. Glinka's supposed debt to folklore made him Russia's first canonical 'national composer'; while A Life took on the status of the quintessential 'Russian opera', its ritual performance on all national occasions practically enforced by Imperial decree. Yet in fact there were relatively few folk melodies (in a noticeable form) in the opera. Glinka had assimilated the folk style and expressed its basic spirit, but the music he wrote was entirely his own. He had fused the qualities of Russian peasant music with the European form. He had shown, in the words of the poet Odoevsky, that 'Russian melody may be elevated to a tragic style'.[126]

In painting, too, there was a new approach to the Russian peasantry. The canons of good taste in the eighteenth century had demanded that the peasant be excluded, as a subject, from all serious forms of art. Classical norms dictated that the artist should present universal themes: scenes from antiquity or the Bible, set in a timeless Greek or Italian landscape. Russian genre painting developed very late, in the final decades of the eighteenth century, and its image of the common man was sentimentalized: plump peasant cherubs in a pastoral scene or sympathetic 'rustic types' with stock expressions to display that they had human feelings, too. It was a visual version of the sentimental novel or the comic opera which had highlighted the serfs' humanity by telling of their love lives and romantic suffering. Yet, in the wake of 1812, a different picture of the peasantry emerged – one that emphasized their heroic strength and human dignity.

This can be seen in the work of Alexei Venetsianov, a quintessential child of 1812. The son of a Moscow merchant (from a family that

6. Alexei Venetsianov: Cleaning Beetroot, *1820*

came originally from Greece), Venetsianov was a draughtsman and a land surveyor for the government before setting up as a painter and engraver in the 1800s. Like many of the pioneers of Russian culture (Musorgsky comes to mind), he received no formal education and remained outside the Academy throughout his life. In 1812 he came to the attention of the public for a series of engravings of the peasant partisans. Selling in huge numbers, they glorified the image of the partisans, drawing them in the form of warriors of ancient Greece and Rome, and from that point on the public called the partisans the 'Russian Hercules'.[127] The war of 1812 formed Venetsianov's views. Although not a political man, he moved in the same circles as the Decembrists and shared their ideals. In 1815 he acquired through his wife a small estate in Tver and, four years later, he retired there, setting up a school for the village children and supporting several peasant artists from his meagre income off the land. One of them was Grigory Soroka, whose tender portrait of his teacher, painted in the 1840s, is a moving testimony to Venetsianov's character.

Venetsianov knew the peasants of his village individually – and in his best portraits, that is how he painted them. He conveyed their personal qualities, just as other portrait painters set out to convey the individual character of noblemen. This psychological aspect was revolutionary for its day, when, with few exceptions, portraitists turned out generic 'peasant types'. Venetsianov focused on the close-up face, forcing viewers to confront the peasant and look him in the eyes, inviting them to enter his inner world. Venetsianov also pioneered the naturalist school of landscape painting in Russia. The character of the Tver countryside – its subdued greens and quiet earth colours – can be seen in all his work. He conveyed the vastness of the Russian land by lowering the horizon to enhance the immensity of the sky over its flat open spaces – a technique derived from icon painting and later copied by epic landscape painters such as Vrubel and Vasnetsov. Unlike the artists of the Academy, who treated landscape as mere background and copied it from European works, Venetsianov painted directly from nature. For *The Threshing Floor* (1820) he had his serfs saw out the end wall of a barn so that he could paint them at work inside it. No other painter brought such realism to his depictions of agricultural life. In *Cleaning Beetroot* (1820) he makes the viewer look at the dirty callused hands and exhausted expressions of the three young female labourers who dominate the scene. It was the first time that such ugly female forms – so foreign to the classical tradition – had appeared in Russian art. Yet these sad figures win our sympathy for their human dignity in the face of suffering. Venetsianov's elevated vision of human toil was most apparent in his many images of peasant women. In perhaps his finest painting, a symbolic study of a peasant with her child, *In the Ploughed Field: Spring* (1827) (plate 4), he combines the distinctive Russian features of his female labourer with the sculptural proportions of an antique heroine. The woman in the field is a peasant goddess. She is the mother of the Russian land.

5

Compared to their parents, the Russian nobles who grew up after 1812 put a higher valuation on childhood. It took a long time for such attitudes to change, but already by the middle decades of the nineteenth century one can discern a new veneration of childhood on the part of those memoirists and writers who recalled their upbringing after 1812. This nostalgia for the age of childhood merged with a new reverence for the Russian customs which they had known as children through their fathers' household serfs.

In the eighteenth century the aristocracy had seen childhood as a preparation for the adult world. It was a stage to be overcome as soon as possible, and children who delayed this transition, like Mitrofan in Fonvizin's *The Minor*, were regarded as simpletons. High-born children were expected to behave like 'little adults' and they were prepared to enter into society from an early age. Girls were taught to dance from eight years old. By the age of ten or twelve they were already going to the 'children's balls' that were run by dancing masters in the fashionable houses, from which, at the age of thirteen or fourteen, they would graduate to their first grown-up ball. Natasha Rostov was relatively old, at eighteen years, when she attended her first ball and danced with Prince Andrei in *War and Peace*. Boys, meanwhile, were signed up for the Guards and dressed in their regimental uniforms long before they were old enough to hold a sword. Volkonsky joined his father's regiment (a sergeant *in absentia*) at the tender age of six. By eight he was a sergeant in the Kherson Grenadiers; by nine, an adjutant to General Suvorov; although, of course, it was only later, at the age of sixteen, that he began active service on the battlefield. Boys destined for the civil service were sent to boarding school at the age of eight or nine, where they were indoctrinated in the service ethic and, like adult state officials, they wore a civil (rather than a school) uniform. School was seen as little more than an apprenticeship for the civil service and, since the student was allowed to join the service on his fifteenth birthday, few noble families thought it necessary to educate their sons beyond that age. Indeed, in so far as the Table of Ranks reinforced the principle of promotion by seniority, any further education was considered disadvantageous: the sooner one got on to the promotion ladder the better.

The memoirist Vasily Selivanov grew up in a household where the seven sons were all prepared for military service from an early age. His father ran the family like a regiment, the sons all ranked by age and under strict instructions to stand up in his presence and call him 'sir'. When Selivanov joined the Dragoons in 1830, at the age of seventeen, the transition from palace to barracks must have felt like going from one home to another.[128] Not all noble families were quite as regimented as the Selivanovs, of course, but in many the relations between parents and their children were conducted on the same basic principles of discipline that ruled the institutions of the army and the state. Such rigour had not always been the case: the domestic life of the noble family in the seventeenth century might have been extremely patriarchal but it was also intimate. Rather, it was copied by the Russians from the West, especially England – although, like much that was brought to Russia in the eighteenth century, it became so ingrained in the nobility that it practically defined that class in the nineteenth century. Noble parents kept their children at arm's length, which often meant the length of the longest corridor, or down the longest staircase to a separate basement floor in the servants' quarters of their house. V. A. Sollogub grew up in a mansion on the Palace Embankment in St Petersburg. The adults lived in the main house while the children were consigned with their nanny and a wet nurse to an annexed wing, and only saw their parents briefly once or twice a day – for example, to thank them for their dinner (but not to eat with them) or to kiss them goodbye when they went away. 'Our lives were entirely separate,' Sollogub recalled, 'and there was never any sign of emotion. We children were allowed to kiss our parents on the hand, but there was no fondling, and we had to address them in French with the formal "*vous*". Children were subjected to a strict domestic code of servility, almost like the laws for serfs'.[129] Nikolai Shatilov, who grew up in a wealthy landowning family of Tula province in the 1860s, was confined as a young boy to a separate apartment in the house, where he lived with his tutor and took all his meals: he did not see his parents 'for months on end'.[130]

Distant fathers were, of course, the norm in nineteenth-century Europe, but there were few cultures where the mother was as remote as she tended to be in the Russian noble family. It was the custom for a noble child to be put into the care of a wet nurse almost from the day they were born. Even as the child grew up there were many noble mothers who were just too busy with their social life, or with other babies, to give them the attention that they must have surely craved. 'Mother was extremely kind, but we hardly ever saw her' is a phrase that crops up often in nineteenth-century memoirs about gentry life.[131] Anna Karenina, although not a model parent, was not exceptional in her ignorance of the routines of her children's nursery ('I'm so useless here').[132]

It was not unusual, then, for the noble child to grow up without any direct parental discipline. Parents often left their children to the care of relatives (typically a spinster aunt or grandmother) or to the supervision of their nannies and the maids and the rest of the domestic staff. Yet the servants were naturally afraid to discipline their master's children (the 'little masters' and the 'little mistresses'), so they tended to indulge them and let them have their way. Boys, in particular, were prone to misbehave ('little monsters'), knowing very well that their parents would defend them if their nanny, a mere serf, dared to complain. Critics of the social system, like the writer Saltykov-Shchedrin, argued that this latitude encouraged noble children to be cruel to serfs; in their adult lives they carried on in the belief that they could lord it over all their serfs and treat them as they liked. It is certainly conceivable that the selfishness and cruelty towards the serfs that ran right through the governing élites of Tsarist Russia went back in some cases to the formative experiences of childhood. For example, if a noble child was sent to the local parish school (a practice that was common in the provinces), he would go with a serf boy, whose sole purpose was to take the whipping for his master's misdemeanours in the class. How could this develop any sense of justice in the noble child?

Yet there were bonds of affection and respect between many noble children and their serfs. Herzen argued that children liked to be with the servants 'because they were bored in the drawing-room and happy in the pantry' and because they shared a common temperament.

This resemblance between servants and children accounts for their mutual attraction. Children hate the aristocratic ideas of the grown-ups and their benevolently condescending manners, because they are clever and understand that in the eyes of grown-up people they are children, while in the eyes of servants they are people. Consequently they are much fonder of playing cards or lotto with the maids than with visitors. Visitors play for the children's benefit with condescension. They give way to them, tease them, and stop playing whenever they feel like it; the maids, as a rule, play as much for their own sakes as for the children's, and that gives the game interest. Servants are extremely devoted to children, and this is not the devotion of a slave, but the mutual affection of the *weak* and the *simple*.[133]

Writing as a socialist, Herzen put down his 'hatred of oppression' to the 'mutual alliance' he had formed with the servants as a child against the senior members of the house. He recalled: 'At times, when I was a child, Vera Artamonovna [his nanny] would say by way of the greatest rebuke for some naughtiness: "Wait a bit, you will grow up and turn into just such another master as the rest." I felt this a horrible insult. The old woman need not have worried herself – just such another as the rest, anyway, I have not become.'[134] Much of this, of course, was written for effect; it made for a good story. Yet other writers similarly claimed that their populist convictions had been formed by their childhood contacts with the serfs.[135]

The high-born Russian boy spent his childhood in the downstairs servants' world. He was cared for by his serf nanny, who slept by his side in the nursery, held him when he cried, and in many cases became like a mother to him. Everywhere he went he was accompanied by his serf 'uncle'. Even when he went to school or enrolled in the army this trusted servant would act as his guardian. Young girls, too, were chaperoned by a 'shaggy footman' – so-called on account of the fur coat he wore over the top of his livery – like the one imagined as 'a huge and matted bear' in Tatiana's dream in *Eugene Onegin*:

> She dare not look to see behind her,
> And ever faster on she reels;
> At every turn he seems to find her,
> The shaggy footman at her heels! . . .[136]

By necessity the children of the servants were the playmates of the high-born child – for in the countryside there would not be other children of a similar social class for miles around. Like many nineteenth-century memoirists, Anna Lelong had fond memories of the games she played with the village girls and boys: throwing games with blocks of wood (*gorodki*); bat-and-ball games played with bones and bits of scrap metal (*babki* and its many variants); clapping-singing-dancing games; and divination games. In the summer she would go swimming with the village children in the river, or she would be taken by her nanny to the villages to play with the younger children as their mothers threshed the rye. Later, in the autumn, she would join the village girls to pick whortleberries and make jam. She loved these moments when she was allowed to enter the peasant world. The fact that it was forbidden by her parents, and that her nanny made her promise not to tell, made it even more exciting for the girl. In the pantry was an atmosphere of warmth and intimacy that was missing in her parents' drawing room. 'I would get up very early and go into the maids' room where they were already at their spinning wheels, and nanny would be knitting socks. I would listen to the stories about peasants being sold, about young boys sent to Moscow or girls married off. There was nothing like this in my parents' house.' Listening to such stories, she 'began to understand what serfdom meant and it made me wish that life was different'.[137]

Herzen wrote that there existed 'a feudal bond of affection' between the noble family and its household serfs.[138] We have lost sight of this bond in the histories of oppression that have shaped our views of serfdom since 1917. But it can be found in the childhood memoirs of the aristocracy; it lives on in every page of nineteenth-century literature; and its spirit can be felt in Russian paintings – none more lyrical than Venetsianov's *Morning of the Lady of the Manor* (1823) (plate 3).

Of all the household servants, those associated with childcare (the maid, the wet nurse and the nanny) were the closest to the family. They formed a special caste that died out suddenly after the emancipation of the serfs in 1861. They were set apart from the other serfs by their fierce devotion and, hard though it may be to understand today, many of them derived all their joy from serving the family. Given special rooms in the main house and treated, on the whole, with kindness and respect, such women became part of the family and many were kept on and provided for long after they had ceased to work. The nostalgia

7. A wet nurse in traditional Russian dress.
Early-twentieth-century photograph

of the nobleman for his childhood was associated with the warmth and tenderness of his relationship with these people.

The wet nurse was a particularly important figure in the Russian noble family. Russians continued to employ a peasant wet nurse long after it had become the conventional wisdom in the rest of Europe for mothers to breastfeed their own infants. Child-rearing handbooks of the early nineteenth century were overtly nationalist in their defence of this habit, claiming that the 'milk of a peasant girl can give lifelong health and moral purity to the noble child'.[139] It was common for the wet nurse to be dressed, and sometimes even painted, in traditional Russian dress – a custom that continued in many families until the revolution of 1917.* Ivan Argunov, the Sheremetevs' artist, depicted several 'unknown peasant girls' who were most probably wet nurses. The fact that a girl like this should become the subject of a portrait painting, commissioned for display in her owner's house, in itself speaks volumes about her position in the culture of the Russian aristocracy. Pavel Sumarokov, recalling daily life among the nobility in the eighteenth century, said that the wet nurse was given pride of place among all the domestic staff. The family would call her by her name and patronymic rather than by the nickname that was given to most serfs. She was also the only servant who was allowed to remain seated in the presence of the mistress or the master of the house.[140] Noble memoirs from the nineteenth century are filled with descriptions of the family's affection for their old wet nurse, who was likely to be treated as a much-loved member of the family and provided with living quarters until she died. Anna Lelong loved her nurse Vasilisia 'more than anyone', and parting from her, as she had to do when she left home to get married, caused her 'dreadful grief'. The intimacy of their relationship, which was 'like that of a mother and a daughter', stemmed from the death of the nurse's infant son. Because of her duties to nurse Anna, she had been obliged to abandon him. Guilt and surrogacy became intertwined, for both Anna and her nurse. Later on, when Anna's husband died, she took it upon herself to care for her old nurse, who came to live with her at the family estate.[141]

But it was the nanny who was closest to the heart of the noble child.

---

* The artist Dobuzhinsky described the spectacular appearance of the traditional wet nurse on the streets of Petersburg before 1917: 'She had a kind of "parade uniform", a pseudo-peasant costume, theatrically designed, which was worn right up to the outbreak of the war in 1914. One often saw a fat, red cheeked wet nurse walking beside her fashionably dressed mistress. She would be dressed in a brocade blouse and cape, and a pink head-dress if the baby was a girl, or a blue one if it was a boy. In the summer the wet nurses used to wear coloured *sarafans* with lots of small gold or glass buttons and muslin balloon sleeves'. (M. V. Dobuzhinskii *vospominaniia* (New York, 1976), p. 34.)

The stereotype of the old-fashioned nanny – the sort that appears in countless works of art from *Eugene Onegin* to *Boris Godunov* – was a simple and kind-hearted Russian peasant woman who got the children up, supervised their play, took them out for walks, fed them, washed them, told them fairy tales, sang them songs and comforted them at night when they woke up with nightmares. More than a surrogate mother, the nanny was the child's main source of love and emotional security. 'Simply and unthinkingly,' reminisced one woman of her noble childhood, 'I imbibed the life-giving fluids of love from my nanny, and they keep me going even now. How many loyal and loving Russian nannies have guarded and inspired the lives of their children, leaving an indelible impression upon them.'[142]

Such indeed was the lasting influence of the nanny's tender care that many nineteenth-century memoirists became obsessed with the nostalgic topic of their nursery years. This was not some arrested development. Rather it was a reflection of the fact that their primary emotions were locked up in that distant chamber of their past. Time and time again these memoirists stress that it was their nanny who taught them how to love and how to live. For some, the key was their nanny's innate kindness, which awoke their moral sensibilities; for others, it was her religious faith, which brought them into contact with the spiritual world. 'How wonderful was our nanny!' Lelong recalled. 'She was intelligent and always serious, and she was very devout; I would often wake up in the nursery at night and see nanny praying by the door of our room, from where she could see the votive lamp. What fantastic fairy tales she told us when we went for a walk in the woods. They made me see the forest world anew, to love nature from a poetic point of view.'[143] The lost idyll of 'a Russian childhood', if ever it existed, was contained in these emotions, which remained associated with the image of the nanny in the adult memory. 'It may seem strange', wrote A. K. Chertkova (the wife of Tolstoy's secretary), 'but forty years have passed since our childhood, and our nanny still remains alive in my memory. The older I become, the clearer is the memory of childhood in my mind, and these recollections are so vivid that the past becomes the present and everything connected in my heart to the memory of my dear good little nanny becomes all the more precious.'[144]

At the age of six or seven the noble child was transferred from the care of a nanny to the supervision of a French or German tutor and then sent off to school. To be separated from one's nanny was to undergo a painful rite of passage from the world of childhood to that of youth and adulthood, as Guards officer Anatoly Vereshchagin recalled. When at the age of six he was told that he would be sent to school, he was 'frightened most of all by the thought of being separated from my nanny. I was so scared that I woke up crying in the night; I would call out for my nanny, and would plead with her not to leave me'.[145] The trauma was compounded by the fact that it entailed a transition from the female-regulated sphere of childhood play to the strict male domain of the tutor and the boarding school; from the Russian-speaking nursery to a house of discipline where the child was forced to speak French. The young and innocent would no longer be protected from the harsh rules of the adult world; he would suddenly be forced to put aside the language that had expressed his childhood feelings and adopt an alien one. To lose nanny was, in short, to be wrenched from one's own emotions as a child. But the separation could be just as difficult on the nanny's side:

Because Fevronia Stepanovna had always spoiled me endlessly, I became a cry-baby, and a proper coward, which I came to regret later when I joined the army. My nanny's influence paralysed the attempts of all my tutors to harden me and so I had to be sent away to boarding school. She found it difficult when I started to grow up and entered into the world of adult men. After cosseting me my whole childhood, she cried when I went swimming in the river with my elder brother and our tutor, or when I went riding, or when I first shot my father's gun. When, years later, as a young officer, I returned home, she got ready two rooms in the house for my return, but they looked like a nursery. Every day she would place two apples by my bed. It hurt her feelings that I had brought my batman home, since she thought it was her duty to serve me. She was shocked to discover that I smoked, and I did not have the heart to tell her that I drank as well. But the greatest shock was when I went to war to fight the Serbs. She tried to dissuade me from going and then, one evening, she said that she would come with me. We would live together in a little cottage and while I went to war she would clean the house and prepare the supper for the evening. Then on holidays we would spend the day together baking pies, as we had always done, and when the war was over we would come back home with medals on my chest. I went to sleep peacefully that night, imagining that war was just as idyllic as she thought it was . . . Yet I needed nanny more than I had thought. When I was nine and our Swiss tutor first arrived, my father said that I had to share a room with my elder brother and this Mr Kaderli, moving out of the room I had shared with my nanny. It turned out that I was completely unable to undress or wash myself or even go to bed without my nanny's help. I did not know how to go to sleep without calling out for her, at least six times, to check that she was there. Getting dressed was just as hard. I had never put my own socks on.[146]

It was not at all unusual for grown men and women to remain in frequent contact with their former nannies; indeed, for them to provide for them in their old age. Pushkin remained close to his old nanny, and he put her image into many of his works. In some ways she was his muse – a fact recognized by many of his friends, so that Prince Viazemsky, for example, signed off his letters to the poet with 'a deep bow of respect and gratitude to Rodionovna!'[147] Pushkin loved his nanny more than anyone. Estranged from his own parents, he always called her 'Mama' and when she died, his was the grief of a son:

> My friend in days devoid of good,
> My ageing and decrepit dove!
> Abandoned in a far-off wood,
> You still await me with your love.
> Beside the window in the hall,
> As if on watch, you sit and mourn,
> At times your knitting needles stall
> In hands now wrinkled and forlorn.
> Through long-deserted gates you peer
> Upon the dark and distant way:
> Forebodings, anguish, cares and fear
> Constrict your weary breast today.[148]

Diaghilev, as well, was famously attached to his nanny. He had never known his mother, who had died when he was born. Nanny Dunia had been born a serf on the Yevreinov estate of his mother's family. She had nursed Diaghilev's mother before coming as part of the dowry to his father's family in Perm. When Diaghilev moved as a student to St Petersburg, his nanny went with him and lived as a housekeeper in his flat. The famous Monday meetings of the 'World of Art' (*Mir iskusstva*) – the circle formed around the journal of that name from which the ideas of the Ballets Russes emerged – were all held in Diaghilev's apartment, where Nanny Dunia presided like a hostess near the *samovar*.[149] The painter Leon Bakst, a regular attender of these meetings, immortalized her image in his famous 1906 portrait of Diaghilev (plate 13).

The nanny was an almost sacred figure in that cult of childhood which the Russian gentry made its own. No other culture has been so sentimental or quite so obsessed about childhood. Where else can one find so many memoirs where the first few years of the writer's life were given so much space? Herzen's, Nabokov's and Prokofiev's – all of them inclined to linger far too long in the nursery of their memory. The essence of this cult was a hypertrophied sense of loss – loss of the ancestral home, loss of the mother or the nanny's tender care, loss of the peasant, child-like Russia contained in fairy tales. Little wonder, then, that the cultural élites became so fixated on folklore – for it took them back to their happy childhoods, to the days when they had listened to their nannies' tales on woodland walks and the nights when they had been sung off to sleep with lullabies. Tolstoy's *Childhood, Boyhood, Youth* (1852–7), Aksakov's *Childhood Years* (1856), Herzen's *Past and Thoughts* (1852–68), Nabokov's *Speak, Memory* (1947) – this is the canon of a literary cult that reinvented childhood as a blissful and enchanted realm:

Happy, happy, irrecoverable days of childhood! How can one fail to love and cherish its memories? Those memories refresh and elevate my soul and are the source of my greatest delight.[150]

The way these Russians wrote about their childhood was extraordinary, too. They all summoned up a legendary world (Aksakov's memoirs were deliberately structured as a fairy tale), mixing myth and memory, as if they were not content to recollect their childhood, but felt a deeper need to retrieve it, even if that meant reinventing it. This same yearning to recover what Nabokov termed 'the legendary Russia of my boyhood' can be felt in Benois and Stravinsky's *Petrushka* (1911). This ballet expressed their shared nostalgia for the sounds and colours which they both recalled from the fairgrounds of their St Petersburg childhoods. And it can be felt in the musical childhood fantasies of Prokofiev, from *The Ugly Duckling* for voice and piano (1914) to the 'symphonic fairy tale' *Peter and the Wolf* (1936), which were inspired by the bedtime tales he had heard as a small boy.

6

'Oh please, Nurse, tell me again how the French came to Moscow.' Thus Herzen starts his sublime memoir *My Past and Thoughts*, one of the greatest works of Russian literature. Born in 1812, Herzen had a special fondness for his nanny's stories of that year. His family had been forced to flee the flames that engulfed Moscow, the young Herzen carried out in his mother's arms, and it was only through a safe conduct from Napoleon himself that they managed to escape to their Yaroslav estate. Herzen felt great 'pride and pleasure at [having] taken part in the Great War'. The story of his childhood merged with the national drama he so loved to hear: 'Tales of the fire of Moscow, of the battle of Borodino, of the Berezina, of the taking of Paris were my cradle songs, my nursery stories, my Iliad and my Odyssey.'[151] For Herzen's generation, the myths of 1812 were intimately linked with their childhood memories. Even in the 1850s children were still brought up on the legends of that year.[152] History, myth and memory were intertwined.

For the historian Nikolai Karamzin, 1812 was a tragic year. While his Moscow neighbours moved to their estates, he refused to 'believe that the ancient holy city could be lost' and, as he wrote on 20 August, he chose instead to 'die on Moscow's walls'.[153] Karamzin's house burned down in the fires and, since he had not thought to evacuate his library, he lost his precious books to the flames as well. But Karamzin saved one book – a bulging notebook that contained the draft of his celebrated *History of the Russian State* (1818–26). Karamzin's masterpiece was the first truly national history – not just in the sense that it was the first by a Russian, but also in the sense that it rendered Russia's past as a national narrative. Previous histories of Russia had been arcane chronicles of monasteries and saints, patriotic propaganda, or heavy tomes of documents compiled by German scholars, unread and unreadable. But Karamzin's *History* had a literary quality that made its twelve large volumes a nationwide success. It combined careful scholarship with the narrative techniques of a novelist. Karamzin stressed the psychological motivations of his historical protagonists – even to the point of inventing them – so that his account became more compelling to a readership brought up on the literary conventions of Romantic texts. Medieval Tsars like Ivan the Terrible or Boris Godunov became tragic figures in Karamzin's *History* – subjects for a modern psychological drama; and from its pages they walked on to the stage in operas by Musorgsky and Rimsky Korsakov.

The first eight volumes of Karamzin's *History* were published in 1818. 'Three thousand copies were sold within a month – something unprecedented in our country. Everyone, even high-born ladies, began to read the history of their country,' wrote Pushkin. 'It was a revelation. You could say that Karamzin discovered ancient Russia as Columbus discovered America.'[154] The victory of 1812 had encouraged a new interest and pride in Russia's past. People who had been raised on the old conviction that there was no history before the reign of Peter the Great began to look back to the distant past for the sources of their country's unexpected strengths. After 1812 history books appeared at a furious pace. Chairs were established in the universities (Gogol held one for a term at St Petersburg). Historical associations were set up, many in the provinces, and huge efforts were suddenly devoted to the rescuing of Russia's past. History became the arena for all those troubling questions about Russia's nature and its destiny. As Belinsky wrote in 1846, 'we interrogate our past for an explanation of our present and a hint of our future.'[155] This historical obsession was reinforced by the failure of the Decembrists. If Russia was no longer to pursue the Western path of history toward a modern constitutional state, as the Decembrists and their supporters had hoped, what then was its proper destiny?

This was the question posed by Pyotr Chaadaev, the Guards officer and foppish friend of Pushkin, in his sensational *First Philosophical Letter* (1836). Chaadaev was another 'child of 1812'. He had fought at Borodino, before resigning from the army, at the height of his career in 1821, to spend the next five years in Europe. An extreme Westernist – to the extent that he converted to the Roman Church – he was thrown into despair by Russia's failure to take the Western path in 1825. This was the context in which he wrote his *Letter* – 'at a time of madness' (by his own admission) when he tried to take his life. 'What have we Russians ever invented or created?' Chaadaev wrote in 1826. 'The time has come to stop running after others; we must take a fresh and frank look at ourselves; we must understand ourselves as we really are; we must stop lying and find the truth.'[156] The *First Letter* was an attempt to reveal this bleak and unpalatable truth. It was more a work of history than of philosophy. Russia, it concluded, stood 'outside of time, without a past or a future', having played no part in the history of the world. The Roman legacy, the civilization of the Western Church and the Renaissance – these had all passed Russia by – and now, after 1825, the country was reduced to a 'cultural void', an 'orphan cut off from the human family' which could imitate the nations of the West but never become one of them. The Russians were like nomads in their land, strangers to themselves, without a sense of their own national heritage or identity.[157]

To the reader in the modern world – where self-lacerating national declarations are made in the media almost every month – the cataclysmic shock of the *First Letter* may be hard to understand. It took away the ground from under the feet of every person who had been brought up to believe in 'European Russia' as their native land. The outcry was immense. Patriots demanded the public prosecution of the 'lunatic' for 'the cruellest insult to our national honour', and, on the orders of the Tsar, Chaadaev was declared insane, placed under house arrest and visited by doctors every day.[158] Yet what he wrote had been felt by every thinking Russian for many years: the overwhelming sense of living in a wasteland or 'phantom country', as Belinsky put it, a country which they feared they might never really know; and the acute fear that, contrary to the *raison d'être* of their civilization, they might never in fact catch up with the West. There were many similar expressions of this cultural pessimism after 1825. The triumph of reaction had engendered a deep loathing of the 'Russian way'. 'Real patriotism', wrote Prince Viazemsky in 1828, 'should consist of hatred for Russia as she manifests herself at the present time.'[159] The literary critic Nadezhdin (who published the *First Letter* in his journal *Telescope*) himself wrote in 1834: 'We [the Russians] have created nothing. There is no branch of learning in which we can show something of our own. There is not a single person who could stand for Russia in the civilization of the world.'[160]

The Slavophiles had an opposite response to the crisis posed by Chaadaev. They first emerged as a distinct grouping in the 1830s, when they launched their public disputes with the Westernists, but they too had their roots in 1812. The horrors of the French Revolution had led the Slavophiles to reject the universal culture of the Enlightenment and to emphasize instead those indigenous traditions that distinguished Russia from the West. This search for a more 'Russian' way of life was a common response to the débâcle of 1825. Once it became clear that Russia would diverge from the Western path, European Russians, like Lavretsky in Turgenev's *Nest of Gentlefolk* (1859), began to explore – and find virtue in – those parts of Russian culture that were different from the West:

The free-thinker began to go to church and to order prayers to be said for him; the European began to steam himself in the Russian bath, to dine at two o'clock, to go to bed at nine, and to be talked to sleep by the gossip of an old butler . . .[161]

The Slavophiles looked first to the virtues they discerned in the patriarchal customs of the countryside – hardly surprising, given that they were born, for the most, to landed families that had lived in the same region for several hundred years. Konstantin Aksakov, the most famous and the most extremist of the Slavophiles, spent practically his entire life in one house, clinging to it, in the words of one contemporary, 'like an oyster to his shell'.[162] They idealized the common folk (*narod*) as the true bearer of the national character (*narodnost'*). Slavophile folklorists such as Pyotr Kireevsky went out to the villages to transcribe the peasant songs, which they thought could be interpreted as historical expressions of the 'Russian soul'. As devout upholders of the Orthodox ideal, they maintained that the Russian was defined by Christian sacrifice and humility. This was the foundation of the spiritual community (*sobornost'*) in which, they imagined, the squire and his serfs were bound together by their patriarchal customs and Orthodox beliefs. Aksakov argued that this 'Russian type' was incarnated in the legendary folk hero Ilia Muromets, who appears in epic tales as protector of the Russian land against invaders and infidels, brigands and monsters, with his 'gentle strength and lack of aggression, yet his readiness to fight in a just defensive war for the people's cause'.* The peasant soldiers of 1812 had shown these very qualities. Myth entering history.

Karamzin's *History* was the opening statement in a long debate on Russia's past and future that would run right through its culture in the nineteenth century. Karamzin's own work was squarely situated in the monarchist tradition, which portrayed the Tsarist state and its noble servitors as a force for progress and enlightenment. The overarching theme of the *History* was Russia's steady advance towards the ideal of a unitary Imperial state whose greatness lay in the inherited wisdom of its Tsar and the innate obedience of its citizens. The Tsar and his nobles initiated change, while 'the people remain silent' ('*narod bezmolvstvuet*'), as Pushkin put it in the final stage direction of *Boris Godunov*. Pushkin shared Karamzin's statist view of Russian history – at least in his later years, after the collapse of his republican convictions (which were in any case extremely dubious) in 1825. In *The History of Pugachev* (1833) Pushkin emphasized the need for enlightened monarchy to protect the nation from the elemental violence ('cruel and merciless') of the Cossack rebel leader Pugachev and his peasant followers. By highlighting the role of paternal noblemen such as General Bibikov and Count Panin, who put down Pugachev yet pleaded with the Empress to soften her regime, Pushkin underscored the national leadership of the old landed gentry from which he was so proud to descend.

In contrast to these views was the democratic trend of Russian history advanced by the Decembrists and their followers. They stressed

---

* Dostoevsky shared this view. The Russians, he wrote in 1876, were 'a people devoted to sacrifice, seeking truth and knowing where truth can be found, as honest and pure in heart as one of their high ideals, the epic hero Ilia Muromets, whom they cherish as a saint' (F. Dostoevsky, *A Writer's Diary*, trans. K. Lantz, 2 vols. (London, 1993), vol. 1, p. 660).

the rebellious and freedom-loving spirit of the Russian people and idealized the medieval republics of Novgorod and Pskov, and the Cossack revolts of the seventeenth and eighteenth centuries, including Pugachev's. They believed that the common people had always been the (hidden) moving force of history – a theory largely shaped by their observation of the peasant soldiers in the war of 1812. In response to Karamzin's famous motto 'The history of the nation belongs to the Tsar', the Decembrist historian Nikita Muraviev began his study with the fighting words: 'History belongs to the people.'[163]

The origins of Russia was a major battlefield in this war between historians. Monarchists subscribed to the so-called Norman theory, originally devised by German historians in the eighteenth century, which maintained that the first ruling princes had arrived in Russia from Scandinavia (in the ninth century) by invitation from the warring Slavic tribes. The only real evidence for this argument was the *Primary Chronicle* – an eleventh-century account of the founding of the Kievan state in 862 – which had probably been written to justify what actually amounted to the Scandinavian conquest of Russia. The theory became increasingly untenable as nineteenth-century archaeologists drew attention to the advanced culture of the Slavic tribes in southern Russia. A picture emerged of a civilization stretching back to the ancient Scythians, the Goths, the Romans and the Greeks. Yet the Norman theory was a good foundation myth for the defenders of autocracy – supposing, as it did, that without a monarchy the Russians were incapable of governance. In Karamzin's words, before the establishment of princely rule, Russia had been nothing but an 'empty space' with 'wild and warring tribes, living on a level with the beasts and birds'.[164] Against that the democrats maintained that the Russian state had evolved spontaneously from the native customs of the Slavic tribes. According to this view, long before the Varangians arrived the Slavs had set up their own government, whose republican liberties were gradually destroyed by the imposition of princely rule. Versions of the argument were made by all those groups who believed in the natural predilection of the Slavic people for democracy: not just the Decembrists but left-wing Slavophiles, Polish historians (who used it to denounce the Tsarist system in Poland), and Populist historians in the Ukraine and (later on) in Russia, too.

Another battlefield was medieval Novgorod – the greatest monument to Russian liberty and, in the Decembrist view, historic proof of the people's right to rule themselves. Along with nearby Pskov, Novgorod was a flourishing civilization connected to the Hanseatic League of German trading towns prior to its conquest by Tsar Ivan III and its subjugation to Muscovy during the late fifteenth century. The Decembrists made a cult of the city republic. As a symbol of the people's long-lost freedoms, they saw its *veche*, or assembly, as a sacred legacy connecting Russia to the democratic traditions of ancient Greece and Rome. The teenage members of the 'holy *artel*' (1814–17) – among them several of the future Decembrists – opened all their meetings with the ceremonial ringing of the *veche* bell. In their manifestos the Decembrists used the terminology of medieval Novgorod, calling the future parliament the 'national *veche*'.[165] The myth of Novgorod took on a new meaning and subversive power after the suppression of their uprising. In 1830 Lermontov wrote a poem entitled *Novgorod* ('Brave sons of the Slavs, for what did you die?'), in which it was left deliberately unclear whether it was the fallen heroes of medieval Novgorod or the freedom fighters of 1825 whose loss was to be mourned. The same nostalgic note was struck by Dimtry Venevitanov in his pro-Decembrist poem *Novgorod* (1826):

> Answer great city:
> Where are your glorious days of liberty,
> When your voice, the scourge of kings,
> Rang true like the bells at your noisy assembly?
> Say, where are those times?
> They are so far away, oh, so far away![166]

The monarchist perception of medieval Novgorod formed a stark contrast. According to Karamzin, Moscow's conquest of the city was a necessary step towards the creation of a unitary state, and was recognized as such by its citizens. This submission was a sign of the Russian people's wisdom, in Karamzin's view: they recognized that freedom was worth nothing without order and security. The Novgorodians were thus the original consenting members in the leviathan of autocracy. They chose the protection of the Tsar in order to save themselves from their own internal squabbles, which had played into the hands of the city's *boyars*, who became despotic and corrupt and who threatened to sell out to the neighbouring state of Lithuania. Karamzin's version was almost certainly closer to the historical truth than the Decembrists' vision of an egalitarian and harmonious republican democracy. Yet it too was a justifying myth. For Karamzin the lesson to be learned from his *History* was clear: that republics were more likely to become despotic than autocracies – and a lesson well worth underlining after the collapse of the French republic into the Napoleonic dictatorship.

The war of 1812 was itself a battlefield for these competing myths of Russian history. This was shown by its commemoration in the nineteenth century. For the Decembrists, 1812 was a people's war. It was the point at which the Russians came of age, the moment when they passed from childhood into adult citizens, and with their triumphant entry into Europe, they should have joined the family of European states. But for the defenders of the status quo, the war symbolized the holy triumph of the Russian autocratic principle, which alone saved Europe from Napoleon. It was a time when the Tsarist state emerged as God's chosen agent in a new historical dispensation.

The regime's image of itself was set in stone with the Alexandrine Column, built, ironically, by the French architect Auguste de Montferrand on Palace Square in Petersburg, and opened on the twentieth anniversary of the battle of Borodino. The angel on the top of the column was given the Tsar Alexander's face.[167] Five years later, work began in Moscow on a larger monument to the divine mission of the Russian monarchy – the grandiose Cathedral of Christ the Saviour on a site overlooking the Kremlin walls. Half war museum and half church, it was intended to commemorate the miraculous salvation of Moscow in 1812. Constantin Ton's design echoed the architectural language of the ancient Russian Church, but enlarged its proportions to an imperial scale. This colossal cathedral was the tallest building in Moscow when it was completed, after fifty years, in 1883, and even today, reconstructed after Stalin had it blown up in 1931 (one death sentence that might be justified on artistic grounds), it still dominates the cityscape.

Throughout the nineteenth century these two images of 1812 – as

8. *Monument to the millennium of Russia in the square in front of St Sophia's Cathedral, Novgorod*

a national liberation or imperial salvation – continued to compete for the public meaning of the war. On the one side was Tolstoy's *War and Peace*, a truly national drama which tells its history from the viewpoint of the noble and the serf. On the other were the monuments in stone, the triumphant arches and gates of victory in the pompous 'Empire style' that trumpeted Russia's imperial might; or the sound of all those cannons in Tchaikovsky's *Overture of 1812*. Even in the early 1860s, when there were high hopes for national unity in the wake of the emancipation of the serfs, these two visions were at loggerheads. The fiftieth anniversary of 1812 coincided with the millennium of the Russian state in 1862. The millennium was due to be commemorated in the spring in (of all symbolic places) Novgorod. But the Emperor Alexander II ordered its postponement to 26 August – the anniversary of the battle of Borodino and the sacred date of his own coronation in 1856. By merging these three anniversaries, the Romanov dynasty was attempting to reinvent itself as a national institution, consecrated by the holy victory of 1812, and one as old as the Russian state itself. The granite monument unveiled in Novgorod was a symbol of this claim. Shaped like the bell of the Novgorod assembly, it was encircled by a band of bas-reliefs with the sculptures of those figures – saints and princes, generals and warriors, scientists and artists – who had shaped a thousand years of Russian history. The great bell was crowned by Mother Russia, bearing in one hand the Orthodox cross and in the other a shield emblazoned with the Romanov insignia. The Decembrists were irate. Volkonsky, who had by now returned from his thirty years of exile, told Tolstoy that the monument had 'trampled on the sacred memory of Novgorod as well as on the graves of all those heroes who fought for our freedom in 1812'.[168]

7

'He is an enthusiast, a mystic and a Christian, with high ideals for the new Russia,' Tolstoy wrote to Herzen after meeting Volkonsky in 1859.[169] A distant cousin of the Decembrist, Tolstoy was extremely proud of his Volkonsky heritage. Having lost his mother at the age of three, he had more than just an academic interest in researching the background of her family: for him, it was an emotional necessity. Sergei Volkonsky was a childhood hero of Tolstoy's (all the Decembrists were idolized by the progressive youths of Tolstoy's age) and in time he became the inspiration for Prince Andrei Bolkonsky in *War and Peace*.[170] Much of Tolstoy's commitment to the peasants, not to mention his desire to become one himself, was inspired by the example of his exiled relative.

In 1859 Tolstoy started a school for peasant children at Yasnaya Polyana, the old Volkonsky estate that had passed down to him on his mother's side. The estate had a special meaning for Tolstoy. He had been born in the manor house – on a dark green leather sofa which he kept throughout his life in the study where he wrote his great novels. He spent his childhood on the estate, until the age of nine, when he moved to Moscow with his father. More than an estate, Yasnaya Polyana was his ancestral nest, the place where his childhood memories were kept, and the little patch of Russia where he felt he most belonged. 'I wouldn't sell the house for anything,' Tolstoy told his brother in 1852. 'It's the last thing I'd be prepared to part with.'[171] Yasnaya Polyana had been purchased by Tolstoy's great-grandmother, Maria Volkonsky, in 1763. His grandfather, Nikolai Volkonsky, had developed it as a cultural space, building the splendid manor house, with its large collection of European books, the landscaped park and lakes, the spinning factory, and the famous white stone entrance gates that served as a post station on the road from Tula to Moscow. As a boy, Tolstoy idolized his grandfather. He fantasized that he was just like him.[172] This ancestor cult, which was at the emotional core of Tolstoy's conservatism, was expressed in Eugene, the hero of his story 'The Devil' (1889):

It is generally supposed that Conservatives are old people, and that those in favour of change are the young. That is not quite correct. Usually Conservatives are young people: those who want to live but who do not think about how to live, and have not time to think, and therefore take as a model for themselves a way of life that they have seen. Thus it was with Eugene. Having settled in the village, his aim and ideal was to restore the form of life that had existed, not in his father's time . . . but in his grandfather's.[173]

Nikolai Volkonsky was brought back to life as Andrei's father Nikolai Bolkonsky in *War and Peace* – the retired general, proud and independent, who spends his final years on the estate at Bald Hill, dedicating himself to the education of his daughter called (like Tolstoy's mother) Maria.

War and Peace was originally conceived as a 'Decembrist novel', loosely based on the life story of Sergei Volkonsky. But the more the writer researched into the Decembrists, the more he realized that their intellectual roots lay in the war of 1812. In the novel's early form (*The Decembrist*) the Decembrist hero returns after thirty years of exile in Siberia to the intellectual ferment of the late 1850s. A second Alexandrine reign has just begun, with the accession of Alexander II to the throne in 1855, and once again, as in 1825, high hopes for political reform are in the air. It was with such hopes that Volkonsky returned to Russia in 1856 and wrote about a new life based on truth:

Falsehood. This is the sickness of the Russian state. Falsehood and its sisters, hypocrisy and cynicism. Russia could not exist without them. Yet surely the point is not just to exist but to exist with dignity. And if we want to be honest with ourselves, then we must recognize that if Russia cannot exist otherwise than she existed in the past, then she does not deserve to exist.[174]

To live in truth, or, more importantly, to live in truth in Russia – these were the questions of Tolstoy's life and work, and the main concerns of *War and Peace*. They were first articulated by the men of 1812.

Volkonsky's release from exile was one of the first acts of the new Tsar. Of the 121 Decembrists who had been sent into exile in 1826, only nineteen lived to return to Russia in 1856. Sergei himself was a broken man, and his health never really recovered from the hardships of Siberia. Forbidden to settle in the two main cities, he was none the less a frequent guest in the Moscow houses of the Slavophiles, who saw his gentle nature, his patient suffering, his simple 'peasant' lifestyle and his closeness to the land as quintessential 'Russian' qualities.[175] Moscow's students idolized Volkonsky. With his long white beard and hair, his sad, expressive face, 'pale and tender like the moon', he was regarded as a 'sort of Christ who had emerged from the Russian wilderness'.[176] A symbol of the democratic cause that had been interrupted by the oppressive regime of Nicholas I, Volkonsky was a living connection between the Decembrists and the Populists, who emerged as the people's champions in the 1860s and 1870s. Volkonsky himself remained true to the ideals of 1812. He continued to reject the values of the bureaucratic state and the aristocracy and, in the spirit of the Decembrists, he continued to uphold the civic obligation to live an honest life in the service of the people, who embodied the nation. 'You

9. Maria Volkonsky and her son Misha. Daguerreotype, 1862.
Maria was suffering from a kidney disease and died a year later

know from experience,' he wrote to his son Misha (now serving in the army in the Amur region) in 1857,

that I have never tried to persuade you of my own political convictions – they belong to me. In your mother's scheme you were directed towards the governmental sphere, and I gave my blessing when you went into the service of the Fatherland and Tsar. But I always taught you to conduct yourself without lordly airs when dealing with your comrades from a different class. You made your own way – without the patronage of your grandmother – and knowing that, my friend, will give me peace until the day when I go to my grave.[177]

Volkonsky's notion of the Fatherland was intimately linked with his idea of the Tsar: he saw the sovereign as a symbol of Russia. Throughout his life he remained a monarchist – so much so indeed that when he heard about the death of Nicholas I, the Tsar who had sent him into exile thirty years before, Volkonsky broke down and cried like a child. 'Your father weeps all day', Maria wrote to Misha, 'it is already the third day and I don't know what to do with him.'[178] Perhaps Volkonsky was grieving for the man he had known as a boy. Or perhaps his death was a catharsis of the suffering he had endured in Siberia. But Volkonsky's tears were tears for Russia, too: he saw the Tsar as the Empire's single unifying force and was afraid for his country now that the Tsar was dead.

Volkonsky's trust in the Russian monarchy was not returned. The former exile was kept under almost constant police surveillance on the orders of the Tsar after his return from Siberia. He was refused the restoration of his princely title and his property. But what hurt him most was the government's refusal to return his medals from the war of 1812.* Thirty years of exile had not changed his love for Russia. He followed the Crimean War between 1853 and 1856 with obsessive interest and was deeply stirred by the heroism of the defenders at Sevastopol (among them the young Tolstoy). The old soldier (at the age of sixty-four) had even petitioned to join them as a humble private in the infantry, and it was only his wife's pleading that eventually

---

* Eventually, after several years of petitioning, the Tsar returned them in 1864. But other forms of recognition took longer. In 1822 the English artist George Dawe was commissioned to paint Volkonsky's portrait for the 'Gallery of Heroes' – 332 portraits of the military leaders of 1812 – in the Winter Palace in St Petersburg. After the Decembrist uprising Volkonsky's portrait was removed, leaving a black square in the line-up of portraits. In 1903 Volkonsky's nephew, Ivan Vsevolozhsky, Director of the Hermitage, petitioned Tsar Nicholas II to restore the picture to its rightful place. 'Yes, of course,' replied the Tsar, 'it was so long ago' (S. M. Volkonskii, *O dekabristakh: po semeinum vospominaniiam* (Moscow, 1994), p. 87).

dissuaded him. He saw the war as a return to the spirit of 1812, and he was convinced that Russia would again be victorious against the French.[179]

It was not. Yet Russia's defeat made more likely Volkonsky's second hope: the emancipation of the serfs. The new Tsar, Alexander II, was another child of 1812. He had been educated by the liberal poet Vasily Zhukovsky, who had been appointed tutor to the court in 1817. In 1822 Zhukovsky had set free the serfs on his estate. His humanism had a major influence on the future Tsar. The defeat in the Crimean War had persuaded Alexander that Russia could not compete with the Western powers until it swept aside its old serf economy and modernized itself. The gentry had very little idea how to make a profit from their estates. Most of them knew next to nothing about agriculture or accounting. Yet they went on spending in the same old lavish way as they had always done, mounting up enormous debts. By 1859, one-third of the estates and two-thirds of the serfs owned by the landed nobles had been mortgaged to the state and noble banks. Many of the smaller landowners could barely afford to feed their serfs. The economic argument for emancipation was becoming irrefutable, and many landowners were shifting willy-nilly to the free labour system by contracting other people's serfs. Since the peasantry's redemption payments would cancel out the gentry's debts, the economic rationale was becoming equally irresistible.*

But there was more than money to the arguments. The Tsar believed that the emancipation was a necessary measure to prevent a revolution from below. The soldiers who had fought in the Crimean War had been led to expect their freedom, and in the first six years of Alexander's reign, before the emancipation was decreed, there were 500 peasant uprisings against the gentry on the land.[180] Like Volkonsky, Alexander was convinced that emancipation was, in Volkonsky's words, a 'ques-

---

* Under the terms of emancipation the peasants were obliged to pay redemption dues on the communal lands which were transferred to them. These repayments, calculated by the gentry's own land commissions, were to be repaid over a 49-year period to the state, which recompensed the gentry in 1861. Thus, in effect, the serfs bought their freedom by paying off their masters' debts. The redemption payments became increasingly difficult to collect, not least because the peasantry regarded them as unjust from the start. They were finally cancelled in 1905.

tion of justice . . . a moral and a Christian obligation, for every citizen who loves his Fatherland'.[181] As the Decembrist explained in a letter to Pushchin, the abolition of serfdom was 'the least the state could do to recognize the sacrifice the peasantry has made in the last two wars: it is time to recognize that the Russian peasant is a citizen as well'.[182]

In 1858 the Tsar appointed a special commission to formulate proposals for the emancipation in consultation with provincial gentry committees. Under pressure from the diehard squires to limit the reform or to fix the rules for the land transfers in their favour, the commission became bogged down in political wrangling for the best part of two years. Having waited all his life for this moment, Volkonsky was afraid that he 'might die before emancipation came to pass'.[183] The old prince was sceptical of the landed gentry, knowing their resistance to the spirit of reform and fearing their ability to obstruct the emancipation or use it to increase their exploitation of the peasantry. Although not invited on to any commission, Volkonsky sketched out his own progressive plans for the emancipation, in which he envisaged a state bank to advance loans to individual peasants to buy small plots of the gentry's land as private property. The peasants would repay these loans by working their allotments of communal land.[184] Volkonsky's programme was not dissimilar to the land reforms of Pyotr Stolypin, the Prime Minister and last reformist hope of Tsarist Russia between 1906 and 1911. Had such a programme been implemented in 1861, Russia might have become a more prosperous place.

In the end the diehard gentry was defeated and the moderate reformists got their way, thanks in no small measure to the personal intervention of the Tsar. The Law of the Emancipation was signed by Alexander on 19 February 1861. It was not as far-reaching as the peasantry had hoped, and there were rebellions in many areas. The Law allowed landowners considerable leeway in choosing the bits of land for transfer to the peasantry – and in setting the price for them. Overall, perhaps half the farming land in European Russia was transferred from the gentry's ownership to the communal tenure of the peasantry, although the precise proportion depended largely on the landowner's will. Owing to the growth of the population it was still far from enough to liberate the peasantry from poverty. Even on the old estates of Sergei Volkonsky, where the prince's influence ensured that nearly all the land was transferred to the peasants, there remained a shortage of agricultural land, and by the middle of the 1870s there were angry demonstrations by the peasantry.[185] None the less, despite its disappointment for the peasantry, the emancipation was a crucial watershed. Freedom of a sort, however limited it may have been in practice, had at last been granted to the mass of the people, and there were grounds to hope for a national rebirth, and reconciliation between the landowners and the peasantry. The liberal spirit of 1812 had triumphed in the end – or so it seemed.

Prince Volkonsky was in Nice when he heard the news of the decree. That evening he attended a thanksgiving service at the Russian church. At the sound of the choir he broke down into tears. It was, he said later, the 'happiest moment of my life'.[186]

Volkonsky died in 1865 – two years after Maria. His health, weakened in exile, was broken by her death, but right to the end his spirit was intact. During these last months he wrote his memoirs. He died, pen in hand, in the middle of a sentence where he started to recount that vital moment after his arrest when he was interrogated by the Tsar: 'The Emperor said to me: "I . . .".'

Towards the end of his memoirs Volkonsky wrote a sentence which the censors cut from the first edition (not published until 1903). It could have served as his epitaph: 'The path I chose led me to Siberia, to exile from my homeland for thirty years, but my convictions have not changed, and I would do the same again.'[187]

3

overleaf:
*St Basil's Cathedral, Red Square, Moscow,
during the late nineteenth century*

MOSCOW!
MOSCOW!

1

'There it is at last, this famous town,' Napoleon remarked as he surveyed Moscow from the Sparrow Hills. The city's palaces and golden cupolas, sparkling in the sun, were spread out spaciously across the plain, and on the far side he could just make out a long black column of people coiling out of the distant gates. 'Are they abandoning all this?' the Emperor exclaimed. 'It isn't possible!'[1]

The French found Moscow empty, like a 'dying queenless hive'.[2] The mass exodus had begun in August, when news of the defeat at Smolensk had arrived in Moscow, and it reached fever pitch after Borodino, when Kutuzov fell back to the outskirts of the city and finally decided to abandon it. The rich (like the Rostovs in *War and Peace*) packed up their belongings and left by horse and cart for their country houses. The poor walked, carrying their children, their chickens crated on to carts, their cows following behind. One witness recalled that the roads as far as Riazan were blocked by refugees.[3]

As Napoleon took up residence in the Kremlin palace, incendiaries set fire to the trading stalls by its eastern wall. The fires had been ordered by Count Rostopchin, the city's governor, as an act of sacrifice to rob the French of supplies and force them to retreat. Soon the whole of Moscow was engulfed in flames. The novelist Stendhal (serving in the Quartermaster's section of Napoleon's staff) described it as a 'pyramid of copper coloured smoke' whose 'base is on the earth and whose spire rises towards the heavens'. By the third day, the Kremlin was surrounded by the flames, and Napoleon was forced to flee. He fought his way 'through a wall of fire', according to Ségur, 'to the crash of collapsing floors and ceilings, falling rafters and melting iron roofs'. All the time he expressed his outrage, and his admiration, at the Russian sacrifice. 'What a people! They are Scythians! What resoluteness! The barbarians!'[4] By the time the fires were burnt out, on 20 September 1812, four-fifths of the city had been destroyed. Re-entering Moscow, Ségur 'found only a few scattered houses standing in the midst of the ruins'.

This stricken giant, scorched and blackened, exhaled a horrible stench. Heaps of ashes and an occasional section of a wall or a broken column alone indicated the existence of streets. In the poorer quarters scattered groups of men and women, their clothes almost burnt off them, were wandering around like ghosts.[5]

All the city's churches and palaces were looted, if not already burned. Libraries and other national treasures were lost to the flames. In a fit of anger Napoleon instructed that the Kremlin be mined as an act of retribution for the fires that had robbed him of his greatest victory. The Arsenal was blown up and part of the medieval walls were destroyed. But the Kremlin churches all survived. Three weeks later, the first snow fell. Winter had come early and unexpectedly. Unable to survive without supplies in the ruined city, the French were forced to retreat.

Tolstoy wrote in *War and Peace* that every Russian felt Moscow to be a mother. There was a sense in which it was the nation's 'home', even for members of the most Europeanized élite of Petersburg. Moscow was a symbol of the old Russia, the place where ancient Russian customs were preserved. Its history went back to the twelfth century, when Prince Dolgoruky of Suzdal built a rough log fortress on the site of the Kremlin. At that time Kiev was the capital of Christian Rus'. But the Mongol occupation of the next two centuries crushed the Kievan states, leaving Moscow's princes to consolidate their wealth and power by collaboration with the khans. Moscow's rise was symbolized by the building of the Kremlin, which took shape in the fourteenth century, as impressive palaces and white-stoned cathedrals with golden onion domes began to appear within the fortress walls. Eventually, as the khanates weakened, Moscow led the nation's liberation, starting with the battle of Kulikovo Field against the Golden Horde in 1380 and ending in the defeat of the khanates of Kazan and Astrakhan in the 1550s, when it finally emerged as the capital of Russia's cultural life.

To mark that final victory Ivan IV ('the Terrible') ordered the construction of a new cathedral on Red Square. St Basil's symbolized the triumphant restoration of the Orthodox traditions of Byzantium. Originally named the Intercession of the Virgin (to mark the fact that the Tatar capital of Kazan had been captured on that sacred feast day in 1552), the cathedral signalled Moscow's role as the capital of a religious crusade against the Tatar nomads of the steppe. This Imperial mission was set out in the doctrine of Moscow as the Third Rome, a doctrine which St Basil's set in stone. After the fall of Constantinople in 1453, Moscow saw itself as the last surviving centre of the Orthodox religion, as the heir to Rome and Byzantium, and as such the saviour of mankind. Moscow's princes claimed the imperial title 'Tsar' (a Russian derivation of 'Caesar'); they added the double-headed eagle of the Byzantine emperors to the figure of St George on their coat of arms. The backing of the Church was fundamental to Moscow's emergence as the mother city of Holy Rus'. In 1326 the Metropolitan had moved the centre of the Russian Church from Vladimir to Moscow and, from that point on, Moscow's enemies were branded the enemies of Christ. The union of Moscow and Orthodoxy was cemented in the churches and the monasteries, with their icons and their frescoes, which remain the glory of medieval Russian art. According to folklore, Moscow boasted 'forty times forty' churches. The actual number was a little over 200 (until the fires of 1812), but Napoleon, it seems, was sufficiently impressed by his hilltop view of the city's golden domes to repeat the mythic figure in a letter to the Empress Josephine.

By razing the medieval city to the ground, the fires carried out what Russia's eighteenth-century rulers always hoped for. Peter the Great had hated Moscow: it embodied the archaic in his realm. Moscow was a centre of the Old Believers – devout adherents of the Russian Orthodox rituals which had been observed before the Nikonian Church reforms of the 1650s (most contentiously, an alteration to the number of fingers used in making the sign of the cross) had brought them into line with those of the Greek Orthodox liturgy. The Old Believers clung to their ancient rituals as the embodiment of their religious faith. They saw the reforms as a heresy, a sign that the Devil had gained a hold on the Russian Church and state, and many of them fled to the remote regions of the north, or even killed themselves in mass suicides, in the belief that the world would end. The Old Believers pinned their faith on Moscow's messianic destiny as the Third Rome, the last true seat of Orthodoxy after the fall of Constantinople. They explained its capture by the Turks as a divine punishment for the reunion of the Greek Orthodox Church with Rome at the Council of Florence in 1439. Fearful and mistrustful of the West, or any innovation from the outside world, they lived in tightly knit patriarchal communities which, like medieval Moscow, were inward-looking and enclosed. They regarded Peter as the Antichrist – his city on the Baltic as a kingdom of the Devil and apocalypse. Many of the darker legends about Petersburg had their origins in the Old Belief.

With the building of St Petersburg, Moscow's fortunes had declined rapidly. Its population had fallen, as half the city's craftsmen, traders and nobility were forced to resettle in the Baltic capital. Moscow had been reduced to a provincial capital (Pushkin compared it to a faded dowager queen in purple mourning clothes obliged to curtsy before a new empress) and until the middle of the nineteenth century it retained the character of a sleepy hollow. With its little wooden houses and narrow winding lanes, its mansions with their stables and enclosed courtyards, where cows and sheep were allowed to roam, Moscow had a distinct rural feel. It was called 'the big village' – a nickname it has retained to this day. As Catherine the Great saw it, though, Moscow was 'the seat of sloth' whose vast size encouraged the nobility to live in 'idleness and luxury'. It was 'full of symbols of fanaticism, churches, miraculous icons, priests and convents, side by side with thieves and brigands',[6] the very incarnation of the old medieval Russia which the Empress wished to sweep away. When in the early 1770s the Black Death swept through the city and several thousand houses needed to be burned, she thought to clear the lot. Plans were drawn up to rebuild the city in the European image of St Petersburg – a ring of squares and plazas linked by tree-lined boulevards, quays and pleasure parks. The architects Vasily Bazhenov and Matvei Kazakov persuaded Catherine to replace the greater part of the medieval Kremlin with new classical structures. Some demolition did take place, but the project was postponed for lack of cash.

After 1812 the centre of the city was finally rebuilt in the European style. The fire had cleared space for the expansive principles of classicism and, as Colonel Skalozub assures us in Griboedov's drama *Woe from Wit*, it 'improved the look of Moscow quite a lot'.[7] Red Square was opened up through the removal of the old trading stalls that had given it the feeling of an enclosed market rather than an open public space. Three new avenues were laid out in a fan shape from the square. Twisting little lanes were flattened to make room for broad straight boulevards. The first of several planned ensembles, Theatre Square, with the Bolshoi Theatre at its centre, was completed in 1824, followed shortly after by the Boulevard and Garden Rings (still today the city's main ring roads) and the Alexander Gardens laid out by the Kremlin's western walls.[8] Private money poured into the building of the city, which became a standard of the national revival after 1812, and it was not long before the central avenues were lined by graceful mansions and Palladian palaces. Every noble family felt instinctively the need to reconstruct their old ancestral home, so Moscow was rebuilt with fantastic speed. Tolstoy compared what happened to the way that ants return to their ruined heap, dragging off bits of rubbish, eggs and corpses, and reconstructing their old life with renewed energy. It showed that there was 'something indestructible' which, though intangible, was 'the real strength of the colony'.[9]

Yet in all this frenzy of construction there was never slavish imitation of the West. Moscow always mixed the European with its own distinctive style. Classical façades were softened by the use of warm pastel colours, large round bulky forms and Russian ornament. The overall effect was to radiate an easygoing charm that was entirely absent from the cold austerity and imperial grandeur of St Petersburg. Petersburg's style was dictated by the court and by European fashion; Moscow's was set more by the Russian provinces. The Moscow aristocracy was really an extension of the provincial gentry. It spent the summer in the country and came to Moscow in October for the winter season of balls and banquets, returning to its estates in the countryside as soon as the roads were passable following the thaw. Moscow was located in the centre of the Russian lands, an economic crossroads between north and south, Europe and the Asiatic steppe. As its empire had expanded, Moscow had absorbed these diverse influences and imposed its own style on the provinces. Kazan was typical. The old khanate capital took on the image of its Russian conqueror – its kremlin, its monasteries, its houses and its churches all built in the Moscow style. Moscow, in this sense, was the cultural capital of the Russian provinces.

But oriental customs and colours and motifs were also to be seen on Moscow's streets. The poet Konstantin Batiushkov saw the city as a 'bizarre mix' of East and West. It was an 'amazing and incomprehensible confluence of superstition and magnificence, ignorance and enlightenment', which led him to the disturbing conclusion that Peter had 'accomplished a great deal – but he did not finish anything'.[10] In the image of Moscow one could still make out the influence of Genghiz Khan. This Asiatic element was a source of magic and barbarity. 'If there were minarets instead of churches', wrote the critic Belinsky, 'one might be in one of those wild oriental cities that Scheherazade used to tell about.'[11] The Marquis de Custine considered that Moscow's cupolas were like 'oriental domes that transport you to Delhi, while donjon-keeps and turrets bring you back to Europe at the time of the crusades'.[12] Napoleon thought its churches were like mosques.[13]

Moscow's semi-oriental nature was given full expression in the so-called neo-Byzantine style of architecture that dominated its reconstruction in the 1830s and 1840s. The term is misleading, for the architecture was in fact quite eclectic, mixing elements of the neo-Gothic and medieval Russian styles with Byzantine and classical motifs. The term was fostered by Nicholas I and his ideologists to signal Russia's cultural turning away from the West in the wake of the suppression of the Decembrists. The Tsar sympathized with a Slavophile world view that associated Russia with the eastern traditions of Byzantium. Churches like the Cathedral of Christ the Saviour, with its onion domes and belltowers, its tent roofs and *kokoshnik* pediments, combined elements of the Greek-Byzantine and medieval Russian styles. With buildings such as this, Moscow's rebirth was soon mythologized as a national renaissance, a conscious rejection of the European culture of St Petersburg in favour of a return to the ancient native traditions of Muscovy.

The opposition between Moscow and St Petersburg was fundamental to the ideological arguments between the Westernizers and the Slavophiles about Russia's cultural destiny. The Westernizers held up Petersburg as the model of their Europe-led ideas for Russia, while the Slavophiles idealized Moscow as a centre of the ancient Russian way of life. The Slavophile ideal of a spiritual community united by homegrown Russian customs seemed to be embodied in the medieval contours of the town – the Kremlin walls so firmly rooted to the ground that they seemed to grow from it. The city's tightly knit communities, its homely character, symbolized the familial spirit of old Rus'.

Moscow's mythic self-image was all about its 'Russian character'.

The Moscow way of life was more provincial, it was closer to the habits of the Russian people than the gentry's way of life in Petersburg. Moscow's palaces resembled small estates. They were spacious and expansive, built for entertaining on a massive scale, with large central courtyards that functioned as farms, with pens for cows and poultry, vegetable allotments, sheds for storing produce brought in from the country for the winter months and, in some of the larger mansions, like Zinaida Volkonsky's on Tverskaya Street, extensive greenhouses for growing exotic winter fruits.* The poet Batiushkov has left a good description of the old-world country atmosphere in a Moscow noble house:

The mansion is built around a big courtyard which is full of litter and firewood; behind there is a garden with vegetables, and at the front a large porch with rails, as they used to have at the country houses of our grandfathers. Entering the house, you will come across the doorman playing cards – he plays from morning until night. The rooms are without wallpaper – the walls are covered in large portraits, on one side with heads of Russian Tsars, and on the other Judith holding the severed head of Holofernes on a large silver dish, and a naked Cleopatra with a snake: marvellous creations by the hand of a domestic servant. We see the table laid with bowls of cabbage soup, sweet pea porridge, baked mushrooms and bottles of *kvas*. The host is dressed in a sheepskin coat, the hostess in a coat; on the right side of the table are the parish priest, the parish teacher and the Holy Fool; on the left – a crowd of children, the old witchdoctor, a French madame and a German tutor.[14]

The interior of the Moscow palace was arranged for private comfort rather than public display. 'All the rooms are furnished with rich carpets,' remarked Batiushkov, 'with mirrors, chandeliers, armchairs and divans – everything designed to make one feel at home.'[15] The Moscow mansion was cosy and domestic, almost bourgeois, by comparison with the more formal palaces of Petersburg. The Empire style, which in Petersburg was principally expressed in a grandiose public architecture, manifested itself in Moscow in the opulence of the orna-

* The ground floor of the Volkonsky (Beloselsky) house was later taken over by the Eliseev shop, the 'Russian Fortnum and Mason', which remains there today.

ment and furnishing of private noble space.[16] The Moscow mansion of the Sheremetev clan, the Staraya Vozdizhenka, had no formal reception rooms as such. The living rooms were cluttered with furniture, plants and ornaments, and the walls all covered with family portraits and icons with their votive lamps.[17] This was where the Muscovite love of comfort met the Victorian aesthetics of the European middle class. The Sheremetevs called their Moscow house the 'family refuge'. Owning as they did their most ancient lands in the Moscow region (including the estate that is occupied today by the city's main airport at Sheremetevo), they thought of the old city as their home. 'All our family traditions, all our historical connections to Russia, drew me back to Moscow,' recalled Sergei Sheremetev, the grandson of Nikolai Petrovich, 'and every time I returned to Moscow I felt spiritually renewed.'[18]

Sergei's feeling was a common one. Many Russians felt that Moscow was a place where they could be more 'Russian', more at ease with themselves. Here was a city that reflected their spontaneous and relaxed character. One that shared their love of the good life. 'Petersburg is our head, Moscow is our heart', went a Russian proverb. Gogol drew the contrast in another way:

Petersburg is an accurate, punctual kind of person, a perfect German, and he looks at everything in a calculated way. Before he gives a party, he will look into his accounts. Moscow is a Russian nobleman, and if he's going to have a good time, he'll go all the way until he drops, and he won't worry about how much he's got in his pockets. Moscow does not like halfway measures . . . Petersburg likes to tease Moscow for his awkwardness and lack of taste. Moscow reproaches Petersburg because he doesn't know how to speak Russian . . . Russia needs Moscow, Petersburg needs Russia.[19]

2

The idea of Moscow as a 'Russian' city developed from the notion of St Petersburg as a foreign civilization. The literary conception of St Petersburg as an alien and an artificial place became commonplace after 1812, as the romantic yearning for a more authentically national way of life seized hold of the literary imagination. But the foreign character of Petersburg had always been a part of its popular mythology. From the moment it was built, traditionalists attacked it for its European ways. Among the Old Believers, the Cossacks and the peasants, rumours spread that Peter was a German, and not the real Tsar, largely on account of the foreigners he had brought to Petersburg and the attendant evils of European dress, tobacco, and the shaving-off of beards. By the middle of the eighteenth century there was a thriving underground mythology of tales and rumours about Petersburg. Stories abounded of the ghost of Peter walking through the streets, of weird mythic beasts hopping over churches, or of all-destroying floods washing up the skeletons of those who had perished in the building of the town.[20] This oral genre later flourished in the literary salons of St Petersburg and Moscow, where writers such as Pushkin and Odoevsky used it as the basis of their own ghost stories from the capital. And so the myth of Petersburg took shape – an unreal city that was alien to Russia, a supernatural realm of fantasies and ghosts, a kingdom of oppression and apocalypse.

Pushkin's *Bronze Horseman* – subtitled a 'Tale of Petersburg' – was the founding text of this literary myth. The poem was inspired by Falconet's equestrian statue of Peter the Great which stands on Senate Square as the city's *genius loci*. Like the poem that would make it so famous, the statue symbolized the dangerous underpinning of the capital's imperial grandeur – on the one hand trumpeting Peter's dazzling achievements in surpassing nature and, on the other, leaving it unclear to what extent he actually controlled the horse. Was he about to fall or soar up into space? Was he urging his mount on or trying to restrain it in the face of some catastrophe? The horseman seemed to teeter on the edge of an abyss, held back only by the taut reins of his steed.[21] The huge granite rock – so wild in its appearance – on which the statue stood, was itself an emblem of the tragic struggle between man and nature. The city hewn in stone is never wholly safe from the incursions of the watery chaos from which it was claimed, and this sense of living on the edge was wonderfully conveyed by Falconet.

In 1909 a technical commission inspected the statue. Engineers bored holes into the bronze. They had to pump out 1,500 litres of water from inside.[22] Without protective dikes, flooding was a constant threat to Petersburg. Pushkin set his poem in 1824, the year of one

10. *Etienne-Maurice Falconet:* The Bronze Horseman.
Monument to Peter the Great, 1782

such flood. *The Bronze Horseman* tells the story of the flood and a sad clerk called Eugene, who finds the house of his beloved, Parasha, washed away. Driven to the verge of madness, Eugene roams the city and, coming across Falconet's horseman, castigates the Tsar for having built a city at the mercy of the flood. The statue stirs in anger and chases the poor clerk, who runs all night in terror of its thundering brass hooves. Eugene's body is finally washed up on the little island where Parasha's house was taken by the flood. The poem can be read in many different ways – as a clash between the state and the individual, progress and tradition, the city and nature, the autocracy and the people – and it was the standard by which all those later writers, from Gogol to Bely, debated the significance of Russia's destiny:

Proud charger, whither art thou ridden?
Where leapest thou? and where, on whom
Wilt plant thy hoof?[23]

For the Slavophiles, Peter's city was a symbol of the catastrophic
rupture with Holy Rus'; for the Westerners, a progressive sign of
Russia's Europeanization. For some, it was the triumph of a civilization, the conquering of nature by order and reason; for others, it was
a monstrous artifice, an empire built on human suffering that was
tragically doomed.

More than anyone, it was Gogol who fixed the city's image as an
alienating place. As a young 'Ukrainian writer' struggling to survive
in the capital, Gogol lived among the petty clerks whose literary *alter
egos* fill his *Tales of Petersburg* (1842). These are sad and lonely
figures, crushed by the city's oppressive atmosphere and doomed, for
the most part, to die untimely deaths, like Pushkin's Evgeny in *The
Bronze Horseman*. Gogol's Petersburg is a city of illusions and deceit.
'Oh have no faith in this Nevsky Prospekt . . . It is all deception, a
dream, nothing is what it seems!' he warns in 'Nevsky Prospekt', the
first of the *Tales of Petersburg*. 'Nevsky Prospekt deceives at all hours
of the day, but the worst time of all is night, when the entire city
becomes a welter of noise and flashing lights . . . and when the Devil
himself is abroad, kindling the street-lamps with one purpose only: to
show everything in a false light.'[24] Hidden in the shadows of this
glittering parade, Gogol's 'little men' scuttle between their offices in
vast ministerial buildings and the equally soulless tenement apartments
in which they live – alone, of course. Gogol's Petersburg is a ghostly
image of the real city, a nightmare vision of a world deprived of grace,
where only human greed and vanity can thrive. In 'The Overcoat', the
last of the *Tales*, the humble civil servant Akaky Akakievich is forced
to scrimp and save to replace his threadbare overcoat that has long
become the joke of his fashionable seniors in the ministry. The new
coat restores his sense of pride and individual worth: it becomes a
symbol of his acceptance by his peers, who throw a champagne party
in celebration. But he is robbed of the prized fur while walking home
across a dark and 'endless square'. His efforts to retrieve it by appealing
to an 'Important Personage' come to naught. He becomes ill and dies,

a tragic figure crushed by a cold and uncaring society. But Akaky's ghost walks the streets of Petersburg. One night it haunts the Important Personage and robs him of his coat.

Dostoevsky said that the whole of Russian literature 'came out from underneath Gogol's "Overcoat"'.[25] His own early tales, especially *The Double* (1846), are very Gogolesque, although in later works, such as *Crime and Punishment* (1866), he adds an important psychological dimension to the capital's topography. Dostoevsky creates his unreal city through the diseased mental world of his characters, so that it becomes 'fantastically real'.[26] In the minds of dreamers like Raskolnikov, fantasy becomes reality, and life becomes a game in which any action, even murder, can be justified. Here is a place where human feelings are perverted and destroyed by human isolation and rationality. Dostoevsky's Petersburg is full of dreamers, a fact which he explained by the city's cramped conditions, by the frequent mists and fog which came in from the sea, by the icy rain and drizzle which made people sick. This was a place of fevered dreams and weird hallucinations, of nerves worn thin by the sleepless White Nights of the northern summer when dreamland and the real world became blurred. Dostoevsky himself was not immune to such flights of fantasy. In 1861 he recalled a 'vision of the Neva' which he himself had had in the early 1840s and included in the short story 'A Weak Heart' (1841). Dostoevsky claimed that it was the precise moment of his artistic self-discovery:

I remember once on a wintry January evening I was hurrying home from the Vyborg side ... When I reached the Neva, I stopped for a minute and threw a piercing glance along the river into the smoky, frostily dim distance, which had suddenly turned crimson with the last purple of a sunset ... Frozen steam poured from tired horses, from running people. The taut air quivered at the slightest sound, and columns of smoke like giants rose from all the roofs on both embankments and rushed upward through the cold sky, twining and untwining on the way, so that it seemed new buildings were rising above the old ones, a new city was forming in the air ... It seemed as if all that world, with all its inhabitants, strong and weak, with all their habitations, the refuges of the poor, or the gilded palaces for the comfort of the powerful of this world, was at that twilight hour like a fantastic vision of fairyland, like a dream which in its turn would vanish and pass away like vapour in the dark blue sky.[27]

3

Moscow, by contrast, was a place of down-to-earth pursuits. With the rise of Petersburg in the eighteenth century, Moscow became the centre of the 'good life' for the nobility. Pushkin said that it attracted 'rascals and eccentrics' – independent noblemen who 'shunned the court and lived without a care, devoting all their passions to harmless scandal-mongering and hospitality'.[28] Moscow was a capital without a court – and without a court to occupy themselves, its grandees gave themselves to sensual amusement. Moscow was famous for its restaurants and clubs, its sumptuous balls and entertainments – in sum, for everything that Petersburg was not. Petersburgers despised Moscow for its sinful idleness. 'Moscow is an abyss of hedonistic pleasure', wrote Nikolai Turgenev, a poet in the circle of the Decembrists. 'All its people do is eat, drink, sleep, go to parties and play cards – and all at the expense of the suffering of their serfs.'[29] Yet no one could deny its Russian character. 'Moscow may be wild and dissolute', wrote F. F. Vigel, 'but there is no point in trying to change it. For there is a part of Moscow in us all, and no Russian can expunge Moscow.'[30]

Moscow was the food capital of Russia. No other city could boast such a range of restaurants. There were high-class dining clubs like the Angleterre, where Levin and Oblonsky have their famous lunch in the opening scene of *Anna Karenina*; business restaurants like the Slavic Bazaar, where merchants made huge deals; fashionable late-night places like the Strelna and the Yar (which Pushkin often mentions in his poetry); coffee houses where women were allowed unaccompanied; eating houses (*karchevnye*) for the common people; and taverns so diverse that every taste was catered for. There were old-fashioned taverns, like the Testov, where parents took their children for a treat; taverns that were famous for their specialities, like Egorov's pancakes or Lopashev's pies; taverns that kept singing birds where hunters liked to meet; and taverns that were well known as places of revelry.[31] Moscow was so rich in its restaurant culture that it even taught the

French a thing or two. When Napoleon's soldiers came to Moscow, they needed to eat fast. '*Bistro!*' they would say, the Russian word for 'fast'.

Moscow was a city of gourmands. It had a rich folklore of the fabulously fat, upon which its own self-image, as the capital of plenty, had been fed. In the early nineteenth century Count Rakhmanov, for example, spent his whole inheritance – said to be in excess of 2 million roubles (£200,000) – in just eight years of gastronomy. He fed his poultry with truffles. He kept his crayfish in cream and parmesan instead of water. And he had his favourite fish, a particularly rare specimen which could be caught only in the Sosna river 300 kilometres away, delivered live to Moscow every day. Count Musin-Pushkin was just as profligate. He would fatten his calves with cream and keep them in cradles like newborn babies. His fowl were fed on walnuts and given wine to drink to enhance the flavour of their meat. Sumptuous banquets had a legendary status in the annals of Moscow. Count Stroganov (an early nineteenth-century ancestor of the one who gave his name to the beef dish) hosted famous 'Roman dinners', where his guests lay on couches and were served by naked boys. Caviare and fruits and herring cheeks were typical hors-d'oeuvres. Next came salmon lips, bear paws and roast lynx. These were followed by cuckoos roasted in honey, halibut liver and burbot roe; oysters, poultry and fresh figs; salted peaches and pineapples. After the guests had eaten they would go into the *banya* and start to drink, eating caviare to build up a real thirst.[32]

Moscow banquets were more notable for their fantastic size than for the refinement of their food. It was not unusual for 200 separate dishes to be presented at a meal. The menu for one banquet shows that guests were served up to 10 different kinds of soup, 24 pies and meat dishes, 64 small dishes (such as grouse or teal), several kinds of roast (lamb, beef, goat, hare and suckling pig), 12 different salads, 28 assorted tarts, cheeses and fresh fruits. When the guests had had enough they retired to a separate room for sweets and sugared fruit.[33] In this society, where prestige meant promotion at court, princes vied with one another in their hospitality. Vast sums were paid for the best serf cooks. Count Sheremetev (Nikolai Petrovich) paid an annual salary of 850 roubles to his senior chef – a huge sum for a serf.[34] Cooks

were regarded by their masters as the equals of artists, and no expense
was spared to have them trained abroad. Princes attained fame for the
dishes first created by their cooks. The illustrious Prince Potemkin, the
most famous of them all, was well known for serving up whole pigs at
his sumptuous feasts: all the innards were removed through the mouth,
the carcass stuffed with sausage, and the whole beast cooked in pastry
made with wine.[35]

It was not only courtiers who ate so well. Provincial families were
just as prone to the consuming passion and, with little else to do on
the estate, eating was, if nothing else, a way to pass the time. Lunch
would last for several hours. First there were the *zakuski* (hors-
d'oeuvres), the cold and then the hot, followed by the soups, the pies,
the poultry dishes, the roast, and finally the fruit and sweets. By then
it was nearly time for tea. There were gentry households where the
whole day was (in Pushkin's words) 'a chain of meals'. The Brodnit-
skys, a middling gentry family in the Ukraine, were typical. When they
got up they had coffee and bread rolls, followed by mid-morning
zakuski, a full six-course lunch, sugared loaves and jams in the afternoon with tea, then poppy seeds and nuts, coffee, rolls and biscuits as
an early evening snack. After that would come the evening meal –
mainly cold cuts from lunch – then tea before they went to bed.[36]

Sumptuous eating of this sort was a relatively new phenomenon.
The food of seventeenth-century Muscovy had been plain and simple
– the entire repertory consisting of fish, boiled meats and domestic
fowl, pancakes, bread and pies, garlic, onion, cucumbers and radishes,
cabbages and beetroot. Everything was cooked in hempseed oil, which
made all the dishes taste much the same. Even the Tsar's table was
relatively poor. The menu at the wedding feast in 1670 of Tsar Alexei
consisted of roast swan with saffron, grouse with lemon, goose giblets,
chicken with sour cabbage and (for the men) *kvas*.[37] It was not until the
eighteenth century that more interesting foods and culinary techniques
were imported from abroad: butter, cheese and sour cream, smoked
meats and fish, pastry cooking, salads and green vegetables, tea and
coffee, chocolates, ice cream, wines and liqueurs. Even the *zakuski*
were a copy of the European custom of hors-d'oeuvres. Although seen
as the most 'Russian' part of any meal (caviare, sturgeon, vodka and
all that), the 'classic *zakuski*', such as fish in aspic, were not in fact

invented until the early nineteenth century. The same was true of Russian cooking as a whole. The 'traditional specialities' that were served in Moscow's restaurants in the nineteenth century – national dishes such as *kulebeika* (a pie stuffed with several layers of fish or meat), carp with sour cream, or turkey with plum sauce – were in fact quite recent inventions: most of them created to appeal to the new taste for old-Russian fashions after 1812. The first Russian cookery book was published as late as 1816, in which it was stated that it was no longer possible to give a full description of Russian cooking: all one could do was try to re-create the ancient recipes from people's memories.[38] Lenten dishes were the only traditional foods that had not yet been supplanted by the European culinary fashions of the eighteenth century. Muscovy had a rich tradition of fish and mushroom dishes, vegetable soups such as *borshcht* (beetroot) and *shchi* (cabbage), recipes for Easter breads and pies, and dozens of varieties of porridges and pancakes (*bliny*) which were eaten during Lent.

Not just nourishment, foodstuffs had an iconic part to play in Russian popular culture. Bread, for example, had a religious and symbolic importance that went far beyond its role in daily life; its significance in Russian culture was far greater than it was in the other Christian cultures of the West. The word for bread (*khleb*) was used in Russian for 'wealth', 'health' and 'hospitality'. Bread played a central role in peasant rituals. Bird-shaped breads were baked in spring to symbolize the return of the migratory flocks. In the peasant wedding a special loaf was baked to symbolize the newly-weds' fertility. At peasant funerals it was the custom to make a ladder out of dough and put it in the grave beside the corpse to help the soul's ascent. For bread was a sacred link between this world and the next. It was connected with the folklore of the stove, where the spirits of the dead were said to live.[39] Bread was often given as a gift, most importantly in the customary offering of bread and salt to visitors. All foodstuffs were used as gifts, in fact, and this was a custom shared by all classes. The eccentric Moscow nobleman Alexander Porius-Vizapursky (even his name was eccentric) made a habit of sending oysters to important dignitaries – and sometimes to people he didn't even know (Prince Dolgorukov once received a parcel of a dozen oysters with a letter from Porius-Vizapursky saying he had called on him to make his acquaintance but had found him not at home). Wildfowl was also a common gift. The poet Derzhavin was well known for sending sandpipers. Once he sent an enormous pie to Princess Bebolsina. When it was cut open it revealed a dwarf who presented her with a truffle pie and a bunch of forget-me-nots.[40] Festive gifts of food were also given to the people by the Tsars. To celebrate victory in the war against the Turks in 1791, Catherine the Great ordered two food mountains to be placed on Palace Square. Each was topped by fountains spouting wine. On her signal from the Winter Palace the general populace was allowed to feast on the cornucopia.[41]

Food also featured as a symbol in nineteenth-century literature. Memories of food were often summoned up in nostalgic scenes of childhood life. Tolstoy's Ivan Ilich concludes on his deathbed that the only happy moments in his life had been when he was a child: all these memories he associates with food – particularly, for some reason, prunes. Gastronomic images were frequently used to paint a picture of the good old life. Gogol's *Evenings on a Farm* is filled with lyrical descriptions of Ukrainian gluttony; Goncharov's Oblomov is always gorging himself on old-fashioned Russian foods – a symbol of his sloth; and then (no doubt in a send-up of this literary tradition) there is Feers, the ancient butler in Chekhov's *The Cherry Orchard* (1904), who still recalls the cherries sent to Moscow from the estate more than fifty years before ('And the dried cherries in those days were soft, juicy, sweet, tasty . . . They knew how to do it then . . . they had a recipe . . .').[42] Moscow itself had a mythical stature in this folklore about food. Ferapont, the butler in Chekhov's *Three Sisters* (1901), tells Andrei, who yearns to go to Moscow and eat at Testov's or some other busy restaurant:

The other day at the office, a contractor was telling me about some business men who were eating pancakes in Moscow. One of them ate forty pancakes and died. It was either forty or fifty, I can't remember exactly.[43]

Bingeing of this sort was often represented as a symbol of the Russian character. Gogol, in particular, used food metaphors obsessively. He often made the link between expansive natures and expansive waists. The Cossack hero of one of his short stories, Taras Bulba (whose name means 'potato' in Ukrainian), is the incarnation of this appetite for life. He welcomes his sons home from the seminary in Kiev with instructions to his wife to prepare a 'proper meal':

We don't want doughnuts, honey buns, poppy cakes and other dainties; bring us a whole sheep, serve a goat and forty-year-old mead! And plenty of vodka, not vodka with all sorts of fancies, not with raisins and flavouring, but pure foaming vodka that hisses and bubbles like mad![44]

It was the test of a 'true Russian' to be able to drink vodka by the bucketful. Since the sixteenth century, when the art of distillation spread to Russia from the West, the custom had been to indulge in mammoth drinking bouts on festive occasions and holidays. Drinking was a social thing – it was never done alone – and it was bound up with communal celebrations. This meant that, contrary to the mythic image, the overall consumption of vodka was not that great (in the year there were 200 fasting days when drinking was prohibited). But when the Russian drank, he drank an awful lot. (It was the same with food – fasting and then feasting – a frequent alternation that perhaps bore some relationship to the people's character and history: long periods of humility and patience interspersed with bouts of joyous freedom and violent release.) The drinking feats of Russian legend were awe-inspiring. At wedding feasts and banquets there were sometimes over fifty toasts – the guests downing the glass in one gulp – until the last man standing became the 'vodka Tsar'.

Deaths from drinking claimed a thousand people every year in Russia between 1841 and 1859.[45] Yet it would be wrong to conclude from this that the Russian drinking problem was an endemic or an ancient one. In fact, it was only in the modern period – starting in the late eighteenth century – that Russian levels of alcohol consumption became a threat to national life; and even then the problem was essentially fabricated by the gentry and the state.* The traditional

---

* Until the second half of the eighteenth century the annual consumption of spirits was around 2 litres for every adult male but by the end of Catherine's reign in the 1790s it had risen to around 5 litres (R. E. F. Smith and D. Christian, *Bread and Salt: A Social and Economic History of Food and Drink in Russia* (Cambridge, 1984), p. 218).

drinking pattern had been set in a context where alcohol was scarce – a rare commodity that could only be afforded on a holiday. But in the latter part of the eighteenth century the gentry distillers who were licensed by the state to manufacture vodka increased their production many times. With the 1775 reform of local government, which transferred the control of the police to gentry magistrates, there was little state control of the booming retail business, legal or illegal, which made vodka traders very rich. Suddenly, there were vodka shops in every town, taverns all over the place, and, other than religious proscription, no more limitations on drinking. The government was conscious of the social costs of increased drunkenness, and the Church was constantly raising the issue, campaigning noisily against the drinking shops. The problem was to modify a drinking pattern that had been formed over many centuries – the habit of overdrinking whenever the Russians drank – or else to reduce the supply of drink. But since the state derived at least a quarter of its total revenues from vodka sales, and the aristocracy had vested interests in the trade, there was little pressure for reform. It was not until the First World War that the state came down on the side of sobriety. But the ban on vodka which it introduced only made the drinking problem worse (for the Russians turned to paraffin and illegal moonshines that were far more dangerous), while the loss of tax revenues from vodka sales was a major contribution to the downfall of the regime in 1917.

'The difference between Moscow and St Petersburg is this. In Moscow, if you have not seen a friend for a few days, you think there's something wrong and send out someone to check that he's not dead. But in Peter, you may not be seen for a year or two and no one will miss you.'[46] Muscovites have always taken comfort from the image of their city as a warm and friendly 'home'. Compared with the cold and formal Petersburg, Moscow prided itself on its relaxed 'Russian' customs and its hospitality. Without a court, or much to occupy them in their offices, Muscovites had little else to do but visit all their friends and do the rounds of parties, feasts and balls. The doors of Moscow's mansions were always open and the Petersburg custom of set times for visits was regarded as absurd. Guests were expected to show up at any time, and on certain days, such as namedays, birthdays or religious holidays, or when someone had arrived from the country or abroad, houses were all come and go.

Moscow was famous for its lavish entertaining. It was not unusual for entire noble fortunes to be spent on it. At its most spectacular, the city's *bon vivants* showed an appetite for gaiety that was unparalleled. Count Yushkov gave eighteen balls in the space of twenty days at his Moscow palace during 1801. Nearby factories had to be closed down because of the hazard of the fireworks, and the music was so loud that the nuns at the neighbouring Novodeviche convent could not sleep – instead of even trying, they gave in to the fun and climbed up on the walls to watch the spectacle.[47] The Sheremetevs were even more renowned for their sumptuous house parties. Several times a year crowds of up to 50,000 guests would make their way from Moscow out to Kuskovo for grand entertainments in the park. The roads would be jammed with carriages and the line would stretch back fifteen miles to the centre of Moscow. Entering the park the guests were met by notices inviting them to make themselves at home and amuse themselves in any way they liked. Choirs sang amid the trees, horn bands played, and the guests were entertained by exotic animals, by operas in the garden and the indoor theatre, by firework displays and *sons et lumières*. On the lake before the house there was even a mock battle between ships.[48]

Less grand houses could be just as generous in their hospitality, sometimes spending all their wealth on social gatherings. The Khitrovos were neither rich nor important, but in nineteenth-century Moscow they were known by everyone for their frequent balls and soirées, which, though not lavish, were always very lively and enjoyable – they were 'typical Moscow'.[49] Another famous hostess in the Moscow style was Maria Rimsky-Korsakov, who became famous for her breakfast parties where Senator Arkady Bashilov, in apron and cap, would serve all the dishes he had cooked himself.[50] Moscow was full of such eccentric hosts – none more so than the super-wealthy playboy Count Prokopy Demidov, whose love of entertaining was notorious. He liked to dress his servants in a special livery, one-half silk and one-half hempen cloth, a stocking on one foot and a bast shoe on the other, to underline their peasant origin. When he entertained he had naked servants take the place of statues in his garden and his house.[51]

The Russian custom of opening one's doors at lunch and dinner time for anyone of rank was an important part of this culture of hospitality. There would be up to fifty guests at every meal in the Fountain House of the Sheremetevs, the grandest of the aristocracy in Petersburg. But in Moscow numbers such as this would be entertained by relatively minor gentry households, while at the grandest houses, such as Stroganov's or Razumovsky's, the numbers were significantly higher. Count Razumovsky was renowned for his open tables. He did not know the names of many of his guests, but since he was extremely keen on chess he was glad always to have new partners to play with. There was an army officer who was so good at chess that he stayed at the count's house for six weeks – even though no one knew his name.[52] Generally it was the custom that, after you had dined at a house once, you would be expected to return there on a regular basis: not to come again would be to give offence. The custom was so widespread that it was quite possible for a nobleman to dine out every day, yet never go so frequently to any house as to outstay his welcome. Grandees like the Sheremetevs, Osterman-Tolstoy and Stroganov acquired permanent hangers-on. General Kostenetsky dined at Count Osterman-Tolstoy's for twenty years – it became such a habit that the count would send his carriage for the general half an hour before every meal. Count Stroganov had a guest whose name he did not learn in nearly thirty years. When one day the guest did not appear, the count assumed he must be dead. It turned out that the man had indeed died. He had been run over on his way to lunch.[53]

As with food and drink, the Russians knew no limits when it came to partying. Sergei Volkonsky, the grandson of the Decembrist, recalled nameday parties that dragged on until dawn.

First there was the tea-drinking, then the supper. The sun set, the moon came up – then there were the games, the gossip and the cards. At around three o'clock the first guests began to leave, but since their drivers were also given alcoholic refreshments, going home that early could be dangerous. I once travelled home from such a nameday party and my carriage toppled over.[54]

The cool light of morning was the enemy of any Moscow host, and there were some who would cover all the windows and stop all the clocks so as not to drive their guests away.[55] From October to the spring, when provincial families with a daughter to marry off would take a house in Moscow for the social season, there were balls and banquets almost every night. Moscow balls were larger than those in Petersburg. They were national rather than society events, and the atmosphere was rather down to earth, with old provincial ladies in their dowdy dresses as much in evidence as dashing young hussars. Yet the champagne flowed all night – and the first guests never left before the morning light. This Moscow lived a nocturnal way of life, its body clock reset to the social whirl. Crawling into bed in the early morning, revellers would breakfast around noon, take their lunch at three or even later (Pushkin made a point of eating lunch at eight or nine in the evening) and go out at ten p.m. Muscovites adored this late-night life – it perfectly expressed their love of living without bounds. In 1850, the government in Petersburg imposed a ban on the playing of live music after four a.m. In Moscow the reaction was practically a *fronde* – a Muscovite rebellion against the capital. Led by Prince Golitsyn, famous for his all-night masquerades, the noblemen of Moscow petitioned Petersburg for a repeal of the ban. There was a lengthy correspondence, letters to the press, and, when their petitions were finally turned down, the Muscovites decided to ignore the rules and party on.[56]

4

In 1874 the Academy of Arts organized a show in remembrance of the artist Viktor Gartman, who had died the previous year, aged thirty-nine. Today Gartman is best known as a friend of Musorgsky, the painter at the centre of his famous piano suite *Pictures at an Exhibition* (1874). Musorgsky was struck down by grief at Gartman's death, and the drinking bouts which led to his own death are dated from this time. He paid his own tribute to his artist friend by composing *Pictures* after visiting the show.[57] Gartman's 'neo-Russian' style had a huge influence on the music of Musorgsky – and indeed on all the trends of nineteenth-century art that took their inspiration from Moscow's cultural world. His architectural drawings were based on years of

11. *Viktor Gartman: design for the Kiev city gate*

study of medieval ornament. The most famous was his fanciful design for the Kiev city gate, shaped in the form of a warrior's helmet with a *kokoshnik* arch, which Musorgsky celebrated in the final picture of the piano suite. One critic called the Gartman design 'marble towels and brick embroideries'.[58]

Moscow was the centre (and the central subject) of this renewal of interest in the ancient Russian arts. The artist Fedor Solntsev played a crucial role, making detailed drawings of the weapons, saddlery, church plate and wall hangings in the Kremlin Armoury, and unearthing many other treasures in the provinces. Between 1846 and 1853 Solntsev published six large volumes of his illustrations called *Antiquities of the Russian State*. They provided artists and designers with a grammar of historic ornament which they could incorporate in their own work. Solntsev himself used these ancient motifs in his restoration of the Kremlin's Terem Palace – an authentic reproduction of the seventeenth-century Moscow style, complete with ceramic-tiled stoves, ornate vaulted ceilings with *kokoshnik* arches and red leather walls and chairs (plate 6). Solntsev's work was carried on by the Stroganov Art School, founded in Moscow in 1860, which encouraged artists to work from ancient Russian church and folk designs. Many of the leading 'Russian style' designers who took the world by storm in the 1900s – Vashkov, Ovchinnikov and the Moscow masters of the Fabergé workshop – had graduated from the Stroganov School.[59] In contrast to the rigid European classicism of the St Petersburg Academy, the atmosphere in Moscow was rather more relaxed and open to the exploration of Russian themes and styles. Artists flocked to Moscow to study its icons, its *lubok* painting and Palekh lacquer work. Three giants of Russian painting, Repin, Polenov and Vasnetsov, all moved there as students from St Petersburg. These old crafts were still alive in Moscow and its environs, whereas they had died out in St Petersburg. There were several *lubok* publishers in Moscow, for example, but none in Petersburg. Icon painters flourished in the towns around Moscow, but there were none in Petersburg. Much of this was explained by the old-style merchant taste that dominated the art market in Moscow. The Moscow School of Painting was also more receptive to these native traditions, and unlike the aristocratic Academy of Arts in St Petersburg, its doors were open to a wide social range of students, who brought with them the outlook of the common folk. The director of the Moscow School called on artists to use folk themes, and on the opening of the Ethnographic Exhibition, in 1867, he lectured on the need to study old folk clothing and embroidery so as to retrieve the ancient Russian style of art that had been buried under Western tastes.[60]

In Gartman's world of architectural design, the mid-century boom in the neo-Russian style was made possible by the abolition of an eighteenth-century law stipulating that buildings in the centre of Moscow should be made from stone with façades in approved European styles. The repeal of this law, in 1858, opened the way for a spate of wooden buildings in the Russian peasant style. More than ever, Moscow took on the appearance of a 'big village'. The historian and Slavophile Pogodin, himself a peasant son and a well-known collector of antique artefacts, commissioned several wooden houses in the peasant style. Wood was declared by nationalists the 'fundamental folk material' and every architect who aspired to be 'national' constructed buildings in that material.[61] Gartman designed the exhibition halls with their wooden folk-style decoration for the Moscow Polytechnic Exhibition which was held in 1872 to mark the bicentenary of Peter the Great's birth. The exhibition heralded a return to the artistic principles of Muscovy. It was housed in the newly opened Russian Museum, opposite St Basil's on Red Square, which had been designed by Vladimir Shervud (an architect of English origin) in the old ecclesiastical style of Moscow. The tall church-like towers of the museum reflected the contours of the neighbouring Kremlin – a symbol of the fact, as Shervud put it, that Orthodoxy was 'the primary cultural element of [Russia's] nationhood'.[62] The neo-Russian style entered its heyday in the 1870s, largely as a result of the growing wealth and status of the Moscow merchant patrons of the arts. Pavel Tretiakov built his famous gallery of Russian art as an annexe to his mansion in the ancient Moscow style. Sergei Shchukin's Moscow villa (which housed his huge collection of French painting) was a neo-Russian fantasy modelled on the seventeenth-century wooden architecture of Yaroslav and Kolomenskoe. The centre of the city, between the Kremlin and Lubianka Square, was entirely reconstructed in the neo-Russian style favoured by the wealthy merchant councillors in Moscow's city hall. New trading rows (later to become the state department store GUM) were constructed on Red Square in the 1880s; followed by a city Duma (to become the Lenin Museum) in 1892. The city's business region was suddenly taken over by ancient tent roofs and *kokoshnik* pediments,

12. *Vladimir Sherwood. Russian Museum, Red Square, Moscow (the Kremlin to the left). Early 1900s*

fancy yellow brickwork and ornate folk designs. Moscow entered the twentieth century with its skyline in the form of the seventeenth.

Musorgsky fell in love with Moscow's 'Russianness'. He had spent nearly all his life in Petersburg. But as an artist he was drawn to the 'realm of fairy tales' which he discovered in the ancient capital. 'You know', he wrote to Balakirev on his first trip to Moscow in 1859, 'I had been a cosmopolitan, but now there's been a sort of rebirth; everything Russian has become close to me and I would be offended if Russia were treated crudely, without ceremony; it's as if at the present time I've really begun to love her.'[63] As a mentor to the young composer, Balakirev was not pleased. For all his pioneering of the nationalist school, Balakirev was a Westernist and a thumping patriot of Petersburg who looked down on Moscow as parochial and archaic; he called it 'Jericho'.[64] Musorgsky's love affair with Moscow, then, seemed almost a desertion from the Balakirev school. It was certainly a sign of the young artist finding his own style and theme. He began to spend his summers on the fabulous estate of the Shilovskys at Glebovo, near Moscow, renewing contact with his own gentry background in that area.* He made new friends in circles outside music where he found a stimulus to his own art: the poet Kutuzov (a descendant of the famous general), the sculptor Antokolsky, the painter Repin, as well as Gartman, who were all receptive to his unschooled style of music, and more tolerant of his alcoholic ways, than the rather staid composers of St Petersburg. Breaking free from the domination of the Balakirev school (which took Liszt and Schumann as the starting point for the development of a Russian style), Musorgsky began to explore a more native musical idiom in his 'village scene' for voice and piano, *Savishna* (1867), in *Boris Godunov* (1868–74) and then in his *Pictures*, which, like Gartman's drawings, reworked Russian folklore in imaginative ways. Moscow thus delivered him from the 'German' orthodoxy of the Balakirev school. It allowed Musorgsky, who had always been perceived as something of an outcast in St Petersburg, to experiment with music from the Russian soil. Gartman's fantastic folk forms were the equivalent of Musorgsky's explorations in music: both were attempts to break free from the formal conventions of European art. Among the pictures at the exhibition there was a design for a clock in the form of Baba Yaga's hut on chicken's legs.† Images like this demanded a new mode of

---

* The Musorgsky family owned 110,000 hectares – eighteen villages – with a total population of 400 serfs prior to the emancipation of 1861 (C. Emerson, *The Life of Musorgsky* (Cambridge, 1999), p. 37).

† In Russian fairy tales the witch Baba Yaga lives deep in the woods in a hut whose legs allow it to rotate to face each unfortunate new visitor.

musical expression, one entirely free from the sonata form of European music, if they were to be redrawn in sound; and this is what Musorgsky's *Pictures* did. They created a new Russian language in music.

'To you, Generalissimo, sponsor of the Gartman Exhibition, in remembrance of our dear Viktor, 27 June, '74.' Thus Musorgsky dedicated *Pictures* to Vladimir Stasov, the critic, scholar and self-appointed champion of the national school in all the Russian arts. Stasov was a huge figure, one might say a tyrant, in the mid-nineteenth-century Russian cultural milieu. He discovered a large number of its greatest talents (Balakirev, Musorgsky, Borodin, Rimsky-Korsakov, Glazunov, Repin, Kramskoi, Vasnetsov and Antokolsky); he inspired many of their works (Borodin's *Prince Igor*, Musorgsky's *Khovanshchina*, Balakirev's *King Lear* and Rimsky's *Sadko* and *Scheherazade*); and he fought their battles in countless thunderous articles and letters to the press. Stasov had a reputation as a brilliant dogmatist. Turgenev carried on a lifelong argument with 'our great all-Russian critic', whom he caricatured in the figure Skoropikhin in his 1877 novel *Virgin Soil* ('He is always foaming and frothing over like a bottle of sour *kvas*'). He also wrote a famous ditty about him:

> Argue with someone more intelligent than you:
> He will defeat you.
> But from your defeat you will learn something useful.

> Argue with someone of equal intelligence:
> Neither will be victorious.
> And in any case you will have the pleasure of the struggle.

> Argue with someone less intelligent:
> Not from a desire for victory
> But because you may be of use to him.

> Argue even with a fool:
> You will not gain glory
> But sometimes it is fun.

> Only do not argue with Vladimir Stasov.[65]

Stasov wanted Russian art to liberate itself from Europe's hold. By copying the West, the Russians could be at best second-rate; but by borrowing from their own native traditions they might create a truly national art that matched Europe's with its high artistic standards and originality. 'Looking at these paintings', Stasov wrote of the Academy Exhibition of 1861, 'it is difficult to guess without a signature or label that they have been done by Russians in Russia. All are exact copies of foreign works.'[66] In his view, art should be 'national' in the sense that it portrayed the people's daily lives, was meaningful to them, and taught them how to live.

Stasov was a towering figure in Musorgsky's life. They first met in 1857, when Stasov was the champion of the Balakirev circle in its revolt against the Petersburg Conservatory. Founded by the pianist Anton Rubinstein in 1861, the Conservatory was dominated by the German conventions of composition developed in the music of Bach, Haydn, Mozart and Beethoven. Its patron was the Grand Duchess Elena Pavlovna, a German by origin and proselytizer of her nation's cultural cause, who secured the court's support after Rubinstein had failed to raise public finance for the Conservatory. Rubinstein was contemptuous of the amateurism of musical life in Russia (he called Glinka a dilettante) and he set about promoting music education on Germanic lines. Russian national music, Rubinstein maintained, was of only 'ethnographic interest', quaint but without artistic value in itself. Balakirev and Stasov were incensed. While they recognized that a standard had been set by the German tradition, as nationalists they worshipped what they perceived as Glinka's 'purely Russian' music (in fact it is steeped in Italian and German influences)[67] and retaliated by accusing Rubinstein of denigrating Russia from the heights of what they called his 'European conservatorial grandeur'.[68] There was an element of xenophobia, even anti-Semitism, in their battles against Rubinstein. They called him 'Tupinstein' ('dull'), 'Dubinstein' ('dumb-head') and 'Grubinstein' ('crude'). But they were afraid that German principles would stifle Russian forms and their fear gave way to foreigner-baiting. In 1862 they established the Free Music School as a direct rival to the Conservatory, setting it the task of cultivating native talent. In Stasov's phrase, it was time for the 'hoopskirts and tailcoats' of the Petersburg élites to make way for the 'long Russian coats' of the provinces.[69] The School became the stronghold of the so-called 'Mighty Five', the *kuchka*, who pioneered the Russian musical style.

The *kuchkist* composers were all young men in 1862. Balakirev was twenty-five, Cui twenty-seven, Musorgsky twenty-three, Borodin the old man at twenty-eight, and Rimsky-Korsakov the baby of them all at just eighteen. All of them were self-trained amateurs. Borodin combined composing with a career as a chemist. Rimsky-Korsakov was a naval officer (his First Symphony was written on a ship). Musorgsky had been in the Guards and then the civil service before taking up music, and even after that, at the height of his success in the 1870s, he was forced by the expense of his drinking habit to hold down a full-time job in the State Forestry Department. In contrast, moreover, to the élite status and court connections of Conservatory composers such as Tchaikovsky, the *kuchkists*, by and large, were from the minor gentry of the provinces. So to some degree their *ésprit de corps* depended on the myth, which they themselves created, of a movement that was more 'authentically Russian', in the sense that it was closer to the native soil, than the classical academy.[70]

But there was nothing mythical about the musical language they developed, which set them poles apart from the conventions of the Conservatory. This self-conscious Russian styling was based on two elements. First they tried to incorporate in their music what they heard in village songs, in Cossack and Caucasian dances, in church chants and (clichéd though it soon became) the tolling of church bells.* 'Once again the sound of bells!' Rimsky once exclaimed after a performance of *Boris Godunov*. He too had often reproduced the sound, in *The Maid of Pskov* (1873), the *Easter Overture* (1888), and his orchestrations of Borodin's *Prince Igor* and Musorsgky's *Khovanshchina*.[71] *Kuchkist* music was filled with imitative sounds of Russian life. It tried to reproduce what Glinka had once called 'the soul of Russian music'

---

* Russian church bells have a special musicality which is unlike the sound of any other bells. The Russian technique of bell-chiming is for the ringers to strike the different bells directly with hammers, or by using short cords attached to the clappers. This encourages a form of counterpoint – albeit with the dissonances which result from the resounding echoes of the bells. The Western technique of ringing bells by swinging them with long ropes from the ground makes such synchronization all but impossible to achieve.

– the long-drawn, lyrical and melismatic song of the Russian peasantry. Balakirev made this possible with his study of the folk songs of the Volga region in the 1860s (the heyday of populism in the arts). More than any previous anthology, his transcriptions artfully preserved the distinctive aspects of Russian folk music:

- its 'tonal mutability': a tune seems to shift quite naturally from one tonic centre to another, often ending up in a different key (usually a second lower or higher) from the one in which the piece began. The effect is to produce a feeling of elusiveness, a lack of definition or of logical progression in the harmony, which even in its stylized *kuchkist* form makes Russian music sound very different from the tonal structures of the West.

- its heterophony: a melody divides into several dissonant voices, each with its own variation of the theme, which is improvised by the individual singers until the end, when the song reverts to a single line.

- its use of parallel fifths, fourths and thirds. The effect is to give to Russian music a quality of raw sonority that is entirely missing in the polished harmonies of Western music.

Secondly the *kuchkists* invented a series of harmonic devices to create a distinct 'Russian' style and colour that was different from the music of the West. This 'exotic' styling of 'Russia' was not just self-conscious but entirely invented – for none of these devices was actually employed in Russian folk or church music:

- the whole-tone scale (C–D–E–F sharp–G sharp–A sharp–C): invented by Glinka and used for the first time in the march of Chernomor, the sorcerer in his opera *Ruslan and Liudmila* (1842), this became the 'Russian' sound of spookiness and evil. It was used by all the major composers from Tchaikovsky (for the apparition of the Countess's ghost in *The Queen of Spades* in 1890) to Rimsky-Korsakov (in all his magic-story operas, *Sadko* (1897), *Kashchei the Immortal* (1902) and *Kitezh* (1907)). The scale is also heard in the music of Debussy, who took it (and much else) from Musorgsky. Later it became a standard device in horror-movie scores.

- the octatonic scale, consisting of a whole tone followed by a semi-tone (C–D–E flat–F–G flat–A flat–B double flat–C double flat): used for the first time by Rimsky-Korsakov in his *Sadko* symphonic suite of 1867, it became a sort of Russian calling card, a *leitmotif* of magic and menace that was used not just by Rimsky but by all his followers, above all Stravinsky in his three great Russian ballets, *The Firebird* (1910), *Petrushka* (1911) and *The Rite of Spring* (1913).

– the modular rotation in sequences of thirds: a device of Liszt's which the Russians made their own as the basis of their loose symphonic-poem type of structure that avoids the rigid (German) laws of modulation in sonata form. Instead of the usual progression to the relative minor in the development section of the sonata form (e.g. C major to A minor), the Russians established a tonic centre in the opening section (say, C major) and then progressed through sequences of thirds (A flat major, F major, D flat major, and so on) in subsequent sections. The effect is to break away from the Western laws of development, enabling the form of a composition to be shaped entirely by the 'content' of the music (its programmatic statements and visual descriptions) rather than by formal laws of symmetry.

This loose structure was especially important in Musorgsky's *Pictures at an Exhibition*, a work that probably did more than any other to define the Russian style. Musorgsky was the most original of the *kuchkist* composers. This was partly because he was the least schooled in European rules of composition. But the main reason was that he consciously rejected the European school and, more than any of the other nationalists, looked to the traditions of the Russian folk as a means of overturning it. There is a sense in which this very Russian figure (lazy, slovenly and heavy-drinking, full of swagger and explosive energy) played the Holy Fool in relation to the West. He rejected out of hand the received conventions of composition drawn up from the music of Bach, Mozart and Haydn. 'Symphonic development, technically understood, is developed by the German, just as his philosophy is', Musorgsky wrote to Rimsky-Korsakov in 1868. 'The German when he thinks first theorises at length and then proves; our Russian brother proves first and then amuses himself with theory.'[72]

Musorgsky's direct approach to life is reflected in his *Pictures*. The suite is a loosely structured series of musical portraits, a gentle amble through a picture gallery, without any sign of the formal ('German') rules of elaboration or development, and little evidence of the Western conventions of musical grammar. At its heart is the magic reach and power of the Russian folk imagination. The opening 'Promenade (*in mode russico*)' is a folk-inspired tune with a metric flexibility, sudden tonal shifts, open fifths and octaves, and a choral heterophony echoing the patterns of the village song. The grotesque and tempestuous 'Baba Yaga' shifts violently between keys, persistently returning to the key of G in that static manner of the Russian peasant song (*nepodvizhnost'*) which, in a musical revolution yet to come, Stravinsky would deploy with such explosive force in *The Rite of Spring*. Musorgsky's final picture, the glorious 'Kiev Gate', religiously uplifting, beautiful and tender, takes its cue from an ancient Russian hymn, the chant of Znamenny, originating from Byzantium and heard here, in the awesome closing moments, resounding to the clangour of the heavy bells. It is a wonderfully expressive moment, a picture of all Russia drawn in sound, and a moving tribute by Musorgsky to his friend.

5

Alongside their interest in its 'Russian style', writers, artists and composers developed an obsession with Moscow's history. One only has to list the great historical operas (from Glinka's *A Life for the Tsar* to Rimsky-Korsakov's *The Maid of Pskov* and Musorgsky's *Boris Godunov* and *Khovanshchina*), the history plays and novels (from Pushkin's *Boris Godunov* to Alexei Tolstoy's trilogy beginning with *The Death of Ivan the Terrible*), the huge proliferation of poetic works on historical themes and the epic history paintings of Surikov and Repin, or Vasnetsov and Vrubel, to see the importance of Moscow's history to the cultural quest for 'Russia' in the nineteenth century. It is no coincidence that nearly all these works concerned the final years of Ivan the Terrible and the so-called 'Time of Troubles' between the reign of Boris Godunov and the foundation of the Romanov dynasty. History was regarded as a battlefield for competing views of Russia and its destiny, and these fifty years were seen as a crucial period in Russia's past. They were a time when everything was up for grabs and the nation was confronted by fundamental questions of identity. Was it to be governed by elected rulers or by Tsars? Was it to be part of Europe or remain outside of it? The same questions were being asked by thinking Russians in the nineteenth century.

Boris Godunov was a vital figure in this national debate. The histories, plays and operas that were written about him were also a discourse on Russia's destiny. The Godunov we know from Pushkin and Musorgsky appeared first in Karamzin's *History*. Karamzin portrayed Godunov as a tragic figure, a progressive ruler who was haunted by the past, a man of immense power and yet human frailty who was undone by the gap between political necessity and his own conscience. But in order to make the medieval Tsar the subject of a modern psychological drama, Karamzin had to invent much of his history.

Boris, in real life, was the orphaned son of an old *boyar* family who had been raised at the Muscovite court as a ward of the Tsar, Ivan the Terrible. The Godunovs became intimate with the Royal Family at a time when noble lineage was viewed as potentially seditious by the Tsar. Engaged in a protracted struggle with noble *boyar* clans, Ivan made a point of promoting loyal servicemen from humble origins like the Godunovs. Boris's sister, Irina Godunova, married Fedor, the Tsar's weak and feeble-minded son. Shortly after, Ivan struck down and killed his eldest son, Ivan the Tsarevich, an episode which gripped the nineteenth-century imagination through Repin's famous painting of the scene, *Ivan the Terrible and His Son Ivan on 16 November 1581* (1885). Dmitry, Ivan's other son, was just two years old when Ivan died in 1584, and his claim to the succession was tenuous at best. He was the child of the Tsar's seventh marriage, but Church law permitted only three. So Fedor was crowned when Ivan died. The practical affairs of government were taken over by Boris Godunov – addressed in official documents as 'the great sovereign's Brother-in-Law, Ruler of the Russian lands'. Boris made a notable success of government. He secured Russia's borders in the Baltic lands, kept in check the Tatar raids from the southern steppe, strengthened ties with Europe and, to secure a stable labour force for the gentry, he laid down the administrative framework of serfdom – a measure which was deeply unpopular with the peasantry. In 1598 Fedor died. Irina refused the crown and went into a convent, overcome with grief at her failure to produce an heir. At the *zemskii sobor*, or 'Assembly of the Land', the Moscow *boyars* voted for Boris to become Tsar – the first elected Tsar in Russian history.

The early years of the Godunov reign were prosperous and peaceful. In many ways Boris was an enlightened monarch – a man ahead of his own time. He was interested in Western medicine, book printing and education, and he even dreamed of founding a Russian university on the European model. But in 1601–3 things went badly wrong. A series of harvest failures led to the starvation of about one-quarter of the peasantry in Muscovy, and since the crisis was made worse by the new laws of serfdom which took away the peasants' rights of movement, the rural protests were aimed against the Tsar. The old princely clans took advantage of the famine crisis to renew their plots against the upstart elected Tsar whose power was a threat to their noble privilege. Boris stepped up his police surveillance of the noble families (especially the Romanovs) and banished many of them to Siberia or to monasteries in the Russian north on charges of treason. Then, in the middle of this political crisis, a young pretender to the Russian throne appeared with an army from Poland – a country always ready to exploit divisions within Russia for territorial gain. The pretender was Grigory Otrepev, a runaway monk who had been at one time in the service of the Romanovs, and he was probably approached by them before his escapade. He claimed to be the Tsarevich Dmitry, Ivan's youngest son. Dmitry had been found with his throat cut in 1591; he was an epileptic and at the time it was established that he had stabbed himself in a fit. But Godunov's opponents always claimed that he had killed the boy to clear his own passage to the Russian throne. The 'False Dmitry' played upon these doubts, claiming he had escaped the plot to murder him. It enabled him to rally supporters against the 'usurper Tsar' among disgruntled peasants and Cossacks on his march towards Moscow. Godunov died suddenly in 1605, as the pretender's forces approached Moscow. According to Karamzin, he died of the 'inner agitation of the soul which is inescapable for a criminal'.[73]

The evidence implicating Godunov in the murder of Dmitry had been fabricated by the Romanovs, whose own claims to the throne had rested on their election by the *boyars*' assembly to restore Russia's unity, following the 'Time of Troubles', a period of civil wars and foreign invasion following the death of Boris Godunov. Perhaps Karamzin should have realized that Godunov was not a murderer. But nearly all the documents which he consulted had been doctored by official clerks or monks, and to challenge the Romanov myth would have got him into trouble with the government. In any case, the murder story was far too good for Karamzin to resist. It allowed him to explore the inner conflicts of Godunov's mind in a way quite unsupported by the evidence. It underpinned his tragic concept of Boris Godunov – a progressive ruler who was haunted by his crime and in the end undone by his own illegitimacy as a Tsar. Karamzin's *History* was dedicated to the Emperor Alexander – the reigning Tsar from the House of Romanov – and its vision was overtly monarchist. The moral lesson which he drew from the Godunov story – that elected rulers are never any good – was carefully attuned to the politics of Alexander's reign. Boris was a Russian Bonaparte.

Pushkin's *Boris Godunov* was very closely based on Karamzin's *History*, sometimes even lifting sections word for word. The conception of the play is firmly royalist – the people play no active part in their own history. That is the meaning of the famous stage direction 'the people remain silent' (*'narod bezmolvstvuet'*) with which the drama ends. Musorgsky, too, who followed Pushkin's text in his first version of the opera (1868–9), portrayed the Russian people as a dark and passive force, mired in the customs and beliefs of the old Russia embodied in Moscow. This conception of the Russians is epitomized in the scene outside St Basil's on Red Square. The starving people gather there and Boris is confronted by the Holy Fool, who by implication condemns the Tsar's crimes. But the crowd remains inert, kneeling in supplication to the Tsar, and even when the Holy Fool says he will not pray for the 'Tsar Herod', the people just disperse. Hence what might have been a signal for revolt is allowed to pass, and the Holy Fool appears not as the people's leader but as a voice of conscience and Boris's remorse.[74] It was only with the addition of the 'Kromy Forest Scene', in the second version of the opera (1871–2), that Musorgsky introduced the theme of conflict between the people and the Tsar. Indeed, this conflict becomes the motive force of the whole drama, and the people the real tragic subject of the opera. In the Kromy scene the people are revealed in rebellion, the crowd mocks the Tsar, and folk song is deployed as the embodiment of the people's voice. Musorgsky was first inspired to insert the scene for musical effect, having been impressed by the choral heterophony of a similar crowd scene in Rimsky-Korsakov's *The Maid of Pskov*. The two men were sharing an apartment (and a piano) at the time and Musorgsky set to work on the Kromy scene just as Rimsky was orchestrating his opera.[75] But the substitution of the Kromy scene for the one before St Basil's (which is what Musorgsky clearly intended) meant a complete switch in the intellectual emphasis of the opera.*

There was no Kromy revolt in Karamzin or Pushkin and, as the Russian music expert Richard Taruskin has brilliantly shown, the Populist redrafting of the opera was rather the result of Musorgsky's friendship with the historian Nikolai Kostomarov, who also helped him in the planning of *Khovanshchina* (1874). Kostomarov viewed the common people as the fundamental force of history. His major work *The Revolt of Stenka Razin* (1859), one of the first fruits of the liberal laws on censorship passed in the early years of Alexander II's reign, had made him a popular and influential figure in the liberal intellectual circles which did so much to advance the Russian arts in the 1860s and 1870s. In *The Time of Troubles* (1866) Kostomarov described how the famine led to bands of migrant serfs rallying behind the False Dmitry in opposition to Boris Godunov:

They were prepared to throw themselves with joy at whoever would lead them against Boris, at whoever would promise them an improvement in their lot. This was not a matter of aspiring to this or that political or social order; the huge crowd of sufferers easily attached itself to a new face in the hope that under a new order things would become better than under the old.[76]

It is a conception of the Russian people – suffering and oppressed, full of destructive and impulsive violence, uncontrollable and unable to control its own destiny – that applies equally to 1917.

---

* So the tendency of modern productions to include both these scenes, though understandable on the basis of the music, contradicts the will of Musorgsky, who physically ripped out the St Basil's scene from the revised version of the score.

'History is my nocturnal friend', Musorgsky wrote to Stasov in 1873; 'it brings me pleasure and intoxication.'[77] It was Moscow that had infected him with the history bug. He loved its 'smell of antiquity' which transported him 'into another world'.[78] For Musorgsky, Moscow was a symbol of the Russian land – it represented a huge weight of inertia in the customs and beliefs of old Russia. Beneath the thin veneer of European civilization that Peter had laid down, the common people were still the inhabitants of 'Jericho'. 'Paper, books, they've gone ahead, but the people haven't moved', the composer wrote to Stasov on the bicentennial jubilee of Peter's birth in 1872. 'Public benefactors are inclined to glorify themselves and to fix their glory in documents, but the people groan, and drink to stifle their groans, and groan all the louder: "*haven't moved!*" '[79] This was the pessimistic vision of old Russia that Musorgsky had expressed in the last prophetic words of the Holy Fool in *Boris Godunov*:

> Darkest dark, impenetrable dark
> Woe, woe to Rus'
> Weep, weep Russian people
> Hungry people.

After *Godunov* he began immediately on *Khovanshchina*, an opera set amid the political and religious struggles in Moscow from the eve of Peter's coronation in 1682 to his violent suppression of the *streltsy* musketeers, the last defenders of the Moscow *boyars* and the Old Belief, who rose up in a series of revolts between 1689 and 1698. More than a thousand musketeers were executed on the Tsar's orders, their mangled bodies displayed as a warning to others, in reprisal for their abortive plot to replace Peter with his sister Sophia, who had ruled as regent in the 1680s when he was still too young to govern by himself. As a punishment for her role in the revolts, Peter forced Sophia to become a nun. The same fate befell his wife, Eudoxia, who had sympathized with the insurrectionaries. The Streltsy revolt and its aftermath marked a crossroads in Russian history, a period when the new dynamic Petrine state clashed with the forces of tradition. The defenders of old Russia were represented in the opera by the hero Prince Khovansky, a Moscow patriarch who was the main leader of the *streltsy* musketeers (*Khovanshchina* means 'Khovansky's rule'); and by the Old Believer Dosifei (a fictional creation named after the last patriarch of the united Orthodox Church in Jerusalem). They are connected by the fictional figure of Marfa, Khovansky's fiancée and a devout adherent to the Old Belief. Marfa's constant prayers and lamentations for Orthodox Russia express the profound sense of loss that lies at the heart of this opera.

The Westernists viewed *Khovanshchina* as a progressive work, a celebration of the passing from the old Moscow to the European spirit of St Petersburg. Stasov, for example, tried to persuade Musorgsky to devote more of Act III to the Old Believers, because this would strengthen their association with 'that side of ancient Russia' that was 'petty, wretched, dull-brained, superstitious, evil and malevolent'.[80] This interpretation was then fixed by Rimsky-Korsakov, who, as the editor of the unfinished score after Musorgsky's death in 1881, moved the prelude ('Dawn over the Moscow River') to the end, so that what in the original version had been a lyrical depiction of the old Moscow now became the sign of Peter's rising sun. All before was night.

This simple message was reinforced by an act of vandalism on Rimsky's part. To the end of the opera's final chorus, a melismatic Old Believers' melody that Musorgsky had transcribed from the singing of a friend, Rimsky added a brassy marching tune of the Preobrazhensky Regiment – the very regiment Peter had established as his personal guard to replace the *streltsy* musketeers (it was Musorgsky's regiment as well). Without Rimsky's programmatic alterations the Old Believers would have had the fifth and final act of the opera to themselves. The fifth act takes its subject from the mass suicides of the Old Believers in response to the suppression of the Streltsy revolt in 1698: some 20,000 Old Believers are said to have gathered in churches and chapels in various remote regions of the Russian north and burned themselves to death. At the end of Musorgsky's original version of the opera the Old Believers marched off to their deaths, singing chants and prayers. The opera had thus ended with a sense of loss at the passing of the old religious world of Muscovy. As far as one can tell, it had been Musorgsky's aim to close *Khovanshchina* in this melancholic vein, in the same pianissimo and pessimistic mood as *Boris Godunov*. He had never felt the need to 'resolve' the opera with a forward-moving plot, like that imposed on it by Rimsky-Korsakov. Deadlock and immobility were Musorgsky's overarching themes. He felt ambivalent about Russia's progress since the fall of Muscovy. He was sympathetic to the idealism of the Old Believers. He thought that only prayer could overcome the sadness and despair of life in Russia. And he held to the conviction that the Old Believers were the last 'authentic Russians', whose way of life had not yet been disturbed by European ways. Such ideas were widely held in the 1860s, not just by the Slavophiles, who idealized the patriarchy of old Muscovy, but by Populist historians such as Kostomarov and Shchapov, who wrote social histories of the schismatics, and by ethnographers who made studies of the Old Believers in Moscow. These views were shared by writers such as Dostoevsky – at that time a member of the 'native soil' movement (*pochvennichestvo*), a sort of synthesis between the Westernizers and the Slavophiles which was immensely influential among writers and critics in the early 1860s. The character Raskolnikov in *Crime and Punishment* has a name that means 'schismatic'.

The painter Vasily Surikov also focused on the history of the Old Believers to explore the clash between the people's native customs and the modernizing state. His two great history paintings, *The Morning of the Execution of the Streltsy* (1881) and *The Boyar's Wife Morozova* (1884) (plate 7) are the visual counterparts of *Khovanshchina*. Surikov was closer to the Slavophiles than Musorgsky, whose mentor Stasov, despite his nationalism, was a confirmed Westernist. Surikov idealized Moscow as a 'legendary realm of the authentic Russian way of life'.[81] He was born in 1848 to a Cossack family in the Siberian town of Krasnoyarsk. Having graduated from the St Petersburg Academy of Arts, he settled down in Moscow, which made him 'feel at home' and inspired him to paint on historical themes. 'When I first stepped out on to Red Square it evoked memories of home, and from that emerged the image of the Streltsy, right down to the composition and the colour scheme.'[82] Surikov spent several years making ethnographic sketches of the Old Believers in the Rogozhskoe and Preobrazhenskoe areas of the city, where much of Moscow's small trade, and about a third of its total population, was crammed into houses in the narrow winding streets. His idea was that history was depicted on the faces of these types. The Old Believers took a shine to him, Surikov recalled, 'because

I was the son of a Cossack and because I didn't smoke'. They over-looked their traditional superstition that to paint a person was a sin, allowing Surikov to sketch them. All the faces in *The Boyar's Wife Morozova* were drawn from living people in Moscow. Morozova herself was modelled on a pilgrim from Siberia. Hence Tolstoy, who was among the first to see the painting, was so full of praise for the crowd figures: 'The artist has caught them splendidly! It is as if they are alive! One can almost hear the words they're whispering.'[83]

When they were exhibited in the 1880s Surikov's two paintings were hailed by the democratic intelligentsia, who saw the Streltsy revolt and the stubborn self-defence of the Old Believers as a form of social protest against Church and state. The 1880s was a time of renewed political repression following the assassination of Alexander II by revolutionary terrorists in March 1881. The new Tsar, Alexander III, was a political reactionary who soon sacked his father's liberal ministers and passed a series of decrees rolling back their reforms: new controls were imposed on local government; censorship was tightened; the personal rule of the Tsar was reasserted through his direct agents in the provinces; and a modern police state began to take shape. In this context the democrats had reason to regard the historical figures of Surikov's paintings as a symbol of their opposition to the Tsarist state. Morozova, in particular, was seen as a popular martyr. This was how the artist had portrayed the famous widow, a scion of the wealthy Moscow *boyar* family and a major patron of the Old Belief at the time of the Nikonian reforms in the mid-seventeenth century. In Surikov's huge painting (it stands several metres high) she is depicted on a sledge, being dragged to prison where she would be tortured until she died, her hand extended upwards in the Old Believers' two-fingered sign of the cross as a gesture of defiance against the state. Morozova appears as a woman of real character and dignity who is prepared to die for an idea. The emotion on her face was drawn directly from contemporary life. In 1881 the artist had been present at the public execution of a female revolutionary – another woman who had been prepared to die for her ideas – and he had been shocked by the 'wild look' on her face as she was marched to the gallows.[84] History was alive on Moscow's streets.

6

Moscow grew into a great commercial centre in the nineteenth century. Within sixty years, the peaceful nest of gentlefolk Napoleon had found was transformed into a bustling metropolis of shops and offices, theatres and museums, with sprawling industrial suburbs that every year drew hordes of immigrants. By 1900, with 1 million people, Moscow was, along with New York, one of the fastest growing cities in the world. Three-quarters of its population had been born elsewhere.[85]

The railways held the key to Moscow's growth. All the major lines converged on the city, the geographic centre between east and west, the agricultural south and the new industrial regions of the north. Financed mainly by Western companies, the railways opened new markets for Moscow's trade and linked its industries with provincial sources of labour and raw materials. Thousands of commuters came in every day by train. The cheap boarding houses in the areas around the city's nine main stations were always overcrowded with casual labourers from the countryside. Moscow, then, emerged as the metropolis of capitalist Russia – a position it still occupies today. Provincial towns like Tver, Kaluga and Riazan, all brought into Moscow's orbit by the train, fell into decay as Moscow's manufacturers sent their goods by rail directly to the local rural markets, and shoppers came themselves to buy in Moscow, where, even taking into account the cost of a third-class railway fare, prices still worked out cheaper than in district towns. Moscow's rise was the demise of its own provincial satellites, which spelt ruin for those gentry farmers, like the Ranevskys in Chekhov's *The Cherry Orchard*, who depended on these towns as consumers of their grain. They were unprepared for the international market which the railways opened up. Chekhov's play begins and ends with a train journey. The railway was a symbol of modernity: it brought in a new life and destroyed the old.*

---

* It is interesting to compare Chekhov's treatment of this symbol with Tolstoy's. For Chekhov, who believed in progress through science and technology (he was, after all, a doctor), the railway was a force of good (for example, in the short story 'Lights') as well as bad (for example, in 'My Life'). But for Tolstoy, a nobleman nostalgic for the simple country life, the railway was a force of destruction. The most important moments in the

Moscow's emergence as an economic giant was associated with its transition from a noble- to a merchant-dominated town. But so, too, was its cultural renaissance in the nineteenth century – a renaissance that made Moscow one of the most exciting cities in the world: as their wealth grew, Moscow's leading merchants grabbed hold of the city's government and patronized its arts.

In the early nineteenth century Moscow's trade was concentrated in the narrow winding streets of the Zamoskvoreche district, opposite the Kremlin on the Moscow river's sleepy southern side. It was a world apart from the rest of Moscow, little touched by modern or European ways, with its patriarchal customs, its strict religious life and Old Beliefs, and its cloistered merchant houses built with their backs to the street. Belinsky called these homes 'fortresses preparing for a siege, their windows shuttered and the gates firmly under lock and key. A knock starts a dog barking.'[86] The appearance of the merchants, with their long *kaftans* and beards, was reminiscent of the peasantry, from which many of them had in fact emerged. The great Moscow textile dynasties – the Riabushinskys and the Tretiakovs, the Guchkovs, Alekseevs and the Vishniakovs – were all descended from serf forebears. For this reason, the Slavophiles idealized the merchants as the bearers of a purely Russian way of life. Slavophiles and merchants joined together in their opposition to free trade, fearing Western goods would swamp the home markets. Outraged by the foreign domination of the railways, they clubbed together to finance the first 'Russian' line, from Moscow to Sergiev Posad, in 1863. It was symbolic that its destination was a monastery, the hallowed shrine, indeed, of the Russian Church, and the spiritual centre of old Muscovy.

The public image of the merchantry was fixed by the plays of Alexander Ostrovsky, himself a child of the Zamoskvoreche – his father had worked in the local judiciary, dealing mainly with the merchantry. After studying law at Moscow University, Ostrovsky

---

tragedy of Anna Karenina are all connected with this metaphor: Anna's first meeting with Vronsky at the Moscow station; Vronsky's declaration of his love for her on the train to Petersburg; and her suicide by throwing herself in front of a train. Here was a symbol of modernity, of sexual liberation and adultery, that led unavoidably to death. All the more ironic and symbolic, then, that Tolstoy himself died in the stationmaster's house at Astapovo (today 'Lev Tolstoy') on a dead-end line to the south of Moscow.

worked as a clerk in the civil courts, so he had direct experience of the scams and squabbles that filled his merchant plays. His first drama, *A Family Affair* (1849), was based on a case in the Moscow courts. It tells the depressing tale of a merchant called Bolshov. To escape his debts he pretends to be bankrupt by transferring all his assets to his daughter and son-in-law, who then run off with the money, leaving Bolshov to go to debtors' jail. The play was banned by the Tsar, who thought its portrait of the merchantry – even if it was based on a story from real life – might prove damaging to its relations with the Crown. Ostrovsky was placed under police surveillance. Sacked from his job in the civil courts, he was forced to earn a living as a dramatist, and he soon turned out a batch of sell-out plays that all dealt with the strange and (at that time) exotic mores of the Moscow business world. The corrupting power of money, the misery of arranged marriages, domestic violence and tyranny, the escape of adultery – these are the themes of Ostrovsky's plays. The most famous is perhaps *The Storm* (1860), which the Czech composer Leoš Janáček would use as the basis for his opera *Katya Kabanova* (1921).

The stereotype of the Russian merchant – greedy and deceitful, narrowly conservative and philistine, the embodiment of everything that was dreary and depressing in provincial towns – became a literary commonplace. In the novels of Turgenev and Tolstoy the traders who swindled the squires of their land symbolized the menace of the new commercial culture to the old-world values of the aristocracy. Take the scene in *Anna Karenina*, for example, where Stiva Oblonsky, the hopelessly spendthrift but endearing nobleman, agrees to sell his forests to a local merchant at far too low a price. When Levin tells Oblonsky of their true value, Oblonsky's sense of honour as a nobleman forces him to go through with the deal, even though he knows that the merchant took advantage of his ignorance. All over Europe it was commonplace for the nineteenth-century cultural élites to hold trade and commerce in contempt, and such attitudes were equally pronounced in the intelligentsia. But nowhere else did they have such an effect as in Russia, where they poisoned the relations of the middle classes with the cultural élites and thereby closed off the possibility of Russia going down the capitalist-bourgeois path – until it was too late. Even as late as the 1890s merchants were excluded from the social circles of Moscow's aristocracy. The governor of the city, the Grand Duke Sergei, would not have a merchant at his ball, even though merchants paid the largest share of the city's taxes and some lent money personally to him. Consequently, many merchants had a deep mistrust of the aristocracy. The textile magnate and patron of the arts Pavel Tretiakov, an old-style Moscow merchant and an Old Believer, forbade his daughter to marry the pianist Alexander Ziloti, on the grounds that he was a nobleman and thus only after her inheritance. He reacted in a similar way to the marriage of his niece to A. I. Tchaikovsky (the composer's brother), another nobleman, and not only that, but a nobleman from Petersburg.

Yet one could also form a brighter view of the Moscow merchants from Ostrovsky's plays. Indeed, for this reason there were merchants like the Botkins, Moscow's tea importers, who patronized his work. Another group who liked Ostrovsky's plays for their positive message about the merchantry were the so-called 'native soil' critics (*pochvenniki*), whose outlet was the journal *Moskvitianin* (*The Muscovite*). The influential critic Apollon Grigoriev was a leading member of the 'native soil' movement, along with the writer Fedor Dostoevsky and his brother Mikhail. Ostrovsky's plays, they said, had spoken a 'new word' on Russian nationality. As a social group that lay somewhere between the peasantry and the educated classes, the merchants, they believed, were uniquely qualified to lead the nation in a way that reconciled its Muscovite and Petrine elements. Ostrovsky's merchants were neither Slavophile nor Westernist, Mikhail Dostoevsky argued in a review of *The Storm*. They had flourished in the European culture of the new Russia, yet had managed to retain the culture of the old; and in this sense, Dostoevsky claimed, the merchants showed the way for Russia to progress without social divisions.[87] This interpretation was a reflection of the 'native soil' ideals of national integration that followed in the wake of the emancipation of the serfs. The decree evoked high hopes of a spiritual rebirth in which the Russian nation, the noble and the peasant, would become reconciled and reunited around the cultural ideals of the intelligentsia. The mixed-class origins of the 'native soil' critics, most of whom were *raznochintsy* types (from a minor noble background, with close connections to the world of trade), perhaps led them to idealize the merchants as the pioneers of a new classless society. Yet the merchants were in fact developing in an interesting way – they were breaking out of the old cultural ghetto of the Zamoskvoreche – and this was reflected in Ostrovsky's later plays. In *The Final Sacrifice* (1878) the usual themes of money and domestic tyranny are almost overshadowed by the appearance of a new generation of merchants' sons and daughters who are European in their ways. When an actress would not play the part of a merchant's wife in the first production of *The Final Sacrifice*, arguing that she did not want to be seen in a peasant shawl, Ostrovsky reassured her that the merchant's wife now dressed more fashionably than the ladies of the aristocracy.[88]

By this time, indeed, there was a group of fabulously wealthy merchant dynasties, many far wealthier than the aristocracy, that had branched out from their family concerns to form vast conglomerates. The Riabushinskys, for example, added glass and paper, publishing and banking, and later motor cars, to their textile factories in Moscow; and the Mamontovs had an immense empire of railways and iron foundries. As they grew in confidence, these familes left behind the narrow cultural world of the Zamoskvoreche. Their sons adopted European ways, entered the professions and civic politics, patronized the arts, and generally competed with the aristocracy for pre-eminence in society. They acquired lavish mansions, dressed their wives in the latest clothes from Paris, gave brilliant parties, and dined at the élite English Club. Some of these young industrial barons were even rich enough to snub the aristocracy. Savva Morozov, the Moscow factory magnate and principal financier of the Moscow Arts Theatre, once received a request from the governor of Moscow to be shown around Morozov's house. Morozov agreed and invited him to come the next day. But when the Grand Duke appeared with his retinue he was greeted by the butler, who informed him that Morozov was away.[89]

Despite the old mistrust between the classes, many of those magnates felt a strong desire for acceptance by the leaders of society. They did not want to join the aristocracy. But they did want to belong to the cultural élite, and they knew that their acceptance depended on their public service and philanthropy – above all, on their support for the arts. This condition was particularly important in Russia, where the cultural influence of the intelligentsia was far stronger than it was in the West. Whereas in America and many parts of Europe, money was enough to become accepted in society, even if the old snobbish attitudes prevailed, Russia never shared the bourgeois cult of money, and its cultural élites were defined by a service ethic that placed a burden on the rich to use their wealth for the people's benefit. Noble clans like the Sheremetevs spent huge sums on charity. In the case of Dmitry Sheremetev these sums represented a quarter of his income, and became a major reason for his growing debts in the middle of the nineteenth century. But Moscow's leading merchants also took their charitable duties very earnestly indeed. Most of them belonged to the Old Belief, whose strict moral code (not unlike that of the Quakers) combined the principles of thrift, sobriety and private enterprise with a commitment to the public good. All the biggest merchant families assigned large chunks of their private wealth to philanthropic projects and artistic patronage. Savva Mamontov, the Moscow railway baron, became an opera impresario and a major patron of the 'World of Art', out of which the Ballets Russes emerged. He had been brought up by his father to believe that 'idleness is vice' and that 'work is not a virtue' but 'a simple and immutable responsibility, the fulfilment of one's debt in life'.[90] Konstantin Stanislavsky, the co-founder of the Moscow Arts Theatre, was brought up with a similar attitude by his father, a Moscow merchant of the old school. Throughout the years from 1898 to 1917, when he acted and directed at the Moscow Arts, he carried on with business at his father's factories. Despite his immense wealth, Stanislavsky could not contribute much to the theatre's funds, because his father had allowed him only a modest income which did not allow him to 'indulge in whims'.[91]

These principles were nowhere more in evidence than in the life and work of Pavel Tretiakov, Russia's greatest private patron of the visual arts. The self-made textile baron came from a family of Old Believer merchants from the Zamoskvoreche. With his long beard, full-length Russian coat and square-toed boots, he cut the figure of an old-school patriarch. But while he adhered throughout his life to the moral code and customs of the Old Belief, he had broken out of its narrow cultural world at an early age. Because his father was opposed to education, he had taught himself by reading books and mixing in the student and artistic circles of Moscow. When he began to collect art, in the mid-1850s, Tretiakov bought mainly Western paintings, but he soon

realized that he lacked the expertise to judge t[...]
avoid the risk of being swindled, he bought o[...]
that point on. Over the next thirty years Tre[...]
1 million roubles on Russian art. His collec[...]
city as the Tretiakov Museum in 1892, inc[...]
Russian easel paintings – far more numerous tha[...]
in the Prado (about 500) or the British ones in the Na[...]
(335). This huge new source of private patronage was a vital bo[...]
the Wanderers – young painters such as Ilya Repin and Ivan Kramskoi
who had broken from the Academy of Arts in the early 1860s and,
like the *kuchkists* under Stasov's influence, had begun to paint in a
'Russian style'. Without the patronage of Tretiakov, the Wanderers
would not have survived these first hard years of independence, when
the private art market beyond the court and the aristocracy was still
extremely small. Their down-to-earth provincial scenes and landscape
paintings appealed to the merchant's ethnocentric taste. 'As for me,'
Tretiakov informed the landscape painter Apollinary Goravsky, 'I want
neither abundant nature scenes, elaborate composition, dramatic lighting, nor any kind of wonders. Just give me a muddy pond and make it
true to life.'[92] The injunction was perfectly fulfilled by Savrasov in his
painting *The Rooks Have Returned* (1871), a poetic evocation of rural
Russia in the early spring thaw, which became Tretiakov's favourite
landscape painting and something of an icon of the Russian School.
Its simple realism was to become a hallmark of the Moscow landscape
school compared to the carefully arranged *veduta* scenes, with their
European styling, stipulated by the Academy in St Petersburg.

Tretiakov in business, the Wanderers in art – each sought to break
free from the bureaucratic controls of St Petersburg; each looked to
Moscow and the provinces for an independent market and identity.
The Wanderers' name (in Russian, *Peredvizhniki*) derived from the
travelling exhibitions organized by their collective in the 1870s.*
Nurtured on the civic and Populist ideals of the 1860s, they toured the
provinces with their exhibitions, usually financed out of their own
pockets, to raise the public's consciousness of art. Sometimes they

---

* The word *Peredvizhniki* came from the *Tovarishchestvo peredvizhnykh khudozhestvennykh vystavok* (Collective of Travelling Art Exhibitions).

country schools or set up their own art schools and museums, with the support of liberal noblemen in local government (the *tvos*) and the Populists. The impact of their tours was enormous. hen the exhibitions came,' recalled a provincial resident, 'the sleepy country towns were diverted for a short while from their games of cards, their gossip and their boredom, and they breathed in the fresh current of free art. Debates and arguments arose on subjects about which the townfolk had never thought before.'[93] Through this mission the Wanderers created a new market for their art. Local merchants funded public galleries that purchased canvases from the Wanderers and their many emulators in provincial towns. In this way the 'national style' of Moscow became the idiom of the provinces as well.

7

Another merchant patron who helped to define the Moscow style in the late nineteenth and early twentieth centuries was the railway magnate Savva Mamontov. A Siberian by birth, Mamontov had moved as a boy to Moscow, where his father was involved as the principal investor in the building of the railway to Sergiev Posad. He fell in love with the place. Its bustling energy was the perfect complement to his creativity and go-ahead panache. Benois (the voice of refined St Petersburg) described Mamontov as 'grandiose and vulgar and dangerous'.[94] He might have been describing Moscow, too.

Mamontov was not just a patron of the arts but an artistic figure in his own right. He studied singing in Milan, acted under Ostrovsky's own direction in *The Storm*, and wrote and directed plays himself. He was strongly influenced by the Populist ideas which circulated around Moscow in his youth. Art was to be for the education of the masses. As a monument to this ideal, he commissioned the artist Korovin to decorate his Moscow railway station (today the Yaroslav) with murals showing rural scenes from the northern provinces where his trains were bound. 'The eyes of the people must be trained to see beauty everywhere, in streets and railway stations,' Mamontov declared.[95] His wife Elizaveta was also influenced by Populist ideas. In 1870 the couple purchased the Abramtsevo estate, set amidst the birchwood forests near Sergiev Posad, sixty kilometres north-east of Moscow, where they set up an artists' colony with workshops to revive the local peasant crafts and manufacture artefacts for sale in Moscow at a special shop. It is ironic that these crafts were dying out as a result of the spread of factory goods by rail. For this was what had made the Mamontovs so rich.

Abramtsevo was located in the heartland of historic Muscovy. It had previously belonged to the Aksakovs, the leading clan of the Slavophiles, and as an artists' colony it attempted to restore the 'authentic' (that is, folk-based) Russian style which the Slavophiles had prized. Artists flocked to it to learn from the old peasant handicrafts and assimilate their style to their own work. Korovin and the two Vasnetsovs, Polenova, Vrubel, Serov and Repin were all active there. Gartman spent a year there before he died, building a workshop and a clinic for the village in the neo-Russian style. Alongside its mission to the peasantry, Abramtsevo was, like everything in which its merchant founder was involved, a commercial enterprise. Its workshops catered to the vibrant market for the neo-Russian style among Moscow's fast expanding middle class. The same was true of other centres, like the Solomenko embroidery workshop, the Talashkino colony and the Moscow *zemstvo* studios, which all likewise combined conservation with commerce. Moscow's middle classes were filling up their houses with the folk-styled tableware and furniture, the embroidery and *objets d'art* that workshops such as these were churning out. At the top end of the market there were spectacular interior designs. Elena Polenova (at Solomenko) built a dining room with elaborate folk wood carvings for the estate of the Moscow textile baroness Maria Yakunchikova (where Chekhov spent the summer of 1903 writing *The Cherry Orchard*). Sergei Maliutin (at the Moscow *zemstvo* studios) designed a similar dining room for the merchant Pertsova. Then there was the folk style, slightly simpler but equally archaic, favoured by the Populist intelligentsia. The artist Vladimir Konashevich recalled having learned to read from a special ABC designed by his father in the 1870s. 'The book was crammed with cart axles, scythes, harrows, hayricks, drying barns and threshing floors.'

In my father's study in front of the writing table stood an armchair whose back was the shaft bow of a harness, and whose arms were two axes. On the seat was a knout whip and a pair of bast shoes carved in oak. The finishing touch was a real little peasant hut which stood on the table. It was made of walnut and full of cigarettes.[96]

Chekhov liked to poke fun at this 'folksy' craze. In his story 'The Grasshopper' (1891) Olga is the wife of a Moscow doctor. She 'plastered all the walls with *lubok* woodcuts, hung up bast shoes and sickles, placed a rake in the corner of the room, and *voila!*, she had a dining room in the Russian style'.[97] Yet Chekhov himself was a purchaser of arts and crafts. At his Yalta house (now a museum) there are two cupboards from Abramtsevo and an armchair like the one described by Konashevich.*

From these arts and crafts, Moscow's artists developed what they called the '*style moderne*', where Russian folk motifs were combined with the styling of European art nouveau. It can be seen in the extraordinary renaissance of Moscow's architecture at the turn of the twentieth century, and perhaps above all in Fedor Shekhtel's splendid mansion for Stepan Riabushinsky, which managed to combine a simple, even austere style with the modern luxuries expected by a rich industrialist. Discreetly hidden from the lavish *style moderne* of its living rooms was an Old Believer chapel designed in the ancient Moscow style. It perfectly expressed the split identity of this merchant caste – on the one hand looking back to the seventeenth century, on the other striding forward to the twentieth. Here indeed was Moscow's paradox – a progressive city whose mythic self-image was in the distant past.

The fashion for old Moscow was also cultivated by the silversmiths and jewellery shops that catered to the city's prosperous merchant class. Craftsmen such as Ivan Khlebnikov and Pavel Ovchinnikov (a former serf of Prince Sergei Volkonsky) produced silver tableware and *samovars*, dishes shaped like ancient Viking ships (*kovshi*), drinking vessels, ornaments and icon covers in the ancient Russian style. These firms were joined by Carl Fabergé, who set up separate workshops in Moscow to produce goods for the rising merchant class. In St Petersburg the Fabergé

---

* There are several similar examples of the armchair in the History Museum of Moscow. All of them were designed by the artist Vasily Shutov.

workshops made gems in the classical and rococo styles. But only Tsars and Grand Dukes could afford to buy such jewels. The Moscow workshops, by contrast, turned out mainly silver objects which were within the financial reach of the middle classes. These Moscow firms all had some artists of extraordinary talent, most of them unknown or neglected to this day. One was Sergei Vashkov, a silver craftsman who made religious objects in the Moscow workshops of the Olovyanishnikovs – and later by commission for Fabergé. Vashkov drew from the simple style of religious art in medieval Russia but he combined this with his own unique version of the *style moderne*, creating sacred objects of a rare beauty and (in a way that was important to the Moscow revival) reuniting church art with the cultural mainstream.

Nicholas II was a major patron of Vashkov and the Moscow workshop of Fabergé.[98] Vashkov designed the silver objects for the mock medieval church in the Fedorov village at Tsarskoe Selo, a sort of Muscovite theme park constructed for the Romanov tercentenary in 1913. This was the high point of the cult of Muscovy. It was engineered by the last Tsar in a desperate effort to invest the monarchy with a mythical historical legitimacy at a time when its right to rule was being challenged by the institutions of democracy. The Romanovs were retreating to the past, hoping it would save them from the future. Nicholas, in particular, idealized the Tsardom of Alexei in the seventeenth century. He saw in it a golden age of paternal rule, when the Tsar had ruled in a mystical union with the Orthodox people, undisturbed by the complications of a modern state. He loathed St Petersburg, with its secular ideas and bureaucracy, its Western culture and intelligentsia, so alien to the 'simple Russian folk', and he tried to Muscovitize it by adding onion domes and *kokoshnik* pediments to the classical façades of its buildings. It was in his reign that the Church of the Spilt Blood was completed on the Catherine Canal. With its onion domes and colourful mosaics, its ornate decorations that contrasted so bizarrely with the classical ensemble in which it was placed, the church was a piece of Moscow kitsch. Yet today tourists flock to it, thinking they are getting something of the 'real' (exotic) Russia so evidently missing in St Petersburg.

Like the church, the Muscovite renaissance in the arts conjured up a land of fairy tales. The retreat to Russian wonderland was a general trend in the final decades of the nineteenth century, when the increased censorship of Alexander III's reign and the early years of Nicholas II's made it hard for the realist school to use art for social or political commentary. And so painters such as Vasnetsov, Vrubel and Bilibin turned to Russian legends as a new way to approach the national theme. Viktor Vasnetsov was the first major artist to make the transition from realist genre painting to fantastic history scenes. He graduated from the Petersburg Academy, but it was his move to Moscow which, by his own admission, accounted for the switch. 'When I came to Moscow, I felt I had come home', he wrote to Stasov. 'The first time I saw the Kremlin and St Basil's, tears welled in my eyes: so forceful was the feeling that they are a part of me.'[99] Vasnetsov depicted monumental figures from the epic folk legends like Ilia Muromets, presenting them as studies of the national character. Nobody in Petersburg would countenance his art. Stasov condemned it for departing from the principles of realism. The Academy denounced it for rejecting classical mythology. Only Moscow welcomed Vasnetsov. The leading Moscow critics had long called on artists to take inspiration from legendary themes, and the Moscow Society of Lovers of Art proved an important outlet for Vasnetsov's epic canvases.[100] Mikhail Vrubel followed Vasnetsov from Petersburg, moving first to Moscow and then Abramtsevo, where he too painted scenes from Russian legends. Like Vasnetsov, Vrubel was inspired by the Moscow atmosphere. 'I am back in Abramtsevo', he wrote to his sister in 1891, 'and again I am enveloped. I can hear that intimate national tone which I so long to capture in my work.'[101]

Vasnetsov and Vrubel brought this land of fairy tales to their colourful designs for Mamontov's Private Opera, which had its origins at Abramtsevo. There was a strong collective spirit within the Abramtsevo circle which expressed itself in the amateur productions at the colony and at the Mamontovs' house in Moscow. Stanislavsky, who was a cousin of Elizaveta Mamontov, recalled that during these productions 'the house would become a tremendous workshop', with actors, artists, carpenters, musicians hurriedly preparing everywhere.[102] At the heart of this collaboration was the ideal of artistic synthesis. Vasnetsov and Vrubel joined with composers such as Rimsky-Korsakov in a conscious effort to unify the arts on the basis of the folk-inspired 'Russian style'. Wagner's idea of the total work of art, the *Gesamtkunstwerk*, was a major influence. Rimsky even planned a Russian version of the *Ring* cycle based on the epic Russian folk legends – with Ilia Muromets as a sort of Slav Siegfried.[103] But Mamontov had also come quite independently to the idea of a total work of art. As he saw it, the opera could not succeed on the basis of good singing and musicianship alone; it had to unite these with its visual and dramatic elements in an organic synthesis. Mamontov established his Private Opera in 1885, three years after the state monopoly of the Imperial Theatre (already an anachronism when private theatres were outlawed in 1803) had finally been lifted by the Tsar. It immediately became the focal point of Moscow's opera world, eclipsing the Bolshoi with its innovative productions of mainly Russian operas. Vasnetsov brought the vibrant primary colours of the folk tradition to the stage for Rimsky's *Snow Maiden*, the big success of the first season. The bulky bulbous form of Tsar Berendei's palace, with its lavishly ornate folk-style decorations and fantastic columns shaped and painted like Russian Easter eggs, was inspired by the wooden palace of Kolomenskoe just outside Moscow. The whole scene conjured up a magic Russian realm, and it left the public, which had never seen such folk art on the stage before, enraptured and amazed.

The height of the company's success came after 1896, when the great bass Shaliapin, still only a young man of twenty-four, signed with Mamontov. Shaliapin's rise had been blocked at the Marinsky Theatre in St Petersburg by senior singers such as Fedor Stravinsky (the composer's father), but Mamontov believed in him and put him in the role of Ivan the Terrible in Rimsky's *Maid of Pskov*, the Private Opera's main production of the 1896–7 season at its new home in the Solodovnikov Theatre in Moscow. It was a sensation. Rimsky was delighted and, having just had *Sadko* turned down by the Marinsky at the express command of Nicholas II (who wanted something 'a bit merrier'),[104] he had no hesitation in throwing in his lot with Mamontov. Rimsky, the young *kuchkist* of the 1860s, had risen to become a pillar of the Russian musical establishment and a professor of the Petersburg Conservatory after 1871; now he too became a convert to Moscow's neo-nationalist school. All his last six major operas were performed by the Private Opera in its distinctive neo-Russian style, including

Sadko and *May Night* (with the 24-year-old Rachmaninov conducting) in 1897, *The Tsar's Bride* in 1899, and *Kashchei the Immortal* in 1902. These were tremendously important productions – their great strength being their visual elements, with colourfully stylized folk-like sets and costumes by Korovin, Maliutin and Vrubel in perfect keeping with the music of these folk-based opera fantasies. They were a major influence on the synthetic ideals of the World of Art movement and the Ballets Russes. Such, indeed, was Mamontov's success that in 1898 he agreed to co-finance the costs of Diaghilev's review the *World of Art*. But then disaster struck. Mamontov was accused of appropriating funds from his railway empire to support the Opera. There was a scandal and a noisy trial in 1900. Mamontov was acquitted of corruption on a wave of public sympathy for a man whose love of art, it was generally concluded, had carried him away. But financially he was ruined. His company collapsed and the Private Opera closed. Mamontov himself was declared bankrupt, and the effects of his Moscow house were sold off by auction in 1903. One of the sale items was a peasant's wooden model of a railway station crafted at Abramtsevo.[105]

8

Private theatrical undertakings were something of a Moscow fashion following the lifting of the state monopoly in 1882. The actress Maria Abramova, for example, set up her own theatre, with the help of merchant patrons, where Chekhov's *Wood Demon* (1889) had its première; and in the 1900s another well-known actress, Vera Komissarzhevskaya, owned a private theatre in St Petersburg. By far the most important of these private ventures was the Moscow Arts Theatre, founded by Vladimir Nemirovich-Danchenko and Konstantin Stanislavsky in 1898. Here Chekhov's last great plays were first performed.

Stanislavsky was born in Moscow to a merchant family which 'had already crossed the threshold of culture', as he would later write. 'They made money in order to spend it on social and artistic institutions.' His maternal grandmother was the French actress Marie Varley, who had made herself a star in Petersburg. But while his parents were rich enough to put on lavish balls, they basically inhabited the old Moscow mercantile world. Stanislavsky's father slept (with his grandfather) in the same bed.[106] As a student Stanislavsky took part in the Mamontov amateur productions. These convinced him that, while huge efforts had been put into the music, the costumes and the sets, very little had been done about the acting, which remained extremely amateurish, not just in the operas but in the theatre, too. He trained himself as an actor by standing for hours before a mirror every day and developing his gestures over several years to make them appear more natural. His famous 'method' (from which 'method acting' was to come) boiled down to a sort of naturalism. It was acting without 'acting' – which fitted in so well with the modern dialogue (where the pauses are as important as the words) and the everyday realities of Chekhov's plays.[107] Later his method was made more systematic through a series of techniques to help the actor convey the inner thoughts and emotions of a part. They were all about recalling moments of intense experience in the actor's own life, supposedly to help him produce the emotion on demand. Mikhail Bulgakov, who wrote a blistering satire of the Moscow Arts in his farcical, unfinished *Black Snow* (1939–), ridiculed these methods in a scene in which the director tries to get an actor to feel what passion is by riding round the stage on a bicycle.

Stanislavsky's vision of an independent theatre brought him together with the playwright and director Vladimir Nemirovich-Danchenko. Both men were committed to the idea that the theatre should reach out to the masses by producing plays about contemporary life. The Moscow Arts was originally called the Accessible Arts Theatre. Cheap seats for students and the poor were mixed in with the expensive ones at the front of the stalls. Even the building, the rundown hermitage in Karetny Row, had a democratic feel. It had previously been used for circuses, and when the actors first moved in there was an all-pervasive smell of beer.[108] After a quick coat of paint, they began in 1898 rehearsals for the opening performances of Alexei Tolstoy's *Tsar Fedor* (1868) and Chekhov's *The Seagull* (1896).

Nemirovich was a great admirer of Chekhov's play. In St Petersburg it had been a disappointment to an audience that expected a comedy. But in the simple, lifelike style of the Moscow Arts' production it was a triumph. 'The public lost all sense of the theatre', wrote Nemirovich: 'the life they now beheld in these simple human contacts on the stage was "real", not theatrical.' People felt 'almost embarrassed to be present', as if they were eavesdropping on a mundane domestic tragedy. There was 'nothing but shattered illusions, and tender feelings crushed by rude reality'.[109] The production relaunched Chekhov's career as a playwright – and he now came home to Moscow as its favourite literary son.

Born in Taganrog, in southern Russia, to a devout, old-style merchant, Anton Chekhov came to Moscow at the age of seventeen and two years later, in 1879, enrolled as a student of medicine at the university. He fell in love with the city from the start. 'I will be a Muscovite for ever', he wrote in a letter of 1881.[110] As a hard-up student, and then as a doctor, Chekhov was acquainted with the city's slums, and he was a lifelong client of its brothels, too. His first literary efforts were as a journalist ('Antosha Chekhonte') for the humorous tabloids and weekly magazines aimed at Moscow's newly literate labourers and clerks. He wrote sketches of street life, vaudeville satires on love and marriage, and stories about doctors and magistrates, petty clerks and actors in Moscow's poor districts. There were many writers of this kind – the most successful being Vladimir Giliarovsky, author of the 1920s classic *Moscow and the Muscovites* (still widely read and loved in Russia today) and something of a mentor to the young Chekhov. But Chekhov was the first major Russian writer to emerge from the penny press (nineteenth-century writers such as Dostoevsky and Tolstoy had written for the serious or 'thick' periodicals that combined literature with criticism and political commentary). His concise written style, for which he is so famed, was fashioned by the need to write for commuters on the train.

Chekhov knew these trains. In 1892 he purchased Melikhovo, a delightful small estate a short journey to the south of Moscow. Moscow often featured as a backdrop to his stories from this period – for example in 'Three Years' (1895) and 'Lady with the Dog' (1899). But the city was now felt by its absence, too. In all his greatest plays Moscow is perceived as a distant ideal realm, a paradise beyond the provinces, where his characters are trapped in a stagnant way of life. Chekhov understood their claustrophobia – he too yearned for city life. 'I miss Moscow', he wrote to Sobolevsky in 1899. 'It's boring without Muscovites, and without Moscow newspapers, and without

SERF ARTISTS. *Nikolai Argunov: Portrait of Praskovya Sheremeteva (1802).*
At the time of this portrait the serf singer's marriage to Count Sheremetev (whose image
is depicted in the miniature) was concealed from the public and the court. Argunov was
the first Russian artist of serf origin to be elected to the Imperial Academy of Arts.

IMAGES OF DOMESTICITY.

Left: *Vasily Tropinin:* Portrait of Pushkin (1827). *Wearing a* khalat, *the writer is portrayed as a European gentleman yet perfectly at ease with the customs of his native land.*

Below: *Alexei Venetsianov:* Morning of the Lady of the Manor (1823), *a picture of what Herzen called the 'feudal bond of affection' between the noble family and its household serfs.*

RUSSIAN PASTORAL. Above: *Venetsianov:* In the Ploughed Field: Spring *(1827), an idealized depiction of the female agricultural labourer in traditional Russian dress.* Below: *Vasily Perov:* Hunters at Rest *(1871). Like Turgenev, Perov portrays hunting as a recreation that brought the social classes together. Here the squire (left) and the peasant (right) share their food and drink.*

MOSCOW RETROSPECT. Above: *The Kremlin's Terem Palace restored in the 1850s by Fedor Solntsev in the seventeenth-century Muscovite style, complete with tiled ovens and kokoshnik-shaped arches. Below: Vasily Surikov:* The Boyar's Wife Morozova (1884). *The faces were all drawn by Surikov from Old Believers living in Moscow.*

The Fabergé Workshop in Moscow crafted objects in a Russian style that was very different from the Classical and Rococo jewels it made in Petersburg. Above: Imperial Presentation Kovsh (an ancient type of ladle) in green nephrite, gold, enamel and diamonds, presented by the Tsar Nicholas II to the French Ambassador in 1906. Below: Silver siren vase by Sergei Vashkov (1908). The female bird wears a kokoshnik and her wings are set with tourmalines.

THE ARTIST AND THE PEOPLE'S CAUSE. *Ilya Repin's* Portrait of Vladimir Stasov *(1873), the nationalist critic whose dogmatic views on the need for art to engage with the people were a towering and, at times, oppressive influence on Musorgsky and Repin.* 'What a picture of the Master you have made!' *the composer wrote.* 'He seems to crawl out of the canvas and into the room.' Below: *Repin:* The Volga Barge Haulers *(1873). Stasov saw the painting as a commentary on the latent force of social protest in the Russian people.* Opposite: *Ivan Kramskoi:* The Peasant Ignatii Pirogov *(1874) – a startlingly ethnographic portrait of the peasant as an individual human being.*

Leon Bakst: Portrait of Diaghilev with his Nanny *(1906).*
Diaghilev had never known his mother, who had died when he was born.

the Moscow church bells which I love so much.' And to Olga Knipper in 1903: 'There's no news. I'm not writing anything. I'm just waiting for you to give me the signal to pack and come to Moscow. "Moscow! Moscow!" These are not the refrain of Three Sisters: they are now the words of One Husband.'[111] In *Three Sisters* (1901) Moscow becomes a symbol for the happiness so lacking in the sisters' lives. They long to go to Moscow, where they lived as children and were happy when their father was alive. But they remain stuck in a provincial town, unable to escape, as youthful hopes give way to the bitter disappointments of middle age. There is no clear explanation for their inertia – a fact which has led critics to lose patience with the play. 'Give the sisters a railway ticket to Moscow at the end of Act One and the play will be over', Mandelstam once wrote.[112] But that is to miss the whole point of the play. The three sisters are suffering from a spiritual malaise, not a geographical displacement. Stifled by the petty routines of their daily life, they strive for a higher form of existence, which they imagine there to be in Moscow, yet in their hearts they know does not exist. The sisters' 'Moscow', then, is not so much a place (they never go there) as a legendary realm – a city of dreams which gives hope and the illusion of meaning to their lives. The real tragedy of the three sisters is voiced by Irena when she comes to realize that this paradise is a fantasy:

I've been waiting all this time, imagining that we'd be moving to Moscow, and I'd meet the man I'm meant for there. I've dreamt about him and I've loved him in my dreams ... But it's all turned out to be nonsense ... nonsense.[113]

Chekhov's Moscow, then, is a symbol of the happiness and better life to come. From Chekhov's point of view, as a Russian and a liberal, its promise was in progress and modernity a far cry from the image of inertia which Musorgsky saw just thirty years before. Chekhov put his faith in science and technology. He was a doctor by training, and by temperament a man who looked to practical solutions rather than to religion or ideologies. In a veiled attack on Tolstoy in 1894, Chekhov wrote that 'there is more love of humanity in electricity and steam than in vegetarianism'.[114] Progress is a constant theme in Chekhov's plays. Noblemen like Astrov in *Uncle Vanya* (1896) or Vershinin in

Three Sisters are constantly speculating about the future of Russia. They hope that one day life will become better and they talk about the need to work towards that end. Chekhov shared these dreamers' hopes, although he was scathing on the subject of intellectuals who did no more than speak about the need to work. Trofimov, the eternal student in *The Cherry Orchard*, is always saying 'we must work', yet he himself has never done a thing. Chekhov thought that well-intentioned chatter was Russia's greatest curse. He worked like one possessed throughout his life. He *believed* in work as the purpose of existence and as a form of redemption: it was at the heart of his own religious faith. 'If you work for the present moment', he wrote in his notebook, 'your work will be worthless. One must work bearing only the future in one's mind.'[115] Perhaps his credo was best expressed by Sonya in the final moving moments of *Uncle Vanya*. There is, she says, no rest from work or suffering, and only in the ideal world is there a better life.

Well, what can we do? We must go on living! We shall go on living, Uncle Vanya. We shall live through a long, long succession of days and tedious evenings. We shall patiently suffer the trials which Fate imposes on us; we shall work for others, now and in our old age, and we shall have no rest. When our time comes we shall die submissively, and over there, in the other world, we shall say that we have suffered, that we've wept, that we've had a bitter life, and God will take pity on us. And then, Uncle dear, we shall both begin to know a life that is bright and beautiful, and lovely. We shall rejoice and look back at all our troubles with tender feelings, with a smile – and we shall have rest. I believe it, Uncle, I believe it fervently, passionately . . . We shall have rest![116]

Chekhov's emphasis on the need to work was more than a Voltairean solution to the quest for meaning in one's life. It was a critique of the landed gentry, which had never really known the meaning of hard work and for this reason was destined for decline. This is the theme of Chekhov's final play, *The Cherry Orchard*, written for the Moscow Arts in 1904. It has often been perceived as a sentimental drama about the passing from an old and charming gentry world to a brash, modern, city-based economy. The plot is, indeed, quite reminiscent of the 'nest of gentry' melodramas that had been in fashion since Turgenev's time. The main characters, the Ranevskys, are forced by debt to sell their prized possession and inheritance (the orchard) to a merchant called Lopakhin, who plans to clear the land and build *dachas* on it for the new middle classes of the towns. Stanislavsky, in the first production, played it as a sentimental tragedy: his actors cried when they first heard the script. No one was prepared to puncture the mystique of 'the good old days' on the estate – a mystique that had grown into a national myth. Journals such as *Bygone Years (Starye gody)* and *Town and Country (Stolitsa i usad'ba)* catered to this cult with their dreamy pictures and nostalgic memoirs about the old gentry way of life. The political agenda of these journals was the preservation of the landowners' estates, not just as a piece of property, an economic system or ancestral home, but as the last remaining outposts of a civilization that was threatened with extinction by the social revolution of the towns. 'Our country nests', Count Pavel Sheremetev told the Moscow *zemstvo*, 'are carrying the ancient torch of culture and enlightenment. God grant them success, if only they are spared the senseless movement to destroy them, supposedly in the interests of social justice.'[117] Had Chekhov's play been written after 1905, when the first agrarian revolution swept through Russia and thousands of those country nests were set alight or ransacked by the peasants, it might have been conceived in this nostalgic way. But Chekhov was insistent that the play should be performed as a comedy, not a sentimental tragedy; and in this conception the play could not have been written later than it was, even if Chekhov had lived for another twenty years. After the 1905 Revolution the passing of the old world was no longer a subject of comedy.

Chekhov called his play a 'piece of vaudeville'.[118] Throughout *The Cherry Orchard* he is subtly ironic and iconoclastic in his treatment of the gentry's 'cultivated ways'. He is sending up the mystique of the 'good old days' on the estate. We are meant to laugh at the clichéd sentimental speeches of Madame Ranevskaya when she waxes lyrical on the former beauty of the old estate or her happy childhood there: a world she had abandoned long ago for France. Her overblown expressions of sadness and nostalgia are belied by the speed with which she recovers and then forgets her grief. This is not a tragedy: it is a satire of the old-world gentry and the cult of rural Russia which grew up around it. What are we to think of Pishchik, for example, the landowner who sings the praises of the 'gentry on the land' and yet at the first opportunity lets some English businessmen have the rights to mine it for some special clay (no doubt to be used for the manufacturing of lavatories in Stoke-on-Trent)? What are we to make of the Ranevskys who set such store by the old paternal ways? Their ancient butler Feers looks back nostalgically to the days of serfdom ('when the peasants belonged to the gentry and the gentry belonged to the peasants'). But he is left behind on the estate when its owners all pack up and go away. Chekhov himself felt nothing but contempt for such hypocrisy. He wrote *The Cherry Orchard* while staying on the estate of Maria Yakunchikova near Moscow. 'A more disgracefully idle, absurd and tasteless life would be hard to find', he wrote. 'These people live exclusively for pleasure.'[119] The merchant Lopakhin, on the other hand, was intended by Chekhov as the hero of the play. He is portrayed as an honest businessman, industrious and modest, kind and generous, with a real nobility of spirit underneath his peasant-like exterior. Although he stands to gain from buying the estate (where his father was a serf), Lopakhin does everything he can to persuade the Ranevskys to develop it themselves, offering to lend them money to help them (and no doubt giving money to them all the time). Here was the first merchant hero to be represented on the Russian stage. From the start Chekhov had the part in mind for Stanislavsky himself, who was of course the son of a merchant family from peasant stock. But mindful of this parallel, Stanislavsky took the role of the feckless noble Gaev, leaving Lopakhin to be played by Leonidov as the usual merchant stereotype – fat and badly dressed (in checkered trousers), speaking boorishly in a loud voice and 'flailing with his arms'.[120] As Meyerhold concluded, the effect was to deprive Chekhov's play of its hero: 'when the curtain falls one senses no such presence and one retains only an impression of "types"'.[121]

The Moscow Arts' production of *The Cherry Orchard*, which became the standard view, has taken us away from the real conception of the play – and from the real Chekhov, too. For everything suggests that, by temperament and background, he identified himself with the outsider crashing through the barriers of society. Like Lopakhin,

Chekhov's father was a merchant who had risen from the enserfed peasantry. He taught himself to play the violin, sang in the church choir, and became the choir master in the Taganrog cathedral in 1864. Chekhov shared his father's industry. He understood that common people could be artists, too. Far from lamenting the old gentry world, his last play embraces the cultural forces that emerged in Moscow on the eve of the twentieth century.

9

On a trip to the city in the 1900s Diaghilev remarked that in the visual arts Moscow produced everything worth looking at. Moscow was the centre of the avant-garde; Petersburg was 'a city of artistic gossiping, academic professors and Friday watercolour classes'.[122] Coming as it did from an arch-patriot of Petrine culture, this was a remarkable acknowledgement. But Moscow really was the place to be in 1900, when the Russian avant-garde first burst on to the scene. Along with Paris, Berlin and Milan, it became a major centre in the world of art, and its extraordinary collection of avant-garde artists were as much influenced by trends in Europe as they were by Moscow's heritage. Its progressive politics, its relaxed atmosphere, its noisy modern ways and new technologies – there was so much in Moscow's cultural milieu to inspire artists in experimental forms. The poet Mikhail Kuzmin, another patriot of Petersburg, noted on a trip to Moscow at this time:

. . . the loud Moscow accent, the peculiar words, the way they clicked their heels as they walked along, the Tatar cheekbones and eyes, the moustaches twirled upwards, the shocking neckties, brightly coloured waistcoats and jackets, the sheer bravado and implacability of their ideas and judgements – all this made me think: new people have come forward.[123]

Moscow's younger generation of merchant patrons embraced and collected modern art. They saw it as an ally of their own campaign to transform the old Russia along modern lines. As young playboys and decadents, these rich merchants' sons moved in the same bohemian circles, the cafés, clubs and parties, as the young artists of the Moscow avant-garde. The poet Andrei Bely recalled sardonically that the Society of Free Aesthetics, the most fashionable of the artists' clubs in Moscow, had been forced to close in 1917 because of an 'excess of lady millionaires'. The merchant couples were everywhere, Bely noted.

The husbands would give subsidies to societies that tried to obtain something from us with the persistence of goats. The wives were languorous and, like Venuses, they would appear from a beautiful gossamer of muslin and diamond constellations.[124]

The most colourful of these younger merchant patrons was Nikolai Riabushinsky, who was famous for his decadent lifestyle – 'I love beauty and I love a lot of women' – and for his outrageous parties at his Moscow mansion, the Black Swan. Riabushinsky promoted avant-garde artists in the journal *Golden Fleece* and its exhibitions between 1908 and 1910. From his patronage stemmed the Blue Rose group of Moscow Symbolist painters who, together with their literary confrères and composers like Alexander Scriabin, sought a synthesis of art with poetry, music, religion and philosophy. Riabushinky also funded the famous 'Jack of Diamonds' exhibitions (1910–14), at which more than forty of the city's youngest and most brilliant artists (Kandinsky, Malevich, Goncharova, Larionov, Lentulov, Rodchenko and Tatlin) declared war on the realist tradition and shocked the public with their art. Exhibits were assembled from a broken table leg, a sheet of iron and bits of a glass jug. Painters decorated their own naked bodies and walked as works of art through Moscow's streets.

The critics fumed with rage. Sergei Yablonovsky said that none of it was art – whereupon Lentulov squeezed out some ochre paint on to a piece of cardboard and hung it in the exhibition he had criticized, with the caption 'Sergei Yablonovsky's Brain'.[125] In other art forms, too, Moscow led the way in experimentation. Meyerhold branched out from the naturalism of the Moscow Arts to experiment with Symbolist drama, establishing his Theatre Studio, with its highly stylized acting, in 1905. Scriabin was the first Russian composer to experiment with what was later known as 'serial music' (Schoenberg, Berg and Webern were doing the same thing). Scriabin was an inspiration to the avant-garde. The young Stravinsky was greatly influenced by Scriabin (and mortified to learn that Scriabin did not know his music when he went to visit him in 1913).[126] In 1962, when Stravinsky revisited Russia for the first time after the 1917 Revolution, he made a pilgrimage to the Scriabin Museum in Moscow and learned that it had become a sort of underground meeting place for avant-garde electronic composers. The writer Boris Pasternak, a Scriabin devotee,* blazed the Futurist trail in poetry along with Vladimir Mayakovsky, his close friend and (from 1906) a fellow Muscovite. They were searching for a new poetic language and they heard it in the discord of the Moscow streets:

> . . .
> A juggler
> pulls rails
> from the mouth of a tram,
> hidden by clock-faces of a tower.
> We are conquered!
> Bathtubs.
> Showers.
> An elevator.
>
> The bodice of a soul is unfastened.
> Hands burn the body.
> Scream, or don't scream:
> 'I didn't mean . . .' –
> torments
> burn
> sharp.
> The prickly wind
> tears out
> a shred of smoky wool

---

* The poet's father, Leonid Pasternak, was a fashionable painter in Moscow and his mother, Rozalia Kaufman, a well-known pianist. Scriabin was a close friend of the family. Under his impact the teenage Boris studied music composition for six years. 'I loved music more than anything else, and I loved Scriabin more than anyone else in the world of music. Scriabin was my god and idol' (F. Bowers, *Scriabin*, 2 vols. (London, 1969), vol. 1, p. 321).

from a chimney.
A bald-head streetlamp
seductively
peels off
a black stocking
from the street.[127]

Malevich called Maytovsky's 'From Street into Street' (1913) the finest illustration of 'versified Cubism'.[128]

Marina Tsvetaeva was equally a poet of Moscow. Her father was Ivan Tsvetaev, sometime professor of Art History at Moscow University and the founding director of the Pushkin Gallery, so, like Pasternak, she grew up in the middle of the Moscow intelligentsia. The spirit of the city breathed in every line of her poetry. She herself once wrote that her early verse was meant to 'elevate the name of Moscow to the level of the name of Akhmatova . . . I wanted to present in myself Moscow . . . not with the goal of conquering Petersburg but of giving Moscow to Petersburg':

> Cupolas blaze in my singing city,
> And a wandering blind man praises the Holy Saviour,
> And I present to you my city of church bells
> – Akhmatova! – and also my heart.[129]

Through their friendship in these years, Tsvetaeva gave Moscow to fellow poet Mandelstam as well. 'It was a magic gift', wrote the poet's wife Nadezhda, 'because with only Petersburg, without Moscow, it would have been impossible to breathe freely, to acquire the true feeling for Russia.'[130]

After 1917 Moscow superseded Petersburg. It became the Soviet capital, the cultural centre of the state, a city of modernity and a model of the new industrial society the Bolsheviks wanted to build. Moscow was the workshop of the avant-garde, the left-wing artists of the Proletkult (Proletarian Culture) and Constructivists like Malevich and Tatlin, Rodchenko and Stepanova, who sought to construct the new Soviet man and society through art. It was a city of unprecedented freedom and experimentation in life as in art, and the avant-garde believed, if only for a few years in the 1920s, that they saw their ideal city taking shape in it. Tatlin's 'tower' – his unrealized design for a monument to the Third International on Red Square – expressed these revolutionary hopes. A giant striding figure to be made out of steel and iron girders, tiered and rounded like the churches of medieval Muscovy, his would-be creation symbolized the city's messianic role, in the words of the refrain of the Internationale, to 'make the world anew'. From the old idea of Moscow as the Third Rome to the Soviet one of it as leader of the Third International, it was but a short step in the city's mission to save humanity.

Soviet Moscow was supremely confident, its confidence reflected in the huge building projects of the 1930s, the mass manufacture of motor cars, the first metros, and the forward-upward images of Socialist Realist 'art'. Moscow's old wooden houses were bulldozed. Churches were destroyed. A vast new parade route was constructed through the centre of the city: the old Tver Boulevard was broadened out (and renamed Gorky Street), a Revolution Square was laid out on the site of the old market, and Red Square was cleared of its market stalls. In this way the Lenin Mausoleum, the sacred altar of the Revolution, became the destination of the mass parades on May Day and Revolution Day. With their armed march past the Kremlin, the citadel of Holy Russia, these parades were imitations of the old religious processions they had replaced. There were even plans to blow up St Basil's cathedral so that the marchers could file past the Revolution's leaders, standing in salute on the Mausoleum's roof, and march off in one unbroken line.

Stalin's Moscow was thus recast as an imperial city – a Soviet Petersburg – and, like that unreal city, it became a subject of apocalyptic myths. In Mikhail Bulgakov's novel *The Master and Margarita* (1940), the Devil visits Moscow and brings its cultural temples crashing down; Satan descends on the city in the person of a magician called Woland, with a band of sorcerers and a supernatural cat called Behemoth. They cause havoc in the capital, exposing it as morally corrupt, before flying off from the Sparrow Hills, where Napoleon (that other devil) had first set his sights on the city. Flying off with them was a young Moscow girl called Margarita, who had sacrificed herself to Woland so as to redeem her beloved Master, the author of a suppressed manuscript about Pontius Pilate and the trial of Christ. As their horses leaped into the air and galloped upwards to the sky, Margarita 'turned round in flight and saw that not only the many-coloured towers but the whole city had long vanished from sight, swallowed by the earth, leaving only mist and smoke where it had been'.[131]

And yet throughout the twentieth century Moscow was still 'home'. It was still the mother city it had always been, and, when Hitler attacked it in the autumn of 1941, its people fought to defend it. There was no question of abandoning the city, as Kutuzov had abandoned it to Napoleon in 1812. A quarter of a million Muscovites dug last-ditch defences, carted food to the soldiers at the front and cared for the injured in their homes. With one last desperate effort the Germans were pushed back from the city's gates – a spot still marked today by a giant iron cross on the road from Moscow to the Sheremetevo airport. It was not the Soviet capital but Mother Moscow which was saved. In the words of Pasternak:

> A haze of legend will be cast
> Over all, like scroll and spiral
> Bedecking gilded boyar chambers
> And the Cathedral of St Basil.

> By midnight denizens and dreamers
> Moscow most of all is cherished.
> Here is their home, the fount of all
> With which this century will flourish.[132]

overleaf:
*A typical one-street village
in central Russia, c. 1910*

THE PEASANT
MARRIAGE

1

In the summer of 1874 thousands of students left their lecture halls in Moscow and St Petersburg and travelled incognito to the countryside to start out on a new life with the Russian peasantry. Renouncing their homes and families, they were 'going to the people' in the hopeful expectation of finding a new nation in the brotherhood of man. Few of these young pioneers had ever seen a village, but they all imagined it to be a harmonious community that testified to the natural socialism of the Russian peasantry. They thus convinced themselves that they would find in the peasant a soul mate and an ally of their democratic cause. The students called themselves the Populists (*narodniki*), 'servants of the people' (the *narod*), and they gave themselves entirely to the 'people's cause'. Some of them tried to dress and talk like peasants, so much did they identify themselves with their 'simple way of life'. One of them, a Jew, even wore a cross in the belief that this might bring him closer to the 'peasant soul'.[1] They picked up trades and crafts to make themselves more useful to the peasantry, and they brought books and pamphlets to teach the peasants how to read. By merging with the people and sharing in the burdens of their lives, these young revolutionaries hoped to win their trust and make them understand the full horror of their social condition.

Yet this was no ordinary political movement. The 'going to the people' was a form of pilgrimage, and the type of person who became involved in it was similar to those who went in search of truth to a monastery. These young missionaries were riddled with the guilt of privilege. Many of them felt a personal guilt towards that class of serfs – the nannies and the servants – who had helped to bring them up in their families' aristocratic mansions. They sought to free themselves from their parents' sinful world, whose riches had been purchased by the people's sweat and blood, and set out for the village in a spirit of repentance to establish a 'New Russia' in which the noble and the peasant would be reunited in the nation's spiritual rebirth. By dedicating themselves to the people's cause – to the liberation of the peasantry from poverty and ignorance and from the oppression of the gentry and the state – the students hoped to redeem their own sin: that of being born into privilege. 'We have come to realize', the prominent Populist theoretician Nikolai Mikhailovsky wrote, 'that our awareness of the universal truth could only have been reached at the cost of the age-old suffering of the people. We are the people's debtors and this debt weighs down our conscience.'[2]

What had given rise to these idealistic hopes was the emancipation of the serfs. Writers such as Dostoevsky compared the Decree of 1861 to the conversion of Russia to Christianity in the tenth century. They spoke about the need for the landlord and the peasant to overcome their old divisions and become reconciled by nationality. For, as Dostoevsky wrote in 1861, 'every Russian is a Russian first of all, and only after that does he belong to a class'.[3] The educated classes were called upon to recognize their 'Russianness' and to turn towards the peasants as a cultural mission – educating them as citizens and reuniting Russia on the basis of a national literature and art.

It was such a vision that inspired the students to go to the people. Brought up as they were in the European world of the noble palace and the university, they were on a journey to an unknown land and a new and moral life based on 'Russian principles'. They saw the emancipation as an exorcism of Russia's sinful past – and out of that a new nation would be born. The writer Gleb Uspensky, who joined the Populists in their 'going to the people', vowed to start a new life in 'the year of '61'. 'It was utterly impossible to take any of my personal past forward . . . To live at all I had to forget the past entirely and erase all the traits which it had instilled in my own personality.'[4]

Some of the Populists who left their parents' homes to live in 'labouring communes' where everything was shared (sometimes including lovers) according to the principles set out by the radical critic Nikolai Chernyshevsky in his seminal novel *What Is to Be Done* (1862). Here was a novel that offered its readers a blueprint of the new society. It became a bible for the revolutionaries, including the young Lenin, who said that his whole life had been transformed by it. Most of these communes soon broke down: the students could not bear the strains of agricultural work, let alone the taste of peasant food, and there were endless squabbles over property and love affairs. But the spirit of the commune, the ascetic lifestyle and materialist beliefs which the students had imbibed from Chernyshevsky, continued to inspire their rejection of the old society. This generation gap was the subject of Turgenev's novel *Fathers and Children* (1862) (often mistranslated as *Fathers and Sons*). It was set in the student protest culture of the early 1860s when the call of youth for direct action in the people's name opened up a conflict with the 'men of the forties', liberal men of letters like Turgenev and Herzen, who were content to criticize the existing state of affairs without addressing the future. Nineteenth-century Russia had its 'sixties' movement, too.

'The peasants have completely overwhelmed us in our literature', wrote Turgenev to Pavel Annenkov in 1858. 'Yet I am beginning to suspect that we still don't really understand them or anything about their lives.'[5] Turgenev's doubts were at the heart of his critique of the student 'nihilists' (as they were called). But they applied equally to the intelligentsia's obsession with the 'peasant question', which dominated Russian culture after 1861. With the emancipation of the serfs, the rest of society was forced to recognize the peasant as a fellow citizen. Suddenly the old accursed questions about Russia's destiny became bound up with the peasant's true identity. Was he good or bad? Could he be civilized? What could he do for Russia? And where did he come from? No one knew the answers. For, in the famous lines of the poet Nekrasov:

> Russia is contained in the rural depths
> Where eternal silence reigns.[6]

Armies of folklorists set out to explore these rural depths. 'The study of the people is the science of our times', declared Fedor Buslaev in 1868.[7] Ethnographic museums were set up in Moscow and St Petersburg – their aim being, in the words of one of their founders, Ivan Beliaev, 'to acquaint the Russians with their own nation'.[8] The public was astounded by the peasant costumes and utensils on display, the photographs and mock-ups of their living quarters in the various regions of the countryside. They seemed to have come from some exotic colony. In almost every field of serious enquiry – geography, philosophy, theology, philology, mythology and archaeology – the question of the peasant was the question of the day.

Writers, too, immersed themselves in peasant life. In the words of Saltykov-Shchedrin, the peasant had become 'the hero of our time'.[9] The literary image of the Russian peasant in the early nineteenth century was by and large a sentimental one: he was a stock character with human feelings rather than a thinking individual. Everything changed in 1852, with the publication of Turgenev's masterpiece, *Sketches from a Hunter's Album*. Here, for the first time in Russian literature, readers were confronted with the image of the peasant as a rational human being, as opposed to the sentient victim depicted in previous sentimental literature. Turgenev portrayed the peasant as a person capable of both practical administration and lofty dreams. He felt a profound sympathy for the Russian serf. His mother, who had owned the large estate in Orel province where he grew up, was cruel and ruthless in punishing her serfs. She had them beaten or sent off to a penal colony in Siberia – often for some minor crime. Turgenev describes her regime in his terrifying story 'Punin and Baburin' (1874), and also in the unforgettable 'Mumu' (1852), where the princess orders a serf's dog to be destroyed because it barks. *Sketches from a Hunter's Album* played a crucial role in changing public attitudes towards the serfs and the question of reform. Turgenev later said that the proudest moment in his life came shortly after 1861, when two peasants approached him on a train from Orel to Moscow and bowed down to the ground in the Russian manner to 'thank him in the name of the whole people'.[10]

Of all those writing about peasants, none was more inspiring to the Populists than Nikolai Nekrasov. Nekrasov's poetry gave a new, authentic voice to the 'vengeance and the sorrow' of the peasantry. It was most intensely heard in his epic poem *Who Is Happy in Russia?* (1863–78), which became a holy chant among the Populists. What attracted them to Nekrasov's poetry was not just its commitment to the people's cause, but its angry condemnation of the gentry class, from which Nekrasov himself came. His verse was littered with colloquial expressions that were taken directly from peasant speech. Poems such as *On the Road* (1844) or *The Peddlers* (1861) were practically transcriptions of peasant dialogue. The men of the forties, such as Turgenev, who were brought up to regard the language of the peasants as too coarse to be 'art', accused Nekrasov of launching an 'assault on poetry'.[11] But the students were inspired by his verse.

The question of the peasant may have been the question of the day. But every answer was a myth. As Dostoevsky wrote:

The question of the people and our view of them . . . is our most important question, a question on which our whole future rests . . . But the people are still a theory for us and they still stand before us as a riddle. We, the lovers of the people, regard them as part of a theory, and it seems not one of us loves them as they really are but only as each of us imagines them to be. And should the Russian people turn out not as we imagined them, then we, despite our love of them, would at once renounce them without regret.[12]

Each theory ascribed certain virtues to the peasant which it then took as the essence of the national character. For the Populists, the peasant was a natural socialist, the embodiment of the collective spirit that distinguished Russia from the bourgeois West. Democrats like Herzen saw the peasant as a champion of liberty – his wildness embodying the spirit of the Russia that was free. The Slavophiles regarded him as a Russian patriot, suffering and patient, a humble follower of truth and justice, like the folk hero Ilia Muromets. They argued that the peasant commune was a living proof that Russia need not look beyond its national borders for guiding moral principles. 'A commune,' declared one of the movement's founding members, Konstantin Aksakov, 'is a union of the people who have renounced their egoism, their individuality, and who express their common accord; this is an act of love, a noble Christian act.'[13] Dostoevsky, too, saw the peasant as a moral animal, the embodiment of the 'Russian soul'; once he even claimed, in a famous argument, that the simple 'kitchen *muzhik*' was morally superior to any bourgeois European gentleman. The peasants, he maintained, 'will show us a new path', and, far from having something to teach them, 'it is *we* who must bow down before the people's truth'.[14]

This convergence on the peasant issue was indicative of a broader national consensus or ideology which emerged in Russia at this time. The old arguments between the Westernizers and the Slavophiles gradually died down as each side came to recognize the need for Russia to find a proper balance between Western learning and native principles. There were hints of such a synthesis as early as 1847, when the doyen of the Westernizers, the radical critic Belinsky, said that, as far as art was concerned, he was 'inclined to side with the Slavophiles' against the cosmopolitans.[15] For their part, the younger Slavophiles were moving to the view in the 1850s that 'the nation' was contained in all classes of society, not just the peasants, as the older ones maintained. Some even argued, in a way that made them virtually indistinguishable from the Westernizers, that the nation's true arena was the civic sphere and that Russia's progress in the world was dependent on the raising of the peasants to that sphere.[16] In short, by the 1860s there was a common view that Russia should evolve along a European path of liberal reform, yet not break too sharply from its unique historical traditions. It was a case of keeping Peter *and* the peasant, too. This was the position of the 'native soil' movement to which Dostoevsky and his brother Mikhail belonged in the 1860s.

Populism was the cultural product of this synthesis and, as such, it became something of a national creed. The romantic interest in folk culture which swept through Europe in the nineteenth century was nowhere felt more keenly than among the Russian intelligentsia. As the poet Alexander Blok wrote (with just a touch of irony) in 1908:

... the intelligentsia cram their bookcases with anthologies of folk-songs, epics, legends, incantations, dirges; they investigate Russian mythology, wedding and funeral rites; they grieve for the people; go to the people; are filled with high hopes; fall into despair; they even give up their lives, face execution or starve to death for the people's cause.[17]

The intelligentsia was defined by its mission of service to the people, just as the noble class was defined by its service to the state; and the intelligentsia lived by the view, which many of its members came to regret, that 'the good of the people' was the highest interest, to which all other principles, such as law or Christian precepts, were subordinate. Such attitudes were so endemic that they were even shared by members of the court, the state administration and the aristocracy. The liberal spirit of reform which had brought about the emancipation continued to inform the government's approach towards the peasantry in the 1860s and 1870s. With the peasant's liberation from the gentry's jurisdiction there was a recognition that he had become the state's responsibility: he had become a citizen.

After 1861 the government set up a whole range of institutions to improve the welfare of its peasant citizens and integrate them into national life. Most of these initiatives were carried out by the new assemblies of local government, the *zemstvos*, established at the district and provincial level in 1864. The *zemstvos* were run by paternal squires of the sort who fill the pages of Tolstoy and Chekhov – liberal, well-meaning men who dreamed of bringing civilization to the backward countryside. With limited resources, they founded schools and hospitals; provided veterinary and agronomic services for the peasantry; built new roads and bridges; invested in local trades and industries; financed insurance schemes and rural credit; and carried out ambitious statistical surveys to prepare for more reforms at a future date.* The optimistic expectations of the *zemstvo* liberals were widely shared by the upper classes of society. There was a general attitude of paternal populism – a sympathy for the people and their cause which induced the high-born from all walks of life to support the students radicals.

The Minister of Justice, in a report to the Tsar, listed a whole catalogue of foolish acts in the 'mad summer' of 1874: the wife of a colonel in the Gendarmes had passed on secret information to her son; a rich landowner and magistrate had hidden one of the leading revolutionaries; a professor had introduced a propagandist to his students; and the families of several state councillors had given warm approval to their children's revolutionary activities.[18] Even Turgenev, who saw the solution to the peasant problem in liberal reform, could not help admiring (and perhaps envying) the idealistic passion of these revolutionaries.[19] He mixed in their circles in France and Switzerland, and he even gave some money to the Populist theorist Pyotr Lavrov

---

* The hopes of the *zemstvo* liberals were never realized. After the assassination of Alexander II in 1881, the powers of the *zemstvos* were severely curtailed by the government of the new Tsar, Alexander III, who looked upon the *zemstvos* as dangerous breeding grounds for radicals. Many of the students who had taken part in the 'going to the people' ended up as *zemstvo* employees – teachers, doctors, statisticians and agronomists whose democratic politics attracted the police. Police raids were carried out on *zemstvo* offices – including even hospitals and lunatic asylums – in the search for such 'revolutionaries'. They even arrested noblewomen for teaching peasant children how to read. (A. Tyrkogo-Williams, *To, chego bol'she ne budet* (Paris, n.d.), p. 253).

(whose writings had inspired the student radicals) so that he could publish his journal *Forwards!* in Europe.[20] In his novel *Virgin Soil* (1877), Turgenev gave a portrait of the types who answered Lavrov's call. Though he saw through the illusions of the Populists, he managed to convey his admiration, too. These 'young people are mostly good and honest', he wrote to a friend on finishing the novel in 1876, 'but their course is so false and impractical that it cannot fail to lead them to complete fiasco'.[21]

Which is just how it turned out. Most of the students were met by a cautious suspicion or hostility on the part of the peasants, who listened humbly to their revolutionary sermons without really understanding anything they said. The peasants were wary of the students' learning and their urban ways, and in many places they reported them to the authorities. Ekaterina Breshkovskaya, later one of Russia's leading socialists, found herself in jail after the peasant woman with whom she was staying in the Kiev region 'took fright at the sight of all my books and denounced me to the constable'.[22] The socialist ideas of the Populists were strange and foreign to the peasantry, or at least they could not understand them in the terms in which they were explained to them. One propagandist gave the peasants a beautiful account of the future socialist society in which all the land would belong to the toilers and nobody would exploit anybody else. Suddenly a peasant triumphantly exclaimed: 'Won't it be just lovely when we divide up the land? I'll hire two labourers and what a life I'll have!'[23] As for the idea of turning out the Tsar, this met with complete incomprehension and even angry cries from the villagers, who looked upon the Tsar as a human god. 'How can we live without a Tsar?' they said.[24]

Rounded up by the police, forced into exile or underground, the Populists returned from their defeat in deep despair. They had invested so much of their own personalities in their idealized conception of the peasantry, they had hung so much of their personal salvation on the 'people's cause', that to see them both collapse was a catastrophic blow to their identity. The writer Gleb Uspensky, to cite an extreme and tragic example, eventually became insane after many years of trying to reconcile himself to the stark reality of peasant life; and many of the Populists were driven to the bottle by this rude awakening. It was suddenly made clear that the idea of the peasantry they had in their minds did not in fact exist – it was no more than a theory and a myth – and that they were cut off from the actual peasants by a cultural, social and intellectual abyss that they could not hope to bridge. Like an unsolved riddle, the peasant remained unknown and perhaps unknowable.

2

In the summer of 1870 Ilia Repin left St Petersburg for 'an undiscovered land'.[25] Together with his brother and a fellow student painter called Fedor Vasilev, he travelled by steamer down the Volga river as far as the town of Stavropol, about 700 kilometres east of Moscow. The young artist's aim was to make a study of the peasants for a painting he had planned of the Volga barge haulers. The idea of the picture had first come to him in the summer of 1868, when he had observed a team of haulers trudging wearily along a river bank near St Petersburg. Repin had originally thought to contrast these sad figures with a well-groomed group of happy picnickers. It would have been a typical example of the sort of expository genre painting favoured by most Russian realists at the time. But he was dissuaded from this propagandist picture by his friend Vasilev, a gifted landscape painter from the Wanderers' school, who persuaded him to depict the haulers on their own.

It took two years to obtain the finance and the permits for their trip – the Tsarist authorities being naturally suspicious of the art students and fearing that they might have revolutionary aims. For three months Repin lived among the former serfs of Shiriayevo, a village overlooking the Volga near Samara. He filled his sketchbooks with ethnographic details of their fishing boats and nets, their household utensils and rag-made shoes and clothes. The villagers did not want to be drawn. They believed that the Devil stole a person's soul when his image was depicted on the page. One day they discovered Repin trying to persuade a group of village girls to pose for him. They accused the painter of the Devil's work and demanded his 'passport', threatening to hand him over to the local constable. The only document which Repin had on him was a letter from the Academy of Arts. The impressive Imperial insignia on the letterhead was enough to restore calm. 'See,' said the village scribe who scrutinized the 'passport', 'he comes to us from the Tsar.'[26]

Eventually the painter found a team of haulers who, for a fee, allowed him to sketch them. For several weeks he lived with these human beasts of burden. As he got to know them, he came to see their individual personalities. One had been an icon painter; another a soldier; and a third, named Kanin, was formerly a priest. Repin was struck by the sheer waste of talent in their bestial servitude. Strapped into their riggings, their noble faces weathered, the haulers were for him 'like Greek philosophers, sold as slaves to the barbarians'.[27] Their bondage was a symbol of the Russian people's oppressed creativity. Kanin, Repin thought, had 'the character of Russia on his face':

There was something eastern and ancient about it . . . the face of a Scyth . . . And what eyes! What depth of vision! . . . And his brow, so large and wise . . . He seemed to me a colossal mystery, and for that reason I loved him. Kanin, with a rag around his head, his clothes in patches made by himself and then worn out, appeared none the less as a man of dignity: he was like a saint.[28]

In the final painting of *The Volga Barge Haulers* (1873) (plate 11) it is this human dignity that stands out above all. The image at the time was extraordinary and revolutionary. Hitherto, even in the paintings of a democratic artist such as Alexei Venetsianov, the image of the peasant had been idealized or sentimentalized. But each of Repin's boatmen had been drawn from life and each face told its own story of private suffering. Stasov saw the painting as a comment on the latent force of social protest in the Russian people, a spirit symbolized in the gesture of one young man readjusting his shoulder strap. But Dostoevsky praised the painting for its lack of crude tendentiousness, seeing it instead as an epic portrait of the Russian character. What Repin meant, however, is more difficult to judge. For his whole life was a struggle between politics and art.

Repin was a 'man of the sixties' – a decade of rebellious questioning in the arts as well as in society. In the democratic circles in which he moved it was generally agreed that the duty of the artist was to focus

13. *Ilia Repin: sketches for* The Volga Barge Haulers, *1870*

the attention of society on the need for social justice by showing how the common people really lived. There was a national purpose in this, too: for, if art was to be true and meaningful, if it was to teach the people how to feel and live, it needed to be national in the sense that it had its roots in the people's daily lives. This was the argument of Stasov, the domineering mentor of the national school in all the arts.

Russian painters, he maintained, should give up imitating European art and look to their own people for artistic styles and themes. Instead of classical or biblical subjects they should depict 'scenes from the village and the city, remote corners of the provinces, the god-forsaken life of the lonely clerk, the corner of a lonely cemetery, the confusion of a market place, every joy and sorrow which grows and lives in peasant huts and opulent mansions'.[29] Vladimir Stasov was the self-appointed champion of civic realist art. He took up the cause of the Wanderers in art, and the *kuchkists* in music, praising each in turn for their break from the European style of the Academy, and pushing each in their own way to become more 'Russian'. Virtually every artist and composer of the 1860s and 1870s found himself at some point in Stasov's tight embrace. The critic saw himself as the driver of a *troika* that would soon bring Russian culture on to the world stage. Repin, Musorgsky and the sculptor Antokolsky were its three horses.[30]

Mark Antokolsky was a poor Jewish boy from Vilna who had entered the Academy at the same time as Repin and had been among fourteen students who left it in protest against its formal rules of classicism, to set up an *artel*, or commune of free artists, in 1863. Antokolsky quickly rose to fame for a series of sculptures of daily life in the Jewish ghetto which were hailed as the first real triumph of democratic art by all the enemies of the Academy. Stasov placed himself as Antokolsky's mentor, publicized his work and badgered him, as only Stasov could, to produce more sculptures on national themes. The critic was particularly enthusiastic about *The Persecution of the Jews in the Spanish Inquisition* (first exhibited in 1867), a work which Antokolsky never really finished but for which he did a series of studies. Stasov saw it as an allegory of political and national oppression – a subject as important to the Russians as to the Jews.[31]

Repin identified with Antokolsky. He, too, had come from a poor provincial family – the son of a military settler (a type of state-owned peasant) from a small town called Chuguev in the Ukraine. He had learned his trade as an icon painter before entering the Academy and, like the sculptor, he felt out of place in the élite social milieu of Petersburg. Both men were inspired by an older student, Ivan Kramskoi, who led the protest in 1863. Kramskoi was important as a portraitist. He painted leading figures such as Tolstoy and Nekrasov, but he also painted unknown peasants. Earlier painters such as Venetsianov had portrayed the peasant as an agriculturalist. But Kramskoi painted him against a plain background, and he focused on the face, drawing viewers in towards the eyes and forcing them to enter the inner world of people they had only yesterday treated as slaves. There were no implements or scenic landscapes, no thatched huts or ethnographic details to distract the viewer from the peasant's gaze or reduce the tension of this encounter. This psychological concentration was without precedent in the history of art, not just in Russia but in Europe, too, where even artists such as Courbet and Millet were still depicting peasants in the fields.

It was through Kramskoi and Antokolsky that Repin came into the circle of Stasov in 1869, at the very moment the painter was preparing his own portrait of the peasantry in *The Volga Barge Haulers*. Stasov encouraged him to paint provincial themes, which were favoured at that time by patrons such as Tretiakov and the Grand Duke Vladimir Alexandrovich, the Tsar's younger son, who, of all people, had commissioned the *Barge Haulers* and eventually put these starving peasants in his sumptuous dining room. Under Stasov's domineering influence, Repin produced a series of provincial scenes following the success of the *Barge Haulers* in 1873. They were all essentially populist – not so much politically but in the general sense of the 1870s, when everybody thought the way ahead for Russia was to get a better knowledge of the people and their lives. For Repin, having just returned from his first trip to Europe in 1873–6, this goal was connected to his cultural rediscovery of the Russian provinces – 'that huge forsaken territory that interests nobody', as he wrote to Stasov in 1876, 'and about which people speak with derision or contempt; and yet it is here that the simple people live, and do so more authentically than we'.[32]

Musorgsky was roughly the same age as Repin and Antokolsky but he had joined Stasov's stable a decade earlier, in 1858, when he was aged just nineteen. As the most historically minded and musically original of Balakirev's students, the young composer was patronized by Stasov and pushed in the direction of national themes. Stasov never let up in his efforts to direct his protégé's interests and musical approach. He cast himself *in loco parentis*, visiting the 'youngster' Musorgsky (then thirty-two) when he shared a room with Rimsky-

Korsakov (then twenty-seven) in St Petersburg. Stasov would arrive early in the morning, help the men get out of bed and wash, fetch their clothes, prepare tea and sandwiches for them, and then, as he put it, when '*we* [got] down to *our* business [my emphasis – O. F.]', he would listen to the music they had just composed or give them new historical materials and ideas for their works.[33] The Populist conception of *Boris Godunov* (in its revised version with the Kromy scene) is certainly in line with Stasov's influence. In a general sense all Musorgsky's operas are 'about the people' – if one understands that as the nation as a whole. Even *Khovanshchina* – which drove Stasov mad with all its 'princely spawn'[34] – carried the subtitle 'A national [people's] music history' ('*narodnaya muzikal'naya drama*'). Musorgsky explained his Populist approach in a letter to Repin, written in August 1873, congratulating him on his *Barge Haulers*:

It is *the people* I want to depict: when I sleep I see them, when I eat I think of them, when I drink I can see them rise before me in all their reality, huge, unvarnished, and without tinsel trappings! And what an awful (in the true sense of that word) richness there is for the composer in the people's speech – as long as there's a corner of our land that hasn't been ripped open by the railway.[35]

And yet there were tensions between Musorgsky and the Populist agenda set out for him by Stasov – tensions which have been lost in the cultural politics that have always been attached to the composer's name.[36] Stasov was crucially important in Musorgsky's life: he discovered him; he gave him the material for much of his greatest work; and he championed his music, which had been unknown in Europe in his lifetime and would surely have been forgotten after his death, had it not been for Stasov. But the critic's politics were not entirely shared by the composer, whose feeling for 'the people', as he had explained to Repin, was primarily a musical response. Musorgsky's populism was not political or philosophical – it was artistic. He loved folk songs and incorporated many of them in his works. The distinctive aspects of the Russian peasant song – its choral heterophony, its tonal shifts, its drawn-out melismatic passages which make it sound like a chant or a lament – became part of his own musical language. Above all, the folk song was the model for a new technique of choral writing which Musorgsky first developed in *Boris Godunov*: building up the different voices one by one, or in discordant groups, to create the sort of choral heterophony which he achieved, with such brilliant success, in the Kromy scene.

Musorgsky was obsessed with the craft of rendering human speech in musical sound. That is what he meant when he said that music should be a way of 'talking with the people' – it was not a declaration of political intent.* Following the mimetic theories of the German literary historian Georg Gervinus, Musorgsky believed that human speech was governed by musical laws – that a speaker conveys emotions and meaning by musical components such as rhythm, cadence, intonation, timbre, volume, tone, etc. 'The aim of musical art', he wrote in 1880, 'is the reproduction in social sounds not only of modes of feeling but of modes of human speech.'[37] Many of his most important compositions, such as the song cycle *Savishna* or the unfinished opera based on Gogol's 'Sorochintsy Fair', represent an attempt to transpose into sound the distinctive qualities of Russian peasant speech. Listen to the music in Gogol's tale:

I expect you will have heard at some time the noise of a distant waterfall, when the agitated environs are filled with tumult and a chaotic whirl of weird, indistinct sounds swirls before you. Do you not agree that the very same effect is produced the instant you enter the whirlpool of a village fair? All the assembled populace merges into a single monstrous creature, whose massive body stirs about the market-place and snakes down the narrow side-streets, shrieking, bellowing, blaring. The clamour, the cursing, mooing, bleating, roaring – all this blends into a single cacophonous din. Oxen, sacks, hay, gypsies, pots, wives, gingerbread, caps – everything is ablaze with clashing colours, and dances before your eyes. The voices drown one another and it is impossible to distinguish one word, to rescue any meaning from this babble; not a single exclamation can be understood with any clarity. The ears are

---

* It is telling, in this context, that the word he used for 'people' was '*liudi*' – a word which has the meaning of individuals – although it has usually been translated to mean a collective mass (the sense of the other word for people – the '*narod*'). J. Leyda and S. Bertensson (eds.), *The Musorgsky Reader: A Life of Modeste Petrovich Musorgsky in Letters and Documents* (New York, 1947), pp. 84–5.

assailed on every side by the loud hand-clapping of traders all over the market-place. A cart collapses, the clang of metal rings in the air, wooden planks come crashing to the ground and the observer grows dizzy, as he turns his head this way and that.[38]

In Musorgsky's final years tensions with his mentor became more acute. He withdrew from Stasov's circle, pouring scorn on civic artists such as Nekrasov, and spending all his time in the alcoholic company of fellow aristocrats such as the salon poet Count Golenishchev-Kutuzov and the arch-reactionary T. I. Filipov. It was not that he became politically right-wing – now, as before, Musorgsky paid little attention to politics. Rather, he saw in their 'art for art's sake' views a creative liberation from Stasov's rigid dogma of politically engaged and idea-driven art. There was something in Musorgsky – his lack of formal schooling or his wayward, almost childlike character – that made him both depend on yet strive to break away from mentors like Stasov. We can feel this tension in the letter to Repin:

So, that's it, glorious lead horse! The *troika*, if in disarray, bears what it has to bear. It doesn't stop pulling . . . What a picture of the Master [Stasov] you have made! He seems to crawl out of the canvas and into the room. What will happen when it has been varnished? Life, power – pull, lead horse! Don't get tired! I am just the side horse and I pull only now and then to escape disgrace. I am afraid of the whip![39]

Antokolsky felt the same artistic impulse pulling him away from Stasov's direction. He gave up working on the *Inquisition*, saying he was tired of civic art, and travelled throughout Europe in the 1870s, when he turned increasingly to pure artistic themes in sculptures like *The Death of Socrates* (1875–7) and *Jesus Christ* (1878). Stasov was irate. 'You have ceased to be an artist of the dark masses, the unknown figure in the crowd', he wrote to Antokolsky in 1883. 'Your subjects have become the "aristocracy of man" – Moses, Christ, Spinoza, Socrates.'[40]

Even Repin, the 'lead horse', began to pull away from Stasov's harnesses: he would no longer haul his Volga barge. He travelled to the West, fell in love with the Impressionists, and turned out French-styled portraits and pretty café scenes which could not have been farther from the Russian national school of utilitarian and thought-provoking art. 'I have forgotten how to reflect and pass judgement on a work of art', Repin wrote to Kramskoi from Paris, 'and I don't regret the loss of this faculty which used to eat me up; on the contrary, I would rather it never return, though I feel that back in my native land it will reclaim its right over me – that is the way things are there.'[41] Stasov condemned Repin for his defection, charging him with the neglect of his artistic duty to the Russian people and his native land. Relations became strained to breaking point in the early 1890s, when Repin rejoined the Academy and reassessed his views of the classical tradition – effectively denying the whole national school. 'Stasov loved his barbarian art, his small, fat, ugly, half-baked artists who screamed their profound human truths', Repin wrote in 1892.[42] For a while the artist even flirted with the World of Art – Benois and Diaghilev, or the 'decadents' as Stasov liked to call them – and their ideal of pure art. But the pull of 'Russia' was too strong – and in the end he patched up his relations with Stasov. However much he loved the light of France, Repin knew that he could not be an artist who was disengaged from the old accursed questions of his native land.

3

In 1855 Tolstoy lost his favourite house in a game of cards. For two days and nights he played *shtoss* with his fellow officers in the Crimea, losing all the time, until at last he confessed to his diary 'the loss of everything – the Yasnaya Polyana house. I think there's no point writing – I'm so disgusted with myself that I'd like to forget about my existence.'[43] Much of Tolstoy's life can be explained by that game of cards. This, after all, was no ordinary house, but the place where he was born, the home where he had spent his first nine years, and the sacred legacy of his beloved mother which had been passed down to him. Not that the old Volkonsky house was particularly impressive when Tolstoy, aged just nineteen, inherited the estate, with its 2,000 acres and 200 serfs, on his father's death in 1847. The paint on the house had begun to flake, there was a leaky roof and a rotten verandah, the paths were full of weeds and the English garden had long gone to seed. But all the same it was precious to Tolstoy. 'I wouldn't sell the house for anything', he had written to his brother in 1852. 'It's the last thing I'd be prepared to part with.'[44] And yet now, to pay his gambling debts, Tolstoy was obliged to sell the house he was born in. He had tried to avoid the inevitable by selling all eleven of his other villages, together with their serfs, their timber stocks and horses, but the sum these had raised was still not quite enough to get him into the black. The house was purchased by a local merchant and dismantled, to be sold in lots.

Tolstoy moved into a smaller house, an annexe of the old Volkonsky manor, and, as if to atone for his sordid game of cards, he set about the task of restoring the estate to a model farm. There had been earlier projects of this kind. In 1847, when he had first arrived as the young landlord, he had set out to become a model farmer, a painter, a musician, a scholar and a writer, with the interests of his peasants close to heart. This was the subject of *A Landowner's Morning* (1852) – the unfinished draft of what was intended to become a grand novel about a landowner (for which read: Tolstoy) who seeks a life of happiness and justice in the country and learns that it cannot be found in an ideal but in constant labour for the good of others less happy than himself. In that first period Tolstoy had proposed to reduce the dues of the serfs on his estate – but the serfs mistrusted his intentions and had turned his offer down. Tolstoy was annoyed – he had under-estimated the gap between nobleman and serf – and he left the country-side for the high life of Moscow, then joined the army in the Caucasus. But by the time of his return in 1856, there was a new spirit of reform in the air. The Tsar had told the gentry to prepare for the liberation of their serfs. With new determination Tolstoy threw himself into the task of living with the peasants in a 'life of truth'. He was disgusted with his former life – the gambling, the whoring, the excessive feasting and drinking, the embarrassment of riches, and the lack of any real work or purpose in his life. Like the Populists with their 'going to the people', he vowed to live a new life, a life of moral truth that was based on peasant labour and the brotherhood of man.

In 1859 Tolstoy set up his first school for the village children in Yasnaya Polyana; by 1862 there were thirteen schools in the locality,

14. *Tolstoy's estate at Yasnaya Polyana, late nineteenth century. The huts and fields in the foreground belong to the villagers*

the teachers being drawn in the main from those students who had been expelled from their universities for their revolutionary views.[45] Tolstoy became a magistrate, appointed by the Tsar to implement the emancipation manifesto, and angered all his colleagues, the leading squires of the Tula area, by siding with the peasants in their claims for land. On his own estate Tolstoy gave the peasants a sizeable proportion of his land – nowhere else in Russia was the manifesto fulfilled in a spirit of such generosity. Tolstoy almost yearned, it seemed, to give away his wealth. He dreamed of abandoning his privileged existence and living like a peasant on the land. For a while he even tried. In 1862 he settled down for good with his new wife, Sonya, at Yasnaya Polyana, dismissed all the stewards, and took charge of the farming by himself. The experiment was a complete failure. Tolstoy did not care for looking after pigs – and ended up deliberately starving them to death. He did not know how to cure hams, how to make butter, when to plough or hoe the fields, and he soon became fed up and ran away to Moscow, or locked himself away in his study, leaving everything to the hired labourers.[46]

The fantasy, however, would not go away. 'Now let me tell you

what I've just decided,' he would tell the village children at his school.
'I am going to give up my land and my aristocratic way of life and
become a peasant. I shall build myself a hut at the edge of the village,
marry a country woman, and work the land as you do: mowing,
ploughing, and all the rest.' When the children asked what he would
do with the estate, Tolstoy said he would divide it up. 'We shall own
it all in common, as equals, you and me.' And what, the children asked,
if people laughed at him and said he had lost everything: 'Won't you
feel ashamed?' 'What do you mean "ashamed"?' the count answered
gravely. 'Is it anything to be ashamed of to work for oneself? Have your
fathers ever told you they were ashamed to work? They have not. What
is there to be ashamed of in a man feeding himself and his family by the
sweat of his brow? If anybody laughs at me, here's what I would say:
there's nothing to laugh at in a man's working, but there is a great deal
of shame and disgrace in his not working, and yet living better than
others. That is what I am ashamed of. I eat, drink, ride horseback, play
the piano, and still I feel bored. I say to myself: "You're a do-nothing." '[47]

Did he really mean it? Was he saying this to give the children pride
in the life of peasant toil that awaited them or was he really planning
to join them? Tolstoy's life was full of contradictions and he never
could decide if he should become a peasant or remain a nobleman. On
the one hand he embraced the élite culture of the aristocracy. *War and
Peace* is a novel that rejoices in that world. There were times while
working on that epic novel – like the day one of the village schools
shut down in 1863 – when he gave up on the peasants as a hopeless
cause. They were capable neither of being educated nor of being
understood. *War and Peace* would depict only 'princes, counts, ministers, senators and their children', he had promised in an early draft,
because, as a nobleman himself, he could no more understand what a
peasant might be thinking than he 'could understand what a cow is
thinking as it is being milked or what a horse is thinking as it is pulling
a barrel'.[48] On the other hand, his whole life was a struggle to renounce
that élite world of shameful privilege and live 'by the sweat of his
own brow'. The quest for a simple life of toil was a constant theme
in Tolstoy's works. Take Levin, for example, the peasant-loving
squire in *Anna Karenina* – a character so closely based on Tolstoy's
life and dreams that he was virtually autobiographical. Who can forget

that blissful moment when Levin joins the peasant mowers in the field and loses himself in the labour and the team?

After breakfast Levin was not in the same place in the string of mowers as before, but found himself between the old man who had accosted him quizzically, and now invited him to be his neighbour, and a young peasant who had only been married in the autumn and who was mowing this summer for the first time.

The old man, holding himself erect, went in front, moving with long, regular strides, his feet turned out and swinging his scythe as precisely and evenly, and apparently as effortlessly, as a man swings his arms in walking. As if it were child's play, he laid the grass in a high, level ridge. It seemed as if the sharp blade swished of its own accord through the juicy grass.

Behind Levin came the lad Mishka. His pleasant boyish face, with a twist of fresh grass bound round his hair, worked all the time with effort; but whenever anyone looked at him he smiled. He would clearly sooner die than own it was hard work for him.

Levin kept between them. In the very heat of the day the mowing did not seem such hard work. The perspiration with which he was drenched cooled him, while the sun, that burned his back, his head, and his arms, bare to the elbow, gave a vigour and dogged energy to his labour; and more and more often now came those moments of oblivion, when it was possible not to think of what one was doing. The scythe cut of itself. Those were happy moments.[49]

Tolstoy loved to be among the peasants. He derived intense pleasure – emotional, erotic – from their physical presence. The 'spring-like' smell of their beards would send him into raptures of delight. He loved to kiss the peasant men. The peasant women he found irresistible – sexually attractive and available to him by his 'squire's rights'. Tolstoy's diaries are filled with details of his conquests of the female serfs on his estate – a diary he presented, according to the custom, to his bride Sonya (as Levin does to Kitty) on the eve of their wedding:*
'21 April 1858. A wonderful day. Peasant women in the garden and by the well. I'm like a man possessed.'[50] Tolstoy was not handsome,

---

* Similar diaries were presented to their future wives by Tsar Nicholas II, the novelist Vladimir Nabokov and the poet Vladimir Khodasevich.

but he had a huge sex drive and, in addition to the thirteen children Sonya bore, there were at least a dozen other children fathered by him in the villages of his estate.

But there was one peasant woman who represented more than a sexual conquest. Aksinia Bazykina was twenty-two – and married to a serf on his estate – when Tolstoy first saw her in 1858. 'I'm in love as never before in my life', he confessed to his diary. 'Today in the wood. I am a fool. A beast. Her bronze flush and her eyes . . . Have no other thought.'[51] This was more than lust. 'It's no longer the feelings of a stag', he wrote in 1860, 'but of a husband for a wife.'[52] Tolstoy, it appears, was seriously considering a new life with Aksinia in some 'hut at the edge of the village'. Turgenev, who saw him often at this time, wrote that Tolstoy was 'in love with a peasant woman and did not want to discuss literature'.[53] Turgenev himself had several love affairs with his own serfs (one even bore him two children), so he must have understood what Tolstoy felt.[54] In 1862, when Tolstoy married Sonya, he tried to break relations with Aksinia; and in the first years of their marriage, when he was working without rest on *War and Peace*, it is hard to imagine his wandering off to find Aksinia in the woods. But in the 1870s he began to see her once again. She bore him a son by the name of Timofei, who became a coachman at Yasnaya Polyana. Long after that, Tolstoy continued to have dreams about Aksinia. Even in the final year of his long life, half a century after their first encounter, he recorded his joy, on seeing the 'bare legs' of a peasant girl, 'to think that Aksinia is still alive'.[55] This was more than the usual attraction of a squire to a serf. Aksinia was Tolstoy's unofficial 'wife', and he continued to love her well into her old age. Aksinia was not beautiful in any conventional sense, but she had a certain quality, a spiritual strength and liveliness, that made her loved by all the villagers. 'Without her', Tolstoy wrote, 'the *khorovod* was not a *khorovod*, the women did not sing, the children did not play'.[56] Tolstoy saw her as the personification of everything that was good and beautiful in the Russian peasant woman – she was proud and strong and suffering – and that is how he drew her in a number of his works. She appears, for example, in 'The Devil', which tells the story of his love affair with her both before and after his marriage. It may be significant that Tolstoy did not know how to end the tale. Two different conclusions were published: one in which the hero kills the peasant woman, the other where he commits suicide.

Tolstoy's own life story was unresolved as well. In the middle of the 1870s, when the 'going to the people' reached its apogee, Tolstoy experienced a moral crisis that led him, like the students, to seek his salvation in the peasantry. As he recounts in *A Confession* (1879–80), he had suddenly come to realize that everything which had provided meaning in his life – family happiness and artistic creation – was in fact meaningless. None of the great philosophers brought him any comfort. The Orthodox religion, with its oppressive Church, was unacceptable. He thought of suicide. But suddenly he saw that there was a true religion in which to place his faith – in the suffering, labouring and communal life of the Russian peasantry. 'It has been my whole life', he wrote to his cousin. 'It has been my monastery, the church where I escaped and found refuge from all the anxieties, the doubts and temptations of my life.'[57]

Yet even after his spiritual crisis Tolstoy was ambivalent: he idealized the peasants and loved to be with them, but for many years he could not bring himself to break from the conventions of society and become one himself. In many ways he only played at being a 'peasant'. When he went out for a walk or rode his horse he put on peasant garb – he was known throughout the world for his peasant shirt and belt, his trousers and bast shoes – but when he went to Moscow, or dined with friends, he dressed in tailored clothes. During the day he would labour in the fields at Yasnaya Polyana – then return to his manor house for a dinner served by waiters in white gloves. The painter Repin visited the writer in 1887 to paint the first in a series of portraits of Tolstoy. A man of genuinely humble origins, Repin was disgusted by the count's behaviour. 'To descend for a day into this darkness of the peasantry's existence and proclaim: "I am with you" – that is just hypocrisy.'[58] Nor, it seems, were the peasants taken in. Four years later, at the height of the famine in 1891, Repin visited the count again. Tolstoy insisted on showing him the 'peasant way' to plough a field. 'Several times', Repin recalled, 'some Yasnaya Polyana peasants walked by, doffed their caps, bowed, and then walked on as if taking no notice of the count's exploit. But then another peasant group appears, evidently from the next village. They stop and stare for a long while. And then a strange thing happens. Never in my life have I seen a clearer expression of irony on a simple peasant's face.'[59]

Tolstoy was aware of the ambiguity, and for years he agonized. As a writer, and a Russian one at that, he felt the artist's responsibility to provide leadership and enlightenment for the people. This was why he had set up the peasant schools, expended his energy on writing country tales, and started a publishing venture ('The Intermediary') to print the classics (Pushkin, Gogol, Leskov and Chekhov) for the growing mass of readers in the countryside. Yet at the same time he was moving to the view that the peasants were the teachers of society and that neither he nor any other scion of the world's immoral civilizations had anything to give. From his teaching at the village schools, he came to the conclusion that the peasant had a higher moral wisdom than the nobleman – an idea he explained by the peasant's natural and communal way of life. This is what the peasant Karataev teaches Pierre in *War and Peace*:

Karataev had no attachments, friendships, or love, as Pierre understood them, but he loved and lived affectionately with everything that life brought him in contact with, particularly with man – not any particular man, but those with whom he happened to be ... To Pierre he always remained ... an unfathomable, rounded, eternal personification of the spirit of simplicity and truth.[60]

With every passing year, Tolstoy strived to live more and more like a peasant. He learned how to make his own shoes and furniture. He gave up writing and spent his time working in the fields. In a turn from his previous life, he even advocated chastity, and became a vegetarian. Sometimes in the evening he would join the pilgrims walking on the road from Moscow to Kiev, which passed by the estate. He would walk with them for miles, returning barefoot in the early morning hours with a new confirmation of his faith. 'Yes, these people know God,' he would say. 'Despite all their superstitions, their belief in St Nicholas-of-the-spring and St Nicholas-of-the-winter, or the Icon of Three Hands, they are closer to God than we are. They lead moral, working lives, and their simple wisdom is in many ways superior to all the artifices of our culture and philosophy.'[61]

4

In 1862, Tolstoy married Sofya (Sonya) Behrs, the daughter of Dr Andrei Behrs, the house doctor of the Kremlin Palace in Moscow, in a ceremony at the Kremlin's Cathedral of the Assumption. Tolstoy drew on this event when he came to write the splendid wedding scene between Kitty and Levin in *Anna Karenina*. As in many gentry weddings of the time, the ceremony combines Orthodox and peasant rituals; and there is an insistence, voiced by Kitty's mother Princess Shcherbatskaya, 'on all the conventions being strictly observed'.[62] Indeed, one can read the scene as an ethnographic document about this special aspect of the Russian way of life.

Every Russian knows the verses from Pushkin's *Eugene Onegin* in which the lovesick Tatiana asks her nurse if she has ever been in love. The peasant woman replies by telling the sad story of how she came to be married, at the age of just thirteen, to an even younger boy she had never seen before:

> 'Oh, come! Our world was quite another!
> We'd never heard of love, you see.
> Why, my good husband's sainted mother
> Would just have been the death of me!'
> 'Then how'd you come to marry, nanny?'
> 'The will of God, I guess . . . My Danny
> Was younger still than me, my dear,
> And I was just thirteen that year.
> The marriage maker kept on calling
> For two whole weeks to see my kin,
> Till father blessed me and gave in.
> I got so scared – my tears kept falling;
> And weeping, they undid my plait,
> Then sang me to the churchyard gate.
>
> 'And so they took me off to strangers . . .
> But you're not even listening, pet.'[63]

The scene encapsulates the contrast between the two different cultures – the European and the folk – in Russian society. Whereas Tatiana looks at marriage through the prism of romantic literature, her nurse regards it from the viewpoint of a patriarchal culture where individual sentiments or choices about love are foreign luxuries. Tolstoy draws the same contrast in Kitty's wedding scene. During the ceremony Dolly thinks back tearfully to her own romance with Stiva Oblonsky and, 'forgetting the present' (meaning all his sexual infidelities), 'she remembered only her young and innocent love'. Meanwhile, in the entrance to the church stands a group of ordinary women who have come in from the street to 'look on breathless with excitement' as the bridal couple take their marriage vows. We listen to them chattering among themselves:

'Why is her face so tear-stained? Is she being married against her will?'
  'Against her will to a fine fellow like that? A prince, isn't he?'
  'Is that her sister in the white satin? Now hear how the deacon will roar: "Wife, obey thy husband!"'
  'Is it the Tchudovsky choir?'
  'No, from the Synod.'
  'I asked the footman. It seems he's taking her straight to his home in the country. They say he's awfully rich. That's why she's being married to him.'
  'Oh no. They make a very well-matched pair.'
. . .
  'What a dear little creature the bride is – like a lamb decked for the slaughter. Say what you like, one does feel sorry for the girl.'[64]

'A lamb decked for the slaughter' is perhaps not how Kitty felt – her love affair with Lovin was a true romance – but, if Sonya's own experience is anything to go by, she might have found some points of contact with these women from the street.

Sonya was eighteen when she married Tolstoy – rather young by European standards but not by Russian ones. Eighteen was in fact the average age of marriage for women in nineteenth-century Russia – far younger than even in those pre-industrial parts of western Europe where women tended to marry relatively early (around the age of twenty-five).[65] (For the past 300 years no other European country has had an average female age at first marriage as low as twenty years – and in this respect Russian marriage more closely fits the Asiatic pattern.)[66] Tatiana's nurse was, therefore, not exceptional in marrying so young, even though thirteen was the youngest she could marry under Russian canon law. Serf owners liked their peasant girls to marry young, so that they could breed more serfs for them; the burden of taxation could be easily arranged so that peasant elders took the same opinion. Sometimes the serf owners enforced early marriages – their bailiffs lining up the marriageable girls and boys in two separate rows and casting lots to decide who would marry whom.[67] Among the upper classes (though not the merchantry) girls married at an older age, although in the provinces it was not unusual for a noble bride to be barely older than a child. Sonya Tolstoy would have sympathized with Princess Raevskaya, who became a widow at the age of thirty-five – by which time she had given birth to seventeen children, the first at the age of just sixteen.[68]

The arranged marriage was the norm in peasant Russia until the beginning of the twentieth century. The peasant wedding was not a love match between individuals ('We'd never heard of love,' recalls Tatiana's nurse). It was a collective rite intended to bind the couple and the new household to the patriarchal culture of the village and the Church. Strict communal norms determined the selection of a spouse – sobriety and diligence, health and child-rearing qualities being more important than good looks or personality. By custom throughout Russia, the parents of the groom would appoint a matchmaker in the autumn courting season who would find a bride in one of the nearby villages and arrange for her inspection at a *smotrinie*. If that was successful the two families would begin negotiations over the bride price, the cost of her trousseau, the exchange of household property and the expenses of the wedding feast. When all this was agreed a formal marriage contract would be sealed by the drinking of a toast which was witnessed by the whole community and marked by the singing of a ceremonial song and a *khorovod*.[69] Judging from the plaintive nature of these songs, the bride did not look forward to her wedding day. There was a whole series of prenuptial songs – most of them laments in which the bride would 'wail', as the nineteenth-century folklorist Dahl described it, 'to mourn the loss of maidenhood'.[70] The prenuptial *khorovod*, which was sung and danced by the village girls in spring, was a sad and bitter song about the life to come in their husband's home:

> They are making me marry a lout
> With no small family.
> Oh! Oh! Oh! Oh! Oh dear me!
> With a father, and a mother
> And four brothers
> And sisters three.
> Oh! Oh! Oh! Oh! Oh dear me!
> Says my father-in-law,
> 'Here comes a bear!'
> Says my mother-in-law,
> 'Here comes a slut!'
> My sisters-in-law cry,
> 'Here comes a do-nothing!'
> My brothers-in-law cry,
> 'Here comes a mischief-maker!'
> Oh! Oh! Oh! Oh! Oh dear me![71]

The bride and groom played a largely passive role in the peasant wedding rituals, which were enacted by the whole community in a highly formalized dramatic performance. The night before the wedding the bride was stripped of the customary belt that protected her maidenly purity and was washed by village girls in the bath house. The bridal shower (*devichnik*) had an important symbolic significance. It was accompanied by ritual songs to summon up the magic spirits of the bath house which were believed to protect the bride and her children. The water from the towel with which the bride was dried was then wrung out and used to leaven dough for the ritual dumplings served to the guests at the wedding feast. The climax of this bath-house rite was the unplaiting of the maiden's single braid, which was then replaited as two braids to symbolize her entry into married life. As in Eastern cultures, the display of female hair was seen as a sexual enticement, and all married Russian peasant women kept their plaited hair hidden underneath a kerchief or head-dress. The bride's virginity was a matter of communal importance and, until it had been confirmed, either by the finger of the matchmaker or by the presence of bloodstains on the sheets, the honour of her household would remain in doubt. At the wedding feast it was not unusual for the guests to act as witnesses to the bride's deflowering – sometimes even for guests to strip the couple and tie their legs together with embroidered towels.

Among the upper classes there were still traces of these patriarchal customs in the nineteenth century, and among the merchants, as anyone familiar with Ostrovsky's plays will know, this peasant culture was very much alive. In the aristocracy arranged marriages remained the norm in Russia long after they had been replaced in Europe by romantic ones; and although romantic love became more influential in the nineteenth century, it never really became the guiding principle. Even among the most educated families, parents nearly always had the final say over the choice of a spouse, and the memoir literature of the time is filled with accounts of love affairs that crashed against their opposition. By the end of the nineteenth century a father would rarely refuse to sanction his child's marriage; yet, in deference to the old custom, it remained accepted practice for the suitor to approach the parents first and ask for their permission to propose.

In the provinces, where the gentry was generally closer to the culture of the peasants, noble families were even slower to assimilate the European notion of romantic love. The marriage proposals were usually handled by the parents of the suitor and the prospective bride. Sergei Aksakov's father was married in this way, his parents having made the proposal to his bride's father.[72] The peasant custom of appointing a matchmaker was also retained by many gentry families in the eighteenth and nineteenth centuries, as was the inspection of the bride – albeit as a customary dinner where the nobleman could get to know the daughter of the house and, if he approved, propose a marriage contract to her parents there and then.[73] Marriage contracts, too, were commonly agreed between the families of a noble bride and groom. When Sergei Aksakov's parents were engaged, in the 1780s, they sealed the marriage contract with a feast that was attended by the whole community – much as was the custom among the peasantry.[74] The noble marriage contract was a complicated thing, recalled Elizaveta Rimsky-Korsakov, who became engaged in the 1790s. It took several weeks of careful preparation while 'the people who knew prices arranged everything', and it needed to be sealed at a large betrothal party, attended by the relatives from both the families, where prayers were said, precious gifts were given as a token of intention and pictures of the bride and groom were swapped.[75]

Moscow was the centre of the marriage market for the gentry from the provinces. The autumn balls in Moscow were a conscious translation of the autumn courtship rituals played out by the peasants and their matchmakers. Hence the advice given to Tatiana's mother in *Eugene Onegin*:

> To Moscow and the marriage mart!
> They've vacancies galore . . . take heart![76]

Pushkin himself met his wife, Natalia Goncharova, who was then aged just sixteen, at a Moscow autumn ball. In Moscow, according to the early nineteenth-century memoirist F. F. Vigel, there was a

whole class of matchmakers to whom noble suitors could apply, giving them the age of their prospective bride and the various conditions of their proposal. These matchmakers would make their business known in the Nobles' Assembly, particularly in the autumn season when noblemen would come from the provinces to find themselves a bride.[77]

In *Anna Karenina* Levin comes to Moscow to court Kitty. The rituals of their wedding draw in equal measure from the Church's sacraments and the pagan customs of the peasantry. Kitty leaves her parents' house and travels with the family icon to the church to meet Levin (who is late, as Tolstoy was at his own wedding, because his man servant had misplaced his shirt). The parents of the bride and groom are absent from the service, as demanded by custom, for the wedding was perceived as the moment when the bridal couple leave their earthly homes and join together in the family of the Church. Like all Russian brides, Kitty is accompanied by her godparents, whose customary role is to help the priest administer this rite of passage by offering the bride and groom the sacred wedding loaf, blessing them with icons and placing on their heads the 'wedding crowns'.

'Put it right on!' was the advice heard from all sides when the priest brought forward the crowns and Shcherbatsky, his hand shaking in its three-button glove, held the crown high above Kitty's head.

'Put it on!' she whispered, smiling.

Levin looked round at her and was struck by her beatific expression. He could not help being infected by her feeling and becoming as glad and happy as she was.

With light hearts they listened to the reading of the Epistle and heard the head-deacon thunder out one last verse, awaited with such impatience by the outside public. With light hearts they drank the warm red wine and water from the shallow cup, and their spirits rose still higher when the priest, flinging back his stole and taking their hands in his, led them round the lectern while a bass voice rang out *'Rejoice, O Isaiah!'* Shcherbatsky and Tchirikov, who were supporting the crowns and getting entangled in the bride's train, smiled too, and were inexplicably happy. They either lagged behind or stumbled on the bride and bridegroom every time the priest came to a halt. The spark of joy glowing in Kitty's heart seemed to have spread to everyone in church. Levin fancied that the priest and deacon wanted to smile as much as he did.

Lifting the crowns from their heads, the priest read the last prayer and congratulated the young couple. Levin glanced at Kitty and thought he had never seen her look like that before, so lovely with the new light of happiness shining in her face. Levin longed to say something to her but did not know whether the ceremony was over yet. The priest came to his aid, saying softly, a smile on his kindly mouth, 'Kiss your wife, and you, kiss your husband,' and took the candles from their hands.[78]

The 'coronation' (*venchane*), as the wedding ceremony was called in Russia, symbolized the grace that the bridal couple received from the Holy Spirit as they founded a new family or domestic church. The crowns were usually made of leaves and flowers. They were crowns of joy and martyrdom, for every Christian marriage involved sacrifice by either side. Yet the crowns had a more secular significance as well: for among the common people the bridal pair were called the 'Tsar' and 'Tsarina', and proverbs said the wedding feast was meant to be *'po tsarskii'* – a banquet fit for kings.[79]

The traditional Russian marriage was a patriarchal one. The husband's rights were reinforced by the teachings of the Church, by custom, by canon and by civil laws. According to the 1835 Digest of Laws, a wife's main duty was to 'submit to the will of her husband' and to reside with him in all circumstances, unless he was exiled to Siberia.[80] State and Church conceived the husband as an autocrat – his absolute authority over wife and family a part of the divine and natural order. 'The husband and the wife are one body,' declared Konstantin Pobedonostsev, the arch-reactionary Procurator-General of the Holy Synod and personal tutor to the last two Tsars. 'The husband is the head of the wife. The wife is not distinguished from her husband. Those are the basic principles from which the provisions of our law proceed.'[81] In fact, Russian women had the legal right to control their property – a right, it seems, that was established in the eighteenth century, and in some respects to do with property they were better off than women in the rest of Europe or America.[82] But women were at a severe disadvantage when it came to inheriting family property; they had no legal right to request a separation or to challenge the authority of their husband; and, short of a severe injury, they had no protection against physical abuse.

'Oh, Oh, Oh, Oh, Oh dear me!' The bridal lament was not unwarranted. The peasant wife was destined for a life of suffering – so much so, indeed, that her life became a symbol of the peasant's misery, used by nineteenth-century writers to highlight the worst aspects of Russian life. The traditional peasant household was much larger than its European counterpart, often containing more than a dozen members, with the wives and families of two or three brothers living under the same roof as their parents. The young bride who arrived in this household was likely to be burdened with the meanest chores, the fetching and the cooking, the washing and the childcare, and generally treated like a serf. She would have to put up with the sexual advances of not just her husband, but his father, too, for the ancient peasant custom of *snokhachestvo* gave the household elder rights of access to her body in the absence of his son. Then there were the wife-beatings. For centuries the peasants had claimed the right to beat their wives. Russian proverbs were full of advice on the wisdom of such violence:

'Hit your wife with the butt of the axe, get down and see if she's breathing. If she is, she's shamming and wants some more.'

'The more you beat the old woman, the tastier the soup will be.'

'Beat your wife like a fur coat, then there'll be less noise.'

'A wife is nice twice: when she's brought into the house [as a bride] and when she's carried out of it to her grave.'[83]

For those who saw the peasant as a natural Christian (that is, practically the whole of the intelligentsia) such barbaric customs presented a problem. Dostoevsky tried to get around it by claiming that the people should be judged by the 'sacred things for which they yearn' rather than 'their frequent acts of bestiality', which were no more than surface covering, the 'slime of centuries of oppression'. Yet even Dostoevsky stumbled when it came to wife-beating:

Have you ever seen how a peasant beats his wife? I have. He begins with a rope or a strap. Peasant life is devoid of aesthetic pleasures – music, theatres, magazines; naturally this gap has to be filled somehow. Tying up his wife or thrusting her legs into the opening of a floorboard, our good little peasant would begin, probably, methodically, cold-bloodedly, even sleepily, with measured blows, without listening to her screams and entreaties. Or rather he does listen – and listens with delight: or what pleasure would there be in beating her? . . . The blows rain down faster and faster, harder and harder – countless blows. He begins to get excited and finds it to his taste. The animal cries of his tortured victim go to his head like vodka . . . Finally, she grows quiet; she stops shrieking and only groans, her breath catching violently. And now the blows come even faster and more furiously. Suddenly he throws away the strap; like a madman he grabs a stick or branch, anything, and breaks it on her back with three final terrifying blows. Enough! He stops, sits down at the table, heaves a sigh, and has another drink.[84]

Wife-beating was a rare phenomenon in the gentry class, but the patriarchal customs of the *Domostroi*, the sixteenth-century manual of the Muscovite household, were still very much in evidence. Alexandra Labzina, the daughter of a minor gentry family, was married off on her thirteenth birthday, in 1771, to a man she only met on her wedding day. Her father having died, and her mother being gravely ill, she was given to her husband with instructions from her mother 'to obey in all things'. It turned out that her husband was a beast, and he treated her with cruelty. He locked her in her room for days on end, while he slept with his niece, or went out for days on drinking-whoring binges with his friends. He forbade her to attend her mother's funeral, or to see her nanny when she became ill. Eventually, like so many of his type, her husband was sent out to administer the mines at Petrozavodsk and later at Nerchinsk, the Siberian penal colony where Volkonsky was exiled. Away from any social censure, his treatment of his wife became increasingly sadistic. One freezing night he locked her naked in the barn while he carried on with prostitutes inside the house. She bore it all with Christian meekness, until he died from syphilis and she returned to Russia, where eventually she married the vice-president of the Academy of Arts.[85]

Labzina's treatment was exceptionally cruel, but the patriarchal culture that had produced it was pretty universal in the provinces until the latter half of the nineteenth century. The landowner Maria Adam, for example, had an aunt in Tambov province who had married a neighbouring landowner in the 1850s. Her husband, it transpired, had only married her to gain possession of her property and, as soon as they were wed, he made her life unbearable. The aunt ran away and sought shelter at her niece's house, but the husband came and found her, threatened to 'skin her alive' and, when his wife's maid intervened, he beat her with his whip. Eventually, after dreadful scenes, Maria took her aunt and the badly beaten maid to appeal for help at the house of the provincial governor, but the governor would not accept the women's evidence and sent them away. For three months they lived at Maria's house, barricaded inside to protect themselves from the husband who came and abused them there every day, until finally, in the liberal atmosphere of 1855, a new governor was appointed who secured the Senate's permission for Maria's aunt to live apart from her husband.[86] Such divorces were very rare indeed – about fifty a year for the whole of Russia in the 1850s, rising to no more than a few hundred in the final decades of the nineteenth century[87] – much fewer than in Europe at the time. Until 1917 the Russian Church retained control of marriage and divorce, and it stubbornly resisted the European trend to relax the divorce laws.

Near the end of Kitty's wedding in *Anna Karenina* the priest motions the bridal pair to a rose silk carpet where they are to perform the sacraments.

Often as they had both heard the saying that the one who steps first on the carpet will be the head of the house, neither Levin nor Kitty could think of that as they took those few steps towards it. They did not even hear the loud remarks and disputes that followed, some maintaining that Levin was first and others insisting that they had both stepped on together.[88]

Tolstoy saw the Kitty–Levin marriage as an ideal Christian love: each lives for the other and, through that love, they both live in God. Tolstoy's own life was a search for just this communion, this sense of belonging. The theme runs right through his literary work. There was a time when he had believed that he might find this community in army life – but he ended up by satirizing military 'brotherhood' and calling for the army to be abolished. Then he looked for it in the literary world of Moscow and St Petersburg – but he ended up by condemning that as well. For a long time he believed that the answer to his problem lay in the sanctity of marriage; so many of his works express that ideal. But here too he failed to find true union. His own selfishness was always in the way. Tolstoy might have pictured his marriage to Sonya as the idyllic attachment of Levin and Kitty, but real life was very different. In the Tolstoy marriage there was never any doubt about who had stepped on to the carpet first. The count was as good as any peasant when it came to his relations with his wife. In the first eight years of their marriage Sonya bore him eight children (according to her diary, he would make sexual demands before she had even healed from giving birth). Sonya served as his private secretary, working for long hours through the night copying out the manuscripts of *War and Peace*. Later Tolstoy would confess that he had 'acted badly and cruelly – as every husband acts towards his wife. I gave her all the hard work, the so-called "women's work", and went hunting or enjoyed myself.'[89] Repulsed by his own behaviour, Tolstoy came to question the romantic basis of marriage. Here was the central theme of all his fiction from *Anna Karenina* to *The Kreutzer Sonata* (1891) and *Resurrection* (1899). Anna is doomed to self-destruction, not so much as a tragic victim of society, but because she is the tragic victim of her own passions (as Tolstoy was of his). Despite her immense suffering and the sacrifice she makes by losing her own child to pursue her love for Vronsky, Anna commits the sin of living to be loved. Tolstoy spelled out his own judgement in an essay called 'On Life', in which he talked about the contradiction of people living only for themselves, looking for their happiness as individuals, whereas it can only be found in living for others. This is the lesson which Levin learns as he settles down to married life with wife and child: happiness depends on a form of love that gives; and we can only find ourselves through a communion with our fellow human beings. Tolstoy had not found this in his own marriage. But he thought he had found it in the peasantry.

5

In 1897 Russian society was engulfed in a storm of debate over a short tale. Chekhov's 'Peasants' tells the story of a sick Moscow waiter who returns with his wife and daughter to his native village, only to find that his poverty-stricken family resent him for bringing another set of mouths to feed. The waiter dies and his widow, who has grown thin and ugly from her short stay in the village, returns to Moscow with these sad reflections on the hopelessness of peasant life:

During the summer and winter months there were hours and days when these people appeared to live worse than cattle, and life with them was really terrible. They were coarse, dishonest, filthy, drunk, always quarrelling and arguing amongst themselves, with no respect for one another and living in mutual fear and suspicion. Who maintains the pub and makes the peasants drunk? The peasant. Who embezzles the village, school and parish funds and spends it all on drink? The peasant. Who robs his neighbour, sets fire to his house and perjures himself in court for a bottle of vodka? Who is the first to revile the peasant at district council and similar meetings? The peasant. Yes, it was terrible living with these people; nevertheless, they were still human beings, suffering and weeping like other people and there was nothing in their lives which did not provide some excuse.[90]

The myth of the good peasant had been punctured by the tale. The peasant was now just a human being, brutalized and coarsened by his poverty, not the bearer of special moral lessons for society. The Populists denounced Chekhov for failing to reflect the spiritual ideals of peasant life. Tolstoy called the story 'a sin before the people' and said that Chekhov had not looked into the peasant's soul.[91] Slavophiles attacked it as a slander against Russia. But the Marxists, whose opinions were beginning to be heard, praised the story for revealing the way the rise of the capitalist town had caused the decline of the village. Reactionaries were pleased with the story, too, because it proved, they said, that the peasant was his own worst enemy.[92]

It may seem odd that a work of literature should cause such huge shock waves throughout society. But Russia's identity was built upon the myth which Chekhov had destroyed. The Populist ideal of the peasantry had become so fundamental to the nation's conception of itself that to question this ideal was to throw the whole of Russia into agonizing doubt. The impact of the story was all the more disturbing for the simple factual style in which it was composed. It seemed not so much a work of fiction as a documentary study: the Tsarist censor had referred to it as an 'article'.[93]

Chekhov's story was the fruit of its author's first-hand knowledge of the peasantry. The villages around his small estate at Melikhovo contained many peasants who went to work as waiters or as other service staff in nearby Moscow. The influence of city life was clearly to be seen in the behaviour of those who stayed behind. Shortly before he wrote the story Chekhov had observed a group of drunken servants in his own kitchen. One of them had married off his daughter, much against her will, in exchange for a bucket of vodka. They were now drinking it.[94] But Chekhov was not shocked by such a scene. Over the years he had come to know the peasants through his work as a doctor. Sickly peasants came to Melikhovo from many miles around, and he treated them free of charge. During the cholera epidemic that followed on the heels of the famine crisis in 1891 he had given up his writing and worked as a doctor for the district *zemstvo* in Moscow. The gruelling work had acquainted him with the squalid conditions in which the poorest peasants lived and died. 'The peasants are crude, unsanitary and mistrustful', Chekhov wrote to a friend, 'but the thought that our labours will not be in vain makes it all unnoticeable.'[95] Five years later, in 1897, Chekhov helped to collect the statistics for the first national census in Russian history. He was horrified by what he learned – that just a few kilometres from Moscow there were villages where six out of every ten infants would die in their first year. Such facts angered him, a 'small deeds' liberal, pushing him politically towards the left. On learning, for example, that the poor discharged from hospital were dying for lack of proper aftercare, Chekhov delivered a tirade to Yezhov, a well-known columnist for the right-wing daily *Novoe vremia*, in which he maintained that, since the rich got richer by turning the poor peasants into drunks and whores, they should be made to meet the costs of their health care.[96]

Beneath all the din surrounding Chekhov's story there was a profound question about Russia's future as a peasant land. The old rural Russia was being swept aside by the advance of the towns, and the nation was divided over it. For the Slavophiles and the Populists, who saw Russia's unique virtues in the old peasant culture and community, the growing subjugation of the village to the town was a national catastrophe. But for Westernists, the liberals and the Marxists, who embraced the city as a modernizing force, the peasantry was backward and bound to die away. Even the government was forced to reassess its peasant policy as the influence of the urban market began to change the countryside. The peasant commune was no longer feeding the growing population of the countryside, let alone providing a marketable surplus for the state to tax; and as the agrarian crisis deepened, it became the organizing kernel of the peasant revolution. Since 1861 the government had left villages in the hands of the communes – believing them to be the bulwarks of the patriarchal order in the countryside: its own state administration stopped at the level of the district towns. But after the 1905 Revolution the government changed its policy. Under Stolypin, Prime Minister between 1906 and 1911, it attempted to break up the village commune, which had organized the peasant war against the manors, by encouraging the stronger peasants to set up private farms on land removed from communal control, and at the same time helping those who were too weak to farm, or deprived of access to the land by the new laws of private property, to move as labourers into the towns.

The root cause of this transformation was the slow decline of peasant farming in the overpopulated central Russian zone. The peasantry's egalitarian customs gave them little incentive to produce anything other than babies. For the commune distributed land among the households according to the number of mouths to feed. The birth rate in Russia (at about fifty births per 1,000 people per year) was nearly twice the European average during the second half of the nineteenth century, and the highest rates of all were in the areas of communal tenure where land holdings were decided according to family size. The astronomical rise of the peasant population (from 50 to 79 million between 1861 and 1897) resulted in a growing shortage of land. By the turn of the century, one in ten peasant households had no land at all; while a further one in five had a tiny plot of little more than one hectare which could barely feed a family, given the primitive methods of cultivation used in the central agricultural zone. The communes kept the open three-field system used in western Europe in medieval times in which two fields were sown and one lay fallow every year. Each household got a certain number of arable strips according to its size and, because the livestock were allowed to graze on the stubble and there were no hedges, all the farmers had to follow the same rotation of crops. As the population grew, the strips of productive arable land became progressively narrower. In the most overcrowded regions these strips were no more than a couple of metres wide, making it impossible to employ modern ploughs. To feed the growing population the communes brought more land under the plough by reducing fallow and pasture lands. But the long-term effect was to make the situation worse – for the soil became exhausted from being overworked, while livestock herds (the main source of fertilizer) were reduced because of the shortage of grazing lands. By the end of the nineteenth century, one in three peasant households did not even own a horse.[97] Millions of peasants were driven off the land by crushing poverty. Some managed to survive through local trades, such as weaving, pottery or carpentry, timber-felling and carting, although many of these handicrafts were being squeezed out by factory competition; or by working as day labourers on the gentry's estates, although the influx of new machines reduced demand for them with every passing year. Others left the overcrowded central areas for the vast and empty steppelands of Siberia, where land was made available to colonists. But most were forced into the towns, where they picked up unskilled jobs in factories or worked as domestic or service staff. Chekhov's waiter had been one of these.

New urban ways were also filtering down to the remote villages. The traditional extended peasant family began to break up as the younger and more literate peasants struggled to throw off the patriarchal tyranny of the village and set up households of their own. They looked towards the city and its cultural values as a route to independence and self-worth. Virtually any urban job seemed desirable compared with the hardships and dull routines of peasant life. A survey of rural schoolchildren in the early 1900s found that half of them wanted to pursue an 'educated profession' in the city, whereas less than 2 per cent held any desire to follow in the footsteps of their peasant parents. 'I want to be a shop assistant,' said one schoolboy, 'because I do not like to walk in the mud. I want to be like those people who are cleanly dressed and work as shop assistants.'[98] Educators were alarmed that, once they had learned to read, many peasant boys, in particular, turned their backs on agricultural work and set themselves above the other peasants by swaggering around in raffish city clothes. Such boys, wrote a villager, 'would run away to Moscow and take any job'.[99] They looked back on the village as a 'dark' and 'backward' world of superstition and crippling poverty – a world Trotsky would describe as the Russia of 'icons and cockroaches' – and they idealized the city as a force of social progress and enlightenment. Here was the basis of the cultural revolution on which Bolshevism would be built. For the Party rank and file was recruited in the main from peasant boys like these; and its ideology was a science of contempt for the peasant world. The revolution would sweep it all away.

Bolshevism was built on the mass commercial culture of the towns. The urban song, the foxtrot and the tango, the gramophone, the fairground entertainment and the cinema – these were its forms after 1917. Yet this urban culture was already attracting peasants in the 1890s, when its presence was first felt in the countryside. The village song was gradually being supplanted by the urban 'cruel romance', or the *chastushka*, a crude rhyming song which was usually accompanied by an accordion (another new invention) in the tavern or streets. Unlike the folk song, whose performance was collective and impersonal, these urban songs were personal in theme and full of individual expression. The folk tale was also dying out, as the new rural readership created by the recent growth of primary schooling turned instead to the cheap urban literature of detective stories and tales of adventure or romance. Tolstoy was afraid that the peasants would be poisoned by the egotistic values of this new book trade. He was concerned that these urban tales had heroes who prevailed by cunning and deceit, whereas the old peasant tradition had upheld moral principles. Joining forces with the publisher Sytin, a humble merchant's son who had become rich by selling such cheap pamphlets in the provinces, Tolstoy set up the Intermediary to publish cheap editions of the Russian classics and simple country tales such as 'How a Little Devil Redeemed a Hunk of Bread' and 'Where There Is God There Is Love' which Tolstoy himself wrote for the new mass peasant readership. Within four years of the publishing house's foundation, in 1884, sales had risen from 400,000 books to a staggering 12 million[100] – book sales that could not be matched by any other country until China under Mao. But sales declined in the 1890s, as more exciting books were brought out in the city, and readers turned away from Tolstoy's 'fairy stories' and 'moralizing tales'.[101]

For the intelligentsia, which defined itself by its cultural mission to raise the masses to its own levels of civilization, this defection was a mortal blow. The peasant had been 'lost' to the crass commercial culture of the towns. The peasant who was meant to bear the Russian soul – a natural Christian, a selfless socialist and a moral beacon to the world – had become a victim of banality. Suddenly the old ideals were crushed, and, as Dostoevsky had predicted, once the champions of 'the people' realized that the people were not as they had imagined them to be, they renounced them without regret. Where before the peasant was the light, now he was the darkening shadow that descended over Russia in the decades leading up to 1917. The educated classes were thrown into a moral panic about what they saw as the peasantry's descent into barbarity.

The 1905 Revolution confirmed all their fears. For years the intelligentsia had dreamed of a genuinely democratic revolution. Since the 1890s liberals and socialists had joined together in their campaign for political reform. They rejoiced in the spring of 1905, when the entire country appeared to be united in the demand for democratic rights. In October 1905, with the Russian empire engulfed by popular revolts, the army crippled by soldiers' mutinies, and his own throne threatened by a general strike, Nicholas II finally gave in to the pressure of his liberal ministers to concede a series of political reforms. The October Manifesto, as these became known, was a sort of constitution – although it was not issued in that name because the Tsar refused to recognize any formal constraints on his autocratic power. The Manifesto granted civil liberties and a legislative parliament (or Duma) elected on a broad franchise. The country celebrated. New political parties were formed. People talked of a new Russia being born. But the political revolution was all the time developing into a social one, as the workers pressed their radical demands for industrial democracy in a growing wave of strikes and violent protests, and the peasantry resumed their age-old struggle for the land, confiscating property and forcing the nobility from their estates. The national unity of 1905 was soon shown to be illusory, as liberals and socialists went their separate ways after October. For the propertied élites, the October Manifesto was the final goal of the revolution. But for the workers and the peasantry, it was only the beginning of a social revolution against all property and privilege. The frightened liberals recoiled from their commitment to the revolution. The growing insubordination of the lower classes, the fighting in the streets, the rural arson and destruction of estates, and the mistrust and the hatred on the faces of the peasants which continued to disturb the landed nobles long after order was bloodily restored – all these destroyed the romance of 'the people' and their cause.

In 1909 a group of philosophers critical of the radical intelligentsia and its role in the Revolution of 1905 published a collection of essays called *Vekhi* (*Landmarks*) in which this disenchantment was power-fully expressed. The essays caused a huge storm of controversy – not least because their writers (former Marxists like Pyotr Struve and Nikolai Berdyaev) had all had spotless (that is, politically radical) credentials – which in itself was symptomatic of the intelligentsia's new mood of doubt and self-questioning. The essays were a fierce attack on the nineteenth-century cult of 'the people' and its tendency to subordinate all other interests to the people's cause. Through this pursuit of material interests the intelligensia was pushing Russia to a second revolution, much more violent and destructive than the first. Civilization was under threat and it was the duty of the educated classes to face this reality:

This is the way we are: not only can we not dream about fusing with the people but we must fear them worse than any punishment by the government, and we must bless that authority which alone with its bayonets and prisons manages to protect us from the popular fury.[102]

There was a general feeling, which the essays had expressed, that the masses would destroy Russia's fragile European civilization and that, come the revolution, Russia would be dragged down to the level of the semi-savage peasantry. Andrei Bely's novel *Petersburg* (1913–14) is filled with images of the city being overrun by Asiatic hordes. Even Gorky, a hero and a champion of the common man, succumbed to the new apocalyptic mood. 'You are right 666 times over', he wrote to a literary friend in 1905, '[the revolution] is giving birth to real barbarians, just like those that ravaged Rome.'[103]

This dark mood was captured in what must surely be the bleakest portrait of rural life in any literature: Ivan Bunin's novella *The Village* (1910). Bunin had experience of peasant life. Unlike Turgenev or Tolstoy, who were scions of the élite aristocracy, Bunin belonged to the minor provincial gentry, who had always lived in close proximity to the peasants and whose lives resembled theirs in many ways. Bunin saw the peasant as the 'national type' and his stories about them were intended to be judgements on the Russian people and their history. He had never had any illusions about the spiritual or noble qualities of the peasants. His diaries are filled with horrific incidents he had seen or heard about in the villages: a woman who was beaten by her drunken husband so that she had to be 'bandaged up like a mummy'; another woman raped so often by her husband that she bled to death.[104] Bunin's early stories dealt with the harsh realities of country life in the 1890s – a decade of famine and flight from the land. They are full of images of destruction and decay: abandoned villages, factories belching blood red smoke, the peasants old or sick. Here Bunin's village was a realm of natural beauty that was being undermined and gradually destroyed by the new industrial economy. After 1905, however, Bunin changed his view of the village. He came to see it not just as a victim, but as the main agent of its own demise. *The Village* is set in 1905 in a place called Durnovo (from the word '*durnoi*', meaning 'bad' or 'rotten'). Its peasants are portrayed as dark and ignorant, thieving and dishonest, lazy and corrupt. Nothing much takes place in Durnovo. There is no plot in Bunin's work. It consists of a description of the dreary existence of a tavern keeper who has just enough intelligence to realize the emptiness of his own life. 'God, what a place! It's a prison!' he concludes. Yet, as Bunin's tale implies, all of peasant Russia is a Durnovo.[105]

The Village gave a huge jolt to society. More perhaps than any other work, it made the Russians think about the hopeless destiny of their peasant land. 'What stunned the reader in this book', wrote one critic, 'was not the depiction of the peasant's material, cultural and legal poverty . . . but the realization that there was no escape from it. The most that the peasant, as depicted by Bunin, was capable of achieving . . . was only the awareness of his hopeless savagery, of being doomed.'[106] Gorky wrote about *The Village* that it had forced society to think seriously 'not just about the peasant but about the question of whether Russia is to be or not to be'.[107]

Like Bunin, Maxim Gorky knew what village life was like: his disenchantment with the peasantry was based on experience. He came from the 'lower depths' himself – an orphan who had survived by scavenging along the banks of the Volga river and roaming round the towns, a street urchin dressed in rags. Tolstoy once said of Gorky that he seemed 'to have been born as an old man' – and indeed Gorky had known more human suffering in his first eight years than the count would see in all his eight decades. Gorky's grandfather's household in Nizhnyi Novgorod, where he had been brought up after the death of his father, was, as he described it in *My Childhood* (1913), a microcosm of provincial Russia – a place of poverty, cruelty and meanness, where the men took to the bottle in a big way and the women found solace in God. All his life he felt a profound loathing for this 'backward' peasant Russia – a contempt that aligned him with the Bolsheviks:

When I try to recall those vile abominations of that barbarous life in Russia, at times I find myself asking the question: is it worth while recording them? And with ever stronger conviction I find the answer is yes, because that was the real loathsome truth and to this day it is still valid. It is that truth which must be known down to the very roots, so that by tearing them up it can be completely erased from the memory, from the soul of man, from our whole oppressive and shameful life.[108]

In 1888, at the age of twenty, Gorky had 'gone to the people' with a Populist called Romas who tried to set up a co-operative and organize the peasants in a village on the Volga near Kazan. The enterprise ended in disaster. The villagers burned them out after Romas failed to heed the threats of the richer peasants, who had close links with the established traders in the nearby town and resented their meddling. Three years later, Gorky was beaten unconscious by a group of peasant men when he tried to intervene on behalf of a woman who had been stripped naked and horsewhipped by her husband and a howling mob after being found guilty of adultery. Experience left Gorky with a bitter mistrust of the 'noble savage'. It led him to conclude that, however good they may be on their own, the peasants left all that was fine behind when they 'gathered in one grey mass':

Some dog-like desire to please the strong ones in the village took possession of them, and then it disgusted me to look at them. They would howl wildly at each other, ready for a fight – and they would fight over any trifle. At these moments they were terrifying and they seemed capable of destroying the very church where only the previous evening they had gathered humbly and submissively, like sheep in a fold.[109]

Looking back on the violence of the revolutionary years – a violence he put down to the 'savage instincts' of the Russian peasantry – Gorky wrote in 1922:

Where then is that kindly, contemplative Russian peasant, the indefatigable searcher after truth and justice, so convincingly and beautifully presented to the world by Russian nineteenth-century literature? In my youth I earnestly sought for such a man throughout the Russian countryside but I did not find him.[110]

6

In 1916 Diaghilev was asked where the Ballets Russes had its intellectual origins. In the Russian peasantry, he replied: 'in objects of utility (domestic implements in the country districts), in the painting on the sleighs, in the designs and the colours of peasant dresses, or the carving around a window frame, we found our motifs, and on this foundation we built'.[111] In fact the Ballets Russes was a direct descendant of the 'going to the people' in the 1870s.

It all began at Abramtsevo, the artists' colony established by the Mamontovs on their estate near Moscow, which soon became the focus for the arts and crafts movement. The railway magnate's wife Elizaveta was a well-known sympathizer of the Populists and, soon after the estate was purchased in 1870, she set up a school and a hospital for the peasants in its grounds. In 1876 a carpentry workshop was added where pupils who had graduated from the school might learn a useful trade. The aim was to revive the peasant handicrafts that were fast disappearing as the railways brought in cheaper factory products from the towns. Artists like Gartman and Elena Polenova took their inspiration from this peasant art and, under Polenova's direction, new workshops were soon set up to cater to the growing middle-class market for pottery and linen in the peasant style. Polenova and her artists would go around the villages copying the designs on the window frames and doors, household utensils and furniture, which they would then adapt for the stylized designs of the craft goods manufactured in the colony's workshops. Polenova collected several thousand peasant artefacts which can still be seen in the Craft Museum at Abramtsevo. She saw these artefacts as the remnants of an ancient Russian style that was still alive, and which gave them, in her view, a value that was higher than the Muscovite designs that had inspired artists in the past. For the latter were a part of a dead tradition that was now as remote to the Russian people as 'the art of Africa or Ancient Greece'.[112] In her own pictures and furniture designs Polenova tried, as she put it, to express 'the vital spirit of the Russian people's poetic view of nature', using animal motifs and floral ornaments which she had sketched from peasant artefacts.[113]

15. *Elena Polenova: 'Cat and Owl' carved door,*
Abramtsevo workshop, early 1890s

Urban fans of this 'neo-national' style took it as a pure and authentic Russian art. Stasov, for example, thought that Polenova's 'Cat and Owl' door could be taken for the work of 'some amazingly talented but anonymous master of our ancient Rus''.[114] But in fact it was a fantasy. By the early 1890s, when the door was carved, Polenova had moved on from copying folk designs to assimilating them to the art nouveau style, which made her work even more appealing to the urban middle class.

Other artists trod the same path from ethnographic to commercial art. At the Solomenko embroidery workshops in Tambov province, for example, the artists' designs were becoming increasingly attuned to the bourgeois tastes of the city women who could afford these luxury goods. Instead of the gaudy colours favoured by the peasants in their own designs (orange, red and yellow), they used the subdued colours (dark green, cream and brown) that appealed to urban tastes. The same change took place at the textile workshops of Talashkino, established by Princess Maria Tenisheva on her estate in Smolensk in 1898. The local peasant women 'did not like our colours', Tenisheva recalled, 'they said they were too "drab"', and she had to pay the weavers bonuses to get them to use them in their work.[115]

The folk-like crafted goods of Sergei Maliutin, the principal artist at Talashkino, were pure invention. Maliutin was the creator of the first *matrioshka*, or Russian nesting doll, in 1891. At that time he was working at the Moscow *zemstvo*'s craft workshops at Sergiev Posad which specialized in making Russian toys. Contrary to the popular belief today, the *matrioshka* has no roots in Russian folk culture at all. It was dreamed up in response to a commission from the Mamontovs to make a Russian version of the Japanese nesting doll. Maliutin created a red-cheeked peasant girl in the shape of a barrel with a chicken underneath her arm. Each smaller doll portrayed a different aspect of peasant life; and at the core was a baby tightly swaddled in the Russian style. The design became immensely popular and by the end of the 1890s several million dolls were being manufactured every year. The myth was then established that the *matrioshka* was an ancient Russian toy.[116] At Talashkino Maliutin also applied his distinctive style to furniture, ceramics, book illustrations, stage designs and buildings. Urban admirers like Diaghilev saw his work as the essence of an 'organic peasant Russianness' which, Diaghilev claimed in one of his most nationalistic utterances, would herald a 'Renaissance of the North'.[117] But the real Russian peasants took a different view. When, in 1902, Tenisheva put on an exhibition of the Talashkino products in Smolensk, less than fifty people came to see it and, as she recalled, the peasants 'viewed our things not with delight but with dumb amazement which we found hard to explain'.[118]

It is not immediately obvious what attracted Diaghilev to the neo-nationalists of Abramtsevo and Talashkino – a marriage that gave birth to the folklore fantasies of the Ballets Russes. In 1898, he delivered a tirade on 'peasant art', attacking artists who thought to 'shock the world' by 'dragging peasant shoes and rags on to the canvas'.[119] By artistic temperament the impresario was aristocratic and cosmopolitan, even if he came from the provincial town of Perm. At his grandfather's house, where he had been brought up from the age of ten, there was an atmosphere of cultivated dilettantism, with regular concerts and literary evenings, in which the young Sergei, with his fluent French and German and his piano-playing skills, was in his element. As a law student at St Petersburg University in the early 1890s, Diaghilev was perfectly at home with young aesthetes such as Alexander Benois, Dmitry Filosofov (Diaghilev's cousin) and Walter ('Valechka') Nouvel. There was a general mood of Populism in these circles, especially at the Bogdanovskoe estate near Pskov which belonged to Filosofov's aunt Anna Pavlovna, a well-known activist for women's liberation and a literary hostess whose salon in St Petersburg was frequently attended by Dostoevsky, Turgenev and Blok. The four students would spend their summers at Bogdanovskoe; and it was then that they first conceived the idea of a magazine to educate the public in the great art of the past. Together with the artist Leon Bakst (an old schoolfriend of Benois, Filosofov and Nouvel at the May Academy in Petersburg) they established the World of Art movement, which arranged concerts, exhibitions and lectures on artistic themes, and founded a magazine of the same name which lasted from 1898 to 1904. Subsidized by Tenisheva and Mamontov, the magazine would come to feature the folk-inspired artists of their colonies alongside modern Western art – the same combination that would later be repeated by Diaghilev and Benois in the Ballets Russes.

The co-founders of the World of Art saw themselves as cosmopolitans of Petersburg (they called themselves the 'Nevsky Pickwickians') and championed the idea of a universal culture which they believed was embodied in that civilization. They identified themselves with the aristocracy, and saw that class as a great repository of Russia's cultural heritage. In a passage of his *Memoirs* that is crucial to an understanding of the World of Art, Benois underlined this point when he reminisced about the Filosofovs, one of Russia's ancient noble families:

Theirs was the class to which all the chief figures of Russian culture in the eighteenth and nineteenth centuries belonged, the class that created the delights of the characteristic Russian way of life. From this class came the heroes and heroines in the novels of Pushkin and Lermontov, Turgenev and Tolstoy. This was the class that achieved all that is peaceful, worthy, durable and meant to last for ever. They set the tempo of Russian life . . . All the subtleties of the Russian psychology, all the nuances of our characteristically Russian moral sensibility arose and matured within this milieu.[120]

Above all, they identified with the artistic values of the aristocracy. They saw art as a spiritual expression of the individual's creative genius, not as a vehicle for social programmes or political ideas, as they believed the Russian arts had become under Stasov's leadership. Their veneration of Pushkin and Tchaikovsky stemmed from this philosophy – not 'art for art's sake', as they frequently insisted, but the belief that ideas should be integrated in the work of art.

Reacting against the nineteenth-century realist tradition, the World of Art group sought to restore an earlier ideal of beauty as the artistic principle of what they envisaged (and successfully promoted) as Russia's cultural renaissance. The classical tradition of St Petersburg was one expression of this ideal. The World of Art circle made a cult of eighteenth-century Petersburg. It was practically defined by nostalgia for a civilization which they sensed was about to pass away. Benois and his nephew Eugene Lanceray each produced a series of prints and lithographs depicting city scenes in the reigns of Peter and Catherine the Great. Benois lamented that the classical ideal of eighteenth-century Petersburg had been abandoned by the vulgar nationalists of the nineteenth century. In the revolutionary year of 1905, Diaghilev mounted an exhibition of eighteenth-century Russian portraits in the Tauride Palace, shortly to become the home of the Duma and the Petrograd Soviet. He introduced the portraits as 'a grandiose summing-up of a brilliant, but, alas, dying period in our history'.[121]

But peasant art could also be regarded as a form of 'classicism' – at least in the stylized forms in which it was presented by the neo-nationalists. It was impersonal, symbolic and austere, strictly regulated by the folk traditions of representation, a mystical expression of the spiritual world yet intimately linked with the collective rituals and practices of village life. Here was an ancient, a different 'world of art', whose principles of beauty could be used to overturn the deadening influence of nineteenth-century bourgeois and romantic art.

For Diaghilev, money played a part. Always keen to spot a new market opportunity, the impresario was impressed by the growing popularity of the neo-nationalists' folk-like art. *Fin-de-siècle* Europe had an endless fascination for 'the primitive' and 'exotic'. The savage of the East was regarded as a force of spiritual renewal for the tired bourgeois cultures of the West. Diaghilev had spotted this trend early on. 'Europe needs our youth and spontaneity', he wrote on his return from a tour there in 1896. 'We must go forth at once. We must show our all, with all the qualities and defects of our nationality.'[122] His instincts were confirmed in 1900 when Russia's arts and crafts made a huge splash at the Paris Exhibition. The centre of attention was Korovin's 'Russian Village', a reconstruction of the wooden architecture he had studied on a trip to the Far North, complete with an ancient *teremok*, or timber tower, and a wooden church, which was built on site by a team of peasants brought in from Russia. The Parisians were enchanted by these 'savage carpenters', with their 'unkempt hair and beards, their broad, child-like smiles and primitive methods', and as one French critic wrote, 'if the objects on display had been for sale, there would not be a single item left'.[123] There was a steady flow of peasant-crafted goods from Russia to the West – so much so that special shops were opened in Paris, London, Leipzig, Chicago, Boston and New York in the 1900s.[124] The Parisian couturier Paul Poiret travelled to Russia in 1912 to buy up peasant garb, from which he drew inspiration for his fashionable clothes. The term '*blouse russe*' echoed round the fashion halls, and models could be seen in clothes which bore the mark of Russian *sarafans* and homespun coats.[125]

But there was more than business to draw Diaghilev to the neo-nationalists. The fact that artists such as Polenova and Maliutin were increasingly rendering their 'peasant art' in the stylized forms of modernism brought them into line with the ethos of the World of Art. Diaghilev was particularly attracted to the paintings of Viktor Vasnetsov, which displayed less folk content than a general sense of peasant colouring. Vasnetsov believed that colour was the key to the Russian people's understanding of beauty, and he developed his own palette from the study of folk art (the *lubok* woodcuts and icons) and peasant artefacts, which he collected on his tours of Viatka province in the 1870s. The artist brought these vibrant primary colours to his brilliant stage designs for Mamontov's production of *The Snow Maiden* (plate 15), a production that became the visual model for Diaghilev and the Ballets Russes.

Vasnetsov's designs were an inspiration for the neo-nationalists who followed in his footsteps from Abramtsevo to the World of Art. Their fairytale-like quality was clearly to be seen in later stage designs for the Ballets Russes by Alexander Golovine (*Boris Godunov*: 1908; *The Firebird*: 1910) and Konstantin Korovin (*Ruslan and Liudmila*: 1909). Even more influential, in the longer term, was Vasnetsov's use of colour, motifs, space and style to evoke the essence of folk art, which would inspire primitivist painters such as Natalia Goncharova, Kazimir Malevich and Marc Chagall. These artists, too, gravitated towards the folk tradition, to the icon and the *lubok* and to peasant artefacts, in their quest for a new poetic outlook on the world. Introducing an exhibition of icons and woodcuts in Moscow in 1913, Goncharova talked about a 'peasant aesthetic' that was closer to the symbolic art forms of the East than the representational tradition of the West. 'This art does not copy or improve on the real world but reconstitutes it.' Here was the inspiration of Goncharova's designs for the Ballets Russes, such as *Le Coq d'Or* of 1914.

The Ballets Russes was meant to be a synthesis of all the arts, and it has often been described as a Russian brand of Richard Wagner's *Gesamtkunstwerk*, in which music, art and drama are united. But in fact that synthesis had less to do with Wagner than with the Russian peasantry. It had its roots in Mamontov's Private Opera which had been founded on the spirit of artistic collaboration at Abramtsevo. The whole purpose of the colony was to bring together all the arts and crafts – to unite life and art – through a collective enterprise which its pioneers equated with their own idealized notion of the peasant commune. What

Photograph by William C. Brumfield

16. *Church at Abramtsevo. Designed by Viktor Vasnetsov, 1881–2*

the artists at Abramtsevo admired most about peasant culture was the synthetic nature of its arts and crafts. Simple artefacts, like textiles or ceramics, brought artistic beauty into people's daily lives. Collective rituals like the *khorovod* were total works of art – little 'rites of spring' – combining folk song and ceremonial dance with real events in village life. The colony was an attempt to re-create this 'world of art'. The whole community – artists, craftsmen and peasant builders – became involved in the building of its church. Artists combined with singers and musicians, costume-makers with set-builders, to stage productions of the opera. This was what Diaghilev meant when he said the Ballets Russes was built on the foundations of peasant arts and crafts.

'I am sending you a proposal', Diaghilev wrote to the composer Anatoly Lyadov in 1909.

I need a *ballet* and a *Russian* one – the *first* Russian ballet, since there is no such thing. There is Russian opera, Russian symphony, Russian song, Russian dance, Russian rhythm – but no Russian ballet. And that is precisely what I need – to perform in May of the coming year in the Paris Grand Opera and in the huge Royal Drury Lane Theatre in London. The ballet needn't be three-tiered. The libretto is ready. Fokine has it. It was dreamed up by us all collectively. It's *The Firebird* – a ballet in one act and perhaps two scenes.[126]

Diaghilev's enthusiasm for the ballet was not always evident. His professional entrée into the art world had been through painting, and his first job in the theatre was a long way from the stage. In 1899 he was employed by Prince Sergei Volkonsky, the grandson of the famous Decembrist, who had just been appointed by the Tsar as Director of the Imperial Theatre in St Petersburg. Volkonsky asked Diaghilev to run the theatre's in-house magazine. Eight years later, when Diaghilev took his first stage productions to the West, it was opera, not ballet, that made up his exotic *saisons russes*. It was only the comparative expense of staging operas that made him look to ballet for a cheap alternative.

The importance of the ballet as a source of artistic innovation in the twentieth century is something that no one would have predicted before its rediscovery by Diaghilev. The ballet had become an ossified art form; in much of Europe it was disregarded as an old-fashioned entertainment of the court. But in Russia it lived on in St Petersburg, where the culture was still dominated by the court. At the Marinsky Theatre, where Stravinsky spent much of his childhood, there were regular Wednesday and Sunday ballet matinées – 'the half-empty auditorium' being made up, in the words of Prince Lieven, of 'a mixture of children accompanied by their mothers or governesses, and old men with binoculars'.[127] Among serious intellectuals the ballet was considered 'an entertainment for snobs and tired businessmen',[128] and with the exception of Tchaikovsky, whose reputation suffered as a consequence of his involvement with the form, the composers for the ballet (such as Pugni, Minkus and Drigo) were mostly foreign hacks.* Rimsky-Korsakov, the ultimate authority on musical taste when Stravinsky studied with him in the early 1900s, was famous for his remark that the ballet was 'not really an art form'.[129]

Benois was the real ballet lover in the World of Art group. It appealed

---

* Cesare Pugni (1802–70), in Russia from 1851; Ludwig Minkus (1826–1907), in Russia from 1850 to 1890; Riccardo Drigo (1846–1930), in Russia from 1879 to 1920.

to his aristocratic outlook, and to his nostalgia for the classical culture of eighteenth-century Petersburg. This retrospective aesthetic was shared by all the founders of the Ballets Russes: Benois, Dobuzhinsky, the critic Filosofov and Diaghilev. The ballets of Tchaikovsky were the incarnation of the classical ideal and, even though they never featured in the *saison russe* in Paris, where Tchaikovsky was the least appreciated of the Russian composers, they were an inspiration to the founders of the Ballets Russes. Tchaikovsky was the last of the great European court composers (he lived in the last of the great European eighteenth-century states). Staunchly monarchist, he was among the intimates of Tsar Alexander III. His music, which embodied the 'Imperial style', was preferred by the court to the 'Russian' harmonies of Musorgsky, Borodin and Rimsky-Korsakov.

The Imperial style was virtually defined by the polonaise. Imported into Russia by the Polish composer Jozek Kozlowski towards the end of the eighteenth century, the polonaise became the supreme courtly form and the most brilliant of all the ballroom genres. It came to symbolize the European brilliance of eighteenth-century Petersburg itself. In *Eugene Onegin* Pushkin (like Tchaikovsky) used the polonaise for the climactic entry of Tatiana at the ball in Petersburg. Tolstoy used the polonaise at the climax of the ball in *War and Peace*, where the Emperor makes his entrance and Natasha dances with Andrei. In *The Sleeping Beauty* (1889) and in his opera *The Queen of Spades* (1890) Tchaikovsky reconstructed the imperial grandeur of the eighteenth-century world. Set in the reign of Louis XIV, *The Sleeping Beauty* was a nostalgic tribute to the French influence on eighteenth-century Russian music and culture. *The Queen of Spades*, based on the story by Pushkin, evoked the bygone Petersburg of Catherine the Great, an era when the capital was fully integrated, and played a major role, in the culture of Europe. Tchaikovsky infused the opera with rococo elements (he himself described the ballroom scenes as a 'slavish imitation' of the eighteenth-century style).[130] He used the story's layers of ghostly fantasy to conjure up a dream world of the past. The myth of Petersburg as an unreal city was thus used to travel back in time and recover its lost beauty and classical ideals.

On the evening of the première of *The Queen of Spades* Tchaikovsky left the Marinsky Theatre and wandered on his own through the streets of Petersburg, convinced that his opera was a dismal failure. Suddenly he heard a group of people walking towards him singing one of the opera's best duets. He stopped them and asked them how they were acquainted with the music. Three young men introduced themselves: they were Benois, Filosofov and Diaghilev, the co-founders of the World of Art. From that moment on, according to Benois, the group was united by their love of Tchaikovsky and his classical ideal of Petersburg. 'Tchaikovsky's music', Benois wrote in his old age, 'was what I seemed to be waiting for since my earliest childhood.'[131]

In 1907 Benois staged a production of Nikolai Cherepnin's ballet *Le Pavillon d'Armide* (based on Gauthier's *Omphale*) at the Marinsky Theatre in St Petersburg. Like *The Sleeping Beauty*, it was set in the period of Louis XIV and was classical in style. The production made a deep impression on Diaghilev. Benois' own sumptuous designs, Fokine's modern choreography, the dazzling virtuosity of Nijinsky's dancing – all this, declared Diaghilev, 'must be shown to Europe'.[132] *Le Pavillon* became the curtain-raiser to the 1909 season in Paris, alongside the Polovtsian dances from Borodin's *Prince Igor* (also choreographed by Fokine), in a mixed programme of Russian classical and nationalist works. The exotic 'otherness' of these *mises-en-scène* caused a sensation. The French loved 'our primitive wildness', Benois later wrote, 'our freshness and our spontaneity'.[133] Diaghilev could see that there was money to be made from the export of more Russian ballets in this vein. And so it was, as he wrote to tell Lyadov, that they cooked up the libretto of *The Firebird*. Diaghilev and Benois and Fokine, with the fabulist Remizov, the painter Golovine, the poet Potemkin and the composer Cherepnin (of *Le Pavillon* fame) dreamt up the whole thing around the kitchen table in the true collective spirit of the Russian tradition. But in the end Lyadov did not want to write the score. It was offered to Glazunov, and then Cherepnin, who turned it down, and then, in a state of utter desperation, Diaghilev resorted to the young, and at that time still little known composer, Igor Stravinsky.

Benois called the ballet a 'fairy tale for grown-ups'. Patched together from various folk tales, its aim was to create what Benois called a 'mysterium of Russia' for 'export to the West'.[134] The real export was the myth of peasant innocence and youthful energy. Each ingredient of the ballet was a stylized abstraction of folklore. Stravinsky's score was littered with borrowings from folk music, especially the peasant wedding songs (*devichniki* and *khorovody*) in the *Ronde des princesses* and the finale. The scenario was a patchwork compilation of two entirely separate peasant tales (for there was no single tale of the Firebird) as retold by Afanasiev and various *lubok* prints from the nineteenth century: the tale of Ivan Tsarevich and the Firebird, and the tale of Kashchei the Immortal. These two stories were rewritten to shift their emphasis from a tale of pagan magic (by the grey wolf of the peasant stories) into one of divine rescue (by the Firebird) consistent with Russia's Christian mission in the world.[135]

In the ballet the Tsarevich is lured into the garden of the monster Kashchey by the beauty of the maiden princess. Ivan is saved from the monster and his retinue by the Firebird, whose airborne powers compel Kashchey and his followers to dance wildly until they fall asleep. Ivan then discovers the enormous egg which contains Kashchey's soul, the monster is destroyed, and Ivan is united with the princess. Reinvented for the stage, the Firebird herself was made to carry far more than she had done in the Russian fairy tales. She was transformed into the symbol of a phoenix-like resurgent peasant Russia, the embodiment of an elemental freedom and beauty, in the pseudo-Slavic mythology of the Symbolists which came to dominate the ballet's conception (as immortalized by Blok's 'mythic bird', which adorned the cover of the *Mir iskusstva* journal in the form of a woodcut by Leon Bakst). The production for the Paris season was a self-conscious package of exotic Russian props – from Golovine's colourful peasant costumes to those weird mythic beasts, the '*kikimora*', '*boliboshki*' and 'two-headed monsters', invented by Remizov for the *Suite de Kashchei* – all of them designed to cater to the *fin-de-siècle* Western fascination with 'primitive' Russia.

But the real innovation of *The Firebird* was Stravinsky's use of folk music. Previous composers of the Russian national school had thought of folklore as purely thematic material. They would frequently cite folk songs but would always subject them to the conventional (and essentially Western) musical language canonized by Rimsky-Korsakov. To their trained ears, the heterophonic harmonies of Russian folk music were ugly and barbaric, and not really 'music' in the proper sense at all, so that it would be highly inappropriate to adopt them as a part of their

17. Gusli *player. The* gusli *was an ancient type of Russian zither, usually five-stringed, and widely used in folk music*

art form. Stravinsky was the first composer to assimilate folk music as an element of style – using not just its melodies but its harmonies and rhythms as the basis of his own distinctive 'modern' style.*

The Firebird was the great breakthrough. But it was only made possible by the pioneering work of two ethnographers, whose musical discoveries were yet another product of the 'going to the people' in the 1870s. The first was by Yury Melgunov, a pianist and philologist who carried out a series of field trips to Kaluga province in the 1870s. On these trips he discovered the polyphonic harmonies of Russian peasant song, and worked out a scientific method of transcribing them. The other was by Evgenia Linyova, who confirmed Melgunov's findings by recording peasant singing with a phonograph on field trips to the provinces. These recordings were the basis of her *Peasant Songs of Great Russia as They Are in the Folk's Harmonization*, published in St Petersburg in 1904–9,[136] which directly influenced the music of Stravinsky in *The Firebird*, *Petrushka* and *The Rite of Spring*. The most important aspect of Linyova's work was her discovery that the voice of the peasant chorus singer was not inflected with individual characteristics, as previously believed by the *kuchkist* composers, but rather strived for a kind of impersonality. In the preface to her *Peasant Songs* she described this last quality:

[A peasant woman called Mitrevna] started singing my favourite song, 'Little Torch', which I had been looking for everywhere but had not yet succeeded in recording. Mitrevna took the main melody. She sang in a deep sonorous voice, surprisingly fresh for a woman so old. In her singing there were absolutely no sentimental emphases or howlings. What struck me was its simplicity. The song flowed evenly and clearly, not a single word was lost. Despite the length of the melody and the slowness of the tempo, the spirit with which she invested the words of the song was so powerful that she seemed at once to be singing and speaking the song. I was amazed at this pure, classical strictness of style, which went so well with her serious face.[137]

---

* Because he had found, in Russian peasant music, his own alternative to the German symphonism of the nineteenth century, Stravinsky did not share the interest of other modernists such as Schoenberg, Berg and Webern in serial (twelve-tone) music. It was only after 1945 that Stravinsky began to develop his own form of serialism.

It was precisely this 'classical' quality that became so central, not just to the music of Stravinsky, but to the whole theory of primitivist art. As Bakst put it, the 'austere forms of savage art are a new way forward from European art'.[138]

In *Petrushka* (1911) Stravinsky used the sounds of Russian life to overturn the entire musical establishment with its European rules of beauty and technique. Here was another Russian revolution – a musical uprising by the lowlife of St Petersburg. Everything about the ballet was conceived in ethnographic terms. Benois' scenario conjured up in detail the vanished fairground world of the Shrovetide carnival of his beloved childhood in St Petersburg. Fokine's mechanistic choreography echoed the jerky ostinato rhythms which Stravinsky heard in vendors' cries and chants, organ-grinder tunes, accordion melodies, factory songs, coarse peasant speech and the syncopated music of village bands.[139] It was a kind of musical *lubok* – a symphonic tableau of the noises of the street.

But of all Stravinsky's Russian ballets, by far the most subversive was *The Rite of Spring* (1913). The idea of the ballet was originally conceived by the painter Nikolai Roerich, although Stravinsky, who was quite notorious for such distortions, later claimed it as his own. Roerich was a painter of the prehistoric Slavs and an accomplished archaeologist in his own right. He was absorbed in the rituals of neolithic Russia, which he idealized as a pantheistic realm of spiritual beauty where life and art were one, and man and nature lived in harmony. Stravinsky approached Roerich for a theme and he came to visit him at the artists' colony of Talashkino, where the two men worked together on the scenario of 'The Great Sacrifice', as *The Rite of Spring* was originally called. The ballet was conceived as a re-creation of the ancient pagan rite of human sacrifice. It was meant to *be* that rite – not to tell the story of the ritual but (short of actual murder) to re-create that ritual on the stage and thus communicate in the most immediate way the ecstasy and terror of the human sacrifice. The ballet's scenario was nothing like those of the romantic story ballets of the nineteenth century. It was simply put together as a succession of ritual acts: the tribal dance in adoration of the earth and sun; the choosing of the maiden for the sacrifice; the evocation of the ancestors by the elders of the tribe which forms the central rite of the sacrifice; and the chosen maiden's sacrificial dance, culminating in her death at the climax of the dance's feverish energy.

The evidence of human sacrifice in prehistoric Russia is by no means clear. Ethnographically it would have been more accurate to base the ballet on a midsummer rite (Kupala) in which Roerich had found some inconclusive evidence of human sacrifice among the Scythians – a fact he publicized in 1898.[140] Under Christianity the Kupala festival had merged with St John's Feast but traces of the ancient pagan rites had entered into peasant songs and ceremonials – especially the *khorovod*, with its ritualistic circular movements that played such a key role in *The Rite of Spring*. The switch to the pagan rite of spring (Semik) was partly an attempt to link the sacrifice with the ancient Slavic worship of the sun god Yarilo, who symbolized the notion of apocalyptic fire, the spiritual regeneration of the land through its destruction, in the mystical world view of the Symbolists. But the change was also based on the findings of folklorists such as Alexander Afanasiev, who had linked these vernal cults with sacrificial rituals involving maiden girls. Afanasiev's *magnum opus*, *The Slavs' Poetic View of Nature* (1866–9), a sort of Slavic *Golden Bough*, became a rich resource for artists like Stravinsky who sought to lend an ethnographic authenticity to their fantasies of ancient Rus'. Musorgsky, for example, borrowed heavily from Afanasiev's descriptions of the witches' sabbath for his *St John's Night on Bald Mountain*. Afanasiev worked on the questionable premise that the world view of the ancient Slavs could be reconstructed through the study of contemporary peasant rituals and folk beliefs. According to his study, there was still a fairly widespread peasant custom of burning effigies, as symbols of fertility, in ritualistic dances marking the commencement of the spring sowing. But in parts of Russia this custom had been replaced by a ritual that involved a beautiful maiden: the peasants would strip the young girl naked, dress her up in garlands (as Yarilo was pictured in the folk imagination), put her on a horse, and lead her through the fields as the village elders watched. Sometimes a dummy of the girl was burned.[141] Here essentially was the scenario of *The Rite of Spring*.

Artistically, the ballet strived for ethnographic authenticity. Roerich's costumes were drawn from peasant clothes in Tenisheva's collection at Talashkino. His primitivist sets were based on archaeol-

18. *Nikolai Roerich: costumes for the Adolescents in the
first production of* The Rite of Spring, *Paris, 1913*

ogy. Then there was Nijinsky's shocking choreography – the real
scandal of the ballet's infamous Paris première at the Théâtre des
Champs-Elysées on 29 May 1913. For the music was barely heard at
all in the commotion, the shouting and the fighting, which broke
out in the auditorium when the curtain first went up. Nijinsky had
choreographed movements which were ugly and angular. Everything
about the dancers' movements emphasized their weight instead of their
lightness, as demanded by the principles of classical ballet. Rejecting
all the basic positions, the ritual dancers had their feet turned inwards,
elbows clutched to the sides of their body and their palms held flat,
like the wooden idols that were so prominent in Roerich's mythic
paintings of Scythian Russia. They were orchestrated, not by steps and
notes, as in conventional ballets, but rather moved as one collective
mass to the violent off-beat rhythms of the orchestra. The dancers
pounded their feet on the stage, building up a static energy which
finally exploded, with electrifying force, in the sacrificial dance. This
rhythmic violence was the vital innovation of Stravinsky's score. Like
most of the ballet's themes, it was taken from the music of the peasantry.[142] There was nothing like these rhythms in Western art music

(Stravinsky said that he did not really know how to notate or bar them) – a convulsive pounding of irregular downbeats, requiring constant changes in the metric signature with almost every bar so that the conductor of the orchestra must throw himself about and wave his arms in jerky motions, as if performing a shamanic dance. In these explosive rhythms it is possible to hear the terrifying beat of the Great War and the Revolution of 1917.

7

The Revolution found Stravinsky in Clarens, Switzerland, where he had been stranded behind German lines since the outbreak of war in 1914. 'All my thoughts are with you in these unforgettable days of happiness', he wrote to his mother in Petrograd on hearing of the downfall of the monarchy in 1917.[143] Stravinsky had high hopes of the Revolution. In 1914 he had told the French writer Romain Rolland that he was 'counting on a revolution after the war to bring down the dynasty and establish a Slavic United States'. He claimed for Russia, as Rolland put it, 'the role of a splendid and healthy barbarism, pregnant with the seeds of new ideas that will change the thinking of the West'.[144] But Stravinsky's disillusionment was swift and emphatic. In the autumn of 1917 his beloved estate at Ustilug was ransacked and destroyed by the peasantry. For years he did not know its fate – though there were signs that it had been destroyed. Rummaging through a bookstall in Moscow in the 1950s, the conductor Gennady Rozhdestvensky found the title page of Debussy's *Preludes* (Book Two) inscribed by the composer 'To entertain my friend Igor Stravinsky': it had come from Ustilug.[145] Not knowing what had happened to the place for all these years could only have intensified Stravinsky's sense of loss. Ustilug was where Stravinsky had spent the happy summers of his childhood years – it was the patch of Russia which he felt to be his own – and his profound loathing of the Soviet regime was intimately linked to the anger which he felt at being robbed of his own past. (Nabokov's politics were similarly defined by his 'lost childhood' at the family estate of Vyra, a vanished world he retrieved through *Speak, Memory*.)

19. *Stravinsky transcribes a folk song sung by a peasant* gusli *player on the porch of the Stravinsky house at Ustilug, 1909. Stravinsky's mother, Anna, holds Theodore, his son*

Stravinsky did the same through his music. Cut off from Russia, he felt an intense longing for his native land. His notebooks from the war years are filled with notations of Russian peasant songs which reappeared in *Four Russian Songs* (1918–19). The final song in this quartet was taken from an Old Believer story about a sinful man who cannot find a path back towards God. Its words read like a lament of the exile's tortured soul: 'Snowstorms and blizzards close all the roads to Thy Kingdom.' Stravinsky seldom talked about this brief and haunting song. Yet his notebooks show that he laboured over it, and that he made frequent changes to the score. The song's five pages are the product of no fewer than thirty-two pages of musical sketching. It suggests how much he struggled to find the right musical expression for these words.[146]

Stravinsky laboured even longer on *The Peasant Wedding* (*Svadebka*), a work begun before the First World War and first performed in Paris (as *Les Noces*) nine years later, in 1923. He worked on it longer than on any other score. The ballet had its origins in his final trip to Ustilug. Stravinsky had been working on the idea of a ballet that would re-create the wedding rituals of the peasantry and, knowing that his library contained useful transcriptions of peasant songs, he made a hurried trip to Ustilug to fetch them just before the outbreak of war. The sources became, for him, a sort of talisman of the Russia he had lost. For several years he worked on these folk songs, trying to distil the essence of his people's musical language, and striving to combine it with the austere style which he had first developed in *The Rite of Spring*. He thinned out his instrumental formula, rejecting the large Romantic orchestra for the small ensemble, using pianos, cimbaloms and percussion instruments to create a simpler, more mechanistic sound. But his truly momentous discovery was that, in contrast to the language and the music of the West, the accents of spoken Russian verse were ignored when that verse was sung. Looking through the song books he had retrieved from Ustilug, Stravinsky suddenly realized that the stress in folk songs often fell on the 'wrong' syllable. 'The recognition of the musical possibilities inherent in this fact was one of the most rejoicing discoveries of my life,' he explained to his musical assistant Robert Craft; 'I was like a man who suddenly finds that his finger can be bent from the second joint as well as from the first.'[147] The freedom of accentuation in the peasant song had a clear affinity with the ever-shifting rhythms of his own music in *The Rite of Spring*; both had the effect of sparkling play or dance. Stravinsky now began writing music for the pleasure of the sound of individual words, or for the joy of puns and rhyming games, like the Russian limericks (*Pribautki*) which he set to music in 1918. But beyond such entertainments, his discovery came as a salvation for the exiled composer. It was as if he had found a new homeland in this common language with the Russian peasantry. Through music he could recover the Russia he had lost.

This was the idea behind *The Peasant Wedding* – an attempt, in his own words, to re-create in art an essential ur-Russia, the ancient peasant Russia that had been concealed by the thin veneer of European civilization since the eighteenth century. It was

the holy Russia of the Orthodox, a Russia stripped of its parasitic vegetation; its bureaucracy from Germany, a certain strain of English liberalism much in fashion with the aristocracy; its scientism (alas!), its 'intellectuals' and their inane and bookish faith in progress; it is the Russia of before Peter the Great and before Europeanism . . . a peasant, but above all Christian, Russia, and truly the only Christian land in Europe, the one which laughs and cries (laughs and cries both at once without always really knowing which is which) in *The Peasant Wedding*, the one we saw awaken to herself in confusion and magnificently full of impurities in *The Rite of Spring*.[148]

Stravinsky had hit upon a form of music that expressed the vital energy and spirit of the people – a truly national music in the Stasovian sense. Stravinsky had drafted the first part of *The Peasant Wedding* by the end of 1914. When he played it to Diaghilev, the impresario broke down in tears and said it was 'the most beautiful and the most purely Russian creation of our Ballet'.[149]

The Peasant Wedding was a work of musical ethnography. In later years Stravinsky tried to deny this. Immersed in the cosmopolitan culture of interwar Paris, and driven by his hatred of the Soviet regime, he made a public show of distancing himself from his Russian heritage. But he was not convincing. The ballet was precisely what Stravinsky claimed that it was not: a direct expression of the music and the culture of the peasantry. Based on a close reading of the folklore sources, and drawing all its music from the peasants' wedding songs, the ballet's whole conception was to re-create the peasant wedding ritual as a work of art on stage.

Life and art were intimately linked. The Russian peasant wedding was itself performed as a series of communal rituals, each accompanied by ceremonial songs, and at certain junctures there were ceremonial dances like the *khorovod*. In the south of Russia, from where Stravinsky's folklore sources were derived, the wedding rite had four main parts. First there was the matchmaking, when two appointed elders, one male and one female, made the first approach to the household of the bride, followed by the inspection of the bride, when by custom she sang her lament for her family and her home. Next came the betrothal, the complex negotiations over the dowry and exchange of property and the sealing of the contract with a vodka toast, which was witnessed by the whole community and marked symbolically by the singing of the song of 'Cosmas and Demian', the patron saints of blacksmiths (for, as the peasants said, all marriages were 'forged'). Then came the prenuptial rituals like the washing of the bride and the *devichnik* (the unplaiting of the maiden's braid), accompanied by more laments, which were followed on the morning of the wedding by the blessing of the bride with the family icon and then, amid the wailing of the village girls, her departure for the church. Finally there was the wedding ceremony itself, followed by the marriage feast. Stravinsky rearranged these rituals into four tableaux in a way that emphasized the coming together of the bride and groom as 'two rivers into one': 1) 'At the Bride's'; 2) 'At the Groom's'; 3) 'Seeing off the Bride'; and 4) 'The Wedding Feast'. The peasant wedding was taken as a symbol of the family's communion in the village culture of these ancient rituals. It was portrayed as a collective rite – the binding of the bridal couple to the patriarchal culture of the peasant community – rather than as a romantic union between two individuals.

It was a commonplace in the Eurasian circles in which Stravinsky moved in Paris that the greatest strength of the Russian people, and the thing that set them apart from the people of the West, was their voluntary surrender of the individual will to collective rituals and forms of life. This sublimation of the individual was precisely what had attracted Stravinsky to the subject of the ballet in the first place – it was a perfect vehicle for the sort of peasant music he had been composing since *The Rite of Spring*. In *The Peasant Wedding* there was no room for emotion in the singing parts. The voices were supposed to merge as one, as they did in church chants and peasant singing, to create a sound Stravinsky once described as 'perfectly homogeneous, perfectly impersonal, and perfectly mechanical'. The same effect was produced by the choice of instruments (the result of a ten-year search for an essential 'Russian' sound): four pianos (on the stage), cimbalom and bells and percussion instruments – all of which were scored to play 'mechanically'. The reduced size and palette of the orchestra (it was meant to sound like a peasant wedding band) were reflected in the muted colours of Goncharova's sets. The great colourist abandoned the vivid reds and bold peasant patterns of her original designs for the minimalist pale blue of the sky and the deep browns of the earth which were used in the production. The choreography (by Bronislava Nijinska) was equally impersonal – the *corps de ballet* moving all as one, like some vast machine made of human beings, and carrying the whole of the storyline. 'There were no leading parts', Nijinska explained; 'each member would blend through the movement into the whole ... [and] the action of the separate characters would be expressed, not by each one individually, but rather by the action of the whole ensemble.'[150] It was the perfect ideal of the Russian peasantry.

5

overleaf:
*Natalia Goncharova: backdrop design
for* The Firebird *(1926)*

IN SEARCH OF THE
RUSSIAN SOUL

1

The monastery of Optina Pustyn nestles peacefully between the pine forests and the meadows of the Zhizdra river near the town of Kozelsk in Kaluga province, 200 kilometres or so south of Moscow. The whitewashed walls of the monastery and the intense blue of its cupolas, with their golden crosses sparkling in the sun, can be seen for miles against the dark green background of the trees. The monastery was cut off from the modern world, inaccessible by railway or by road in the nineteenth century, and pilgrims who approached the holy shrine, by river boat or foot, or by crawling on their knees, were often overcome by the sensation of travelling back in time. Optina Pustyn was the last great refuge of the hermitic tradition that connected Russia with Byzantium, and it came to be regarded as the spiritual centre of the national consciousness. All the greatest writers of the nineteenth century – Gogol, Dostoevsky and Tolstoy among them – came here in their search for the 'Russian soul'.

The monastery was founded in the fourteenth century. But it did not become well known until the beginning of the nineteenth century, when it was at the forefront of a revival in the medieval hermitic tradition and a hermitage, or skete, was built within its walls. The building of the skete was a radical departure from the Spiritual Regulations of the Holy Synod, which had banned such hermitages since 1721. The Spiritual Regulations were a sort of constitution of the Church. They were anything but spiritual. It was the Regulations which established the subordination of the Church to the Imperial state. The Church was governed by the Holy Synod, a body of laymen and clergy appointed by the Tsar to replace the Patriarchate, which was abolished in 1721. The duty of the clergy, as set out in the Regulations, was to uphold and enforce the Tsar's authority, to read out state decrees from the pulpit, to carry out administrative duties for the state, and inform the police about all dissent and criminality, even if such information had been obtained through the confessional. The Church, for the most part, was a faithful tool in the hands of the Tsar. It was not in its interests to rock the boat. During the eighteenth century a large proportion of its lands had been taken from it by the state, so the Church was dependent on the state's finances to support the parish clergy and their families.* Impoverished and venal, badly educated and proverbially fat, the parish priest was no advertisement for the established Church. As its spiritual life declined, people broke away from the official Church to join the Old Believers or the diverse sects which flourished from the eighteenth century by offering a more obviously religious way of life.

Within the Church, meanwhile, there was a growing movement of revivalists who looked to the traditions of the ancient monasteries like Optina for a spiritual rebirth. Church and state authorities alike were wary of this revivalist movement in the monasteries. If the monastic clergy were allowed to set up their own communities of Christian brotherhood, with their own pilgrim followings and sources of income, they could become a source of spiritual dissent from the established doctrines of Church and state. There would be no control on the social influence or moral teaching of the monasteries. At Optina, for example, there was a strong commitment to give alms and spiritual comfort to the poor which attracted a mass following. None the less, certain sections of the senior clergy displayed a growing interest in the mystical ideas of Russia's ancient hermits. The ascetic principles of Father Paissy, who led this Church revival in the latter part of the eighteenth century, were in essence a return to the hesychastic path of Russia's most revered medieval monks.

Hesychasm has its roots in the Orthodox conception of divine grace. In contrast to the Western view that grace is conferred on the virtuous or on those whom God has so ordained, the Orthodox religion regards grace as a natural state, implied in the act of creation itself, and therefore potentially available to any human being merely by virtue of having been created by the Lord. In this view the way the believer approaches God is through the consciousness of his own spiritual personality and by studying the example of Christ in order to cope better with the dangers that await him on his journey through life. The hesychastic monks believed that they could find a way to God in their own hearts – by practising a life of poverty and prayer with the spiritual

---

* Unlike their Catholic counterparts, Russian Orthodox priests were required to marry. Only the monastic clergy were not.

guidance of a 'holy man' or 'elder' who was in touch with the 'energies' of God. The great flowering of this doctrine came in the late fifteenth century, when the monk Nil Sorsky denounced the Church for owning land and serfs. He left his monastery to become a hermit in the wilderness of the Volga's forest lands. His example was an inspiration to thousands of hermits and schismatics. Fearful that Sorsky's doctrine of poverty might provide the basis for a social revolution, the Church suppressed the hesychastic movement. But Sorsky's ideas re-emerged in the eighteenth century, when clergymen like Paissy began to look again for a more spiritual church.

Paissy's ideas were gradually embraced in the early decades of the nineteenth century by clergy who saw them as a general return to 'ancient Russian principles'. In 1822, just over one hundred years after it had been imposed, the ban on sketes was lifted and a hermitage was built at Optina Pustyn, where Father Paissy's ideas had their greatest influence. The skete was the key to the renaissance of the monastery in the nineteenth century. Here was its inner sanctuary where up to thirty hermits lived in individual cells, in silent contemplation and in strict obedience to the elder, or *starets*, of the monastery.[1] Three great elders, each a disciple of Father Paissy and each in turn renowned for his devout ways, made Optina famous in its golden age: Father Leonid was the elder of the monastery from 1829; Father Makary from 1841; and Father Amvrosy from 1860 to 1891. It was the charisma of these elders that made the monastery so extraordinary – a sort of 'clinic for the soul' – drawing monks and other pilgrims in their thousands from all over Russia every year. Some came to the elder for spiritual guidance, to confess their doubts and seek advice; others for his blessing or a cure. There was even a separate settlement, just outside the walls of the monastery, where people came to live so that they could see the elder every day.[2] The Church was wary of the elders' popularity. It was fearful of the saint-like status they enjoyed among their followers, and it did not know enough about their spiritual teachings, especially their cult of poverty and their broadly social vision of a Christian brotherhood, to say for sure that they were not a challenge to the established Church. Leonid met with something close to persecution in his early years. The diocesan authorities tried to stop the crowds of pilgrims from visiting the elder in the monastery. They put

20. *Hermits at a monastery in northern Russia. Those standing have taken the vows of the schema (skhima), the strictest monastic rules in the Orthodox Church. Their habits show the instruments of the martyrdom of Christ and a text in Church Slavonic from Luke 9:24*

up Father Vassian, an old monk at Optina (and the model for Father Ferrapont in *The Brothers Karamazov*), to denounce Leonid in several published tracts.[3] Yet the elders were to survive as an institution. They were held in high esteem by the common people, and they gradually took root in Russia's monasteries, albeit as a spiritual force that spilled outside the walls of the official Church.

It was only natural that the nineteenth-century search for a true Russian faith should look back to the mysticism of medieval monks. Here was a form of religious consciousness that seemed to touch a chord in the Russian people, a form of consciousness that was somehow more essential and emotionally charged than the formalistic religion of the official Church. Here, moreover, was a faith in sympathy with the Romantic sensibility. Slavophiles like Kireevsky, who began the pilgrimage of intellectuals to Optina, discovered a reflection of their own Romantic aversion to abstract reason in the anti-rational approach to the divine mystery which they believed to be the vital feature of the Russian Church and preserved at its purest in the monasteries. They saw the monastery as a religious version of their own striving for community – a sacred microcosm of their ideal Russia – and on that basis they defined the Church as a spiritual union of the Orthodox, the true community of Christian love that was only to be found in the Russian Church. This was a Slavophile mythology, of course, but there was a core of mysticism in the Russian Church. Unlike the Western Churches, whose theology is based on a reasoned understanding of divinity, the Russian Church believes that God cannot be grasped by the human mind (for anything we can know is inferior to Him) and that even to discuss God in such human categories is to reduce the Divine Mystery of His revelation. The only way to approach the Russian God is through the spiritual transcendence of this world.[4]

This emphasis on the mystical *experience* of the Divinity was associated with two important features of the Russian Church. One was the creed of resignation and withdrawal from life. The Russian monasteries were totally devoted to the contemplative life and, compared to their counterparts in western Europe, they played little part in public life. Orthodoxy preached humility and, more than any other Church, it made a cult of passive suffering (the first saints of the Russian Church, the medieval princes Boris and Gleb, were canonized because they let themselves be slaughtered without resistance). The second consequence of this mystical approach was the burden that it placed on ritual and art, on the emotional experience of the liturgy, as a spiritual entry to the divine realm. The beauty of the church – the most striking outward feature of the Orthodox religion – was its fundamental argument as well. According to a story in the *Primary Chronicle*, the first recorded history of Kievan Rus', compiled by monks in the eleventh century, the Russians were converted to Byzantine Christianity by the appearance of the churches in Constantinople. Vladimir, the pagan prince of Kievan Rus' in the tenth century, sent his emissaries to visit various countries in search of the True Faith. They went first to the Muslim Bulgars of the Volga, but found no joy or virtue in their religion. They went to Rome and Germany, but thought their churches plain. But in Constantinople, the emissaries reported, 'we knew not whether we were in heaven or on earth, for surely there is no such splendour or beauty anywhere on earth'.[5]

The Russian Church is contained entirely in its liturgy, and to understand it there is no point reading books: one has to go and see the Church at prayer. The Russian Orthodox service is an emotional experience. The entire spirit of the Russian people, and much of their best art and music, has been poured into the Church, and at times of national crisis, under the Mongols or the Communists, they have always turned to it for support and hope. The liturgy has never become the preserve of scholars or the clergy, as happened in the medieval West. This is a people's liturgy. There are no pews, no social hierarchies, in a Russian church. Worshippers are free to move around – as they do constantly to prostrate and cross themselves before the various icons – and this makes for an atmosphere that is not unlike a busy market square. Chekhov describes it in his story 'Easter Night' (1886):

Nowhere could the excitement and commotion be felt as keenly as in the church. At the door there was a relentless wrestle going on between the ebb and flow. Some people were coming in, and others were going out, but then they were soon coming back again, just to stand for a while before leaving again. There were people scuttling from one place to another, and then hanging about as if they were looking for something. Waves started at the door and rippled through the church, disturbing even the front rows where there were serious worthy people standing. There could be no question of any concentrated praying. There was no praying at all in fact, just a kind of sheer, irrepressible childlike joy looking for a pretext to burst forth and be expressed in some kind of movement, even if it was only the shameless moving about and the crowding together.

You are struck by the same same kind of extraordinary sense of motion in the Easter service itself. The heavenly gates stand wide open in all the side-altars, dense clouds of smoky incense hang in the air around the candelabra; wherever you look there are lights, brightness and candles spluttering every-where. There are no readings planned; the energetic, joyful singing does not stop until the end; after each song in the canon the clergy change their vestments and walk around with the censor, and this is repeated every ten minutes almost.[6]

Anyone who goes to a Russian church service is bound to be impressed by the beauty of its chants and choral song. The entire liturgy is sung – the sonorous bass voice of the deacon's prayers interspersed with canticles from the choir. Orthodoxy's ban on instru-mental music encouraged a remarkable development of colour and variety in vocal writing for the Church. The polyphonic harmonies of folk song were assimilated to the *znamenny* plainchants – so called because they were written down by special signs (*znameni*) instead of Western notes – which gave them their distinctive Russian sound and feel. As in Russian folk song, too, there was a constant repetition of the melody, which over several hours (the Orthodox service can be interminably long) could have the effect of inducing a trance-like state of religious ecstasy. Churches famous for their deacons and their choirs drew huge congregations – Russians being drawn to the spiritual impact of liturgical music, above all. Part of this, however, may have been explained by the fact that the Church had a monopoly on the composition of sacred music – Tchaikovsky was the first to challenge it when he wrote the *Liturgy of St John Chrysostom* in 1878 – so that it was not until the final decades of the nineteenth century that the public could hear sacred music in a concert hall. Rachmaninov's *Vespers*, or *All Night Vigil* (1915), was intended to be used as a part of the liturgy. The summation of Rachmaninov's religious faith, it was based on a detailed study of the ancient chants and in this sense it can stand not simply as a work of sacred art but also as the synthesis of an entire culture of religious life.

Russians pray with their eyes open – their gaze fixed on an icon. For contemplating the icon is itself perceived as a form of prayer. The icon is a gateway to the holy sphere, not a decoration or instruction for the poor, as sacred images became in western Europe from medieval times. In contrast to the Catholics, the Orthodox confess, not to a priest, but to the icon of Christ with a priest in attendance as a spiritual guide. The icon is the focal point of the believer's religious emotion – it links him to the saints and the Holy Trinity – and for this reason it is widely seen by Russians as a sacred object in itself. Even an 'outsider' like Kireevsky, who had been a convert to the Roman Church, felt himself attracted to the icon's 'marvellous power'. As he told Herzen:

I once stood at a shrine and gazed at a wonder-working icon of the Mother of God, thinking of the childlike faith of the people praying before it; some women and infirm old men knelt, crossing themselves and bowing down to the earth. With ardent hope I gazed at the holy features, and little by little the secret of their marvellous power began to grow clear to me. Yes, this was not just a painted board – for centuries it had absorbed these passions and these hopes, the prayers of the afflicted and unhappy; it was filled with the energy of all these prayers. It had become a living organism, a meeting place between the Lord and men. Thinking of this, I looked once more at the old men, at the women and the children prostrate in the dust, and at the holy icon – and then I too saw the animated features of the Mother of God, and I saw how she looked with love and mercy at these simple folk, and I sank on my knees and meekly prayed to her.[7]

Icons came to Russia from Byzantium in the tenth century, and for the first two hundred years or so they were dominated by the Greek style. But the Mongol invasion in the thirteenth century cut off Russia from Byzantium; and the monasteries, which were largely left alone and even flourished at this time, began to develop their own style. The Russian icon came to be distinguished by qualities that guided the worshipper at prayer: a simple harmony of line and colour and a captivating use of 'inverse perspective' (where lines seem to converge on a point in front of the picture) to draw the viewer into the picture space and to symbolize the fact, in the words of Russia's greatest icon scholar Leonid Ouspensky, that 'the action taking place before our eyes is outside the laws of earthly existence'.[8] That style reached its supreme heights in Andrei Rublev's icons of the early fifteenth century – an era coinciding with Russia's triumph over Tatar rule, so that this flowering of sacred art became a cherished part of national identity. Rublev's icons came to represent the nation's spiritual unity. What defined the Russians – at this crucial moment when they were without a state – was their Christianity. Readers may recall the last, symbolic scene of Andrei Tarkovsky's film about the icon painter, *Andrei Rublev* (1966), when a group of craftsmen cast a giant bell for the ransacked church of Vladimir. It is an unforgettable image – a symbol of the way in which the Russians have endured through their spiritual strength and creativity. Not surprising, then, that the film was suppressed in the Brezhnev years.

It is hard to overstress the importance of the fact that Russia received its Christianity from Byzantium and not from the West. It was in the spirit of the Byzantine tradition that the Russian Empire came to see itself as a theocracy, a truly Christian realm where Church and state were united. The god-like status of the Tsar was a legacy of this tradition.[9] After the fall of Constantinople to the Turks, the Russian Church proclaimed Moscow to be the Third Rome – the direct heir to Byzantium and the last remaining seat of the Orthodox religion, with a messianic role to save the Christian world. This Byzantine inheritance was strengthened by the marriage of Ivan III to Sofia Paleologue, the niece of Byzantium's last Emperor, Constantine, in 1472. The ruling princes of Muscovy adopted the title 'Tsar' and invented for themselves a legendary descent from the Byzantine and Roman emperors. 'Holy Russia' thus emerged as the providential land of salvation – a messianic consciousness that became reinforced by its isolation from the West.

With Byzantium's decline, Russia was cut off from the mainstream of Christian civilization and, by the end of the fifteenth century, it was the only major kingdom still espousing Eastern Christianity. As a consequence, the Russian Church grew introspective and withdrawn, more intolerant of other faiths, and more protective of its national rituals. It became a state and national Church. Culturally the roots of this went deep into the history of Byzantium itself. Unlike the Western Church, Byzantium had no papacy to give it supranational cohesion.

It had no lingua franca like Latin – the Russian clergy, for example, being mostly ignorant of Greek – and it was unable to impose a common liturgy or canon law. So from the start the Orthodox community was inclined to break down into independent Churches along national lines (Greek, Russian, Serbian, etc.) – with the result that religion reinforced, and often became synonymous with, national identity. To say 'Russian' was to say 'Orthodox'.

The rituals of the Church were the basis of these national differences. There was one essential doctrine – set long ago by the Church Fathers – but each national Church had its own tradition of rituals as a community of worshippers. For the Western reader, accustomed to conceive of religious differences in terms of doctrine and moral attitudes, it may be difficult to understand how rituals can define a national group. But rituals are essential to the Orthodox religion – indeed, the very meaning of the concept 'Orthodox' is rooted in the idea of the 'correct rituals'. This explains why Orthodoxy is so fundamentally conservative – for purity of ritual is a matter of the utmost importance to the Church – and why indeed its dissenting movements have generally opposed any innovations in the liturgy, the Old Believers being the most obvious case in point.

The whole of Russian life in the eighteenth and nineteenth centuries was permeated with religious rituals. At birth the Russian child would be baptized and given a saint's name. The annual celebration of a person's saint's day was even more important than that of their birthday. Every major event in a Russian's life – entry into school and university, joining the army or civil service, purchasing an estate or house, marriage and death – received some form of blessing from a priest. Russia had more religious holidays than any other Christian country. But no other Church was so hard on the stomach. There were five weeks of fasting during May and June, two weeks in August, six weeks leading up to Christmas Eve, and seven weeks during Lent. The Lenten fast, which was the one fast kept by all classes of society, began after Shrovetide, the most colourful of the Russian holidays, when everybody gorged themselves on pancakes and went for sleigh rides or tobogganing. Anna Lelong, who grew up on a medium-sized estate in Riazan province in the 1840s, recalled the Shrovetide holiday as a moment of communion between lord and serf.

At around 2 p.m. on the Sunday of Shrovetide, horses would be harnessed up to two or three sleighs and a barrel would be put on the driver's seat of one of them. Old Vissarion would stand on it, dressed up in a cape made of matting and a hat decorated with bast leaves. He would drive the first sleigh and behind him would be other sleighs on which our servants crowded, singing songs. They would ride round the whole village and mummers from other villages would join them on their sleighs. A huge convoy would build up and the whole procession lasted until dusk. At around seven our main room would fill with people. The peasants had come to 'bid farewell' before the Lenten journey. Each one had a bundle in his hands with various offerings, such as rolls or long white loaves, and sometimes we children were given spiced cakes or dark honey loaves. We would exchange kisses with the peasants and wish each other well for the Lenten period. The offerings were put in a large basket and the peasants were given vodka and salted fish. On Sunday only our own Kartsevo peasants came to say goodbye, and peasants from other nearby villages would come on the Saturday. When the peasants left, the room would have to be sealed tightly as it smelt of sheepskin coats and mud. Our last meal before Lent began with special pancakes called 'tuzhiki'. We had fish soup, and cooked fish which was also given to the servants.[10]

In Moscow there would be skating on the ice of the Moscow river, where a famous fairground with circuses and puppet shows, acrobats and jugglers would draw huge crowds of revellers. But the aspect of the city would change dramatically on the first day of Lent. 'The endless ringing of bells called everyone to prayer', recalled Mikhail Zernov. 'Forbidden food was banished from all houses and a mushroom market started up on the banks of the Moscow river, where one could buy everything one needed to survive the fast – mushrooms, pickled cabbage, gherkins, frozen apples and rowanberries, all kinds of bread made with Lenten butter, and a special type of sugar with the blessing of the Church.'[11] During Lent there were daily services. With every passing day the religious tension mounted, until its release in Easter week, recalled Zernov.

On the eve of Easter Moscow broke out of its ordered services and a screaming, raving market opened on Red Square. Ancient pagan Rus' was greeting the arrival of warm days and throwing down the gauntlet to orderly Orthodox piety. We went every year to take part in this traditional Moscow celebration with our father. Even from far away, as you approached Red Square, you could hear the sounds of whistles, pipes and other kinds of homemade instruments. The whole square was full of people. We moved among the puppet booths, the tents and stalls that had appeared overnight. Our religious justification was buying willow branches for the All Night Vigil to mark Jesus's entry into Jerusalem. But we preferred the other stalls which sold all kinds of weird and useless things, such as 'sea dwellers' living in glass tubes filled with coloured liquid, or monkeys made from wool. It was difficult to see how they connected with Palm Sunday. There were colourful balloons with wonderful designs, and Russian sweets and cakes which we were not allowed. Nor could we go to see the woman with moustaches, or the real mermaids, or the calves with a double head.[12]

The Easter service is the most important service, and the most beautiful, in the Russian Church. As Gogol once remarked, the Russians have a special interest in celebrating Easter – for theirs is a faith based on hope. Shortly before midnight every member of the congregation lights a candle and, to the subdued singing of the choir, leaves the church in a procession with icons and banners. There is an atmosphere of rising expectation, suddenly released at the stroke of midnight, when the church doors open and the priest appears to proclaim in his deep bass voice 'Christ is risen!' – to which he receives the response from the thronging worshippers: 'He is risen indeed!' Then, as the choir chants the Resurrection Chant, the members of the congregation greet one another with a three-fold kiss and the words 'Christ is risen!' Easter was a truly national moment – a moment of communion between the classes. The landowner Maria Nikoleva recalled Easter with her serfs:

The peasants would come directly from church to exchange Easter greetings. There would be at least 500 of them. We would kiss them on the cheek and give them each a piece of *kulich* [Easter cake] and an egg. Everyone had the right to wander all over our house on that day and I do not remember anything going missing or even being touched. Our father would be in the front room, where he received the most important and respected peasants, old men and elders. He would give them wine, pie, cooked meat and in the maids' room our nanny would give out beer or homebrew. We received so many kisses from faces with beards that were not always very clean that we had to wash quickly so we wouldn't get a rash.[13]

The procession of the icons on the Easter Monday, in which icons were brought to every house for a blessing, was another ritual of communion. Vera Kharuzina, the first woman to become a professor of ethnography in Russia, has left us with a wonderful description of an icon being received in a wealthy merchant household in Moscow during the 1870s:

There were so many people who wanted to receive the Icon of the Heavenly Virgin and the Martyr that a list was always made up and an order given out to set the route of the procession round the city. My father always went to work early, so he preferred to invite the icon and the relics either early in the morning or late at night. The icon and the relics came separately and almost never coincided. But their visits left a deep impression. The adults in the house would not go to bed all night. Mother would just lie down for a while on the sofa. My father and my aunt would not eat anything from the previous evening onwards so as to be able to drink the holy water on an empty stomach. We children were put to bed early, and got up a long time before the arrival. The plants would be moved from the corner in the front room and a wooden divan put in their place, on which the icon could rest. A table would be placed in front of the divan and on it a snow white table cloth. A bowl of water would be placed on it for blessing, a dish with an empty glass, ready for the priest to pour holy water into it, candles and incense. The whole house would be tense with expectation. My father and my aunt would pace from window to window, waiting to see the carriage arrive. The icon and the relics would be transported about the city in a special carriage, which was extremely solid and cumbersome. The housekeeper would be standing in the hall, surrounded by her servants, who were ready to carry out her requests. The doorman would be looking out for the guests and we knew he would run to the front door as soon as he saw the carriage in the lane and knock hard in order to warn us of its arrival. Then we would hear the thunder of six strong horses approaching the gates. A young boy as postilion would sit at the front and a sturdy man would be posted at the back. Despite the severe frost at that time of year, both would travel with their heads uncovered. A cluster of people led by our housekeeper would take the heavy icon and carry it up the front steps with difficulty. Our whole family would greet the icon in the doorway, genuflecting before it. A stream of frosty air would blow in from outside through the open doors, which we found bracing. The service of prayer would begin and the servants, accompanied by their relatives sometimes, would crowd at the door. Aunt would take the glass of holy water standing in the dish from the priest. She would take the glass to everyone to sip from, and they would also dip their fingers in the water in the dish and touch their faces with it. Our housekeeper would follow the priest around the room with the aspergillum and the bowl of holy water. Meanwhile everyone would go up to touch the icon – at first father and mother, then our aunt, and then we children. After us came the servants and those with them. We would take holy cotton wool from bags attached to the icon and wipe our eyes with it. After the prayers, the icon would be taken through the other rooms and outside again into the courtyard. Some people would prostrate themselves before it. The people carrying the icon would step over them. The icon would be taken straight out into the street and passers-by would be waiting to touch it. That moment of common brief prayer would join us to those people – people we did not even know and would probably never see again. Everyone would stand and cross themselves and bow as the icon was put back in the carriage. We would stand at the front door with our fur coats over our shoulders, then we would rush back into the house so as not to catch cold. There was still a festive mood in the house. In the dining room everything would be ready for tea, and aunt would sit by the *samovar* with a joyful expression.[14]

Religious rituals were at the heart of the Russian faith and national consciousness. They were also the main cause of a schism in the Orthodox community that split the Russian nation into two. In the 1660s the Russian Church adopted a series of reforms to bring its rituals closer to the Greek. It was thought that over time there had been deviations in the Russian liturgy which needed to be brought back into line. But the Old Believers argued that the Russian rituals were in fact holier than those of the Greek Church, which had fallen from grace by merging with Rome at the Council of Florence in 1439. In the Old Believers' view the Greeks had been punished for this act of apostasy by the loss of Constantinople in 1453, when the centre of Orthodoxy had passed to Moscow. To the Western reader the schism may appear to be about some obscure points of ritual (the most contentious reform altered the manner of making the sign of the cross from two to three fingers) that pale into insignificance when compared with the great doctrinal disputes of Western Christendom in the sixteenth and seventeenth centuries. But in Russia, where faith and ritual and national consciousness were so closely associated, the schism assumed eschatological proportions. As the Old Believers saw it, the reforms were the work of the Antichrist, and a sign that the end of the world was near. During the last decades of the seventeenth century dozens of communities of Old Believers rose up in rebellion: as the forces of the state approached they shut themselves inside their wooden churches and burned themselves to death rather than defile themselves before Judgement Day by coming into contact with the Antichrist. Many others followed the example of the hermits and fled to the remote lakes and forests of the north, to the Volga borderlands, to the Don Cossack regions in the south, or to the forests of Siberia. In places like the shores of the White Sea they set up their own utopian communities, where they hoped to live in a truly Christian realm of piety and virtue untouched by the evil of the Russian Church and state. Elsewhere, as in Moscow in the eighteenth and nineteenth centuries, they tended to remain in particular neighbourhoods like the Zamoskvoreche. The Old Believers were a broad social movement of religious and political dissent. Their numbers grew as the spiritual life of the established Church declined and it became subordinated to the state in the eighteenth century. By the beginning of the twentieth century their numbers peaked at an estimated 20 million, though their continued persecution by Church and state makes it difficult to say with any certainty that there were not still more in the wilderness.[15]

In many ways the Old Believers remained more faithful than the established Church to the spiritual ideals of the common people, from which they drew their democratic strength. The nineteenth-century historian Pogodin once remarked that, if the ban on the Old Belief was lifted by the state, half the Russian peasants would convert to it.[16] Against the emerging Tsarist doctrine of an autocratic Christian state the Old Believers held up the ideal of a Christian nation which seemed to strike a chord with those who felt alienated from the secular and Westernizing state. Old Believer communities were strictly regulated by the rituals of their faith and the patriarchal customs of medieval Muscovy. They were simple farming communities, in which the honest virtues of hard work, thrift and sobriety were rigidly enforced and indoctrinated in the young. Many of the country's most successful peasant farmers, merchants and industrialists were brought up in the Old Belief.

Persecuted by the government for much of their history, the Old Believers had a strong libertarian tradition which acted as a magnet for the discontented and the dispossessed, for oppressed and marginalized groups, and above all for the Cossacks and members of the peasantry who resented the encroachments of the state against their customs and their liberties. The Old Believers refused to shave off their beards or put on Western clothes, as Peter the Great had demanded in the 1700s. They played a major role in the Cossack rebellions of the 1670s (led by Stenka Razin) and the 1770s (led by Emelian Pugachev). There was a strong anarchistic and egalitarian element in the Old Believer communities – especially in those which worshipped without priests (the *bezpoptsy*) on the reasoning that all priestly hierarchies were a corruption of the Church. At the heart of these communities was the ancient Russian quest for a truly spiritual kingdom on this earth. It had its roots in the popular belief, which was itself an early form of the national consciousness, that such a sacred kingdom might be found in 'Holy Rus''.

This utopian search was equally pursued by diverse peasant sects and religious wanderers, which also rejected the established Church and state: the 'Flagellants' or *Khlysty* (probably a corruption of *Khristy*, meaning 'Christs'), who believed that Christ had entered into living individuals – usually peasants who were seized by some mysterious spirit and wandered round the villages attracting followers (Rasputin was a member of this sect); the 'Fighters for the Spirit' (*Dukhobortsy*), who espoused a vague anarchism based on Christian principles and evaded all state taxes and military dues; the 'Wanderers' (*Stranniki*), who believed in severing all their ties with the existing state and society, seeing them as the realm of the Antichrist, and wandered as free spirits across the Russian land; the 'Milk-drinkers' (*Molokane*), who were convinced that Christ would reappear in the form of a simple peasant man; and, most exotic of them all, the 'Self-castrators' (*Skoptsy*), who believed that salvation came only with the excision of the instruments of sin.

Russia was a breeding ground for Christian anarchists and utopians. The mystical foundation of the Russian faith and the messianic basis of its national consciousness combined to produce in the common people a spiritual striving for the perfect Kingdom of God in the 'Holy Russian land'. Dostoevsky once maintained that 'this ceaseless longing, which has always been inherent in the Russian people, for a great universal church on earth', was the basis of 'our Russian socialism'.[17] And there was a sense in which this spiritual quest lay at the heart of the popular conception of an ideal Russian state where truth and justice (*pravda*) were administered. It was no coincidence, for example, that the Old Believers and sectarians were commonly involved in social protests – the Razin and Pugachev revolts, or the peasant demonstrations of 1861, when many former serfs, disappointed by the limited provisions of the emancipation, refused to believe that the Decree had been passed by the 'truly holy Tsar'. Religious dissent and social protest were bound to be connected in a country such as Russia, where popular belief in the god-like status of the Tsar played such a mighty and oppressive role. The peasantry believed in a Kingdom of God on this earth. Many of them conceived of heaven as an actual place in some remote corner of the world, where the rivers flowed with milk and the grass was always green.[18] This conviction inspired dozens of popular legends about a real Kingdom of God hidden somewhere in the Russian land. There were legends of the Distant Lands, of the Golden Islands, of the Kingdom of Opona, and the Land of Chud, a sacred kingdom underneath the ground where the 'White Tsar' ruled according to the 'ancient and truly just ideals' of the peasantry.[19]

The oldest of these folk myths was the legend of Kitezh – a sacred city that was hidden underneath the lake of Svetloyar (in Nizhegorod province) and was only visible to the true believers of the Russian faith. Holy monks and hermits were said to be able to hear its ancient churches' distant bells. The earliest oral versions of the legend went back to the days of Mongol rule. Kitezh was attacked by the infidels and at the crucial moment of the siege it magically disappeared into the lake, causing the Tatars to be drowned.

Over the centuries the legend became mixed with other stories about towns and monasteries concealed underground, magic realms and buried treasure under the sea, and legends of the folk hero Ilia Muromets. But in the early eighteenth century the Old Believers wrote the legend down, and it was in this form that it was disseminated in the nineteenth century. In the Old Believers' version, for instance, the Kitezh tale became a parable of the truly Christian Russia that was concealed from the Russia of the Antichrist. However, among the peasantry it became a vehicle for dissident beliefs that looked towards a spiritual community beyond the walls of the established Church. Throughout the nineteenth century pilgrims came to Svetloyar in their thousands to set up shrines and pray in hopeful expectation of a resurrection from the lake. The height of the season was the summer solstice, the old pagan festival of Kupala, when thousands of pilgrims would populate the forests all around the lake. The writer Zinaida Gippius, who visited the scene in 1903, described it as a kind of 'natural church' with little groups of worshippers, their icons posted to the trees, singing ancient chants by candlelight.[20]

Another of these utopian beliefs, no less tenacious in the popular religious consciousness, was the legend of Belovode, a community of Christian brotherhood, equality and freedom, said to be located in an archipelago between Russia and Japan. The story had its roots in a real community that had been established by a group of serfs who had fled to the mountainous Altai region of Siberia in the eighteenth century. When they did not return, the rumour spread that they had found the Promised Land. It was taken up, in particular, by the Wanderers, who believed in the existence of a divine realm somewhere at the edge of the existing world, and parties of the sect would journey to Siberia in search of it.[21] The legend grew in status after 1807, when a guidebook to Belovode was published by a monk who claimed to have been there and, although his directions on how to get there were extremely vague, hundreds of peasants set off each year by horse and cart or riverboat to find the legendary realm. The last recorded journeys, in the 1900s, seem to have been prompted by a rumour that Tolstoy had been to Belovode (a group of Cossacks visited the writer to see if this was true).[22] But long after this, Belovode remained in the people's dreams. The painter Roerich, who took an interest in the legend and visited the Altai in the 1920s, claimed to have met peasants there who still believed in the magic land.

2

'I stopped at the Hermitage at Optina', Gogol wrote to Count A. P. Tolstoy, 'and took away with me a memory that will never fade. Clearly, grace dwells in that place. You can feel it even in the outward signs of worship. Nowhere have I seen monks like those. Through every one of them I seemed to converse with heaven.' During his last years Gogol came to Optina on several occasions. He found comfort and spiritual guidance for his troubled soul in the tranquillity of the monastery. He thought he had found there the divine Russian realm for which he had searched all his life. Miles away from the monastery, he wrote to Tolstoy, 'one can smell the perfume of its virtues in the air: everything becomes hospitable, people bow more deeply, and brotherly love increases'.[23]

Nikolai Gogol came from a devout family in the Ukraine. Both his parents were active in the Church, and at home they kept to all the fasts and religious rituals. There was a tinge of mysticism in the Gogol household which helps to account for the writer's life and art. Gogol's parents met when his father had a vision in the local church: the Mother of God had appeared before him and, pointing to the young girl standing next to him, had said that she would become his wife, which indeed she did.[24] Like his parents, Gogol was not satisfied by the observance of the Church's rituals. From an early age he felt a need to experience the divine presence as a drama in his soul. In 1833 he wrote to his mother:

[in my childhood] I looked at everything with an impartial eye; I went to church because I was ordered to, or was taken; but once I was there I saw nothing but the chasuble, the priest and the awful howling of the deacons. I crossed myself because I saw everyone else crossing themselves. But one time – I can vividly remember it even now – I asked you to tell me about the Day of Judgement, and you told me so well, so thoroughly and so touchingly about the good things which await people who have led a worthy life, and you described the eternal torments awaiting sinners so expressively and so fearsomely that it stunned me and awoke in me all my sensitivity. Later on it engendered the most lofty thoughts in me.[25]

Gogol never had religious doubts, as Tolstoy and Dostoevsky did. The torments of his final years arose only from doubts about his own merits before God. But the intense nature of the writer's faith could not be contained within any Church. In some ways, as he himself acknowledged, his faith had much in common with the Protestant religion, in the sense that he believed in a personal relationship with Jesus Christ.[26] Yet in the six years which Gogol spent in Rome, from 1836 to 1842, he also became close to the Catholic tradition, and if he chose not to convert to Rome, it was only, in his words, because he saw no difference between the two creeds: 'Our religion is just the same thing as Catholicism – and there is no need to change from the one to the other.'[27] In the final version of *Dead Souls*, which he never published, Gogol planned to introduce the figure of a priest who would embody Orthodox and Catholic virtues. He seems to have been searching for a Christian brotherhood that would unite all the people in a spiritual Church. This is what he thought he had found at Optina and in the idea of the 'Russian soul'.

Gogol's fiction was the arena of this spiritual search. Contrary to the view of many scholars, there was no real divide between the 'literary works' of Gogol's early period and the 'religious works' of his final years, although he did reveal a more explicit interest in religious issues later on. All Gogol's writings have a theological significance – they were indeed the first in a national tradition that granted fiction the status of religious prophecy. Many of his stories are best read as religious allegories. Their grotesque and fantastic figures are not intended to be realistic – any more than icons aim to show the natural world. They are designed to let us contemplate another world where good and evil battle for man's soul. In Gogol's early stories this religious symbolism is embedded in biblical motifs and sometimes quite obscure religious metaphors. 'The Overcoat', for example, has echoes of the life of St Acacius – a hermit (and tailor) who died after years of torment by his elder, who later repented of his cruelty. This explains the hero's name, Akaky Akakievich – a humble civil servant of St Petersburg who dies unloved, robbed of his precious overcoat, but who then returns to haunt the city as a ghost.[28] After the 'failure' of *The Government Inspector* (1836) – a play intended as a moral parable but which the public took as a hilarious satire – Gogol sought to drive his religious message home. The work to which he then devoted all his energies was envisaged as a three-part novel called *Dead Souls* – an epic 'poem' in the style of Dante's *Divine Comedy* – in which the providential plan for Russia was at last to be revealed. The grotesque imperfections of provincial Russia exposed in the first, and only finished (1842) volume of the novel – where the adventurer Chichikov travels through the countryside swindling a series of moribund squires out of the legal title to their deceased serfs (or 'souls') – were to be negated by Gogol's lofty portrait of the 'living Russian soul' which he was intending for the second and third parts. Even the roguish Chichikov would eventually be saved, ending up as a paternal landowner, as Gogol moved towards the Slavic idyll of Christian love and brotherhood. The whole conception of the 'poem' was Russia's resurrection and its spiritual ascent on an 'infinite ladder of human perfection' – a metaphor he took from the parable of Jacob's ladder in the Book of Genesis.[29]

Gogol's divine vision was inspired by his champions, the Slavophiles, whose fantasy of Russia as a holy union of Christian souls was naturally attractive to a writer so disturbed by the soulless individualism of modern society. The Slavophile idea was rooted in the notion of the Russian Church as a free community of Christian brotherhood – a *sobornost'* (from the Russian word '*sobor*', which was used for both 'cathedral' and 'assembly') – as outlined by the theologian Aleksei Khomiakov in the 1830s and 1840s. Khomiakov came to his conception from a mystical theology. Faith could not be proved by reasoning, he said. It had to be arrived at by experience, by feeling from within the Truth of Christ, not by laws and dogmas. The True Church could not persuade or force men to believe, for it had no authority except the love of Christ. As a freely chosen community, it existed in the spirit of Christian love that bound the faithful to the Church – and this spirit was its only guarantee.

The Slavophiles believed that the True Church was the Russian one. Unlike the Western churches, which enforced their authority through laws and statist hierarchies like the Papacy, Russian Orthodoxy, as they saw it, was a truly spiritual community, whose only head was Christ. To be sure, the Slavophiles were critical of the established Church, which in their view had been spiritually weakened by its close alliance with the Tsarist state. They espoused a social Church, some would say a socialistic one, and many of their writings on religion were banned as a result (Khomiakov's theological writings were not published until 1879).[30] The Slavophiles were firm believers in the liberation of the serfs: for only the communion of fully free and conscious individuals could create the *sobornost'* of the True Church. They placed their faith in the Christian spirit of the Russian people, and this was the spirit which defined their Church. The Slavophiles believed that the Russian people were the only truly Christian people in the world. They pointed to the peasantry's communal way of life ('a Christian union of love and brotherhood'), to their peaceful, gentle nature and humility, to their immense patience and suffering, and to their willingness to sacrifice their individual egos for a higher moral good – be that for the commune, the nation or the Tsar. With all these Christian qualities, the Russians were far more than a nationality – they bore a divine mission in the world. In the words of Aksakov, 'the Russian people is not just a people, it is a humanity'.[31]

Here was the vision of the 'Russian soul' – of a universal spirit that would save the Christian world – which Gogol tried to picture in the second and third volumes of *Dead Souls*. The concept of a national soul or essence was commonplace in the Romantic age, though Gogol was the first to give the 'Russian soul' this messianic turn. The lead came from Germany, where Romantics like Friedrich Schelling developed the idea of a national spirit as a means to distinguish their own national culture from that of the West. In the 1820s Schelling had a godlike status in Russia, and his concept of the soul was seized upon by intellectuals who sought to contrast Russia with Europe. Prince Odoevsky, the archpriest of the Schelling cult in Russia, argued that the West had sold its soul to the Devil in the pursuit of material progress. 'Your soul has turned into a steam engine', he wrote in his novel *Russian Nights* (1844); 'I see screws and wheels in you but I don't see life.' Only Russia, with her youthful spirit, could save Europe now.[32] It stands to reason that young nations like Germany and Russia that lagged behind the industrializing West would have recourse to the idea of a national soul. What such nations lacked in economic progress they could more than make up for in the spiritual virtues of the unspoilt countryside. Nationalists attributed a creative spontaneity and fraternity to the simple peasantry that had long been lost in the bourgeois culture of the West. This was the vague Romantic sense in which the idea of the Russian soul began to develop from the final decades of the eighteenth century. In his essay 'On the Innate Qualities of the Russian Soul' (1792), Pyotr Plavilshikov maintained, for example, that in its peasantry Russia had a natural creativity that had more potential than the science of the West. Carried away by national pride, the playwright even claimed some unlikely firsts:

One of our peasants has made a tincture which all the learning of Hippocrates and Galen failed to find. The bone setter of the village Alekseevo is famous among pioneers of surgery. Kulibin and the mechanic Sobakin from Tver are marvels in mechanics ... What the Russian cannot grasp will for ever be unknown to men.[33]*

After the triumph of 1812 the idea of the peasant's soul, of his selfless virtue and self-sacrifice, began to be linked to the notion of Russia as the saviour of the West. This was the mission that Gogol first developed in *Dead Souls*. In his earlier story 'Taras Bulba' (1835) Gogol had attributed to the Russian soul a special kind of love that only Russians felt. 'There are no bonds more sacred than those of comradeship!' Taras Bulba tells his fellow Cossacks:

The father loves his child, the mother loves her child, a child loves its mother and father. But this is not the same, my brothers; a beast also loves its young. But the kinship of the spirit, rather than the blood, is something only known to man. Men have been comrades in other lands too, but there have never been comrades such as those in the Russian land ... No, brothers, to love as the Russian soul loves – that does not mean to love with the head or with some other part of you, it means to love with everything that God has given you.[34]

---

* Such claims were often made by Russian nationalists. In the 1900s, when a practical joker let loose a report that an old Russian peasant had flown several kilometres on a homemade aeroplane, this was taken as a proof that the patriarchal system of Russia was not only better than the West's – it was cleverer as well (B. Pares, *Russia* (Harmondsworth, 1942), p. 75).

The closer Gogol came to the Slavophiles, the more convinced he was that this Christian brotherhood was Russia's unique message to the world. Here was the providential plan for the 'Russian soul' which Gogol hinted at in the unforgettable *troika* passage at the end of the first volume of *Dead Souls*:

Is it not like that that you, too, Russia, are speeding along like a spirited *troika* that nothing can overtake? The road is like a cloud of smoke under you, the bridges thunder, and everything falls back and is left far behind. The spectator stops dead, struck dumb by the divine miracle: it is not a flash of lightning thrown down by heaven. What is the meaning of this terrifying motion? And what mysterious force is hidden in these horses the like of which the world has never seen? Oh horses, horses – what horses! Are whirlwinds hidden in your manes? Is there some sensitive ear, alert to every sound, concealed in your veins? They have caught the sound of the familiar song from above, and at once they strain their chests of brass and barely touching the ground with their hoofs are transformed almost into straight lines, flying through the air, and the *troika* rushes on full of divine inspiration. Russia, where are you flying to? Answer! She gives no answer. The bells fill the air with their wonderful tinkling; the air is torn asunder, it thunders and is transformed into wind; everything on earth is flying past, and, looking askance, other nations and states draw aside and make way for her.[35]

The 'Russian principle' of Christian love, to be revealed by Gogol in the second and third volumes, would save humanity from the selfish individualism of the West. As Herzen put it after reading Gogol's novel, '*in potentia* there is a great deal in the Russian soul'.[36]

The longer Gogol worked on his novel, the greater was his sense of a divine mission to reveal the sacred truth of the 'Russian soul'. 'God only grant me the strength to finish and publish the second volume', he wrote to the poet Nikolai Yazykov in 1846. 'Then they will discover that we Russians have much that they never even guessed about, and that we ourselves do not want to recognize.'[37] Gogol looked for inspiration to the monasteries – the place where he believed this hidden Russian spirit was to be revealed. What he most admired in the hermits of Optina was their apparent ability to master their own passions and cleanse their souls of sin. It was in such discipline that he saw the solution to Russia's spiritual malaise. Once again it was the Slavophiles who pointed Gogol towards Optina. Kireevsky had been there many times to see Father Makary in the 1840s, when the two men had brought out a life of Father Paissy and translated the works of the Church Fathers from the Greek.[38] Like all the Slavophiles who followed him, Kireevsky believed that the hermits of Optina were the true embodiment of Orthodoxy's ancient spiritual traditions, the one place where the 'Russian soul' was most alive, and by the time Gogol returned to Moscow from abroad, its salons were all filled with Optina devotees.

Dead Souls was conceived as a work of religious instruction. Its written style is imbued with the spirit of Isaiah, who prophesied the fall of Babylon (an image Gogol often used for Russia in his letters while working on the second volume of *Dead Souls*).[39] As he struggled with the novel Gogol was swept up by the religious fervour of his own prophecy. He plunged into the writings of the seventh-century hermit John of Sinai, who had talked about the need to purify one's soul and climb a ladder of spiritual perfection (an image Gogol used in his letters to his friends where he said that he was only on the bottom rungs).[40] Constant prayer was Gogol's only comfort and, as he believed, the spiritual source from which he would get the strength to complete his divine mission in *Dead Souls*. 'Pray for me, for the sake of Christ Himself', he wrote to Father Filaret at Optina Pustyn in 1850.

Ask your worthy superior, ask all of the brotherhood, ask all of those who pray most fervently and who love to pray, ask them all to pray for me. My path is a difficult one, and my task is such that without God's help at every minute and hour of the day, my pen will not move . . . He, the Merciful, has the power to do anything, even to turn me, a writer black like coal, into something white and pure enough to speak about the holy and the beautiful.[41]

The trouble was that Gogol could not picture this holy Russia, the realm of Christian brotherhood which he believed it was his divine task to reveal. This, the most pictorial of all the Russian writers, could not conjure up an image of this place – or at least not one that satisfied his critical judgement as a writer. However hard he tried to paint an ideal picture of his Russian characters – an icon, if you like, of the Russian soul – Gogol's observations of reality were such that he could not help but burden them with grotesque features derived from their natural habitat. As he himself despaired of his own religious vision, 'this is all a dream and it vanishes as soon as one shifts to what it really is in Russia'.[42]

Sensing he had failed in his fictional endeavour, Gogol sought instead to drive his message home in *Selected Passages from Correspondence with Friends* (1846), a pedantic moral sermon on the divine principle contained in Russia which was meant to serve as a sort of ideological preface to the unfinished volumes of *Dead Souls*. Gogol preached that Russia's salvation lay in the spiritual reform of every individual citizen. He left untouched the social institutions. He neglected the questions of serfdom and the autocratic state, ludicrously claiming that both were perfectly acceptable so long as they were combined with Christian principles. Progressive opinion was outraged – it seemed a defection from their sacred ideals of progress and political commitment to the people's cause. In an open letter of 1847 Belinsky launched a devastating attack on the writer whom he had championed (mistakenly, perhaps) as a social realist and advocate of political reform:

Yes, I did love you, with all the passion a man tied by blood ties to his country can feel for a man who was its hope, its glory and its pride, one of its great leaders on the path of consciousness, progress and development . . . Russia sees her salvation not in mysticism, asceticism or piety, as you suggest, but in education, civilization and culture. She has no need of sermons (she has heard too many), nor prayers (she has mumbled them too often), but of the awakening in the people of human dignity, a sense lost for centuries in the mud and filth.[43]

The Slavophiles, who were no less committed to reform, threw their hands up in despair. 'My friend', Sergei Aksakov wrote to Gogol, 'if your aim was to cause a scandal, to make your friends and foes stand up and unite against you, then you have simply achieved this. If this publication was one of your jokes, it has succeeded beyond anyone's wildest dreams: everyone is mystified.'[44] Even Father Makary, Gogol's mentor at Optina, could not endorse *Selected Passages*. The elder thought that Gogol had not understood the need for humility. He had set himself up as a prophet and had prayed with all the fervour of a fanatic, but, without the truth or inspiration of the Holy Ghost, that was 'not enough for religion'. 'If a lamp is to shine', he wrote to Gogol in September 1851, 'it is not enough that its glass merely be washed clean: its candle must be lit within.'[45] Nor could Makary agree with the writer's social quietism. For the calling of his monastery was to alleviate the suffering of the poor. Makary's criticisms were a crushing blow for Gogol, all the more so since he must have realized that they were fair: he did not feel that divine inspiration in his soul. As soon as he received Makary's letter Gogol broke off all relations with Optina. He saw that he had failed in his divine calling as a writer-prophet. He felt himself unworthy before God and began to starve himself to death. Instructing his servant to burn the manuscript of his unfinished novel, he took to his deathbed. The last words he uttered as he died, aged forty-three, on 24 February 1852, were, 'Bring me a ladder. Quickly, a ladder!'[46]

3

In his letter to Gogol, Belinsky had acknowledged that the Russian peasant was full of pious reverence and fear of God. 'But he utters the name of God while scratching his backside. And he says about the icon: "It's good for praying – and you can cover the pots with it as well." Look carefully', the literary critic concluded, 'and you will see that the Russians are by nature an atheistic people with many superstitions but not the slightest trace of religiosity.'[47]

Doubts about the Christian nature of the peasant soul were by no means confined to the socialist intelligentsia for whom Belinsky spoke. The Church itself was increasingly concerned by the image of a heathen peasantry. Parish priests drew a dismal picture of religious ignorance in the countryside. 'Out of one hundred male peasants', wrote I. S. Belliutsin in the 1850s,

a maximum of ten can read the Creed and two or three short prayers (naturally, without the slightest idea or comprehension of what they have read). Out of one thousand men, at most two or three know the Ten Commandments; so far as the women are concerned, nothing even needs to be said here. And this is Orthodox Rus'! What a shame and disgrace! And our pharisees dare to shout for everyone to hear that only in Russia has the faith been preserved undefiled, in Rus', where two-thirds of the people have not the slightest conception of the faith![48]

For the parish priest it was an uphill task to lead his peasant flock towards a conscious knowledge of the faith – even more to defend it from the secular ideas that came in from the towns. It was partly that the priest himself was barely literate. Most priests were the sons of other parish priests. They were brought up in the countryside, and few had received more than a little education in a local seminary. The peasants did not hold their priests in high esteem. They saw them as servants of the gentry and the state, and their humble, even squalid, way of life did not earn the peasantry's respect. The clergy were unable to support themselves on the meagre salaries they received from the state, or from the farming of their own small chapel plots. They relied heavily on collecting fees for their services – a rouble or so for a wedding, a bottle of vodka for a funeral – and, as a consequence, the peasants came to see them less as spiritual guides than as a class of tradesmen in the sacraments. The peasant's poverty and the priest's proverbial greed often made for lengthy haggling over fees, with peasant brides left standing for hours in the church, or the dead left unburied for several days, until a compromise was found.

In this precarious situation the priest was obliged to live on the constantly shifting border between the Church's idea of faith and the semi-pagan version of the peasantry. He would use the icons, the candles and the cross to ward away the demons and the evil spirits who, the peasants were convinced, were able to cast spells on their cattle and crops, make women infertile, bring misfortune or disease, or come back as apparitions of the dead to haunt their houses. For all the claims of the Slavophiles and the intense devotion of the Old Believers, the Russian peasant had never been more than semi-attached to the Orthodox religion. Only a thin coat of Christianity had been painted over his ancient pagan folk culture. To be sure, the Russian peasant displayed a great deal of external devotion. He crossed himself constantly, pronounced the Lord's name in every other sentence, always observed the Lenten fast, went to church on religious holidays, and was even known to go on pilgrimages from time to time to the holy shrines. He thought of himself, first of all, as 'Orthodox', and only later (if at all) as 'Russian'. Indeed, if one could travel back in time and ask the inhabitants of a nineteenth-century Russian village who they thought they were, the most likely answer would be: 'We are Orthodox, and we are from here.' The religion of the peasants was a long way from the bookish Christianity of the clergy. Being illiterate, the average nineteenth-century Russian peasant knew very little of the Gospels, for there was no real tradition of preaching in the countryside. Even peasant readers had little means of access to the Russian Bible (which did not exist in a complete published version until the middle of the 1870s). The Lord's Prayer and the Ten Commandments were unknown to the average peasant. He vaguely understood the concepts of heaven and hell, and he no doubt hoped that his lifelong observance of the Church's rituals would save his soul. But other abstract notions were a foreign land to him. He thought of God as a human being, and could not understand him as an abstract spirit that was invisible. In *My Universities* (1922) Gorky describes a peasant he encountered in a village near Kazan who

pictured God as a large, handsome old man, the kindly, clever master of the universe who could not conquer evil only because: 'He cannot be everywhere at once, too many men have been born for that. But he will succeed, you see. But I can't understand Christ at all! He serves no purpose as far as I'm concerned. There is God and that's enough. But now there's another! The son, they say. So what if he's God's son. God isn't dead, not that I know of.'[49]

This was the way the peasant thought of saints and natural gods as well: the two, in fact, were frequently combined or interchangeable in the peasant's Christian-pagan religion. There was Poludnitsa, goddess of the harvest, worshipped through the placement of a sheaf of rye behind the icon in the peasant's house; Vlas, the protector of the herds, who became in Christian times St Vlasius; and Lada, the deity of good fortune (an attribute much needed on the Russian roads), who featured with St George and St Nicholas in peasant wedding songs. The Christianization of the pagan gods was also practised in the Russian Church itself. At the core of the Russian faith is a distinctive stress on motherhood which never really took root in the West. Where the Catholic tradition stressed Mary's purity, the Russian Church emphasized her divine motherhood – the *bogoroditsa* – which practically assumed the status of the Trinity in the Russian religious consciousness. This cult of motherhood can easily be seen in the way that Russian icons tend to show the Madonna's face pressed maternally against her infant's head. It was, it seems, a conscious plan on the part of the Church to appropriate the pagan cult of Rozhanitsa, the goddess of fertility, and the ancient Slavic cult of the damp Mother Earth, or the goddess known as Mokosh, from which the myth of 'Mother Russia' was conceived.[50] In its oldest peasant form, the Russian religion was a religion of the soil.

Russia's Christian rituals and ornaments were similarly influenced by pagan practices. From the sixteenth century, for example, the procession of the Cross in the Russian Church moved in clockwise circles with the sun (as it did in the Western Church). In the Russian case it has been suggested that this was in imitation of the pagan circle dance (*khorovod*) which moved in the direction of the sun to summon up its magic influence (as late as the nineteenth century there were peasant proverbs advising on the wisdom of ploughing in the direction of the sun's movement).[51] The onion dome of the Russian church was also modelled on the sun. Its inner 'sky', or ceiling, usually depicted the Holy Trinity at the centre of a sun that radiated twelve apostolic rays.[52] Medieval Russian churches and religious manuscripts were often decorated with plant motifs and other ornaments, such as rosettes, rhomboids, swastikas and petals, crescent moons and trees, that were derived from pagan animistic cults. No doubt most of these symbols had long lost their original iconographic significance, but the frequency with which they reappeared in the folk designs of the nineteenth century, in wooden carvings and embroidery, suggests that they continued to serve in the peasant consciousness as a gateway to the supernatural sphere.

Embroidered towels and belts had a sacred function in peasant culture – they were often draped around the icon in the 'holy corner' of the peasant hut – and individual patterns, colours and motifs had symbolic meanings in various rituals. The twisting threaded pattern, for example, symbolized the creation of the world ('the earth began to twist and it appeared', the peasants said).[53] The colour red had a special magic power: it was reserved for belts and towels that were used in sacred rituals. In Russian the word for 'red' (*krasnyi*) is connected with the word for 'beautiful' (*krasivyi*) – which explains, among many other things, the naming of Red Square. It was equally the colour of fertility – which was regarded as a sacred gift. There were different belts for every stage of life. Newborn babies were tied up with a belt. Boys were given a red 'virgin belt'. Bridal couples girded themselves with embroidered linen towels. And by custom a pregnant woman stepped on a red belt before giving birth.[54] It was important for a dead man to be buried with a belt, ideally the one that he was given at his birth, to symbolize the end of the life cycle and the return of his soul to the spirit world.[55] According to folklore, the Devil was afraid of a man with a belt; not to wear a belt was regarded as a sign of belonging to the underworld. Hence Russian demons and mermaids were always portrayed beltless. A sorcerer would remove his belt when he entered into conversation with the spirit world.

These old pagan rituals were by no means confined to the peasantry. Many of them had become a part of national custom and were even found among the upper classes, who prided themselves on their modern attitudes. The Larin family in Pushkin's *Eugene Onegin* were typical in this respect:

> Amid this peaceful life they cherished,
> They held all ancient customs dear;
> At Shrovetide feasts their table flourished
> With Russian pancakes, Russian cheer;
> Twice yearly too they did their fasting;
> Were fond of songs for fortune-casting,
> Of choral dances, garden swings.
> At Trinity, when service brings
> The people, yawning, in for prayer,
> They'd shed a tender tear or two
> Upon their buttercups of rue.[56]

It was not unusual for a gentry family to observe all the strictest rituals of the Church and, without any sense of contradiction, to hold simultaneously to pagan superstitions and beliefs that any European would have dismissed as the nonsense of serfs. Fortune-telling games and rituals were almost universal among the aristocracy. Some families would employ a sorcerer to divine the future by interpreting their dreams. Others relied on their maids to read the signs from the tea-leaves.[57] Yuletide fortune-telling was a serious affair and, as Anna Lelong remembered, its rituals were a part of the all-night vigil on New Year's Eve:

There was always an all-night vigil and prayers on New Year's Eve. Dinner was at nine, and afterwards there would be fortune-telling in the dining room. Twelve cups would be made by hollowing out onions – one for every month – and salt would be sprinkled in them. Then they would be put in a circle on the table marking a different month on each. We children would be given two glasses – we would pour water into them and then drop egg white into them. We would then get up on New Year's morning very early and go into the dining-room, which stank of onion. We would look into our glasses and see fantastic shapes that had been made by the egg-white – churches, towers or castles. Then we would try to create some kind of pleasant meaning out of them. The grown-ups looked at the onion cups and worked out which month would be particularly rainy or snowy depending on whether the salt in the onion was dry or not. People took all this very seriously and we would make a note of what resulted. We also predicted whether the harvesting of grain would be wet or not. There was an order then to clear everything away and the stoves were heated, all the windows opened, and some kind of powder burned which gave off a nice smell. We were not taken to church that morning. We would spend it playing with our puppets, with bits of food for their banquet given to us by the servants in the kitchen.[58]

Peasant superstitions were also widely found among the aristocracy, even among those who would shudder at the thought of sharing any other customs with the peasantry. Stravinsky, for example, who was the perfect European gentleman, always kept a talisman that had been given to him at his birth. Diaghilev was full of superstitions which he had inherited from his peasant nanny. He did not like being photographed; he would become alarmed if someone placed his hat on the table (which meant that he would lose money) or on the bed (which meant that he would become ill); the sight of a black cat, even on the Champs-Elysées in Paris, filled him with horror.[59]

The peasant nanny was without a doubt the main source of these superstitions, and such was her importance in the nobleman's upbringing that they often loomed much larger in his consciousness than all the teachings of the Church. Pushkin's upbringing, for example, was Orthodox but only in a superficial way. He was taught to pray, and he went to church; but otherwise he was a Voltairean who held firmly to the secular beliefs of the Enlightenment throughout his life.[60] However, from his nanny he inherited superstitions that had their origins in the medieval age. He was struck down by foreboding when a fortune-teller told him that he would be killed by a tall blond man (true, as it turned out), and he was notoriously superstitious about hares (a fact that may have saved his life in 1825 when a hare crossed his path on his estate near Pskov and made him superstitious about travelling to Petersburg to join the Decembrists on Senate Square).[61]

Superstitions about death were particularly common in the aristocracy. Gogol never used the word 'death' in his letters, fearing it might bring about his own. This was, in fact, a widely held belief. It may perhaps explain why Tolstoy gave the nameless pronoun 'it' to the idea of death in those brilliant passages where he explores the experience of dying in *The Death of Ivan Ilich* and in the scene of Andrei's death in *War and Peace*.[62] Tchaikovsky, who was terrified of death (a fact often overlooked by those who claim that he committed suicide to cover up a homosexual affair), shared this common phobia. The composer's friends were careful not to mention words like 'cemetery' or 'funeral' in his presence, knowing that they threw him into a panic.[63]

Orthodox and pagan – yet a rationalist: an educated Russian could be all these things. It was part of the Russian condition to master such conflicting strands within oneself and fashion out of them a sensibility, ways of living, of looking at the world that were perfectly at ease with each other. Stravinsky, for example, though more chameleon-like than most, found an intellectual home in French Catholicism in the 1920s. Yet at the same time he became more emotionally attached than ever to the rituals of the Russian Church. He attended services at the

Orthodox Church in Paris on a regular basis from 1926; he collected Russian icons for his home in Paris and faithfully observed the Russian rituals in his private worship there; he even planned to build a Russian chapel at his house. There was no contradiction in this combination – at least not one that Stravinsky ever felt. Indeed, it was quite common for the cosmopolitan élites into which Stravinsky had been born to live in several different faiths. Some were drawn to the Roman Church, particularly those (like Zinaida Volkonsky when she moved to Italy in the 1830s) who found its internationalism more in keeping with their own world view than the ethnocentric Russian Church. Others were more drawn to Lutheranism, particularly if, like many of the aristocracy, they were of Russian–German parentage. It is difficult to say what was more important in the evolution of this complex religious sensibility, the relatively superficial nature of the aristocracy's religious upbringing which allowed space for other beliefs or the multinational influences on that class, but either way it made for a culture that was far more complex than the type we might imagine from the mythic image of the 'Russian soul'.

4

In 1878 Dostoevsky made the first of several trips to Optina Pustyn. It was a time of profound grief in the writer's life. His favourite child Aleksei (Alyosha) had just died of epilepsy, an illness he had inherited from his father, and, on the urging of his wife, Dostoevsky visited the monastery for spiritual comfort and guidance. The writer was working on the last of his great novels, *The Brothers Karamazov* (1880), which at that time he was planning as a novel about children and childhood.[64] Many of the scenes he witnessed at Optina would reappear in it, and the long discourse of the elder Zosima on the social ideal of the Church, which really should be read as Dostoevsky's own *profession de foi*, was borrowed from the writings of the monastery, with long parts lifted almost word for word from *The Life of the Elder Leonid* (1876) by Father Zedergolm.[65] The character of Zosima was mainly based on the elder Amvrosy, whom Dostoevsky saw on three occasions, once, most memorably, with a crowd of pilgrims who had come to see him at the monastery.[66] The novelist was struck by the charismatic power of the elder and, in one of the novel's early chapters, 'Devout Peasant Women', he re-creates a scene which takes us to the heart of the Russian faith. Zosima gives comfort to a desperate peasant woman who is also grieving for a little son:

'And here's one from a long way off,' he said, pointing to a woman who was still quite young, but thin and worn out, with a face that was not so much sunburnt as blackened. She was kneeling and staring motionless at the elder. There was almost a frenzied look in her eyes.

'From a long way off, Father, from a long way off,' the woman said in a sing-song voice . . . 'Two hundred miles from here – a long way, Father, a long way.'

She spoke as though she were keening. There is among the peasants a silent and long-enduring sorrow. It withdraws into itself and is still. But there is also a sorrow that has reached the limit of endurance: it will then burst into tears and from that moment break out into keening. This is especially so with women. But it is not easier to bear than a silent sorrow. The keening soothes it only by embittering and lacerating the heart still more. Such sorrow does not desire consolation and feeds upon the sense of its hopelessness. The keening is merely an expression of the constant need to reopen the wound . . .

'What is it you're weeping for?'

'I'm sorry for my little boy, Father. He was three years old – three years in another three months he would have been, I'm grieving for my little boy, Father, for my little boy – the last I had left. We had four, Nikita and I, four children, but not one of them is alive, Father, not one of them, not one. I buried the first three, I wasn't very sorry for them, I wasn't, but this last one I buried and I can't forget him. He seems to be standing before me now – he never leaves me. He has dried up my soul. I keep looking at his little things, his little shirt or his little boots, and I wail. I lay out all that's left of him, every little thing. I look at them and wail. I say to my husband, to Nikita, let me go, husband, I'd like to go on a pilgrimage. He's a driver, Father. We're not poor people, Father. We're our own masters. It's all our own, the horses and the carriage. But what do we want it all for now? My Nikita has taken to drinking without me, I'm sure he has, he used to before: I had only to turn my back, and he'd weaken. But now I'm no longer thinking of him. It's over two months since I left home. I've forgotten everything, I have, and I don't want to remember. And what will my life with him be like now? I've done with him, I have, I've done with them all. I don't want to see my house again and my things again. I hope I'll never see them again!'

'Now listen to me, Mother,' said the elder. 'Once, a long time ago, a great saint saw a woman like you in church. She was weeping for her little infant child, her only one, whom God had also taken. "Don't you know," said the saint to her, "how bold and fearless these little ones are before the throne of our Lord? There's none bolder or more fearless than they in the Kingdom of Heaven: Thou, O Lord, hast given us life, they say to God, and no sooner had we looked upon it than Thou didst take it away. And so boldly and fearlessly do they ask and demand an explanation that God gives them at once the rank of angels. And therefore," said the saint, "you, too, Mother, rejoice and do not weep, for your little one is now with the Lord in the company of his angels." That's what the saint said to the weeping mother in the olden days. And he was a great saint and he would not have told her an untruth . . . I shall mention your little boy in my prayers. What was his name?'

'Aleksei, Father.'

'A sweet name. After Aleksei the man of God?'

'Of God, Father, of God. Aleksei the man of God.'

'He was a great saint! I shall mention him in my prayers, Mother, I shall. And I shall mention your sorrow in my prayers, too, and your husband that he may live and prosper. Only you should not have left your husband. You must go back to him and look after him. Your little boy will look down on you and, seeing that you've forsaken his father, he will weep over you both: why do you destroy his bliss? For don't forget, he's living, he's living, for the soul lives for ever, and though he is no longer in the house, he's always there unseen beside you. How do you expect him to come home if you say you hate your house? To whom is he to go, if he won't find you, his father and mother, together? You see him in your dreams now and you grieve, but if you go back he will send you sweet dreams. Go to your husband, Mother, go back to him today.'[67]

Dostoevsky was a man who yearned for faith. But the death of little children was a fact he could not accept as a part of the divine plan. His notebooks from when he was working on *The Brothers Karamazov* are filled with agonizing commentaries on incidents of awful cruelty to children which he had read about in the contemporary press. One of these true stories appears at the centre of *The Brothers Karamazov* and its discourse about God. It involved a general whose hunting dog was wounded when a serf boy on his estate threw a stone. The general had the serf boy arrested, stripped naked in front of the other villagers, and, to the cries of his desperate mother, torn to shreds by a pack of hunting dogs. This incident is cited by Ivan, the rationalist philosopher among the three Karamazov brothers, to explain to Alyosha, his younger brother and a novice at the monastery, why he cannot believe in the existence of a God if his truth entails the suffering of little innocents.

'I say beforehand that the entire truth is not worth such a price. I do not want a mother to embrace the torturer who had her child torn to pieces by his dogs ... Is there in the whole world a being who could or would have the right to forgive? I don't want harmony. I don't want harmony, out of a love for mankind, I don't want it.'[68]

In a letter to a friend Dostoesvky said that Ivan's argument was 'irrefutable'.[69] In terms of moral feeling it was unacceptable to leave such torture unavenged, and even Alyosha, who tries to follow Christ's example of forgiveness, agrees with Ivan that the general should be shot. Here was the fundamental question which Dostoevsky posed, not just in this novel, but in all his life and art: How could one believe in God when the world created by him was so full of suffering? It was a question he was bound to ask when he looked at the society in which he lived. How could God have made Russia?

Dostoevsky came, in his own words, from a 'pious Russian family' where 'we knew the Gospel almost from the cradle'.[70] The teaching of the Gospels always remained at the core of Dostoevsky's personality and even when, in the 1840s, he became a socialist, the type of socialism to which he subscribed had a close affinity with Christ's ideals. He agreed with Belinsky that if Christ appeared in Russia he 'would join the socialists'.[71] In 1849 Dostoevsky was arrested as a member of a radical underground movement which met at the house of the young socialist Mikhail Petrashevsky in St Petersburg. His offence was to have read out Belinsky's by-then famous but forbidden letter to Gogol of 1847 in which the literary critic had attacked religion and called for social reform in Russia. It was even forbidden to circulate or read handwritten copies of the letter as Dostoevsky did. Dostoevsky and his comrades were condemned to death, but at the final moment, when they were on the parade ground waiting to be shot, they received a reprieve from the Tsar. Dostoevsky's sentence was commuted to four years of prison labour in Siberia, followed by service as a private soldier in a front-line Siberian regiment.

Dostoevsky's years in the Omsk prison camp were to be the turning point of his life. They brought him face to face with the roughest and most brutal of the common people and gave him what he thought of as a special insight into the hidden depths of the Russian soul. 'All in all, the time hasn't been lost', he wrote to his brother in 1854. 'I have learned to know, if not Russia, then at least her people, to know them, as perhaps very few know them.'[72] What Dostoevsky found among his fellow convicts was a level of depravity that shook him from his old intelligentsia belief in the people's innate goodness and perfectibility. In this underworld of murderers and thieves he found not a shred of human decency – only greed and guile, violent cruelty and drunkenness, and hostility to himself as a gentleman. But the most depressing aspect of it all, as he describes it in *The House of the Dead* (1862), was an almost total absence of remorse.

I have already said that for a period of several years I saw among these people not the slightest trace of repentance, not one sign that their crime weighed heavily on their conscience, and that the majority of them consider themselves to be completely in the right. This is a fact. Of course, vanity, bad examples, foolhardiness and false shame are the causes of much of it. On the other hand, who can say that he has fathomed the depths of these lost hearts and has read in them that which is hidden from the whole world? It must surely have been possible over so many years to have noticed something, to have caught at least some feature of these hearts that bore witness to inner anguish, to suffering. But this was absent. Yet, it seems that crime cannot be comprehensible from points of view that are already given, and that its philosophy is rather more difficult than is commonly supposed.[73]

This dark vision of the human psyche was the inspiration for the murderers and thieves who populate the pages of Dostoevsky's post-Siberian novels, beginning with *Crime and Punishment* (1866).

And yet at the depths of his despair came a vision of redemption to restore the writer's faith. The revelation appeared, as if by a miracle, at Easter time, if we are to believe Dostoevsky's own later recollection in *A Writer's Diary*.[74] The prisoners were drinking, fighting and carousing, and Dostoevsky was lying down on his plank bed to escape. Suddenly, a long-forgotten incident from his childhood came into his mind. When he was aged nine he was staying at his family's country home, and one August day he wandered off alone into the woods. He heard a sound, thought that someone shouted 'There's a wolf!' and ran terrified into a nearby field, where one of his father's serfs, a peasant called Marey, took pity on the boy and tried to comfort him:

'Why you took a real fright, you did!' he said, wagging his head. 'Never mind, now, my dear. What a fine lad you are!'

He stretched out his hand and suddenly stroked my cheek.

'Never mind, now, there's nothing to be afraid of. Christ be with you. Cross yourself, lad.' But I couldn't cross myself; the corners of my mouth were trembling, and I think that particularly struck him. He quietly stretched out a thick, earth-soiled finger with a black nail and gently touched it to my trembling lips.

'Now, now,' he smiled at me with a broad, almost maternal smile. 'Lord, what a dreadful fuss. Dear, dear, dear!'[75]

Remembering this 'maternal' act of kindness magically transformed Dostoevsky's attitude towards his fellow prisoners.

And so when I climbed down from my bunk and looked around, I remember I suddenly felt I could regard these unfortunates in an entirely different way and that suddenly, through some sort of miracle, the former hatred and anger in my heart had vanished. I went off, peering intently into the faces of those I met. This disgraced peasant, with shaven head and brands on his cheek, drunk and roaring out his hoarse, drunken song – why he might also be that very same Marey; I cannot peer into his heart, after all.[76]

Suddenly it seemed to Dostoevsky that all the Russian convicts had some tiny glimmer of goodness in their hearts (although, always the nationalist, he denied its existence in the Polish ones). Over Christmas some of them put on a vaudeville, and at last, in a gesture of respect, they sought his help as an educated man. The convicts might be thieves, but they also gave their money to an Old Believer in the prison camp, who had earned their trust and whose saintliness they recognized. Now, to Dostoevsky, the convicts' ability to preserve any sense of decency, in the dreadful conditions of the camp, seemed little short of miraculous, and the best proof there could be that Christ was alive in the Russian land. On this vision Dostoevsky built his faith. It was not much to build on. From the distant memory of a single peasant's kindness, he made a leap of faith to the belief that all Russian peasants harboured Christ's example somewhere in their souls. Not that he had any illusions about the way the peasants actually lived their lives (his horrific description of 'how a peasant beats his wife' is clear evidence of that). But he saw this barbarism as the 'filth' of centuries of oppression concealing, like a 'diamond', the peasant's Christian soul. 'One must know', he wrote,

how to segregate the beauty in the Russian peasant from the layers of barbarity that have accumulated over it . . . Judge the Russian people not by the abominations they so frequently commit, but by those great and sacred things for which, even in their abominations, they constantly yearn. Not all the people are villains; there are true saints, and what saints they are: they are radiant and illuminate the way for all! . . . Do not judge our People by what they are, but by what they would like to become.[77]

Dostoevsky was released and allowed to return to St Petersburg in 1859, three years after Volkonsky was set free by the 'Tsar Liberator' Alexander II. The educated circles of the capital were in a state of high excitement when Dostoevsky arrived from Siberia. The emancipation of the serfs, which was in its final stages of preparation, had given rise to hopes of a national and spiritual rebirth. The landlord and the peasant were to be reconciled on Russian-Christian principles. Dostoevsky compared the Decree to Russia's original conversion to Christianity in 988. He belonged at this time to the group of writers known as the 'native soil' movement (*pochvennichestvo*). They called on the intelligentsia (and on Russia's writers in particular) to turn toward the peasants, not just to discover their own nationality and express it in their art but, more importantly, in that truly 'Russian' spirit of Christian brotherhood, to bring their Western learning to the backward villages.

For Dostoevsky, in particular, this turning towards 'Russia' became his defining credo. He was a repentant nihilist, as he described himself, an unhappy atheist who longed to find a Russian faith. In the early 1860s he mapped out a series of novels to be called 'The Life of a Great Sinner'. It would chart the spiritual journey of a Western-educated Russian man who had lost his faith and led a life of sin. He would go in search of truth to a monastery, become a Slavophile, join the Khlysty sect, and at the end he would find 'both Christ and the Russian land, the Russian Christ and the Russian God'. It was to be a 'gigantic novel', Dostoevsky wrote to the poet Apollon Maikov in December 1868: 'please don't tell anyone, but this is how it is for me: to write this last novel, even if it kills me – and I'll get it all out'.[78] Dostoevsky never wrote 'The Life of a Great Sinner'. But his four great novels – *Crime and Punishment, The Idiot, The Devils* and *The Brothers Karamazov* – were all variations on its theme.

Like his sinner, Dostoevsky struggled over faith. 'I am a child of the age', he wrote in 1854, 'a child of unbelief and scepticism.'[79] His novels are filled with figures, like himself, who yearn for a religion in the face of their own doubts and reasoning. Even the believers, such as Shatov in *The Devils* (1872), can never quite commit to an unambiguous belief in God. 'I believe in Russia,' Shatov tells Stavrogin.

'I believe in the Greek Orthodox Church. I – I believe in the body of Christ – I believe that the second coming will take place in Russia – I believe,' he murmured in a frenzy.

'But in God? In God?'

'I – I *shall* believe in God.'[80]

Dostoevsky's novels can be read as an open discourse between reason and belief in which the tension between the two is never quite resolved.[81] According to Dostoevsky, truth is contained in reason *and* belief – one cannot be undermined by the other – and all true belief must be maintained in the face of all reason. There is no rational answer to Ivan's arguments against a God that allows little children to suffer. Nor is there a reasonable response to the arguments of the Grand Inquisitor, the subject of Ivan's poetic fantasy in *The Brothers*

Karamazov, who arrests Christ when he reappears in Counter-reformation Spain. Interrogating his prisoner, the Grand Inquisitor argues that the only way to prevent human suffering is, not by Christ's example, which ordinary mortals are too weak to follow, but by the construction of a rational order which can secure, by force if necessary, the peace and happiness that people really want. But Dostoevsky's faith was not of the sort that could be reached by *any* reasoning. He condemned as 'Western' all faiths which sought a reasoned under-standing of Divinity or which had to be enforced by papal laws and hierarchies (and in this sense the Legend of the Grand Inquisitor was itself intended by Dostoevsky as an argument against the Roman Church). The 'Russian God' in which Dostoevsky believed could only be arrived at by a leap of faith: it was a mystical belief outside of all reasoning. As he wrote in 1854, in one of the rare statements of his own religious credo, 'if someone proved to me that Christ was outside the truth, and it *really* was that the truth lay outside Christ, I would prefer to remain with Christ rather than with the truth'.[82]

In Dostoevsky's view, the ability to continue to believe in the face of overwhelming scientific evidence was a peculiarly Russian gift. There is a scene in *The Brothers Karamazov* where Karamazov's servant Smerdyakov is holding forth on the question of God at a family dinner. In a confused effort to refute the Gospels, Smerdyakov says that nobody can move a mountain to the sea – except 'perhaps two hermits in the desert'.

'One moment!' screamed Karamazov in a transport of delight. 'So you think there are two men who can move mountains, do you? Ivan, make a note of this extraordinary fact, write it down. There you have the Russian all over!'[83]

Like Karamazov, Dostoevsky took delight in this 'Russian faith', this strange capacity to believe in miracles. It was the root of his nationalism and his messianic vision of the 'Russian soul' as the spiritual saviour of the rationalistic West, which ultimately led him, in the 1870s, to write in the nationalist press about the 'holy mission' of 'our great Russia' to build a Christian empire on the continent. The simple Russian people, Dostoevsky claimed, had found the solution to the intellectual's torment over faith. They needed their belief, it was central to their lives, and it gave them strength to go on living and endure their suffering. This was the source of Dostoevsky's faith as well – the urge to go on believing, despite his doubts, because faith was necessary for life; rationalism led only to despair, to murder or to suicide – the fate of all the rationalists in his novels. Dostoevsky's answer to the voice of doubt and reason was a sort of existential *'credo ergo sum'* that took its inspiration from those 'Russian types' – hermits, mystics, Holy Fools and simple Russian peasants – imaginary and real, whose faith stood beyond reasoning.

Dostoevsky's Orthodoxy was inseparable from his belief in the redemptive quality of the Russian peasant soul. In all his novels the quest of the 'Great Sinner' for a 'Russian faith' is intimately linked to the idea of salvation through reconciliation with the native soil. Dostoevsky's own salvation came to him in the Siberian prison camp where for the first time he came into close contact with the common Russian people, and this theme of penance and redemption was a leitmotif in all his later works. It is the central theme of *Crime and Punishment*, a murder novel which conceals a political subplot. Its main protagonist, Raskolnikov, tries to justify his senseless murder of the old pawnbroker Alyona Ivanovna using the same utilitarian reasoning as that used by the nihilists and revolutionaries: that the old woman had been 'useless' to society and that he, meanwhile, was poor. He thus persuades himself that he killed the pawnbroker for altruistic reasons, just as the revolutionaries legitimized their crimes, when in fact, as he comes to realize with the help of his lover and spiritual guide, the prostitute Sonya, he killed her to demonstrate his superiority. Like Caesar and Napoleon, he had believed himself exempt from the rules of ordinary morality. Raskolnikov confesses to his crime. He is sentenced to seven years' hard labour in a Siberian prison camp. One warm Easter Day Sonya comes to him. By some strange force, 'as though something had snatched at him', Raskolnikov is hurled to Sonya's feet, and in this act of repentance, she understands that he has learned to love. It is a moment of religious revelation:

Her eyes began to shine with an infinite happiness; she had understood, and now she was in no doubt that he loved her, loved her infinitely, and that at last it had arrived, that moment . . .

They tried to speak, but were unable to. There were tears in their eyes. Both of them looked pale and thin; but in these ill, pale faces there now gleamed the dawn of a renewed future, a complete recovery to a new life.[84]

Strengthened by Sonya's love, he turns for moral guidance to the copy of the Gospels which she had given him, and resolves to use his time in prison to start on the road to that new life.

The suffering of such convicts had long been seen by Russian writers as a form of spiritual redemption. The journey to Siberia became a journey towards God. Gogol, for example, had envisaged that in the final volume of *Dead Souls* the old rogue Chichikov would see the light in a Siberian penal colony.[85] Among the Slavophiles, the Decembrist exiles had the status of martyrs. They venerated Sergei Volkonsky as an 'ideal Russian type', in the words of Ivan Aksakov, because he 'accepted all his suffering in the purest Christian spirit'.[86] Maria Volkonsky was practically worshipped in the democratic circles of the mid-nineteenth century, where everybody knew by heart the poem by Nekrasov ('Russian Women') which compared Maria to a saint. Dostoevsky shared this veneration of the Decembrists and their suffering wives. During his own journey to Siberia, in 1850, his convoy had been met by the Decembrist wives in the Tobolsk transit camp. Even after a quarter of a century, in his recollection of this encounter in *A Writer's Diary*, his attitude towards them was deeply reverential:

We saw the great martyresses who had voluntarily followed their husbands to Siberia. They gave up everything: their social position, wealth, connections, relatives, and sacrificed it all for the supreme moral duty, the *freest* duty that can ever exist. Guilty of nothing, they endured for twenty-five long years everything that their convicted husbands endured. Our meeting went on for an hour. They blessed us on our new journey; they made the sign of the cross over us and gave each of us a copy of the Gospels, the only book permitted in the prison. This book lay under my pillow during the four years of my penal servitude.[87]

In 1854 Dostoevsky wrote to one of these Decembrist wives, Natalia Fonvizina, with the first clear statement of the new faith he had found from his revelation in the prison camp at Omsk.

What struck the writer most about these women was the voluntary nature of their suffering. At the centre of his faith was the notion of humility, which Dostoevsky argued was the truly Christian essence of the Russian peasantry – their 'spiritual capacity for suffering'.[88] It was the reason why they felt a natural tenderness towards the weak and poor, even towards criminals, whom villagers would help with gifts of food and clothes as they passed in convoy to Siberia. Dostoevsky explained this compassion by the idea that the peasants felt a 'Christian sense of common guilt and responsibility towards their fellow-men'.[89] This Christian sense emerged as the central theme of *The Brothers Karamazov*. At the heart of the novel stand the teachings of the elder Zosima – that 'we are all responsible for each other', even for the 'murderers and robbers in the world', and that we must all share in our common suffering. The Kingdom of Heaven, Zosima concludes, will become a reality only when everybody undergoes this 'change of heart' and the 'brotherhood of man will come to pass'.[90]

Dostoevsky places Zosima's own conversion precisely at that moment when he realizes his guilt and responsibility toward the poor. Before he became a monk Zosima had been an army officer. He had fallen in love with a society beauty, who had rejected him for another man. Zosima provoked his rival to a duel. But the night before the duel a revelation came to him. In the evening Zosima had been in a foul mood. He had struck his batman twice about the face with all his strength, drawing blood, while the serf just stood there 'stiffly to attention, his head erect, his eyes fixed blankly on me as though on parade, shuddering at every blow but not daring to raise his hands to protect himself'. That night Zosima slept badly. But the next morning he woke with a 'strange feeling of shame and disgrace', not at the prospect of shedding blood in that day's duel, but at the thought of his wanton cruelty to the poor batman the evening before. Suddenly he realized that he had no right to be waited on 'by a man like me created in God's image'. Filled with remorse, he rushed to his servant's little room and went down on his knees to beg for his forgiveness. At the duel he let his rival shoot, and, when he missed, Zosima fired his own shot into the air and apologized to him. That day he resigned from his regiment and went into the monastery.[91]

Dmitry Karamazov, another dissolute army officer, experiences a similar revelation and, in the end, comes to repent for the guilt of social privilege. Wrongly convicted of his father's murder, Dmitry wants nevertheless to suffer in Siberia to purify himself and expiate the sins of other men. Suffering thus awakens consciousness. The revelation comes to Dmitry in a dream. During the hearings before his trial he falls asleep and finds himself in a peasant's hut. He cannot understand why the peasants are so poor, why the mother cannot feed her baby, which continually cries. He wakes up from the dream transformed, 'his face radiant with joy', having at last felt a 'change of heart', and expressing his compassion for his fellow men.[92] He knows that he is not guilty of his father's murder, but is, he feels, to blame for the suffering of the peasants, his own serfs. Nobody can understand why Dmitry keeps muttering about the 'poor baby' or that it is the reason he 'must go to Siberia!'[93] But all is revealed at his trial:

And what does it matter if I spend twenty years in the mines hacking out ore with a hammer? I'm not afraid of that at all. It's something else that I fear now – that the new man that has arisen within me may depart. One can find a human heart there also, in the mines, under the ground, next to you, in another convict and murderer, and make friends with him. For there too one can live and love and suffer! One can breathe new light into the frozen heart of such a convict. One can wait on him for years and years and at last bring up from the thieves' kitchen to the light of day a lofty soul, a soul that has suffered and has become conscious of its humanity, to restore life to an angel, bring back a hero! And there are so many of them, hundreds of them, and we are all responsible for them! Why did I dream of that 'baby' just then? 'Why is the baby poor?' That was a sign to me at that moment! It's for the 'baby' that I'm going. For we are all responsible for all. For all the 'babies', for there are little children and big children. All of us are 'babies'. And I'll go there for all, for someone has to go for all.[94]

Dostoevsky believed in a Church of social action and responsibility. He was critical of the official Church, which had allowed itself to become shackled by the Petrine state since the eighteenth century and, as a consequence, had lost its spiritual authority. He called on the

Church to become more active in society. It had, he said, lost sight of its pastoral role and had shown itself to be indifferent to Russia's major problem, the suffering of the poor. Such views were widely shared by lay theologians, like the Slavophile Khomiakov, and even by some priests in the Church hierarchy, whose writings were an influence on Dostoevsky.[95] There was a common feeling that the Church was losing ground to the socialist intelligentsia and to the various sectarians and mystics who were searching for a more meaningful and socially responsible spiritual community.

Dostoevsky's writings must be seen in this context. He, too, was searching for such a Church, a Christian brotherhood like the Slavophiles' *sobornost'*, that would transcend the walls of the monastery and unite all the Russians in a living community of believers. His utopia, a socio-mystical ideal, was nothing less than a theocracy. Dostoevsky advanced this idea in *The Brothers Karamazov* – in the scene where Ivan gains the approbation of the elder Zosima for his article proposing the radical expansion of the jurisdiction of the ecclesiastical courts. This was a subject of considerable topical importance at the time of the novel's publication. Ivan argues that, contrary to the pattern of Western history, where the Roman Church was absorbed by the state, the idea of Holy Russia was to raise the state to the level of a Church. Ivan's reforms of the courts would substitute the moral sanction of the Church for the coercive power of the state: instead of punishing its criminals, society should seek to reform their souls. Zosima rejoices at this argument. No criminal can be deterred, he argues, let alone reformed, by 'all these sentences of hard labour in Siberian prisons'. But unlike the foreign criminal, Zosima maintains, even the most hardened Russian murderer retains sufficient faith to recognize and repent of his crime; and through this spiritual reformation, the elder predicts, not only would a member of the living Church be saved but 'perhaps also the number of crimes themselves would diminish to a quite unbelievable extent'.[96] From Dostoevsky's *Notebooks* it is clear that he shared the elder's theocratic vision (which was closely based on the writings of Optina's Father Zedergolm) of a 'single universal and sovereign Church' that was destined to appear on the Russian land. 'The star will shine in the East!'[97]

According to Dostoevsky's friend and fellow writer Vladimir Soloviev, *The Brothers Karamazov* was planned as the first of a series of novels in which the writer would expound his ideal of the Church as a social union of Christian love.[98] One can see this vision unfolding in the final scene of *The Brothers Karamazov*, where Alyosha (who has left the monastery and gone into the world) attends the funeral of the poor child Ilyusha, struck down by tuberculosis. After the service, he gathers around him a group of boys who had followed him in caring for the dying boy. There are twelve of these apostles. They gather at the stone where Ilyusha's father had wanted to bury his son. In a farewell speech of remembrance, Alyosha tells the children that the spirit of the dead boy will live on for ever in their hearts. It will be a source of kindness in their lives and it will remind them, as Alyosha tells them, 'How good life is when you do something that is good and just!'[99] Here was a vision of a Church that lived outside the walls of any monastery, a Church that reached out to the heart of every child; a Church in which, as Alyosha had once dreamed, ' "there will be no more rich or poor, exalted nor humbled, but all men will be as the children of God and the real Kingdom of Christ will arrive" '.[100]

The censors banned large parts of Dostoevsky's novel, claiming that such passages had more to do with socialism than with Christ.[101] It is perhaps ironic for a writer who is best known as an anti-socialist, but Dostoevsky's vision of a democratic Church remained close to the socialist ideals which he espoused in his youth. The emphasis had changed – as a socialist he had believed in the moral need for the transformation of society, whereas as a Christian he had come to see that spiritual reform was the only way to effect social change – but essentially his quest for Truth had always been the same. Dostoevsky's whole life can be seen as a struggle to combine the teaching of the Gospels with the need for social justice on this earth, and he thought he found his answer in the 'Russian soul'. In one of his final writings Dostoevsky summarized his vision of the Russian Church:

I am speaking now not about church buildings and not about sermons: I am speaking about our Russian 'socialism' (and, however strange it may seem, I am taking this word, which is quite the opposite of all that the Church represents, to explain my idea), whose purpose and final outcome is the establishment of the universal church on earth, insofar as the earth is capable of containing it. I am speaking of the ceaseless longing, which has always been inherent in the Russian people, for a great, general, universal union of brotherhood in the name of Christ. And if this union does not yet exist, if the Church has not yet been fully established – not merely in prayers alone, but in fact – then the instinct for this Church and the ceaseless longing for it . . . is still to be found in the hearts of the millions of our people. It is not in Communism, not in mechanical forms that we find the socialism of the Russian people: they believe that salvation is ultimately to be found in worldwide union in the name of Christ. That is our Russian socialism![102]

5

At 4 a.m. on 28 October 1910 Tolstoy crept out of his house at Yasnaya Polyana, took a carriage to the nearby station, and bought a third-class railway ticket to Kozelsk, the station for the monastery at Optina Pustyn. At the age of eighty-two, with just ten days to live, Tolstoy was renouncing everything – his wife and children, his family home in which he had lived for nearly fifty years, his peasants and his literary career – to take refuge in the monastery. He had felt the urge to flee many times before. Since the 1880s he had got into the habit of setting out at night to walk with the pilgrims on the Kiev road that passed by his estate – often not returning until breakfast time. But now his urge was to leave for good. The endless arguments with his wife Sonya, largely over his religious views, had made life at home unbearable. He wanted peace and quiet in his final days.

Tolstoy did not know where he was going. He left in a hurry, without plans. But something drew him to Optina. Perhaps it was *The Brothers Karamazov*, which Tolstoy had just read for the first time; or perhaps it was the presence of his sister Marya, the last survivor of his happy childhood, who was living out her last days at the nearby Shamordino convent under the direction of Optina's monks. The monastery was not far from his estate at Yasnaya Polyana, and on several occasions over the previous thirty years he had walked there like a peasant to calm his troubled mind by talking about God with the elder Amvrosy. The ascetic life of the Optina hermits was an inspiration to Tolstoy: so much so that *Father Sergius* (1890–98) – his story of an aide-de-camp-turned-hermit from Optina who struggles to find God through prayer and contemplation and at last finds peace as a humble pilgrim on the road – can be read as a monologue on Tolstoy's own religious longing to renounce the world. Some say that Tolstoy was searching at Optina for a final reconciliation with the Church – that he did not want to die before his excommunication (imposed by the Church in 1901) had been rescinded. Certainly, if there was a site where such a reconciliation could have taken place, it was Optina, whose mystical approach to Christianity, uncluttered as it was by the rituals and institutions of the Church, was very close to Tolstoy's own religious faith. But it seems more likely that Tolstoy was driven by the need to 'go away'. He wanted to escape from the affairs of this world to prepare his soul for the journey to the next.

To judge from *A Confession*, Tolstoy's turn to God was a sudden one – the result of a moral crisis in the latter half of the 1870s. This, too, is the view of most scholars, who draw a sharp distinction between the literary Tolstoy of the pre-crisis decades and the religious thinker of the post-crisis years. But in fact the search for faith was a constant element of Tolstoy's life and art.[103] His whole identity was bound up in the quest for spiritual meaning and perfection, and he took his inspiration from the life of Christ. Tolstoy thought of God in terms of love and unity. He wanted to belong, to feel himself a part of a community. This was the ideal he sought in marriage and in his communion with the peasantry. For Tolstoy, God is love: where there is love, there is God. The divine core of every human being is in their compassion and ability to love. Sin is loss of love – a punishment itself – and the only way to find redemption is through love itself. This theme runs through all Tolstoy's fiction, from his early story 'Family Happiness' (1859) to his final novel, *Resurrection* (1899). It is misleading to see these literary works as somehow separate from his religious views. Rather, as with Gogol, they are allegories – icons – of these views. All Tolstoy's characters are searching for a form of Christian love, a sense of relatedness to other human beings that alone can give a meaning and a purpose to their lives. That is why Anna Karenina – isolated and thrown back completely on herself – is destined to perish in Tolstoy's universe; or why his most exalted figures, such as Princess

Maria or the peasant Karataev in *War and Peace*, show their love by suffering for other human beings.

Tolstoy had a mystical approach to God. He thought that God could not be comprehended by the human mind, but only felt through love and prayer. For Tolstoy, prayer is a moment of awareness of divinity, a moment of ecstasy and freedom, when the spirit is released from the personality and merges with the universe.[104] Not a few Orthodox theologians have compared Tolstoy's religion to Buddhism and other oriental faiths.[105] But in fact his mystical approach had more in common with the hermits' way of prayer at Optina. Tolstoy's division from the Russian Church, however, was a fundamental one, and not even Optina could satisfy his spiritual requirements. Tolstoy came to reject the doctrines of the Church – the Trinity, the Resurrection, the whole notion of a divine Christ – and instead began to preach a practical religion based on Christ's example as a living human being. His was a form of Christianity that could not be contained by any Church. It went beyond the walls of the monastery to engage directly with the major social issues – of poverty and inequality, cruelty and oppression – which no Christian in a country such as Russia could ignore. Here was the religious basis of Tolstoy's moral crisis and renunciation of society from the end of the 1870s. Increasingly persuaded that the truly Christian person had to live as Jesus taught in the Sermon on the Mount, Tolstoy vowed to sell his property, to give away his money to the poor, and to live with them in Christian brotherhood. Essentially his beliefs amounted to a kind of Christian socialism – or rather anarchism, insofar as he rejected all forms of Church and state authority. But Tolstoy was not a revolutionary. He rejected the violence of the socialists. He was a pacifist. In his view, the only way to fight injustice and oppression was by obeying Christ's teachings.

The Revolution of 1917 has obscured from our view the threat which Tolstoy's simple reading of the Gospels posed to Church and state. By the time of his excommunication in the 1900s, Tolstoy had a truly national following. His Christian anarchism was hugely appealing to the peasantry, and as such it was perceived as a major threat to the established Church, even to the Tsar. Any social revolution in Russia was bound to have a spiritual base, and even the most atheistic socialists were conscious of the need to give religious connotations to their stated goals.* 'There are two Tsars in Russia', wrote A. S. Suvorin, editor of the conservative newspaper *Novoe vremia*, in 1901: 'Nicholas II and Leo Tolstoy. Which one is stronger? Nicholas II can do nothing about Tolstoy; he cannot shake his throne. But Tolstoy, undoubtedly, is shaking his.'[106] It would not have come to this, if the tsarist authorities had left Tolstoy alone. Few people read his religious writings of the 1880s, and it was only in the 1890s, when the Church began to denounce him for trying to bring down the government, that mass illegal printings of these works began to circulate in the provinces.[107] By 1899, when Tolstoy published *Resurrection*, he was better known as a social critic and religious dissident than as a writer of fiction. It was the novel's religious attack on the institutions of the tsarist state – the Church, the government, the judicial and penal systems, private property and the social conventions of the aristocracy – that made it, by a long way, his best selling novel in his own lifetime.[108] 'All of Russia is feeding on this book', an ecstatic Stasov wrote to congratulate Tolstoy. 'You cannot imagine the conversations and debates it is provoking ... This event has had no equal in all the literature of the nineteenth century.'[109] The more the Church and the state attacked Tolstoy, the greater was the writer's following, until he was finally excommunicated in 1901. The intention of the excommunication had been to provoke a wave of popular hatred against Tolstoy, and there were reactionaries and Orthodox fanatics who responded to the call. Tolstoy received death threats and abusive letters, and the Bishop of Kronstadt, who was notorious for his support of the extreme

---

* The Bolsheviks made the most political capital out of socialism's religious resonance. S. G. Strumilin, in a pamphlet for the rural poor in 1917, compared socialism to the work of Christ and claimed that it would create a 'terrestrial kingdom of fraternity, equality and freedom' (S. Petrashkevich [Strumilin], *Pro zemliu i sotsializm: slovo sotsialdemokrata k derevenskoi bednote* (Petrograd, 1917), pp. 1–2). The cult of Lenin, which took off in August 1918, after he had been wounded in an assassination attempt, carried explicit religious overtones. Lenin was depicted as a Christ-like figure, ready to die for the people's cause, and, because the bullets had not killed him, blessed by miraculous powers. *Pravda* (meaning Truth and Justice), the title of the Party's newspaper, had an obvious religious meaning in the peasant consciousness – as did the Red Star, for, according to folklore, the maiden Pravda wore a burning star on her forehead which lit up the whole world and brought it truth and happiness.

nationalists, even wrote a prayer for the writer's death which was circulated widely in the right-wing press.[110] Yet for every threatening message, Tolstoy received a hundred letters of support from villages across the land. People wrote to tell him of abuses in their local government, or to thank him for his condemnation of the Tsar in his famous article 'I Cannot Remain Silent', written in response to the execution of the revolutionaries since 1905. Millions of people who had never read a novel suddenly began to read Tolstoy's. And every-where the writer went, huge crowds of well-wishers would appear – many more, it was remarked by the police amidst the celebrations for Tolstoy's eightieth birthday in 1908, than turned out to greet the Tsar.

Tolstoy gave all the money he had made from *Resurrection* to the Dukhobors. The Dukhobors were Tolstoyans before Tolstoy. The religious sect went back to the eighteenth century, if not earlier, when its first communities of Christian brotherhood were established. As pacifists who rejected the authority of Church and state, they had suffered persecution from the very start of their existence in Russia, and in the 1840s they had been forced to settle in the Caucasus. Tolstoy first became interested in the Dukhobors in the early 1880s. The influence of their ideas on his writings is palpable. All the core elements of 'Tolstoyism' – the idea that the Kingdom of God is within oneself, the rejection of the doctrines and rituals of the established Church, the Christian principles of the (imagined) peasant way of life and community – were also part of Dukhobor belief. In 1895 the sect staged a series of mass demonstrations against military conscription. Thousands of Tolstoyans (or pacifists who called themselves by that name) flocked to join their protest in the Caucasus, many of them merging with the Dukhobors. Tolstoy himself publicized their cause, writing several hundred letters to the press and eventually securing and largely paying for their resettlement in Canada (where their dissent proved just as troublesome to the government).[111]

Tolstoy was in close contact with many other sects. There was a natural affinity between his living Christianity and the sects' searching for a True Church in the Russian land: both came from social visions of utopia. 'Tolstoyism' was itself a kind of sect – or at least its enemies thought so. There were prolonged discussions between Tolstoy's followers and the main religious sects about organizing a united move-ment under Tolstoy's leadership.[112] This was a major challenge to the Church. The number of sectarians had grown dramatically, from somewhere in the region of 3 million members in the eighteenth century to perhaps 30 million in the first decade of the twentieth century, although some scholars thought that fully one-third of the Russian population (about 120 million) was sectarian.[113] New sects were formed, or discovered, every year, as the Populist intelligentsia began to study them in the final decades of the nineteenth century. Then, in the 1900s, the theosophists, the anthroposophists, the Symbolists, Rasputinites and mystics of all types started to see in these sects an answer to their yearning for a new and more 'essential' kind of Russian faith. The established Church was in danger of imploding. Politically shackled to the state, its parish life inert, if not spiritually dead, the Church could not prevent its peasant flock from running off to join sects, or fleeing to the city and the socialists, in their search for truth and justice on this earth.

If Tolstoy's Christian anarchism was motivated by the yearning to belong to a free community of Christian love and brotherhood, the personal root of his religion was a fear of death which became more intense with every passing year. Death was an obsession throughout his life and art. He was a child when his parents died; and then as a young man he lost his brother Dmitry as well – a haunting episode he pictured in the death scene of Nikolai Levin, Konstantin's brother, in *Anna Karenina*. Tolstoy desperately tried to rationalize death as a part of life. 'People who fear death, fear it because it appears to them as emptiness and blackness', he wrote in 'On Life' (1887), 'but they see emptiness and blackness because they do not see life.'[114] Then, under Schopenhauer's influence perhaps, he came to regard death as the dissolution of one's personality in some abstract essence of the uni-verse.[115] But none of it was convincing to those who knew him well. As Chekhov put it in a letter to Gorky, Tolstoy was terrified of his own death, but he did not want to admit it, so he calmed himself by reading the Scriptures.[116]

In 1897 Tolstoy paid a visit to Chekhov. The playwright was gravely ill. His long illness from tuberculosis had taken a sudden and dramatic turn for the worse, with a massive haemorrhaging of the lungs, and

Chekhov, who had hitherto ignored his condition, was finally obliged to call for the doctors. When Tolstoy arrived at the clinic, six days after the haemorrhage, he found Chekhov sitting up in bed in a cheerful mood, laughing and joking, and coughing blood into a large beer glass. Chekhov was aware of the danger he was in – he was a doctor, after all – but he kept his spirits up, and even talked of plans for the future. Tolstoy, Chekhov noted with his usual cutting wit, was 'almost disappointed' not to find his friend at the point of death. It was clear that Tolstoy had come with the intention of talking about death. He was fascinated by the way that Chekhov seemed to accept death and just get on with life, and, envious of this calm attitude perhaps, he wanted to know more. Soon Tolstoy touched on the topic which is generally taboo around the bed of someone who is gravely ill. As Chekhov lay there spitting blood, he harangued him with a lecture about death and the afterlife. Chekhov listened attentively, but in the end he lost patience and started arguing. He viewed the mysterious force, in which Tolstoy thought the dead would be dissolved, as a 'formless frozen mass', and told Tolstoy that he did not really want that kind of eternal life. In fact, Chekhov said, he did not understand life after death. He saw no point in thinking about it, or in comforting oneself, as he put it, with 'delusions of immortality'.[117] Here was the crucial difference between the two men. When Tolstoy thought of death his mind turned to another world, while Chekhov's always returned to this one. 'It is frightening to become nothing,' he told his friend and publisher A. S. Suvorin in the clinic after Tolstoy left. 'They take you to the cemetery, return home, begin drinking tea, and say hypocritical things about you. It's ghastly to think about it!'[118]

It was not that Chekhov was an atheist – although in the last years of his life he claimed to have no faith.[119] His religious attitudes were in fact very complex and ambivalent. Chekhov had grown up in a religious family and throughout his life he retained a strong attachment to the rituals of the Church. He collected icons. At his house in Yalta there was a crucifix on his bedroom wall.[120] He liked reading about the Russian monasteries and the lives of saints.[121] From his correspondence we learn that Chekhov loved to hear church bells, that he often went to church and enjoyed the services, that he stayed at monasteries, and that on more than one occasion he even thought of becoming a monk himself.[122] Chekhov saw the Church as an ally of the artist, and the artist's mission as a spiritual one. As he once said to his friend Gruzinsky, 'the village church is the only place where the peasant can experience something beautiful'.[123]

Chekhov's literary works are filled with religious characters and themes. No other Russian writer, with the possible exception of Leskov, wrote so often or with so much tender feeling about people worshipping, or about the rituals of the Church. Many of Chekhov's major stories (such as 'The Bishop', 'The Student', 'On the Road' and 'Ward No. 6') are profoundly concerned with the search for faith. Chekhov himself had religious doubts – he once wrote that he would become a monk if the monasteries took people who were not religious and he did not have to pray.[124] But he clearly sympathized with people who had faith or spiritual ideals. Perhaps Chekhov's view is best expressed by Masha, when she says in *Three Sisters*, 'It seems to me that a man must have faith, or be seeking it, otherwise his life is empty, quite empty.'[125] Chekhov was not overly concerned with the abstract question about the existence of a God. As he told Suvorin, a writer should know better than to ask such things.[126] But he did embrace the concept of religion as a way of life – a basic moral code – which is what it was for him and what he thought it was for the simple Russian man.[127]

In his early story 'On the Road' (1886) Chekhov discusses this Russian need for faith. The scene is a highway inn where some travellers are sheltering from bad weather. A young noblewoman gets into a conversation with a gentleman called Likharev. She wants to know why famous Russian writers all find faith before they die. 'As I understand it,' replies Likharev, 'faith is a gift of the spirit. It is a talent: you have to be born with it.'

'As far as I can judge, speaking for myself, and from all that I have seen, this talent is present in the Russian people to the highest degree. Russian life represents an endless series of beliefs and enthusiasms, but it has not, if you ask my advice, it has not yet gone anywhere near not believing or rejecting belief. If a Russian person does not believe in God, it means he believes in something else.'[128]

This was close to Chekhov's view – and he himself was very Russian in this sense. Chekhov might have had his own doubts about the existence of a God. But he never once lost sight of the need for Russians to believe. For without faith in a better world to come, life in Chekhov's Russia would be unendurable.

The need to believe was as central to his art as it was to the Russian way of life. Chekhov's plays abound in characters (Dr Astrov in *Uncle Vanya*, Vershinin in *Three Sisters*, Trofimov in *The Cherry Orchard*) who place their faith, as Chekhov himself did, in the ability of work and science to improve life for humanity. They are filled with characters who reconcile themselves to suffer and endure in the Christian hope of a better life to come. As Sonya puts it in those famous (and already cited) closing lines of *Uncle Vanya*: 'When our time comes we shall die submissively, and over there, in the other world, we shall say that we have suffered, that we've wept, that we've had a bitter life, and God will take pity on us.'[129] Chekhov saw the artist as a fellow sufferer – as somebody who worked for a spiritual end. In 1902 he wrote to Diaghilev:

Modern culture is but the beginning of a work for a great future, a work which will go on, perhaps, for ten thousand years, in order that mankind may, even in the remote future, come to know the truth of a real God – that is, not by guessing, not by seeking in Dostoevsky, but by perceiving clearly, as one perceives that twice two is four.[130]

Death is felt in all of Chekhov's works, and in many of his later stories the approach of death is the major theme. Chekhov had confronted death throughout his life – first as a doctor and then as a dying man – and perhaps because he was so close to it he wrote about the subject with a fearless honesty. Chekhov understood that people die in a very ordinary way – for the most part they die thinking about life. He saw that death is simply part of the natural process – and when death came to him, he met it with the dignity and courage, and the same love of life, he had always shown. In June 1904 he booked into a hotel at Badenweiler, Germany, with his wife Olga. 'I am going away to die,' Chekhov told a friend on the eve of their departure. 'Everything is finished.'[131] On the night of 2 July he woke in a fever, called for a doctor and told him loudly, '*Ich sterbe*' ('I am dying'). The doctor tried to calm him and went away. Chekhov ordered a bottle of champagne, drank a glass, lay down on his bed, and passed away.[132]

For Tolstoy, death was no such easy thing. Terrified of his own mortality, he attached his religion to a mystical conception of death as a spiritual release, the dissolution of the personality into a 'universal soul'; yet this never quite removed his fear. No other writer wrote so often, or so imaginatively, about the actual moment of dying – his depictions of the deaths of Ivan Ilich and of Prince Andrei in *War and Peace* are among the best in literature. But these are not just deaths. They are final reckonings – moments when the dying re-evaluate the meaning of their lives and find salvation, or some resolution, in a spiritual truth.[133] In *The Death of Ivan Ilich* (1886) Tolstoy shows a man, a senior judge, who comes to realize the truth about himself as he lies on his deathbed looking back on his life. Ivan Ilich sees that he has existed entirely for himself and that his life has therefore been a waste. He has lived for his career as a judge, but he cared no more for the people who appeared before him than the doctor treating him cares for him now. He has organized his life around his family, but he does not love them, and nor does it appear that they love him, for none of them will recognize the fact that he is dying and try to comfort him. The only real relationship which Ivan Ilich has is with his servant Gerasim, a 'fresh young peasant lad' who looks after him, sits with him at night and brings him comfort by holding up his legs. Gerasim does all of this as a simple act of kindness for a man who, he knows, is about to die, and his recognition of this fact is itself of immense comfort to the dying man. 'The awful, terrible act of his dying was', Ivan Ilich sees,

reduced by those about him to the level of a fortuitous, disagreeable and rather indecent incident (much in the same way as people behave with someone who goes into a drawing-room smelling unpleasantly) – and this was being done in the name of the very decorum he had served all his life long. He saw that no one felt for him, because no one was willing even to appreciate his situation. Gerasim was the only person who recognized the position and was sorry for him. And that was why Ivan Ilich was at ease only when Gerasim was with him . . . Gerasim alone told no lies; everything showed that he alone understood the facts of the case, and did not consider it necessary to disguise them, and simply felt sorry for the sick, expiring master. On one occasion when Ivan Ilich was for sending him away to bed he even said straight out:

'We shall all of us die, so what's a little trouble?' meaning by this that he did not mind the extra work because he was doing it for a dying man and hoped someone would do the same for him when his time came.[134]

A simple peasant has given to this judge a moral lesson about truth and compassion. He has shown him how to live and how to die – for the peasant's acceptance of the fact of death enables Ivan Ilich, at the final conscious moment of his life, to overcome his fear.

The Death of Ivan Ilich was based upon the death of Tolstoy's friend, Ivan Ilich Mechnikov, an official in the judicial service, whose brother furnished Tolstoy with a detailed account of his final days.[135] It was not uncommon for the Russian upper classes to draw comfort from their servants' presence at the moment of their death. From diaries and memoirs it would seem that, far more than the priest who came to take confession and administer last rites, the servants helped the dying overcome their fears with their simple peasant faith which 'enabled them to look death in the face'.[136] The fearless attitude of the peasant towards death was a commonplace of nineteenth-century Russian literature. 'What an astonishing thing is the death of a Russian peasant!' wrote Turgenev in *Sketches from a Hunter's Album*. 'His state of mind before death could be called neither one of indifference, nor one of stupidity; he dies as if he is performing a ritual act, coldly and simply.'[137] Turgenev's hunter encounters several peasants at the point of death. One, a woodcutter called Maxim who is crushed by a falling tree, asks his team-mates to forgive him, and then, just before he breathes his last, asks them to make sure that his wife receives a horse for which he has put down money. Another is informed in a country hospital that he has only a few days to live. The peasant thinks about this for a bit, scratches the nape of his neck and puts his cap on, as if to depart. The doctor asks him where he is going.

'Where to? It's obvious where to – home, if things are that bad. If things are like that, there's a lot to be put in order.'

'But you'll do yourself real harm, Vasily Dmitrich. I'm surprised that you even got here at all. Stay here, I beg you.'

'No, Brother Kapiton Timofeich, if I'm going to die, I'll die at home. If I died here, God knows what a mess there'd be at home.'[138]

The same peasant attitudes were noted by Tolstoy in *Three Deaths* (1856), by Leskov in *The Enchanted Pilgrim* (1873), by Saltykov-Shchedrin in *Old Days in Poshekhonie* (1887) and by practically every major Russian writer thereafter, so that in the end the stoicism of the peasants assumed the status of a cultural myth. This was the form in which it was repeated by Alexander Solzhenitsyn in *Cancer Ward* (1968), in the scene in which Yefrem remembers how 'the old people used to die back home on the Kama'.

They didn't puff themselves up or fight against it or brag that they were going to die – they took death calmly. They didn't shirk squaring things up, they prepared themselves quietly and in good time, deciding who should have the mare, who the foal, who the coat and who the boots, and they departed easily, as if they were just moving into a new house. None of them would be scared by cancer. Anyway, none of them got it.[139]

But attitudes like this were not just literary invention. They were documented in the memoir sources, medical reports and ethnographic studies of the nineteenth and the early twentieth centuries.[140] Some put down the peasants' resignation to a serf-like fatalism in which death was viewed as a release from suffering. When they talked about their lot, the peasants often referred to the afterlife as a 'kingdom of liberty' where their ancestors lived in 'God's freedom'.[141] This was the idea behind Turgenev's *Sketches*, in the story 'Living Relic', where a sick peasant woman yearns for death to end her suffering. Like many of her class, she believes that she will be rewarded for her suffering in Heaven and this makes her unafraid to die. Others explained such peasant fatalism as a form of self-defence. Death was such a common fact of village life that, to a degree, the peasant must have become hardened towards it. In a society where nearly half the children died before the age of five there had to be some way of coping with the grief. Doctors often noted that the parents of a village child would not react emotionally to its death, and in many of the poorest regions, where there were too many mouths to feed, women would even thank

God for taking it away.[142] There were peasant proverbs to advance the view that 'It's a good day when a child dies'.[143] Infanticide was not uncommon, especially at times of economic hardship, and with children who were illegitimate it was practically the norm.[144]

The desperate peasant woman in *The Brothers Karamazov* who has lost her boy is told by Zosima that God has taken him and given him the rank of an angel. In peasant Russia it was generally believed, in the words of a villager from Riazan province, that 'the souls of little children go straight up to heaven'.[145] Such thoughts must have been of real comfort. For the peasantry believed in a universe where the earth and spirit worlds were intimately linked in one continuum. The spirit world was a constant presence in their daily lives, with demons and angels at every turn. The fortunes of the souls of their kin were a matter of the highest importance. There were good and bad spirits in the Russian peasant world, and how a person died determined whether his spirit would also be good or bad. The peasant thought it was essential to prepare for death, to make the dying comfortable, to pray for them, to end all arguments with them, to dispose properly of their property, and to give them a Christian burial (sometimes with a candle and a bread ladder to help them on their way) in order that their souls could rise up peacefully to the spirit world.[146] Those who died dissatisfied would return to haunt the living as demons or diseases. Hence, in many places it became the custom to bury murder victims, those who died by suicide or poisoning, deformed people and sorcerers and witches outside the boundaries of the cemetery.

During a severe harvest failure it was even known for the peasants to exhume the corpses of those whose evil spirits were thought to be to blame.[147] In the peasant belief system the spirits of the dead led an active life. Their souls ate and slept, they felt cold and pain, and they often came back to the family household, where by custom they took up residence behind the stove. It was important to feed the dead. All sorts of food would be left around the house where the spirit of the dead was believed to remain for forty days. Water and honey were mandatory, in popular belief, but vodka, too, was often left out to prepare the soul for its long journey to the other world. In some places they left money out, or placed it in the grave, so that the spirit of the dead person could buy land in the next world to feed itself.[148]

At set times of the year, but especially at Easter and Pentecost, it was important for the family to give remembrance to the dead and feed their souls, in graveside picnics, with ritual breads and pies and decorated eggs. Breadcrumbs would be scattered on the graves to feed the birds – symbols of the souls that rose up from the ground and flew around the village during Easter time – and if the birds arrived it was taken as a sign that the spirits of the dead were alive and well.[149] Dostoevsky was borrowing from this ancient custom in *The Brothers Karamazov* when he made Ilyusha, the dying little boy, ask his father to scatter bread around his grave 'so that the sparrows may fly down, and I shall hear and it will cheer me up not to be lying alone'.[150] The Russian grave was much more than a place of burial. It was a sacred site of social interchange between the living and the dead.

One of the last utterances Tolstoy made, as he lay dying in the stationmaster's little house at Astapovo, was 'What about the peasants? How do peasants die?' He had thought a lot about the question, and had long believed that the peasants died in a different way from the educated classes, a way that showed they knew the meaning of their lives. The peasants died accepting death, and this was the proof of their religious faith. Tolstoy meant to die in that way, too.[151] Many years before, he had written in his diary: 'When I am dying I should like to be asked whether I still see life as before, as a progression towards God, an increase of love. If I should not have the strength to speak, and the answer is yes, I shall close my eyes; if it is no, I shall look up.'[152] No one thought of asking him the question at the moment of his death, so we shall never know how he crossed the frontier which had brought him so much agony and so much doubt. There was no reconciliation with the Church, despite Tolstoy's flight to Optina. The Holy Synod tried to win him back and even sent one of the Optina monks to Astapovo, where Tolstoy became stranded, too ill to go on, after he had left the monastery. But the mission failed – none of Tolstoy's family would even let the monk see the dying man – and so in the end the writer was denied a Christian burial.[153]

But if the Church refused to say a mass for the dead man, the people said one for him in another way. Despite the attempts of the police to stop them, thousands of mourners made their way to Yasnaya Polyana, where amid scenes of national grief that were not to be found on the death of any Tsar, Tolstoy was buried in his favourite childhood spot. It was a place in the woods where, many years before, his brother Nikolai had buried in the ground a magic stick on which he had written the secret about how eternal peace would come and evil would be banished from the world. As Tolstoy's coffin was lowered into the ground, the mourners started singing an ancient Russian chant, and someone shouted, in defiance of the police who had been instructed to impose the Church's excommunication of the writer to the end, 'On your knees! Take off your hats!'[154] Everyone obeyed the Christian ritual and, after hesitating for a moment, the police kneeled down too and removed their caps.

overleaf:
Scythian figures: late-nineteenth-century archaeological engraving

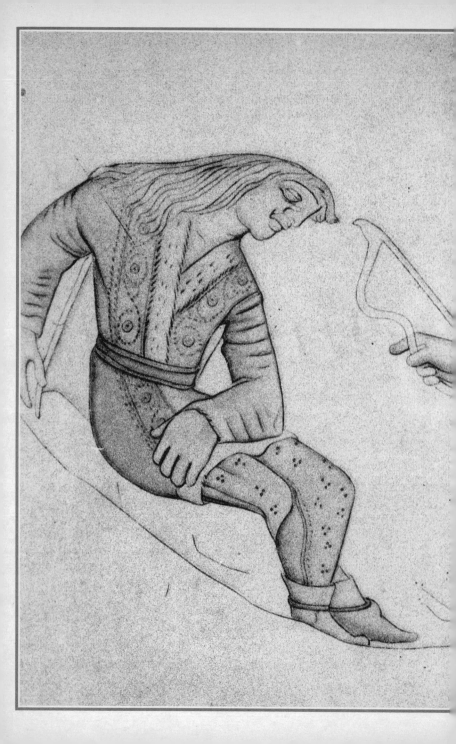

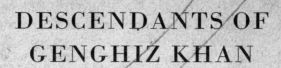

DESCENDANTS OF
GENGHIZ KHAN

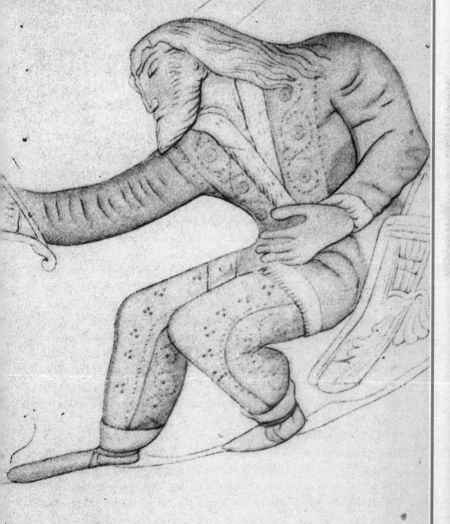

1

Before he turned to art Kandinsky thought he might become an anthropologist. As a student reading law at Moscow University, he had fallen
ill in his final year, and to recuperate he had set off on a trip to the
remote Komi region, 800 kilometres north-east of Moscow, to study
the beliefs of its Finno-Ugric tribes. Travelling by train as far as
Vologda, where the railway stopped, he then sailed east along the
Sukhona river, entering the forests of 'another world', as he recalled,
where the people still believed in demons and spirits. Anthropologists
had long marked out the Komi region as a meeting point between
Christianity and the old shamanic paganism of the Asiatic tribes. It
was a 'wonderland' where 'the people's every action is accompanied
by secret magic rituals'.[1] The trip left an indelible impression on
Kandinsky. The shamanism he discovered there became one of the
major inspirations for his abstract art.[2] 'Here I learned how to look at
art', he would later write – 'how to turn oneself around within a
painting and how to live in it.'[3]

Kandinsky's journey east was a journey back in time. He was looking
for the remnants of the paganism which Russian missionaries had
described in that region from medieval times. There were ancient
records of the Komi people worshipping the sun, the river and the
trees; of frenzied whirling dances to summon up their spirits; and there
were legendary tales about the Komi shamans who beat their drums
and flew off on their horse-sticks to the spirit world. Six hundred years
of church-building had given no more than a gloss of Christianity to
this Eurasian culture. The Komi people had been forcibly converted
to the Christian faith by St Stephan in the fourteenth century. The area
had been colonized by Russian settlers for several hundreds years, and
the culture of the Komi, from their language to their dress, bore a close
resemblance to the Russian way of life.

Ust-Sysolsk, the region's capital, where Kandinsky lived for three
summer months in 1889, looked much like any Russian town. It
consisted of a small classical ensemble of administrative buildings in
the centre of a sprawling settlement of log-built peasant huts. As
Kandinsky did his fieldwork, recording the beliefs of the old people

21. *Group of Komi people in typical clothing, c. 1912*

and looking for motifs of shamanistic cults in their folk art, he soon
found traces of this ancient pagan culture concealed underneath the
Russian one. None of the Komi would describe themselves as anything
but Orthodox (at least not to someone from Moscow), and in their
public rituals they had a Christian priest. But in their private lives, as
Kandinsky ascertained, they still looked to the old shamans. The Komi

people believed in a forest monster called 'Vörsa'. They had a 'living soul' they called an 'ort', which shadowed people through their lives and appeared before them at the moment of their death. They prayed to the spirits of the water and the wind; they spoke to the fire as if they were speaking to a living thing; and their folk art still showed signs of worshipping the sun. Some of the Komi people told Kandinsky that the stars were nailed on to the sky.[4]

Scratching the surface of Komi life Kandinsky had revealed its Asian origins. For centuries the Finno-Ugric tribes had intermingled with the Turkic peoples of northern Asia and the Central Asian steppe. Nineteenth-century archaeologists in the Komi region had unearthed large amounts of ceramic pottery with Mongolian ornament. Kandinsky found a chapel with a Mongolian roof, which he sketched in his journal of the trip.[5] Nineteenth-century philologists subscribed to the theory of a Ural-Altaic family of languages that united the Finns with the Ostiaks, the Voguls, Samoyeds and Mongols in a single culture stretching from Finland to Manchuria. The idea was advanced in the 1850s by the Finnish explorer M. A. Castren, whose journeys to the east of the Urals had uncovered many things he recognized from home.[6] Castren's observations were borne out by later scholarship. There are shamanistic motifs, for example, in the Kalevala, or 'Land of Heroes', the Finnish national epic poem, which may suggest a historical connection to the peoples of the East, although the Finns themselves regard their poem as a Baltic Odyssey in the purest folk traditions of Karelia, the region where Finland and Russia meet.[7] Like a shaman with his horse-stick and drum, its hero Väinämöinen journeys with his kantele (a sort of zither) to a magic underworld inhabited by spirits of the dead. One-fifth of the Kalevala is composed in magic charms. Not written down until 1822, it was usually sung to tunes in the pentatonic ('Indo-Chinese') scale corresponding to the five strings of the kantele, which, like its predecessor, the five-stringed Russian gusli, was tuned to that scale.[8]

Kandinsky's exploration of the Komi region was not just a scientific quest. It was a personal one as well. The Kandinskys took their name from the Konda river near Tobolsk in Siberia, where they had settled in the eighteenth century. The family was descended from the Tungus tribe, who lived along the Amur river in Mongolia. Kandinsky was proud of his Mongol looks and he liked to boast that he was a descendant of the seventeenth-century Tungus chieftain Gantimur. During the eighteenth century the Tungus had moved north-west to the Ob and Konda rivers. They intermingled with the Ostiaks and the Voguls, who traded with the Komi and with other Finnic peoples on the Urals' western side. Kandinsky's ancestors were among these traders, who would have intermarried with the Komi people, so it is possible that he had Komi blood as well.[9]

Many Russian families had Mongol origins. 'Scratch a Russian and you will find a Tatar,' Napoleon once said. The coats of arms of Russian families – where Muslim motifs such as sabres, arrows, crescent moons and the 8-pointed star are much in evidence – bear witness to this Mongol legacy. There were four main groups of Mongol descendants. First there were those descended from the Turkic-speaking nomads who had swept in with the armies of Genghiz Khan in the thirteenth century and settled down in Russia following the break-up of the 'Golden Horde', the Russian name for the Mongol host with its gleaming tent encampment on the Volga river, in the fifteenth century. Among these were some of the most famous names in Russian history: writers like Karamzin, Turgenev, Bulgakov and Akhmatova; philosophers like Chaadaev, Kireevsky, Berdiaev; statesmen like Godunov, Bukharin, Tukhachevsky; and composers like Rimsky-Korsakov.[*] Next were the families of Turkic origin who came to Russia from the west: the Tiutchevs and Chicherins, who came from Italy; or the Rachmaninovs, who had arrived from Poland in the eighteenth century. Even the Kutuzovs were of Tatar origin (*qutuz* is the Turkic word for 'furious' or 'mad') – an irony in view of the great general Mikhail Kutuzov's status as a hero made of purely Russian

---

[*] The name Turgenev derives from the Mongol word for 'swift' (*türgen*); Bulgakov from the Turkic word 'to wave' (*bulgaq*); Godunov from the Mongol word *gödön* ('a stupid person'); and Korsakov from the Turkic word *qorsaq*, a type of steppeland fox. Akhmatova was born Anna Gorenko. She changed her name to Akhmatova (said to be the name of her Tatar great-grandmother) when her father said he did not want a poet in his family. Akhmatova claimed descent from Khan Akhmat, a direct descendant of Genghiz Khan and the last Tatar khan to receive tribute from the Russian princes (he was assassinated in 1481). Nadezhda Mandelstam believed that Akhmatova had invented the Tatar origins of her great-grandmother (N. Mandelstam, *Hope Abandoned* (London, 1989), p. 449).

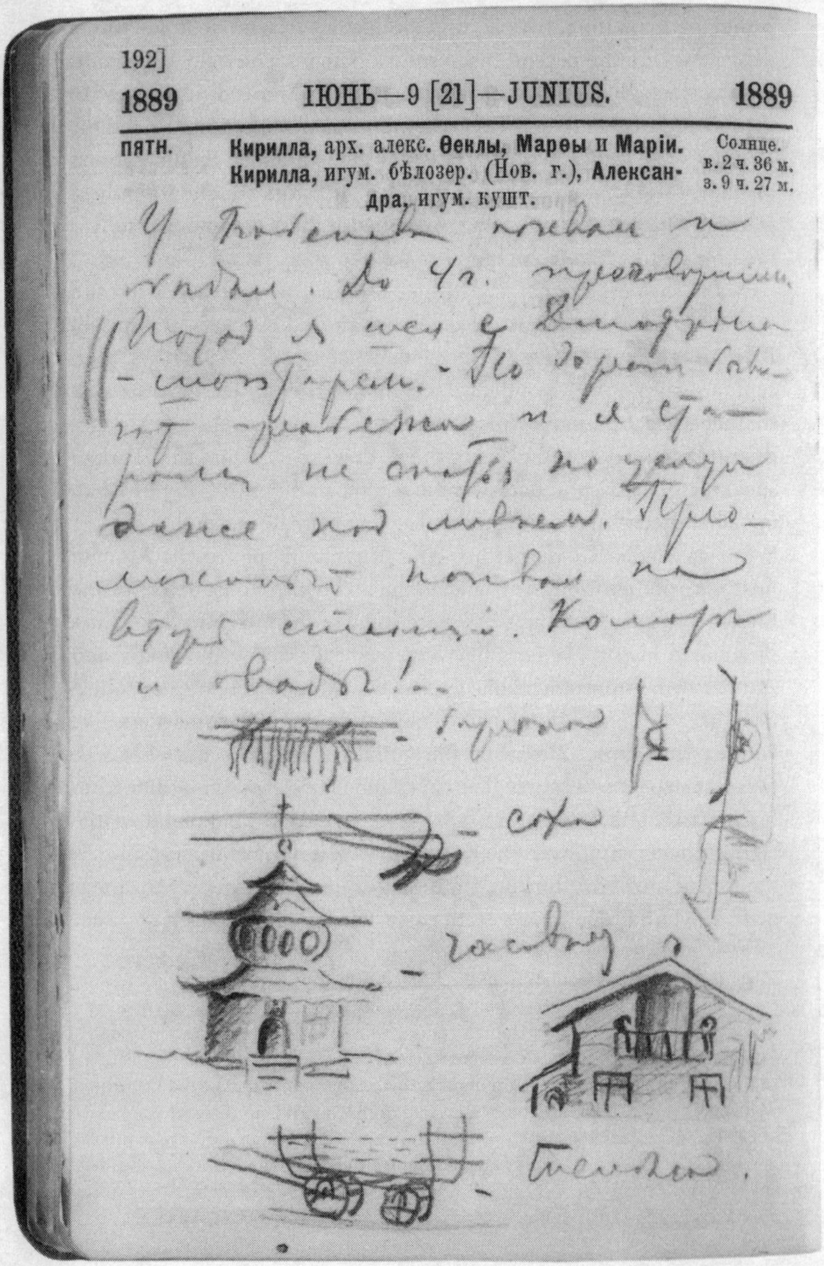

192]

1889 ІЮНЬ—9 [21]—JUNIUS. 1889

ПЯТН. **Кирилла,** арх. алекс. **Ѳеклы, Марѳы** и **Маріи. Кирилла,** игум. бѣлозер. (Нов. г.), **Александра,** игум. кушт.

Солнце. в. 2 ч. 36 м. з. 9 ч. 27 м.

stuff. Families of mixed Slav and Tatar ancestry made up a third category. Among these were some of Russia's grandest dynasties – the Sheremetevs, Stroganovs and Rostopchins – although there were many at a lower level, too. Gogol's family, for instance, was of mixed Polish and Ukrainian descent but it shared a common ancestry with the Turkic Gogels, who derived their surname from the Chuvash word *gögül* – a type of steppeland bird (Gogol was renowned for his bird-like features, especially his beaky nose). The final group were Russian families who changed their names to make them sound more Turkic, either because they had married into a Tatar family, or because they had bought land in the east and wanted smooth relations with the native tribes. The Russian Veliaminovs, for example, changed their name to the Turkic Aksak (from *aqsaq*, meaning 'lame') to facilitate their purchase of enormous tracts of steppeland from the Bashkir tribes near Orenburg: and so the greatest family of Slavophiles, the Aksakovs, was founded.[10]

Adopting Turkic names became the height of fashion at the court of Moscow between the fifteenth and seventeenth centuries, when the Tatar influence from the Golden Horde remained very strong and many noble dynasties were established. During the eighteenth century, when Peter's nobles were obliged to look westwards, the fashion fell into decline. But it was revived in the nineteenth century – to the point where many pure-bred Russian families invented legendary Tatar ancestors to make themselves appear more exotic. Nabokov, for example, claimed (perhaps with tongue in cheek) that his family was descended from no less a personage than Genghiz Khan himself, who 'is said to have fathered the Nabok, a petty Tatar prince in the twelfth century who married a Russian damsel in an era of intensely artistic Russian culture'.[11]

After Kandinsky had returned from the Komi region he gave a lecture on the findings of his trip to the Imperial Ethnographic Society in St Petersburg. The auditorium was full. The shamanistic beliefs of the Eurasian tribes held an exotic fascination for the Russian public at

22. (opposite) *Vasily Kandinsky: sketches of buildings in the Komi region, including a church with a Mongolian-type roof. From the Vologda Diary of 1889*

23. *Masked Buriat shaman with drum, drumstick and horse-sticks.*
Note the iron on his robe. Early 1900s

this time, when the culture of the West was widely seen as spiritually dead and intellectuals were looking towards the East for spiritual renewal. But this sudden interest in Eurasia was also at the heart of an urgent new debate about the roots of Russia's folk culture.

In its defining myth Russia had evolved as a Christian civilization.

Its culture was a product of the combined influence of Scandinavia and Byzantium. The national epic which the Russians liked to tell about themselves was the story of a struggle by the agriculturalists of the northern forest lands against the horsemen of the Asiatic steppe – the Avars and Khazars, Polovtsians and Mongols, Kazakhs, Kalmyks and all the other bow-and-arrow tribes that had raided Russia from the earliest times. This national myth had become so fundamental to the Russians' European self-identity that even to suggest an Asiatic influence on Russia's culture was to invite charges of treason.

In the final decades of the nineteenth century, however, cultural attitudes shifted. As the empire spread across the Asian steppe, there was a growing movement to embrace its cultures as a part of Russia's own. The first important sign of this cultural shift had come in the 1860s, when Stasov tried to show that much of Russia's folk culture, its ornament and folk epics (*byliny*), had antecedents in the East. Stasov was denounced by the Slavophiles and other patriots. Yet by the end of the 1880s, when Kandinsky made his trip, there was an explosion of research into the Asiatic origins of Russia's folk culture. Archaeologists such as D. N. Anuchin and N. I. Veselovsky had exposed the depth of the Tatar influence on the Stone Age culture of Russia. They had equally revealed, or at least suggested, the Asiatic origins of many folk beliefs among the Russian peasants of the steppe.[12] Anthropologists had found shamanic practices in Russian peasant sacred rituals.[13] Others pointed out the ritual use of totems by the Russian peasantry in Siberia.[14] The anthropologist Dmitry Zelenin maintained that the peasants' animistic beliefs had been handed down to them from the Mongol tribes. Like the Bashkirs and the Chuvash (tribes of Finnish stock with a strong Tatar strain), the Russian peasants used a snake-like leather charm to draw a fever; and like the Komi, or the Ostiaks and the Buriats in the Far East, they were known to hang the carcass of an ermine or a fox from the portal of their house to ward away the 'evil eye'. Russian peasants from the Petrovsk region of the Middle Volga had a custom reminiscent of the totemism practised by many Asian tribes. When a child was born they would carve a wooden figurine of the infant and bury it together with the placenta in a coffin underneath the family house. This, it was believed, would guarantee a long life for the child.[15] All these findings raised disturbing questions about the identity of the Russians. Were they Europeans or Asians? Were they the subjects of the Tsar or descendants of Genghiz Khan?

2

In 1237 a vast army of Mongol horsemen left their grassland bases on the Qipchaq steppe to the north of the Black Sea and raided the principalities of Kievan Rus'. The Russians were too weak and internally divided to resist, and in the course of the following three years every major Russian town, with the exception of Novgorod, had fallen to the Mongol hordes. For the next 250 years Russia was ruled, albeit indirectly, by the Mongol khans. The Mongols did not occupy the central Russian lands. They settled with their horses on the fertile steppelands of the south and collected taxes from the Russian towns, over which they exerted their domination through periodic raids of ferocious violence.

It is hard to overstress the sense of national shame which the 'Mongol yoke' evokes in the Russians. Unless one counts Hungary, Kievan Rus' was the only major European power to be overtaken by the Asiatic hordes. In terms of military technology the Mongol horsemen were far superior to the forces of the Russian principalities. But rarely did they need to prove the point. Few Russian princes thought to challenge them. It was as late as 1380, when the power of the Mongols was already weakening, that the Russians waged their first real battle against them. And even after that it took another century of in-fighting between the Mongol khans – culminating in the breakaway of three separate khanates from the Golden Horde (the Crimean khanate in 1430, the khanate of Kazan in 1436, and that of Astrakhan in 1466) – before the Russian princes found the wherewithal to fight a war against each one in turn. By and large, then, the Mongol occupation was a story of the Russian princes' own collaboration with their Asiatic overlords. This explains why, contrary to national myth, relatively few towns were destroyed by the Mongols; why Russian arts and crafts, and even major projects such as the building of churches, showed no signs of slowing down; why trade and agriculture carried on as normal; and why in the period of the Mongol occupation there was no great migration by the Russian population from the southern regions closest to the Mongol warriors.[16]

According to the national myth, the Mongols came, they terrorized and pillaged, but then they left without a trace. Russia might have succumbed to the Mongol sword, but its Christian civilization, with its monasteries and churches, remained unaffected by the Asiatic hordes. This assumption has always remained central to the Russians' identity as Christians. They may live on the Asiatic steppe but they face towards the West. 'From Asia', wrote Dmitry Likhachev, the leading twentieth-century cultural historian of Russia, 'we received extraordinarily little' – and his book, called *Russian Culture*, has nothing more to say on the Mongol legacy.[17] This national myth is based on the idea of the Mongols' cultural backwardness. They ruled by terror, bringing (in Pushkin's famous phrase) 'neither algebra nor Aristotle' with them when they came to Russia, unlike the Moors when they conquered Spain. They plunged Russia into its 'Dark Age'. Karamzin, in his *History of the Russian State*, did not write a thing about the cultural legacies of Mongol rule. 'For how', he asked, 'could a civilized people have learned from such nomads?'[18] The great historian Sergei Soloviev devoted just three pages to the cultural influence of the Mongols in his 28-volume *History of Russia*. Even Sergei Platonov, the leading nineteenth-century Mongol scholar, suggested that the Mongols had no influence on Russian cultural life.

In fact the Mongol tribes were far from backward. If anything, particularly in terms of their military technology and organization, they were considerably in advance of the Russian people whose lands they mastered for so long. The Mongols had a sophisticated system of administration and taxation, from which the Russian state would develop its own structures, and this is reflected in the Tatar origins of many related Russian words like *dengi* (money), *tamozhna* (customs) and *kazna* (treasury). Archaeological excavations near the Mongol capital of Sarai (near Tsaritsyn, today Volgograd, on the Volga river) showed that the Mongols had the capacity to develop large urban settlements with palaces and schools, well laid-out streets and hydraulic systems, craft workshops and farms. If the Mongols did not occupy the central part of Russia, it was not, as Soloviev suggested, because they were too primitive to conquer or control it, but because, without rich pastures or trade routes, the northern forest lands were of little benefit to their nomadic life. Even the taxes which they levied on the Russians, although burdensome to the peasantry, were insignificant compared to the riches they derived from their silk-route colonies in the Caucasus, Persia, Central Asia and northern India.

The Mongol occupation left a profound mark on the Russian way of life. As Pushkin wrote to Chaadaev in 1836, it was then that Russia became separated from the West. That history posed a fundamental challenge to the Russians' European self-identification:

Of course the schism separated us from the rest of Europe and we took no part in any of the great events which stirred her; but we have had our own mission. It was Russia who contained the Mongol conquest within her vast expanses. The Tatars did not dare cross our western frontiers and so leave us in the rear. They retreated to their deserts, and Christian civilization was saved. To this end we were obliged to lead a completely separate existence which, while it left us Christians, almost made us complete strangers in the Christian world . . . The Tatar invasion is a sad and impressive history . . . Do you not discern something imposing in the situation of Russia, something that will strike the future historian? Do you think he will put us outside Europe? . . . I do not by any means admire all that I see around me . . . but I swear to you that not for anything in the world would I change my country for another, nor have any history other than that of our ancestors, such as it has been given us by God.[19]

Pushkin's willingness to embrace this legacy was exceptional, given the taboo which Asia represented to the educated classes of Russia at that time. Perhaps it was explained by Pushkin's origins – for he himself was of African descent on his mother's side. Pushkin was the great-grandson of Abram Gannibal, an Abyssinian who had been found at the palace of the Ottoman sultan in Istanbul and purchased by the Russian ambassador as a present for Peter the Great. A favourite at Peter's court, Gannibal was sent to study in Paris. He rose to become a major-general under the Empress Elizabeth, who granted him an estate with 1,400 serfs at Mikhailovskoe, near Pskov. Pushkin took much pride in his great-grandfather – he had inherited his African lips and thick black curly hair. He wrote an unfinished novel, *The Negro of Peter the Great* (1827), and in the opening chapter of *Eugene Onegin* he appended a long footnote on his ancestry to the line (no doubt composed to necessitate the note) 'Beneath the sky of my Africa'.[20] But Russian Europhiles like Chaadaev found nothing to impress them in the Mongol legacy. Seeking to explain why their country took a separate path from Western Europe, many Russians blamed the despotism of the Mongol khans. Karamzin pointed to the Mongols for the degeneration of Russia's political morals. The historian V. O. Kliuchevsky described the Russian state as 'an Asiatic structure, albeit one that has been decorated by a European façade'.[21]

The Asiatic character of Russia's despotism became a commonplace of the nineteenth-century democratic intelligensia and was also later used as an explanation for the Soviet system. Herzen said that Nicholas I was 'Genghiz Khan with a telegraph' – and, continuing in that tradition, Stalin was compared to Genghiz Khan with a telephone. The Russian autocratic tradition had many roots, but the Mongol legacy did more than most to fix the basic nature of its politics. The khans demanded, and mercilessly enforced, complete submission to their will from all their subjects, peasants and noblemen alike. Moscow's princes emulated the behaviour of the khans when they ousted them from the Russian lands and succeeded them as Tsars in the sixteenth century. Indeed, they justified their new imperial status not just on the basis of their spiritual descent from Byzantium but also on the basis of their territorial inheritance from Genghiz Khan. The title 'Tsar' had been used by the last khan of the Golden Horde and for a long time the Russian terms for Tsar and khan were interchangeable. Even Genghiz Khan was rendered Genghiz Tsar.[22]

As the Golden Horde broke up and the Tsarist state pushed east, many of the Mongols who had served the khan remained in Russia and entered into service in the court of Muscovy. Genghiz Khan's descendants held a prominent position in the Moscow court and, by any estimate, a sizeable proportion of the Russian aristocracy had the great khan's blood running through their veins. There were at least two Tsars who were descended from the Golden Horde. One was Simeon Bekbulatovich (also known as Sain Bulat), who was Tsar of part of Russia for the best part of a year, in 1575. The grandson of a khan of the Golden Horde, Bekbulatovich had joined the Moscow court and risen through its ranks to become a retainer of Ivan IV ('the Terrible'). Ivan set Bekbulatovich to rule over the *boyars*' domains while he himself retreated to the countryside, taking the title 'Prince of Moscow'. The appointment was a temporary and tactical man-oeuvre on Ivan's part to tighten his control of his rebellious guards, the *oprichnina*. Bekbulatovich was only nominally in charge. But Ivan's choice was clearly motivated by the high prestige which the Golden Horde retained within society. At the end of his short 'reign', Ivan rewarded Bekbulatovich with a rich estate of 140,000 hectares along with the title of the Grand Prince of Tver. But under Boris Godunov Bekbulatovich was accused of treason, deprived of his estate and forced into the monastery of St Cyril, near Belo Ozero. Boris Godunov was the other Tsar descendant of the Golden Horde – the great-great-great-great-grandson of a Tatar khan named Chet who had entered the service of the Moscow princes in the middle of the fourteenth century.[23]

It was not just Mongol nobles who settled down in Russia. The Mongol invasion involved a huge migration of nomadic tribes who had been forced to find new pastures on the steppe through the over-population of Mongolia. The whole Eurasian steppe, from the Ukraine to Central Asia, was engulfed by incoming tribes. Many of the immi-grants became absorbed in the settled population and stayed behind in Russia when the Golden Horde was pushed back to Mongolia. Their Tatar names are still marked on maps of southern Russia and the Volga lands: Penza, Chembar, Ardym, Anybei, Kevda, Ardatov and Alatyr. Some of the settlers were cohorts of the Mongol army stationed as administrators in the southern borderlands between the Volga and the river Bug. Others were traders or artisans who went to work in the Russian towns, or poor nomads who were forced to become peasant farmers when they lost their herds. There was such a heavy influx of these Tatar immigrants, and so much intermingling with the native population over several centuries, that the idea of a peasantry of purely Russian stock must be seen as no more than myth.

The Mongol influence went deep into the roots of Russian folk culture. Many of the most basic Russian words have Tatar origins – *loshad* (horse), *bazar* (market), *ambar* (barn), *sunduk* (chest) and several hundred more.[24] As already noted, imported Tatar words were particularly common in the languages of commerce and administration, where the descendants of the Golden Horde dominated. By the fifteenth century the use of Tatar terms had become so modish at the court of Muscovy that the Grand Duke Vasily accused his courtiers of 'excessive love of the Tatars and their speech'.[25] But Turkic phrases also left their mark on the language of the street – perhaps most notably in those 'davai' verbal riffs which signal the intention of so many daily acts: 'davai poidem' ('Come on, let's go'), 'davai posidim' ('Come on, let's sit down'), and 'davai popem' ('Come on, let's get drunk').

Russian customs were equally influenced by the Tatar immigration, although this is easier to establish at the level of the court and high society, where Russian customs of hospitality were clearly influenced by the culture of the khans, than it is at the level of the common Russian folk. None the less, the archaeologist Veselovsky traced the Russian folk taboos connected with the threshold (such as not to step on it or not to greet a person across it) to the customs and beliefs of the Golden Horde. He also found a Mongol origin for the Russian peasant custom of honouring a person by throwing them into the air – a ceremony performed by a crowd of grateful peasants on Nabokov's father after he had settled a dispute on the estate.[26]

From my place at table I would suddenly see through one of the west windows a marvellous case of levitation. There, for an instant, the figure of my father in his wind-rippled white summer suit would be displayed, gloriously sprawling in midair, his limbs in a curious casual attitude, his handsome, imperturbable features turned to the sky. Thrice, to the mighty heave-ho of his invisible tossers, he would fly up in this fashion, and the second time he would go higher than the first and then there he would be, on his last and loftiest flight, reclining, as if for good, against the cobalt blue of the summer noon, like one of those paradisiac personages who comfortably soar, with such a wealth of fold in their garments, on the vaulted ceiling of a church while below, one by one, the wax tapers in mortal hands light up to make a swarm of minute flames in the midst of incense, and the priest chants of eternal repose, and funeral lilies conceal the face of whoever lies there, among the swimming lights, in the open coffin.[27]

There is also reason to suppose that the shamanistic cults of the Mongol tribes were incorporated in the Russian peasant faith, as

Kandinsky and his fellow anthropologists had argued at the end of the nineteenth century (although it is telling that they found no trace of the Muslim religion which the Golden Horde adopted in the fourteenth century).* Many of the peasant sects, the 'Wailers' and the 'Jumpers', for example, used techniques that were highly reminiscent of the Asian shamans' to reach a trance-like state of religious ecstasy.[28]

The Holy Fool (*yurodivyi*) was probably descended from the Asian shamans, too, despite his image as the quintessential 'Russian type' in many works of art. It is difficult to say where the Holy Fools came from. There was certainly no school for Holy Fools and, like Rasputin (who was in his way a sort of Holy Fool), they seem to have emerged as simple men, with their own techniques of prophecy and healing, which enabled them to set out on their life of religious wandering. In Russian folklore, the 'fool for the sake of Christ', or Holy Fool for short, held the status of a saint – though he acted more like an idiot or madman than the self-denying martyr demanded by St Paul. Widely deemed to be clairvoyant and a sorcerer, the Holy Fool dressed in bizarre clothes, with an iron cap or harness on his head and chains beneath his shirt. He wandered as a poor man round the countryside, living off the alms of the villagers, who generally believed in his supernatural powers of divination and healing. He was frequently received and given food and lodgings in the households of the provincial aristocracy.

The Tolstoy family retained the services of a Holy Fool at Yasnaya Polyana. In his semi-fictional, semi-autobiographical *Childhood*, Tolstoy recounts a memorable scene in which the children of the household hide in a dark cupboard in Fool Grisha's room to catch a glimpse of his chains when he goes to bed:

Almost immediately Grisha arrived with his soft tread. In one hand he had his staff, in the other a tallow candle in a brass candlestick. We held our breaths.

'Lord Jesus Christ! Most Holy Mother of God! To the Father, the Son and the Holy Ghost . . .' he kept saying, drawing the air into his lungs and speaking

---

* Long after shamanism became fashionable, the Muslim impact on Russian culture remained taboo. Even in St Petersburg, a city founded on the principle of religious tolerance, there was no mosque until 1909.

with the different intonations and abbreviations peculiar to those who often repeat these words.

With a prayer he placed his staff in a corner of the room and inspected his bed; after which he began to undress. Unfastening his old black girdle, he slowly divested himself of his tattered nankeen coat, folded it carefully and hung it over the back of a chair . . . His movements were deliberate and thoughtful.

Clad only in his shirt and undergarment he gently lowered himself on the bed, made the sign of the cross all round it, and with an effort (for he frowned) adjusted the chains beneath his shirt. After sitting there for a while and anxiously examining several tears in his linen he got up and, lifting the candle with a prayer to the level of the glass case where there were some icons, he crossed himself before them and turned the candle upside down. It spluttered and went out.

An almost full moon shone in through the windows which looked towards the forest. The long white figure of the fool was lit up on one side by its pale silvery rays; from the other its dark shadow, in company with the shadow from the window-frames, fell on the floor, on the walls and up to the ceiling. Outside in the courtyard the watchman was striking on his iron panel.

Folding his huge hands on his breast, Grisha stood in silence with bowed head before the icons, breathing heavily all the while. Then with difficulty he sank to his knees and began to pray.

At first he softly recited familiar prayers, only emphasizing certain words; then he repeated them, but louder and with much animation. Then he began to pray in his own words, making an evident effort to express himself in Church Slavonic. Though incoherent, his words were touching. He prayed for all his benefactors (as he called those who received him hospitably), among them for our mother and us; he prayed for himself, asking God to forgive him his grievous sins, and he kept repeating: 'Oh God, forgive my enemies!' He rose to his feet with a groan and repeating the same words again and again, fell to the floor and again got up despite the weight of his chains, which knocked against the floor every time with a dry harsh sound . . .

For a long time Grisha continued in this state of religious ecstasy, improvising prayers. Now he would repeat several times in succession *Lord, have mercy* but each time with renewed force and expression. Then he prayed *Forgive me, O Lord teach me how to live . . . teach me how to live, O Lord* so feelingly that he might be expecting an immediate answer to his petition.

The piteous sobs were all that we could hear . . . He rose to his knees, folded his hands on his breast and was silent.[29]

Writers and artists portrayed the Holy Fool as an archetype of the simple Russian believer. In Pushkin's and in Musorgsky's *Boris Godunov* the Holy Fool appears as the Tsar's conscience and as the voice of the suffering people. Prince Myshkin, the epileptic, Christ-like hero of *The Idiot*, is called a Holy Fool by the wealthy merchant Rogozhin; and Dostoevsky clearly wanted to create in him a genuinely Christian individual who, like the Holy Fool, is driven to the margins of society. In his painting *In Russia* (1916) Mikhail Nesterov portrayed the Holy Fool as the unofficial spiritual leader of the Russian people. Yet the Fool's untutored and largely improvised sacraments probably owed more to the Asian shamans than they did to the Russian Church. Like a shaman, the Holy Fool performed a sort of whirling dance with strange shrieks and cries to enter into a state of religious ecstasy; he used a drum and bells in his magic rituals; and he wore his chains in the belief, which was shared by Asian shamans, that iron had a supernatural quality. Like a shaman, too, the Holy Fool frequently employed the image of the raven in his rituals – a bird with a magic and subversive status in Russian folklore. Throughout the nineteenth century the peasants of the Volga region saw the Cossack rebel leaders Pugachev and Razin in the form of giant ravens in the sky.[30]

Many common elements of Russian clothing were also Asiatic in their origins – a fact reflected in the Turkic derivation of the Russian words for clothes like *kaftan*, *zipun* (a light coat), *armiak* (heavy coat), *sarafan* and *khalat*.[31] Even the Tsar's crown or Cap of Monomakh – by legend handed down from Byzantium – was probably of Tatar origin.[32] The food of Russia, too, was deeply influenced by the cultures of the East, with many basic Russian dishes, such as *plov* (pilaff), *lapsha* (noodles) and *tvorog* (curd cheese) imported from the Caucasus and Central Asia, and other eating habits, like the Russian taste for horsemeat and *koumis* (fermented mare's milk) no doubt handed down from the Mongol tribes. In contrast to the Christian West and most Buddhist cultures of the East, there was no religious sanction against eating horsemeat in Russia. Like the Mongol tribes, the Russians even bred a type of horse specifically to eat or (in the Volga region) to milk for *koumis*. Such practices were practically unknown in western Europe – at least until the nineteenth century, when French social reformers began to advocate the eating of horsemeat as a solution to the problems of poverty and malnutrition. But even then there was something of a stigma attached to eating horses. The practice of breeding horses for meat was regarded as barbaric in the West.[33]

All the major tribes of Central Asia – the Kazakhs, the Uzbeks, the Kalmyks and Kirghiz – were offshoots of the Golden Horde. With the dissolution of the Horde in the fifteenth century, they had remained on the Russian steppe and became the allies or the subjects of the Tsar. The ancestors of the Kazakhs – Islamic-Turkic Mongols – left the Golden Horde in the fifteenth century. Gradually they became closer to the Russians as they were forced out of the richest steppeland pastures by their rival tribes, the Dzhungars and the Uzbeks. The Uzbeks also came out of the Horde in the fifteenth century. They settled down to an agricultural life on the fertile plain of Ferghana, inheriting the riches of the old Iranian oasis towns between the Oxus and Jaxartes rivers (the heritage of Tamerlane), on which basis they went on to found the Uzbek states of Bukhara, Khiva and Khokand and established trade relations with the Tsar. As for the Kalmyks, they were western Mongols (Oirats) who had left the Mongol army and stayed put on the steppe when the Golden Horde dissolved (the Turkic verb *kalmak* – from which the Kalmyks get their name – means 'to stay'). Driven west by other tribes, they settled with their herds near Astrakhan on the northern Caspian shores and became the main suppliers of the Russian cavalry, driving 50,000 horses every year to Moscow until the trade declined in the eighteenth century.[34] Russian settlers drove the Kalmyks off the Volga steppe in the early decades of the nineteenth century. Most of the tribesmen moved back east, but others settled in Russia, where they took up trades or farming, and converted to the Orthodox belief. Lenin was descended from one of these Kalmyks. His paternal grandfather, Nikolai Ulianov, was a Kalmyk son from Astrakhan. This Mongol descent was clearly visible in Lenin's looks.

3

To commemorate the defeat of the Mongol khanates of Kazan and Astrakhan Ivan the Terrible ordered the construction of a new cathedral on Red Square in Moscow. St Basil's, as it was to become popularly known in honour of the city's favourite Holy Fool, was completed in 1560, just five years after its construction had begun. The cathedral was far more than a symbol of Russia's victory over the Mongol khanates. It was a triumphant proclamation of the country's liberation from the Tatar culture that had dominated it since the thirteenth century. With its showy colours, its playful ornament and outrageous onion domes, St Basil's was intended as a joyful celebration of the Byzantine traditions to which Russia now returned (although, to be truthful, there was nothing so ornate in the Orthodox tradition and the mosque-like features of the cathedral were probably derived from an oriental style).

The cathedral was originally named the Intercession of the Virgin – to mark the fact that Kazan was captured on that sacred feast day (Pokrova) in 1552. Moscow's victory against the Tatars was conceived as a religious triumph, and the empire which that victory launched was in many ways regarded as an Orthodox crusade. The conquest of the Asiatic steppe was portrayed as a holy mission to defend the Church against the Tatar infidels. It was set out in the doctrine of Moscow as the Third Rome – a doctrine which St Basil's cast in stone – whereby Russia came to see itself as the leader of a truly universal Christian empire built on the traditions of Byzantium. Just as the mighty Russian state was built on the need to defend its Christian settlers on the heathen steppe, so the Russian national consciousness was forged by this religious war against the East. In the Russian mind this religious boundary was always more important than any ethnic one, and the oldest terms for a foreigner (for example, *inoverets*) carry connotations of a different faith. It is equally telling that the word in Russian for a peasant (*krestianin*), which in all other European languages stems from the idea of the country or the land, is connected with the word for a Christian (*khristianin*).

From the capture of Kazan in 1552 to the revolution in 1917, the

Russian Empire grew at the fantastic rate of over 100,000 square kilometres every year. The Russians were driven east by fur, the 'soft gold' that accounted for one-third of the Imperial coffers at the height of the fur trade in the seventeenth century.[35] Russia's colonial expansion was a massive hunt for bears and minks, sables, ermine, foxes and otters. Close on the heels of the fur trappers came the Cossack mercenaries, such as those commanded by the Russian hero Ermak, who seized the ore-rich mines of the Urals for his patron Stroganov and finally defeated the khanate of Siberia in 1582. Then came the Tsar's troops, who constructed fortresses and exacted tributes from the native tribes, followed shortly after by the Church's missionaries, who set out to deprive them of their shamanistic cults. Surikov's enormous painting *Ermak's Conquest of Siberia* (1895) – a crowded battlescene between the icon-bearing, musket-firing Cossacks and the heathen bow-and-arrow tribesmen with their shamans beating drums – did more than any other work of art to fix this mythic image of the Russian empire in the national consciousness. As Surikov portrayed it, the real point of the conquest was to undermine the shamans who enjoyed a divine status in the Asiatic tribes.

This religious conquest of the Asiatic steppe was far more fundamental to the Russian empire than the equivalent role such missions played in the overseas empires of the European states. The explanation for this is geography. There was no great ocean to divide Russia from its Asian colonies: the two were part of the same land mass. The Ural mountains, which officially divided the European steppe from the Asiatic one, were physically no more than a series of big hills with large tracts of steppeland in between, and the traveller who crossed them would have to ask his driver where these famous mountains were. So without a clear geographical divide to distinguish them from their Asian colonies, the Russians looked instead to cultural categories. This became especially important in the eighteenth century, when Russia sought to redefine itself as a European empire with a presence in the West. If Russia was to be styled as a Western state, it needed to construct a clearer cultural boundary to set itself apart from this 'Asiatic other' in the Orient. Religion was the easiest of these categories. All the Tsar's non-Christian tribes were lumped together as 'Tartars', whatever their origins or faith, Muslim, shamanic or Buddhist. To reinforce this 'good and evil' split, the word 'Tartar' was deliberately misspelled (with the extra 'r') to bring it into line with the Greek word for 'hell' (*tartarus*). More generally, there was a tendency to think of all of Russia's newly conquered territories (Siberia, the Caucasus and Central Asia) as one undifferentiated 'east' – an '*Aziatshchina*' – which became a byword for 'oriental langour' and 'backwardness'. The image of the Caucasus was orientalized, with travellers' tales of its wild and savage tribes. Eighteenth-century maps consigned the Caucasus to the Muslim East, though geographically it was in the south, and historically it was an ancient part of the Christian West. In Georgia and Armenia the Caucasus contained Christian civilizations which went back to the fourth century, five hundred years before the Russians converted to Christianity. They were the first states in Europe to adopt the Christian faith – before even the conversion of Constantine the Great and the foundation of the Byzantine empire.

Nowhere were the Russians more concerned to erect cultural boundaries than in Siberia. In the eighteenth-century imagination the Urals were built up into a vast mountain range, as if shaped by God on the middle of the steppe to mark the eastern limit of the civilized world.* The Russians on the western side of these mountains were Christian in their ways, whereas the Asians on the eastern side were described by Russian travellers as 'savages' who needed to be tamed.[36] To Asianize its image, Russian atlases in the eighteenth century deprived Siberia of its Russian name (*Sibir'*) and referred to it instead as the 'Great Tatary', a title borrowed from the Western geographic lexicon. Travel writers wrote about its Asiatic tribes, the Tungus and the Yakuts and the Buriats, without ever mentioning the settled Russian population in Siberia, even though it was already sizeable. In this way, which came to justify the whole colonial project in the east, the steppe was reconstructed in the Russian mind as a savage and exotic wilderness whose riches were untapped. It was 'our Peru' and 'our India'.[37]

This colonial attitude was further strengthened by the economic decline of Siberia in the eighteenth and early nineteenth centuries. As

---

* The cultural importance of the Ural mountains for Russia's European self-identification has persisted to this day – as testified by the notion of a Europe 'from the Atlantic to the Urals' advanced by Gorbachev.

fashions in Europe changed and the fur trade declined in importance, and efforts by the Russian state to develop mining failed to compensate for the loss of revenues, so the promise of a virgin continent suddenly became supplanted by the bleak image of a vast wasteland. 'Nevsky Prospekt, on its own, is worth at least five times as much as the whole of Siberia', wrote one bureaucrat.[38] Russia would be better off, another writer thought in 1841, if the 'ocean of snow' that was Siberia could be replaced by a real sea, which would at least enable more convenient maritime trade with the Far East.[39] This pessimistic vision of Siberia was reinforced by its transformation into one vast prison camp. The term 'Siberia' became synonymous in colloquial expressions with penal servitude, wherever it occurred, with savage cruelty (*sibirnyi*) and a harsh life (*sibirshchina*).[40] In the poetic imagination the unforgiving nature of Siberia was itself a kind of tyranny:

> The gloomy nature of these lands
> Is always harsh and wild,
> The angry river roars
> Storms often rage,
> And the clouds are dark.
>
> Fearing the winters,
> Endless and icy,
> Nobody will visit
> This wretched country,
> This vast prison house for exiles.[41]

This Siberia was a region of the mind, an imaginary land to which all the opposites of European Russia were consigned. Its boundaries were in constant flux. For the city-bound élites of the early nineteenth century, 'Siberia' began where their own little 'Russia' – St Petersburg or Moscow and the road to their estate – gave way to a world they did not know. Katenin said that Kostroma, just 300 kilometres to the north-east of Moscow, was 'not far from Siberia'. Herzen thought that Viatka, several hundred kilometres to the west of the Urals, was in Siberia (and in a sense it was, for he was exiled there in 1835). Vigel thought that Perm – a little further east but still not within view of the

Ural mountains – was 'in the depths of Siberia'. Others thought that Vladimir, Voronezh or Riazan, all within a day or so's coach ride from Moscow, were the start of the 'Asiatic steppe'.[42]

But Russian attitudes toward the East were far from being all colonial. Politically, Russia was as imperialist as any Western state. Yet culturally there was a deep ambivalence, so that in addition to the usual Western stance of supcriority towards the 'Orient' there was an extraordinary fascination and even in some ways an affinity with it.* Much of this was a natural consequence of living on the edge of the Asiatic steppe, torn between the counter-pulls of East and West. This ambiguous geography was a source of profound insecurity – mainly in relation to the West, though such feelings were always the mainspring of Russia's wavering attitude towards the East as well. The Russians might define themselves as Europeans in relation to Asia, but they were 'Asiatics' in the West. No Western writer failed to score this point. According to the Marquis de Custine, the centre of St Petersburg was the only European part of the Tsar's vast empire, and to go beyond the Nevsky Prospekt was to venture into the realm of the 'Asiatic barbarism by which Petersburg is constantly besieged'.[43] Educated Russians themselves cursed their country's 'Asiatic backwardness'. They craved to be accepted as equals by the West, to enter and become part of the mainstream of European life. But when they were rejected or they felt that Russia's values had been underestimated by the West, even the most Westernized of Russia's intellectuals were inclined to be resentful and to lurch towards a chauvinistic pride in their country's threatening Asiatic size. Pushkin, for example, was a thorough European in his upbringing and, like all the men of the Enlightenment, he saw the West as Russia's destiny. Yet when Europe denounced Russia for its suppression of the Polish insurrection in 1831, he wrote a nationalistic poem, 'To the Slanderers of Russia', in which he emphasized the Asiatic nature of his native land, 'from the cold cliffs of Finland to the fiery cliffs of Colchis' (the Greek name for the Caucasus).

---

* This makes Russia an extremely big exception to Edward Said's provocative argument in *Orientalism*: that the arrogant European sense of cultural superiority imposed on the 'Orient' an 'antitype' or 'other' which underwrote the West's conquest of the East (E. Said, *Orientalism* (New York, 1979)). Said does not refer to the Russian case at all.

There was far more, however, than simply resentment of the West in this Asiatic orientation. The Russian empire grew by settlement, and the Russians who moved out into the frontier zones, some to trade or farm, others to escape from Tsarist rule, were just as likely to adopt the native culture as they were to impose their Russian way of life on the local tribes. The Aksakovs, for example, who settled on the steppes near Orenburg in the eighteenth century, used Tatar remedies when they fell ill. These entailed drinking *koumis* from a horse-skin bag, using special herbs and going on a diet of mutton fat.[44] Trade and intermarriage were universal forms of cultural interchange on the Siberian steppe, but the further east one went the more likely it became that the Russians were the ones who would change their ways. In Yakutsk, for example, in north-east Siberia, 'all the Russians spoke in the Yakut language', according to one writer in the 1820s.[45] Mikhail Volkonsky, the son of the Decembrist, who played a leading role in the Russian conquest and settlement of the Amur basin in the 1850s, recalls stationing a detachment of Cossacks in a local village to teach Russian to the Buriats. One year later Volkonsky returned to see how the Cossacks were getting on: none of the Buriats could converse in Russian yet, but all 200 Cossacks spoke fluent Buriat.[46]

Such a thing would never have occurred in the overseas empires of the European states, at least not once their mode of operation had been switched from trade to colonial mastery. For, with a few exceptions, the Europeans did not need to settle in their colonies (and did not have to take much interest in their cultures) to siphon off their wealth. But such things were almost bound to happen in a territorial empire as enormous as the Tsar's, where the Russian settlers in the remotest regions, six months' journey from the capital, were often forced to adopt local ways. The Russian Empire developed by imposing Russian culture on the Asian steppe, but in that very process many of the colonizers became Asian, too. One of the consequences of this encounter was a cultural sympathy towards the colonies that was rarely to be found in colonizers from the European states. It was frequently the case that even the most gung-ho of the Tsar's imperialists were enthusiasts and experts about oriental civilizations. Potemkin, Prince of Tauride, for example, revelled in the ethnic mix of the Crimea, which he wrested from the last of the Mongol khanates in 1783. To celebrate the victory he built himself a palace in the Moldavian-Turkish style, with a dome and four minaret towers, like a mosque.[47] Indeed, it was typical, not just of Russia but of eighteenth-century Europe as a whole, that precisely at that moment when Russian troops were marching east and crushing infidels, Catherine's architects at Tsarskoe Selo were building Chinese villages and pagodas, oriental grottoes, and pavilions in the Turkish style.[48]

A living embodiment of this dualism was Grigory Volkonsky, the father of the famous Decembrist, who retired as a hero of Suvorov's cavalry to become Governor of Orenburg between 1803 and 1816. Orenburg was a vital stronghold of the Russian Empire at this time. Nestled in the southern foothills of the Ural mountains, it was the gateway into Russia for all the major trade routes between Central Asia and Siberia. Every day a thousand camel caravans with precious goods from Asia, cattle, carpets, cottons, silks and jewels, would pass through Orenburg on their way to the markets of Europe.[49] It was the duty of the governor to tax, protect and promote this trade. Here Volkonsky was extremely successful, developing new routes to Khiva and Bukhara, important cotton kingdoms, which opened up the way to Persia and India.[50] But Orenburg was also the last outpost of the Imperial state – a fortress to defend the Russian farmers on the Volga steppelands from the nomadic tribes, the Nogai and the Bashkirs, the Kalmyks and Kirghiz, who roamed the arid steppes on its eastern side.

During the course of the eighteenth century the Bashkir pastoralists had risen up in a series of revolts against the Tsarist state, as Russian settlers had begun to move on to their ancient grazing lands. Many of the Bashkirs joined the Cossack leader Pugachev in his rebellion against the harsh regime of Catherine the Great in 1773–4. They besieged Orenburg (a story told by Pushkin in *The Captain's Daughter*) and captured all the other towns between the Volga and the Urals, plundering property and terrorizing the inhabitants. After the suppression of the rebellion, the Tsarist authorities reinforced the town of Orenburg. From this fortress they carried out a brutal campaign of pacification against the steppeland tribes. This campaign was continued by Volkonsky, who also had to cope with a serious uprising by the Ural Cossacks. In his dealings with them both he was extremely harsh. On Volkonsky's order several hundred Bashkir and Cossack rebel leaders were publicly flogged and branded on their foreheads or sent off to the penal camps in the Far East. Among the Bashkirs, the governor became known as 'Volkonsky the Severe'; he was a demon figure in the folklore of the Cossacks, who still sang songs about him in the 1910s.[51] Yet Volkonsky was by no means all severe. By nature he was soft and kind-hearted, according to his family, with a poetic spirit and a passion for music, intensely Christian in his private life. Among the citizens of Orenburg, he had the reputation of an eccentric. It was perhaps the consequence of a shrapnel wound he had received in the war against the Turks which left him with strange voices in his head. In mid-winter, when the temperature in Orenburg would sink as low as −30 degrees centigrade, he would walk about the streets in his dressing gown, or sometimes only dressed in his underpants, proclaiming that Suvorov (who had died ten years before) was 'still alive' in him. In this state he would set off to the market and hand out food and money to the poor, or go entirely naked into church to pray.[52]

Despite his brutal treatment of the Bashkir population, Volkonsky was an expert on their Turkic culture. He learned their Turkic language and spoke with the local tribesmen in their native tongue.[53] He travelled widely throughout Central Asia and wrote extensively about its flora and fauna, its customs and its history and ancient cultures in his private diaries and letters home. He thought the Tobol river, on the eastern side of the Ural mountains, was 'the best corner of all Russia'.[54] He was a connoisseur of oriental shawls, carpets, chinaware and jewellery, which friends from Petersburg would commission him to buy.[55] During his last years in Orenburg he even came to lead a semi-oriental life. 'I love this place', he wrote to his nephew Pavel Volkonsky, the Emperor Alexander's Chief-of-Staff. 'I love its nomadic way of life.'[56] Volkonsky lived like a Persian sultan in his exotic palace, surrounded by a retinue of Kirghiz and Kalmyk household serfs whom he regarded as his 'second family'.[57] He also kept a secret harem of Bashkir 'wives'.[58] Volkonsky mixed in a large society of Tatar tribesmen, whom he liked to refer to as 'my natives'.[59] Abandoning his Imperial uniform, he would receive the Kirghiz khans in a Mongol ceremonial uniform, or even in a *khalat*.[60] All the years he lived in Orenburg, Volkonsky never said he missed St Petersburg, and throughout this time he went back only once. 'The quiet life of the Asian steppe suits my temperament', he wrote to his daughter Sofia. 'You may consider me an Asiatic – perhaps I even count myself as one.'[61]

4

'A fairytale land from *The Thousand and One Nights*,' proclaimed Catherine the Great on her first trip to the newly annexed Tatar lands of the Crimea in 1783.[62] Literature and empire had a close relationship in the Russian conquest of the Orient. The marvels of these places were such a fertile source for the imagination that many statesmen came to view them through their images in literature and art. Eighteenth-century tales, starting with the Russian translation of *The Thousand and One Nights* (1763–71), portrayed the Orient as a hedonistic kingdom of sensual luxury and indolence, seraglios and sultans, as everything, in fact, that the austere north was not. These themes reappeared in the oriental dream worlds of the nineteenth century.

This 'Orient' was not a place that could be found on any map. It was in the south, in the Caucasus and the Crimea, as well as in the east. The two compass points of south and east became combined in an imaginary 'Orient' – an exotic counter-culture in the Russian imagination – and it was made up as a sort of pot-pourri from many different cultural elements. In Borodin's *Prince Igor*, for example, the melismatic music of the Polovtsian Dances, which came to represent the quintessential sound of the Orient, was actually drawn from Chuvash, Bashkir, Hungarian, Algerian, Tunisian and Arabian melodies. It even contained slave songs from America.[63]

Long before the Russians ever knew their colonies as ethnographic facts, they had invented them in their literature and arts. The Caucasus occupied a special place in the Russian imagination, and for much of the nineteenth century, as the Tsar's armies struggled to control its mountainous terrain and fought a bloody war against its Muslim tribes, Russian writers, artists and composers identified with it in a romantic way. The Caucasus depicted in their works was a wild and dangerous place of exotic charm and beauty, where the Russians from the north were strikingly confronted by the tribal cultures of the

Muslim south. It was Pushkin who did more than anyone to fix the Russian image of the Caucasus. He reinvented it as the 'Russian Alps', a place for contemplation and recuperation from the ills of urban life, in his poem *The Prisoner of the Caucasus* – a sort of *Childe Harold* of the Orient. The poem served as a guidebook for several generations of Russian noble families who travelled to the Caucasus for a spa cure. By the 1830s, when Lermontov set his novel *A Hero of Our Times* in the spa resort of Piatigorsk, the 'Caucasian cure' had become so fashionable among the upper classes that the annual trek southwards was even being compared to the pilgrimage of Muslims to Mecca.[64] Some travellers were disappointed not to find the wild, exotic spirit of Pushkin's poem in the grey and prosaic actuality of the Russian garrison towns where, for safety's sake, they were obliged to stay. Such was the craving for adventure and romance that even a patently second-rate (and today almost entirely forgotten) belletrist like Alexander Bestuzhev-Marlinsky was widely hailed as a literary genius (the 'Pushkin of prose') simply on account of his Caucasian tales and travelogues.[65]

This fascination with the Caucasus centred on more than a search for exotic charm, at least as far as Russia's writers were concerned. Pushkin's generation was deeply influenced by the 'southern theory' of Romanticism expounded by Sismondi in his *De la littérature du Midi de l'Europe* (1813), which portrayed the ancient Arabs as the original Romantics. For Russia's young Romantics, who were looking for a source to distinguish Russian culture from the West, Sismondi's theory was a revelation. Suddenly, it seemed, the Russians had their own 'south' in the Caucasus, a unique colony of Muslim–Christian culture whose possession brought them closer to the new Romantic spirit than any of the nations of the West. In his essay *On Romantic Poetry* (1823) the writer Orest Somov claimed that Russia was the birthplace of a new Romantic culture because through the Caucasus it had taken in the spirit of Arabia. The Decembrist poet Vilgem Kiukhelbeker called for a Russian poetry that combined 'all the mental treasures of both Europe and Arabia'.[66] Lermontov once said that Russian poetry would find its destiny by 'following the East instead of Europe and the French'.[67]

The Cossacks were a special caste of fiercely Russian soldiers living since the sixteenth century on the empire's southern and eastern frontiers in their own self-governing communities in the Don and Kuban regions along the Terek river in the Caucasus, on the Orenburg steppe and, in strategically important settlements, around Omsk, lake Baikal and the Amur river in Siberia. These ur-Russian warriors were semi-Asiatic in their way of life, with little to distinguish them from the Tatar tribesmen of the eastern steppes and the Caucasus, from whom indeed they may have been descended ('Cossack' or 'quzzaq' is a Turkic word for horseman). Both the Cossack and the Tatar tribesman displayed a fierce courage in the defence of their liberties; both had a natural warmth and spontaneity; both loved the good life. Gogol emphasized the 'Asiatic' and 'southern' character of the Ukrainian Cossacks in his story 'Taras Bulba': in fact, he used these two terms interchangeably. In a related article ('A Look at the Making of Little Russia', that is, Ukraine) he spelled out what he meant:

The Cossacks are a people belonging to Europe in terms of their faith and location, but at the same time totally Asiatic in their way of life, their customs and their dress. They are a people in which two opposite parts of the world, two opposing spirits have strangely come together: European prudence and Asiatic abandon; simplicity and cunning; a strong sense of activity and a love of laziness; a drive towards development and perfection and at the same time a desire to appear scornful of any perfection.[68]

As a historian Gogol tried to link the nature of the Cossacks to the periodic waves of nomadic in-migration that had swept across the steppe since 'the Huns in ancient times'. He maintained that only a warlike and energetic people such as the Cossacks was able to survive on the open plain. The Cossacks rode 'in Asiatic fashion across the steppe'. They rushed with the 'swiftness of a tiger out of hiding places when they launched a raid'.[69] Tolstoy, who had come to know the Cossacks as an officer in the army, also thought of them as semi-Asiatic in character. In *The Cossacks* (1863) Tolstoy showed in ethnographic detail that the Russian Cossacks on the northern side of the Terek river lived a way of life that was virtually indistinguishable from that of the Chechen hill tribes on the Terek's southern side.

When Pushkin travelled to the Caucasus, in the early 1820s, he thought of himself as going to a foreign land. 'I have never been beyond my own unbounded Russia', he wrote in *A Journey to Arzrum* (1836).[70] But Lermontov, who went there a decade later, embraced the Caucasus as his 'spiritual homeland' and asked its mountains to bless him 'as a son':

> At heart I am yours
> Forever and everywhere yours![71]

The mountains were the inspiration and indeed the setting of many his works, including his greatest masterpiece, *A Hero of Our Times*, the first really world-class Russian prose novel. Born in Moscow in 1814, Lermontov had suffered from rheumatic fevers as a boy and so he was taken on a number of occasions to the spa resort of Piatigorsk. The wild romantic spirit of its mountain scenery left a lasting imprint on the young poet. In the early 1830s he was a student of oriental literature and philosophy at Moscow University. From that time he was strongly drawn to the fatalistic outlook which he saw as Russia's inheritance from the Muslim world (an idea he explores in the final chapter of *A Hero of Our Times*). Lermontov took a keen interest in Caucasian folklore, especially the legends told by Shora Nogmov, a mullah-turned-Guards-officer from Piatigorsk, about the exploits of the mountain warriors. One of these tales inspired him to write his first major poem, *Izmail Bey*, in 1832 (though it was not passed for publication until many years later). It told the story of a Muslim prince surrendered as a hostage to the Russian troops in their conquest of the Caucasus. Brought up as a Russian nobleman, Izmail Bey abandons his commission in the Russian army and takes up the defence of his Chechen countrymen, whose villages are destroyed by the Tsarist troops. Lermontov himself was enrolled in the Guards to fight these mountain tribes, and to some degree he identified with Izmail Bey, feeling much the same divided loyalties. The poet fought with extraordinary courage against the Chechens at Fort Grozny, but he was repulsed by the savage war of terror he witnessed against the Chechen strongholds in the mountain villages. In *Izmail Bey* Lermontov concludes with a bitter condemnation of the Russian Empire which the Tsarist censor's pen could not disguise:

Where are the mountains, steppes and oceans
Yet to be conquered by the Slavs in war?
And where have enmity and treason
Not bowed to Russia's mighty Tsar?
Circassian fight no more! Likely as not,
Both East and West will share your lot.
The time will come: you'll say, quite bold,
'I am a slave but my Tsar rules the world.'
The time will come: the North will be graced
By an awesome new Rome, a second Augustus.

Auls are burning, their defenders mastered,
The homeland's sons have fallen in battle.
Like steady comets, fearful to the eyes,
A glow is playing across the skies,
A beast of prey with bayonet, the victor
Charges into a peaceful house,
He kills the children and the old folks,
And with his bloody hand he strokes
The unmarried girls and young mothers.
But a woman's heart can match her brother's!
After those kisses, a dagger's drawn,
A Russian cowers, gasps – he's gone!
'Avenge me comrade!' And in just a breath
(A fine revenge for a murderer's death)
The little house now burns, a delight to their gaze,
Circassian freedom set ablaze![72]

Lermontov was an accomplished watercolourist and in one self-portrait he paints himself with a Circassian sword gripped firmly in his hand, his body wrapped in a Caucasian cloak, and the cartridge cases worn by mountain tribesmen fixed on to the front of his Guards uniform. This same mixed identity, semi-Russian and semi-Asiatic, was assigned by Lermontov to Pechorin, the subject of *A Hero of Our Times*. Restless, cynical and disillusioned with the high society of St Petersburg, Pechorin undergoes a transformation when he is transferred, as a Guards officer, to the Caucasus. He falls in love with Bela,

*24. Watercolour copy of a lost self-portrait with Circassian sword and cloak
by Mikhail Lermontov, 1837*

the daughter of a Circassian chief, learns her Turkic language, and wears Circassian dress to declare his love for her. At one point the narrator compares him to a Chechen bandit. This, it seems, was the essential point: there was no clear boundary between the 'civilized' behaviour of the Russian colonists and the 'barbarous' acts of the Asiatic tribes.

Lermontov was not the only Russian to adopt the Caucasus as his 'spiritual home'. The composer Balakirev was another 'son of the mountains'. The founder of the 'Russian music school' came from ancient Tatar stock, and he was proud of it, judging from the frequency with which he posed for portraits in Caucasian costumes.[73] 'The Circassians', he wrote to Stasov in 1862, 'beginning with their costume (I know no better dress than that of the Circassians) are as much to my taste as to Lermontov's.'[74] Rimsky-Korsakov described Balakirev as 'half-Russian and half-Tatar in his character'. Stravinsky recalled him as a 'large man, bald, with a Kalmyk head and the shrewd, sharp-eyed look of a Lenin'.[75] In 1862 Balakirev toured the Caucasus. He fell in love with the region's wild landscape. It summoned up the spirit of his favourite poet, Lermontov. 'Of all things Russian', he wrote to Stasov from Piatigorsk, 'Lermontov affects me most of all.'[76]

Balakirev attempted to evoke this love for the writer in his symphonic poem *Tamara* (1866–81), based upon Lermontov's poem of that name. Lermontov's *Tamara* (1841) retold the folk story of a Georgian queen whose seductive voice lured lovers to her castle in the mountains overlooking the Terek river. After a night of orgiastic dancing she would throw the bodies of the lovers she had murdered from the tower of the castle into the river far below. It was the spirit of Tamara's 'whirling dance', as Stasov was to put it, which Balakirev tried to re-create in the frenzied music of his piano suite:

> And strange wild sounds
> All night were heard from there
> As if in this empty tower
> A hundred horny young men and girls
> Came together on a wedding night
> Or on the feast of a great funeral.[77]

The musical devices which Balakirev used were mostly from the common stock of 'oriental sounds' – sensuous chromatic scales, syncopated dance-like rhythms and languorous harmonies designed to conjure up the exotic world of hedonistic pleasure which people in the West had long associated with the Orient. But Balakirev also introduced a stunning new device which he had picked up from his transcriptions of Caucasian folk songs. For Balakirev had noticed that in all these songs the harmonies were based on the pentatonic (or five-tone) scale common to the music of Asia. The distinctive feature of the pentatonic or 'Indo-Chinese' scale is its avoidance of semitones and thus of any clear melodic gravitation towards any particular tone. It creates the sense of 'floating sounds' which is characteristic of South-east Asian music in particular. *Tamara* was the first major piece of Russian music to make extensive use of the pentatonic scale. Bala-kirev's innovation was akin to the discovery of a new artistic language with which to give Russian music its 'Eastern feel' and make it so distinct from the music of the West. The pentatonic scale would be used in striking fashion by every Russian composer who followed in the Balakirev 'national school', from Rimsky-Korsakov to Stravinsky.

This oriental element was one of the hallmarks of the Russian music school developed by the *kuchkists* – the 'Mighty Handful' (*kuchka*) of nationalist composers which included Balakirev, Musorgsky, Borodin and Rimsky-Korsakov. Many of the *kuchkists'* quintessential 'Russian' works – from Balakirev's fantasy for piano *Islamei* (a cornerstone of the Russian piano school and a 'must perform' at the Tchaikovsky Piano Competition) to Borodin's *Prince Igor* and Rimsky-Korsakov's *Scheherazade* – were composed in this oriental style. As the founding father of the school, Balakirev had encouraged the use of Eastern themes and harmonies to distinguish this self-conscious 'Russian' music from the German symphonism of Anton Rubinstein and the Conservatory. The 'First Russian Symphony' of Rimsky-Korsakov – which was in fact composed more than twelve years after the *Ocean Symphony* of Rubinstein – earned its nickname because of its use of Russian folk and oriental melodies, which Rimsky's teacher, Balakirev, had transcribed in the Caucasus. 'The symphony is good', wrote the composer César Cui to Rimsky in 1863. 'We performed it a few days ago at Balakirev's – to the great pleasure of Stasov. It is really Russian. Only a Russian could have composed it, because it lacks the slightest trace of any stagnant Germanness [*nemetschina*].'[78]

Along with Balakirev, Stasov was the major influence on the devel-opment of a Russian-oriental musical style. Many of the pioneering *kuchkist* works which shaped that style, including *Prince Igor* and *Scheherazade*, were dedicated to the nationalist critic. In 1882 Stasov wrote an article on 'Twenty-five Years of Russian Art', in which he tried to account for the profound influence of the Orient on Russian composers:

Some of them personally saw the Orient. Others, although they had not travelled to the East, had been surrounded with Oriental impressions all their lives. Therefore, they expressed them vividly and strikingly. In this they shared a general Russian sympathy with everything Oriental. Its influence has pervaded Russian life and given to its arts a distinctive colouring . . . To see in this only a strange whim and capriciousness of Russian composers . . . would be absurd.[79]

For Stasov the significance of the Eastern trace in Russian art went far beyond exotic decoration. It was a testimony to the historical fact of Russia's descent from the ancient cultures of the Orient. Stasov believed that the influence of Asia was 'manifest in all the fields of Russian culture: in language, clothing, customs, buildings, furniture and items of daily use, in ornaments, in melodies and harmonies, and in all our fairy tales'.[80]

Stasov had first outlined the argument in his thesis on the origins of Russian ornament during the 1860s.[81] Analysing medieval Russian Church manuscripts, he had linked the ornamentation of the lettering to similar motifs (rhomboids, rosettes, swastikas and chequered patterns, and certain types of floral and animal design) from Persia and Mongolia. Comparable designs were found in other cultures of Byzantium where the Persian influence was also marked; but whereas the Byzantines had borrowed only some of the Persian ornaments, the Russians had adopted nearly all of them, and to Stasov this suggested that the Russians had imported them directly from Persia. Such an argument is difficult to prove – for simple motifs like these are found all over the world. But Stasov focused on some striking similarities. There was, for example, a remarkable resemblance in the ornamental image of the tree, which Stasov thought was linked to the fact that both the Persians and the pagan Russians had 'idealized the tree as a sacred cult'.[82] In both traditions the tree had a conic base, a spiral round the trunk, and bare branches tipped with magnoliaceous flowers. The image appeared frequently in pagan rituals of the tree cult, which, as Kandinsky had discovered, was still in evidence among the Komi

25. *Vladimir Stasov: study of the Russian letter 'B' (Б) from a fourteenth-century manuscript of Novgorod*

people in the last decades of the nineteenth century. Stasov even found it as the calligraphic trunk of the letter 'B' in a fourteenth-century Gospel from Novgorod, where a man kneels in prayer at the base of the tree. Here is a perfect illustration of the complex mix of Asian, pagan and Christian elements which make up the main strands of Russian folk culture.

Stasov turned next to the study of the *byliny*, the epic songs which contained Russia's oldest folk myths and legends, claiming that these too were from Asia. In his *Origins of the Russian Byliny* (1868) he argued that the *byliny* were Russified derivatives of Hindu, Buddhist or Sanskrit myths and tales, which had been brought to Russia by armies, merchants and nomadic immigrants from Persia, India and Mongolia. Stasov's argument was based upon the theory of cultural borrowing – at that time just recently advanced by the German philologist Theodor Benfey. During the last decades of the nineteenth century Benfey's theory was increasingly accepted by those folklorists in the West (Gödeke and Köhler, Clouston and Liebrecht) who maintained that European folk tales were secondary versions of oriental originals. Stasov was the first to make a detailed argument for Benfey's case. His argument was based on a comparative analysis of the *byliny* with the texts of various Asian tales – especially the ancient Indian stories of the *Mahabharata*, the *Ramayana* and the *Panchantra*, which had been translated into German by Benfey in 1859.

Stasov paid particular attention to the narrative details, the symbols and the motifs of these ancient tales (not perhaps the strongest basis from which to infer a cultural influence, for basic similarities of plot and character can easily be found in folk tales from around the world).* Stasov concluded, for example, that the Russian legend of *Sadko* (where a merchant goes to an underwater kingdom in search of wealth) was derived from the Brahmin story of the *Harivansa* (where the flight to the underworld is a spiritual journey in search of truth). According to Stasov, it was only in the later versions of the Russian tale (those that date from after the fifteenth century) that the religious element was supplanted by the motif of commercial wealth. It was at this time that the legend was transposed on to the historical figure of Sadko – a wealthy member of a seafaring guild in Novgorod who had endowed a church of St Boris and St Gleb in the twelfth century.[83]

Similarly, Stasov argued that the folk heroes (*bogatyrs*) of the *byliny* were really the descendants of the oriental gods. The most famous of these *bogatyrs* was Ilia Muromets – a brave and honest warrior who championed the people's cause against such enemies as *Solovei Razboinik*, the 'Nightingale Robber', who was usually recast with Tatar features in the later versions of this Russian tale. Stasov drew attention to the supernatural age of Ilia Muromets – several hundred years by logical deduction from the details of the tale. This suggested that

---

* There is some historical evidence to support Stasov's thesis, however. Indian tales were certainly transported by migrants to South-east Asia, where these tales are widely known today; and the *Ramayana* tale was known from translations in Tibet from at least the thirteenth century (see J. W. de Jong, *The Story of Rama in Tibet: Text and Translation of the Tun-huang Manuscripts* (Stuttgart, 1989)).

Muromets was descended from the mythic kings who reigned over India for centuries, or from the oriental gods who transcended human time.[84] The word '*bogatyr*' was itself derived from the Mongol term for 'warrior' (*bagadur*), according to Stasov. He drew on evidence from European philologists, who had traced the word's etymological relatives to all those countries that had once been occupied by the Mongol hordes: *bahadir* (in Persian), *behader* (in Turkish), *bohater* (in Polish), *bator* (in Magyar), etc.[85]

Finally, Stasov analysed the ethnographic details of the texts – their place names, number systems, scenery and buildings, household items and furniture, clothing, games and customs – all of which suggested that the *byliny* had come, not from the northern Russian forests, but rather from the steppe.

If the *byliny* really did grow out of our native soil in ancient times, then, however much they were later altered by the princes and the Tsars, they should still contain the traces of our Russian land. So we should read in them about our Russian winters, our snow and frozen lakes. We should read about our Russian fields and meadows; about the agricultural nature of our people; about our peasant huts and generally about the native, always wooden buildings and utensils; about our Russian hearth and the spiritual beliefs that surround it; about the songs and rituals of the village chorus; about the way we worship our ancestors; about our belief in mermaids, goblins, house spirits and various other superstitions of pagan Rus'. Everything, in short, should breathe the spirit of our country life. But none of this is in the *byliny*. There is no winter, no snow or ice, as if these tales are not set in the Russian land at all but in some hot climate of Asia or the East. There are no lakes or mossy river banks in the *byliny*. Agricultural life is never seen in them. There are no wooden buildings. None of our peasant customs is described. There is nothing to suggest the Russian way of life and what we see instead is the arid Asian steppe.[86]

Stasov caused considerable outrage among the Slavophiles and other nationalists with his Asiatic theory of the *byliny*. He was accused of nothing less than 'slandering Russia'; his book was denounced as a 'source of national shame', its general conclusions as 'unworthy of a Russian patriot'.[87] It was not just that Stasov's critics took offence at his 'oriental fantasy' that 'our culture might have been descended from the barbarous nomads of the Asian steppe'.[88] As they perceived it, Stasov's theory represented a fundamental challenge to the nation's identity. The whole philosophy of the Slavophiles had been built on the assumption that the nation's culture grew from its native soil. For over thirty years they had lavished their attentions on the *byliny*, going round the villages and writing down these tales in the firm belief that they were true expressions of the Russian folk. Tales such as *Sadko* and *Ilia Muromets* were sacred treasures of the people's history, the Slavophiles maintained, a fact which was suggested by the very word *bylina*, which was, they said, derived from the past tense of 'to be' (*byl*).[89]

One of the strongholds of the Slavophiles was the 'mythological school' of folklorists and literary scholarship which had its origins in the European Romantic movement of the early nineteenth century. Stasov's fiercest critics belonged to the school, which numbered the most venerable folklorists, such as Buslaev and Afanasiev, among its followers. The exponents of the mythological theory worked on the rather questionable assumption that the ancient beliefs of the Russian people could be reconstructed through their contemporary life and art. For Buslaev, the songs about Sadko were 'the finest living relics of our people's poetry which have been preserved in all their purity and without the slightest trace of outside influence'. Ilia Muromets was a real folk hero of the ancient past 'who embodies, in their purest form, the spiritual ideals of the people'.[90] In the early 1860s the *byliny* had suddenly become a new and vital piece of evidence for the mythological school. For it had been revealed by Pavel Rybnikov that they were still a living and evolving form. Rybnikov was a former civil servant who had been exiled to the countryside of Olonets, 200 kilometres to the north-east of Petersburg, as a punishment for his involvement in a revolutionary group. Like so many of the Tsar's internal exiles, Rybnikov became a folklorist. Travelling around the villages of Olonets, he recorded over thirty different singers of the *byliny*, each with his own versions of the major tales such as *Ilia Muromets*. The publication of these *Songs*, in four volumes between 1861 and 1867, sparked a huge debate about the character and origins of Russia's folk culture which, if one is to judge from Turgenev's novel *Smoke* (1867), even engulfed the émigré community in Germany. Suddenly the origins of the *byliny* had become the battleground for opposing views of Russia and its cultural destiny. On the one side there was Stasov, who argued that the pulse of ancient Asia was still beating in the Russian villages; and on the other the Slavophiles, who saw the *byliny* as living proof that Russia's Christian culture had remained there undisturbed for many centuries.

This was the background to the intellectual conflicts over the conception of *Sadko* (1897), the opera by Rimsky-Korsakov. The evolution of the opera was typical of the collectivist traditions of the *kuchkist* school. The original idea had been given by Stasov to Balakirev as early as 1867; Balakirev passed it on to Musorgsky; and Musorgsky handed it to Rimsky-Korsakov. It is easy to see why Rimsky should have been attracted to the story of the opera. Like Sadko, Rimsky was a sailor (a former naval officer, to be precise) and musician who came from Novgorod. Moreover, as Stasov wrote to him with his draft scenario in 1894, the subject would allow the composer to explore 'the magic elements of Russian pagan culture which are so strongly felt in your artistic character'.[91] In the standard versions of the *bylina* Sadko is a humble minstrel (*skomorokh*) who plays the *gusli* and sings of setting sail for distant lands in search of new markets for the town. None of the merchant élites will back him, so Sadko sings his songs to Lake Ilmen, where the Sea Princess appears and declares her love for him. Sadko journeys to the underwater world, where the Sea King, delighted by the minstrel's singing, rewards him with his daughter's hand in marriage. At their wedding there is such wild dancing to the tunes played by Sadko that it causes hurricanes and a violent sea storm, which sinks all the ships from Novgorod. When the storm subsides, Sadko is washed up, with a net of golden fish, on the shores of lake Ilmen. He returns to Novgorod, gives away his money to the merchants ruined by the storm, and endows the church of St Boris and St Gleb.

For Stasov this *bylina* was the perfect vehicle for his cultural politics. The spirit of rebellion which Sadko showed against the Novgorod élites symbolized the struggle of the Russian school against the musical establishment. But more importantly, as Stasov hoped, the opera was a chance to draw attention to the Eastern elements of the Sadko tale. As Stasov explained in his draft scenario for Rimsky-Korsakov, *Sadko* was full of shamanistic magic, and this pointed to its Asian provenance, in particular to the Brahmin *Harivansa* tale. The *skomorokh*, in

Stasov's view, was a Russian descendant of the Asian shamans (a view, incidentally, which many modern scholars share).[92] Like a shaman, the *skomorokh* was known to wear a bearskin and a mask, to bang his *gusli* like a drum, and to sing and dance himself into a trance-like frenzy, chanting magic charms to call upon the spirits of the magic world.[93] In the draft scenario Stasov underlined these shamanistic powers by having Sadko's music serve as the main agency of transcendental flight to the underwater world and back again; and, as he emphasized to Rimsky-Korsakov, it was the 'magic effect of his music that should be seen to cause the sea-storm, which sinks all the ships'.* Sadko's odyssey was to be portrayed as a shamanistic flight to a dreamworld, a 'spiritual voyage into his own being', as Stasov mapped it out for the composer, and the hero of the opera should return to Novgorod 'as if waking from a dream'.[94]

There was good reason for Stasov to look to Rimsky as the ideal composer for the opera. Rimsky had in the past been interested in Stasov's Eastern version of Sadko. In 1867 he had composed the symphonic suite *Sadko*, a work whose debt to Balakirev's *Tamara* ('far from completed at the time but already well-known to me from the fragments played by the composer') was candidly acknowledged by Rimsky in his *Reminiscences*.[95] Sadko's whirling dance is practically identical to the Tamara theme, and, like Balakirev, Rimsky used the pentatonic scale to create an authentic oriental feel.† However, by the time of his *Sadko* opera, Rimsky had become a professor at the Conservatory and, like many professors, was rather too conformist to experiment again with pentatonic harmonies or oriental programmes for the plot. Besides, Rimsky by this stage was much more interested in the Christian motifs of the *bylina*. It was an interest which reflected his increasing preoccupation with the Christian ideal of Russia – an ideal he expressed in his last great opera, *The Legend of the Invisible City of Kitezh and the Maiden Fevroniya* (1907). Rimsky rejected the draft scenario which Stasov, in his usual cajoling manner, had insisted

---

* According to A. N. Afanasiev, the great nineteenth-century scholar of mythology, Sadko was the pagan god of wind and storms among the ancient Slavs (see his *Poeticheskie vozzreniia slavian na prirodu*, 3 vols. (Moscow, 1865–9), vol. 2, p. 214).
† Sadko's dance is even written in Balakirev's favourite key of D flat major.

he adopt (the only place where Rimsky gave way to Stasov was in the opening civic scene: it enabled him to begin *Sadko* with the large set-piece for orchestra and chorus that had become an almost mandatory feature for Russian nationalist opera). There was nothing in the music to re-create the Eastern feel of the symphonic suite – other than the common stock of ornamental features which composers in the past had used to evoke the 'exotic Orient' (Rimsky used it here to summon up the other-worldly Sea Kingdom). With the help of the Slavophile folklorists who had criticized Stasov, Rimsky made *Sadko* a 'Russian opera', with a civic Christian message for the public at the end. At the height of the wedding scene the Sea King calls upon the seas to overflow and 'destroy the Orthodox people!' But just then a Russian pilgrim (St Nicholas of Mozhaisk in the *bylina*) appears on the scene to break the Sea King's spell and send Sadko back to Novgorod. By a miracle the Sea Princess is transformed into the river Volkhova, providing Novgorod with an outlet to the sea. Her disappearance is meant to represent the demise of paganism and the triumph of the Christian spirit in Russia – a spirit symbolized by the building of the church of St Boris and St Gleb.

In the end, it seems, the conception of *Sadko* as a story linking Russia to the Asian steppe was far too controversial to produce on stage. *Sadko*, after all, was a national myth – as important to the Russians as *Beowulf* is to the English or the *Kalevala* to the Finns. The only place where Asia left its imprint on the opera was in Stasov's design for the title page of the score. Stasov used the motifs of medieval manuscripts which he identified as clearly oriental in origin. The middle letter 'D' is formed into the shape of a *skomorokh* with his *gusli*. He sits there like an idol or a buddha of the East. The rosette underneath the letter 'S' was taken from a portal in the palace of Isphahan.[96] The opera's Christian message was subtly undermined by its very first utterance.

5

In April 1890 Chekhov left from Moscow on a three-month trek to Sakhalin, a barren devil's island in the Okhotsk sea, 800 kilometres north of Japan, where the Tsarist government sentenced some of its

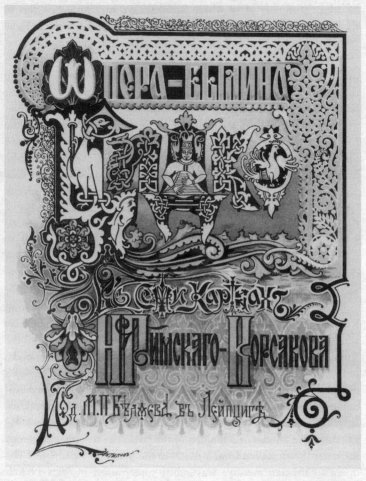

26. *Vladimir Stasov: title page of Rimsky-Korsakov's opera score* Sadko *(1897). The title features an authentic fourteenth-century Novgorodian capital 'D' (Д) formed around a* skomorokh *or minstrel playing the* gusli

most dangerous criminals to penal servitude. Few of Chekhov's friends could understand why the newly famous writer should abandon every- thing for such a long and miserable trip, especially in view of his own poor health. Chekhov himself told Suvorin that he was 'departing totally convinced that my journey will yield a valuable contribution neither to literature nor to science'.[97] But self-deprecation was natural to him. Whether he was driven by the end of a romance,* the need to find new inspiration for his work, the recent death of his brother Nikolai from tuberculosis, or simply the desire to escape from the oppressive atmosphere of his own illness, it would appear that Chekhov felt a desperate need to get away and achieve something 'serious' before he died.

One of Chekhov's heroes was the traveller and writer Nikolai Przhevalsky, who had opened up the world of Central Asia and Tibet to the Russian reading public when Chekhov was a boy. On Przhevalsky's death, Chekhov wrote a eulogy which tells us a great deal about his state of mind. 'One Przhevalsky', Chekhov wrote,

is worth dozens of scholarly institutions and hundreds of fine books . . . In our sick times, when European societies are seized by indolence, heroes are as necessary as the sun. Their personalities are living proof that besides people who out of boredom write trifling tales, unneeded plans and dissertations, there are people with a clear faith and objective who perform great feats.[98]

Chekhov wanted to become a Przhevalsky – to carry out some obvious achievement for humanity and write something of greater consequence than the 'trifling tales' he had penned so far. He read a huge amount in preparation for the trip, researching everything from the geology to the penal settlement of the remote island, to the point where he complained that he was being driven to insanity: *Mania Sachalinosa*.[99]

Chekhov's original aim, as far as one can tell from his correspondence, was to 'repay a little of my debt to the science of medicine' by focusing attention on the treatment of the prisoners in Sakhalin, 'I regret that I am not a sentimentalist', he wrote to Suvorin,

otherwise I would say that we should go on pilgrimages to places like Sakhalin, as the Turks go to Mecca. From the books I have read, it is clear that we have allowed millions of people to rot in prisons, to rot for no purpose, without

---

* With Lidya Avilova (a married woman).

any care, and in a barbarous way . . . All of us are guilty, but none of this has anything to do with us, it is just not interesting.[100]

During the three months he spent on Sakhalin, Chekhov interviewed several thousand prisoners, working up to eighteen hours every day and recording all the details on a database of cards which he had printed up for his research. Officials were amazed by the ease with which he gained the convicts' trust, a capacity he had perhaps developed from his work as a doctor. It gave to his findings, which he wrote up in a simple factual style in *The Island of Sakhalin* (1893–4), the unmistakable authority of truth. In one of the final chapters of that work Chekhov gave an unforgettable description of the brutal beatings which were meted out on an almost casual basis to male and female prisoners alike.

The executioner stands to one side and strikes in such a way that the lash falls across the body. After every five strokes he goes to the other side and the prisoner is permitted a half-minute rest. [The prisoner] Prokhorov's hair is matted to his forehead, his neck is swollen. After the first five or ten strokes his body, covered by scars from previous beatings, turns blue and purple, and his skin bursts at each stroke.

Through the shrieks and cries there can be heard the words, 'Your worship! Your worship! Mercy, your worship!'

And later, after twenty or thirty strokes, he complains like a drunken man or like someone in delirium:

'Poor me, poor me, you are murdering me . . . Why are you punishing me?'

Then follows a peculiar stretching of the neck, the noise of vomiting. A whole eternity seems to have passed since the beginning of the punishment. The warden cries, 'Forty-two! Forty-three!' It is a long way to ninety.[101]

The passage made such an impression on the Russian public that it helped to bring about the eventual abolition of corporal punishment – first for women (in 1897) and then for men (in 1904). The campaign was led by members of the medical profession, with Chekhov in a vocal role.[102]

A stirring indictment of the tsarist penal system, *Sakhalin* is also a masterpiece of travel writing whose extraordinary feel for the land-scape and the wildlife of the Siberian steppe remains unsurpassed.

Let it be said without offence to the jealous admirers of the Volga that I have never in my life seen a more magnificent river than the Yenisey. A beautifully dressed, modest, melancholy beauty the Volga may be, but, at the other extreme, the Yenisei is a mighty, raging Hercules, who does not know what to do with his power and youth. On the Volga a man starts out with spirit, but finishes up with a groan which is called a song; his radiant golden hopes are replaced by an infirmity which it is the done thing to term 'Russian pessimism', whereas on the Yenisei life commences with a groan and finishes with the kind of high spirits which we cannot even dream about. Shortly after the Yenisei the celebrated taiga commences. At first one is really a little disappointed. Along both sides of the road stretch the usual forests of pine, larch, spruce and birch. There are no trees of five arm-girths, no crests, at the sight of which one's head spins; the trees are not a whit larger than those that grow in the Moscow Sokolniki. I had been told that the taiga was soundless, and that its vegetation had no scent. This is what I had been expecting, but, the entire time I travelled through the taiga, birds were pouring out songs and insects were buzzing; pine-needles warmed by the sun saturated the air with the thick fragrance of resin, the glades and edges of the forest were covered with delicate pale-blue, pink and yellow flowers, which caress not merely the sense of sight. The power and enchantment of the taiga lie not in titanic trees or the silence of the graveyard, but in the fact that only birds of passage know where it ends.[103]

As he sailed down the Amur passing Russian villages that had been settled only forty years before, he had the impression that he was 'no longer in Russia, but somewhere in Patagonia, or Texas; without even mentioning the distinctive, un-Russian scenery, it seemed to me the entire time that the tenor of our Russian life is completely alien to the native of Amur, that Pushkin and Gogol are not understood here and therefore not necessary, that our history is boring, and that we who arrive from European Russia seem like foreigners'.[104] The Russian prisoners were overwhelmed by this same sense of estrangement, so much so that, according to Chekhov, the convicts who attempted to escape the island were motivated chiefly by the physical yearning to see their native land:

First and foremost an exile is spurred to leave Sakhalin by his passionate love for his home district. If you listen to the convicts – what happiness it is, what joy, to live in one's own place in one's own country! They talk about Sakhalin, the land here, the people, the trees and the climate, with scornful laughter, with exasperation and loathing, while in European Russia everything is wonderful and enchanting; the most daring thinking cannot acknowledge that in European Russia there might be unhappy people, since to live somewhere in the Tula or Kursk region, to see log cabins every day, and to breathe Russian air already by itself constitutes the supreme happiness. God knows, a person might suffer poverty, sickness, blindness, dumbness and disgrace from the people around, just as long as God permits him to die at home.[105]

The visual engagement with the landscape of Sakhalin is so intense that it seems at times as if Chekhov's words are surrogates for paint:

If a landscape painter should happen to come to Sakhalin, then I recommend the Arkovo Valley to his notice. This spot, besides the beauty of its location, is extremely rich in hues and tints, so that it is difficult to get by without the hackneyed simile of a multicoloured carpet or a kaleidoscope. Here there is dense, sappy verdure with giant burdocks glittering from the rain that has only just fallen; beside it, in an area no larger than a few square feet or so, there is the greenery of rye, then a scrap of land with barley, and then burdocks again, with a space behind it covered with oats, after that beds of potatoes, two immature sunflowers with drooping heads, then, forming a little wedge, a deep-green patch of hemp; here and there plants of the umbelliferous family similar to candelabras proudly hold up their heads, and this whole diversity of colour is strewn with pink, bright-red and crimson specks of poppies. On the road you meet peasant women who have covered themselves against the rain with big burdock leaves, like headscarves, and because of this look like green beetles. And the sides of the mountains – well, maybe they are not the mountains of the Caucasus, but they are mountains all the same.[106]

There was in fact a landscape painter who had meant to go with Chekhov on the trip to Sakhalin. Isaak Levitan was a close friend of the writer. Exact contemporaries, they had known each other since their teenage years, when Levitan met Chekhov's brother at art school. Born into a poor Jewish family in Lithuania, Levitan was orphaned by the time he met the Chekhovs, who adopted him as a brother and a friend. Levitan and Chekhov shared the same passions – hunting, fishing, womanizing, brothels – and perhaps it was because he knew his friend so well that, when the artist fell in love with Chekhov's sister, the writer told Maria not to marry him.[107] The two men were such close friends, they shared so much in common in artistic temperament, that their lives and art were intertwined in many different ways. Levitan appears in various forms in Chekhov's works – perhaps most famously (and almost at the cost of their friendship) in 'The Grasshopper' as the lecherous artist Ryabovsky who has an affair with a married woman to whom he teaches art. Many of the scenes in *The Seagull* – the suicide attempt by the playwright Treplyov, the killing of the bird – were taken directly from Levitan's own life.[108]

Levitan's approach to landscape painting was very similar to Chekhov's own depictions of nature. Both men shared a passion for the humble, muddy countryside of Moscow's provinces, whose melancholic poetry was captured perfectly in both their works. Each admired deeply the other's work. Many of Levitan's paintings are the prototypes for Chekhov's best descriptions of the countryside, while Levitan thought this passage from the story 'Fortune' (1887) was 'the height of perfection' in landscape art:[109]

A large flock of sheep was spending the night by the wide steppe road that is called the main highway. Two shepherds were watching over them. One was an old man of about eighty, who was toothless, with a face which shook, and who was lying on his stomach by the edge of the road, with his elbows resting on dusty plants. The other was a young lad with thick black brows and no moustache, dressed in the sort of cloth from which they make cheap bags, and lying on his back with his hands behind his head looking up at the sky, where stars were twinkling and the Milky Way stretched out right over his face . . . The sheep slept. Silhouettes of the sheep which were awake could be seen here and there against the grey background of the dawn, which was already beginning to cover the eastern part of the sky; they were standing up and had their heads lowered, thinking about something . . . In the sleepy, still air there was a monotonous humming sound which you cannot get away from on a summer night on the steppe. Crickets chirped without stopping, quails sang and young nightingales whistled lazily about a mile away from the flock in a gully where a stream ran and where willows grew . . . It was already getting light. The Milky Way was pale and melting away little by little like snow, losing its definition. The sky became cloudy and dull, so that you could not determine whether it was clear or completely filled with clouds, and it was only by the clear and glossy strip towards the east and the occasional star here and there that you could work out what was going on ... And when the sun began to scorch the earth, promising a long, unvanquished sultriness, everything that had moved during the night and emitted sounds now sank into somnolence.[110]

What Chekhov most admired in Levitan's art (and Levitan in Chekhov's) was its spiritual response to the natural world. Levitan's landscapes evoke reflective moods and emotions, even when their subjects are the most mundane. In this respect he was very much the pupil of his teacher Savrasov, whose famous painting *The Rooks Have Returned* (1871) was a perfect illustration of the poetry contained in the most ordinary provincial scene. Chekhov found in Levitan the sort of images he wanted to create in his reader's mind. In 'Three Years' (1895) he gives a description of Levitan's painting *A Quiet Dwelling* (1891) which captures perfectly the effect which Chekhov himself wanted to achieve:

In Easter week the Laptevs went to the School of Art to see a picture exhibition ... Julia stopped by a small landscape and idly looked at it. The foreground was a stream crossed by a wooden bridge with a path merging into dark grass on the far side. On the right was part of a wood with a bonfire near it – there must be grazing horses and watchmen hereabouts. Far away the sunset's last fires smouldered. Julia imagined going over the bridge, and then further and further down the path. It was quiet there, sleepy landrails cried. A light winked far away. Suddenly she vaguely felt that she had often seen them long ago – those clouds spanning the red of the sky, that wood, those fields. She felt lonely, she wanted to walk on, on, on down the path. There, at the sunset's end, lay reflected an eternal, unearthly something.[111]

Chekhov knew the works of Monet and Cézanne; none the less, he considered Levitan the greatest landscape painter of his day.[112] Throughout his life he bitterly regretted that he had not bought his favourite Levitan painting, *The Village* (1888). As he told a journalist in 1904, it was just a 'village that was dull and miserable, God-forsaken and lifeless, but the picture imparts such an inexpressible charm that you can't take your eyes off it; you just want to keep looking and looking at it. No one has managed to achieve the simplicity and purity of conception which Levitan achieved at the end of his life and I do not know if anyone else will ever achieve anything like it.'[113]

In 1886 Levitan made the first of several trips to the Volga steppe. These marked the start of a new epic style in his landscape painting, completely different from the intimate and lyrical approach to nature in his earlier landscapes of the Moscow provinces. The first of these epic canvases was *Evenings on the Volga* (1888), where the steppe-land's broad expanse is suggested indirectly by the dominating presence of the sky. Chekhov, too, was inspired by a visit to the Volga steppe-lands at this time. His approach to landscape in 'The Steppe' (1887), the first story to bring him literary fame, was very similar to Levitan's:

A wide boundless plain encircled by a chain of low hills lay stretched before the travellers' eyes. Huddling together and peeping out from behind one another, these hills melted together into rising ground, which stretched right to the very horizon and disappeared into the violet distance; one drives on and on and cannot discern where it begins or where it ends . . .[114]

Enthused by the steppe, the two men thought of travelling together to Siberia, and Chekhov included his friend in his plans for the trip to Sakhalin. Levitan was in the entourage of friends and family who accompanied the writer on the first leg of his trip. But he did not go with Chekhov to Siberia, deciding in the end that he could not leave his lover and her husband for that long. Chekhov was annoyed at Levitan (it was perhaps the cause of his cruel satire in 'The Grass-hopper' which broke off their relations for three years). In several letters from Siberia Chekhov told his sister that the artist was a fool to miss out on the scenery of the Yenisel, on the unknown forests and the mountains of Baikal: 'What ravines! What cliffs!'[115]

Like Chekhov, Levitan was drawn towards Siberia's penal history. In his *Vladimirka* (1892) (plate 23) he combined landscape art with a social history of the steppe. It was Levitan's attempt to achieve in painting what Chekhov had achieved in *Sakhalin*. The idea of the painting had come to Levitan on a hunting trip with his lover, the young artist Sofya Kuvshinnikova (the one described by Chekhov in

'The Grasshopper'). The painter had chanced upon the famous high-way near Boldino in Vladimir province. Levitan had just been staying with Chekhov and Chekhov had told him of his trip to Sakhalin, so perhaps this influenced the way he saw the road.[116] 'The scene was pregnant with a wondrous silence', recalled Kuvshinnikova.

The long white line of the road faded as it disappeared among the forests on the blue horizon. In the distance one could just make out the figures of two pilgrims ... Everything was calm and beautiful. All of a sudden, Levitan remembered what sort of road this was. 'Stop,' he said. 'This is the Vladimirka, the one on which so many people died on their long walk to Siberia.' In the silence of this beautiful landscape we were suddenly overwhelmed by an intense feeling of sadness.[117]

Looking at this scene, as Levitan portrayed it, one cannot fail to feel the desolation – it is haunted by the suffering of those distant prisoners, by people like Volkonsky, who for three hot summer months had dragged his heavy chains along the Vladimirka to Siberia.

Chekhov's 'Steppe' is also dominated by this atmosphere of suffering. Its boundless space seems inescapable – a prison in itself. The landscape in the story is stifling and oppressive, without sound or movement to disrupt the tedium. Time seems to come to a standstill, the scenery never changes, as four men cross the steppe in a 'shabby covered chaise'. Everything is subdued by a feeling of stagnation and desolation. Even the singing of a woman in the distance sounds so sad that it 'made the air more suffocating and stagnant'.[118]

Chekhov's ambiguity toward the steppe – seeing both the beauty and the bleak monotony of its vast space – was shared by many artists and writers. There were many, on the one hand, who took pride and inspiration from the grandeur of the steppe. In the epic history paintings of Vasnetsov and Vrubel, for example, the heroic stature of the legendary figures of the Russian past is thrown into relief by the monumental grandeur of the steppe. In Vasnetsov's painting *After Igor's Battle with the Polovtsians* (1880), the notion of the epic is carried entirely by the vastness of the steppe, for what commands the eye is the lowered line of the horizon. Similarly, in his *Bogatyrs* (1898), it is the landscape which is the real subject of the painting, rather than the legendary warriors from which it takes its name. This is emphasized by the central *bogatyr*, who puts his hand against his brow to gaze farther into the distance. Vrubel's panneau of the legendary ploughman *Mikula Selianovich* (1896) is similar in this respect – the strangely inert peasant figure is raised to epic status by his relationship with the landscape. For these artists the national character had been shaped by the open plain: the Russians were as 'broad and unrestrained' in nature as the boundless steppe. This was the view which Gogol took in his 'Thoughts on Geography', published in his collection *Arabesques* in 1835. He also expounded it in his story 'Taras Bulba', where the vast size of the steppe is used as a projection of the Cossacks' open nature and expansiveness. Many artists thought that the boundless plains were a spur to contemplation and religious hope – its infinite horizon forcing people to look upwards to the sky.[119] Chekhov, too, was inclined to fantasize that 'giants with immense strides such as Ilia Muromets' were still alive and that, if they were, 'how perfectly in keeping with the steppe . . . they would have been!'[120]

On the other hand, the sheer monotony of the never-ending steppe drove many Russian poets to despair. Mandelstam called it the 'water-melon emptiness of Russia' and Musorgsky, 'the All-Russian bog'.[121] At such moments of despair these artists were inclined to view the steppe as a limitation on imagination and creativity. Gorky thought that the boundless plain had

the poisonous peculiarity of emptying a man, of sucking dry his desires. The peasant has only to go out past the bounds of the village and look at the emptiness around him to feel in a short time that this emptiness is creeping into his very soul. Nowhere around can one see the results of creative labour. The estates of the landowners? But they are few and inhabited by enemies. The towns? But they are far away and not much more cultured. Round about lie endless plains and in the centre of them, insignificant, tiny man abandoned on this dull earth for penal labour. And man is filled with the feeling of indifference killing his ability to think, to remember his past, to work out his ideas from experience.[122]

But it was not just the peasant who became more dull from living on the steppe. The gentry did as well. The loneliness of living in a country house, miles away from any neighbours in that social class, the lack of stimulation, the interminable hours without anything to do but stare out of the windows at the endless plain: is it any wonder that the gentry became fat and sluggish on the steppe? Saltykov-Shchedrin gives a wonderful description of this mental slumber in *The Golovlyov Family* (1880):

[Arina] spent most of the day dozing. She would sit in her armchair by the table where her grubby playing-cards were laid out and doze. Then she would wake with a start, look through the window and vacantly stare at the seemingly boundless fields, stretching away into the remote distance . . . All around lay fields, fields without end, with no trees on the horizon. However, since Arina had lived almost solely in the country since childhood, this miserable landscape did not strike her as in the least depressing; on the contrary, it even evoked some kind of response in her heart, stirring sparks of feeling still smouldering there. The better part of her being had lived in those bare endless fields and instinctively her eyes sought them out at every opportunity. She would gaze at the fields receding into the distance, at rain-soaked villages resembling black specks on the horizon, at white churches in village graveyards, at multi-coloured patches of light cast on the plain by clouds wandering in the rays of the sun, at a peasant she had never seen before, who was in fact walking between the furrows but who seemed quite still to her. As she gazed she would think of nothing – rather, her thoughts were so confused they could not dwell on anything for very long. She merely gazed and gazed, until a senile drowsiness began to hum in her ears again, veiling the fields, churches, villages and that distant, trudging peasant in mist.[123]

The Russians have a word for this inertia – *Oblomovshchina* – from the idle nobleman in Goncharov's *Oblomov* who spends the whole day dreaming and lying on the couch.* Thanks to the literary critic Nikolai Dobroliubov, who first coined the term soon after the book's publication in 1859, *Oblomovshchina* came to be regarded as a national disease. Its symbol was Oblomov's dressing gown (*khalat*).

---

* Though Gogol, too, had referred to such Russian 'lie-a-beds' in the second volume of *Dead Souls* (N. Gogol, *Dead Souls*, trans. D. Magarshack (Harmondsworth, 1961), p. 265).

Dobroliubov even claimed that the 'most heartfelt striving of all our Oblomovs is their striving for repose in a dressing gown'.[124] Goncharov made a careful point of emphasizing the Asian origin of his hero's dressing gown. It was 'a real oriental dressing-gown, without the slightest hint of Europe, without tassels, without velvet trimmings', and in the true 'Asiatic fashion' its sleeves 'got wider from the shoulders to the hands'.[125] Living 'like a sultan', surrounded by his serfs, and never doing anything that they could be commanded to do instead for him, Oblomov became a cultural monument to Russia's 'Asiatic immobility'. Lenin used the term when he grew frustrated with the unreformability of Russian social life. 'The old Oblomov is with us', he wrote in 1920, 'and for a long while yet he will still need to be washed, cleaned, shaken and given a good thrashing if something is to come of him.'[126]

6

In 1874 the Ministry of Internal Affairs in St Petersburg hosted an extraordinary exhibition by the artist Vasily Vereshchagin, whose enormous battle scenes of the Turkestan campaign had recently returned with high acclaim from a European tour. Huge crowds came to see the exhibition (30,000 copies of the catalogue were sold in the first week) and the building of the Ministry became so cramped that several fights broke out as people jostled for a better view. Vereshchagin's pictures were the public's first real view of the Imperial war which the Russians had been fighting for the past ten years against the Muslim tribes as the Tsar's troops conquered Turkestan. The Russian public took great pride in the army's capture of the khanates of Kokand, Bukhara and Khiva, followed by its conquest of Tashkent and the arid steppe of Central Asia right up to the borders with Afghanistan and British India. After its defeat in the Crimean War, the campaign showed the world that Russia was a power to be reckoned with. But Vereshchagin's almost photographic battle images revealed a savagery which had not been seen by civilians before. It was not clear who was more 'savage' in his pictures of the war: the Russian troops or their Asiatic opponents. There was 'something fascinating, something deeply horrifying, in the wild energy of these canvases', concluded one reviewer in the press. 'We see a violence that could not be French or even from the Balkans: it is half-barbarian and semi-Asiatic – it is a Russian violence.'[127]

It had not originally been the painter's aim to draw this parallel. Vereshchagin started out as an official war artist, and it was not part of his remit to criticize the conduct of the Russian military. He had been invited by General Kaufman, the senior commander of the Turkestan campaign, to join the army as a surveyor, and had fought with distinction (the only Russian painter ever to be honoured with the Order of St George) before receiving the commission from the Grand Duke Vladimir (the same who had bought Repin's *The Volga Barge Haulers*) for the Asian battle scenes.[128] But his experience of the war in Turkestan had given rise to doubts about the 'civilizing mission' of the Russian Empire in the East. On one occasion, after the Russian troops had massacred the people of a Turkmen village, Vereshchagin dug their graves himself. None of his compatriots would touch the dead.[129] Vereshchagin came to see the war as a senseless massacre. 'It is essential to underline that both sides pray to the same God', he advised his friend Stasov on a piece he was preparing for the exhibition, 'since this is the tragic meaning of my art.'[130] The message of Vereshchagin's epic canvases was clearly understood. He portrayed the Asian tribesmen, not as savages, but as simple human beings who were driven to defend their native land. 'What the public saw', Stasov later wrote, 'was both sides of the war – the military conquest and the human suffering. His paintings were the first to sound a loud protest against the barbarism of the Imperial war.'[131]

There was a huge storm of controversy. Liberals praised the artist for his stance against all war.* Conservatives denounced him as a 'traitor to Russia', and mounted a campaign to strip him of his Order of St George.[132] General Kaufman became so enraged when he saw the artist's pictures that he began to shout and swear at Vereshchagin and

---

* Even Kaiser Wilhelm II, the most militarist of the German Emperors, told Vereshchagin at his Berlin exhibition in 1897: '*Vos tableaux sont la meilleure assurance contre la guerre*' (F. I. Bulgakov, *V. V. Vereshchagin i ego proizvedeniia* (St Petersburg, 1905), p. 11).

physically attacked him in the presence of his fellow officers. The General Staff condemned his paintings as a 'slander against the Imperial army', and called for them to be destroyed; but the Tsar, ironically, was on the liberals' side. Meanwhile, the right-wing press was outraged by the fact that Vereshchagin had been offered a professorship by the Imperial Academy of Arts (and even more outraged when the artist turned it down). Critics attacked his 'barbarous art' on the racist grounds that no real Russian worth the name could paint such tribesmen as equal human beings. 'It is an offence', argued a professor in the journal *Russian World*, 'to think that all these works were painted by a man who calls himself a European! One can only suppose that he ceased to be a Russian when he painted them; he must have taken on the mind of one of his Asian savages.'[133]

As his opponents knew, Vereshchagin was of Tatar origin. His grandmother had been born into a Turkmen tribe.[134] For this reason he felt a close affinity for the landscape and the people of the Central Asian steppe. 'I insist', he once wrote to Stasov, 'that I only learned to paint when I went to Turkestan. I had more freedom for my studies there than I would have had if I had studied in the West. Instead of the Parisian attic, I lived in a Kirghiz tent; instead of the paid model, I drew real people.'[135] Stasov claimed that Vereshchagin's feeling for the Central Asian steppe 'could only have been felt by an artist from Russia (not a European) who had lived among the people of the East'.[136]

Bitter and depressed by the campaign against him in the nationalist press, Vereshchagin fled St Petersburg, where the police had refused to protect him from threats against his life. He left Russia well before the exhibition's end. Vereshchagin travelled first to India, where he felt, as he wrote to tell Stasov, 'that something draws me ever farther to the East'. Then he trekked through the Himalayas, pointing out in sketches which he sent back to his friend 'the architectural similarities between Tibet and ancient Rus''.[137] Stasov was forbidden to display these sketches in the public library of St Petersburg (even though he was its chief librarian).[138] Under pressure from the right-wing press, a warrant for the arrest of the exiled painter was despatched to the border with Mongolia.[139] The warrant was issued from the very building where Vereshchagin's paintings were displayed, until they were purchased by Tretiakov (no academy would accept them). Banned for twenty years from his native land, Vereshchagin spent the remainder of his life in western Europe, where his paintings were acclaimed. But he always longed to return to the East, and he finally did so in 1904, when Admiral Makarov invited him to join the fleet as an artist during the war against Japan. He was killed three months later on the *Petropavlovsk* when a bomb explosion sank the ship, drowning all on board.

In Russia's educated circles the military conquest of the Central Asian steppe produced two opposing reactions. The first was the sort of imperialist attitude which Vereshchagin's paintings had done so much to offend. It was based on a sense of racial superiority to the Asiatic tribes, and at the same time a fear of those same tribes, a fear of being swamped by the 'yellow peril' which reached fever pitch in the war against Japan. The second reaction was no less imperialist but it justified the empire's eastern mission on the questionable grounds that Russia's cultural homeland was on the Eurasian steppe. By marching into Asia, the Russians were returning to their ancient home. This rationale was first advanced in 1840 by the orientalist Grigoriev. 'Who is closer to Asia than we are?' Grigoriev had asked. 'Which of the European races retained more of the Asian element than the Slavic races did, the last of the great European peoples to leave their ancient homeland in Asia?' It was 'Providence that had called upon the Russians to reclaim the Asian steppe'; and because of 'our close relations with the Asiatic world', this was to be a peaceful process of 'reunion with our primeval brothers', rather than the subjugation of a foreign race.[140] During the campaign in Central Asia the same thesis was advanced. The Slavs were returning to their 'prehistoric home', argued Colonel Veniukov, a geographer in Kaufman's army, for 'our ancestors had lived by the Indus and the Oxus before they were displaced by the Mongol hordes'. Veniukov maintained that Central Asia should be settled by the Russians. The Russian settlers should be encouraged to intermarry with the Muslim tribes to regenerate the 'Turanian' race that had once lived on the Eurasian steppe. In this way the empire would expand on the 'Russian principle' of 'peaceful evolution and assimilation' rather than by conquest and by racial segregation, as in the empires of the European states.[141]

The idea that Russia had a cultural and historic claim in Asia became a founding myth of the empire. During the construction of the

Trans-Siberian Railway in the 1890s, Prince Ukhtomsky, the press baron and adviser to the young Tsar Nicholas II, advocated the expansion of the empire across the whole of the Asian continent, reasoning that Russia was a sort of 'older brother' to the Chinese and the Indians. 'We have always belonged to Asia,' Ukhtomsky told the Tsar. 'We have lived its life and felt its interests. We have nothing to conquer.'[142]

Inspired by the conquest of Central Asia, Dostoevsky, too, advanced the notion that Russia's destiny was not in Europe, as had so long been supposed, but rather in the East. In 1881 he told the readers of his *Writer's Diary*:

Russia is not only in Europe but in Asia as well . . . We must cast aside our servile fear that Europe will call us Asiatic barbarians and say that we are more Asian than European . . . This mistaken view of ourselves as exclusively Europeans and not Asians (and we have never ceased to be the latter) . . . has cost us very dearly over these two centuries, and we have paid for it by the loss of our spiritual independence . . . It is hard for us to turn away from our window on Europe; but it is a matter of our destiny . . . When we turn to Asia, with our new view of her, something of the same sort may happen to us as happened to Europe when America was discovered. For, in truth, Asia for us is that same America which we still have not discovered. With our push towards Asia we will have a renewed upsurge of spirit and strength . . . In Europe we were hangers-on and slaves, while in Asia we shall be the masters. In Europe we were Tatars, while in Asia we can be Europeans. Our mission, our civilizing mission in Asia will encourage our spirit and draw us on; the movement needs only to be started.[143]

This quotation is a perfect illustration of the Russians' tendency to define their relations with the East in reaction to their self-esteem and status in the West. Dostoevsky was not actually arguing that Russia is an Asiatic culture; only that the Europeans thought of it as so. And likewise, his argument that Russia should embrace the East was not that it should seek to be an Asiatic force: but, on the contrary, that only in Asia could it find new energy to reassert its Europeanness. The root of Dostoevsky's turning to the East was the bitter resentment which he, like many Russians, felt at the West's betrayal of Russia's Christian cause in the Crimean War, when France and Britain had sided with the Ottomans against Russia to defend their own imperial interests. In the only published verse he ever wrote (and the poetic qualities of 'On the European Events of 1854' are such that one can see why this was so) Dostoevsky portrayed the Crimean War as the 'crucifixion of the Russian Christ'. But, as he warned the Western readers of his poem, Russia would arise and, when she did so, she would turn toward the East in her providential mission to Christianize the world.

> Unclear to you is her [Russia's] predestination!
> The East – is hers! To her a million generations
> Untiringly stretch out their hands . . .
> And the resurrection of the ancient East
> By Russia (so God had commanded) is drawing near.[144]

A resentful contempt for Western values was a common Russian response to the feeling of rejection by the West. During the nineteenth century the 'Scythian temperament' – barbarian and rude, iconoclastic and extreme, lacking the restraint and moderation of the cultivated European citizen – entered the cultural lexicon as a type of 'Asiatic' Russianness that insisted on its right to be 'uncivilized'. This was the sense of Pushkin's lines:

> Now temperance is not appropriate
> I want to drink like a savage Scythian.[145]

And it was the sense in which Herzen wrote to Proudhon in 1849:

But do you know, Monsieur, that you have signed a contract [with Herzen to co-finance a newspaper] with a barbarian, and a barbarian who is all the more incorrigible for being one not only by birth but by conviction? . . . A true Scythian, I watch with pleasure as this old world destroys itself and I don't have the slightest pity for it.[146]

The 'Scythian poets' – as that loose group of writers which included Blok and Bely and the critic Ivanov-Razumnik called themselves – embraced this savage spirit in defiance of the West. Yet at the same time their poetry was immersed in the European avant-garde. They took their name from the ancient Scyths, the nomadic Iranian-speaking tribes that had left Central Asia in the eighth century BC and had ruled the steppes around the Black and Caspian seas for the next 500 years. Nineteenth-century Russian intellectuals came to see the Scyths as a sort of mythical ancestor race of the eastern Slavs. In the final decades of the century archaeologists such as Zabelin and Veselovsky led huge excavations of the Scythian *kurgans*, the burial mounds which are scattered throughout southern Russia, the south-eastern steppe, Central Asia and Siberia, in an effort to establish a cultural link between the Scyths and the ancient Slavs. In 1897, the artist Roerich, who was a fully-trained archaeologist before he became famous for his Scythian designs for *The Rite of Spring*, worked with Veselovsky on the excavation of the Maikop *kurgan* in the Crimea. The gold and silver treasures which they excavated there can still be seen today in the Hermitage Museum in St Petersburg.[147]

As a student of archaeology, Roerich had been deeply influenced by the ideas of Stasov on the Eastern origins of Russian culture. In 1897, he made plans for a series of twelve paintings on the founding of Russia in the ninth century. Only one of these paintings was ever completed – *The Messenger: Tribe Has Risen against Tribe* (1897), which Roerich submitted as his graduation project at the Academy – but it is a good example of the ethnographic programme which he planned to execute. Roerich checked on every minor detail of the way of life of the early Slavs by writing to Stasov. Not that much was known about the early Slavs. So there was artistic licence to extrapolate these details from the archaeology of the ancient Scyths and other Eastern tribes, on the assumption, as Stasov wrote to Roerich, that 'the ancient East means ancient Russia: the two are indivisible'.[148] Asked about designs for window frames, Stasov replied, for example, that there was no record of Russian ornament before the eleventh century. He advised the artist to make friezes up from motifs found in ancient Asia and in the Near East.[149]

This imaginary quality was also to be found in Roerich's paintings of the Stone Age in Russia. Roerich idealized the prehistoric world of this Scythia-cum-Rus' as a perfect realm of spiritual beauty where man and nature lived in harmony, and life and art were one. In his essay 'Joy in Art' (1909), in which he describes the ancient Slav spring ritual of human sacrifice upon which *The Rite of Spring* was based, Roerich argues that this prehistoric Russia could not be known thorugh ethnographic facts: it could only be approached through artistic intuition or religious faith. This was the spirit of his Stone Age paintings such as *The Idols* (1901) (plate 17), which, for all their look of archaeological authenticity, were really no more than abstract or iconic illustrations of his mystical ideals. The same was true of his designs for Diaghilev and the Ballets Russes. The Asiatic image of ancient Scythian Rus' was conjured up by Roerich in the set designs and costumes for *The Rite of Spring* and Rimsky's opera *The Snow Maiden* (plate 18). Set in the mythic world of Russia's Scythian past, the designs for both these works combined motifs from medieval Russian ornament with ethnographic details (such as the heavy jewellery or the Tatar-like head-dress of the village girls) to suggest the semi-Asian nature of the early Slavs. It is easy to forget that, in the controversy surrounding the first performance of *The Rite of Spring*, it was the Asiatic look of Roerich's costumes which was seen by many critics as the ballet's most shocking element.[150]

The Scythian poets were fascinated by this prehistoric realm. In their imaginations the Scyths were a symbol of the wild rebellious nature of primeval Russian man. They rejoiced in the elemental spirit ('*stikhiia*') of savage peasant Russia, and convinced themselves that the coming revolution, which everybody sensed in the wake of the 1905 one, would sweep away the dead weight of European civilization and establish a new culture where man and nature, art and life, were one. Blok's famous poem *The Scythians* (1918) was a programmatic statement of this Asiatic posturing towards the West:

> You are millions, we are multitudes
> And multitudes and multitudes.
> Come fight! Yes, we are Scythians,
> Yes, Asiatics, a slant-eyed greedy tribe.

It was not so much an ideological rejection of the West as a threatening embrace, an appeal to Europe to join the revolution of the 'savage hordes' and renew itself through a cultural synthesis of East and West: otherwise it ran the risk of being swamped by the 'multitudes'. For centuries, argued Blok, Russia had protected a thankless Europe from the Asiatic tribes:

> Like slaves, obeying and abhorred,
> We were the shield between the breeds
> Of Europe and the raging Mongol horde.

But now the time had come for the 'old world' of Europe to 'halt before the Sphinx':

> Yes, Russia is a Sphinx. Exulting, grieving,
> And sweating blood, she cannot sate
> Her eyes that gaze and gaze and gaze
> At you with stone-lipped love and hate.

Russia still had what Europe had long lost – 'a love that burns like fire' – a violence that renews by laying waste. By joining the Russian Revolution, the West would experience a spiritual renaissance through peaceful reconciliation with the East.

> Come to us from the horrors of war,
> Come to our peaceful arms and rest.
> Comrades, before it is too late,
> Sheathe the old sword, may brotherhood be blest.

But if the West refused to embrace this 'Russian spirit', Russia would unleash the Asiatic hordes against it:

> Know that we will no longer be your shield
> But, careless of the battle cries,
> We shall look on as the battle rages
> Aloof, with indurate and narrow eyes

> We shall not move when the savage Hun
> Despoils the corpse and leaves it bare,
> Burns towns, herds the cattle in the church,
> And the smell of white flesh roasting fills the air.[151]

The inspiration of Blok's apocalyptic vision (and of much else besides in the Russian avant-garde) was the philosopher Vladimir Soloviev. The opening lines of his memorable poem 'Pan-Mongolism' (1894) were used by Blok for the epigraph of *The Scythians*. They perfectly expressed the ambivalent unease, the fear and fascination, which Blok's generation felt about the East:

> Pan-Mongolism! What a savage name!
> Yet it is music to my ears.[152]

In his last major essay, *Three Conversations on War, Progress and the End of History* (1900), Soloviev described a vast Asiatic invasion of Europe under the banner of the Antichrist. For Soloviev this 'yellow peril' was an awesome threat. But for the Scythians it represented renewal. Mixed with Russia's European culture, the elemental spirit of the Asiatic steppe would reunite the world.

Andrei Bely was another disciple of Soloviev. In *Petersburg* Bely maps a city living on the edge of a huge catastrophe. Set in the midst of the 1905 Revolution, when Russia was at war with Japan, its Petersburg is swept by howling winds from the Asiatic steppe that almost blow the city back into the sea. The novel builds on the nineteenth-century vision of an all-destroying flood, which was a constant theme in the literary myth of the Russian capital. Built in defiance of the natural order, on land stolen from the sea, Peter's stone creation was, it seemed, an invitation to Nature's revenge. Pushkin was the first of many Russian writers to develop the diluvial theme, in *The Bronze Horseman*. Odoevsky used it, too, as the basis of his story 'A Joker from the Dead' in *Russian Nights*.*

By the middle of the nineteenth century the notion of the flood had become so integral to the city's own imagined destiny that even Karl Bruillov's famous painting *The Last Days of Pompeii* (1833) was

---

* The story of a beautiful princess who abandons her young lover to marry a middle-aged official. One stormy autumn night they attend a ball in St Petersburg, where she has a fainting fit. In her dreams the Neva breaks its banks. Its waters flood the ballroom, bringing in a coffin whose lid flies open to reveal her dead lover. The palace walls come crashing down, and Petersburg is swept into the sea.

viewed as a warning to St Petersburg.* Slavophiles like Gogol, a close friend of Bruillov, saw it as a prophecy of divine retribution against Western decadence. 'The lightning poured out and flooded everything', commented Gogol, as if to underline that the city on the Neva lived in constant danger of a similar catastrophe.[153] But Westernists like Herzen drew the parallel as well: 'Pompeii is the Muse of Petersburg!'[154] As the year 1917 approached, the flood became a revolutionary storm. Everybody was aware of imminent destruction. This was expressed in all the arts – from Benois' illustrations for *The Bronze Horseman* (1905–18), which seemed to presage the impending revolution in the swirling sea and sky, to the violent ('Scythian') rhythms of *The Rite of Spring* and the poetry of Blok:

> And over Russia I see a quiet
> Far-spreading fire consume all.[155]

Bely portrays Petersburg as a fragile Western civilization precariously balanced on the top of the savage 'Eastern' culture of the peasantry. Peter the Great – in the form of the Bronze Horseman – is recast as the Antichrist, the apocalyptic rider spiralling towards the end of time and dragging Russia into his vortex. The bomb which structures the thin plot (a student is persuaded by the revolutionaries to assassinate his father, a high-ranking bureaucrat) is a symbol of this imminent catastrophe.

The novel takes division as its central theme. The city is divided into warring class-based zones, and the two main characters, the senator Apollon Apollonovich Ableukhov and his student revolutionary son Nikolai Apollonovich, are on opposing sides of the barricades. Like Russia itself, the Ableukhovs are made up of discordant elements from Europe and Asia. They are descended from the Mongol horsemen who rode into Russia with Genghiz Khan; however Europeanized they might appear, this Asiatic element is still within them. Nikolai is a

---

* Apocalyptic fantasies of modern technological cities destroyed by Nature obsessed the literary imagination in nineteenth-century Europe (see G. Steiner, *In Bluebeard's Castle: Some Notes Towards the Redefinition of Culture* (New Haven, 1971), pp. 20–24).

follower of Kant but 'entirely Mongol' in his way of life, so that 'his soul is divided in two halves'. Apollon is a typically European bureaucrat, who thinks on rational lines and likes well-ordered city grids. But he has a morbid fear of the Asiatic steppe, where he was once nearly frozen as a boy, and he thinks he hears the thundering sound of horses' hoofs as Mongol tribesmen ride in from the plain.

He had a fear of space. The landscape of the countryside actually frightened him. Beyond the snows, beyond the ice, and beyond the jagged line of the forest the blizzard would come up. Out there, by a stupid accident, he had nearly frozen to death. That had happened some fifty years ago. While he had been freezing to death, someone's cold fingers, forcing their way into his breast, had harshly stroked his heart, and an icy hand led him along. He had climbed the rungs of his career with that same incredible expanse always before his eyes. There, from there an icy hand beckoned. Measureless immensity flew on: the Empire of Russia.

Apollon Apollonovich Ableukhov ensconced himself behind city walls for many years, hating the orphaned distances of the provinces, the wisps of smoke from tiny villages, and the jackdaw. Only once had he risked transecting these distances by express train: on an official mission from Petersburg to Tokyo. Apollon Apollonovich did not discuss his stay in Japan with anyone. He used to say to the Minister: 'Russia is an icy plain. It is roamed by wolves!' And the Minister would look at him, stroking his well-groomed grey moustache with a white hand. And he said nothing, and sighed. On the completion of his official duties he had been intending to . . .

But he died.

And Apollon Apollonovich was utterly alone. Behind him the ages stretched into immeasurable expanses. Ahead of him an icy hand revealed immeasurable expanses. Immeasurable expanses flew to meet him.

Oh, Rus', Rus'!

Is it you who have set the winds, storms and snows howling across the steppe? It seemed to the senator that from a mound a voice was calling him. Only hungry wolves gather in packs out there.[156]

This agoraphobic fear of Asia reaches fever pitch in a nightmare vision of his revolutionary son:

Nikolai Apollonovich was a depraved monster . . . he was in China, and there Apollon Apollonovich, the Emperor of China, ordered him to slaughter many thousands (which was done). In more recent times thousands of Tamerlane's horsemen had poured down on Rus'. Nikolai Apollonovich had galloped into this Rus' on a charger of the steppes. He was then incarnated in the blood of a Russian nobleman. And he reverted to his old ways: he slaughtered thousands there. Now he wanted to throw a bomb at his father. But his father was Saturn. The circle of time had come full turn. The kingdom of Saturn had returned.[157]

The thunder of those chargers from the steppe was the approaching sound of 1917. For in the minds of Russia's Europeans, the destructive violence of the revolution was an Asiatic force.

Among the scattered émigrés who fled Soviet Russia was a group of intellectuals known as the Eurasianists. Stravinsky found himself at the centre of their circle in Paris in the 1920s; his friends the philosopher Lev Karsavin and the brilliant music critic Pierre Souvchinsky (Karsavin's son-in-law) were leading members of the group. But Eurasianism was a dominant intellectual trend in all the émigré communities. Many of the best-known Russian exiles, including the philologist Prince N. S. Trubetskoi, the religious thinker Father George Florovsky, the historian George Vernadsky and the linguistic theorist Roman Jakobson, were members of the group. Eurasianism was essentially a phenomenon of the emigration insofar as it was rooted in the sense of Russia's betrayal by the West in 1917–21. Its largely aristocratic followers reproached the Western powers for their failure to defeat the Bolsheviks in the Revolution and civil war, which had ended with the collapse of Russia as a European power and their own expulsion from their native land. Disillusioned by the West, but not yet hopeless about a possible future for themselves in Russia, they recast their homeland as a unique ('Turanian') culture on the Asiatic steppe.

The founding manifesto of the movement was *Exodus to the East*, a collection of ten essays published in Sofia in 1921, in which the Eurasianists foresaw the West's destruction and the rise of a new civilization led by Russia or Eurasia. At root, argued Trubetskoi, the author of the most important essays in the collection, Russia was a steppeland Asian culture. Byzantine and European influences, which had shaped the Russian state and its high culture, barely penetrated to the lower strata of Russia's folk culture, which had developed more through contact with the East. For centuries the Russians had freely intermingled with the Finno-Ugric tribes, the Mongolians and other nomad peoples from the steppe. They had assimilated elements of their languages, their music, customs and religion, so that these Asiatic cultures had become absorbed in Russia's own historical evolution.

Trubetskoi drew on Russian geography, where the Eurasianist idea had a long pedigree. In the final decades of the nineteenth century, the geologist Vladimir Lamansky had shown that the soil structure was the same on either side of the Ural mountains: there was one vast steppe stretching from the western borders of the Russian Empire to the Pacific. Building on the work of Lamansky, the Eurasianist geographer Savitsky showed that the whole land mass of Eurasia was one continuum in biogeographic terms. It was made up of a series of parallel zones that ran like ribbons latitudinally across the continent – completely unaffected by the Ural mountains – from the plains of Hungary to Mongolia. Savitsky grouped these strips into four categories – starting with the tundra of the north, followed by the forest, the steppe and then the desert in the extreme south. There was nothing exceptional in this geography, but it served as a sort of 'scientific' basis for more daring arguments about the Eastern influence on Russia's folk culture.

In his essay 'On the Higher and Lower Strata of Russian Culture' (1921), Trubetskoi set out to prove the Asian influence on Russian music, dancing and psychology. He argued that Russian folk music was essentially derived from the pentatonic scale – an argument he based on the observation of the simplest peasant songs. Folk dance, too, according to Trubetskoi, had much in common with the dancing of the East, especially that of the Caucasus. Russian dancing was in lines and circles, rather than in pairs, as in the Western tradition. Its rhythmic movements were performed by the hands and shoulders as well as by the feet. The male dancing was virtuosic, as exemplified by the Cossack dance, with heels hitting fingers and high jumps. There was nothing like this in the Western tradition – with the single exception of Spanish dancing (which Trubetskoi put down to the Moorish influence). Female dancing also showed an Eastern character, with great importance placed on keeping the head still and on subtle doll-like movements by the rest of the body. All these cultural forms were seen by Trubetskoi as the Russian manifestations of a distinctively Eastern inclination for schematic formulae. This 'Eastern psyche' was manifested in the Russian people's tendency to contemplation, in their fatalistic attitudes, in their love of abstract symmetry and universal laws, in their emphasis on religious ritual, and in their *'udal'* or fierce bravery. According to Trubetskoi these mental attributes were not shared by the Slavs in Eastern Europe, suggesting, in his view, that they must have come to Russia from Asia rather than from Byzantium. The 'Turanian psychology' had penetrated into the Russian mind at a subconscious level and had left a profound mark on the national character. Even Russian Orthodoxy, although superficially derived from Byzantium, was 'essentially Asiatic in its psychological structures', insofar as it depended on 'a complete unity between ritual, life and art'. For Trubetskoi this unity explained the quasi-religious nature of state authority in Russia and the readiness of the Russians to submit themselves to it. Church, state and nation were indivisible.[158]

Such ideas had little in the way of ethnographic evidence to support them. They were all polemic and resentful posturing against the West. In this respect they came from the same stable as that notion first advanced by Dostoevsky that the empire's destiny was in Asia (where the Russians could be 'Europeans') rather than in Europe (where they were 'hangers-on'). Yet because of their emotive power, Eurasianist ideas had a strong cultural impact on the Russian emigration of the 1920s, when those who mourned the disappearance of their country from the European map could find new hope for it on a Eurasian one. Stravinsky, for one, was deeply influenced by the mystical views of the Eurasianists, particularly the notion of a natural Russian ('Turanian') inclination for collectivity, which the music of such works as *The Peasant Wedding*, with its absence of individual expression in the singing parts and its striving for a sparse, impersonal sound, was intended to reflect.[159] According to Souvchinsky, the rhythmic immobility (*nepodvizhnost'*) which was the most important feature of Stravinsky's music in *The Peasant Wedding* and *The Rite of Spring* was 'Turanian' in character. As in the Eastern musical tradition, Stravinsky's music developed by the constant repetition of a rhythmic pattern, with variations on the melody, rather than by contrasts of musical ideas, as in the Western tradition. It was this rhythmic immobility which created the explosive energy of Stravinsky's 'Turanian' music. Kandinsky strived for a similar effect of built-up energy in the geometric patterning of lines and shapes, which became the hallmark of his abstract art.

7

'In their primitive habitat I found something truly wonderful for the first time in my life, and this wonderment became an element of all my later works.'[160] So Kandinsky recalled the impact of his encounter with the Komi people on his evolution towards abstract art.

The link between the 'primitive' and modern abstract art is not unique to the Russian avant-garde. Throughout the Western world there was a fascination with the life and art of tribes in distant colonies, of prehistoric cultures, peasants and even children, whose primal forms of expression were an inspiration to artists as diverse as Gauguin and Picasso, Kirchner and Klee, Nolde and Franz Marc. But whereas Western artists had to travel to Martinique or other far-off lands for their savage inspiration, the Russians' 'primitives' were in their own back yard. It gave their art an extraordinary freshness and significance.

The Russian Primitivists (Malevich and Kandinsky, Chagall, Goncharova, Larionov and Burliuk) took their inspiration from the art of Russian peasants and the tribal cultures of the Asiatic steppe. They saw this 'barbarism' as a source of Russia's liberation from the stranglehold of Europe and its old artistic norms. 'We are against the West,' declared Larionov. 'We are against artistic societies which lead to stagnation.'[161] The avant-garde artists grouped around Larionov and his wife Goncharova looked to Russian folk and oriental art as a new outlook on the world. Goncharova talked about a 'peasant aesthetic' that was closer to the symbolic art forms of the East than the representational tradition of the West. She reflected this symbolic quality (the quality of icons) in the monumental peasants, whom she even gave an Asiatic look, in such works as *Haycutting* (1910). All these artists embraced Asia as a part of Russia's cultural identity. 'Neoprimitivism is a profoundly national phenomenon', wrote the painter Shevchenko. 'Russia and the East have been indissolubly linked from as early as the Tatar invasions, and the spirit of the Tatars, of the East, has become so rooted in our life that at times it is difficult to distinguish where a national feature ends and where an Eastern influence begins . . . Yes we are Asia and are proud of this.' Shevchenko made a detailed case for Russian art originating in the East. Comparing Russian folk with Indo-Persian art, he claimed that one could 'see their common origin'.[162]

Kandinsky himself was a great admirer of Persian art and equated its ideals of simplicity and truth with 'the oldest icons of our Rus''.[163] Before the First World War, Kandinsky lived in Munich, where he and Marc were the co-editors of *The Blue Rider* almanac. Alongside the works of Europe's leading artists, *The Blue Rider* featured peasant art and children's drawings, folk prints and icons, tribal masks and totems – anything, in fact, that reflected the ideal of spontaneous expression and vitality which Kandinsky placed at the heart of his artistic philosophy. Like the Scythians, Kandinsky at this time was moving to the idea of a synthesis between Western, primitive and oriental cultures. He looked to Russia as the Promised Land (and returned to it after 1917). This search for synthesis was the key theme in Kandinsky's early (so-called 'Russian') works (which were still pictorial rather than abstract). In these paintings there is in fact a complex mix of Christian, pagan and shamanic images from the Komi area. In *Motley Life* (1907) (plate 19), for example, the scene is clearly set in the Komi capital of Ust-Sysolk, at the confluence of the Sysola and Vychegda rivers (a small log structure in the upper right-hand corner of the canvas, just below the hilltop monastery, confirms the locale: the Komi used these huts on stilts as storage sheds). On the surface this appears to be a Russian-Christian scene. But, as Kandinsky suggests in the title *Motley Life*, underneath the surface there is a collision of diverse beliefs. The red squirrel in the tree, directly at the visual centre of the painting and echoing the golden dome of the chapel to the right, is an emblem of the forest spirits, to whom the Komi people offered squirrel pelts as a sacrifice. The old man in the foreground may have the appearance of a Christian pilgrim, but his supernaturally coloured beard (a pale green) may also mark him out as a sorcerer, while his stick and musical accomplice, in the form of the piper to his right, suggest shamanic lore.[164]

Several of Kandinsky's early works narrate the story of St Stephan's confrontation with the Komi shaman Pam on the banks of the Vychegda river. According to legend, Pam led the resistance of the Komi people to the fourteenth-century Russian missionary. In a public debate by the riverside Pam based his defence of the pagan religion on the notion that the shamans were better than the Christians at hunting bears and other forest animals. But Stephan challenged him to a 'divine trial by fire and water', inviting Pam to walk through a burning hut and dive into the icy river. The shaman was forced to concede defeat. In Kandinsky's version of the legend, as portrayed in *All Saints II* (1911) (plate 20), Pam escapes from persecution in a boat. He wears a pointed 'sorcerer's hat'. A mermaid swims alongside the boat; another sits on the rock to its right. Standing on the rock are a pair of saints. They, too, wear sorcerer's caps, but they also have haloes to symbolize the fusion of the Christian and the pagan traditions. On the left St Elijah rides his *troika* through a storm – blown by the piper in the sky – a reference to the Finno-Ugric god the 'Thunderer', whose place Elijah took in the popular religious imagination. St Simon stands on a column in the bottom right-hand corner of the painting. He is another compound figure, combining elements of the blacksmith Simon, who builds an iron pillar to survey the world in the Russian peasant tale of 'The Seven Simons', and St Simeon the Stylite, who spent his life in meditation on top of a pillar and became the patron saint of all blacksmiths. Finally, the figure in the foreground, seated on a horse with his arms outstretched, is the World-watching Man. He is seen here in a double form: as the shaman riding his horse to the spirit world and as St George.[165] This figure reappears throughout Kandinsky's work, from his first abstract canvas, *Composition II*, in 1910, to his final painting, *Tempered Elan*, in 1944. It was a sort of symbolic signature of his shaman *alter ego* who used art as his magic instrument to evoke a higher spiritual world.

The shaman's oval drum is another leitmotif of Kandinsky's art. The circle and the line which dominate Kandinsky's abstract schemata were symbols of the shaman's drum and stick. Many of his paintings, like *Oval No. 2* (1925) (plate 21), were themselves shaped like drums. They were painted with hieroglyphs invented by Kandinsky to emulate the symbols he had seen on the drums of Siberian shamans: a hooked curve and line to symbolize the horse, circles for the sun and moon, or beaks and eyes to represent the bird form which many shamans used as a dance head-dress (plate 22).[166] The hooked curve and line was a double cipher. It stood for the horse-stick on which the shaman rode to the spirit world in seances. Buriat shamans hit their sticks (called 'horses') while they danced: the tops were shaped like horses' heads, the bottom ends like hoofs. Among Finno-Ugric tribes the shaman's drum itself was called a 'horse' and was equipped with reins, while the drumstick was referred to as a 'whip'.[167]

In eastern Europe the hobby horse has a preternatural pedigree which belies its benign status in the Western nursery. The Hungarian *taltos*, or sorcerer, rode with magic speed on a reed horse – a reed between his legs – which in turn became the model of a peasant toy. In the *Kalevala* the hero Väinämöinen travels to the north on a straw stallion – as emulated by generations of Finnish boys and girls. In Russia the horse has a special cultural resonance as a symbol of the country's Asiatic legacy – the successive waves of invasion by nomadic horsemen of the steppe, from the Khazars to the Mongols, which have shaped the course of Russian history. The horse became the great poetic metaphor of Russia's destiny. Pushkin started it with *The Bronze Horseman*.

> Where will you gallop, charger proud,
> Where next your plunging hoofbeats settle?[168]

For the Symbolist circles in which Kandinsky moved, the horse was a symbol of the Asiatic steppe upon which Russia's European civilization had been built. It featured constantly in Symbolist paintings (perhaps most famously in Petrov-Vodkin's *Bathing the Red Horse* (1912) (plate 25) and it was a leitmotif of Scythian poetry, from Blok's 'Mare of the Steppes' to Briusov's 'Pale Horseman'. And the hoofbeat sound of Mongol horses approaching from the steppe echoes throughout Bely's *Petersburg*. To attribute a 'dark side' to the hobby horse in Russia, where children no doubt rode it in all innocence, would be absurd. But from an early age Russians were aware of what it meant to 'gallop on a charger of the steppes'. They felt the heavy clatter of the horses' hooves on the Asiatic steppeland beneath their feet.

7

overleaf:
Anna Akhmatova at the Fountain House

RUSSIA THROUGH
THE SOVIET LENS

1

Akhmatova arrived at the Fountain House, the former palace of the Sheremetevs, when she went to live there with her second husband, Vladimir Shileiko, in 1918. The house remained as it had always been, a sanctuary from the destruction of the war and revolution that had transformed Petersburg in the four years since it had been renamed Petrograd;* but, like the city (which had lost its status as the capital), the beauty of the palace was a retrospective one. Its last owner, Count Sergei, the grandson of Praskovya and Nikolai Petrovich, had preserved the house as a family museum. He himself had written several books on the history of the Sheremetev clan. During the February Revolution of 1917, when crowds came to the house and demanded arms to help them in their struggle against the Tsar's last loyalist troops, the count had opened the collection cabinets of Field Marshal Boris Petrovich, the founder of the palace, and handed out to them some picks and axes from the sixteenth century.[1] To save his home from the violence of the mob, he turned it over to the state, signing an agreement with the newly installed Soviet government to preserve the house as a museum, before his family fled abroad. The old Sheremetev servants were kept on, and Shileiko, a brilliant young scholar of Middle Eastern archaeology who had been a tutor to the last count's grandsons and a close friend of the family, was allowed to keep his apartment in the northern wing. Akhmatova had known Shileiko since before the war, when he was a minor poet in her bohemian circle at the 'Stray Dog' club with Mandelstam and her previous husband, the poet Nikolai Gumilev. The Fountain House was more than just the scene of her romance with Shileiko – it drew her to him in a spiritual way. The Sheremetev motto, *'Deus conservat omnia'* ('God preserves all'), inscribed on the coat of arms at the Fountain House, where she would live for over thirty years,

---

* After the outbreak of the First World War the German-sounding name of St Petersburg was changed to the more Slavic Petrograd to appease patriotic sentiment. The city kept that name until 1924, when, after Lenin's death, it was renamed Leningrad.

became the guiding redemptive principle of Ahkmatova's life and art.

Although she was only twenty-nine when she moved to the Shereme-tev palace, Akhmatova, like her new home, was from a vanished world. Born in 1889, she had gone to school at Tsarskoe Selo, where, like Pushkin, she imbibed the spirit of French poetry. In 1911 she went to Paris, where she became friends with the painter Amedeo Modigliani, whose drawing of her, one of many, hung in her apartment at the Fountain House until 1952. Her early poetry was influenced by the Symbolists. But in 1913 she joined Gumilev and Mandelstam in a new literary group, the Acmeists, who rejected the mysticism of the Symbolists and returned to the classical poetic principles of clarity, concision and the precise expression of emotional experience. She won immense acclaim for her love poetry in *Evening* (1912), and then *Rosary* (1914): the accessibility and simplicity of her verse style made her poetry easy to commit to memory; and its female voice and sensi-bility, at that time a novelty in Russia, made it hugely popular with women in particular. Akhmatova had many female imitators of her early style – a fact she would deplore in later years. As she wrote in 'Epigram' (1958):

> I taught women to speak . . .
> But Lord, how to make them cease![2]

On the eve of the First World War, Akhmatova was at the height of her success. Tall and astonishingly beautiful, she was surrounded by friends, lovers and admirers. Freedom, merriment and a bohemian spirit filled these years. She and Mandelstam would make each other laugh 'so much that we fell down on the divan, which sang with all its springs'.[3] And then, at once, with the outbreak of the war, 'we aged a hundred years', as she put it in her poem 'In Memoriam, 19 July, 1914' (1916):

> We aged a hundred years, and this
> Happened in a single hour:
> The short summer had already died,
> The body of the ploughed plains smoked.

Suddenly the quiet road burst into colour,
A lament flew up, ringing, silver . . .
Covering my face, I implored God
Before the first battle to strike me dead.

Like a burden henceforth unnecessary,
The shadows of passion and songs vanished
    from my memory.
The Most High ordered it – emptied –
To become a grim book of calamity.[4]

After all the horrors of the First World War and the Russian Revolution, Akhmatova's intimate and lyrical style of poetry seemed to come from a different world. It appeared old-fashioned, from another century.

The February Revolution had swept away, not just the monarchy, but an entire civilization. The liberals and moderate socialists like Alexander Kerensky, who formed the Provisional Government to steer the country through to the end of the First World War and the election of a Constituent Assembly, had assumed that the Revolution could be confined to the political sphere. But almost overnight all the institutions of authority collapsed – the Church, the legal system, the power of the gentry on the land, the authority of the officers in the army and the navy, deference for senior figures – so that the only real power in the country passed into the hands of the local revolutionary committees (that is, the Soviets) of the workers, peasants and soldiers. It was in their name that Lenin's Bolsheviks seized power in October 1917 and instituted their Dictatorship of the Proletariat. They consolidated their dictatorship by leaving the war and buying peace with Germany. The cost of the treaty of Brest-Litovsk, signed in March 1918, was one-third of the Russian Empire's agricultural land and more than half its industrial base, as Poland, the Baltic territories and most of the Ukraine were given nominal independence under German protection. Soviet Russia, as a European power, was reduced to a status comparable to that of seventeenth-century Muscovy. From the remnants of the Imperial army, the Bolsheviks established the Red Army to fight against

the Whites (a motley collection of monarchists, democrats and socialists opposed to the Soviet regime) and the interventionary forces of
Britain, France, Japan, the USA and a dozen other western powers
which supported them in the civil war of 1918–21.

Popularly seen as a war against all privilege, the practical ideology
of the Russian Revolution owed less to Marx – whose works were
hardly known by the semi-literate masses – than to the egalitarian
customs and utopian yearnings of the peasantry. Long before it was
written down by Marx, the Russian people had lived by the idea that
surplus wealth was immoral, all property was theft, and that manual
labour was the only true source of value. In the Russian peasant
mind there was Christian virtue in being poor – a fact the Bolsheviks
exploited brilliantly when they called their newspaper *The Peasant
Poor* (*Krestianskaia bednota*). It was this striving for *pravda*, for truth
and social justice, that gave the Revolution its quasi-religious status in
the popular consciousness: the war on private wealth was a bloody
purgatory on the way to a heaven on earth.

By giving institutional form to this crusade, the Bolsheviks were
able to draw on the revolutionary energies of those numerous elements
among the poor who derived satisfaction from seeing the rich and
mighty destroyed, regardless of whether such destruction brought
about any improvement in their own lot. They licensed the Red Guards
and other self-appointed groups of armed workers to raid the houses
of 'the rich' and confiscate their property. They rounded up the leisured
classes and forced them to do jobs such as clearing snow or rubbish
from the streets. Akhmatova was ordered to clean the streets around
the Fountain House.[5] House Committees (usually made up of former
porters and domestic servants) were instructed to move the urban
poor into the apartments of the old privileged élites. Palaces like the
Fountain House were sub-divided and made into apartment blocks.
Soon after their seizure of power, the Bolsheviks unleashed a campaign
of mass terror, encouraging the workers and the peasants to denounce
their neighbours to Revolutionary Tribunals and the local Cheka, or
political police. Almost anything could be construed as 'counter-
revolutionary' – hiding property, being late for work, drunkenness or
hooligan behaviour – and the prisons were soon filled. Most of those

arrested by the Cheka in the early years of the Bolshevik regime had been denounced by their neighbours – often as a result of some vendetta. In this climate of mass terror no private space was left untouched. People lived under constant scrutiny, watched all the time by the House Committees, and always fearful of arrest. This was not a time for lyric poetry.

Akhmatova was dismissed as a figure from the past. Left-wing critics said her private poetry was incompatible with the new collectivist order. Other poets of her generation, such as Pasternak, were able to adapt to the new conditions of the Revolution. Or, like Mayakovsky, they were made for it. But Akhmatova was rooted in a classical tradition that had been thrown out in 1917, and she found it hard to come to terms – as did Mandelstam – with her new Soviet environment. She wrote very little in the early Soviet years. Her energy was consumed by the struggle to survive the harsh conditions of the civil war in Petrograd, where chronic shortages of food and fuel reduced the population by more than half, as people died or fled the hungry city for the countryside. Trees and wooden houses were chopped down for firewood; horses lay dead in the middle of the road; the waters of the Moika and Fontanka were filled with rubbish; vermin and diseases spread; and the daily life of the Tsars' capital appeared to return to the prehistoric age, as desperate people scavenged for a piece of bread to eat or a stick of wood to burn.[6]

> And confined to this savage capital,
> We have forgotten forever
> The lakes, the steppes, the towns,
> And the dawns of our great native land.
> Day and night in the bloody circle
> A brutal languor overcomes us . . .
> No one wants to help us
> Because we stayed home,
> Because, loving our city
> And not winged freedom,
> We preserved for ourselves
> Its palaces, its fire and water.

A different time is drawing near,
The wind of death already chills the heart,
But the holy city of Peter
Will be our unintended monument.[7]

For the old intelligentsia conditions were particularly harsh. In the Dictatorship of the Proletariat they were put to the bottom of the social pile. Although most were conscripted by the state for labour teams, few had jobs. Even if they received food from the state, it was the beggarly third-class ration, 'just enough bread so as not to forget the smell of it', in the words of Zinoviev, the Party boss of Petrograd.[8] Gorky took up the defence of the starving Petrograd intelligentsia, pleading with the Bolsheviks, among whom he was highly valued for his left-wing commitment before 1917, for special rations and better flats. He established a writers' refuge, followed later by a House of Artists, and set up his own publishing house, called World Literature, to publish cheap editions of the classics for the masses. World Literature provided work for a vast number of writers, artists and musicians as translators and copy editors. Indeed, many of the greatest names of twentieth-century literature (Zamyatin, Babel, Chukovsky, Khodasevich, Mandelstam, Piast', Zoshchenko and Blok and Gumilev) owed their survival of these hungry years to Gorky's patronage.

Akhmatova also turned to Gorky for help, asking him to find her work and get her a ration. She was sharing Shileiko's tiny food allowance, which he received as an assistant in the Department of Antiquities at the Hermitage. They had no fuel to burn, dysentery was rife among the inhabitants of the Fountain House, and, extravagant though it may appear, they had a St Bernard dog to feed which Shileiko had found abandoned and which, in the spirit of the Sheremetev motto, they had decided to keep. Gorky told Akhmatova that she would only get the most beggarly of rations for doing office work of some kind, and then he took her to see his valuable collection of oriental rugs. According to Nadezhda Mandelstam, 'Akhmatova looked at Gorky's carpets, said how nice they were, and went away empty-handed. As a result of this, I believe, she took a permanent dislike to carpets. They smelled too much of dust and a kind of prosperity strange in a city that was dying so catastrophically.'[9] Perhaps Gorky was afraid to help

Akhmatova; perhaps he disliked her and her poetry. But in 1920 she did at last find work as a librarian in the Petrograd Agronomic Institute, and perhaps Gorky helped.

In August 1921, Akhmatova's former husband Nikolai Gumilev was arrested by the Petrograd Cheka, jailed for a few days, and then shot without trial on charges, which were almost certainly false, of belonging to a monarchist conspiracy. Gumilev was the first great poet to be executed by the Bolsheviks, although many more would soon follow. With his death, there was a feeling in the educated classes that a boundary had been crossed: their civilization had passed away. The moving poems of Akhmatova's collection *Anno Domini MCMXXI* (*In the Year of Our Lord 1921*) were like a prayer, a requiem, for her ex-husband and the values of his age.

> The tear-stained autumn, like a widow
> In black weeds, clouds every heart . . .
> Recalling her husband's words,
> She sobs without ceasing.
> And thus it will be, until the most quiet snow
> Takes pity on the sorrowful and weary one . . .
> Oblivion of pain and oblivion of bliss –
> To give up life for this is no small thing.[10]

Akhmatova had no hopes for the Revolution – she had only fears. Yet she made it clear that she thought it was a sin for poets to leave Russia after 1917:

> I am not with those who abandoned their land
> To the lacerations of the enemy.
> I am deaf to their coarse flattery,
> I won't give them my songs.
>
> But to me the exile is forever pitiful,
> Like a prisoner, like someone ill.
> Dark is your road, wanderer,
> Like wormwood smells the bread of strangers.

> But here, in the blinding smoke of the conflagration
> Destroying what's left of youth,
> We have not deflected from ourselves
> One single stroke.
>
> And we know that in the final accounting,
> Each hour will be justified . . .
> But there is no people on earth more tearless,
> More simple and more full of pride.[11]

Like all of Russia's greatest poets, Akhmatova felt the moral obligation to be her country's 'voice of memory'.[12] But her sense of duty transcended the national; she felt a Christian imperative to remain in Russia and to suffer with the people in their destiny. As did many poets of her generation, she considered the Revolution as a punishment for sin, and believed it was her calling to atone for Russia's transgressions through the prayer of poetry. Akhmatova was a poet of redemption, the 'last great poet of Orthodoxy', according to Chukovsky, and the theme of sacrifice, of suffering for Russia, appears throughout her work.[13]

> Give me bitter years of sickness,
> Suffocation, insomnia, fever,
> Take my child and my lover,
> And my mysterious gift of song –
> This I pray at your liturgy
> After so many tormented days,
> So that the stormcloud over darkened Russia
> Might become a cloud of glorious rays.[14]

The Fountain House had a special place in Akhmatova's universe. She saw it as a blessed place, the spiritual kernel of St Petersburg, which became the Ideal City of her poetry. In several of her poems she compared St Petersburg ('the holy city of Peter') to Kitezh, the legendary city which had preserved its sacred values from the Mongol infidels by vanishing beneath lake Svetloyar to a spiritual realm.[15] The Fountain House was another world enclosed by water. Its inner sanctum represented the European civilization, the vanished universal culture for which Akhmatova nostalgically yearned.* Akhmatova was drawn to the history of the house. She saw herself as its guardian. In her first autumn there she managed to establish that the oak trees in the garden were older than St Petersburg itself. They were longer lasting than any government.[16] She researched the history of the Sheremetev clan, and in particular she felt a close attachment to Praskovya, who shared her 'gift of song' and lived, like her, *persona non grata*, in the Fountain House.

> What are you muttering, midnight?
> In any case, Parasha is dead,
> The young mistress of the palace.[17]

The cultural history of the palace was a true inspiration to Akhmatova. She sensed the presence of the great Russian poets who had been connected with the house: Tiutchev (a friend of Count Sergei); Viazemsky, who had visited the house (though Akhmatova was mistaken in her belief that he had died in the room where she lived);† and Pushkin, above all, the poet she adored, who was a friend of Praskovya's son, Dmitry Sheremetev, the father of the last owner of the house. Rejected by Soviet publishers because they found her verse too esoteric, Akhmatova was drawn even closer to Pushkin from the middle of the 1920s. He, too, had been censored, albeit by the Tsar one hundred years earlier, and her identification with him gave a unique edge to her scholarship on Pushkin, the subject of some of her best writing from this period. As a

---

* During his famous meeting with the poet at the Fountain House in 1945, the philosopher Isaiah Berlin asked Akhmatova whether the Renaissance was a real historical past to her, inhabited by imperfect human beings, or an idealized image of an imaginary world. 'She replied that it was of course the latter; all poetry and art, to her, was – here she used an expression once used by Mandelstam – a form of nostalgia, a longing for a universal culture, as Goethe and Schlegel had conceived it, of what had been transmuted into art and thought . . .' (I. Berlin, 'Meetings with Russian Writers in 1945 and 1956', in *Personal Impressions* (Oxford, 1982), p. 198).

† The room contained a desk with the name Prince Viazemsky written on it, but it belonged to the poet's son, who had died in that room in 1888. The poet died in Baden-Baden ten years earlier (N. I. Popova and O. E. Rubinchuk, *Anna Akhmatova i fontanny dom* (St Petersburg, 2000), pp. 36–8).

27. *Akhmatova and Punin in the courtyard*
of the Fountain House, 1927

fellow poet, she could draw attention to the way he had defied the authorities by writing about politics and other moral issues in disguised literary forms – much as she was doing in her writing on Pushkin.

Akhmatova and Shileiko were divorced in 1926. He had been a jealous husband, jealous not just of her other lovers but of her talent, too (once in anger he had even burned her poetry). Akhmatova moved out of the Fountain House, but soon returned to live there with her new lover, Nikolai Punin, and his wife (from whom he was separated) in their apartment in its southern wing. Punin was an art critic, a leading figure in the Futurist movement, but, unlike many of the Futurists, he knew the cultural value of the poets of the past. In one courageous article, in 1922, he had even spoken out against Trotsky, who had written an attack in *Pravda* against the poetry of Akhmatova and Tsvetaeva ('internal and external émigrées') as 'literature irrelevant to October'.[18] It was a warning of the terror to come.* 'What', asked Punin, 'if Akhmatova put on a leather jacket and a Red Army star, would she then be relevant to October?' If Akhmatova was to be rejected, 'why allow the works of Bach?'[19]

Despite his commitment to the Futurist group of left-wing artists, Punin's apartment in the Fountain House retained the atmosphere of pre-revolutionary Petersburg. There were always visitors, late night talks around the kitchen table, people sleeping on the floor. Apart from Punin's former wife, her mother and daughter and a houseworker called Annushka, there were always people staying in the tiny four-roomed flat. By Soviet standards this was far more cubic space than the Punins were entitled to, and in 1931 Annushka's son and his new wife, an illiterate peasant girl who had come to Petrograd as a factory worker, were moved in by the Housing Committee, and the flat was reassigned as a communal one.[20] Cramped conditions and the crippling poverty of living on Punin's meagre wages (for Akhmatova herself was earning nothing in the 1930s) imposed a strain on their relationship. There were frequent arguments over food and money which would often spill into the corridor so that neighbours overheard.[21] Lydia Chukovskaya describes visiting Akhmatova at the Fountain House in 1938, just before she broke up with Punin:

I climbed the tricky back staircase that belonged to another century, each step as deep as three. There was still some connection between the staircase and her, but then! When I rang the bell a woman opened the door, wiping soap suds from her hands. Those suds and the shabby entrance hall, with its scraps

---

* Trotsky's two articles were published just a fortnight after the expulsion from the country of several hundred leading intellectuals (accused of being 'counter-revolutionaries') in September 1922.

of peeling wallpaper, were somehow quite unexpected. The woman walked ahead of me. The kitchen; washing on lines, its wetness slapping one's face. The wet washing was just like the ending of a nasty story, like something out of Dostoevsky, perhaps. Beyond the kitchen, a little corridor, and to the left, a door leading to her room.[22]

2

The Fountain House was only one of many former palaces to be converted into communal apartments after 1917. The Volkonsky mansion in Moscow, where Princess Zinaida Volkonsky had held her famous salon in the 1820s, was similarly turned into workers' flats. The Soviet writer Nikolai Ostrovsky lived in one of them in the last years of his life, from 1935 to 1936, after the success of his Socialist Realist novel, *How the Steel Was Tempered* (1932), which sold more than 2 million copies in its first three years and in 1935 earned its author the highest Soviet honour, the Order of Lenin.[23] Meanwhile, Zinaida's great-nephew, Prince S. M. Volkonsky, the grandson of the Decembrist, lived in a workers' communal apartment in the suburbs of Moscow between 1918 and 1921.[24]

Nothing better illustrates the everyday reality of the Revolution than this transformation of domestic space. The provincial gentry were deprived of their estates, their manor houses burned or confiscated by the peasant communes or the local Soviet, and the rich were forced to share their large apartments with the urban poor or to give up rooms to their old domestic servants and their families. This Soviet 'war against the palaces' was a war on privilege and the cultural symbols of the Tsarist past. But it was also part of a crusade to engineer a more collective way of life which lay at the heart of the cultural revolution in the Soviet Union. By forcing people to share communal flats, the Bolsheviks believed that they could make them communistic in their basic thinking and behaviour. Private space and property would disappear, the patriarchal ('bourgeois') family would be replaced by communist fraternity and organization, and the life of the individual would become immersed in the community.

In the first years of the Revolution the plan entailed the socialization of the existing housing stock: families were assigned to a single room, and sometimes even less, in the old apartment blocks, sharing kitchens and bathrooms with other families. But from the 1920s, new types of housing were designed to bring about this transformation in mentality. The most radical Soviet architects, like the Constructivists in the Union of Contemporary Architects, proposed the complete obliteration of the private sphere by building commune houses (*dom kommuny*) where all property, including even clothes and underwear, would be shared by the inhabitants, where domestic tasks like cooking and childcare would be assigned to teams on a rotating basis, and where everybody would sleep in one big dormitory, divided by gender, with private rooms set aside for sexual liaisons.[25]

Few houses of this sort were ever built, although they loomed large in the utopian imagination and futuristic novels such as Zamyatin's *We* (1920). Most of the projects which did materialize, like the Narkomfin (Ministry of Finance) house, designed by the Constructivist Moisei Ginzburg and built in Moscow between 1928 and 1930, tended to stop short of the full communal form, with private living spaces and communalized blocks for laundries and bath houses, dining rooms and kitchens, nurseries and schools.[26] But the aim remained to marshal architecture in a way that would induce the individual to move away from private ('bourgeois') forms of domesticity to a more collective way of life. Architects envisaged a utopia where everybody lived in huge communal houses, stretching high into the sky, with large green open spaces surrounding them (much like those conceived by Le Corbusier or the garden city movement in Europe at that time), and everything provided on a social basis, from entertainment to electricity. They conceived of the city as a vast laboratory for organizing the behaviour and the psyche of the masses, as a totally controlled environment where the egotistic impulses of individual people could be remoulded rationally to operate as one collective body or machine.[27]

It had always been the aim of the Bolsheviks to create a new type of human being. As Marxists, they believed that human nature was a product of historical development, and could thus be transformed by a revolution in the way that people lived. Lenin was deeply influenced by the ideas of the physiologist Ivan Sechenov, who maintained that the brain was an electromechanical device responding to external stimuli. Sechenov's materialism was the starting point for I. P. Pavlov's research on the conditioned reflexes of the brain (dogs' brains in particular), which was heavily supported by the Soviet government despite Pavlov's well-known anti-Soviet views. This was where science and socialism met. Lenin spoke of Pavlov's work as 'hugely significant for our revolution'.[28] Trotsky waxed lyrical on the 'real scientific possibility' of reconstructing man:

What is man? He is by no means a finished or harmonious being. No, he is still a highly awkward creature. Man, as an animal, has not evolved by plan but spontaneously, and has accumulated many contradictions. The question of how to educate and regulate, of how to improve and complete the physical and spiritual construction of man, is a colossal problem which can only be understood on the basis of socialism. We can construct a railway across the Sahara, we can build the Eiffel Tower and talk directly with New York, but surely we cannot improve on man. Yes we can! To produce a new, 'improved version' of man – that is the future task of communism. And for that we first have to find out everything about man, his anatomy, his physiology and that part of his physiology which is called his psychology. Man must look at himself and see himself as a raw material, or at best as a semi-manufactured product, and say: 'At last, my dear *homo sapiens*, I will work on you.'[29]

The artist also had a central role to play in the construction of Soviet man. It was Stalin who first used the famous phrase, in 1932, about the artist as the 'engineer of the human soul'. But the concept of the artist as engineer was central to the whole of the Soviet avant-garde (not just those artists who toed the Party line), and it applied to many of the left-wing and experimental groups which dedicated their art to the building of a New World after 1917: the Constructivists, the Futurists, the artists aligned to Proletkult and the Left Front (LEF), Vsevolod Meyerhold in the theatre, or the Kinok group and Eisenstein in cinema – all broadly shared the communist ideal. All these artists were involved in their own revolutions against 'bourgeois' art, and they were convinced that they could train the human mind to see the world in a more socialistic way through new art forms. They viewed the brain as a complex piece of machinery which they could recondition through reflexes provoked by their mechanistic art (cinematic montage, biomechanics in the theatre, industrial art, etc.). Since they believed that consciousness was shaped by the environment, they focused on forms of art, like architecture and documentary film, photomontage and poster art, designs for clothes and fabrics, household objects and furniture, which had a direct impact on people's daily lives.

The Constructivists were in the forefront of this movement to bring art into union with life. In their founding manifestos, written during 1921, they detached themselves from the history of art, rejecting easel painting and other such artistic modes as individualistic and irrelevant to the new society; as 'constructors' and 'technicians', they declared their commitment, by contrast, to the design and production of practical objects which they believed could transform social life.[30] To this end, Varvara Stepanova and Vladimir Tatlin designed workers' clothes and uniforms. Stepanova's designs, which were strongly geometric and impersonal, broke down the divisions between male and female clothes. Tatlin's designs subordinated the artistic element to functionality. A man's spring coat, for example, was designed to be light yet retain heat, but it was made out of undyed material and lacked decorative design.[31] Alexander Rodchenko and Gustav Klutsis used photomontage to smuggle agitation into commercial advertisements and even packaging. El Lissitzky (a late convert to the production art of the Constructivists) designed simple, lightweight furniture capable of being mass produced for standard use. It was versatile and movable, as necessitated by the ever-changing circumstances of the communal house. His folding bed was a good example of the Constructivist philosophy. It was highly practical, a real space-saver in the cramped Soviet apartments, and at the same time, insofar as it enabled the single person to change his sleeping place and sleeping partner, it was designed to be instrumental in the communistic movement to break down the conjugal relations of the bourgeois family.[32]

The Proletkult (Proletarian Culture) movement was equally committed to the idea of the artist fostering new forms of social life. 'A new science, art, literature, and morality', wrote one of its founders, Pavel Lebedev–Poliansky, in 1918, 'is preparing a new human being with a new system of emotions and beliefs.'[33] The roots of the movement went back to the 1900s when the Forward (Vperedist) group of the Social Democrats (Gorky, Bogdanov and Anatoly Lunacharsky) had set up schools in Italy for workers smuggled out of Russia. The object was to educate a tier of 'conscious proletarian socialists', a sort of working-class intelligentsia, who would then spread their knowledge to other workers and thereby ensure that the revolutionary movement created its own cultural revolution. In the Vperedists' view the organic development of a working-class culture was an essential prerequisite for the success of a socialist and democratic revolution, because knowledge was the key to power and, until the masses controlled it, they would be dependent on the bourgeoisie. The Vperedists clashed bitterly with Lenin, who was dismissive of the workers' potential as an independent cultural force, but after 1917, when the leading Bolsheviks were preoccupied with the more pressing matter of the civil war, cultural policy was left largely in their hands. Lunacharsky became the evocatively titled Commissar of Enlightenment, while Bogdanov assumed the leadership of the Proletkult movement. At its peak, in 1920, Proletkult claimed over 400,000 members in its factory clubs and theatres, artists' workshops and creative writing groups, brass bands and choirs, organized into some 300 branches spread across the Soviet territory. There was even a Proletarian University in Moscow and a *Socialist Encyclopaedia*, whose publication was seen by Bogdanov as a preparation for the future proletarian civilization, just as, in his view, Diderot's *Encyclopédie* had been an attempt by the rising bourgeoisie of eighteenth-century France to prepare its own cultural revolution.[34]

As one might expect in such a broad movement, there was a great diversity of views on the proper content of this revolutionary culture. The main ideological division concerned the relationship between the new and old, the Soviet and the Russian, in the proletarian civilization. On the extreme left wing of Proletkult there was a strong iconoclastic trend that revelled in the destruction of the old world. 'It's time for bullets to pepper museums', declared Mayakovsky, the founder of LEF, a loose association of Futurists and Constructivists which sought to link the avant-garde with Proletkult and the Soviet state. He dismissed the classics as 'old aesthetic junk' and punned that Rastrelli, the great palace-builder of St Petersburg, should be put against the wall (*rasstreliat'* in Russian means to execute). Much of this was intellectual swagger, like these lines from the poem 'We' by Vladimir Kirillov, the Proletkult poet:

> In the name of our tomorrow we will burn Raphael,
> Destroy the museum, and trample over Art.[35]

Yet there was also the utopian faith that a new culture would be built on the rubble of the old. The most committed members of the Proletkult were serious believers in the idea of a purely Soviet civilization that was entirely purged of historical and national elements. This 'Soviet culture' would be internationalist, collectivist and proletarian. There would be a proletarian philosophy, proletarian science and proletarian arts. Under the influence of such ideas, experimental forms of art appeared. There were films without professional actors (using 'types' selected from the streets), orchestras without conductors and 'concerts in the factory', with sirens, whistles, hooters, spoons and washboards as the instruments. Shostakovich (perhaps with tongue in cheek) introduced the sound of factory whistles in the climax of his Second Symphony ('To October') in 1927.

But was it possible to construct a new culture without learning from the old? How could one have a 'proletarian culture', or a 'proletarian intelligentsia', unless the proletariat was first educated in the arts and sciences of the old civilization? And if they were so educated, would they, or their culture, still be proletarian? The more moderate members of the Proletkult were forced to recognize that they could not expect to build their new culture entirely from scratch and that, however utopian their plans, much of their work would consist of educating workers in the old culture. After 1921, once the Bolshevik victory in the civil war was assured, official policy encouraged something of a rapprochement with the 'petty-bourgeois' (that is, peasant and small-trading) sector and what remained of the intelligentsia, through the New Economic Policy (NEP).

Lenin, a conservative in artistic matters, had always been appalled by the cultural nihilism of the avant-garde. He once confessed to Klara Zetkin, the German communist, that he could not understand or derive any pleasure from works of modern art. His cultural politics were firmly based on the Enlightenment ideals of the nineteenth-century intelligentsia, and he took the view that the Revolution's task was to raise the working class to the level of the old élite culture. As he put it to Zetkin, 'We must preserve the beautiful, take it as a model, use it as a starting point, even if it is "old". Why must we turn away from the truly beautiful just because it is "old"? Why must we bow low in front of the new, as if it were God, only because it is "new"?[36]

But pressure on the Proletkult came from below as well as above. Most of the workers who visited its clubs wanted to learn French, or how to dance in pairs; they wanted to become, as they put it, more 'kul'turny' ('cultured'), by which they understood more 'refined'. In their habits and artistic taste, the Russian masses appeared to be resistant to the experiments of the avant-garde. There was little real enthusiasm for communal housing, which never escaped its associations with grim necessity. Even the inhabitants of commune houses rarely used their social space: they would take their meals from the canteen to their beds rather than eat them in the communal dining room.[37] In the Moscow Soviet's model commune house, built in 1930, the residents put up icons and calendars of saints on the dormitory walls.[38] The unlifelike images of the avant-garde were just as alien to a people whose limited acquaintance with the visual arts was based on the icon. Having decorated the streets of Vitebsk for the first anniversary of the October Revolution, Chagall was asked by local officials: 'Why is the cow green and why is the house flying through the sky, why? What's the connection with Marx and Engels?'[39] Surveys of popular reading habits in the 1920s show that the workers continued to prefer the adventure stories of the sort they had read before 1917, and even the nineteenth-century classics, to the 'proletarian poetry' of the avant-garde.[40] Just as unsuccessful was the new music. At one 'concert in the factory' there was such a cacophonous din from all the sirens and the hooters that even the workers failed to recognize the tune of what was meant to be the anthem of their proletarian civilization: it was the Internationale.[41]

3

'For us the most important of all the arts is cinema,' Lenin is reported to have said.[42] He valued film above all for its propaganda role. In a country such as Russia, where in 1920 only two out of every five adults could read,[43] the moving picture was a vital weapon in the battle to extend the Party's reach to the remote countryside, where makeshift cinemas were established in requisitioned churches and village halls. Trotsky said the cinema would compete with the tavern and the church: it would appeal to a young society, whose character was formed, like a child's, through play.[44] The fact that in the early 1920s nearly half the audience in Soviet cinemas was aged between ten and fifteen years (the age when political ideas start to form in a person's mind) was one of the medium's greatest virtues as far as its patrons in the Kremlin were concerned.[45] Here was the art form of the new socialist society – it was technologically more advanced, more democratic, and more 'true to life' than any of the arts of the old world.

'The theatre is a game. The cinema is life', wrote one Soviet critic in 1927.[46] It was the realism of the photographic image that made film the 'art of the future' in the Soviet Union.[47] Other art forms represented life; but only cinema could capture life and reorganize it as a new reality. This was the premise of the Kinok group, formed in 1922 by the brilliant director Dziga Vertov, his wife, the cine newsreel editor Elizaveta Svilova, and his brother, Mikhail Kaufman, a daring cameraman who had been with the Red Army in the civil war. All three were involved in making propaganda films for Soviet agitprop. Travelling by special 'agit-trains' around the front-line regions in the civil war, they had noticed how the villagers to whom they showed their films were free from expectations of a narrative. Most of them had never seen a film or play before. 'I was the manager of the cinema carriage on one of the agit-trains', Vertov later wrote. 'The audience was made up of illiterate or semi-literate peasants. They could not even read the subtitles. These unspoiled viewers could not understand the theatrical conventions.'[48] From this discovery, the Kinok group became convinced that the future of the cinema in Soviet Russia was to be found in non-fiction films. The basic idea of the group was signalled by its name. The word *Kinok* was an amalgam of *kino* (cinema) and *oko* (eye) – and the *kinoki*, or 'cine-eyes', were engaged in a battle over sight. The group declared war on the fiction films of the studios, the 'factory of dreams' which had enslaved the masses to the bourgeoisie, and took their camera out on to the streets to make films whose purpose was to 'catch life as it is' – or rather, insofar as their aim was 'to see and show the world in the name of the proletarian revolution', to catch life as it ought to be.[49]

This manipulative element was the fundamental difference between the *kinoki* and what would become known as *cinema verité* in the Western cinematic tradition: *cinema verité* aspired to a relatively objective naturalism, whereas (their claims to the contrary notwithstanding) the *kinoki* arranged their real-life images in a symbolic way. Perhaps it was because their visual approach was rooted in the iconic tradition of Russia. The Kinok group's most famous film, *The Man with a Movie Camera* (1929), is a sort of symphony of images from one day in the ideal Soviet metropolis, starting with early morning scenes of different types of work and moving through to evening sports and recreations. It ends with a visit to the cinema where *The Man with a Movie Camera* is on the screen. The film is full of such visual jokes and tricks, designed to debunk the fantasies of fiction film. Yet what emerges from this playful irony, even if it takes several viewings to decode, is a brilliant intellectual discourse about seeing and reality. What do we see when we look at a film? Life 'as it is' or as it is acted for the cameras? Is the camera a window on to life or does it make its own reality?

Vertov, like all the Soviet avant-garde directors, wanted cinema to change the way its viewers saw the world. To engineer the Soviet consciousness, they hit upon a new technique – montage. By intercutting shots to create shocking contrasts and associations, montage aimed to manipulate the audience's reactions, directing them to the ideas the director wanted them to reach. Lev Kuleshov was the first director to use montage in the cinema – long before it was adopted in the West. He came to the technique by accident, when the chronic shortages of film stock in the civil war led him to experiment with making new movies by cutting up and rearranging bits of old ones. The scarcity of film compelled all the early Soviet directors to plan out scenes on paper first (storyboarding). This had the effect of reinforcing the intellectual composition of their films as a sequence of symbolic movements and gestures. Kuleshov believed that the visual meaning of the film was best communicated by the arrangement (montage) of the frames, and not by the content of the individual shots, as practised in the silent films and even in the early montage experiments of D. W. Griffith in America. According to Kuleshov, it was through the montage of contrasting images that cinema could create meaning and emotions in the audience. To demonstrate his theory he intercut a single neutral close-up of the actor Ivan Mozzukhin with three different visual sequences: a bowl of steaming soup, a women's body laid out in a coffin, and a child at play. It turned out that the audience interpreted the meaning of the close-up according to the context in which it was placed, seeing hunger in Mozzukhin's face in the first sequence, grief in the second, and joy in the third, although the three shots of him were identical.[50] All the other great Soviet film directors of the 1920s used montage: Dziga Vertov, Vsevolod Pudovkin, Boris Barnet and, in its most intellectualized form, Sergei Eisenstein. Montage was so central to the visual effect of Soviet experimental cinema that its exponents were afraid that their medium would be destroyed by the arrival of film sound. The essence of film art, as these directors saw it, lay in the orchestration of the visual images and the use of movement and of mimicry to suggest emotions and ideas. The introduction of a verbal element was bound to reduce film to a cheap surrogate for the theatre. With the advent of sound, Eisenstein and Pudovkin proposed to use it 'contrapuntally', contrasting sound with images as an added element of the montage.[51]

Montage required a different kind of acting, capable of conveying the meaning of the film quickly and economically. Much of the theory behind this new acting was derived from the work of François Delsarte and Emile Jacques Dalcroze, who had developed systems of mime, dance and rhythmic gymnastics (eurhythmics). The system was based on the idea that combinations of movements and gestures could be used to signal ideas and emotions to the audience, and this same idea was applied by Kuleshov to both the training of the actors and the montage editing for cinema.

The Delsarte–Dalcroze system had been brought to Russia by Prince Sergei Volkonsky in the early 1910s. The grandson of the Decembrist had been Director of the Imperial Theatre between 1899 and 1901, but was sacked after falling out with the prima ballerina (and mistress of the Tsar) Mathilde Kshesinskaya. The cause of his dismissal was a farthingale. Kshesinskaya had refused to wear one in the ballet *Kamargo* and, when Volkonsky had fined her, she persuaded the Tsar to dismiss him from his post. Volkonsky might have saved his career by rescinding the fine, but, like his grandfather, he was not the type to be diverted from what he saw as his professional duty by an order from the court.[52] The one real legacy of Volkonsky's brief tenure was the discovery of Diaghilev, whom he promoted to his first position in the theatre world as the editor and publisher of the Imperial Theatre's annual review.* After 1901 Volkonsky became one of Russia's most important art and theatre critics. So when he began to propagandize the Delsarte–Dalcroze system, even setting up his own school of rhythmic gymnastics in Petersburg, he drew many converts from the Russian theatre, including Diaghilev and his Ballets Russes. The essence of Volkonsky's teaching was the conception of the human body as a dynamo whose rhythmic movements can be trained subconsciously to express the emotions required by a work of art.† Volkonsky conceived of the human body as a machine which obeys 'the general laws of mechanics', but which is 'oiled and set in motion by feeling'.[53] After 1917, this idea was taken up in Soviet film and theatre circles, where similar theories of 'biomechanics' were championed by the great avant-garde director Meyerhold. In 1919 Volkonsky set up a Rhythmic Institute in Moscow. Until he was forced to flee from Soviet Russia in 1921, he also taught his theories at the First State School of Cinema, where Kuleshov was one of the directors to be influenced by them. In Kuleshov's own workshop, established in Moscow in 1920, actors were trained in a lexicon of movements and gestures based on the rhythmic principles of Volkonsky.[54]

Many of the most important Soviet directors of the avant-garde graduated from the Kuleshov workshop, among them Pudovkin, Barnet and Eisenstein. Born in Riga in 1898, Sergei Eisenstein was the son of a famous *style moderne* architect of Russian–German–Jewish

---

* Diaghilev was dismissed when Volkonsky left the Imperial Theatre. Diaghilev's dismissal meant he was ruled out for any future job in the Imperial Theatre, so in a sense it could be said that Volkonsky had a hand in the foundation of the Ballets Russes.

† The theory was not dissimilar to Gordon Craig's conception of the actor as a 'supermarionette', with the one important distinction that the movements of Craig's actor were choreographed by the director, whereas Volkonsky's actor was supposed to internalize these rhythmic impulses to the point where they became entirely unconscious. See further M. Yampolsky, 'Kuleshov's Experiments and the New Anthropology of the Actor', in R. Taylor and I. Christie, *Inside the Film Factory: New Approaches to Russian and Soviet Cinema* (London, 1991), pp. 32–3.

ancestry. In 1915 he went to Petrograd to study to become a civil engineer. It was there in 1917 that, as a 19-year-old student, he became caught up in the revolutionary crowds which were to become the subject of his history films. In the first week of July Eisenstein took part in the Bolshevik demonstrations against the Provisional Government, and he found himself in the middle of the crowd when police snipers hidden on the roofs above the Nevsky Prospekt opened fire on the demonstrators. People scattered everywhere. 'I saw people quite unfit, even poorly built for running, in headlong flight', he recalled.

Watches on chains were jolted out of waistcoat pockets. Cigarette cases flew out of side pockets. And canes. Canes. Canes. Panama hats . . . My legs carried me out of range of the machine guns. But it was not at all frightening . . . These days went down in history. History for which I so thirsted, which I so wanted to lay my hands on![55]

Eisenstein would use these images in his own cinematic re-creation of the scene in *October* (1928), sometimes known as *Ten Days That Shook the World*.

Enthused by the Bolshevik seizure of power, Eisenstein joined the Red Army as an engineer on the northern front, near Petrograd. He was involved in the civil war against the White Army of General Yudenich which reached the city's gates in the autumn of 1919. Eisenstein's own father was serving with the Whites as an engineer. Looking back on these events through his films, Eisenstein saw the Revolution as a struggle of the young against the old. His films are imbued with the spirit of a young proletariat rising up against the patriarchal discipline of the capitalist order. The bourgeois characters in all his films, from the factory bosses in his first film *Strike* (1924) to the well-groomed figure of the Premier Kerensky in *October*, bear a close resemblance to his own father. 'Papa had 40 pairs of patent leather shoes', Eisenstein recalled. 'He did not acknowledge any other sort. And he had a huge collection of them "for every occasion". He even listed them in a register, with any distinguishing feature indicated: "new", "old", "a scratch". From time to time he held an inspection and roll-call.'[56] Eisenstein once wrote that the reason he came to support the Revolution 'had little to do with the real miseries of social injustice . . . but directly and completely with what is surely the prototype of every social tyranny – the father's despotism in a family'.[57]

But his commitment to the Revolution was equally connected with his own artistic vision of a new society. In a chapter of his memoirs, 'Why I Became a Director', he locates the source of his artistic inspiration in the collective movement of the Red Army engineers building a bridge near Petrograd:

An ant hill of raw fresh-faced recruits moved along measured-out paths with precision and discipline and worked in harmony to build a steadily growing bridge which reached across the river. Somewhere in this ant hill I moved as well. Square pads of leather on my shoulders supporting a plank, resting edgeways. Like the parts of a clockwork contraption, the figures moved quickly, driving up to the pontoons and throwing girders and handrails festooned with cabling to one another – it was an easy and harmonious model of *perpetuum mobile*, reaching out from the bank in an ever-lengthening road to the constantly receding edge of the bridge . . . All this fused into a marvellous, orchestral, polyphonic experience of something being done . . . Hell, it was good! . . . No: it was not patterns from classical productions, nor recordings of outstanding performances, nor complex orchestral scores, nor elaborate evolutions of the *corps de ballet* in which I first experienced that rapture, the delight in the movement of bodies racing at different speeds and in different directions across the graph of an open expanse: it was in the play of intersecting orbits, the ever-changing dynamic form that the combination of these paths took and their collisions in momentary patterns of intricacy, before flying apart for ever. The pontoon bridge . . . opened my eyes for the first time to the delight of this fascination that was never to leave me.[58]

Eisenstein would try to re-create this sense of poetry in the crowd scenes which dominate his films, from *Strike* to *October*.

In 1920, on his return to Moscow, Eisenstein joined Proletkult as a theatre director and became involved in the Kuleshov workshop. Both led him to the idea of *typage* – the use of untrained actors or 'real types' taken (sometimes literally) from the street. The technique was used by Kuleshov in *The Extraordinary Adventures of Mr West in the Land of the Bolsheviks* (1923) and, most famously, by Eisenstein himself in *The Battleship Potemkin* (1925) and *October*. Proletkult would exert a lasting influence on Eisenstein, particularly on his treatment of the masses in his history films. But the biggest influence on Eisenstein was the director Meyerhold, whose theatre school he joined in 1921.

Vsevolod Meyerhold was a central figure in the Russian avant-garde. Born in 1874 to a theatre-loving family in the provincial city of Penza, Meyerhold had started as an actor in the Moscow Arts Theatre. In the 1900s he began directing his own experimental productions under the influence of Symbolist ideas. He saw the theatre as a highly stylized, even abstract, form of art, not the imitation of reality, and emphasized the use of mime and gesture to communicate ideas to the audience. He developed these ideas from the traditions of the Italian *commedia dell'arte* and the Japanese kabuki theatre, which were not that different from the practices of Delsarte and Dalcroze. Meyerhold staged a number of brilliant productions in Petrograd between 1915 and 1917 and he was one of the few artistic figures to support the Bolsheviks when they nationalized the theatres in November 1917. He even joined the Party in the following year. In 1920 Meyerhold was placed in charge of the theatre department in the Commissariat of Enlightenment, the main Soviet authority in education and the arts. Under the slogan 'October in the Theatre' he began a revolution against the old naturalist conventions of the drama house. In 1921 he established the State School for Stage Direction to train the new directors who would take his revolutionary theatre out on to the streets. Eisenstein was one of Meyerhold's first students. He credited Meyerhold's plays with inspiring him to 'abandon engineering and "give myself" to art'.[59] Through Meyerhold, Eisenstein came to the idea of the mass spectacle – to a theatre of real life that would break down the conventions and illusions of the stage. He learned to train the actor as an athlete, expressing emotions and ideas through movements and gestures; and, like Meyerhold, he brought farce and pantomime, gymnastics and circus tricks, strong visual symbols and montage to his art.

Eisenstein's style of film montage also reveals Meyerhold's stylized approach. In contrast to the montage of Kuleshov, which was meant to affect the emotions subliminally, Eisenstein's efforts were explicitly didactic and expository. The juxtaposition of images was intended to engage members of the audience in a conscious way – and draw them towards the correct ideological conclusions. In *October*, for example, Eisenstein intercuts images of a white horse falling from a bridge into the Neva river with scenes showing Cossack forces suppressing the workers' demonstrations against the Provisional Government in July 1917. The imagery is very complex. The horse had long been a symbol of apocalypse in the Russian intellectual tradition. Before 1917 it had been used by the Symbolists to represent the Revolution, whose imminence they sensed. (Bely's *Petersburg* is haunted by the hoofbeat sound of Mongol horses approaching from the steppe.) The white horse in particular was also, paradoxically, an emblem of the Bonapartist tradition. In Bolshevik propaganda the general mounted on a white horse was a standard symbol of the counter-revolution. After the suppression of the July demonstrations, the new premier of the Provisional Government, Alexander Kerensky, had ordered the arrest of the Bolshevik leaders, who had aimed to use the demonstrations to launch their own putsch. Forced into hiding, Lenin denounced Kerensky as a Bonapartist counter-revolutionary, a point reinforced in the sequence of *October* which intercuts scenes of Kerensky living like an emperor in the Winter Palace with images of Napoleon. According to Lenin, the events of July had transformed the Revolution into a civil war, a military struggle between the Reds and the Whites. He campaigned for the seizure of power by claiming that Kerensky would establish his own Bonapartist dictatorship if the Soviet did not take control. All these ideas are involved in Eisenstein's image of the falling horse. It was meant to make the audience perceive the suppression of the July demonstrations, as Lenin had described it, as the crucial turning point of 1917.

A similarly conceptual use of montage can be found in the sequence, ironically entitled 'For God and Country', which dramatizes the march of the counter-revolutionary Cossack forces led by General Kornilov against Petrograd in August 1917. Eisenstein made a visual deconstruction of the concept of a 'God' by bombarding the viewer with a chain of images (icon–axe–icon–sabre–a blessing–blood) which increasingly challenge that idea.[60] He also used montage to extend time and increase the tension – as in *The Battleship Potemkin* (1925), in the famous massacre scene on the steps of Odessa in which the action is slowed down by the intercutting of close-ups of faces in the crowd with repeated images of the soldiers' descent down the stairs.* The scene, by the way, was entirely fictional: there was no massacre on the Odessa steps in 1905 – although it often appears in the history books.

Nor was this the only time when history was altered by the mythic images in Eisenstein's films. When he arrived at the Winter Palace to shoot the storming scene for *October*, he was shown the left ('October') staircase where the Bolshevik ascent had taken place. But it was much too small for the mass action he had in mind, so instead he shot the scene on the massive Jordan staircase used for state processions during Tsarist times. The Jordan staircase became fixed in the public mind as the October Revolution's own triumphant route. Altogether Eisenstein's *October* was a much bigger production than the historical reality. He called up 5,000 veterans from the civil war – far more than the few hundred sailors and Red Guards who had taken part in the palace's assault in 1917. Many of them brought their own guns with live ammunition and fired bullets at the Sèvres vases as they climbed the stairs, wounding several people and arguably causing far more casualties than in 1917. After the shooting, Eisenstein recalled being told by an elderly porter who swept up the broken china: 'Your people were much more careful the first time they took the palace.'[61]

Meanwhile, Meyerhold was storming barricades with his own revolution in the theatre. It began with his spectacular production of Vladimir Mayakovsky's *Mystery Bouffe* (1918; revived in 1921) – a cross between a mystery play and a street theatre comedy which dramatized the conquest of 'the clean' (the bourgeois) by 'the unclean' (the proletariat). Meyerhold removed the proscenium arch, and instead of a stage constructed a monumental platform projecting deep into the auditorium. At the climax of the spectacle he brought the audience on to the platform to mingle, as if in a city square, with the actors in their costumes, the clowns and acrobats, and to join with them in tearing up the curtain, which was painted with symbols – masks and wigs – of the old theatre.[62] The war against theatrical illusion was summed up in the prologue to the play: 'We will show you life that's real – but

---

* Usually described as 'temporal expansion through overlapping editing'. See D. Bordwell and K. Thompson, *Film Art, An Introduction*, 3rd edn (New York, 1990), p. 217.

28. *Liubov Popova: stage design for Meyerhold's 1922 production
of the* Magnanimous Cuckold

in this spectacle it will become transformed into something quite
extraordinary.'[63] Such ideas were far too radical for Meyerhold's political patrons and in 1921 he was dismissed from his position in the
commissariat. But he continued to put on some truly revolutionary
productions. In his 1922 production of Belgian playwright Fernand
Crommelynck's *Magnanimous Cuckold* (1920) the stage (by the Constructivist artist Liubov Popova) became a kind of 'multi-purpose

461

scaffolding'; the characters were all in overalls and identified themselves by performing different circus tricks. In Sergei Tretiakov's 1923 play *The Earth Rampant*, adapted from *La Nuit* by Marcel Martinet, a drama about the mutiny of the French troops in the First World War, there were cars and machine-guns, not just on the stage but in the aisles as well. The lighting was provided by huge searchlights at the front of the stage, and actors in real soldiers' uniforms passed through the audience to collect money for a Red Army plane.[64]

Some of Meyerhold's most interesting techniques were close to those of the cinema, in which he also worked as a director (he made two films before 1917) and (thanks to his impact on directors like Eisenstein and Grigory Kozintsev) arguably had his greatest influence.[65] In his 1924 production of Ostrovsky's *The Forest*, for example, Meyerhold used montage by dividing the five acts into thirty-three small episodes with pantomimic interludes to create contrasts of tempo and mood. In other productions, most notably that of Gogol's *The Government Inspector* in 1926, he placed certain actors on a little stage trolley and wheeled it to the front of the main stage to simulate the cinematic idea of a close-up. He was deeply influenced by movie actors such as Buster Keaton and, above all, Charlie Chaplin, whose films were shown in cinemas right across the Soviet Union. Chaplin's emphasis on mime and gesture made him close to Meyerhold's theatrical ideal.[66]

That ideal was expressed by the system known as 'biomechanics', which was not unlike the reflexology and rhythmic gymnastics of the Delsarte–Dalcrozean school, insofar as it approached the actor's body as a biomechanical device for the physical expression of emotions and ideas. Meyerhold would have his actors trained in the techniques of the acrobatic circus, fencing, boxing, ballet and eurhythmics, gymnastics and modern dance so that they could tell a story through the supple movements of their whole bodies or even just their faces.[67] The system was consciously opposed to the Stanislavsky method (in which Meyerhold was trained at the Moscow Arts Theatre between 1898 and 1902), in which the actor was encouraged to identify with the inner thoughts and feelings of his character by recalling moments of intense experience in his own life. In place of such free expressivity, Meyerhold insisted on the actors' rhythmic regimentation. He was very interested in the Red Army's programme of physical culture (synchronized gymnastics and all that) and in 1921 he even took command of a special theatre section for physical culture in the Commissariat of Enlightenment, which aimed to use the army's system of gymnastics for the 'scientific organization of labour' in an experimental military settlement.[68] This aspect of labour management was the crucial difference between biomechanics and the Delsarte–Dalcrozean school. Meyerhold envisaged the actor as an artist-engineer who organizes the 'raw material' of his own body on the scientific principles of time and motion. He saw his system as the theatrical equivalent of 'scientific management' in industry. Like all the Bolsheviks, he was particularly influenced by the theories of the American engineer F. W. Taylor, who used 'time and motion' studies to divide and automate the labour tasks of industry.

Lenin was a huge fan of Taylorism. Its premise that the worker was the least efficient part of the whole manufacturing process accorded with his view of the Russian working class. He saw Taylorism's 'scientific' methods as a means of discipline that could remould the worker and society along more controllable and regularized lines. All this was of a piece with the modernist belief in the power of machines to transform man and the universe. Meyerhold's enthusiasm for mechanics was widely shared by the avant-garde. One can see it in the Futurists' idealization of technology; in the fascination with machines which pervades the films of Eisenstein and Vertov; in the exaltation of factory production in left-wing art; and in the industrialism of the Constructivists. Lenin encouraged the cult of Taylor and of another great American industrialist, Henry Ford, inventor of the egalitarian Model 'T', which flourished throughout Russia at this time: even remote villagers knew the name of Henry Ford (some of them believed he was a sort of god who organized the work of Lenin and Trotsky).

The most radical exponent of the Taylorist idea was Aleksei Gastev, the Bolshevik engineer and poet who envisaged the mechanization of virtually every aspect of life in Soviet Russia, from methods of production to the thinking patterns of the common man. A friend of Meyerhold, Gastev may have been the first person to use the term 'biomechanics', sometime around 1922.[69] As a 'proletarian poet' (the 'Ovid of engineers, miners and metalworkers', as he was described by fellow poet Nikolai Aseev),[70] Gastev conjured up the vision of a future communist society in which man and machine merged. His verse reverberates to the thunderous sounds of the blast furnace and the factory siren. It sings its liturgy to an 'iron messiah' who will reveal the brave new world of the fully automated human being.

As head of the Central Institute of Labour, established in 1920, Gastev carried out experiments to train the workers so that they would end up acting like machines. Hundreds of identically dressed trainees would be marched in columns to their benches, and orders would be given out by buzzes from machines. The workers were trained to hammer correctly, for instance, by holding a hammer attached to and moved by a special machine, so that they internalized its mechanical rhythm. The same process was repeated for chiselling, filing and other basic skills. Gastev's aim, by his own admission, was to turn the worker into a sort of 'human robot' – a word, not coincidentally, derived from the Russian (and Czech) verb 'to work': *rabotat'*. Since Gastev saw machines as superior to human beings, he thought bio-mechanization would represent an improvement in humanity. Indeed, he saw it as the next logical step in human evolution. Gastev envisaged a utopia where 'people' would be replaced by 'proletarian units' identified by ciphers such as 'A, B, C, or 325, 075, 0, and so on'. These automatons would be like machines, 'incapable of individual thought', and would simply obey their controller. A 'mechanized collectivism' would 'take the place of the individual personality in the psychology of the proletariat'. There would no longer be a need for emotions, and the human soul would no longer be measured 'by a shout or a smile but by a pressure gauge or a speedometer'.[71] This was the Soviet paradise Zamyatin satirized in his novel *We*, which depicts a futuristic world of rationality and high technology, with robot-like beings who are known by numbers instead of names and whose lives are controlled in every way by the One State and its Big Brother-like ruler, the Benefactor. Zamyatin's novel was the inspiration of George Orwell's *1984*.[72]

Thanks to the influence of Meyerhold, two great artists were brought into the orbit of the cinema. One was Dmitry Shostakovich, who worked at Meyerhold's theatre from 1928 to 1929, during which time, influenced no doubt by its production of *The Government Inspector*, he composed his Gogolian opera *The Nose* (1930). In his student days, between 1924 and 1926, Shostakovich had worked as a piano accompanist for silent movies at the Bright Reel cinema on Nevsky Prospekt in Leningrad.[73] It set the pattern for his life – composing for the cinema to earn some extra money and keep himself out of trouble (in total he would score the music for over thirty films).[74]

Writing for the screen had a major influence on Shostakovich's composing style, as it did on the whole Soviet music school.[75] The big film sound of the Soviet orchestra and the need for tuneful melodies to appeal to the masses are obvious enough. With the exception of Myaskovsky, no composer in the twentieth century wrote more symphonies than Shostakovich; none wrote better tunes than Prokofiev – in both cases certainly an effect of writing for the cinema. Films using montage, in particular, demanded new techniques of musical composition to reflect their polyphonic dramaturgy. They required a new rhythmic treatment and faster harmonic shifts to deal with their constant cross-cutting between the frames,* the sharp joins between the scenes, and to highlight the associations between themes and visual images. These cinematic qualities are discernible in many of Shostakovich's works – notably the music for *The Nose* and his Third ('May Day') Symphony (1930), with its fast-paced montage of musical tableaux. Shostakovich once explained that in writing his film music he did not follow the standard Western principle of illustration or accompaniment, but sought rather to connect a series of sequences with one musical idea – so that in this sense it was the music which revealed the 'essence and the idea of the film'.[76] The music was to be an added element of the montage. This ideal was best expressed in Shostakovich's first film score, for *The New Babylon* (1929), a cinematic reconstruction of the revolutionary events of the Paris Commune in 1871. As its director Kozintsev explained, the purpose of the music was not just to reflect or illustrate the action but to take an active part in it by communicating to the audience the film's underlying emotions.[77]

Meyerhold's other new recruit to the cinema was the poet Mayakovsky, who wrote some thirteen film scenarios and (a man of

---

* Soviet films that used montage had a far higher number of different shots (in *October*, for example, there were 3,200 shots) compared to the average (around 600) in conventional Hollywood films during the 1920s.

extraordinary looks) starred in several films as well. Meyerhold and Mayakovsky had been close friends since before the war. They shared the same far-left outlook on politics and theatre which found expression in their partnership on *Mystery Bouffe*. Mayakovsky played the part of the 'Person of the Future' – a proletarian *deus ex machina* who appeared on stage hanging from the ceiling – in the first (1918) production of his play. It was, he said, referring to himself and Meyerhold, 'our revolution in poetry and theatre. The mystery is the greatness of the action – the bouffe the laughter in it.'[78] Mayakovsky spread his talents wide: to his poetry and his work in theatre and the cinema, he added journalism, writing radio songs and satires, drawing cartoons with brief captions for the *lubok*-like propaganda posters of the Russian Telegraph Agency (ROSTA) and creating advertising jingles for state stores and slogans for the banners which appeared on every street. His poetry was immersed in politics, even his intimate love lyrics to his mistress Lily Brik, and a good deal of his best-known verse, like the allegory *150,000,000* (1921), a Soviet parody of the *bylina*, which tells the story of the battle between Ivan, the leader of the 150 million Russian workers, and the Western capitalist villain Woodrow Wilson, was agitational. Mayakovsky's terse, iconoclastic style was tailor-made for political effect in a country such as Russia where the *lubok* and *chastushka* (a simple, often bawdy, rhyming song) had real roots in the mass consciousness, and he imitated both these literary forms.

> Forward, my country,
> > move on faster!
> Get on with it,
> > sweep away the antiquated junk!
> Stronger, my commune,
> > strike at the enemy,
> Make it die out,
> > that monster, the old way of life.[79]

Mayakovsky embraced revolution as a quickening of time. He longed to sweep away the clutter of the past, the 'petty-bourgeois' domesticity of the 'old way of life' (*byt*), and to replace it with a higher and more spiritual existence (*bytie*).* The battle against *byt* was at the heart of the Russian revolutionary urge to establish a more communistic way of life.[80] Mayakovsky hated *byt*. He hated all routine. He hated all the banal objects in the 'cosy home': the *samovar*, the rubber plant, the portrait of Marx in its little frame, the cat lying on old copies of *Izvestiia*, the ornamental china on the mantelpiece, the singing canaries.

> From the wall Marx watches and watches
> And suddenly
> Opening his mouth wide,
> He starts howling:
> The Revolution is tangled up in philistine threads
> More terrible than Wrangel† is philistine *byt*
> Better
> To tear off the canaries' heads –
> So communism
> Won't be struck down by canaries.[81]

In much of his writing Mayakovsky talked of his desire to escape this humdrum world of material things ('it will turn us all into philistines') and to fly away, like a figure from Chagall, to a higher spiritual realm. This is the theme of his long poem *Pro eto* (*About This*) (1923), written in the form of a love song to Lily Brik, with whom he was living, on and off, in Petersburg and Moscow in a *ménage à trois* with her husband, the left-wing poet and critic Osip Brik. In his autobiography Mayakovsky records that he wrote the poem 'about our way of life in general but based on personal material'. He said it was a poem 'about *byt*, and by this I mean a way of life which has not changed at all and which is our greatest enemy'.[82] *Pro eto* chronicles Mayakovsky's response to a two-month separation imposed by Lily Brik in December 1922. In it, the hero, a poet living all alone in his

---

* The word *byt* ('way of life') derived from the verb *byvat'*, meaning to happen or take place. But, from the nineteenth century, *bytie* took on the positive idea of 'meaningful existence' which became central to the Russian intellectual tradition, while *byt* became increasingly associated with the negative aspects of the 'old' way of life.

† Leader of the White armies in southern Russia during the civil war.

29. *Alexander Rodchenko: illustration from*
Mayakovsky's Pro eto *(1923)*

tiny room while his lover Lily carries on with her busy social and
domestic life, dreams about a poem he wrote before 1917 in which a
Christ-like figure, a purer version of his later self, prepares for the
coming revolution. The despairing hero threatens to commit suicide
by jumping from a bridge into the Neva river: his love for Lily compli-

cates his own crisis of identity, because in his imagination she is tied to the 'petty-bourgeois' *byt* of Russia in the NEP, which has diverted him from the ascetic path of the true revolutionary. This betrayal leads to a dramatic staging of the narrator's crucifixion, which then gives way to the redemptive vision of a future communist utopia, where love is no longer personal or bodily in form but a higher form of brotherhood. At the climax of the poem the narrator catapults himself a thousand years into the future, to a world of communal love, where he pleads with a chemist to bring him back to life:

> Resurrect me –
> > I want to live my share!
> Where love will not be – a servant
> of marriages,
> > lust,
> > > money.
> Damning the bed,
> > arising from the couch,
> love will stride through the universe.[83]

4

In 1930, at the age of thirty-seven, Mayakovsky shot himself in the communal flat in which he had lived, near the Lubianka building in Moscow, when the Briks would not have him. Suicide was a constant theme in Mayakovsky's poetry. The poem he wrote for his suicide note quotes (with minor alterations) from an untitled and unfinished poem written probably in the summer of 1929:

> As they say,
> > a bungled story.
> Love's boat
> > smashed
> > against existence.
> And we are quits
> > with life.

So why should we
idly reproach each other
with pain and insults?
To those who remain – I wish happiness.[84]

The Briks explained his suicide as the 'unavoidable outcome of Mayakovsky's hyperbolic attitude to life'.[85] His transcendental hopes and expectations had crashed against the realities of life. Recent evidence has led to claims that Mayakovsky did not kill himself. Lily Brik, it has been revealed, was an agent of the NKVD, Stalin's political police, and informed it of the poet's private views. In his communal flat there was a concealed entrance through which someone could have entered Mayakovsky's room, shot the poet and escaped unnoticed by neighbours. Notes discovered in the archives of his close friend Eisenstein reveal that Mayakovsky lived in fear of arrest. 'He had to be removed – so they got rid of him,' concluded Eisenstein.[86]

Suicide or murder, the significance of the poet's death was clear: there was no longer room in Soviet literature for the individualist. Mayakovsky was too rooted in the pre-revolutionary age, and his tragedy was shared by all the avant-garde who, like him, threw in their lot with the new society. The last works of Mayakovsky had been viciously attacked by the Soviet authorities. The press condemned *The Bedbug* (1929), a dazzling satire on Soviet manners and the new bureaucracy, with a sparkling score by Shostakovich which added to the montage by having several bands play different types of music (from classical to foxtrot) on and off the stage.[87] They said the play had failed to portray the Soviet future in heroic terms. 'We are brought to the conclusion', complained one reviewer, 'that life under socialism will be very dull in 1979' (it was, it turned out, an accurate portrayal of the Brezhnev years).[88] His next play, *The Bath House*, which opened in Meyerhold's theatre in Moscow just one month before the poet's death, was an awful flop, and its hilarious critique of Soviet bureaucrats again roundly condemned in the press. But the final straw was Mayakovsky's retrospective exhibition of his artwork, which he put on in Moscow in March 1930. The exhibition was consciously avoided by the artistic intelligentsia; the poet Olga Berggolts, who went to visit Mayakovsky there, recalls the sight of the 'tall man with a sad and austere face, his arms folded behind him, as he paced the empty rooms'.[89] At an evening devoted to the exhibition, Mayakovsky said that he could no longer achieve what he had set out do – 'to laugh at things I consider wrong . . . and to bring the workers to great poetry, without hack writing or a deliberate lowering of standards'.[90]

The activities of RAPP (the Russian Association of Proletarian Writers) made life impossible for non-proletarian writers and 'fellow travellers' like Mayakovsky, who disbanded LEF, the Left Front, and joined RAPP in a last desperate bid to save himself in the final few weeks of his life. Formed in 1928 as the literary wing of Stalin's Five-year Plan for industry, RAPP saw itself as the militant vanguard of a cultural revolution against the old intelligentsia. 'The one and only task of Soviet literature', its journal declared in 1930, 'is the depiction of the Five-year Plan and the class war.'[91] The Five-year Plan was intended as the start of a new revolution which would transform Russia into an advanced industrialized state and deliver power to the working class. A new wave of terror began against the so-called 'bourgeois' managers in industry (that is, those who had held their jobs since 1917), and this was followed by a similar assault on 'bourgeois specialists' in the professions and the arts. Supported by the state, RAPP attacked the 'bourgeois enemies' of Soviet literature which it claimed were hidden in the left-wing avant-garde. Just five days before his death, Mayakovsky was condemned at a RAPP meeting at which his critics demanded proof that he would still be read in twenty years.[92]

By the beginning of the 1930s, any writer with an individual voice was deemed politically suspicious. The satirists who flourished in the relatively liberal climate of the 1920s were the first to come under attack. There was Mikhail Zoshchenko, whose moral satires on the empty verbiage of the Soviet bureaucracy and the cramped conditions of communal flats were suddenly considered anti-Soviet in the new political climate of the Five-year Plan, when writers were expected to be positive and the only acceptable subject for satire were the foreign enemies of the Soviet Union. Then there was Mikhail Bulgakov, whose Gogolian satires about censorship (*The Crimson Island*), daily life in Moscow in the NEP (*Adventures of Chichikov*), Soviet xenophobia (*Fatal Eggs*) and his brilliant comic novel *The Heart of a Dog* (where a Pavlov-like experimental scientist transplants the brain and sexual organs of a dog into a human being) were not only banned from publication but forbidden to be read when passed as manuscripts from hand to hand. Finally, there was Andrei Platonov, an engineer and utopian communist (until he was expelled from the Bolshevik Party in 1926) whose own growing doubts about the human costs of the Soviet experiment were reflected in a series of extraordinary dystopian satires: *The Epifan Locks* (1927), a timely allegory on the grandiose but ultimately disastrous canal-building projects of Peter the Great; *Chevengur* (also 1927), a fatal odyssey in search of the true communist society; and *The Foundation Pit* (1930), a nightmare vision of collectivization in which the foundation pit of a huge communal home for the local proletariat turns out to be a monumental grave for humanity. All three were condemned as 'counter-revolutionary' and banned from publication for over sixty years.

RAPP's 'class war' reached fever pitch, however, in 1929 with its organized campaign of vilification against Zamyatin and Pilnyak. Both writers had published works abroad which had been censored in the Soviet Union: Zamyatin's *We* appeared in Prague in 1927; and Pilnyak's *Red Mahogany*, a bitter commentary on the decline of the revolutionary ideals of the Soviet state, was published in Berlin in 1929. But the attack on them had a significance beyond the condemnation of particular works. Boris Pilnyak, who was chairman of the Board of the All-Russian Writers' Union and so effectively the Soviet Union's Writer Number One, was perhaps the widest read and most widely imitated serious prose writer in the country.* His persecution was an advance warning of the strict obedience and conformity which the Soviet state would demand of all its writers from the start of the first Five-year Plan.

For the Five-year Plan was not just a programme of industrialization. It was nothing less than a cultural revolution in which all the arts were called up by the state in a campaign to build a new society. According to the plan, the primary goal of the Soviet writer was to raise the workers' consciousness, to enlist them in the 'battle' for 'socialist construction' by writing books with a social content which they could

---

* Pilnyak's best-known novels are *The Naked Year* (1921), *Black Bread* (1923) and *Machines and Wolves* (1924).

understand and relate to as positive ideals. For the militants of RAPP this could only be achieved by writers like Gorky, with his impeccably proletarian background, not by left-wing 'bourgeois' writers who were deemed no more than 'fellow travellers'. Between 1928 and 1931 some 10,000 'shock authors', literary confrères of the 'shock workers' who would lead the charge to meet the Plan, were plucked from the shop-floor and trained by RAPP to write workers' stories for the Soviet press.[93]

Gorky was hailed as the model for this Soviet literature. In 1921, horrified by the Revolution's turn to violence and dictatorship, Gorky fled to Europe. But he could not bear the life of an exile: he was disillusioned by the rise of fascism in his adopted homeland of Italy; and he convinced himself that life in Stalin's Russia would become more bearable once the Five-year Plan had swept aside the peasant backwardness which in his view had been the cause of the Revolution's failure. From 1928 Gorky began to spend his summers in the Soviet Union and in 1931 Gorky returned home for good. The prodigal son was showered with honours: streets, buildings, farms and schools were named after him; a trilogy of films was made about his life; the Moscow Arts Theatre was renamed the Gorky Theatre; and his native city (Nizhnyi Novgorod) was renamed after him. He was also appointed head of the Writers' Union, the post previously held by Pilnyak.

Gorky had initially supported the RAPP campaign of promoting worker authors as a temporary experiment, but he quickly realized that the quality of the writing was not good. In April 1932 the Central Committee passed a resolution to abolish RAPP, together with all other independent literary groups, and placed them under the cen-tralized control of the Writers' Union. Gorky's influence was instru-mental in this sudden change of direction, but things did not quite turn out as he had planned. Gorky's intention had been two fold: to halt the destructive 'class war' led by RAPP; and to restore to Soviet literature the aesthetic principles established by Tolstoy. In October 1932, a famous meeting attended by Stalin and other Kremlin leaders, as well as fifty writers and other functionaries, took place at Gorky's Moscow house. It was at this meeting that the doctrine of Socialist Realism was formulated, although at the time it was not clear to Gorky that it would become a regimented orthodoxy for all artists in the

Soviet Union. Gorky's understanding was that Socialist Realism would unite the critical realist traditions of nineteenth-century literature with the revolutionary romanticism of the Bolshevik tradition. It was to combine the depiction of the humble everyday reality of life in the Soviet Union with a vision of the Revolution's heroic promise. But in Stalin's version of the doctrine, as defined at the First Congress of the Writers' Union in 1934, it meant that the artist was to portray Soviet life, not as it was in reality, but as it should become:

Socialist Realism means not only knowing reality as it is, but knowing where it is moving. It is moving towards socialism, it is moving towards the victory of the international proletariat. And a work of art created by a Socialist Realist is one which shows where that conflict of contradictions is leading which the artist has seen in life and reflected in his work.[94]

In this formula the artist was to produce a panegyric or iconic form of art which conformed strictly to the Party's narrative of socialist development.[95] Whereas the *kinoki* and other avant-garde artists of the 1920s had sought to expand their audience's vision of freedom and possibility, now artists were to fix that vision in ways strictly prescribed by the state. The new Soviet writer was no longer the creator of original works of art, but a chronicler of tales which were already contained in the Party's own folklore.[96] There was a sort of 'master plot' which Soviet writers were to use in shaping their own novels and characters. In its classic form, as set out in Gorky's early novel *Mother* (1906), the plot was a Bolshevik version of the *Bildungsroman*: the young worker hero joins the class struggle and through the tutelage of senior Party comrades he arrives at a higher consciousness, a better understanding of the world around him and the tasks ahead for the Revolution, before dying a martyr to the cause. Later novels added elements to this master plot: Dmitry Furmanov's *Chapaev* (1923) fixed the model of the civil war hero; while Fedor Gladkov's *Cement* (1925) and Ostrovsky's *How the Steel Was Tempered* raised the communist production worker to Promethean status, capable of conquering every-thing before him, even the most untamed forces of the natural world, as long as he allows the Party to direct his energies. But basically the story that the novelist could tell was strictly circumscribed by the

Party's mythic version of its own revolutionary history; even senior writers were forced to change their works if they did not adhere to this doxology.*

To the sophisticated Western reader this no doubt seems a horrible perversion of the role of literature. But it did not appear so in Stalin's Russia, where the overwhelming mass of the reading public was new to the conventions of literary fiction, and there was less awareness of the difference between the real world and the world of books. People approached literature, as they had perhaps once approached the icons or the stories of the saints, in the conviction that it held up moral truths for the guidance of their lives. The German writer Lion Feuchtwanger commented on this peculiar characteristic of the Soviet reading public when he visited Moscow in 1937:

Among Soviet people the thirst for reading is totally unimaginable. Newspapers, journals, books – all this is absorbed without quenching the thirst to the tiniest degree. Reading is one of the main activities of daily life. But for the reader in the Soviet Union there are, as it were, no clear divisions between the reality in which he lives and the world he reads about in books. The reader treats the heroes of his books as if they are actual people. He argues with them, denounces them, and he even reads realities into the events of the story and its characters.[97]

Isaiah Berlin noted the same attitudes to literature on his visit to the Soviet Union in 1945:

The rigid censorship which, with so much else, suppressed pornography, trash and low-grade thrillers such as fill railway bookstalls in the West, served to make the response of Soviet readers and theatre audiences purer, more direct and naïve than ours; I noticed that at performances of Shakespeare or Sheridan or Griboedov, members of the audience, some of them obviously country folk, were apt to react to the action on the stage or to lines spoken by the

---

* The most famous example is Alexander Fadeev. In 1946 he won the Stalin Prize for *The Young Guard*, a semi-factual novel about the underground youth organization in occupied Ukraine during the Second World War. Attacked in the press for under-rating the role of the Party leadership, Fadeev was forced to add new material to his novel. This enlarged version, published in 1951, was then hailed as a classic Socialist Realist text.

actors . . . with loud expressions of approval or disapproval; the excitement generated was, at times, very strong and, to a visitor from the West, both unusual and touching.[98]

In the cinema the state's concern for art to play a morally didactic role was crucial to the rise of the Socialist Realist film. With the start of the Five-year Plan the Party expressed its impatience with the avant-garde directors, whose intellectual films never really drew a mass audience. Surveys showed that the Soviet public preferred foreign films, action-packed adventures or romantic comedies to the propaganda films of Vertov or Eisenstein.[99] In 1928 a Party Conference on Cinema was held at which there were louds calls for film to play a more effective role in mobilizing mass enthusiasm for the Five-year Plan and the class war. The avant-garde directors of the 1920s – Vertov, Pudovkin, Kuleshov – were all condemned as 'formalists', intellectuals who were more concerned with cinema as art than with making films that could 'be understood by the millions'.[100] Eisenstein's *October*, which had been released on the eve of the conference, was bitterly attacked for its 'formalist' preoccupation with montage, for the lack of any individual heroes in the film which made it hard for a mass audience to identify with, for the *typage* casting of the Lenin character (played by a worker named Nikandrov), whose woodenness did so much to offend Party sensibilities, and – of special offence to Stalin, who ordered that his image be cut out after previewing the film at the studio – for the fact that it depicted Trotsky, the military leader of the October insurrection, who had been kicked out of the Party just three months before the conference began.[101]

But there were just as many criticisms of the leadership of Sovkino, the Soviet film trust under the command of Lunacharsky's Commissariat, for failing to provide an attractive and more healthy Soviet alternative to the cheap entertainment films imported from abroad. As a propaganda weapon of the state, the Soviet cinema needed to be popular. 'Our films must be 100 percent ideologically correct and 100 percent commercially viable,' declared one Party official.[102]

In 1930 Sovkino was finally disbanded, together with the independent studios which had flourished in the 1920s, and the Soviet cinema was nationalized as one vast state enterprise under the centralized direction of Soiuzkino (All-Union Soviet Film Trust). Its chief apparat-chik, Boris Shumiatsky, became the ultimate authority in the world of Soviet cinema (until his own arrest and execution as a 'Trotskyite' in 1938), although Stalin, who loved the cinema and frequently watched movies in his Kremlin cinema, kept a beady eye on the latest films and often intervened in their production.* Shumiatsky ran a sort of 'Soviet Hollywood', with huge production studios in Moscow, Kiev, Lenin-grad and Minsk reeling off a succession of smash-hit Soviet musicals, romantic comedies, war adventures and Western-modelled frontier films ('Easterns') like *Chapaev* (1934), Stalin's favourite film.† Shumi-atsky drew up a Five-year Plan for the cinema which called for no less than 500 films to be made in 1932 alone. All of them were to conform to the new ideological directives, which demanded optimistic pictures about Soviet life with positive individual heroes drawn from the ranks of the proletariat. Party-controlled producers and script departments were placed in charge of the production to ensure that all this entertain-ment was politically correct. 'Life is getting gayer, comrades,' Stalin famously remarked. But only certain types of laughter were allowed.

This was the climate to which Eisenstein returned in 1932. For the previous three years he had been abroad – a semi-dissident ambassador of the Soviet cinema. He travelled to Europe and on to Hollywood to learn about the new techniques of sound, signing up for several films he never made. He enjoyed the freedom of the West, and he was no doubt fearful of going back to Russia, where Shumiatsky's attacks on the 'formalists' were at their most extreme when directed against him. Stalin accused Eisenstein of defecting to the West. The NKVD bullied his poor mother into begging Eisenstein to return home, threatening her with some form of punishment if he failed to do so. In the first two years after his return Eisenstein had several film proposals turned

---

* In 1938, in the final stages of the editing of Eisenstein's *Alexander Nevsky*, Stalin asked to see the rough cuts. The film-maker hurried to the Kremlin and, in his haste, left behind one reel. Stalin loved the film but, since no one dared to inform him that it was incomplete, it was released without the missing reel (J. Goodwin. *Eisenstein, Cinema and History* (Urbana, 1993), p. 162).

† Stalin could apparently recite long passages of the dialogue by heart. See R. Taylor and I. Christie (eds.), *The Film Factory: Russian and Soviet Cinema Documents, 1896–1939* (London, 1994), p. 384.

down for production by Soiuzkino. He withdrew to a teaching post at the State Film School and, although he lavished praise (in his public statements) on the mediocre films that were churned out at that time, he stood firm by the films which he had made, courageously refusing to denounce himself, as he was called upon to do, at the Party's Second Conference on Cinema in 1935.[103]

Under pressure to produce a film which conformed to the Socialist Realist mould, Eisenstein accepted a commission from the Komsomol (the Communist Youth League) in 1935. He was to realize a film scenario that took its title, although not much else, from Turgenev's 'Bezhin Meadow', a story about peasant boys discussing supernatural signs of death which formed one of the *Sketches from a Hunter's Album*. The film was actually inspired by the story of Pavlik Morozov, a boy hero who, according to the version of his life propagandized by the Stalinist regime, had been murdered by the 'kulaks' of his remote Urals village after he had denounced his own father, the chairman of the village Soviet, as a kulak opponent of the Soviet campaign for collectivization.* By 1935, the Morozov cult was at its height: songs and poems, even a cantata with full orchestra and chorus, had been written about him. This no doubt persuaded Eisenstein that it was safe to make a film about him. But his conception of the film was deemed unacceptable. He turned it from a story about individuals to a conflict between types, between old and new, and, in a scene that showed the communists dismantling a church to break the resistance of the kulak saboteurs, he came dangerously close to suggesting that collectivization had been something destructive. In August 1936, with most of the film already shot, Eisenstein was ordered by Shumiatsky to rewrite the script. With the help of the writer Isaac Babel he recommenced shooting in the autumn. The church scene was cut and a speech in tribute to Stalin was added. But then, in March 1937, Shumiatsky ordered all work on the film stopped. In an article in *Pravda* he accused Eisenstein of depicting collectivization as an elemental conflict between good and evil, and

---

* In fact Morozov was murdered by the NKVD, which then executed thirty-seven kulak villagers, falsely charged with the boy's murder for propaganda purposes. For the full story, see Y. Druzhnikov, *Informer 001: The Myth of Pavlik Morozov* (New Brunswick, 1997).

denounced the film for its 'formalist' and religious character.[104] Eisenstein was forced to publish a 'confession' of his mistakes in the press, although it was penned in such a way as to be read by those whose opinions mattered to him as a satirical attack on his Stalinist masters. The negatives of the film were burned – all, that is, except a few hundred stills of extraordinary photographic beauty which were found in Eisenstein's personal archive following his death in 1948.[105]

The suppression of *Bezhin Meadow* was part of the continuing campaign against the artistic avant-garde. In 1934, at the First Writers' Congress, Party leader Karl Radek, a former Trotskyite who was now making up for his past errors by proving himself the good Stalinist, condemned the writings of James Joyce – a huge influence on Eisenstein and all the Soviet avant-garde. Radek described *Ulysses* as 'a dung heap swarming with maggots and photographed by a movie camera through a microscope'.[106] This no doubt held a reference to the famous maggot scene in *The Battleship Potemkin*, in which Eisenstein zooms in on the offending larvae by filming them through the monocle of the commanding officer. Then, in January 1936, *Pravda* published a diatribe against Shostakovich's opera *Lady Macbeth of Mtsensk*, which had been a great success, with hundreds of performances in both Russia and the West since its première in Leningrad in 1934. The unsigned article, 'Chaos Instead of Music', was evidently written with the full support of the Kremlin, and evidence suggests, as it was rumoured at the time, that Andrei Zhdanov, the Party boss in Leningrad, wrote it on the personal instructions of Stalin, who, just a few days before the article appeared, had seen the opera and clearly hated it.[107]

From the first moment, the listener is shocked by a deliberately dissonant, confused stream of sound. Fragments of melody, embryonic phrases appear – only to disappear again in the din, the grinding, and the screaming ... This music ... carries into the theatre ... the most negative features of 'Meyerholdism' infinitely multiplied. Here we have 'leftist' confusion instead of natural, human music ... The danger of this trend to Soviet music is clear. Leftist distortion in opera stems from the same source as the leftist distortion in painting, poetry, teaching and science. Petty-bourgeois innovations lead to a break with real art, real science and real literature ... All this is primitive and vulgar.[108]

This was not just an attack on Shostakovich, although, to be sure, its effect on him was devastating enough that he never dared again to write an opera. It was an attack on all modernists – in painting, poetry and theatre, as well as in music. Meyerhold, in particular, who was brave and self-assured enough to speak out publicly in defence of Shostakovich and against the Party's stifling influence on art, was subjected to denunciations of a feverish intensity. He was condemned in the Soviet press as an 'alien', and even though he tried to save himself by staging the Socialist Realist classic *How the Steel Was Tempered* in 1937, his theatre was closed down at the beginning of the following year. Stanislavsky came to his old student's aid, inviting him to join his Opera Theatre in March 1938, although artistically the two directors were poles apart. When Stanislavsky died that summer, Meyerhold became the theatre's artistic director. But in 1939 he was arrested, tortured brutally by the NKVD to extract a 'confession', and then, in the arctic frost of early 1940, he was shot.[109]

This renewed assault against the avant-garde involved a counter-revolution in cultural politics. As the 1930s wore on, the regime completely abandoned its commitment to the revolutionary idea of establishing a 'proletarian' or 'Soviet' form of culture that could be distinguished from the culture of the past. Instead, it promoted a return to the nationalist traditions of the nineteenth century, which it reinvented in its own distorted forms as Socialist Realism. This reassertion of the 'Russian classics' was a fundamental aspect of the Stalinist political programme, which used culture to create the illusion of stability in the age of mass upheaval over which it reigned, and which championed its version of the nationalist school in particular to counter-act the influence of the 'foreign' avant-garde. In all the arts the nineteenth-century classics were now held up as the model which Soviet artists were expected to follow. Contemporary writers like Akhmatova could not find a publisher, but the complete works of Pushkin and Turgenev, Chekhov and Tolstoy (though not Dostoevsky),* were

---

* Dostoevsky was despised (though not read) by Lenin, who once famously dismissed his novel *The Devils*, which contains a devastating critique of the Russian revolutionary mentality, as a 'piece of reactionary trash'. Apart from Lunacharsky, none of the Soviet leadership favoured his retention in the literary canon, and even Gorky wanted to get rid of him. Relatively few editions of Dostoevsky's works were therefore published in

issued in their millions as a new readership was introduced to them. Landscape painting, which had been a dying art in the 1920s, was suddenly restored as the favoured medium of Socialist Realist art, particularly scenes that illustrated the heroic mastery of the natural world by Soviet industry; all of it was styled on the landscape painters of the late nineteenth century, on Levitan or Kuindzhi or the Wanderers, with whom some of the older artists had even studied in their youth. As Ivan Gronsky once remarked (with the bluntness one might expect from the editor of *Izvestiia*), 'Socialist Realism is Rubens, Rembrandt and Repin put to serve the working class.'[110]

In music, too, the regime put the clock back to the nineteenth century. Glinka, Tchaikovsky and the *kuchkists*, who had fallen out of favour with the avant-garde composers of the 1920s, were now held up as the model for all future music in the Soviet Union. The works of Stasov, who had espoused the cause of popular nationalist art in the nineteenth century, were now elevated to the status of scripture. Stasov's championing of art with a democratic content and progressive purpose or idea was mobilized in the 1930s as the founding argument of Socialist Realist art. His opposition to the cosmopolitanism of Diaghilev and the European avant-garde was pressed into the service of the Stalinist regime in its own campaign against the 'alien' modernists.* It was a gross distortion of the critic's views. Stasov was a Westernist. He sought to raise Russia's culture to the level of the West's, to bring it into contact as an equal with the West, and his nationalism was never exclusive of Europe's influence. But in the hands

---

the 1930s – about 100,000 copies of all his works were sold between 1938 and 1941, compared with about 5 million copies of Tolstoy's. It was only in the Khrushchev thaw that print runs of Dostoevsky's works were augmented. The 10-volume 1956 edition of Dostoevsky's works published to commemorate the seventy-fifth anniversary of his death ran to 300,000 copies – though this was still extremely small by Soviet standards (V. Seduro, *Dostoevski in Russian Literary Criticism, 1846–1956* (New York, 1957), p. 197; and same author, *Dostoevski's Image in Russia Today* (Belmont, 1975), p. 379).
* For example, in the foreword to the 3-volume 1952 edition of Stasov's works (V. V. Stasov, *Sobranie sochinenii v 3-kh tomakh, 1847–1906* (Moscow, 1952)) the Soviet editors made the extraordinary announcement that 'the selection of materials has been determined by our attempt to show Stasov in the struggle against the cosmopolitanism of the Imperial Academy, where the prophets of 'Art for Art's sake', aestheticism, formalism and decadence in art were to be found in the nineteenth century'.

of the Soviet regime he became a Russian chauvinist, an enemy of Western influence and a prophet of the Stalinist belief in Russia's cultural superiority.

In 1937 Soviet Russia marked the centenary of Pushkin's death. The whole country was involved in festivities: small provincial theatres put on plays; schools organized special celebrations; Young Communists went on pilgrimages to places connected with the poet's life; factories organized study groups and clubs of 'Pushkinists'; collective farms held Pushkin carnivals with figures dressed as characters from Pushkin's fairy tales (and in one case, for no apparent reason, the figure of Chapaev with a machine-gun); scores of films were made about his life; libraries and theatres were established in his name; and streets and squares, theatres and museums, were renamed after the poet.[111] The boom in Pushkin publishing was staggering. Nineteen million copies of his works sold in the jubilee alone, and tens of millions of subscriptions were taken for the new edition of his complete works which had been planned for 1937 – though because of the purges and the frequent losses of staff in which they resulted it was only finished in 1949. The cult of Pushkin reached fever pitch when *Pravda* declared him a 'semi-divine being' and the Central Committee issued a decree in which he was heralded as the 'creator of the Russian literary language', the 'father of Russian literature' and even as 'the founder of Communism'.[112] In an article entitled 'Pushkin Our Comrade', the writer Andrei Platonov maintained that Pushkin had been able to foresee the October Revolution because the spirit of the Russian people had burned like a 'red hot coal' within his heart; the same spirit had flickered through the nineteenth century and flared up anew in Lenin's soul.[113] As Pushkin was a truly national poet whose writing spoke to the entire people, his homeland, it was claimed by *Pravda*, was not the old Russia but the Soviet Union and all humanity.[114]

'Poetry is respected only in this country', Mandelstam would tell his friends in the 1930s. 'There's no place where more people are killed for it.'[115] At the same time as it was erecting monuments to Pushkin, the Soviet regime was murdering his literary descendants. Of the 700 writers who attended the First Writers' Congress in 1934, only fifty survived to attend the Second in 1954.[116] Stalin was capricious in his persecution of the literary fraternity. He saved Bulgakov, he cherished

Pasternak (both of whom could be construed as anti-Soviet), yet without a moment's hesitation he condemned Party hacks and left-wing writers from the ranks of RAPP. Stalin was not ignorant of cultural affairs. He read serious literature (the poet Demian Bedny hated lending books to him because he returned them with greasy fingermarks).[117] He knew the power of poetry in Russia, and feared it. Stalin kept a jealous eye on the most talented or dangerous writers: even Gorky was placed under constant surveillance. But after 1934, when full-scale terror was unleashed, he moved towards more drastic measures of control. The turning point was the murder in 1934 of Sergei Kirov, the Party boss in Leningrad. It is probable that Kirov had been killed on Stalin's orders: he was more popular than Stalin in the Party, in favour of more moderate policies, and there had been plots to put him into power. But in any case, Stalin exploited the murder to unleash a campaign of mass terror against all the 'enemies' of Soviet power, which culminated in the show trials of the Bolshevik leaders Bukharin, Kamenev and Zinoviev in 1936–8 and subsided only when Russia entered the Second World War in 1941. Akhmatova called the early 1930s the 'vegetarian years', meaning they were relatively harmless in comparison with the 'meat-eating' years that were to come.[118]

Mandelstam was the first to be taken. In November 1933 he had written a poem about Stalin which had been read in secret to his friends. It is the simplest, most straightforward, verse he ever wrote, a fact his widow Nadezhda would explain as demonstrating Mandelstam's concern to make the poem comprehensible and accessible to all. 'It was, to my mind, a gesture, an act that flowed logically from the whole of his life and work . . . He did not want to die before stating in unambiguous terms what he thought about the things going on around us.'[119]

> We live, deaf to the land beneath us,
> Ten steps away no one hears our speeches,
> All we hear is the Kremlin mountaineer,
> The murderer and peasant-slayer.
> His fingers are fat as grubs
> And the words, final as lead weights, fall from his lips,
> His cockroach whiskers leer

And his boots gleam.
Around him a rabble of thin-necked leaders –
Fawning half-men for him to play with.
They whinny, purr or whine
As he prates and points a finger,
One by one forging his laws, to be flung
Like horseshoes at the head, the eye or the groin.
And every killing is a treat
For the broad-chested Ossete.[120]

Akhmatova was visiting the Mandelstams in Moscow in May 1934 when the secret police burst into the flat. 'The search went on all night', she wrote in a memoir about Mandelstam. 'They were looking for poetry, and walked across manuscripts that had been thrown out of the trunk. We all sat in one room. It was very quiet. On the other side of the wall, in Kirsanov's flat, a ukulele was playing . . . They took him away at seven in the morning.'[121] During his interrogations in the Lubianka, Mandelstam made no attempt to conceal his Stalin poem (he even wrote it out for his torturers) – for which he might well have expected to be sent straight to the gulags in Siberia. Stalin's resolution, however, was to 'isolate but preserve': at this stage, the poet was more dangerous to him dead than alive.[122] The Bolshevik leader Nikolai Bukharin had intervened on Mandelstam's behalf, warning Stalin that 'poets are always right, history is on their side'.[123] And Pasternak, though obviously careful not to compromise himself, had done his best to defend Mandelstam when Stalin called him at home on the telephone.[124]

The Mandelstams were exiled to Voronezh, 400 kilometres south of Moscow, returning to the Moscow region (but still barred from the capital itself) in 1937. Later that autumn, without a place to live, they visited Akhmatova in Leningrad, sleeping on the divan in her room at the Fountain House. During this last visit Akhmatova wrote a poem for Osip Mandelstam, the person whom she thought of almost as her twin. It was about the city they both loved:

Not like a European capital
With the first prize for beauty –

> But like stifling exile to the Yenisei,
> Like a transfer to Chita,
> To Ishim, to waterless Irghiz,
> To renowned Atbasar,
> To the outpost Svobodny,
> To the corpse stench of rotting bunks –
> So this city seemed to me
> On that midnight, pale blue –
> This city, celebrated by the first poet,
> By us sinners and by you.[125]

Six months later Mandelstam was re-arrested and sentenced to five years' penal labour in Kolyma, eastern Siberia – in effect a death sentence in view of his poor health. On his way there he passed the Yenisei river, the towns of Chita and Svobodny, and ended up in a camp near Vladivostok, where he died of a heart attack on 26 December 1938.

In her memoir about Mandelstam, Akhmatova recalls the final time she saw her friend, stripped of everything, on the eve of his arrest: 'For me he is not only a great poet but a great human being who, when he found out (probably from Nadya) how bad it was for me in the House on the Fontanka, told me when he was saying goodbye at the Moscow train station in Leningrad: "Annushka" [which he had never used before], always remember that my house – is yours." '[126]

Mandelstam's seditious poem also played a role in the arrest of Lev Gumilev, Akhmatova's son, in 1935. Since the death of his father, in 1921, Lev had lived with relatives in the town of Bezhetsk, 250 kilometres north of Moscow, but in 1929 he moved into the Punin apartment at the Fountain House and, after several applications (all turned down on account of his 'social origins'), he was finally enrolled, in 1934, as a history student at Leningrad University. One spring evening at the Fountain House Lev recited the Mandelstam poem, which by that time he, like many people, knew by heart. But among his student friends that night was an informant of the NKVD, who came to arrest him, along with Punin, in October 1935. Akhmatova was driven to a frenzy. She rushed to Moscow and, with the help of Pasternak, who wrote personally to Stalin, secured Lev's release. It was not the first time, nor the last, that Lev would be arrested. He had never been involved in anti-Soviet agitation. Indeed, his sole crime was to be the son of Gumilev and Akhmatova; if he was arrested it was only as a hostage to secure his mother's acquiescence to the Soviet regime. The mere fact of her close relationship with Mandelstam was enough to make the authorities suspicious of her.

Akhmatova herself was being closely watched by the NKVD during 1935. Its agents followed her and photographed her visitors as they came in and out of the Fountain House, in preparation, as archives have now revealed, for her arrest.[127] Akhmatova was conscious of the danger she was in. After Lev's arrest she had burned a huge pile of her manuscripts in full expectation of another raid on the Punin apartment.[128] Like all communal blocks, the Fountain House was full of NKVD informants – not paid-up officials, but ordinary residents who were themselves afraid and wished to demonstrate their loyalty, or who bore a petty grudge against their neighbours or thought that by denouncing them they would get more living space. The cramped conditions of communal housing brought out the worst in those who suffered them. There were communal houses where everyone got along, but in general the reality of living together was a far cry from the communist ideal. Neighbours squabbled over personal property, foodstuffs that went missing from the shared kitchen, noisy lovers or music played at night, and, with everybody in a state of nervous paranoia, it did not take much for fights to turn into denunciations to the NKVD.

Lev was re-arrested in March 1938. For eight months he was held and tortured in Leningrad's Kresty jail, then sentenced to ten years' hard labour on the White Sea Canal in north-west Russia.* This was at the height of the Stalin Terror, when millions of people disappeared. For eight months Akhmatova went every day to join the long queues at the Kresty jail, now just one of Russia's many women waiting to hand in a letter or a parcel through a little window and, if it was accepted, to go away with joy at the knowledge that their loved one must be still alive. This was the background to her poetic cycle *Requiem* (written between 1935 and 1940; first published in Munich in 1963).

---

* The sentence was later changed to five years' labour in the gulag at Norilsk.

As Akhmatova explained in the short prose piece 'Instead of a Preface' (1957):

In the terrible years of the Yezhov terror, I spent seventeen months in the prison lines of Leningrad. Once, someone 'recognized' me. Then a woman with bluish lips standing behind me, who, of course, had never heard me called by name before, woke up from the stupor to which everyone had succumbed and whispered in my ear (everyone spoke in whispers there):
    'Can you describe this?'
    And I answered, 'Yes I can.'
    Then something that looked like a smile passed over what had once been her face.[129]

In *Requiem* Akhmatova became the people's voice. The poem represented a decisive moment in her artistic evolution – the moment when the lyric poet of private experience became, in the words of *Requiem*, the 'mouth through which a hundred million scream'.[130] The poem is intensely personal. Yet it gives voice to an anguish felt by every person who had lost someone.

> This was when the ones who smiled
> Were the dead, glad to be at rest.
> And like a useless appendage, Leningrad
> Swung from its prisons.
> And when, senseless from torment,
> Regiments of convicts marched,
> And the short songs of farewell
> Were sung by locomotive whistles.
> The stars of death stood above us
> And innocent Russia writhed
> Under bloody boots
> And under the tyres of the Black Marias.[131]

This was when Akhmatova's decision to remain in Russia began to make sense. She had shared in her people's suffering. Her poem had become a monument to it – a dirge for the dead sung in whispered incantations among friends; and in some way it redeemed that suffering.

No, not under the vault of alien skies,
And not under the shelter of alien wings –
I was with my people then,
There, where my people, unfortunately, were.[132]

5

Some time at the end of the 1940s Akhmatova was walking with
Nadezhda Mandelstam in Leningrad when she suddenly remarked:
'To think that the best years of our life were during the war when so
many people were being killed, when we were starving and my son
was doing forced labour.'[133] For anyone who suffered from the Terror
as she did, the Second World War must have come as a release. As
Gordon says to Dudorov in the epilogue of *Doctor Zhivago*, 'When
war broke out its real dangers and its menace of death were a blessing
compared with the inhuman power of the lie, a relief because it broke
the spell of the dead letter.'[134] People were allowed and had to act in
ways that would have been unthinkable before the war. They organized
themselves for civilian defence. By necessity, they spoke to one another
without thinking of the consequences. From this spontaneous activity
a new sense of nationhood emerged. As Pasternak would later write,
the war was 'a period of vitality and in this sense an untrammelled,
joyous restoration of the sense of community with everyone'.[135] His
own wartime verse was full of feeling for this community, as if the
struggle had stripped away the state to reveal the core of Russia's
nationhood:

> Through the peripeteia of the past
> And the years of war and poverty
> Silently I came to recognize
> The inimitable features of Russia
>
> Overcoming my feelings of love
> I observed in worship
> Old women, residents
> Students and locksmiths[136]

As the German armies crossed the Soviet border, on 22 June 1941, Vyacheslav Molotov, the Foreign Minister, gave a radio address in which he spoke of the impending 'patriotic war for homeland, honour and freedom'.[137] The next day the main Soviet army newspaper, *Krasnaia zvezda*, referred to it as a 'holy war'.[138] Communism was conspicuously absent from Soviet propaganda in the war. It was fought in the name of Russia, of the 'family of peoples' in the Soviet Union, of Pan-Slav brotherhood, or in the name of Stalin, but never in the name of the communist system. To mobilize support, the Stalinist regime even embraced the Russian Church, whose patriotic message was more likely to persuade a rural population that was still recovering from the disastrous effects of collectivization. In 1943, a patriarch was elected for the first time since 1917; a theological academy and several seminaries were re-opened; and after years of persecution the parish churches were allowed to restore something of their spiritual life.[139] The regime glorified the military heroes of Russian history – Alexander Nevsky, Dmitry Donskoi, Kuzma Minin and Dmitry Pozharsky, Alexander Suvorov and Mikhail Kutuzov – all of whom were summoned as an inspiration for the nation's self-defence. Films were made about their lives, military orders were created in their names. History became the story of great leaders rather than the charting of the class struggle.

Russia's artists enjoyed a new freedom and responsibility in the war years. Poets who had been regarded with disfavour or banned from publication by the Soviet regime suddenly began to receive letters from the soldiers at the front. Throughout the years of the Terror they had never been forgotten by their readers; nor, it would seem, had they ever really lost their spiritual authority. In 1945, Isaiah Berlin, on a visit to Russia, was told that

the poetry of Blok, Bryusov, Sologub, Esenin, Tsvetaeva, Mayakovsky, was widely read, learnt by heart and quoted by soldiers and officers and even political commissars. Akhmatova and Pasternak, who had for a long time lived in a kind of internal exile, received an amazingly large number of letters from the front, quoting from both published and unpublished poems, for the most part circulated privately in manuscript copies; there were requests for autographs, for confirmation of the authenticity of texts, for expressions of the author's attitude to this or that problem.[140]

Zoshchenko received about 6,000 letters in one year. Many of them came from readers who said they often thought of suicide and looked to him for spiritual help.[141] In the end the moral value of such writers could not fail to impress itself on the Party's bureaucrats, and conditions for these artists gradually improved. Akhmatova was allowed to publish a collection of her early lyrics, *From Six Books*. Huge queues formed to buy it on the day when it appeared, in a small edition of just 10,000 copies, in the summer of 1940, whereupon the Leningrad authorities took fright and, on the orders of Party Secretary Andrei Zhdanov, had the book withdrawn from circulation.[142]

In her patriotic poem 'Courage' (published in the Soviet press in February 1942) Akhmatova presented the war as a defence of the 'Russian word' – and the poem gave courage to the millions of soldiers who went into battle with its words on their lips:

> We know what lies in balance at this moment,
> And what is happening right now.
> The hour for courage strikes upon our clocks,
> And courage will not desert us.
> We're not frightened by a hail of lead,
> We're not bitter without a roof overhead –
> And we will preserve you, Russian speech,
> Mighty Russian word!
> We will transmit you to our grandchildren
> Free and pure and rescued from captivity
> Forever![143]

In the first months of the war Akhmatova joined the Civil Defence in Leningrad. 'I remember her near the old iron railings of the House on the Fontanka', wrote the poet Olga Berggolts. 'Her face severe and angry, a gas mask strapped over her shoulder, she took her turn on the fire watch like a regular soldier.'[144] As the German armies circled in on Leningrad, Berggolts's husband, the literary critic Georgy Makogonenko, turned to Akhmatova to raise the spirits of the city by talking to its people in a radio broadcast. For years her poetry had been forbidden by the Soviet authorities. Yet, as the critic explained later, the very name Akhmatova was so synonymous with the spirit of the city that even Zhdanov was prepared to bow to it in this hour of need. Akhmatova was sick, so it was agreed to record her speech in the Fountain House. Akhmatova's address was proud and courageous. She appealed to the city's entire legacy – not just to Lenin but to Peter the Great, Pushkin, Dostoevsky and Blok, too. She ended with a stirring tribute to the women of the old capital:

Our descendants will honour every mother who lived at the time of the war, but their gaze will be caught and held fast by the image of the Leningrad woman standing during an air raid on the roof of a house, with a boat-hook and fire-tongs in her hand, protecting the city from fire; the Leningrad girl volunteer giving aid to the wounded among the still smoking ruins of a building. . . No, a city which has bred women like these cannot be conquered.[145]

Shostakovich also took part in the radio broadcast. He and Akhmatova had never met, even though they loved each other's work and felt a spiritual affinity.* Both felt profoundly the suffering of their city, and expressed that suffering in their own ways. Like Akhmatova, Shostakovich had joined the Civil Defence, as a fireman. Only his bad eyesight had prevented him from joining up with the Red Army in the first days of the war. He turned down the chance to leave the besieged city in July, when the musicians of the Conservatory were evacuated to Tashkent in Uzbekistan. In between the fire fighting, he began composing marches for the front-line troops, and in the first two weeks of September, as the bombs began to fall on Leningrad, he worked by candlelight, in a city now deprived of electricity, to finish what would be his Seventh Symphony. As one might expect from his Terror-induced caution and St Petersburg reserve, Shostakovich was rather circumspect in his radio address. He simply told the city that he was about to complete a new symphony. Normal life was going on.[146]

---

* Akhmatova rarely missed a Shostakovich première. After the first performance of his Eleventh Symphony ('The Year 1905') in 1957, she compared its hopeful revolutionary songs, which the critics had dismissed as devoid of interest (this was the time of the Khrushchev thaw), to 'white birds flying against a terrible black sky'. The next year she dedicated the Soviet edition of her *Poems*: 'To Dmitry Dmitrievich Shostakovich, in whose epoch I lived on earth'. The two eventually met in 1961. 'We sat in silence for twenty minutes. It was wonderful,' recalled Akhmatova (E. Wilson, *Shostakovich: A Life Remembered* (London, 1994), pp. 319, 321).

Later that same day, 16 September 1941, the Germans broke through to the gates of Leningrad. For 900 days they cut the city off from virtually all its food and fuel supplies; perhaps a million people, or one third of the pre-war population, died by disease or starvation, before the siege of Leningrad was at last broken in January 1944. Akhmatova was evacuated to Tashkent soon after the German invasion; Shostakovich to the Volga city of Kuibyshev (now known by its pre-revolutionary name of Samara), where he completed the final movement of the Seventh Symphony on a battered upright piano in his two-room apartment. At the top of the first page he scribbled in red ink: 'To the city of Leningrad'. On 5 March 1942 the symphony received its première in Kuibyshev. It was performed by the orchestra of the Bolshoi Theatre, which had also been evacuated to the Volga town. Broadcast by radio throughout the land, it transmitted, in the words of the violinist David Oistrakh, who was listening in Moscow, 'the prophetic affirmation ... of our faith in the eventual triumph of humanity and light'.[147] The Moscow première later that month was broadcast globally, its drama only highlighted by an air raid in the middle of the performance. Soon the symphony was being performed throughout the Allied world, a symbol of the spirit of endurance and survival, not just of Leningrad but of all countries united against the fascist threat, with sixty-two performances in the USA alone during 1942.[148]

The symphony was resonant with themes of Petersburg: its lyrical beauty and classicism, evoked nostalgically in the moderato movement (originally entitled 'Memories'); its progressive spirit and modernity, signalled by the harsh Stravinskian wind chords of the opening adagio; and its own history of violence and war (for the Boléro-like march of the first movement is not just the sound of the approaching German armies, it comes from within). Since the Stalinist assault against his music in 1936, Shostakovich had developed a sort of double-speak in his musical language, using one idiom to please his masters in the Kremlin and another to satisfy his own moral conscience as an artist and a citizen. Outwardly he spoke in a triumphant voice. Yet beneath the ritual sounds of Soviet rejoicing there was a softer, more melancholic voice – the carefully concealed voice of satire and dissent only audible to those who had felt the suffering his music expressed. These two voices are clearly audible in Shostakovich's Fifth Symphony (the composer's 'Socialist Realist' rejoinder to those who had attacked *Lady Macbeth*), which received a half-hour ovation of electrifying force when it was first performed in the Great Hall of the Leningrad Philharmonia in November 1937.[149] Beneath the endless fanfares trumpeting the triumph of the Soviet state in the finale, the audience had heard a distant echo of the funeral march from Mahler's First Symphony and, whether they recognized the march or not, they must have felt its sadness – for nearly everyone in that audience would have lost someone in the Terror of 1937 – and they responded to the music as a spiritual release.[150] The Seventh Symphony had the same overwhelming emotional effect.

For it to achieve its symbolic goal, it was vital for that symphony to be performed in Leningrad – a city which both Hitler and Stalin loathed. The Leningrad Philharmonic had been evacuated and the Radio Orchestra was the only remaining ensemble in the city. The first winter of the siege had reduced it to a mere fifteen players, so extra musicians had to be brought out of retirement or borrowed from the army defending Leningrad. The quality of playing was not high, but that hardly mattered when the symphony was finally performed in the bombed-out Great Hall of the Philharmonia on 9 August 1942 – the very day when Hitler had once planned to celebrate the fall of Leningrad with a lavish banquet at the Astoria Hotel. As the people of the city congregated in the hall, or gathered around loudspeakers to listen to the concert in the street, a turning point was reached. Ordinary citizens were brought together by music; they felt united by a sense of their city's spiritual strength, by a conviction that their city would be saved. The writer Alexander Rozen, who was present at the première, describes it as a kind of national catharsis:

Many people cried at the concert. Some people cried because that was the only way they could show their joy; others because they had lived through what the music was expressing with such force; others cried from grief for the people they had lost; or just because they were overcome with the emotion of being still alive.[151]

The war was a period of productivity and relative creative liberty for Russia's composers. Inspired by the struggle against Hitler's armies, or perhaps relieved by the temporary relaxation of the Stalinist Terror, they responded to the crisis with a flood of new music. Symphonies and songs with upbeat martial tunes for the soldiers to march to were the genres in demand. There was a production line of music of this sort. The composer Aram Khachaturian recalled that in the first few days after the invasion by the German troops a sort of 'song head-quarters' was set up at the Union of Composers in Moscow.[152] But even serious composers felt compelled to respond to the call.

Prokofiev was particularly eager to prove his commitment to the national cause. After eighteen years of living in the West, he had returned to the Soviet Union at the height of the Great Terror, in 1936, when any foreign connections were regarded as a sign of potential treachery. Prokofiev appeared a foreigner. He had lived in New York, Paris, Hollywood, and had become comparatively wealthy from his compositions for the Ballets Russes, the theatre and the cinema. With his colourful and fashionable clothes, Prokofiev cut a shocking figure in the grey atmosphere of Moscow at that time. The pianist Sviatoslav Richter, then a student at the Conservatory, recalled him wearing 'checkered trousers with bright yellow shoes and a reddish-orange tie'.[153] Prokofiev's Spanish wife, Lina, whom he had brought to Moscow and had then abandoned for a student at the Literary Institute, was arrested as a foreigner in 1941, after she had refused to follow him and his new mistress when they left Moscow for the Caucasus.* Prokofiev was attacked as a 'formalist', and much of his more experimental music, like his score for Meyerhold's 1937 production of Pushkin's *Boris Godunov*, remained unperformed. What saved him, however, was his amazing talent for composing tunes. His Fifth Symphony (1944) was filled with expansive and heroic themes that perfectly expressed the spirit of the Soviet war effort. The huge scale of its register, with its thick bass colours and Borodin-esque harmonies, summoned up the grandeur of the Russian land. This same epic quality was to be found in *War and Peace* – an opera whose theme was obviously suggested by the striking parallels between Russia's war

---

* Sentenced to twenty years' hard labour in Siberia, Lina Prokofiev was released in 1957. After many years of struggling for her rights as a widow she was finally allowed to return to the West in 1972. She died in London in 1989.

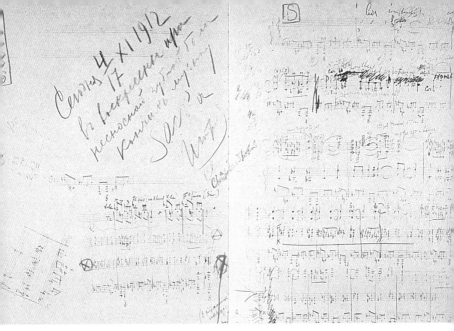

FOLKLORE FANTASIES. The Rite of Spring *(1913): the original score by Igor Stravinsky. Below: Viktor Vasnetsov: set design for Mamontov's production of Rimsky-Korsakov's opera* The Snow Maiden *(Abramtsevo, 1881). Vasnetsov's designs, with their folk-like use of colour, became a visual model for the Ballets Russes and primitivist painters such as Goncharova, Malevich and Chagall.*

SCYTHIAN RUSSIA. The Rite of Spring *was conceived by Nikolai Roerich as the re-enactment of an ancient ('Scythian') ritual of human sacrifice. A trained archaeologist, Roerich designed the sets and costumes of* The Rite of Spring. *These were reproduced by the Joffrey Ballet for its revival of the original ballet in 1987 (above). The rhythm of the music and the choreography emphasized the dancers' weight and immobility, a sense conveyed by Roerich in his many paintings of Scythian Russia.* Below: *Roerich:* The Idols *(1901).*

Roerich: costume designs for The Snow Maiden *(Chicago, 1921). A disciple of Stasov, Roerich believed in the Asiatic origins of Russian folk culture, as suggested here by the heavy jewellery and the Tatar-like headgear.*

PAGAN RUSSIA. *Vasily Kandinsky: Motley Life (1907). Ostensibly a Russian-Christian scene, the painting is filled with pagan symbols from the Komi region, which Kandinsky had explored as an anthropologist. Below: Kandinsky: All Saints II (1911) tells the story of the confrontation between St Stephan and the Komi shaman Pam. Like Pam (seen escaping persecution in a boat) the two saints (standing on the rock) wear sorcerer's caps but they also have halos to symbolize the fusion of the Christian and the pagan traditions.*

THE ARTIST AS SHAMAN. Left: *Kandinsky: Oval No. 2 (1925). The oval shapes and hieroglyphia of Kandinsky's abstract paintings were largely copied from the symbols he had seen on the drums of Siberian shamans. A hooked curve and line symbolized a horse, circles symbolized the sun and moon, while beaks and eyes were meant to represent the bird-like headdress worn by many shamans for their dance rituals (below).*

RUSSIA AND THE ASIATIC STEPPE. *Isaak Levitan:*
Vladimirka *(1892). This was the road on which Russia's convicts travelled
to their penal exile in Siberia. Below: Vasily Vereshchagin: Surprise Attack
(1871). An official war artist with Russia's army on the Turkestan
campaign, Vereshchagin's canvases were perceived as an attack on the
savage Russian violence against the Asian tribes.*

HORSES AND APOCALYPSE. *From Pushkin's* Bronze Horseman, *the horse became the great poetic metaphor of Russia's destiny and a symbol of apocalypse. Kuzma Petrov-Vodkin:* Bathing the Red Horse *(1912), a work strongly influenced by the Russian icon tradition. Below: Kazimir Malevich:* Red Cavalry *(1930).*

Nathan Altman: Portrait of Anna Akhmatova *(1914).*

against Napoleon and the war against Hitler. The first version of the opera, composed in the autumn of 1941, paid as much attention to intimate love scenes as it did to battle scenes. But following criticism from the Soviet Arts Committee in 1942, Prokofiev was forced to compose several revised versions where, in direct contravention of Tolstoy's intentions, the heroic leadership and military genius of (the Stalin-like) Kutuzov was highlighted as the key to Russia's victory, and the heroic spirit of its peasant soldiers was emphasized in large choral set pieces with Russian folk motifs.[154]

As he was working on the score of *War and Peace* Prokofiev was asked by Eisenstein to compose the music for his film *Ivan the Terrible*, released in 1944. Cinema was the perfect medium for Prokofiev. His ability to compose tunes to order and deliver them on time was phenomenal. For Prokofiev the cinema became a sort of Soviet version of the operatic tradition in which he had been schooled under Rimsky Korsakov at the Conservatory. It gave new inspiration to his classical symphonism, allowing him free rein once again to write big tunes for grand *mises-en-scène*. Prokofiev's collaboration with Eisenstein had begun in 1938, when, after the disaster of *Bezhin Meadow*, the film director was given one more chance to please Stalin with an epic history film, *Alexander Nevsky* (1938), about the prince of Novgorod who had defended Russia from the Teutonic knights in the thirteenth century. Prokofiev was asked by Eisenstein to write the score for his first film in sound. Under the influence of Meyerhold, the two were moving at this time toward the idea of a synthesis of images and sound – an essentially Wagnerian conception which they would apply to opera as well as to film.*

This theatrical ideal lies at the heart of their conception of *Alexander Nevsky* and *Ivan the Terrible*. These two epic film dramas are essentially cinematic versions of the great nineteenth-century history operas. In *Ivan*, especially, the scenes are structured like an opera, and Prokofiev's brilliant score would not be out of place in any opera house. The

---

* The two men worked together with Meyerhold on the production of Prokofiev's opera *Semyon Kotko* in 1939. The next year, following the signing of the Nazi–Soviet pact, Eisenstein produced *Die Walküre* at the Bolshoi in Moscow. See further R. Bartlett, *Wagner and Russia* (Cambridge, 1995), pp. 271–81.

film opens with an overture whose stormy leitmotif is clearly borrowed from Wagner's *Die Walküre*. There are orchestrated arias and choral songs; liturgical chants; even, quite incongruously, a polonaise; and symphonic leitmotifs, or the sound of bells, which carry the emotions of the 'music drama', as Eisenstein describes it in a note outlining his new Wagnerian cinema. In the final colour scenes, where music, dance and drama are combined, there is even an attempt to reach a complete harmony of sound and colour, as Wagner had once dreamed.[155]

For Eisenstein these films represented a volte-face in artistic principles: the avant-garde of the 1920s had tried to take the theatre out of cinema, and now here he was putting it back in. Montage was abandoned for a clear sequential exposition of the theme through the combined effect of images and sound. In *Alexander Nevsky*, for example, the central idea of the film, the emotive clash between the peaceful Russians and the Teutonic invaders, is conveyed by the programmatic music as much as by the visual imagery. Eisenstein re-cut the film to synchronize the visual with the tonal images. In the famous battle scene on ice he even shot the film to match the score.[156] Stalin was delighted with *Alexander Nevsky*. Its emotional power was perfectly harnessed to the propaganda message of heroic leadership and patriotic unity which the Soviet regime needed to boost national morale on the outbreak of war. Indeed, the subject of the film had such an obvious parallel with the Nazi threat that its screening was postponed following the signing of the Nazi–Soviet pact in 1939.

Stalin saw Ivan the Terrible as a medieval prototype of his own statesmanship. In 1941, as Soviet Russia went to war, it seemed a good moment to remind the nation of the lessons Stalin drew from Ivan's reign: that force, even cruelty, were needed to unite the state and drive the foreigners and traitors from the land. The official cult of Ivan took off in the wake of the Great Terror (as if to justify it) in 1939. 'Our benefactor thinks that we have been too sentimental', Pasternak wrote to Olga Freidenberg in February 1941. 'Peter the Great is no longer an appropriate model. The new passion, openly confessed, is for Ivan the Terrible, the *oprichnina*, and cruelty. This is the subject for new operas, plays and films.'[157] One month earlier, Zhdanov had commissioned Eisenstein to make his film. But Eisenstein's conception of *Ivan the Terrible* was far removed from the official one. The first part of the film to emerge in his imagination was the confession scene (planned for the third and final part of the film), in which Ivan kneels beneath the fresco of the Last Judgement in the Cathedral of the Assumption and offers his repentance for the evils of his reign while a monk reads out an endless list of people executed on the Tsar's command.[158]

From the start, then, *Ivan* was conceived as a tragedy, a Soviet version of *Boris Godunov* which would contain a terrifying commentary on the human costs of tyranny. However, because everybody knew what Stalin did with people who made parables like this, the film's tragic nature and contemporary theme could not be revealed until the end.[159] In Part One of the film Eisenstein depicts the heroic aspects of Ivan: his vision of a united state; his fearless struggle against the scheming *boyars*; his strong authority and leadership in the war against the Tatars of Kazan. Stalin was delighted, and Eisenstein was honoured with the Stalin Prize. But at a banquet to celebrate his triumph Eisenstein collapsed with a heart attack. Earlier that day he had put the final touches to Part Two of his epic film (not publicly released until 1958). He knew what lay in store. In Part Two the action switches from the public sphere to Ivan's inner world. The Tsar now emerges as a tormented figure, haunted by the terror to which he is driven by his own paranoia and his isolation from society. All his former allies have abandoned him, there is no one he can trust, and his wife has been murdered in a *boyars'* plot. The parallels between Ivan and Stalin were unmissable. Stalin, too, had lost his wife (she had killed herself in 1932) and the effect of her death on his own mental condition, which doctors had already diagnosed as paranoia and schizophrenia, no doubt contributed to the terror he unleashed.[160]

When Stalin saw the film he reacted violently. 'This is not a film – it is some kind of nightmare!'[161] In February 1947 Stalin summoned Eisenstein to a late-night interview in the Kremlin at which he delivered a revealing lecture on Russian history. Eisenstein's Ivan was weak-willed and neurotic, like Hamlet, he said, whereas the real Tsar had been great and wise in 'preserving the country from foreign influence'. Ivan had been 'very cruel', and Eisenstein could 'depict him as a cruel man, but', Stalin explained, you have to show why he had to be cruel. One of Ivan the Terrible's mistakes was to stop short of cutting up the five key feudal clans. Had he destroyed these five clans, there would have been no Time of Troubles. And when Ivan the Terrible had someone executed, he would spend a long time in repentance and prayer. God was a hindrance to him in this respect. He should have been more decisive.[162]

Part Two of *Ivan* was banned by Stalin, but Eisenstein was permitted to resume production on Part Three on the understanding that he incorporate approved material from the previous film in it. On Stalin's instructions, he even promised to shorten Ivan's beard. At a screening of Part Two at the State Institute of Cinema, Eisenstein gave a speech in which he criticized himself for the 'formalistic deviations' of his film. But he told his friends that he would not change his film. 'What re-shooting?' he said to one director. 'Don't you realize that I'd die at the first shot?'[163] Eisenstein, who had never lacked bravura, was evidently preparing an artistic rebellion, culminating in the confession scene of the film's third and final part, a terrifying commentary on Stalin's madness and his sins:

Tsar Ivan bangs his forehead against the flagstones in a rapid sequence of genuflections. His eyes swim with blood. The blood blinds him. The blood enters his ears and deafens him. He sees nothing.[164]

When they shot the scene the actor Mikhail Kuznetsov asked Eisenstein what was going on. 'Look, 1,200 *boyars* have been killed. The Tsar *is* "Terrible"! So why on earth is he repenting?' Eisenstein replied: 'Stalin has killed more people and he does not repent. Let him see this and then he will repent.'[165]

Eisenstein took inspiration from Pushkin, whose own great drama *Boris Godunov* had served as a warning against tyranny in the wake of the suppression of the Decembrist revolt by Tsar Nicholas I. But there is a deeper sense in which his brave defiance as an artist was rooted in the whole of the Russian humanist tradition of the nineteenth century. As he explained to a fellow director, who had pointed out the connection to *Boris Godunov*:

'Lord, can you really see it? I'm so happy, so happy! Of course it is Boris Godunov: "Five years I have governed in peace, but my soul is troubled . . ."' I could not make a film like that without the Russian tradition – without that great tradition of conscience. Violence can be explained, it can be legalized, but it can't be justified. If you are a human being, it has to be atoned. One man may destroy another – but as a human being I must find this painful, because man is the highest value . . . This, in my opinion, is the inspiring tradition of our people, our nation, and our literature.[166]

Eisenstein did not have enough strength to complete his film. The heart attack had crippled him. He died in 1948.

6

The Leningrad to which Akhmatova returned in 1944 was a shadow of its former self. For her it was a 'vast cemetery, the graveyard of her friends', Isaiah Berlin wrote: 'it was like the aftermath of a forest fire – the few charred trees made the desolation still more desolate'.[167] Before the war she had been in love with a married man, Vladimir Garshin, a medical professor from a famous nineteenth-century literary family. He had helped her through her son's arrest and her first heart attack in 1940. On Akhmatova's return to Leningrad she was expecting to be with him again. But when he met her at the station there was something wrong. During the siege Garshin had become the chief coroner of Leningrad, and the daily horror which he experienced in the starving city, where cannibalism became rife, stripped away his sanity. In October 1942 his wife had collapsed from hunger on the street and died. He had recognized her body in the morgue.[168] When Garshin met Akhmatova at the station, it was only to tell her that their love affair was over. Akhmatova returned to the Fountain House. The palace had been half-destroyed by a German bomb. Her old apartment had large cracks in the walls, the windows were all smashed, and there was no running water or electricity. In November 1945, her son Lev came to live with her, having been released from the labour camp to fight in the war, and he resumed his studies at the university.

During that same month Akhmatova received an English visitor. In

1945 Isaiah Berlin had just arrived as First Secretary of the British Embassy in Moscow. Born in Riga in 1909, the son of a Russian-Jewish timber merchant, Berlin had moved in 1916 with his family to Petersburg, where he had witnessed the February Revolution. In 1919 his family returned to Latvia, then emigrated to England. By the time of his appointment to the Moscow embassy Berlin was already established as a leading scholar for his 1939 book on Marx. During a visit to Leningrad, Berlin was browsing in the Writers' Bookshop on the Nevsky Prospekt when he 'fell into casual conversation with someone who was turning over the leaves of a book of poems'.[169] That someone turned out to be the well-known literary critic Vladimir Orlov, who told Berlin that Akhmatova was still alive and residing in the Fountain House, a stone's throw away. Orlov made a telephone call and at three o'clock that afternoon he and Berlin climbed the stairs to Akhmatova's apartment.

It was very barely furnished – virtually everything in it had, I gathered, been taken away – looted or sold – during the siege; there was a small table, three or four chairs, a wooden chest, a sofa and, above the unlit stove, a drawing by Modigliani. A stately, grey-haired lady, a white shawl draped about her shoulders, slowly rose to greet us. Anna Andreevna Akhmatova was immensely dignified, with unhurried gestures, a noble head, beautiful, somewhat severe features, and an expression of immense sadness.[170]

After conversing for a while, Berlin suddenly heard someone shouting his name outside. It was Randolph Churchill, Winston's son, whom Berlin had known as an undergraduate at Oxford and who had come to Russia as a journalist. Churchill needed an interpreter and, hearing that Berlin was in the city, had tracked him down to the Fountain House. But since he did not know the exact location of Akhmatova's apartment he 'adopted a method which had served him well during his days in Christ Church'. Berlin rushed downstairs and left with Churchill, whose presence might be dangerous for Akhmatova. But he returned that evening and spent the night in conversation with Akhmatova – who, perhaps, fell in love with him. They spoke about Russian literature, about her loneliness and isolation, and about her friends from the vanished world of Petersburg before the Revolution, some of whom he had since met as émigrés abroad. In her eyes, Berlin was a messenger between the two Russias which had been split apart in 1917. Through him she was able to return to the European Russia of St Petersburg – a city from which she felt she had lived apart as an 'internal exile' in Leningrad. In the cycle *Cinque*, among the most beautiful poems she ever wrote, Akhmatova evokes in sacred terms the feeling of connection she felt with her English visitor.

> Sounds die away in the ether,
> And darkness overtakes the dusk.
> In a world become mute for all time,
> There are only two voices: yours and mine.
> And to the almost bell-like sound
> Of the wind from invisible Lake Ladoga,
> That late-night dialogue turned into
> The delicate shimmer of interlaced rainbows.[171]

'So our nun now receives visits from foreign spies,' Stalin remarked, or so it is alleged, when he was told of Berlin's visit to the Fountain House. The notion that Berlin was a spy was absurd, but at that time, when the Cold War was starting and Stalin's paranoia had reached extreme proportions, anyone who worked for a Western embassy was automatically considered one. The NKVD stepped up its surveillance of the Fountain House, with two new agents at the main entrance to check specifically on visitors to Akhmatova and listening devices planted clumsily in holes drilled into the walls and ceiling of her apartment. The holes left little heaps of plaster on the floor, one of which Akhmatova kept intact as a warning to her guests.[172] Then, in August 1946, Akhmatova was attacked in a decree by the Central Committee which censored two journals for publishing her work. A week later Andrei Zhdanov, Stalin's chief of ideology, announced her expulsion from the Writers' Union, delivering a vicious speech in which he described Akhmatova as a 'left-over from the old aristocratic culture' and (in a phrase that had been used by Soviet critics in the past) as a 'half-nun, half-harlot or rather harlot-nun whose sin is mixed with prayer'.[173]

Akhmatova was deprived of her ration card and forced to live off food donated by her friends. Lev was barred from taking his degree at the university. In 1949, Lev was re-arrested, tortured into making a confession and sentenced to ten years in a labour camp near Omsk. Akhmatova became dangerously ill. With rumours circulating of her own arrest, she burned all her manuscripts at the Fountain House. Among them was the prose draft of a play about a woman writer who is tried and sentenced to prison by a writers' tribunal. It was an allegory on her own tormented position. Because the tribunal consciously betrays the freedom of thought for which, as fellow writers, they are meant to stand, its literary bureaucrats are far more terrifying than the state's police.[174] It is a sign of her utter desperation that, in an attempt to secure her son's release, she even wrote a poem in tribute to Stalin.* Lev was only released, after Stalin's death, in 1956. Akhmatova believed that the cause of his arrest had been her meeting with Berlin in 1945. During his interrogation Lev was questioned several times about the 'English spy' – on one occasion while his head was being smashed against a prison wall.[175] She even managed to convince herself (if no one else) that their encounter was the cause of the Cold War. She 'saw herself and me as world-historical personages chosen by destiny to begin a cosmic conflict', Berlin wrote.[176]

Berlin always blamed himself for the suffering he had caused.[177] But his visit to the Fountain House was not the cause of the attack on Akhmatova, nor of Lev's arrest, though it served as a pretext for both. The Central Committee decree was the beginning of a new onslaught on the freedom of the artist – the last refuge of freedom in the Soviet Union – and Akhmatova was the obvious place to start. For the intelligentsia she was the living symbol of a spirit which the regime could neither destroy nor control: the spirit of endurance and human dignity that had given them the strength to survive the Terror and the war. Zoshchenko believed that the decree had been passed after Stalin had been told of a literary evening at the Polytechnic Museum in Moscow during 1944 at which Akhmatova had received an ovation from a 3,000-strong audience. 'Who organized this standing ovation?' Stalin was said to have asked – a question so in keeping with his character that nobody could possibly have made it up.[178]

* She later requested that it be omitted from her collected works.

Attacked by the same decree as Akhmatova was Mikhail Zoshchenko. Like Akhmatova, he was based in Leningrad, a city whose spiritual autonomy made Stalin suspicious. The suppression of these two writers was a way of demonstrating to the Leningrad intelligentsia its place in society. Zoshchenko was the last of the satirists – Mayakovsky, Zamyatin and Bulgakov had all perished – and a major thorn in Stalin's side. The immediate cause of the attack was a children's story, 'Adventures of a Monkey', published in *Zvezda* (one of the journals censured in the decree) in 1946, in which a monkey that has escaped from the zoo is retrained as a human being. But Stalin had been irritated by Zoshchenko's stories for some years. He recognized himself in the figure of the sentry in 'Lenin and the Guard' (1939), in which Zoshchenko portrays a rude and impatient 'southern type' (Stalin was from Georgia) with a moustache, whom Lenin treats like a little boy.[179] Stalin never forgot insults such as this. He took a personal interest in the persecution of Zoshchenko, whom he regarded as a 'parasite', a writer without positive political beliefs whose cynicism threatened to corrupt society. Zhdanov used the same terms in his vicious speech which followed the decree. Barred from publication, Zoshchenko was forced to work as a translator and to resume his first career as a shoemaker, until Stalin's death in 1953, when he was re-admitted to the Writers' Union. But by this stage Zoshchenko had fallen into such a deep depression that he produced no major writings before his death in 1958.

The attack against Akhmatova and Zoshchenko was soon followed by a series of decrees in which a rigid Party line was laid down by Zhdanov for all the other arts. The influence of Zhdanov was so dominant that the post-war period became known as the *Zhdanovshchina* ('Zhdanov's reign'). Even though he died in 1948, his cultural policies remained in force until (and in some ways long after) the Khrushchev thaw. Zhdanov's ideology reflected the Soviet triumphalism which had emerged in the communist élites following the victory against Hitler and the military conquest of eastern Europe in 1945. The Cold War led to renewed calls for iron discipline in cultural affairs. The terror of the state was now principally directed at the intelligentsia, its purpose being to impose an Orwellian conformity to the Party's ideology on all the arts and sciences. Zhdanov launched a series of violent attacks against 'decadent Western influences'. He led a new campaign against the 'formalists', and a blacklist of composers (including Shostakovich, Khachaturian and Prokofiev), who were charged with writing music that was 'alien to the Soviet people and its artistic taste', was published by the Central Committee in February 1948.[180] For the composers named it meant the sudden loss of jobs, cancellation of performances and their virtual disappearance from the Soviet repertoire. The declared aim of this new purge was to seal off Soviet culture from the West. Tikhon Khrennikov, the Zhdanovite hardliner at the head of the Composers' Union, stamped out any signs of foreign or modernist (especially Stravinsky's) influence on the Soviet musical establishment. He rigidly enforced the model of Tchaikovsky and the Russian music school of the nineteenth century as the starting point for all composers in the Soviet Union.

Immense national pride in the cultural and political superiority of Soviet Russia went hand in hand with anti-Western feeling during the Cold War. Absurd claims for Russia's greatness began to appear in the Soviet press. 'Throughout its history', declared *Pravda*, 'the Great Russian people have enriched world technology with outstanding discoveries and inventions.'[181] Absurd claims were made for the superiority of Soviet science under the direction of Marxist-Leninist ideology, which led to the promotion of frauds and cranks like the pseudo-geneticist Timofei Lysenko, who claimed to have developed a new strain of wheat that would grow in the Arctic frost. The aeroplane, the steam engine, the radio, the incandescent bulb – there was scarcely an invention or discovery which the Russians did not claim as their own. Cynics even joked that Russia was the homeland of the elephant.*

This triumphalism also found expression in the architectural style which dominated plans for the reconstruction of Soviet cities after 1945. 'Soviet Empire' combined the neoclassical and Gothic motifs of the Russian Empire style that had flourished in the wake of 1812 with the monumental structures that trumpeted the magnificence of

---

* Andrei Sakharov records a joke in scientific circles at that time. A Soviet delegation attends a conference on elephants and delivers a 4-part report: (1) Classics of Marxism-Leninism-Stalinism on Elephants; (2) Russia – the Elephant's Homeland; (3) The Soviet Elephant: The Best Elephant in the World; and (4) The Belorussian Elephant – Little Brother to the Russian Elephant (A. Sakharov, *Memoirs* (London, 1990), p. 123).

the Soviet achievement. 'Stalin's cathedrals', the seven elephantine wedding-cake-like structures (such as the Foreign Ministry and the Moscow University ensemble on the Lenin Hills) which shot up around Moscow after 1945, are supreme examples of this ostentatious form. But metro stations, 'palaces of culture', cinemas and even circuses were also built in the Soviet Empire style, with massive forms, classical façades and porticoes, and neo-Russian historical motifs. The most striking example is the Moscow metro station Komsomolskaia-Kol'tsevaia, built in 1952. Its huge subterranean 'Hall of Victory', conceived as a monument to Russia's military heroes of the past, was a model of the Russian baroque. Its decorative motifs were largely copied from the Rostov Kremlin Church.[182]

Soviet pride in Russian culture knew no bounds in the post-war period. The Russian ballet was pronounced the best, the Russian classics in literature and music the most popular in the world. Russia's cultural domination was also imposed on the satellite regimes of eastern Europe and on the republics of the Soviet Union, where Russian became a compulsory language in all schools and children were brought up on Russian fairy tales and literature. Soviet 'folk' choirs and dancing troupes made frequent tours to eastern Europe, whose own state-sponsored 'folk' ensembles (the Lado and the Kolo in Yugoslavia, the Mazowsze in Poland, the Sluk in Czechoslovakia and the Hungarian State Ensemble) sprang up on the Soviet design.[183] The stated aim of these 'folk' groups was to promote regional and national cultures within the Soviet bloc. Soviet policy, since 1934, had been to foster cultures that were 'national in form and socialist in content'.[184] But these groups had little real connection with the folk culture they were meant to represent. Made up of professionals, they performed a type of song and dance which bore the clear hallmarks of the ersatz folk songs performed by Red Army ensembles, and their national character was reflected only in their outward forms (generic 'folk costumes' and melodies).

The long-term plan of Soviet policy was to channel these 'folk cultures' into higher forms of art on the lines set out (or so it was believed) by the Russian nationalists of the nineteenth century. Russian composers were assigned by Moscow to the Central Asian and Caucasian republics to set up 'national operas' and symphonic traditions in places where there had been none before. The European opera house and concert hall arrived in Alma Ata and Tashkent, in Bukhara and Samarkand, as pillars of this imported Soviet-Russian culture; and soon they were filled with the strange sound of a wholly artificial 'national music' which was based on native tribal melodies notated in the European style then placed in the musical framework of the Russian national movement of the nineteenth century.

The Russian composer Reinhold Gliere (the composition teacher of the young Prokofiev) wrote the first 'national opera' of Azerbaijan, mixing old Azeri melodies with European forms and harmonies. Gliere also composed the first Uzbek opera, *Gulsara* (1937), an epic Soviet tale of women's liberation from the old patriarchal way of life, with Uzbek folk tunes harmonized and orchestrated in the style of Berlioz. The Kirghiz opera was established by two Muscovites (Vladimir Vlasov and Vladimir Fere) who orchestrated Kirghiz melodies (notated by the Kirghizian Abdilas Maldybaev) in their own imaginary Kirghiz national style with lots of raw and open harmonies. The Russian founder of the Kazakh national opera, Evgeny Brusilovsky, continued writing Kazakh opera until the 1950s, long after a new generation of native-born composers had emerged from the conservatory in Alma Ata. The campaign against the 'formalists' encouraged many composers to flee Moscow and Petersburg for the relatively liberal atmosphere of these remote republics. Alexander Mosolov, perhaps better known as a composer of experimental music in the 1920s, moved via the gulag to Turkmenistan, where he remained until his death in 1973, a composer of national Turkmen music in the style of Borodin. Maximilian Steinberg, Stravinsky's closest rival in St Petersburg in the 1900s and teacher to the leading avant-garde composers (including Shostakovich) in the early 1920s, ended his career as People's Artist of the Uzbek Soviet Socialist Republic.[185]

As the Cold War became more intense, and Stalin's own paranoic fear of 'internal enemies' and 'spies' increased, his regime's suspicions of all foreign influence turned to hatred of the Jews. This anti-Semitism was thinly veiled by Soviet (that is, Russian) patriotic rhetoric, but there was no mistaking that the victims of the vicious inquisition against 'cosmopolitanism' were predominantly Jewish. In January 1948, the well-known Jewish actor Solomon Mikhoels, chairman of the Jewish Anti-Fascist Committee (JAFC), was killed by state security troops. The assassination was carried out on the strict personal instructions of Stalin, who, three days before the brutal killing, had summoned all the members of the Politburo, denounced Mikhoels in a fit of rage and, in a way that suggests that this was to be a symbolic murder,* specified that 'Mikhoels must be struck on the head with an axe, wrapped up in a wet quilted jacket and run over by a truck'.[186]

The murder of Mikhoels was linked to the arrest of several dozen leading Jews accused of taking part in an American-Zionist conspiracy organized by the JAFC against the Soviet Union.† The JAFC had been established on Stalin's orders in 1941 to mobilize Jewish support abroad for the Soviet war campaign. It received enthusiastic support from the left-wing Jewish community in Palestine, so much so that Stalin even thought he might turn the new state of Israel into the main sphere of Soviet influence in the Middle East. But Israel's growing links with the USA after 1948 unleashed Stalin's lifelong hatred of the Jews.[187] The JAFC was abolished, its members all arrested and accused of plotting to turn the Crimea into an American–Zionist base for an attack on the Soviet Union. Thousands of Jews were forcibly evicted from the regions around Moscow and despatched as 'rootless parasites' to the Siberian wilderness, where a special 'Jewish Autonomous Region' had been established in Birobidzhan: it was a sort of Soviet version of Hitler's Madagascar, where the Nazis had once thought to export the Jews. In November 1948 the Central Committee decided that all the Jews in the Soviet Union would have to be resettled in Siberia.[188]

In the cultural sphere the 'ugly distortions' of the avant-garde were put down to the influence of Jews like Eisenstein, Mandelstam,

---

* Stalin's father had been murdered by an axe wrapped in a quilted jacket; and his likely killer, an Armenian criminal who had worked with Stalin for the Tsarist secret police in Tiflis in the 1900s, was killed on Stalin's orders, sixteen years later in 1922, when he was run over by a truck (R. Brackman, *The Secret File of Joseph Stalin: A Hidden Life* (London, 2001), pp. 38–43).

† Even two of Stalin's own relatives by marriage, Anna Redens and Olga Allilueva, were arrested for their Jewish connections. Explaining the arrest of her two aunts to his own daughter, Stalin said: 'They knew too much. They blabbed a lot' (S. Allilueva, *Only One Year* (New York, 1969), p. 154).

Chagall. The offensive was personally instigated by Stalin. He even studied linguistics, and wrote at length about it in *Pravda* during 1949, with the aim of denouncing the 'Jewish' theory, originally advanced by Niko Marr in the 1900s, that the Georgian language had Semitic origins.[189] In 1953 Stalin ordered the arrest of several Jewish doctors who worked for the Kremlin on trumped-up charges (the so-called 'Doctors' Plot') of having poisoned Zhdanov and another Politburo member, A. S. Shcherbakov.* The tirade in the press against the 'murderers in white coats' produced a wave of anti-Jewish hatred, and many Jews were evicted from their jobs and homes. Jewish scientists, scholars and artists were singled out for attacks as 'bourgeois nationalists', even if (as was so often the case) they were more Russian than Jewish. The fact that they had 'Jew' written in their Soviet passports was enough to condemn them as Zionists.†

Jewish film directors (Leonid Trauberg, Dziga Vertov, Mikhail Romm) were accused of making 'anti-Russian' films and forced out of their studios. Vasily Grossman's novel *Stalingrad*, based on his work as a war correspondent, was banned principally because its central character was a Russian Jew. *The Black Book* (first published in Jerusalem in 1980), Grossman's still-unrivalled memoir-based account of the Holocaust on Soviet soil, which he assembled for the Literary Commission of the JAFC, was never published in the Soviet Union. When Grossman started writing in the 1930s, he thought of himself as a Soviet citizen. The Revolution had brought to an end the Tsarist persecution of the Jews. But in his last novel, the epic wartime story *Life and Fate* (first published in Switzerland in 1980), he portrayed the Nazi and Soviet regimes, not as opposites, but as mirror images of each other. Grossman died in 1964, a quarter of a century before his

---

* One of these prominent doctors was Isaiah Berlin's uncle Leo, who was accused of passing Kremlin secrets to the British through his nephew on his visit to Moscow in 1945. Severely beaten, Leo attempted suicide and eventually 'confessed' to having been a spy. He was held in prison for a year and released in 1954, shortly after Stalin's death. One day, while still weak from his time in prison, he saw one of his torturers in the street ahead of him, collapsed from a heart attack and died (M. Ignatieff, *Isaiah Berlin: A Life* (London, 1998), pp. 168–9).

† All citizens of the USSR had a Soviet passport. But inside the passport there was a category that defined them by 'nationality' (ethnicity).

masterpiece was published in his native land. He had asked to be buried in a Jewish cemetery.[190]

'I had believed that after the Soviet victory, the experience of the thirties could not ever come again, yet everything reminded me of the way things had gone then', wrote Ilya Ehrenburg (one of the few senior Jewish intellectuals to emerge unscathed from the Stalin era) in *Men, Years – Life* (1961–6).[191] Coming as it did after the release of the war years, this new wave of terror must have felt in some ways more oppressive than the old; to try to survive such a thing the second time around must have been like trying to preserve one's very sanity. Ehrenburg visited Akhmatova at the Fountain House in 1947.

She was sitting in a small room where her portrait by Modigliani hung on the wall and, sad and majestic as ever, was reading Horace. Misfortunes crashed down on her like avalanches; it needed more than common fortitude to preserve such dignity, composure and pride.[192]

Reading Horace was one way of keeping sane. Some writers turned to literary scholarship or, like Kornei Chukovsky, to writing children's books. Others, like Pasternak, turned to translating foreign works.

Pasternak's Russian translations of Shakespeare are works of real artistic beauty, if not entirely true to the original. He was Stalin's favourite poet, far too precious to arrest. His love of Georgia and translations of Georgian poetry endeared him to the Soviet leader. But even though he lived amid all the creature comforts of a Moscow gentleman, Pasternak was made to suffer from the Terror in a different way. He bore the guilt for the suffering of those writers whom he could not help through his influence. He was tortured by the notion that his mere survival somehow proved that he was less than honourable as a man – let alone as a great writer in that Russian tradition which took its moral values from the Decembrists. Isaiah Berlin, who met Pasternak on several occasions in 1945, recalled that he 'kept returning to this point, and went to absurd lengths to deny that he was capable of [some squalid compromise with the authorities] of which no one who knew him could begin to conceive him to be guilty'.[193]

Pasternak refused to attend the meeting of the Writers' Union at which Akhmatova and Zoshchenko were denounced. For this he was expelled from the Union's board. He went to see Akhmatova. He gave her money, which may have led to the attack on him in *Pravda* as 'alien' and 'remote from Soviet reality'.[194] After all his optimism in the war Pasternak was crushed by the return to the old regime of cruelty and lies. He withdrew from the public scene and worked on what he now regarded as his final message to the world: his great novel *Doctor Zhivago*. Set amidst the horrific chaos of the Russian Revolution and the civil war, it is no coincidence that the novel's central theme is the importance of preserving the old intelligentsia, represented by Zhivago. In many ways the hero's younger brother, the strange figure called Evgraf, who has some influence with the revolutionaries and often helps his brother out of dire straits by making calls to the right people, is the very type of saviour figure that Pasternak himself would have liked to have been. Pasternak regarded the novel as his greatest work (much more important than his poetry), his testament in prose, and he was determined that it should be read by the widest possible audience. His decision to publish it abroad, after it was delayed and then turned down by the journal *Novyi mir*, was his final act of rebellion against the bullying of the Soviet regime.*

Shostakovich found another way to save his sanity. In 1948 he was dismissed from his teaching posts at the conservatories in Moscow and Leningrad – his pupils were also forced to repent for having studied with the 'formalist'. Fearing for his family, Shostakovich admitted his 'mistakes' at a Congress of Composers in April: he promised to write music which 'the People' could enjoy and understand. For a while, Shostakovich contemplated suicide. His works were banned from the concert repertoire. But, as in former times, he found a refuge and an outlet in the cinema. Between 1948 and 1953, Shostakovich wrote the music for no less than seven films.[195] 'It allows me to eat', he wrote to his friend Isaak Glickman, 'but it causes me extreme fatigue.'[196] He

---

* Smuggled out of Russia and first published in Italy in 1957, *Doctor Zhivago* became an international bestseller, and Pasternak was nominated for the Nobel Prize in 1958, but under pressure from the Writers' Union, and a storm of nationalist abuse against him in the Soviet press, he was forced to refuse the prize. Pasternak died in 1960.

told fellow composers that it was 'unpleasant' work, to be done 'only in the event of extreme poverty'.[197] Shostakovich needed all the money he could earn from this hack work. But he also had to show that he was taking part in the 'creative life of the Party'. Five of the film scores he composed in these years were awarded the prestigious Stalin Prize, and two of his songs from Alexandrov's *Meeting on the Elbe* (1948) became hits, with enormous record sales. The composer's own political rehabilitation and a modicum of material comfort for his family were secured.

Yet all the time Shostakovich was writing secret music 'for the drawer'. Some of it was musical lampoon, like *Rayok*, or *The Peep Show*, a cantata satire on the Zhdanov era, with music set to the pompous speeches of the Soviet leaders, which finally received its première in Washington in 1989.* More than any other artist, Shostakovich laughed (inside) to save his sanity: that was why he so loved the writings of Gogol and Zoshchenko. But most of the music which he composed at this time was deeply personal, especially that music with a Jewish theme. Shostakovich identified with the suffering of the Jews. To some extent he even assumed a Jewish identity – choosing to express himself as a composer in a Jewish idiom and incorporating Jewish melodies in his compositions. What Shostakovich liked about the music of the Jews, as he himself explained in a revealing interview, was its 'ability to build a jolly melody on sad intonations. Why does a man strike up a jolly song? Because he feels sad at heart.'[198] But using Jewish music was a moral statement, too: it was the protest of an artist who had always been opposed to fascism in all its forms.

Shostakovich first used Jewish themes in the finale of the Second Piano Trio (1944), dedicated to his closest friend, the musicologist Ivan Sollertinsky, who had died in February 1944. It was composed just as the reports were coming in of the Red Army's capture of the Nazi death camps at Majdanek, Belzec and Treblinka. As Stalin

---

* It is not entirely clear when Shostakovich wrote *Rayok*. Sketches of it seem to date from 1948, but with the constant threat of a house search, it seems unlikely that he would have dared to compose the full score until after Stalin's death (see further M. Yakubov, 'Shostakovich's Anti-formalist *Rayok*: A History of the Work's Composition and Its Musical and Literary Sources', in R. Bartlett (ed.), *Shostakovich in Context* (Oxford, 2000), pp. 135–58).

initiated his own campaign against the Jews, Shostakovich voiced his protest by adopting Jewish themes in many of his works: the song cycle *From Jewish Poetry* (1948), courageously performed at private concerts in his flat at the height of the Doctors' Plot; the Thirteenth Symphony (1962), the 'Babi Yar' with its requiem, the words composed by the poet Yevtushenko, for the Jews of Kiev who were murdered by the Nazis in 1941; and virtually all the string quartets from No. 3 (in 1946) to the unforgettable No. 8 (in 1961). The official dedication of the Eighth Quartet was 'To the Victims of Fascism', but, as Shostakovich told his daughter, it was really 'dedicated to myself'.[199] The Eighth Quartet was Shostakovich's musical autobiography – a tragic summing up of his whole life and the life of his nation in the Stalinist era. Throughout this intensely personal work, which is full of self-quotation, the same four notes recur (D–E flat–C–B) which, in the German system of musical notation, make up four letters of the composer's name (D-S-C-H). The four notes are like a dirge. They fall like tears. In the fourth and final movement the grief becomes unbearable as these four notes are symbolically combined with the workers' revolutionary funeral lament, 'Tortured by a Cruel Bondage', which Shostakovich sings here for himself.

7

On 4 October 1957 the first beeps from space were heard as Sputnik I made its pioneering flight. A few weeks later, just in time for the fortieth anniversary of the October Revolution, the dog Laika ventured into space in Sputnik II. With this one small step, it suddenly appeared that the Soviet Union had leaped ahead of the Western world in science and technology. Khrushchev made the most of the success, claiming that it heralded the triumph of the communist idea. The next year a red flag was planted on the surface of the moon, and then, in April 1961, Yury Gagarin became the first man to leave the earth's atmosphere.

The Soviet system was defined by its belief in science and technology. After 1945 the regime made a huge investment in the scientific establishment, promoting not just nuclear physics and other disciplines that were useful to the military but academic sciences and mathematics, too. The state made science a top priority, elevating scientists to a status on a par with that of senior industrial managers and Party officials. The whole Marxist core of the system's ideology was an optimistic faith in the power of man's reason to banish human suffering and master the forces of the universe. The Soviet regime had been founded on the sort of futuristic visions imagined by Jules Verne and H. G. Wells, whose writings were more popular in Russia than in any other country of the world. Wells was one of the first Western writers to visit Soviet Russia, in 1919, and even then, in the midst of the country's devastation from civil war, he found Lenin in the Kremlin dreaming about journeys into space.[200]

Russia had its own prodigious range of science fiction which, unlike that of the West, formed part of its mainstream literature from the very start. Science fiction served as an arena for utopian blueprints of the future society, such as the 'Fourth Dream' in Chernyshevsky's novel *What Is to Be Done?* (1862), from which Lenin drew his communist ideals. It was a testing ground for the big moral ideas of Russian literature – as in Dostoevsky's science-fiction tale, 'The Dream of a Ridiculous Man' (1877), in which the vision of salvation through scientific and material progress advanced by Chernyshevsky is dispelled in a dream of utopia on a perfect twin of earth: the cosmic paradise soons breaks down into a society of masters and slaves, and the narrator wakes up from his dream to see that the only true salvation is through Christian love of one's fellow human beings.

Mixing science fiction with mystical belief was typical of the Russian literary tradition, where the path to the ideal was so often seen in terms of the transcendence of this world and its mundane realities. The Russian Revolution was accompanied by a huge upsurge of apocalyptic science fiction. Bogdanov, the Bolshevik co-founder of Proletkult, took the lead with his science-fiction novels, *Red Star* (1908) and *Engineer Menni* (1913), which portrayed the communist utopia on the planet Mars sometime in the middle of the third millennium. This cosmic vision of socialist redemption fuelled the boom of science fiction writing in the 1920s, from Platonov's utopian tales to Aleksei Tolstoy's bestselling novels *Aelita* (1922) and *The Garin Death Ray* (1926), which returned to the Martian theme of science in the service of the proletariat. Like its nineteenth-century antecedents, this fantastic literature was a vehicle for the great philosophical and moral questions about science and conscience. Zamyatin's science fiction drew from the Russian tradition to develop a humanist critique of the Soviet technological utopia. His dystopian novel *We* derived much of its moral argument from Dostoevsky. The central conflict of the novel, between the rational, all-providing high-tech state and the beautiful seductress I-330, whose deviant and irrational need for freedom threatens to subvert the power of that absolutist state, is a continuation of the discourse which stands at the centre of 'The Grand Inquisitor' in *The Brothers Karamazov* about the unending conflict between the human needs for security and liberty.*

Science fiction largely disappeared in the 1930s and 1940s. Socialist Realism left no space for utopian dreams, or any form of moral ambiguity, and the only science fiction that was not stamped out was that which extolled Soviet technology. But the space programme of the 1950s led to a resurgence of science fiction in the Soviet Union, and Khrushchev, who was a devotee of the genre, encouraged writers to return to the traditions of the pre-Stalin years.

Ivan Efremov's *Andromeda* (1957) was perhaps the most important work in this new wave, and certainly one of the bestselling (with over 20 million copies sold in the Soviet Union alone). Set in a distant future, when the earth has been united with the other galaxies in a universal civilization, it portrays a cosmic paradise in which science plays a discreet role in providing for all human needs; but what emerges above all else as the purpose of existence is the eternal need of human beings for ethical relationships, freedom, beauty and creativity. Efremov was bitterly attacked by communist hardliners: his emphasis on spiritual values was uncomfortably close to a fundamental challenge

---

* It may be that the title of Zamyatin's novel *We* was drawn at least in part from Dostoevsky – in particular from Verkhovensky's words to Stavrogin (in *The Devils*, trans. D. Magarshack (Harmondsworth, 1971), p. 423) where he describes his vision of the future revolutionary dictatorship ('[W]e shall consider how to erect an edifice of stone . . . *We* shall build it, we, we alone!'). Perhaps more obviously, the title may have been a reference to the revolutionary cult of the collective (the Proletkult poet Kirillov even wrote a poem by the title of 'We'). See further G. Kern, *Zamyatin's* We: *A Collection of Critical Essays* (Ann Arbor, 1988), p. 63.

to the whole materialist philosophy of the Soviet regime. But he was not alone. Science fiction was rapidly becoming the principal arena for liberal, religious and dissident critiques of the Soviet world view. In Daniel Granin's *Into the Storm* (1962), the physicist hero is a humanist, a Pyotr Kapitsa or an Andrei Sakharov, who understands the need to harness science to spiritual human goals. 'What,' he asks, 'distinguishes people from animals? Atomic energy? The telephone? I say – moral conscience, imagination, spiritual ideals. The human soul will not be improved because you and I are studying the earth's magnetic fields.'[201]

The science fiction novels of the Strugatsky brothers (Arkady and Boris) were subversively conceived as contemporary social satire in the manner of Gogol and, drawing much from Dostoevsky, as an ideological critique of the Soviet materialist utopia. That, to be sure, is how they were received by millions of readers in the Soviet Union who had grown accustomed from years of censorship to read all literature as allegory. In *Predatory Things of the Century* (1965) the Strugatskys portrayed a Soviet-like society of the future, where nuclear science and technology have delivered every conceivable power to the omnipresent bureaucratic state. Since there is no longer any need for work or independent thought, the people are transformed into happy morons. Sated with consumer goods, the citizens have become spiritually dead. This same idea was taken up by the dissident writer Andrei Sinyavsky in his *Unguarded Thoughts* (1966), a collection of aphoristic essays which renounce science and materialism for a Russian faith and native soil-type nationalism that could have come directly from the pages of Dostoevsky.

Science fiction films were equally a vehicle for challenging Soviet materialism. In Romm's *Nine Days* (1962), for example, some scientists engage in long debates about the moral questions posed by atomic energy. They philosophize about the means and ends of science as a whole – to the point where this very verbal film begins to resemble a scene out of Dostoevsky in which characters discuss the existence of a God. In Andrei Tarkovsky's masterpiece *Solaris* (1972) the exploration of outer space becomes a moral and spiritual quest for self-knowledge, love and faith. The cosmic traveller, a scientist called Chris, journeys to a space station in the distant galaxies where scientists have been researching the mysterious regenerative powers of a huge burning star. His journey becomes a more personal quest, as Chris rediscovers his capacity to love, when Hari, his ex-lover, whom he had driven to suicide through his emotional coldness, is brought back to life, or a mirage of it, by the powers of the star. Hari's sacrifice (she destroys herself again) releases Chris from his emotional dependence on her and allows him to return to earth (an oasis which appears in the burning star). In a spirit of atonement he kneels before his father to beg forgiveness for his sins. The earth thus emerges as the proper destination of all journeys into space. Man ventures out not to discover new worlds but to find a replica of earth in space. This affirmation of the human spirit is wonderfully conveyed in the scene on the space station where Hari looks at Bruegel's painting *Hunters in the Snow* which helps her to recall her former life on earth. The camera scans in detail over Bruegel's painting as Bach's F minor Choral Prelude, interspersed with the sounds of the forest and the chimes of the Rostov bells, rejoices in the beauty of our world. *Solaris* is not a story about space in the literal sense of Stanley Kubrick's *2001*, with which it is so frequently compared. Whereas Kubrick's film looks at the cosmos from the earth, Tarkovsky's looks from the cosmos at the earth. It is a film about the human values in which every Christian culture, even Soviet Russia's, sees its redemption.

In his cinematic credo, *Sculpting in Time* (1986), Tarkovsky compares the artist to a priest whose mission it is to reveal the beauty that is 'hidden from the eyes of those who are not searching for the truth'.[202] Such a statement is in the tradition of the Russian artist stretching back to Dostoevsky, Tolstoy and beyond – to the medieval icon painters such as the one whose life and art Tarkovsky celebrated in his masterpiece, *Andrei Rublev* (1966). Tarkovsky's films are like icons, in effect. To contemplate their visual beauty and symbolic imagery, as one is compelled to do by the slowness of their action, is to join in the artist's own quest for a spiritual ideal. 'Art must give man hope and faith', the director wrote.[203] All his films are about journeys in search of moral truth. Like Alyosha in *The Brothers Karamazov*, Andrei Rublev abandons the monastery and goes into the world to *live* the truth of Christian love and brotherhood among his fellow Russians under Mongol rule. 'Truth has to be lived, not taught. Prepare for battle!'

Tarkovsky said that Hermann Hesse's line from *The Glass Bead Game* (1943) 'could well have served as an epigraph to *Andrei Rublev*'.[204]

The same religious theme is at the centre of *Stalker* (1979), which, in Tarkovsky's own description, he meant to be a discourse on 'the existence of God in man'.[205] The stalker of the film's title guides a scientist and a writer to 'the zone', a supernatural wilderness abandoned by the state after some industrial catastrophe. He is straight out of the Russian tradition of the Holy Fool. He lives alone in poverty, despised by a society where everyone has long ceased to believe in God, and yet he derives a spiritual power from his religious faith. He understands that the heart of 'the zone' is just an empty room in a deserted house. But, as he tells his travelling companions, the basis of true faith is the *belief* in the Promised Land: it is the journey and not the arrival. The need for faith, for something to believe in outside of themselves, had defined the Russian people, in their mythic understanding of themselves, since the days of Gogol and the 'Russian soul'. Tarkovsky revived this national myth as a counter to the value system of the Soviet regime, with its alien ideas of rational materialism. 'Modern mass culture', Tarkovsky wrote, 'is crippling people's souls, it is erecting barriers between man and the crucial questions of his existence, his consciousness of himself as a spiritual being.'[206] This spiritual consciousness, he believed, was the contribution Russia might give to the West – an idea embodied in the last iconic image of his film *Nostalgia* (1983), in which a Russian peasant house is portrayed inside a ruined Italian cathedral.

It may seem extraordinary that films like *Stalker* and *Solaris* were produced in the Brezhnev era, when all forms of organized religion were severely circumscribed and the deadening orthodoxy of 'Developed Socialism' held the country's politics in its grip. But within the Soviet monolith there were many different voices that called for a return to 'Russian principles'. One was the literary journal *Molodaia gvardiia* (*Young Guard*), which acted as a forum for Russian nationalists and conservationists, defenders of the Russian Church, and neo-Populists like the 'village prose writers' Fedor Abramov and Valentin Rasputin, who painted a nostalgic picture of the countryside and idealized the honest working peasant as the true upholder of the Russian soul and its mission in the world. *Molodaia gvardiia* enjoyed

30. 'The Russian house inside the Italian cathedral'. Final shot from
Andrei Tarkovsky's Nostalgia (1983)

the support of the Party's senior leadership throughout the 1970s.*
Yet its cultural politics were hardly communist; and at times, such as
in its opposition to the demolition of churches and historic monuments,
or in the controversial essays it published by the nationalist painter
Ilya Glazunov which explicitly condemned the October Revolution as
an interruption of the national tradition, it was even anti-Soviet. The
journal had links with opposition groups in the Russian Church, the
conservation movement (which numbered several million members in

* It had the political protection of Politburo member Mikhail Suslov, Brezhnev's chief
of ideology. When Alexander Yakovlev attacked *Molodaia gvardiia* as anti-Leninist
on account of its nationalism and religious emphasis, Suslov succeeded in winning
Brezhnev over to the journal's side. Yakovlev was sacked from the Party's Propaganda
Department. In 1973, he was dismissed from the Central Committee and appointed
Soviet ambassador to Canada (from where he would return to become Gorbachev's
chief ideologist).

the 1960s) and the dissident intelligentsia. Even Solzhenitsyn came to its defence when it was attacked by the journal *Novy mir* (the very journal which had made his name by publishing *One Day in the Life of Ivan Denisovich* in 1962).[207] In the 1970s Russian nationalism was a growing movement, which commanded the support of Party members and dissidents alike. There were several journals like *Molodaia gvardiia* – some official, others dissident and published underground (*samizdat*) – and a range of state and voluntary associations, from literary societies to conservation groups, which forged a broad community on 'Russian principles'. As the editor of the *samizdat* journal *Veche* put it in his first editorial in 1971: 'In spite of everything, there are still Russians. It is not too late to return to the homeland.'[208]

What, in the end, was 'Soviet culture'? Was it anything? Can one ever say that there was a specific Soviet genre in the arts? The avant-garde of the 1920s, which borrowed a great deal from Western Europe, was really a continuation of the modernism of the turn of century. It was revolutionary, in many ways more so than the Bolshevik regime, but in the end it was not compatible with the Soviet state, which could never have been built on artists' dreams. The idea of constructing Soviet culture on a 'proletarian' foundation was similarly unsustainable – although that was surely the one idea of culture that was intrinsically 'Soviet': factory whistles don't make music (and what, in any case, is 'proletarian art'?). Socialist Realism was also, arguably, a distinctively Soviet art form. Yet a large part of it was a hideous distortion of the nineteenth-century tradition, not unlike the art of the Third Reich or of fascist Italy. Ultimately the 'Soviet' element (which boiled down to the deadening weight of ideology) added nothing to the art.

The Georgian film director Otar Ioseliani recalls a conversation with the veteran film-maker Boris Barnet in 1962:

He asked me: 'Who are you?' I said, 'A director' . . . 'Soviet', he corrected, 'you must always say "Soviet director". It is a very special profession.' 'In what way?' I asked. 'Because if you ever manage to become honest, which would surprise me, you can remove the word "Soviet".'[209]

8

From beneath such ruins I speak,
From beneath such an avalanche I cry,
As if under the vault of a fetid cellar
I were burning in quicklime.
I will pretend to be soundless this winter
And I will slam the eternal doors forever,
And even so, they will recognize my voice,
And even so they will believe in it once more.[210]

Anna Akhmatova was one of the great survivors. Her poetic voice was irrepressible. In the last ten years of her long life, beginning with the release of her son from the gulag in 1956, Akhmatova enjoyed a relatively settled existence. She was fortunate enough to retain her capacity for writing poetry until the end.

In 1963 she wrote the last additions to her masterpiece, *Poem without a Hero*, which she had started writing in 1940. Isaiah Berlin, to whom she read the poem at the Fountain House in 1945, described it as a 'kind of final memorial to her life as a poet and the past of the city – St Petersburg – which was part of her being'.[211] The poem conjures up, in the form of a carnival procession of masked characters which appears before the author at the Fountain House, a whole generation of vanished friends and figures from the Petersburg that history left behind in 1913. Through this creative act of memory the poetry redeems and saves that history. In the opening dedication Akhmatova writes,

....
. . . and because I don't have enough paper,
I am writing on your first draft.[212]*

* Akhmatova informed several friends that the first dedication was to Mandelstam. When Nadezhda Mandelstam initially heard her read the poem and asked her to whom the dedication was addressed, Akhmatova replied 'with some irritation': 'Whose first draft do you think I can write on?' (Mandelstam, *Hope Abandoned*, p. 435).

The poem is full of literary references, over which countless scholars have puzzled, but its essence, as suggested by the dedication, is foretold by Mandelstam in a prayer-like poem which Akhmatova quotes as an epigraph to the third chapter of her own poem.

> We shall meet again in Petersburg
> as though we had interred the sun in it
> and shall pronounce for the first time
> that blessed, senseless word.
> In the black velvet of the Soviet night,
> in the velvet of the universal void
> the familiar eyes of blessed women sing
> and still the deathless flowers bloom.[213]

Akhmatova's *Poem* is a requiem for those who died in Leningrad. That remembrance is a sacred act, in some sense an answer to Mandelstam's prayer. But the poem is a resurrection song as well – a literal incarnation of the spiritual values that allowed the people of that city to endure the Soviet night and meet again in Petersburg.

Akhmatova died peacefully in a convalescent home in Moscow on 5 March 1966. Her body was taken to the morgue of the former Sheremetev Alms House, founded in the memory of Praskovya, where she was protected by the same motto that overlooked the gates of the Fountain House: '*Deus conservat omnia*'. Thousands of people turned out for her funeral in Leningrad. The baroque church of St Nicholas spilled its dense throng out on to the streets, where a mournful silence was religiously maintained throughout the requiem. The people of a city had come to pay their last respects to a citizen whose poetry had spoken for them at a time when no one else could speak. Akhmatova had been with her people then: 'There, where my people, unfortunately, were.' Now they were with her. As the cortège passed through Petersburg on its way to the Komarovo cemetery, it paused before the Fountain House, so that she could say a last farewell.

8

overleaf:
Igor and Vera Stravinsky arriving at Sheremetevo Airport in Moscow,
21 September 1962

RUSSIA ABROAD

1

Homesickness! that long
Exposed weariness!
It's all the same to me now
Where I am altogether lonely

Or what stones I wander over
Home with a shopping bag to
A house that is no more mine
Than a hospital or a barracks.

It's all the same to me, a captive
Lion – what faces I move through
Bristling, or what human crowd will
Cast me out as it must –

Into myself, into my separate internal
World, a Kamchatka bear without ice.
Where I fail to fit in (and I'm not trying) or
Where I'm humiliated it's all the same.

And I won't be seduced by the thought of
My native language, its milky call.
How can it matter in what tongue I
Am misunderstood by whomever I meet

(Or by what readers, swallowing
Newsprint, squeezing for gossip?)
They all belong to the twentieth
Century, and I am before time,

Stunned, like a log left
Behind from an avenue of trees.
People are all the same to me, everything
Is the same, and it may be that the most

> Indifferent of all are those
> Signs and tokens which once were
> Native but the dates have been
> Rubbed out: the soul was born somewhere,
>
> But my country has taken so little care
> Of me that even the sharpest spy could
> Go over my whole spirit and would
> Detect no birthmark there!
>
> Houses are alien, churches are empty
> Everything is the same:
> But if by the side of the path a
> Bush arises, especially
> > a rowanberry . . .[1]

The rowanberry tree stirred up painful memories for the exiled poet Marina Tsvetaeva. It was a reminder of her long-lost childhood in Russia and the one native 'birthmark' that she could neither disguise nor bury underneath these lines of feigned indifference to her native land. From her first attempts at verse, Tsvetaeva adopted the rowan-berry tree as a symbol of her solitude:

> The red mound of a rowanberry kindled,
> Its leaves fell, and I was born.[2]

From such associations the homesick exile constitutes a homeland in his mind. Nostalgia is a longing for particularities, not some devotion to an abstract fatherland. For Nabokov, 'Russia' was contained in his dreams of childhood summers on the family estate: mushroom-hunting in the woods, catching butterflies, the sound of creaking snow. For Stravinsky it was the sounds of Petersburg which he also recalled from his boyhood: the hoofs and cart wheels on the cobblestones, the cries of the street vendors, the bells of the St Nicholas Church, and the buzz of the Marinsky Theatre where his musical persona was first formed. Tsvetaeva's 'Russia', meanwhile, was conjured up by the mental image of her father's Moscow house at Three Ponds Lane. The house was stripped apart for firewood in the cold winter of 1918. But after nearly twenty years of exile, when she returned to it in 1939, she found her favourite rowanberry growing as before. The tree was all that remained of her 'Russia', and she begged Akhmatova not to tell a soul of its existence, unless 'they find out and cut it down'.[3]

Of the many factors that lay behind Tsvetaeva's return to Stalin's Russia, the most important was her desire to feel the Russian soil beneath her feet. She needed to be near that rowanberry tree. Her return was the outcome of a long and painful struggle within herself. Like most émigrés, she was torn between two different notions of her native land. The first was the Russia that 'remains inside yourself': the written language, the literature, the cultural tradition of which all Russian poets felt themselves a part.[4] This interior Russia was a country that was not confined to any territory. 'One can live outside of Russia and have it in one's heart,' Tsvetaeva explained to the writer Roman Gul. It was a country that one could 'live in anywhere'.[5] As Khodasevich put it when he left for Berlin in 1922, this was a 'Russia' that could be encapsulated in the works of Pushkin and 'packed up in a bag'.

> All I possess are eight slim volumes,
> And they contain my native land.[6]

The other Russia was the land itself – the place that still contained memories of home. For all her declarations of indifference, Tsvetaeva could not resist its pull. Like an absent lover, she ached for its physical presence. She missed the open landscape, the sound of Russian speech, and this visceral web of associations was the inspiration of her creativity.

Three million Russians fled their native land between 1917 and 1929. They made up a shadow nation stretching from Manchuria to California, with major centres of Russian cultural life in Berlin, Paris and New York. Here were the remnants of a vanished world: former advisers to the Tsar and government officials lived from the sale of their last jewels; ex-landowners worked as waiters; ruined businessmen as factory hands; officers of the defeated White armies worked by night as taxi drivers and by day composed their memoirs about the mistakes of the White Army leader, General Denikin. Large families, like the Sheremetevs, were fragmented as their members fled in all directions. The main branch of the Sheremetevs left in 1918, travelling to Paris and then to New York. But others fled to South America, Belgium, Greece and Morocco.

Berlin was the first major centre of the emigration. It was a natural crossroads between Russia and Europe. The post-First World War economic crisis and the collapse of the mark made the city relatively inexpensive for those Russians who arrived with jewels or Western currency, and in the suburbs of the ruined middle classes a large but cheap apartment could be easily obtained. In 1921 the Soviet government lifted its controls on exit visas as part of its New Economic Policy. At that time Germany was the only major European country to have diplomatic and commercial relations with Soviet Russia. Still paying for the war through reparations and trade embargoes imposed by the victorious Western governments, it looked to Soviet Russia as a trading partner and a diplomatic friend. Half a million Russians crowded into Charlottenburg and the other southwestern suburbs of the German capital in the early 1920s. Berliners dubbed the city's major shopping street, the Kurfürstendamm, the 'Nepskii Prospekt'. Berlin had its own Russian cafés, its own Russian theatres and bookshops, its own Russian cabaret. In the suburbs there were Russian grocers, Russian launderettes, Russian pawn shops and Russian antique stores. There was even a Russian orchestra. And a Russian football team (with a young Vladimir Nabokov playing in goal).[7]

Berlin was the undisputed cultural capital of the Russian émigré community. Its musical talent was extraordinary: Stravinsky, Rachmaninov, Heifetz, Horowitz and Nathan Milstein could have shared the stage in any concert there. By the time Tsvetaeva arrived, in 1922, Berlin had become the adopted home of some of the most brilliant literary talents of the Russian avant-garde (Khodasevich, Nabokov, Berberova, Remizov). The city had an astounding eighty-six Russian-language publishers – comfortably outnumbering the German ones – while its Russian newspapers were sold throughout the world.[8]

Berlin was also a halfway house between Soviet Russia and the West for writers such as Gorky, Bely, Pasternak, Aleksei Tolstoy and Ilya

Ehrenburg, who were yet to make up their minds where they wanted to be based. It became a meeting place for writers from the Soviet Union, their literary confrères from the West, and the already-established Russian émigré community. Publishing costs in Berlin were extremely low – so low that several Soviet publishers and periodicals set up offices in the German capital. In the Russian Berlin of the early 1920s there was still no clear divide between Soviet and émigré culture. The city was the centre of the left-wing avant-garde, among whom the idea of a common Russian culture uniting Soviet Russia with the emigration remained strongest after 1917. Such ideas were generally rejected in the other major centres of the emigration. But Berlin was different – and for a brief period it was possible for writers to move freely between Moscow and Berlin. The climate changed in the middle of the decade when a group of émigrés known as *Smena vekh* (Change of Landmarks) began to campaign for a permanent return to the Soviet Union and established their own journal *Nakanune* (*On the Eve*) with Soviet backing. The turning point came in 1923, when the historical novelist Aleksei Tolstoy defected back to Moscow. In the ensuing scandal the Berlin émigré community became sharply polarized between left and right – between those who wanted to build bridges to the Soviet homeland and those who wanted to burn them.

During the middle of the 1920s the German mark was stabilized, the economy began to recover, and Berlin suddenly became expensive for the Russian émigrés. Its Russian population halved as the émigrés dispersed across the continent. Tsvetaeva and her husband, Sergei Efron, left for Prague so that he could study at the Charles University. Prague was a centre of Russian scholarship. Tomáš Masaryk, the first President of Czechoslovakia, was a distinguished Russian scholar. The Czechs welcomed the 'White Russians' as their fellow Slavs and allies in the Russian civil war. In 1918 a legion of Czech nationalists had fought alongside the anti-Bolsheviks in the hope of getting Russia to rejoin the war against the Central Powers.* After the establishment of

* As nationalists fighting for independence from the Austro-Hungarian Empire, the 35,000 soldiers of the Czech Legion wanted to return to the battlefields in France to continue their own struggle against Austria. Rather than run the risk of crossing enemy lines, they resolved to travel eastwards, right around the world, reaching Europe via Vladivostok and the USA. But as they moved east along the Trans-Siberian Railway

an independent Czechoslovakia that year, the government in Prague gave grants to Russian students like Efron.

In 1925, Tsvetaeva and Efron moved on to Paris. If Berlin was the cultural centre of Russia Abroad, Paris was its political capital. The post-war Versailles Conference had attracted delegates from all the major parties and would-be governments of Russia-in-exile. By the middle of the 1920s Paris was a hotbed of political intrigue, with Russian factions and movements of all types vying for attention from the Western governments and for the support of the wealthy Russian émigrés who tended to live there. Tsvetaeva and Efron stayed with their two young children in the cramped apartment of Olga Chernov, former wife of Viktor Chernov, the veteran Socialist Revolutionary leader who had been chairman of the short-lived Constituent Assembly which had been closed down by the Bolsheviks in January 1918. In the 'Little Russia' that formed around the Rue Daru, the Efrons regularly came across the other fallen heroes of the Revolution: Prince Lvov, Prime Minister of the first Provisional Government; Pavel Miliukov, its Foreign Minister; and the dashing young Alexander Kerensky, another former Prime Minister whom Tsvetaeva had compared to her idol Bonaparte in that fateful summer of 1917.

> And someone, falling on the map,
> Does not sleep in his dreams.
> There came a Bonaparte
> In my country.[9]

By the end of the 1920s Paris had become the undisputed centre of the Russian emigration in Europe. Its status was confirmed in the years

---

they soon became bogged down in petty fighting with the local Soviets, who tried to seize their arms. The Czechs ended up joining forces with the Socialist Revolutionaries, who had fled from Moscow and St Petersburg to the Volga provinces to rally the support of the peasantry against the Bolshevik regime and the ending of the war following the closure of the Constituent Assembly in January 1918. On 8 June the Czech Legion captured the Volga city of Samara, where a government composed of former members of the Constituent Assembly was in tenuous control until its defeat by the Red Army the following October, when the Czech Legion broke up and lost the will to fight, following the declaration of Czech independence on 28 October 1918.

of the depression, as Russians fled to the French capital from Hitler's Germany. The literary and artistic life of Russian Paris flourished in the cafés of the sixteenth *arrondissement*, where artists such as Goncharova and her husband Mikhail Larionov, Benois, Bakst and Alexandra Exter mixed with Stravinsky and Prokofiev and writers like Bunin and Merezhkovsky, or Nina Berberova and her husband Khodasevich, who had moved there from Berlin in 1925.

As most of the exiles saw it, Russia had ceased to exist in October 1917. '*Sovdepia*', as they contemptuously referred to Soviet Russia (from the acronym for Soviet department), was in their view an impostor unworthy of the name. Stravinsky always said that when he went into exile he did not so much leave as 'lose' Russia for good.[10] In her 'Poems to a Son', written in the early 1930s, Tsvetaeva concluded that there was no Russia to which she could return:

> With a lantern search through
> The whole world under the moon.
> That country exists not
> On the map, nor yet in space.
>
> Drunk up as though from the
> Saucer: the bottom of it shines!
> Can one return to a
> House which has been razed?[11]

The idea of Russia as an optical illusion, as something that had vanished like a childhood memory, was a central theme of Russian verse abroad. As Georgy Ivanov put it:

> Russia is happiness, Russia is all light.
> Or perhaps Russia disappeared into the night.
>
> And on the Neva the sun does not go down,
> And Pushkin never died in our European town,
>
> And there is no Petersburg, no Kremlin in Moscow –
> Only fields and fields, snow and yet more snow.[12]

For Tsvetaeva the mirage of Russia was the fading memory of her dismantled house at Three Ponds Lane. For Nabokov, in his poem 'The Cyclist' (1922), it was the dream of a bike ride to Vyra, his family's country house, which always promised to appear round the next bend – yet never did.[13] This nostalgic longing for an irretrievable patch of one's own childhood is beautifully evoked by Nabokov in *Speak, Memory* (1951). To be cut off from the place of one's childhood is to watch one's own past vanish into myth.

Tsvetaeva was the daughter of Ivan Tsvetaev, Professor of Art History at Moscow University and founding director of Moscow's Museum of Fine Arts (today known as the Pushkin Gallery). Like Tatiana in Pushkin's *Eugene Onegin*, the young poet lived in a world of books. 'I am all manuscript,' Tsvetaeva once said.[14] Pushkin and Napoleon were her first romantic attachments and many of the real people (both men and women) with whom she fell in love were probably no more than projections of her literary ideals. She called these affairs '*amitiés littéraires*' – and the objects of her affections included the poets Blok and Bely, Pasternak and Mandelstam. It was never clear to what degree the passion was in her own mind. Efron was the exception – the single lasting human contact in her tragic life and the one person she could not live without. So desperate was her longing to be needed that for him she was prepared to ruin her own life. They met in 1911 when he was still at school, and she barely out of it, on a summer holiday in the Crimea. Efron was a beautiful young man – slender-faced with enormous eyes – and she cast him as her 'Bonaparte'. The two shared a romantic attachment to the idea of the Revolution (Efron's father had been a terrorist in the revolutionary underground). But when the Revolution finally arrived they both sided with the Whites. Tsvetaeva was repulsed by the crowd mentality, which seemed to her to trample individuals underfoot. When Efron left Moscow to join Denikin's army in south Russia, she portrayed him as her hero in *The Camp of Swans* (1917–21).

> White guards: Gordian knot
> Of Russian valour.
> White Guards: white mushrooms
> Of the Russian folksong.

31. *Sergei Efron and Marina Tsvetaeva, 1911*

> White Guards: white stars,
> Not to be crossed from the sky.
> White Guards: black nails
> In the ribs of the Antichrist.[15]

For the next five years, from 1918 to 1922, the young couple lived apart. Tsvetaeva pledged that, if both of them survived the civil war, she would follow Efron 'like a dog', living wherever he chose to live. While Efron was fighting for Denikin's armies in the south, Tsvetaeva stayed in Moscow. She grew prematurely old in the daily struggle for bread and fuel. Prince Sergei Volkonsky, who became a close friend during those years, recalled her life in the 'unheated house, sometimes without light, a bare apartment . . . little Alya sleeping behind a screen surrounded by her drawings . . . no fuel for the wretched stove, the electric light dim . . . The dark and cold came in from the street as though they owned the place.'[16] The desperate hunt for food exposed Tsvetaeva to the brutalizing effect of the Revolution. It seemed to her that the common people had lost all sense of human decency and tenderness. Despite her love of Russia, the revelation of this new reality made her think about emigrating. The death of her younger daughter, Irina, in 1920 was a catastrophic shock. 'Mama could never put it out of her mind that children can die of hunger here', her elder daughter, Alya, later wrote.[17] Irina's death intensified Tsvetaeva's need to be with Efron. There was no news of him after the autumn of 1920, when the defeated White armies retreated south through the Crimea and crowded on to ships to flee the Bolsheviks. She said she would kill herself if he was not alive. At last, Efron was located in Constantinople. She left Moscow to join him in Berlin.

Tsvetaeva describes leaving Russia as a kind of death, a parting of the body from the soul, and she was afraid that, separated from the country of her native tongue, she would not be capable of writing poetry. 'Here a broken shoe is unfortunate or heroic', she wrote to Ehrenburg shortly before her departure from Moscow, 'there it's a disgrace. People will take me for a beggar and chase me back where I came from. If that happens I'll hang myself.'[18]

The loss of Russia strengthened Tsvetaeva's concern with national themes. During the 1920s she wrote a number of nostalgic poems. The best were collected in *After Russia* (1928), her last book to be published during her lifetime:

> My greetings to the Russian rye,
> To fields of corn higher than a woman.[19]

Increasingly she also turned to prose ('emigration makes of me a prose writer'[20]) in a series of intensely moving recollections of the Russia she had lost. 'I want to resurrect that entire world', she explained to a fellow émigrée, 'so that all of them should not have lived in vain, so that I should not have lived in vain.'[21] What she longed for, in essays like 'My Pushkin' (1937), was the cultural tradition that made up the old Russia in her heart. This was what she meant when she wrote in 'Homesickness' that she felt

> Stunned, like a log left
> Behind from an avenue of trees.[22]

As an artist she felt she had been orphaned by her separation from the literary community founded by Pushkin.

Hence her intense, almost daughterly, attraction to Sergei Volkonsky, the eurhythmic theorist and former director of the Imperial Theatre who was forced to flee from Soviet Russia in 1921. In Paris Volkonsky became a prominent theatre critic in the émigré press. He lectured on the history of Russian culture in universities throughout Europe and the USA. But it was his link to the cultural tradition of the nineteenth century that made him so attractive to Tsvetaeva. The prince was the grandson of the famous Decembrist; his father had been a close friend of Pushkin. And he himself had met the poet Tiutchev in his mother's drawing room. There was even a connection between the Volkonskys and the Tsvetaev family. As Ivan Tsvetaev mentioned in his speech at the opening of the Museum of Fine Arts in 1912, the idea of founding such a museum in Moscow had first been voiced by the prince's great-aunt, Zinaida Volkonsky.[23] Tsvetaeva fell in love with Volkonsky – not in a sexual way (Volkonsky was almost certainly homosexual) but in the heady fashion of her *amitiés littéraires*. After several barren years, lyric poetry began to flow from Tsvetaeva again. In the cycle of poems *The Disciple* (1921–2) she cast herself at the feet of a prophet (the 'father') who linked her with the wisdom and the values of the past. The poem 'To the Fathers' was dedicated to 'the best friend of my life', as she described Volkonsky to Evgenia Chirikova, 'the most intelligent, fascinating, charming, old-fashioned, curious and – most brilliant person in the world. He is 63 years old. Yet when you see him you forget how old you are. You forget where you are living, the century, the date.'[24]

> In the world which roars:
> 'Glory to those who are to come!'
> Something in me whispers:
> 'Glory to those who have been!'[25]

Volkonsky dedicated his own *Memoirs* (1923) to Tsvetaeva – recompense, perhaps, for the fact that she had typed out its two thick volumes for the publisher. She saw his recollections as a sacred testament to the nineteenth-century tradition that had been broken in 1917.

To mark their publication she wrote an essay called 'Cedar: An Apology'. The title had been taken from the Prince's nickname, given to him because he had planted cedars on his favourite patch of land (today it is a forest of 12,000 hectares) at the family estate in Borisoglebsk, Tambov province.

The cedar is the tallest of trees, the straightest too, and it comes from the North (the Siberian cedar) and the South as well (the Lebanese). This is the dual nature of the Volkonsky clan: Siberia and Rome [where Zinaida settled as an émigrée]![26]

In the preface to his memoirs Volkonsky voiced the exile's agony:

Motherland! What a complex idea, and how difficult to catch. We love our motherland – who does not? But what is it we love? Something that existed? Or something that will be? We love our country. But where is our country? Is it any more than a patch of land? And if we are separated from that land, and yet in our imagination we can re-create it, can we really say that there is a motherland; and can we really say that there is exile?[27]

2

Russian émigré communities were compact colonies held together by their cultural heritage. The first generation of Russian exiles after 1917 was basically united by the hope and conviction that the Soviet Union would not last and that they would eventually return to Russia. They compared their situation to that of the nineteenth-century political exiles who had gone abroad to fight the Tsarist regime from the relative freedom of Europe and then returned to their native land. Living as they did in constant readiness for their own return, they never really unpacked their suitcases. They refused to admit that they were anything but temporary exiles. They saw it as their task to preserve the old traditions of the Russian way of life – to educate their children in Russian-language schools, to keep alive the liturgy of the Russian Church, and to uphold the values and achievements of Russian culture in the nineteenth century – so that they could restore all these institutions when they returned home. They saw themselves as the guardians of the true Russian way of life which was being undermined by the Soviet regime.

In the 'Little Russias' of Berlin, Paris and New York the émigrés created their own mythic versions of the 'good Russian life' before 1917. They returned to a past that never was – a past, in fact, that had never been as good, or as 'Russian', as that now recalled by the émigrés. Nabokov described the first generation of exiles from Soviet Russia as 'hardly palpable people who imitated in foreign cities a dead civiliz-ation, the remote, almost legendary, almost Sumerian mirages of St Petersburg and Moscow, 1900–1916 (which even then, in the twenties and thirties, sounded like 1916–1900 BC)'.[28] There were literary soirées in private rooms and hired halls, where faded actresses provided nostalgic echoes of the Moscow Arts Theatre and mediocre authors 'trudged through a fog of rhythmic prose'.[29] There were mid-night Easter masses in the Russian church; summer trips to Biarritz ('as before'); and weekend parties at Chekhovian houses in the south of France which recalled a long-gone era of the 'gentry idyll' in the Russian countryside. Russians who before the Revolution had assumed foreign ways, or had never gone to church, now, as exiles, clung to their native customs and Orthodox beliefs. There was a revival of the Russian faith abroad, with much talk among the émigrés of how the Revolution had been brought about by European secular beliefs, and a level of religious observance which they had never shown before 1917. The exiles stuck to their native language as if to their personality. Nabokov, who had learned to read English before he could read Russian, became so afraid of losing his command of the Russian language when he was at Cambridge University in the early 1920s that he resolved to read ten pages of Dahl's *Russian Dictionary* every day.

This accentuation of their Russianness was reinforced by a mutual animosity between the exiles and their hosts. The French and the Germans, in particular, looked upon the Russians as barbaric parasites on their own war-torn economies; while the Russians, who were destitute but on the whole much better read than either the French or the Germans, thought themselves a cut above such 'petty bourgeois' types (according to Nabokov, the Russians of Berlin mixed only with the Jews). In a passage of *Speak, Memory* that still smacks of such attitudes Nabokov claims that the only German in Berlin he ever got to know was a university student,

well-bred, quiet, bespectacled, whose hobby was capital punishment ... Although I have lost track of Dietrich long ago, I can well imagine the look of calm satisfaction in his fish-blue eyes as he shows nowadays (perhaps at the very minute I am writing this) a never-expected profusion of treasures to his thigh-clapping, guffawing co-veterans – the absolutely *wunderbar* pictures he took during Hitler's reign.[30]

The sheer volume of artistic talent in the émigré communities was bound to divide them from the societies in which they found themselves. 'The ghetto of emigration was actually an environment imbued with a greater concentration of culture and a deeper freedom of thought than we saw in this or that country around us,' Nabokov reminisced in an interview in 1966. 'Who would want to leave this inner freedom in order to enter the outer unfamiliar world?'[31] There was, moreover, a political division between the mainly left-wing intellectuals of the West and those Russians who had fled the Bolsheviks. Berberova maintained that there was 'not one single writer of renown who would have been for us [the émigrés]' – and it is hard to disagree. H. G. Wells, George Bernard Shaw, Romain Rolland, Thomas Mann, André Gide, Stefan Zweig all declared their support for the Soviet regime; while others, such as Hemingway or the Bloomsbury set, were basically indifferent to what was going on inside the Soviet Union.

Isolated in this way, the émigrés united around the symbols of Russian culture as the focus of their national identity. Culture was the one stable element they had in a world of chaos and destruction – the only thing that remained for them of the old Russia – and for all their political squabbles, the thing that gave the émigrés a sense of common purpose was the preservation of their cultural heritage. The 'Little Russias' of the emigration were intellectual homelands. They were not defined by attachment to the soil or even to the history of the real Russia (there was no period of Russian history around which they could agree to unite: for the émigré community contained both monarchists and anti-monarchists, socialists and anti-socialists).

In these societies literature became the *locus patriae*, with the 'thick' literary journal as its central institution. Combining literature with social commentary and politics, these journals organized their readers in societies of thought, as they had done in Russia before 1917. Every major centre of the emigration had its thick journals, and each journal was in turn associated with the literary clubs and cafés which represented the different shades of political opinion. The biggest-selling journal was published in Paris – *Sovremenny zapiski* (*Contemporary Annals*), a title which was meant as a reference to the two most prestigious liberal journals of the nineteenth century: *Sovremennik* (*The Contemporary*) and *Otechestvennye zapiski* (*Annals of the Fatherland*). Its stated mission was the preservation of Russia's cultural heritage. This meant keeping to the well-tried names that had been established before 1917 – writers such as Ivan Bunin, Aleksei Remizov and (the queen of literary Paris) Zinaida Gippius – which made it very hard for younger or more experimental writers such as Nabokov and Tsvetaeva. There was enough demand for the reassuring presence of the Russian classics to sustain a score of publishers.[32]

Pushkin became a sort of figurehead of Russia Abroad. His birthday was celebrated as a national holiday in the absence of any other historical event the émigrés could agree to commemorate. There was much in Pushkin with which the émigrés could identify: his liberal-conservative (Karamzinian) approach to Russian history; his cautious support of the monarchy as a bulwark against the anarchistic violence of the revolutionary mob; his uncompromising individualism and belief in artistic liberty; and his 'exile' from Russia (in his case, from Moscow and St Petersburg). It is perhaps no coincidence that the emigration spawned some of the most brilliant Pushkin scholars of the twentieth century – among them Nabokov, with his 4-volume annotated English translation of *Eugene Onegin*.[33]

Among the Parisian émigrés Bunin was revered as the heir to this literary heritage, a living affirmation that the realist tradition of Turgenev and Tolstoy continued on in the diaspora. As Bunin himself put it in a celebrated speech of 1924, it was 'The Mission of the Emigration' to act for the 'True Russia' by protecting this inheritance from the modernist corruptions of left-wing and Soviet art. The mantle of national leadership had been conferred on Bunin, as a writer, only after 1917. Before the Revolution he had not been placed by many in the highest class: his prose style was heavy and conventional compared to the favoured writers of the avant-garde. But after 1917 there was a revolution in the artistic values of the émigrés. They came to reject the literary avant-garde, which they associated with the revolutionaries, and, once they found themselves abroad, they took great comfort in the old-fashioned 'Russian virtues' of Bunin's prose. As one critic put it, Bunin's works were the 'repository of a covenant', a 'sacred link' between the emigration and the Russia that was lost. Even Gorky, in Berlin, would abandon everything and lock himself away to read the latest volume of Bunin's stories as soon as it arrived in the mail from Paris. As an heir to the realist tradition, Gorky thought of Bunin as the last great Russian writer in the broken line of Chekhov and Tolstoy.[34] In 1933 Bunin was awarded the Nobel Prize, the first Russian writer to be honoured in this way. Coming as it did at a time when Stalin was putting Soviet culture into chains, the award was perceived by the émigrés as a recognition of the fact that the True Russia (as defined by culture) was abroad. Gippius, who was somewhat prone to hero-worship, called Bunin 'Russia's prime minister in exile'. Others hailed him as the 'Russian Moses' who would lead the exiles back to their promised land.[35]

The Russia Bunin re-creates in his stories is a dreamland. In 'The Mowers' (1923) and 'Unhurried Spring' (1924) he conjures up a vision of the old rural Russia that had never been – a sunny happy land of virgin forests and boundless steppes where the peasants were hard-working and happy in their work, in harmony with nature and their fellow farmers – the nobility. There could not have been a starker contrast with Bunin's dark portrayal of provincial rot in *The Village*, the novel that had first brought him to fame in 1910, nor a more ironic one. For Bunin was now escaping to precisely the sort of rural fantasy which he himself had done so much to puncture in his earlier work. In exile, his literary mission was to contrast the idyll he imagined in the Russian countryside with the evil of the cities where Bolshevism had corrupted the good old Russian ways. But the land he portrayed was, in his own admission, 'an Elysium of the Past', a shift 'into a kind of dream',[36] and not an actual place to which the exiles could return. Retreating into a legendary past is perhaps a natural response of the artist who is dislocated from his native land. Nabokov even took artistic inspiration from the experience of exile. But for Bunin it must have been particularly difficult to write when he was cut off from his own country. How could a realist write about a Russia that no longer was?

Emigration tends to breed conservatives in art. Retrospection and nostalgia are its moods. Even Stravinsky found himself moving away from the ultra-modernism of *The Rite of Spring*, the last major work of his 'Russian period', to the neoclassicism of the Bach-like works of his Parisian exile. Others became stuck in the style they had developed in their native land – unable to move on in the new world. This was true of Rachmaninov. Like Bunin's writing, his music remained trapped in the late Romantic mode of the nineteenth century.

Sergei Rachmaninov had learned composition at the Moscow Conservatory at a time when Tchaikovsky was its musical hero, and it was Tchaikovsky who had made the deepest impact on his life and art. In exile in New York after 1917, Rachmaninov remained untouched by the avant-garde – the last of the Romantics in the modern age. In a revealing interview in 1939, which the composer forbade to be published in his own lifetime, he explained to Leonard Liebling of *The Musical Courier* his feelings of estrangement from the world of modernism. His musical philosophy was rooted in the Russian spiritual tradition, where the role of the artist was to create beauty and to speak the truth from the depths of his heart.

I felt like a ghost wandering in a world grown alien. I cannot cast out the old way of writing, and I cannot acquire the new. I have made intense efforts to feel the musical manner of today, but it will not come to me . . . I always feel that my own music and my reactions to all music remain spiritually the same, unendingly obedient in trying to create beauty . . . The new kind of music seems to come not from the heart but from the head. Its composers think rather than feel. They have not the capacity to make their works exalt – they mediate, protest, analyse, reason, calculate and brood, but they do not exalt.[37]

In his last major interview, in 1941, Rachmaninov revealed the spiritual connection between this outpouring of emotion and his Russianness.

I am a Russian composer, and the land of my birth has influenced my temperament and outlook. My music is a product of the temperament, and so it is

Russian music. I never consciously attempt to write Russian music, or any other kind of music. What I try to do when writing down my music is to say simply and directly what is in my heart.[38]

The 'Russianness' of Rachmaninov's music, a kind of lyrical nostalgia, became the emotional source of his musical conservatism in exile.

Being out of step had always been a part of his persona. Born in 1873 to an ancient noble family from Novgorod province, Rachmaninov had been an unhappy child. His father had walked out on the family and left his mother penniless when he was only six. Two years later the young boy was sent to study music in St Petersburg. He invested his emotions in his music. He came to view himself as an outsider, and that Romantic sense of alienation became fused with his identity as an artist and later as an émigré. Exile and isolation as a theme figured in his music from an early stage. It was even there in his graduation piece from the Conservatory, a one-act opera called *Aleko* (1892), based on Pushkin's 'Gypsies', in which the Russian hero of the poem is rejected by the gypsies and banished to the life of a lonely fugitive. Rachmaninov's best-known music before 1917 was already marked by a precocious nostalgia for his native land: the *Vespers* (1915), with their conscious imitation of the ancient church plainchants; *The Bells* (1912), which allowed him to explore that Russian sound; and above all the piano concertos. The haunting opening theme of the Third Piano Concerto (1909) is liturgical in manner and very similar to the Orthodox chant from the vesper service used at the Pechersk monastery in Kiev, although Rachmaninov himself denied that it had any religious source. Rachmaninov had never been a regular churchgoer and after his marriage to his first cousin, Natalia Satina, a marriage forbidden by the Russian Church, he ceased to go at all. Yet he felt a deep attachment to the rituals and the music of the Church, especially the sound of Russian bells, which reminded him of his childhood in Moscow. This became a source of his nostalgia after 1917.

The other source of Rachmaninov's nostalgia was his longing for the Russian land. He yearned for one patch of land in particular: his wife's estate at Ivanovka, five hundred kilometres south-east of Moscow, where he had spent his summers from the age of eight, when the Rachmaninovs were forced to sell their own estate. Ivanovka contained his childhood and romantic memories. In 1910, the estate became his own through marriage and he moved there with Natalia. Ivanovka was the place where he composed nearly all his works before 1917. 'It had no special wonders – no mountains, ravines or ocean views', Rachmaninov remembered in 1931. 'It was on the steppe, and instead of the boundless ocean there were endless fields of wheat and rye stretching to the horizon.'[39] This is the landscape whose spirit is expressed in Rachmaninov's music. 'The Russians', he explained to an American magazine (and he was clearly thinking mainly of himself), 'feel a stronger tie to the soil than any other nationality. It comes from an instinctive inclination towards quietude, tranquillity, admiration of nature, and perhaps a quest for solitude. It seems to me that every Russian is something of a hermit.'[40] In 1917 the Ivanovka peasants forced Rachmaninov to abandon his home. 'They often got drunk and ran round the estate with flaming torches,' recalled one of the villagers. 'They stole the cattle and broke into the stores.' After his departure – first for Sweden and then for the USA – the house was looted and burned down.[41] For Rachmaninov, the loss of Ivanovka was equated with the loss of his homeland, and the intense pain of exile which he always felt was mingled with its memory.

Financial hardship forced Rachmaninov, at the age of forty-five, to start a new career as a piano virtuoso, touring Europe or the US every year. His peripatetic lifestyle left little time for composition. But he himself put his failure to compose down to his painful separation from the Russian soil: 'When I left Russia, I left behind the desire to compose: losing my country, I lost myself also.'[42]

In America, where they bought their first home in 1921, and then in France and Switzerland from 1930, the Rachmaninovs tried to re-create the special Russian atmosphere of Ivanovka, holding house parties for their Russian friends: Bunin, Glazunov, Horowitz, Nabokov, Fokine and Heifetz – all were frequent guests. They spoke in Russian, employed Russian servants, Russian cooks, a Russian secretary, consulted Russian doctors and scrupulously observed all the Russian customs such as drinking tea from a *samovar* and attending midnight mass. Their country house in France, at Clairefontaine near Paris, was purchased because it bordered on a secluded pine wood like the one in which Rachmaninov had liked to walk at Ivanovka. The

Russian atmosphere the couple re-created there was described by their American friends, the Swans, who visited them in 1931:

The chateau-like house, Le Pavilion, protected from the street by a solid wrought fence, lent itself well to this Russian life on a large scale ... The wide steps of the open veranda led into the park. The view was lovely: an unpretentious green in front of the house, a tennis court tucked away among shrubs, sandy avenues flanked with tall, old trees, leading into the depths of the park, where there was a large pond. The whole arrangement was very much like that of an old Russian estate ... A small gate opened into the vast hunting grounds: pine woods with innumerable rabbits. Rachmaninov loved to sit under the pine trees and watch the pranks of the rabbits. In the morning the big table in the dining room was set for breakfast. As in the country in Russia, tea was served and with it cream, ham, cheese, hard-boiled eggs. Everybody strolled in leisurely. There were no rigid rules or schedules to disturb the morning sleep.[43]

Gradually, as the old routines of Ivanovka were resumed, Rachmaninov returned to composing music once again – full-blown nostalgic works like the Third Symphony (1936). Western critics were surprised by the conservatism of the symphony's harmonic language, comparing it to the romanticism of a bygone age. But this was to miss its Russianness. The Third Symphony was a retrospective work – a farewell to the Russian tradition – and its whole purpose was to *dwell* on the spirit of the past. At a rehearsal of the *Three Russian Songs* (1926) in the USA in the 1930s Rachmaninov implored the chorus to slow down. 'I beg you,' he told the singers, 'do not spoil it for a devout Russian Orthodox churchman. Please, sing more slowly.'[44]

3

'Our tragedy', wrote Nina Berberova of the younger exiled writers in the 1920s, was 'our inability to evolve in terms of style.'[45] The renewal of style entailed a fundamental problem for the émigrés. If their purpose as Russian artists was to preserve their national culture, how could they evolve stylistically without adapting to their new environment and hence, in some ways, abandoning Russia? The problem mainly affected the younger generation – writers like Nabokov who had 'emerged naked from the Revolution'.[46] Older writers like Bunin brought with them to the West an established readership and written style from which they could not break. There was too much pressure on them to continue in the comforting traditions of the past – to churn out plays and stories about nests of Russian gentlefolk – and those who tried to break away were little prized or understood. Tsvetaeva's tragedy – to lose the readership that had sustained her as the rising star of the pre-revolutionary avant-garde – was yet another variant of this experience.

> Scattered in bookshops, greyed by dust and time,
> Unseen, unsought, unopened, and unsold,
> My poems will be savoured as are rarest wines –
> When they are old.[47]

Even Miliukov, former statesman, historian and editor of the Parisian journal *Poslednie novosti*, said, 'I don't understand Tsvetaeva.'[48] But for writers like Nabokov who had yet to find their feet there was little point or prospect in returning to the past. The old generation was dying out and the new becoming less Russian by the day as it assimilated into the mainstream of European culture. To create a new readership such writers had to break out of the mould.

Nabokov was the first major writer to complete this literary metamorphosis. According to Berberova, he was the only Russian-language writer of her generation with the genius to create not just a new style of writing but a new reader, too. 'Through him we learned to identify not with his fictional heroes' – as the nineteenth-century writers expected of their readers – 'but with the author, with Nabokov, and his existential themes became our theme as well.'[49] Nabokov always claimed that his writings were not about Russia or the émigrés. But exile was their central theme. And even if he saw that as a universal theme, a metaphor of the human condition, the appearance of Nabokov's writings in the Berlin of the 1920s was received by the Russian émigrés as an affirmation of their own national identity. Nabokov's writings were proof that 'Russia' (as embodied in its culture) was still with them in the West. As Berberova put it, with the publication of his first great novel, *The Luzhin Defence*, in 1930, 'a great Russian writer had been born, like a phoenix from the ashes of the Revolution and exile. Our existence acquired a new meaning. All my generation were justified. We were saved.'[50]

Exile was Nabokov's omnipresent theme, though he discovered the 'sorrows and delights of nostalgia' long before the Revolution had removed the scenery of his early years.[51] Nabokov was born in 1899, the elder son of a highly cultured and prominently liberal aristocratic family from St Petersburg who fled Russia in 1919. His grandfather, Dmitry Nabokov, had been Minister of Justice in the final years of Alexander II's reign, when the Emperor had considered the adoption of a liberal constitution in the European mould. Until his dismissal in 1885, he had opposed the attempts by Alexander III to overturn the liberal judicial reforms of 1864. The writer's father, V. D. Nabokov, was a well-known liberal lawyer and an influential member of the Kadet (Constitutional Democratic) Party in the First Duma of 1906. He had drafted the abdication manifesto of the Grand Duke Mikhail, briefly invited to assume the throne in the February Revolution of 1917, which brought the monarchy to an official end. He had also been head of the Chancellery in the Provisional Government, a sort of executive secretary to the cabinet, and had played a leading role in formulating the electoral system of the Constituent Assembly. The Bolshevik seizure of power forced the Nabokovs to leave Russia, moving first to London and then to Berlin, where the writer's father was the editor of the newspaper *Rul'* until his assassination by a Russian monarchist in 1922. Throughout his career as a Russian writer in Europe Nabokov kept the pen name 'Sirin' (the name of a legendary bird of paradise in Russian mythology) to set himself apart from his famous father in the émigré community.

The Nabokov family was strongly Anglophile. Its mansion in St Petersburg was filled with 'the comfortable products of Anglo-Saxon civilization', Nabokov wrote in *Speak, Memory*:

Pears' soap, tar-black when dry, topaz-like when held to the light between wet fingers, took care of one's morning bath. Pleasant was the decreasing weight of the English collapsible tub when it was made to protrude a rubber underlip and disgorge its frothy contents into the slop pail. 'We could not improve the cream, so we improved the tube,' said the English toothpaste. At breakfast, Golden Syrup imported from London would entwist with its glowing coils the revolving spoon from which enough of it had slithered on to a piece of Russian bread and butter. All sorts of snug, mellow things came in a steady procession from the English shop on Nevski Avenue: fruitcakes, smelling salts, playing cards, picture puzzles, striped blazers, talcum-white tennis balls.[52]

Nabokov was taught to read English before he could read his native tongue. He and his brother and sister were looked after by 'a bewildering sequence of English nurses and governesses', who read them *Little Lord Fauntleroy*; and later by a mademoiselle who read to the children *Les Malheurs de Sophie*, *Le Tour du Monde en Quatre-vingts Jours* and *Le Comte de Monte Cristo*. In a sense Nabokov was brought up as an émigré. As a schoolboy he would set himself apart, imagining himself as an 'exiled poet who longed for a remote, sad and – unquenchable Russia'.[53] Pushkin was Nabokov's inspiration. Many of the heroes in his novels were meant to be the poet in disguise. Nabokov saw himself as Pushkin's heir. So much so, in fact, that when, at the age of eighteen, Nabokov found himself a refugee in the Crimea, where his family had fled the Bolsheviks, he took inspiration from the image of himself as a romantic exile, wandering in the footsteps of Pushkin, who had been sent into exile a hundred years before. His first published collections of poems, *The Empyrean Path* (1923), contains an epigraph from Pushkin's poem 'Anon' on the title page.

From the Crimea the family sailed to England, where Nabokov completed his education at Trinity College, Cambridge, between 1919 and 1922. The reality of post-war England was a long way from the Anglo-Saxon dreamworld of the Nabokov mansion in St Petersburg. The rooms at Trinity were cold and damp, the food unspeakable, and the student clubs were full of naive socialists, like the pipe-smoking 'Nesbit' in *Speak, Memory* who saw only bad in Russia's past and only good in the Bolsheviks.* Nabokov grew homesick. 'The story of my college years in England is really the story of my trying to become

---

* Nabokov later identified R. A. ('Rab') Butler, the future Tory Deputy Prime Minister and 'a frightful bore', as the man behind the mask of R. Nesbit Bain in *Speak, Memory* (B. Boyd, *Nabokov: The Russian Years* (London, 1990), p. 168).

a Russian writer', he recalled. 'I had the feeling that Cambridge and all its famed features – venerable elms, blazoned windows, loquacious tower clocks – were of no consequence in themselves but existed merely to frame and support my rich nostalgia.'[54]

The focus of Nabokov's longing for Russia was the family estate at Vyra, near St Petersburg. It contained his childhood memories. In *Speak, Memory* he claimed to have felt his first pangs of nostalgia at the tender age of five, when, on holiday in Europe, 'I would draw with my forefinger on my pillow the carriage road sweeping up to our Vyra house.'[55] The pain of losing Vyra was acute – perhaps more acute than the loss of much of the family wealth or the loss of his homeland, which Nabokov hardly knew, apart from Vyra and St Petersburg. In *Speak, Memory* he emphasizes the point.

The following passage is not for the general reader, but for the particular idiot who, because he lost a fortune in some crash, thinks he understands me.

My old (since 1917) quarrel with the Soviet dictatorship is wholly unrelated to any question of property. My contempt for the émigré who 'hates the Reds' because they 'stole' his money and land is complete. The nostalgia I have been cherishing all these years is a hypertrophied sense of lost childhood, not sorrow for lost banknotes.

And finally: I reserve for myself the right to yearn after an ecological niche:

> ... Beneath the sky
> Of my America to sigh
> For *one* locality in Russia.

The general reader may now resume.[56]

From the gloom of Cambridge – where the porridge at breakfast in Trinity College was 'as grey and dull as the sky above Great Court' – he wrote to his mother, who had settled in Berlin, in October 1920:

Mother, dear, yesterday I woke up in the middle of the night and asked someone – I don't know whom – the night, the stars, God: will I really never return, is it really all finished, wiped out, destroyed? Mother, we must return, mustn't we, it cannot be that all this has died, turned to dust – such an idea could drive one mad. I would like to describe every little bush, every stalk in our divine park at Vyra – but no one can understand this. How little we valued our paradise! – we should have loved it more pointedly, more consciously.[57]

This nostalgia for Vyra was the inspiration for *Speak, Memory*, in which he lovingly describes its 'every little bush' in an effort to recover his childhood memories and desires. It was a sort of Proustian discourse on the sinuosity of time and consciousness. Nabokov's 'memory' was a creative act, a reanimation of the past which blended with the present through association, and was then transfigured into personality and art. He once wrote that the exile has a sharper sense of time. His extraordinary capacity to re-create through words the sensations of the past was surely his own exile's dividend.

Exile is a leitmotif throughout Nabokov's works. *Mary*, his first novel, published in Berlin in 1926, was intended as a portrait of the émigré condition, even if Nabokov, in his introduction to the English version in 1970, stressed its autobiographical nature. Ganin, the hero, in yearning for Mary, becomes an emblem of the exile's dream: the hope of retrieving and reliving the lost happiness of his youth in Russia. In *Glory* (1932) the hero, Martin Edelweiss, a Russian émigré from the Crimea who is studying at Cambridge University, dreams of returning to Russia. His fantasies take shape as he travels to Berlin and ventures through the woods to cross the Russian border, never to return. The subject of *The Gift* (1938) is equally the 'gloom and glory of exile'.[58] It is the theme of all Nabokov's Russian-language novels (of which there are nine). Their tragic characters are émigrés, lost and isolated in a foreign world or haunted by a past which is irretrievable except through the creative memory of fantasy or art. In *The Gift* its hero, the writer Fedor Godunov-Cherdyntsev, re-creates the literary life of Russia through his poetry. In *Glory* and *Pale Fire* (written in English in 1962) the hero lives in a dreamworld Russia to escape the misery of his exile. Nabokov's thoughts about the 'distant Northern land' he called Zembla in *Pale Fire* reveal the writer's response to exile:

1. The image of Zembla must creep up on the reader very gradually . . .

4. Nobody knows, nobody should know – even Kinbote hardly knows – if Zembla really exists.

5. Zembla and its characters should remain in a fluid misty condition . . .

6. We do not even know whether Zembla is pure invention or a kind of lyrical simile of Russia (Zembla: *Zemlya* [the Russian word for 'land']).[59]

In the first of Nabokov's English-language novels, *The Real Life of Sebastian Knight* (1941), the exile theme appears in a different form: the split identity. The hero, Sebastian, is the subject of a biography, ostensibly written by his brother, who gradually emerges as the real Sebastian. This sense of confusion and inner division was experienced by many émigrés. Khodasevich writes very movingly about it in 'Sorrento Photographs' (in his collection of poems *European Nights* (1922–7)), in which he compares the exile's divided consciousness, the confusion in his mind of images from his two lives at home and abroad, to the double exposure of a film.

Nabokov's switch from writing in Russian to writing in English is a complicated story intimately linked with his adoption of a new (American) identity. It must have been a painful switch, as Nabokov, who was famous for his showmanship, always liked to stress. It was, he said, 'like learning to handle things after losing seven or eight fingers in an explosion'.[60] Throughout his life Nabokov complained about the handicap of writing in English – perhaps too often to be totally believed (he once confessed in a letter to a friend that his 'best work was written in English').[61] Even at the height of his literary prowess he argues, in his 1956 afterword to *Lolita*, that it had been his 'private tragedy' to

abandon my natural idiom, my untrammelled, rich and infinitely docile Russian tongue for a second-rate brand of English, devoid of any of those apparatuses – the baffling mirror, the black velvet backdrop, the implied associations and traditions – which the native illusionist, frac-tails flying, can magically use to transcend the heritage in his own way.[62]

But even if such claims were a form of affectation, his achievement is undeniable. It is extraordinary that a writer who has been hailed as the supreme stylist of the modern English language should have written it as a foreigner. As his wife Vera put it, not only had he 'switched from a very special and complex brand of Russian, all his own, which he had perfected over the years into something unique and peculiar to him', but he had embraced 'an English which he then proceeded to wield and bend to his will until it, too, became under his pen something it had never been before in its melody and flexibility'. She came to the conclusion that what he had done was substitute for his passionate affair with the Russian language *un mariage de raison* which 'as it sometimes happens with a *mariage de raison* – became in turn a tender love affair'.[63]

Until the Revolution destroyed his plans, Nabokov had set out to become the next Pushkin. In later life he played upon this image of the stymied genius, even if in fact his English writing style, which he had developed since the age of five, had always been as good as, if not better than, his Russian one. But once he was in exile Nabokov had a sense of writing in a void. Liberated from the Soviet regime, he began to feel that the freedom he enjoyed was due to his working *in vacuo* – without readers or a public context in which to write – so that 'the whole thing acquired a certain air of fragile unreality'.[64] (Tsvetaeva expressed a similar despair – although in her case, without another language to fall back on, it signalled a more profound private tragedy: 'From a world where my poems were as necessary as bread I came into a world where no one needs poems, neither my poems nor any poems, where poems are needed like – dessert: if anyone – needs – dessert . . .')[65]

The need for an audience was the fundamental motive of Nabokov's switch. As he himself explained, a writer 'needs some reverberation, if not a response'.[66] His Russian-language reading public was reduced in size with every passing year, as the children of the émigrés became assimilated into the culture in which they lived. It was virtually impossible for a young Russian writer like Nabokov to make a living from writing alone, and the competition was intense. 'To get into literature is like squeezing into an overcrowded trolley car. And once inside, you do your best to push off any new arrival who tries to hang on', complained another writer, Georgy Ivanov.[67]

Berlin was a particularly difficult place to live, as thousands of Russians fled the city after Hitler's rise to power in 1933. The Nabokovs stayed in the German capital. They lived in poverty – Vera working as a secretary and Nabokov giving private lessons in English and in French. But it was obvious that they, too, would have to leave. Vera was Jewish, and in 1936 the man who had assassinated Nabokov's father, Sergei Taboritsky, was appointed second-in-command of Hitler's department for émigré affairs. Nabokov searched in desperation for an academic post in London or New York, anywhere but Hitler's Germany, and settled in the end for a move to Paris in 1938. From there the Nabokovs made arrangements to go to New York in the spring of 1940, just two weeks before the Germans reached Paris. In their studio apartment near the Bois de Boulogne Nabokov locked himself in the bathroom, laid a suitcase across the bidet and typed out his entry ticket to the English literary world: *The Real Life of Sebastian Knight*, published in New York in 1941.

Nabokov's passage to New York had been arranged by Alexandra Tolstoy, the novelist's daughter and the head of the Tolstoy Foundation, which had just been set up to look after the interests of Russian émigrés in America. The outbreak of the Second World War had brought about a flood of well-known refugees from Hitler's Europe: Einstein, Thomas Mann, Huxley, Auden, Stravinsky, Bartók and Chagall – all made new homes for themselves in the USA. New York was swollen with Russian émigrés. The literary capital of Russia in America, its daily Russian newspaper, *Novoe russkoe slovo* (*New Russian Word*) had a national readership of half a million. The Nabokovs settled in 'a dreadful little flat' on West 87th Street, near Central Park. As a writer Nabokov was not well known among the émigrés in the USA. Until the scandal and success of *Lolita*, completed in 1952 but not published until 1955, he struggled to survive from his writing. Like the hero of his novel *Pnin* (1957), he was forced to make his living from temporary lecturing jobs at, among other universities, Stanford, Wellesley and Cornell. Not that his financial hardship reduced Nabokov's considerable pride. When Rachmaninov sent the struggling writer some of his old clothes, Nabokov, who was something of a dandy and the son of possibly the best-dressed man in the entire history of St Petersburg,* returned the suits to the composer, complaining that they had been tailored 'In the period of the Prelude'.[68]

'America is my home now,' Nabokov said in interviews in 1964.

---

* Nabokov *père* was famous for his finely tailored English suits, which he wore, without self-consciousness, in the Duma assembly, where many of the rural deputies were dressed in peasant clothes (A. Tyrkova-Williams, *Na putiakh k svobode* (New York, 1952), p. 270). His sartorial extravagance was a common source of anecdotes in pre-revolutionary Petersburg. It was even said that he sent his underpants to England to be washed.

'I am an American writer.'[69] Despite his sometimes rather scathing portraits of the USA (most notoriously in *Lolita*), it appears the sentiment was genuinely held. Nabokov liked to play the real American. Having lost the Nabokov inheritance in the Old World way, through revolution, he had earned his fortune in the New World way: by hard work and brains.[70] The bounty of *Lolita* was a badge of his success as an American, and he wore it with great pride. 'This is the only known case in history when a European pauper ever became his own American uncle', writes an envious but admiring reviewer of the Russian writer and émigré Vadim (read: Nabokov) in *Look at the Harlequins!* (1974).[71] Nabokov would not tolerate any criticism of America. He was a patriot. Throughout his life he kept the oath which he had sworn when he became a US citizen in 1945. When Gallimard produced a cover design for the French edition of *Pnin* showing the professor standing on the US flag, Nabokov objected to the Stars and Stripes 'being used as a floor coverage or a road surfacing'.[72]

Nabokov's anti-Soviet politics were at the core of his Americanism. He thought McCarthy was probably right about the existence of Communist spies in the US government. He despised the liberals who harboured sympathies for the Soviet Union. He refused to have anything to do with Soviet Russia – even at the height of the Second World War when it was an ally of the West. When Nabokov learned, in 1945, that Vasily Maklakov, the official representative of the Russian émigrés in France, had attended a luncheon at the Soviet embassy in Paris, and had drunk a toast 'to the motherland, to the Red Army, to Stalin', he wrote in anger to a friend:

I can understand denying one's principles in *one* exceptional case: if they told me that those closest to me would be tortured or spared according to my reply, I would immediately consent to anything, ideological treachery or foul deeds and would even apply myself lovingly to the parting on Stalin's backside. Was Maklakov placed in such a situation? Evidently not.

All that remains is to outline a classification of the emigration. I distinguish five main divisions:

1. The philistine majority, who dislike the Bolsheviks for taking from them their little bit of land or money, or twelve Ilf-and-Petrov chairs.

2. Those who dream of pogroms and a Rumanian Tsar, and now fraternize with the Soviets because they sense in the Soviet Union the Soviet Union of the Russian people.

3. Fools.

4. Those who ended up across the border by inertia, vulgarians and careerists who pursue their own advantage and lightheartedly serve any leader at all.

5. Decent freedom-loving people, the old guard of the Russian intelligentsia, who unshakeably despise violence against language, against thought, against truth.[73]

Nabokov placed himself in the final category. In his courses on Russian literature he refused to lecture on any literature since 1917, although in his classes at Cornell he made a concession for Akhmatova and the poetry of Pasternak.* Nabokov maintained that the communist regime had prevented the development of an 'authentic literature'.[74] He was equally hostile to the realist tradition of the nineteenth century which looked to literature for social content and ideas – a tradition which he rightly saw as a predecessor of the Soviet approach to literature. It was on this basis that he criticized both *Dr Zhivago* ('dreary conventional stuff'), which competed with *Lolita* at the top of the bestseller lists in 1958, and Solzhenitsyn's *The Gulag Archipelago* (1973–5) ('a kind of juicy journalese, formless, wordy and repetitious')[75] – although there must have been some jealousy at work

---

* Nabokov was normally dismissive of Akhmatova and of the many female imitators of her early style. In *Pnin* the professor's estranged wife Liza sings out 'rhythmically, in long-drawn, deep-voiced tones' a cruel parody of Akhmatova's verse:

> 'I have put on a dark dress
> And am more modest than a nun;
> An ivory crucifix
> Is over my cold bed,
>
> But the lights of fabulous orgies
> Burn through my oblivion,
> And I whisper the name George –
> Your golden name!'

(V. Nabokov, *Pnin* (Harmondsworth, 2000), p. 47). Akhmatova was deeply offended by the parody, which had played upon the 'half-harlot, half-nun' image used by Zhdanov in 1948 (L. Chukovskaia, *Zapiski ob Anne Akhmatovoi*, 2 vols. (Paris, 1980), vol. 2, p. 383).

there as well (for unlike Pasternak and Solzhenitsyn, Nabokov never won the Nobel Prize). And yet, despite his political denials, he felt a deep attachment to the Russian tradition. He longed to write another novel in his native tongue. He felt that there was something of his tragic hero Pnin – the bumbling, noble-hearted émigré professor of Russian who cannot quite adapt to his American environment – not only in himself but in all the best émigrés.

In 1965 Nabokov worked on a Russian translation of *Lolita*. In the afterword to the English edition he had referred to his switch from Russian into English as a 'private tragedy'. But he now began his afterword to the Russian edition by confessing that the process of translating his prose back again had been disillusioning:

Alas, that 'marvellous Russian language' that I thought awaited me some-where, blossoming like a faithful springtime behind a tightly locked gate whose key I had kept safe for so many years, proved to be nonexistent, and beyond the gate are nothing but charred stumps and the hopeless autumnal vista, and the key in my hand is more like a jimmy.[76]

The Russian language had moved on since Nabokov left his native land, and 'the baffling mirror, the black velvet backdrop, the implied associations and traditions' which he had used like a magician in his early Russian novels were now lost on his Soviet audience.

4

When the poet Zinaida Gippius and her husband Dmitry Merezhkov-sky arrived in Paris in 1919 they opened the door of their flat with their own key and found everything in place: books, linen, kitchenware.[77] Exile was a return to their second home. For many of the old St Peters-burg élite, coming to Paris was like returning to the old cosmopolitan lifestyle that they themselves had imitated in St Petersburg. The Grand Duke Alexander Mikhailovich, brother-in-law to the last Tsar, arrived in Paris in the same year as the Merezhkovskys and made like a homing pigeon for the Ritz Hotel – his bills paid courtesy of a rare collection of Tsarist coins with which he had fled from his native land. This Paris was not so much a 'Little Russia' as a microcosm (and continuation) of the extraordinary cultural renaissance in St Petersburg between 1900 and 1916. Diaghilev, Stravinsky, Benois, Bakst, Shaliapin, Goncharova, Koussevitsky and Prokofiev – they all made Paris home.

The effect of the arrival of such émigrés was to accentuate two related facets of Russia's cultural image in the West. The first of these was a renewed appreciation of the European character of Russian culture as manifested in the so-called 'neoclassical' style of Stravinsky, Prokofiev and the Ballets Russes. Stravinsky himself disliked the term, claiming that it meant 'absolutely nothing' and that music, by its very nature, could not express anything at all.[78] But his neoclassicism was itself a statement of artistic principles. It was a conscious rejection of the Russian peasant music of his early neo-nationalist phase, of the violent Scythian rhythms in *The Rite of Spring* which had erupted in the Revolution of 1917. Forced into exile, Stravinsky now clung nostalgically to the ideal of beauty embodied in the classical inheritance of his native Petersburg. He borrowed from Bach and Pergolesi and, above all, from the Italo-Slavs (Berezovsky, Glinka and Tchaikovsky) who had shaped a particular strand of the Russian musical style in the eighteenth and nineteenth centuries.

An important aspect of this renewed engagement with the Imperial past was Diaghilev's promotion of Tchaikovsky's ballets in Paris. Before 1917 Tchaikovsky had been regarded in the West as the least interesting of the Russian composers. His music, in the words of the French critic Alfred Bruneau in 1903, was 'devoid of the Russian character that pleases and attracts us in the music of the New Slavic school'.[79] Seen as a pale imitation of Beethoven and Brahms, it lacked the exotic Russian character which the West expected from the Ballets Russes; Tchaikovksy's ballets did not feature in the *saisons russes*. But after 1917 a nostalgia for the old Imperial St Petersburg and its classical traditions, which Tchaikovsky's music epitomized, led to a conscious effort by the Paris émigrés to redefine themselves by this identity. Diaghilev revived *The Sleeping Beauty* (1890) for the Paris season of 1921. Stravinsky, who re-orchestrated parts of the score, wrote an open letter to the London *Times* in which he saluted the ballet as 'the most authentic expression of the epoch in our Russian life that we call the "Petersburg period"'. This tradition, Stravinsky now maintained, was just as

Russian as the folk-based culture which before 1914 the Ballets Russes had pedalled to the West in the form of works like his own *Firebird*:

> The music of Tchaikovsky, which does not seem obviously Russian to everyone, is often more profoundly Russian than that which long ago received the superficial label of Muscovite picturesqueness. This music is every bit as Russian as Pushkin's verse or Glinka's songs. Without specifically cultivating 'the Russian peasant soul' in his art, Tchaikovsky imbibed unconsciously the true national sources of our race.[80]

The second cultural feature of the émigrés in Paris was their reassertion of the aristocratic values that lay at the heart of the Petrine Imperial legacy. Beneath the surface gloss of its Slav exotica, this aristocratism constituted the essential spirit of the World of Art. This, too, was rooted in the music of Tchaikovsky, which had first brought together the three co-founders of the World of Art, Benois, Filosofov and Diaghilev, in the early 1890s. What they loved about the ballets of Tchaikovsky, as Benois was to put it in his *Reminiscences* in 1939, was their 'aristocratic spirit' which remained 'untouched by any democratic deviations' such as were to be found in utilitarian forms of art.[81] These were precisely the 'Art for Art's sake' values which the émigrés in Paris came to prize above all. They made a cult of the Alexandrine age with its high French Empire style and *raffiné* artistic aristocracy exemplified by Pushkin. Harking back to these old certainties was a natural response by the émigrés. The Revolution had destroyed the aristocratic civilization from which most of them had come, forcing them to find a second home in Europe. To some degree, despite Nabokov's claims to the contrary, they were shaken, too, by the loss of status they had enjoyed as members of their country's propertied élite. With their Nansen (League of Nations) passports* and their Alien

---

* The Russian passports of the émigrés were no longer valid after the formation of the Soviet Union: Russia as a country had ceased to exist. In place of their old papers the émigrés and other stateless persons were issued with temporary 'Nansen' passports (named after the polar explorer Fridtjof Nansen, the League of Nations High Commissioner for Refugees). The carriers of these flimsy passports suffered long delays and hostile questioning by functionaries throughout the West whenever they travelled or registered for work.

Registration Cards, landowners' sons like Stravinsky and Nabokov resented being treated by the Western states as 'second-class citizens'.[82]

The Ballets Russes was the centre of Russian cultural life in Paris. It was a sort of Parisian embassy of the Petersburg renaissance headed by Ambassador Diaghilev. After its wartime tours of America he had brought the company to France in the hope of reuniting his winning team of artists and of ending its perpetual cash flow crises by tapping the French market for the Russian arts that had done so well for it before the war. Fokine having settled in America, Diaghilev needed a new choreographer to carry on that distinctive Russian balletic tradition that went back to the school of Petipa. He found it in Georges Balanchine (né Georgy Balanchivadze). Born in 1904 in St Petersburg, the son of a Georgian composer, Balanchine had trained at Petipa's Imperial Ballet Academy and worked in the troupe of the Marinsky Theatre in St Petersburg before going on tour to Europe in 1924. Diaghilev perceived Balanchine as a vital link with the Petersburg traditions, and the first thing he asked him after Balanchine's dancers had run through a few routines they had brought with them from Russia was whether he could transfer them to the stage.[83] Balanchine's affinity for the music of Stravinsky made him the ideal choice for Diaghilev, whose plans for Paris had Stravinsky's ballets centre stage. The first collaboration between Stravinsky and Balanchine, *Apollon Musagète* (1928), was the start of a lifelong partnership between composer and choreographer. It was a partnership that would ensure the survival of the modern ballet – Diaghilev's invention – as an art form.

The Ballets Russes of the 1920s was defined by the principles of neoclassicism. In dance this entailed a return to the Apollonian rigour of the classical academy: an abstract, almost architectural, design in the manoeuvres of the ensemble; the rehabilitation of the male dancer in heroic mode; and the sacrifice of plot to the sensual connections between music, colour and movement. In music it entailed a renunciation of the Russian nationalist school and a stylized imitation of the classical (and predominantly Italian) traditions of Petersburg – as, for example, in Stravinsky's *commedia dell'arte Pulcinella* (1920) and his one-act *opéra bouffe* entitled *Mavra* (1922), which was dedicated to the memory of Pushkin, Glinka and Tchaikovsky.

This re-engagement with the classical tradition was an obvious re-action by the émigrés. After the chaos and destruction of the revo-lutionary period, they longed for some sense of order. They looked back to the European values and inheritance of Petersburg to redefine themselves as Europeans and to shift their 'Russia' west. They wanted to recover the old certainties from underneath the rubble of St Petersburg.

With the death of Diaghilev, in 1929, the Ballets Russes split up. The impresario had always been the inspiration of the group. He possessed the sort of presence that gave people a feeling of anticlimax when he left the room. So when he left the world it was almost bound to happen that his stars should go their separate ways. Many worked in the various 'Ballet Russes' touring companies that inherited the repertoire and glamour of the original Diaghilev organization: Fokine, Massine, Benois, Nijinska, Balanchine. Others, like Anna Pavlova, struck out on their own, establishing small companies that carried on Diaghilev's experimentalist tradition. In England his alumni laid the foundations of the British ballet: Ninette de Valois and the Vic–Wells Ballet (which later became the Royal Ballet), the Ballet Rambert and the Markova–Dolin Ballet were all descendants of the Ballets Russes. Balanchine transported the Diaghilev tradition to America, where he set up the New York City Ballet in 1933.

Paris was an outlet to the West, a door through which exiled Russians reached a new homeland. Most of those who made their home in Paris in the 1920s ended up by fleeing to America as the threat of war approached in the 1930s. The main attraction of America was its freedom and security. Artists like Stravinsky and Chagall escaped from Hitler's Europe to work in peace in the United States. For Strav-insky, this was not a question of politics: he publicly supported the Italian fascists ('I have an overpowering urge to render homage to your Duce. He is the saviour of Italy and – let us hope of Europe', he had told an Italian newspaper in the early 1930s);[84] and although he loathed the Nazis (they attacked his music), he was careful to put space between himself and his German-Jewish contacts after 1933. It was more a question of his own convenience: he loved order and needed it to work.

The composer Nicolas Nabokov (a cousin of the writer) recalls a revealing incident. Shortly after his arrival in America, Stravinsky became worried by the possibility of revolution there. He asked an acquaintance whether this was likely and, when he was told that it was possible, he asked in 'an appalled and indignant tone': 'But where will I go?'[85] Having lived through the Russian Revolution, Stravinsky's deepest political instinct was a fear of disorder.

After teaching for a year at Harvard University, he found his refuge in Los Angeles, where he purchased his first house, a small suburban villa in West Hollywood which would remain his home for the next thirty years. Los Angeles had attracted many artists from Europe, largely on account of its film industry; the German writer Thomas Mann described wartime Hollywood as a 'more intellectually stimulating and cosmopolitan city than Paris or Munich had ever been'.[86] Among the Stravinskys' friends were Bertolt Brecht and Charlie Chaplin, René Clair and Greta Garbo, Max Reinhardt and Alma Mahler (married to Franz Werfel), Lion Feuchtwanger and Erich Maria Remarque. Such cosmopolitanism made the United States a natural home for many of the Russian émigrés. Its 'melting pot' of nations, in New York and Los Angeles especially, was reminiscent of the cultural milieu in which they had lived in Petersburg. America enabled them to develop as international artists not troubled, as they had been in Europe, by irksome questions of national identity.

This sense of wanting to be rid of Russia – of wanting to break free to a new identity – was expressed by Nabokov in his poem 'To Russia' (1939), written just before his own departure from Paris for the USA.

Will you leave me alone? I implore you!
Dusk is ghastly. Life's noises subside.
I am helpless. And I am dying
Of the blind touch of your whelming tide.

He who freely abandons his country
on the heights to bewail it is free.
But now I am down in the valley
and now do not come close to me.

I'm prepared to lie hidden forever
and to live without a name. I'm prepared,
lest we only in dreams come together,
all conceivable dreams to forswear;

to be drained of my blood, to be crippled,
to have done with the books I most love,
for the first available idiom
to exchange all I have: my own tongue.

But for that, through the tears, oh, Russia,
through the grass of two far-parted tombs,
through the birch tree's tremulous macules,
through all that sustained me since youth,

with your blind eyes, your dear eyes, cease looking
at me, oh, pity my soul,
do not rummage around in the coalpit,
do not grope for my life in this hole

because years have gone by and centuries,
and for sufferings, sorrow, and shame,
too late – there is no one to pardon
and no one to carry the blame.[87]

Stravinsky's exodus to America followed a similar emotional path. He wanted to forget about the past and move on. His childhood was a painful memory. He had lost his father, two brothers and a daughter before he 'lost' Russia in 1917. He needed to put Russia behind him. But it would not let him be. As an émigré in France, Stravinsky tried to deny his own Russianness. He adopted a sort of European cosmopolitanism which at times became synonymous, as it had once been in St Petersburg itself, with an aristocratic hauteur and contempt for what was thought of as 'Russia' in the West (that is, the version of peasant culture which he had imitated in *The Firebird* and *The Rite of Spring*). 'I don't think of myself as particularly Russian,' he told a Swiss journalist in 1928. 'I am a cosmopolitan.'[88] In Paris

Stravinsky mixed in the fashionable circles of Cocteau and Proust, Poulenc and Ravel, Picasso and Coco Chanel. Chanel became his lover and transformed him from the rather unattractive and self-effacing man who had arrived in Paris in 1920 into the *homme dur et monoclé*, elegantly dressed in finely tailored suits and drawn (with Asiatic eyes) by Picasso.

Stravinsky made a very public show of distancing himself from the peasant Russia that had inspired his earlier works. It had turned into the Red Russia he despised – the Russia which had betrayed him. He denied the influence of folklore on his work. He claimed (mendaciously) that the ancient Russian setting of *The Rite of Spring* was an incidental choice that followed from the music, which he had composed first, without regard for the folklore.[89] He similarly denied the Russian roots of *The Peasant Wedding* – a work entirely based on musical folklore. 'I borrowed nothing from folk pieces', he wrote in his *Chronique de ma vie* in 1935. 'The recreation of a country wedding ritual, which in any case I had never seen, did not enter my mind. Ethnographic questions were of very little interest to me.'[90] Perhaps he was trying to distinguish his own music from the ersatz folklore (one should really call it 'fakelore') of the Stalinist regime, with its pseudo folk-dance troupes and *balalaika* orchestras, its Red Army choirs which dressed up in generic 'folk' costumes and played the role of happy peasants while the real peasants starved or languished in the gulags in the wake of Stalin's war to force them all into collective farms. But the lengths to which he went to erase his Russian roots suggest a more violent, personal reaction.

The music of Stravinsky's neoclassical period was an expression of his 'cosmopolitan' identity. There is almost nothing evidently 'Russian' – and certainly no musical folklore – in jazz-inspired works such as the Octet for Wind (1923), or in classically formed works like the Piano Concerto (1924); and even less in later works like *Dumbarton Oaks* (1937) or the Symphony in C (1938). The fact that he chose Latin – rather than his native Russian or adopted French – as the language of his 'opera-oratorio' *Oedipus Rex* (1927) lends further weight to this idea. Nicolas Nabokov, who spent the Christmas of 1947 with the Stravinskys in Hollywood, was struck by the apparent thoroughness of the composer's break with his native land. 'For

Stravinsky, Russia is a language which he uses with superb, gourmand-like dexterity; it is a few books; Glinka and Tchaikovsky. The rest either leaves him indifferent or arouses his anger, contempt and violent dislike.'[91] Stravinsky had an amazing chameleon-like capacity to adapt and make himself at home in foreign habitats. This, too, was perhaps a product of his Petersburg background. His son recalled that 'every time we moved house for a few weeks my father always managed to give an air of permanence to what was in fact very temporary . . . All his life, wherever he might be, he always managed to surround himself with his own atmosphere.'[92]

In 1934 the composer became a citizen of France – a decision he explained by claiming he had found his 'intellectual climate' in Paris, and by what he called 'a kind of shame towards my mother-land'.[93] Yet despite his French passport and his orchestrated image as an Artist of the World, Stravinsky harboured deeply felt emotions for the country of his birth. He was far more rooted in his native culture than he readily acknowledged; and these feelings were expressed in a concealed way within his works. Stravinsky felt pro-found nostalgia for St Petersburg – a city that was 'so much a part of my life', he wrote in 1959, 'that I am almost afraid to look further into myself, lest I discover how much of me is still joined to it'.[94] So painful was its memory that in 1955 the composer refused an invitation to Helsinki on the grounds that it was 'too near a certain city that I have no desire to see again'.[95] Yet he loved Rome, and Venice too, because they reminded him of Petersburg. Stravinsky's sublimated nostalgia for the city of his birth is clearly audible in his Tchaikovskian ballet *The Fairy's Kiss* (1928). He was equally nostalgic about Ustilug, the family's estate in Volhynia, where he had composed *The Rite of Spring*. Ustilug was a subject he would not discuss with anyone.[96] It was an immeasurable source of pain to him that he did not know what had happened to the house where he had spent his happiest childhood days. Yet the fact that he laboured longer on *The Peasant Wedding* than on any other score is an indication of his feelings for the place. The work was based on sources he had retrieved from the house on his final visit there.

Throughout his life in exile Stravinsky remained emotionally attached to the rituals and the culture of the Russian Church – even if in France he became attracted intellectually to the Catholic tradition, which he celebrated in his *Symphony of Psalms* (1930). In the mid-1920s, after nearly thirty years of non-observance, Stravinsky resumed an active life in the Orthodox community, in part under the influence of his wife Katya, who became increasingly devout during the long illness from which she eventually died in 1939. As an artist and as an émigré, Stravinsky found solace in the discipline and order of the Russian Church. 'The more you cut yourself off from the canons of the Christian Church,' he told an interviewer while at work on the *Symphony of Psalms*, 'the more you cut yourself off from the truth.'

These canons are as true for the composition of an orchestra as they are for the life of an individual. They are the only place where order is practised to the full: not a speculative, artificial order, but the divine order which is given to us and which must reveal itself as much in the inner life as in its exteriorization in painting, music, etc. It's the struggle against anarchy, not so much disorder as the absence of order. I'm an advocate of architecture in art, since architecture is the embodiment of order; creative work is a protest against anarchy and nonexistence.[97]

Stravinsky became a regular attender at services in the Russian church in the Rue Daru. He surrounded himself with the paraphernalia of Orthodox worship – his homes in Nice and Paris were filled with icons and crosses. He dated his musical sketches by the Orthodox calendar. He corresponded with Russian priests in all the major centres of the emigration, and the Russian priest in Nice became 'practically a member' of his household there.[98] Stravinsky claimed that the strongest pull of the Russian Church was 'linguistic': he liked the sound of the Slavonic liturgy.[99] It comes across in his Slavonic chants for the Russian church. *

This desire to return to the religion of his birth was connected to a profound love of Russia, too. Throughout his life Stravinsky adhered to the Russian customs of his childhood in pre-revolutionary Petersburg. Even in Los Angeles, his home remained an outpost of the old Russia.

---

* Before switching to Latin he had intended to set the *Symphony of Psalms* in Slavonic, too.

The living room was filled with Russian books and ornaments, pictures and icons. The Stravinskys mixed with Russian friends. They employed Russian servants. They spoke Russian in their home. Stravinsky spoke in English or in French only if he had to, and then in a thick accent. He drank tea in the Russian way – in a glass with jam. He ate his soup from the same spoon with which as a child he had been fed by his *babushka*.[100]

Chagall was another Artist of the World who concealed a Russian heart. Like Stravinsky, he invented his own image as a cosmopolitan. He liked to claim that the questions of identity which critics always asked ('Are you a Jewish artist? A Russian? Or a French?') did not actually bother him. 'You talk, I will work,' he used to say.[101] But such statements cannot be taken at face value. Chagall made up his own biography – and he frequently changed it. The major decisions of his life were taken, he claimed, on the basis of his own convenience as a practising artist. In 1922 he emigrated from Soviet Russia because conditions there made it hard for him to work. In western Europe, by contrast, he was already famous and he knew that he could become rich. There is no evidence to suggest that he was affected by the Bolshevik destruction of the synagogues and a good deal of the Jewish quarter in his home town of Vitebsk.[102] In 1941, when Chagall fled Paris for America, the danger from the Nazis was real enough – though here again he justified the move in terms of personal convenience. Throughout his life Chagall remained a wanderer, never settling down in any land, or calling it his own. Like the subjects of his paintings, he lived with his feet off the ground.

None the less, the unanswered question of his nationality was central to the painter's life and art. Of the diverse elements that were fused together in his personality (Jewish, Russian, French, American and international), it was the Russian that meant the most to him. 'The title "A Russian Painter"', Chagall once remarked, 'means more to me than any international fame. In my pictures there is not one centimetre free from nostalgia for my native land.'[103] Chagall's homesickness was focused on Vitebsk, the half-Jewish half-Russian town on the border between Russia and Belarus, where he had grown up, the son of a petty trader, in the 1890s. In 1941 it was overrun by the Nazis and all its Jewish inhabitants were killed. Three years later Chagall wrote a moving lamentation 'To My Native Town, Vitebsk' that was published as a letter in *The New York Times*.

It is a long time since I last saw you, and found myself among your fenced streets. You didn't ask in pain, why I left you for so many years when I loved you. No, you thought: the lad's gone off somewhere in search of brilliant unusual colours to shower like snow or stars on our roofs. But where will he get them from? Why can't he find them nearer to hand? In your ground I left the graves of my ancestors and scattered stones. I did not live with you and yet there was not a single one of my pictures in which your joys and sorrows were not reflected. All through these years I had one constant worry: does my native town understand me?[104]

Vitebsk was the world Chagall idealized. It was not so much a place as a mythical ideal, the artistic site of his childhood memories. In his fanciful paintings he re-created Vitebsk as a world of dreams. The muddy streets of the real town were magically transformed into colours reminiscent of a festive set for Mother Goose. Such was the demand for his Vitebsk theme, and the ruthlessness with which Chagall exploited it, that critics accused him of merchandizing his own exotica as art. Picasso said he was a businessman. The painter Boris Aronson complained that Chagall was 'always doing a *Fiddler on the Roof*'.[105] Yet, however much he might have traded on the Vitebsk theme, his homesickness was genuine enough.

Jews in Israel could not understand how Chagall could be so nostalgic about life in Russia. Wasn't it a country of pogroms? But Vitebsk was a town where the Jews had not just co-existed with the Russians; they were beneficiaries of Russian culture, as well. Like Mandelstam, a Polish-Russian Jew, Chagall had identified with the Russian tradition: it was the means of entry to the culture and values of Europe. Russia was a big, cosmopolitan civilization before 1917. It had absorbed the whole of Western culture, just as Chagall, as a Jew, had absorbed the culture of Russia. Russia liberated Jews like Chagall from the provincial attitudes of their home towns and connected them with the wider world.[106] Only Russia could inspire feelings such as these. None of the other East European civilizations was large enough to provide the Jews with a cultural homeland.

5

When Tsvetaeva moved to Paris in 1925 it had been in the hope that she would find a broader readership for her verse. In Prague she had struggled to keep 'body and pen together', as Nabokov would so memorably describe the predicament of the émigré writers.[107] She scraped by through translation work and hand-outs from her friends. But the constant struggle put a strain on her relations with Efron, a perpetual student who could not find a job, and with her daughter and her newborn son.

Efron began to drift away from her – no doubt losing patience with her constant love affairs – and became involved in politics. In Paris he immediately threw himself into the Eurasian movement, whose conception of Russia as a separate Asiatic or Turanian continent had already taken hold of Stravinsky. By the middle of the 1920s the movement had begun to split. Its right wing flirted with the fascists, while its left wing, towards which Efron veered, favoured an alliance with the Soviet regime as champion of their imperial ideals for Russia as the leader of a separate Eurasian civilization in hostile opposition to the West. They put aside their old opposition to the Bolshevik regime, recognizing it (mistakenly perhaps) as the popular, and therefore rightful, victor of the civil war, and espoused its cause as the only hope for the resurrection of a Great Russia. Efron was a vocal advocate of a return to the motherland. He wanted to expiate his 'guilt' for having fought on the White side in the civil war by laying down his life for the Soviet (read: the Russian) people's cause. In 1931 Efron applied to return to Stalin's Russia. His well-known feelings of homesickness for Russia turned him into an obvious target for the NKVD, which had a policy of playing on such weaknesses to infiltrate the émigré community. Efron was recruited as an NKVD agent on the promise that eventually he would be allowed to return to Soviet Russia. During the 1930s he became the leading organizer of the Parisian Union for a Return to the Motherland. It was a front for the NKVD.

Efron's politics placed enormous strain on his relationship with Tsvetaeva. She understood his need to return home but she was equally aware of what was happening in Stalin's Russia. She accused her husband of naivety: he closed his eyes to what he did not want to see. They argued constantly – she warning him that if he went back to the Soviet Union he would end up in Siberia, or worse, and he retorting that he would 'go wherever they send me'.[108] Yet Tsvetaeva knew that, if he went, she would follow her husband, as ever, 'like a dog'.

Efron's activities made Tsvetaeva's own position in émigré society untenable. It was assumed that she herself was a Bolshevik, not least because of her continued links with 'Soviet writers' such as Pasternak and Bely, who like her had their roots in the pre-revolutionary avant-garde. She found herself ever more alone in a community that increasingly shunned any contact with the Soviet world. 'I feel that I have no place here', she wrote to the Czech writer Anna Teskova. The French were 'sociable but superficial' and 'interested only in themselves', while 'from the Russians I am separated by my poetry, which nobody understands; by my personal views, which some take for Bolshevism, others for monarchism or anarchism; and then again – by all of me'.[109] Berberova described Tsvetaeva as an 'outcast' in Paris: 'she had no readers' and there was 'no reaction to what she wrote'.[110] *After Russia*, the last collection of her poetry to be published during her lifetime, appeared in Paris in 1928. Only twenty-five of its hundred numbered copies were bought by subscription.[111] In these final years of life abroad Tsvetaeva's poetry shows signs of her growing estrangement and solitude.

> Just say: enough of torment – take
> A garden – lonesome like myself.
> (But do not stand near by, Yourself!)
> A garden, lonesome, like Myself.[112]

'Everything is forcing me towards Russia', she wrote to Anna Teskova in 1931. 'Here I am unnecessary. There I am impossible.'[113] Tsvetaeva became increasingly frustrated with the editors of the émigré periodicals – professors and politicians like Miliukov who failed to understand her prose and hacked it into pieces to conform to the neat, clean style of their journals. Her frustration drove her to form an over-rosy view of literary life in the Soviet Union. She talked herself into believing that she was 'needed' there, that she would be able to be published once again, and that she could find a new circle of writer friends who would 'look on me as one of their own'.[114] With every passing year she felt the 'milky call' of her native tongue, which she knew was so essential, not just to her art but to her very identity. This physical longing for Russia was far stronger and more immediate than any intellectual rationalization for her continued exile: that Russia was contained inside herself and, like a suitcase filled with Pushkin's works, could be taken anywhere. 'The poet', she concluded, 'cannot survive in emigration: there is no ground on which to stand – no medium or language. There are – no roots.'[115] Like the rowanberry tree, her art needed to be rooted in the soil.

In 1937 Efron was exposed as a Soviet agent and implicated in the assassination of a Soviet spy who had refused to return to the Soviet Union. Pursued by the French police, Efron fled to the Soviet Union, where Alya had already settled earlier that year. Now Tsvetaeva could not remain in France. Shunned by everyone, her life there became impossible. Berberova saw her for the last time in the autumn of 1938. It was the funeral of Prince Sergei Volkonsky – at the moment when his coffin was carried out of the church on the Rue François Gérard. 'She stood at the entrance, her eyes full of tears, aged, almost grey, hands crossed on her bosom . . . She stood as if infected with plague: no one approached her. Like everyone else I walked by her.'[116] On 12 June 1939, Tsvetaeva and her son left by boat from Le Havre for the Soviet Union. The evening before her departure she wrote to Teskova: 'Goodbye! What comes now is no longer difficult, what comes now is fate.'[117]

Pasternak had warned Tsvetaeva: 'Don't come back to Russia – it's cold, there is a constant draught.' It was an echo of her own prophetic fear

That the Russian draught should blow away my soul![118]

But she was like her husband: she did not hear what she did not want to hear.

Many of the exiles who returned to Stalin's Russia did so in the knowledge, or with the intuition, that they were going back to a life of slavery. It was a mark of their desperate situation in the West, of their longing for a social context in which they could work, that they were prepared to close their eyes to the harsh realities of the 'new life' in the Soviet Union. Homesickness overcame their basic instinct of survival.

Maxim Gorky was the first major cultural figure to discover the perils of return. The writer, who had championed the Revolution's cause in his early novels like *Mother*, became disillusioned by its violence and chaos during 1917. He had looked to socialism as a force of cultural progress and enlightenment bringing Russia closer to the ideals of the West. But instead of heralding a new civilization, the street fighting that brought Lenin into power also brought the country, as Gorky had warned, to the brink of a 'dark age' of 'Asiatic barbarism'. The people's class hatred and desire for revenge, stoked up by the rhetoric of the Bolsheviks, threatened to destroy all that was good. The savage terror of the civil war, followed by the famine in which millions perished, seemed a gruesome proof of Gorky's prophecy. Bravely, he spoke out against the Leninist regime between 1917 and 1921, when, profoundly shaken by everything he had seen in those years, he left Russia for Berlin. Unable to live in Soviet Russia, neither could Gorky bear to live abroad. For several years, he wavered in this schizophrenic state, homesick for Russia and yet too sick of it to return home. From Berlin, he wandered restlessly through the spa towns of Germany and Czechoslovakia before settling in the Italian resort of Sorrento. 'No, I cannot go to Russia', he wrote to Romain Rolland in 1924. 'In Russia I would be the enemy of everything and everyone, it would be like banging my head against a wall.'[119]

On Lenin's death in 1924, however, Gorky revised his attitude. He was overwhelmed with remorse for having broken off with the Bolshevik leader and convinced himself, as Berberova put it, 'that Lenin's death had left him orphaned with the whole of Russia'.[120] His eulogistic *Memories of Lenin* was the first step towards his reconciliation with Lenin's successors in the Kremlin. He began to think about the idea of returning to the Soviet Union but put off a decision, perhaps afraid of what he might find there. Meanwhile, his two epic novels, *The Artamonov Business* (1925) and *The Life of Klim Samgin* (1925–36) did poorly in the West, where his didactic style no longer found favour. The rise of fascism in his adopted homeland of Italy made Gorky question all his earlier ideals – ideals that had formed the basis of his opposition to the Bolsheviks – about Europe as a historic force of moral progress and civilization. The more disillusioned he became with fascist Europe the more he was inclined to extol Soviet Russia as a morally superior system. In 1928 Gorky returned on the first of a series of summer trips to the Soviet Union, settling there for good in 1931. The prodigal son was showered with honours; he was given as his residence the famous Riabushinsky mansion (built by Shekhtel) in Moscow; two large country *dachas*; private servants (who turned out to be Lubianka spies); and supplies of special foods from the same NKVD department that catered for Stalin. All of this was given with the aim of securing Gorky's political support and of presenting him as a Soviet author to the Western world.[121] At that time opinion in the West was equally divided over whether Gorky or Bunin should win the Nobel Prize. Once the Kremlin took up Gorky's cause, the competition between the two writers became a broader political struggle over who should have the right to speak in the name of the cultural tradition that went back to Pushkin and Tolstoy – Moscow or the Paris émigrés?

The Soviet regime to which Gorky had returned was deeply split between the Stalinists and the so-called Rightists, like Tomsky and Bukharin, who opposed Stalin's murderous policies of collectivization and industrialization. To begin with, Gorky occupied a place somewhere between the two: he broadly supported Stalin's goals while attempting to restrain his extremist policies. But increasingly he found himself in opposition to the Stalinist regime. Gorky had never been the sort of person who could remain silent when he did not like something. He had opposed Lenin and his reign of terror, now he was a thorn in Stalin's side as well. He protested against the persecution of Zamyatin, Bulgakov and Pilnyak – though he failed to draw attention to the arrest of Mandelstam in 1934. He voiced his objections to the cult of Stalin's personality and even refused a commission from the Kremlin to write a hagiographic essay about him. In his diaries of the 1930s – locked up in the NKVD archives on his death – Gorky compared Stalin to a 'monstrous flea' which propaganda and mass fear had 'enlarged to incredible proportions'.[122]

The NKVD placed Gorky under close surveillance. There is evidence that Gorky was involved in a plot against Stalin with Bukharin and Kirov, the Party boss of Leningrad who was assassinated, perhaps on Stalin's orders, in 1934. Gorky's death in 1936 may also have been a consequence of the plot. For some time he had been suffering from chronic influenza caused by lung and heart disease. During the Bukharin show trial of 1938 Gorky's doctors were found guilty of the writer's 'medical murder'. Perhaps Stalin used the writer's natural death as a pretext to destroy his political enemies, but Gorky's involvement with the opposition makes it just as likely that Stalin had him killed. It is almost certain that the NKVD murdered Gorky's son, Maxim Peshkov, in 1934; and this may have been part of a plan to weaken Gorky.[123] Certainly the writer's death came at a highly convenient time for Stalin – just before the show trials of Zinoviev and Kamenev, which Gorky had intended to expose as a sham in the Western press. Gorky's widow was adamant that her husband had been killed by Stalin's agents when she was asked about this in 1963. But the truth will probably never be known.[124]

Prokofiev was the other major figure to return to Stalin's Russia – at the height of the Great Terror in 1936. The composer had never been known for his political acumen but the unhappy timing of his return was, even by his standards, the outcome of extraordinary naivety. Politics meant little to Prokofiev. He thought his music was above all that. He seemed to believe that he could return to the Soviet Union and remain unaffected by Stalin's politics.

Perhaps it was connected with his rise to fame as an infant prodigy in St Petersburg. The child of prosperous and doting parents, Prokofiev had had instilled in him from an early age an unshakeable belief in his own destiny. By the age of thirteen, when he entered the St Petersburg Conservatory, he already had four operas to his name. Here was the Russian Mozart. In 1917 he escaped the Revolution by travelling with his mother to the Caucasus and then emigrated via Vladivostok and Japan to the United States. Since Rachmaninov had recently arrived in America, the press inevitably made comparisons between the two. Prokofiev's more experimental style made him second best in the view of the generally conservative American critics. Years later, Prokofiev recalled wandering through New York's Central Park and

thinking with a cold fury of the wonderful American orchestras that cared nothing for my music . . . I arrived here too early; this *enfant* – America – still had not matured to an understanding of new music. Should I have gone back *home*? But how? Russia was surrounded on all sides by the forces of the Whites, and anyway, who wants to return *home* empty-handed?[125]

According to Berberova, Prokofiev had been heard to say on more than one occasion: 'There is no room for me here while Rachmaninov is alive, and he will live another ten or fifteen years. Europe is not enough for me and I do not wish to be second in America.'[126]

In 1920 Prokofiev left New York and settled in Paris. But with Stravinsky already ensconced there, the French capital was even harder for Prokofiev to conquer. The patronage of Diaghilev was all-important in Paris – and Stravinsky was the impresario's 'favourite son'. Prokofiev liked to write for the opera, an interest that stemmed from his love for setting Russian novels to music: *War and Peace*, Dostoevsky's *Gambler* and Briusov's *Fiery Angel* were all turned into operas by him. But Diaghilev had famously declared that the opera was an art form that was 'out of date'.[127] The Ballets Russes had been founded on the search for a non-verbal synthesis of the arts – dance, mime and music and the visual arts but not literature. Stravinsky, by contrast, was committed to the ballet, an art form that enjoyed enormous kudos in the West as quintessentially 'Russian'. Encouraged by Diaghilev, Prokofiev composed the music for three ballets in the 1920s. *The Buffoon* (1921) was a moderate success – though it rankled with Stravinsky, who subsequently plotted to turn the arbiters of musical taste in Paris (Nadia Boulanger, Poulenc and Les Six) against Prokofiev. The second, *The Steel Step* (1927), which handled Soviet themes, was denounced by the Paris émigrés as 'Kremlin propaganda', though in fact its idea was Diaghilev's. Only the last of Prokofiev's ballets, *The Prodigal Son* (1929), was an unqualified success. Its theme was close to the composer's heart.

Prokofiev became a lonely figure in Paris. He had a small circle of Russian friends which included the composer Nicolas Nabokov, the conductor Sergei Koussevitsky and the poet Konstantin Balmont. For seven years he laboured on his opera *The Fiery Angel* (1927), a work he always thought of as his masterpiece but which he never saw performed. Its central theme – the unconquerable divide between two worlds – spoke in many ways of his own separation from Russia.

Isolated from the émigré community in Paris, Prokofiev began to develop contacts with the Soviet musical establishment. In 1927 he accepted an invitation from the Kremlin to make a concert tour of the Soviet Union. On his return to Petersburg he was overcome by emotion. 'I had somehow managed to forget what Petersburg was really like', he recorded in his diary of the trip. 'I had begun to think that its European charm would pale in comparison with the West and that, on the contrary, Moscow was something unique. Now, however, the grandeur of the city took my breath away.'[128] The lavish production of his *Love for Three Oranges* (1919) in the Marinsky Theatre made him feel that he had at last been recognized as Russia's greatest living composer. The Soviet authorities pulled out all the stops to lure him back for good. Lunacharsky, the commissar of culture who had allowed him to go abroad in 1917 ('You are a revolutionary in music, we are revolutionaries in life . . . I shall not stop you'),[129] now tried to persuade the composer to return to Soviet Russia by citing Mayakovsky's famous open 'Letter-Poem' to Gorky (1927), in which he had asked him why he lived in Italy when there was so much work to do in Russia. Mayakovsky was an old acquaintance of Prokofiev; on the eve of Prokofiev's departure for America Mayakovsky had dedicated a volume of his poems 'To the World President of Music from the World President of Poetry: to Prokofiev'. Another of his old friends, the avant-garde director Meyerhold, talked enthusiastically of new collaborations to realize the Russian classics on the stage. Missing these old allies was a crucial factor in Prokofiev's decision to return. 'Foreign company does not inspire me', he confessed in 1933,

because I am a Russian, and that is to say the least suited of men to be an exile, to remain myself in a psychological climate that isn't of my race. My compatriots and I carry our country about with us. Not all of it, but just enough for it to be faintly painful at first, then increasingly so, until at last it breaks us down altogether . . . I've got to live myself back into the atmosphere of my homeland. I've got to see real winters again, and springs that burst into being from one moment to the next. I've got to hear the Russian language echoing in my ears. I've got to talk to people who are my own flesh and blood, so that they can give me something I lack here – their songs – my songs.[130]

From 1932 Prokofiev began to spend half the year in Moscow; four years later he moved his wife and two sons there for good. He was afforded every luxury – a spacious apartment in Moscow with his own furniture imported from Paris and the freedom to travel to the West (at a time when Soviet citizens were despatched to the gulag for ever having spoken to a foreigner). With his uncanny talent for writing tunes, Prokofiev was commissioned to compose numerous scores for the Soviet stage and screen, including his *Lieutenant Kije* suite (1934) and *Romeo and Juliet* (1935–6). Prizes followed – he was awarded the prestigious Stalin Prize on no less than five occasions between 1942 and 1949 – and even though he knew that they were window-dressing, he was flattered by the recognition of his native land.

Still, in spite of all the accolades, Prokofiev's working life at home became steadily more difficult. Attacked as a 'formalist' in the campaign which began, in 1936, with the suppression of Shostakovich's opera *Lady Macbeth of Mtsensk*, Prokofiev retreated by turning his attention to music for the young: *Peter and the Wolf* (1936) is a product (and perhaps an allegory) of the Terror years (the hunt for the wolf has overtones of the assault on the 'enemies of the people'). Many of his more experimental works remained unperformed: the huge *Cantata for the Twentieth Anniversary of the October Revolution* (1937); the music for Meyerhold's 1937 Pushkin centenary production of *Boris Godunov*; even the opera *War and Peace* was not staged in Russia (in its final version) until 1959. After 1948, when Zhdanov renewed the Stalinist assault against the 'formalists', nearly all the music which Prokofiev had written in Paris and New York was banned from the Soviet concert repertory.

Prokofiev spent his last years in virtual seclusion. Like Shostakovich, he turned increasingly to the intimate domain of chamber music, where he could find expression for his private sadness. The most moving of all these works is the Violin Sonata in D Major (ironically awarded the Stalin Prize in 1947). Prokofiev told the violinist David Oistrakh that its haunting opening movement was meant to sound 'like the wind in a graveyard'.[131] Oistrakh played the sonata at Prokofiev's funeral, a sad affair that was scarcely noticed by the Soviet public. Stalin had died on the same day as Prokofiev, 5 March 1953. There were no flowers left to buy, so a single pine branch was placed on the composer's grave.

Tsvetaeva returned to live with Efron and their son and daughter in a *dacha* near Moscow in 1939. Having hoped to rediscover the sort of writers' circles that she had left behind nearly twenty years before, it was a shock to find herself almost completely isolated on her return to Russia. As Nadezhda Mandelstam recalled, under Stalin 'it had become a matter of second nature to ignore people who had returned from the West'.[132] Everything about Tsvetaeva made her dangerous to know – or be seen to know. She seemed alien and outmoded, a figure of the past, from another world. Few people recalled her poetry.

Two months after their return, Tsvetaeva's daughter Alya was arrested and accused of spying for the Western powers in league with the Trotskyites. Shortly after, they arrested Efron as well. Tsvetaeva joined the women in the prison queues whose dreadful burden was recorded by Akhmatova. Tsvetaeva never saw her husband or daughter again. She did not even find out what had become of them.* With her son, she was taken in by Efron's sister in Moscow. Thin and exhausted, her face grey and colourless, she scraped a living by translating poetry. Finally, after Pasternak had come to her aid, she moved to a village near the writers' colony at Golitsyno, on the road between Moscow and Minsk, where she found a job as a dishwasher and was allowed to take her meals. Some of the older writers there still recalled her poetry and treated her with a respect bordering on awe. But from the viewpoint of official Soviet literature Tsvetaeva had ceased to exist long ago. Her last book in Russia had been published in 1922 – and in the climate of 1939 there was very little chance that her poems would be published there again. She submitted a collection of her verse to the state publishers in 1940, but instead of her more patriotic or civic verse she chose to include many of her poems from the period when Efron was fighting for the Whites. Unsurprisingly, the collection was turned down as anti-Soviet. It was typical of Tsvetaeva's wilful refusal to compromise. She was incapable of reining herself in, even if at the risk of disaster for herself. She could not come to terms with the age in which she was compelled to live.

Shortly before she left France, Tsvetaeva had told a friend that, if she could not write in the Soviet Union, she would kill herself.

---

* Alya served eight years in a labour camp. Efron was shot in 1941.

Tsvetaeva was increasingly fixated on the idea of her suicide. She had often used it as a threat. After 1940 she wrote little verse, and the few lines that she wrote were full of death:

> It's time to take off the amber,
> It's time to change the language,
> It's time to extinguish the lantern
> Above the door.[133]

Her last poem, written in March 1941, was addressed to the young and handsome poet Arseny Tarkovsky (the father of the future film director), with whom she had been in love. It was a ghostly refrain which spoke about her own sense of abandonment, not just by Tarkovsky, but by all those unnamed friends whom she referred to here as the 'six souls':

> I am no one: not a brother, not a son, not a husband,
> Not a friend – and still I reproach you:
> You who set the table for six – *souls*
> But did not seat me at the table's end.[134]

Tsvetaeva's son Mur was her last hope and emotional support. But the teenager was struggling to break free from his mother's suffocating hold. In August 1941, as the Germans swept through Russia towards Moscow, the two were evacuated to the small town of Elabuga, in the Tatar republic near Kazan. They rented half a room in a little wooden house. Tsvetaeva had no means of support. On Sunday 30 August her landlords and her son went off fishing for the day. While they were away she hanged herself. She left a note for Mur:

Murlyga! Forgive me, but to go on would be worse. I am gravely ill, this is not me anymore. I love you passionately. Do understand that I could not live anymore. Tell Papa and Alya, if you ever see them, that I loved them to the last moment and explain to them that I found myself in a trap.[135]

Tsvetaeva was buried in an unmarked grave. Nobody attended her funeral, not even her son.

6

In 1962 Stravinsky accepted a Soviet invitation to visit the country of his birth. It was exactly fifty years since he had left Russia and there was a complicated tangle of emotions behind his decision to return. As an émigré he had always given the impression of violently rejecting his own Russian past. He told his close friend and musical assistant, the conductor Robert Craft, that he thought about his childhood in St Petersburg as a 'period of waiting for the moment when I could send everyone and everything connected with it to hell'.[136] Much of this antipathy was an émigré's reaction to the Soviet regime, which had rejected his music and deprived the composer of his native land. The mere mention of the Soviet Union was enough to send him into a rage. In 1957, when a hapless German waiter came up to his table and asked if he was proud of the Russians because of the recent Sputnik breakthrough into space, Stravinsky became 'furious in equal measure with the Russians for having done it and with the Americans for not having done it'.[137]

He was particularly scathing about the Soviet musical academy, where the spirit of the Rimsky-Korsakovs and Glazunovs who had howled abuse at *The Rite of Spring* was still alive and kicking against the modernists. 'The Soviet virtuoso has no literature beyond the nineteenth century,' Stravinsky told a German interviewer in 1957. Soviet orchestras, if asked to perform the music of Stravinsky or 'the three Viennese' (Schoenberg, Berg and Webern) would be 'unable to cope with the simplest problems of rhythmic execution that we introduced to music fifty years ago'.[138] His own music had been banned from the Soviet concert repertory since the beginning of the 1930s, when Stravinsky was denounced by the Soviet musical establishment as 'an artistic ideologist of the Imperialist bourgeoisie'.[139] It was a sort of musical Cold War.

But after Stalin's death the climate changed. The Khrushchev 'thaw' had brought an end to the Zhdanovite campaign against the so-called 'formalists' and had restored Shostakovich to his rightful place at the head of the Soviet musical establishment. Young composers were emerging who took inspiration from Stravinsky's work

(Edison Denisov, Sofya Gubaidulina and Alfred Schnittke). A brilliant generation of Soviet musicians (Oistrakh, Richter, Rostropovich, the Beethoven Quartet) was becoming well known through recordings and tours in the West. Russia, in short, appeared to be returning to the centre of the European music world – the place it had occupied when Stravinsky had left in 1912.

Despite his own denials, Stravinsky had always regretted the circumstances of his exile from Russia. He bore the severance from his past like an open wound. The fact that he turned eighty in 1962 must have played a part in his decision to return. As he grew older, he thought more of his own childhood. He often slipped into childish Russian phrases and diminutives. He re-read the books he had read in Russia – like Gorky's *Mother*. 'I read it when it was first published [in 1906] and am trying again now,' he told Craft, 'probably because I want to go back into myself.'[140] Stravinsky told the US press that his decision to go to the Soviet Union was 'due primarily to the evidence I have received of a genuine desire or need for me by the younger generation of Russian musicians'.[141] Perhaps there was a desire on Stravinsky's part to secure his legacy in the country of his birth. Yet, despite his claims that nostalgia played no role in his intended visit, that sentiment was surely at its heart. He wanted to see Russia before he died.

On 21 September 1962, the Stravinskys landed in a Soviet plane at Sheremetevo. Straining to catch a glimpse of the forests turning yellow, the meadows, fields and lakes as the plane came in to land, Stravinsky was choking with excitement and emotion, according to Craft, who accompanied the couple throughout their trip. When the plane came to a halt and the hatch was opened, Stravinsky emerged and, standing at the top of the landing stairs, bowed down low in the Russian tradition. It was a gesture from another age, just as Stravinsky's sunglasses, which now protected him from the television lights, symbolized another kind of life in Hollywood. As he descended, Stravinsky was surrounded by a large welcoming committee, out of which emerged Maria Yudina, a stout woman with Tatar eyes (or so it seemed to Craft) who introduced herself to the composer as his niece. Also there was the daughter of Konstantin Balmont, the poet who had introduced Stravinsky to the ancient pagan world of *The Firebird* and *The Rite of Spring*. She presented Craft with a 'birch-bark basket containing a twig, a leaf, a blade of wheat, an acorn, some moss, and other souvenirs of the Russian earth' which the young American did 'not greatly need at that moment'. For these two women a lifelong dream was coming true. Craft compared the atmosphere to a child's birthday party: 'everyone, not least I.S. [Stravinsky] himself, is bursting with relief'.[142]

The trip released a huge outpouring of emotion in Stravinsky. In the fifteen years that Robert Craft had known him he had never realized how important Russia was to the composer, or how much of it was still inside his heart. 'Only two days ago, in Paris, I would have denied that I.S. . . . . could ever be at home here again . . . Now I see that half a century of expatriation can be, whether or not it has been, forgotten in a night.'[143] It was not to the Soviet Union that Stravinsky had returned, but to Russia. When Khrennikov, the head of the Soviet Composers' Union, met him at the airport, Stravinsky refused to shake hands with the old Stalinist and offered him his walking stick instead.[144] The next day, the Stravinskys drove with Craft to the Sparrow Hills, from where Napoleon had first surveyed Moscow, and as they looked down on the city, they were, Craft thought, 'silent and more moved than I have ever seen them'.[145] At the Novodeviche monastery the Stravinskys were visibly 'disturbed not for any religious or political reason but simply because the Novodeviche is the Russia that they knew, the Russia that is still a part of them'. Behind the ancient walls of the monastery was an island of old Russia. In the gardens women in black kerchiefs and worn-out coats and shoes were tending the graves, and in the church a priest was leading a service where, as it seemed to Craft, the 'more fervent members [of the congregation] lie kow-tow, in the totally prostrate position that I.S. used to assume during his own devotions in the Russian Church in Hollywood'.[146] Despite all the turmoil that the Soviet Union had gone through, there were still some Russian customs that remained unchanged.

The same was true of the musical tradition, as Robert Craft found out when he rehearsed the Moscow National Orchestra in the Tchaikovsky Hall of the Conservatory for a performance of *The Rite of Spring*.

The orchestral ensemble is good, quick to adopt my alien demands of phrasing and articulation, and harder-working than European orchestras in general.

The *Sacre*, played with an emotion I can describe only as non-Gallic and un-Teutonic, is an entirely different piece. The sound does not glitter as it does with American orchestras, and it is less loud, though still deafening in this very live room . . . This sobriety is very much to I.S.'s taste . . . Another satisfying oddity is the bass drum, which is open on one side as if sawed in two; the clear, *secco* articulation from the single head makes the beginning of *Danse de la terre* sound like the stampede I.S. says he had in mind . . . I.S. notes that the bassoon timbre is different than in America, and that 'The five *fagiotti* at the end of the *Evocation des ancêtres* sound like the *cinq vieillards* I had imagined.'[147]

Stravinsky took delight in this distinct orchestral sound. It brought his Russian ballets back to life.

He also rejoiced in his rediscovery of spoken Russian. From the moment he arrived back on Russian soil he slipped easily into modes of speech and conversation, using terms and phrases, even long-forgotten childhood expressions, he had not employed for over fifty years. When he spoke in Russian, he had always seemed to Craft 'a different person'; but now, 'speaking it with musicians who call him "Igor Fedorovich" which quickly established that family feeling peculiar to Russians – he is more buoyant than I can remember him'.[148] Craft was struck by the transformation in Stravinsky's character. Asked whether he believed that he was now seeing 'the true Stravinsky', the American replied that 'all I.S.s are true enough . . . but my picture of him is finally being given its background, which does wash out a great deal of what I had supposed to be "traits of character" or personal idiosyncrasies'.[149] Craft wrote that, as a result of the visit to Russia, his ear became attuned to the Russian elements of Stravinsky's music during the post-Russia years. The Russianness of Stravinsky's later compositions is not immediately obvious. But it is there – in the rhythmic energy and the chant-like melodies. From the *Symphony of Psalms* to the *Requiem* (1966) his musical language retains a Russian core.[150] As he himself explained to the Soviet press:

I have spoken Russian all my life, I think in Russian, my way of expressing myself is Russian. Perhaps it may not be noticeable in my music on a first hearing, but it is inherent in my music and part of its hidden character.[151]

There was much of Russia in Stravinsky's heart. It was made up of more than the icons in his house, the books he read, or the favourite childhood spoon from which he ate. He retained a physical sensation and memory of the land, Russian habits and customs, Russian ways of speech and social interaction, and all these feelings came flooding back to him from the moment he set foot on his native soil. A culture is more than a tradition. It cannot be contained in a library, let alone the 'eight slim volumes' which the exiles packed up in their bags. It is something visceral, emotional, instinctive, a sensibility that shapes the personality and binds that person to a people and a place. The Western public saw Stravinsky as an exile visiting the country of his birth. The Russians recognized him as a Russian coming home.

Stravinsky barely knew Moscow. He had only been there once on a short day trip sixty years or so before.[152] His return to Petersburg, the city of his birth, was even more emotional. At the airport the Stravinskys were welcomed by an elderly gentleman who began to weep. Craft recalls the encounter:

It is Vladimir Rimsky-Korsakov [the son of the composer], and I.S. has failed to recognize him, for the given reason that he has a moustache instead of, as when last seen (1910), a beard; but the real reason, I.S. tells me later, is that 'He said "Igor Fedorovich" instead of "Gima"'. He always called us, me and my brother, "Gury and Gima".'[153]

In the few days since arriving in Russia Stravinsky had stepped back some fifty years. His face rippled with pleasure on recognizing the Marinsky Theatre (at that time renamed the Kirov) where, as a boy, he had sat in his father's box and watched the ballet. He remembered the winged cupids in the box, the ornate blue and gold decoration of the auditorium, the glittering chandeliers, the richly perfumed audience, and on one occasion, in 1892, as he had stepped out of the box into the foyer at a gala performance of Glinka's *Ruslan and Liudmila* (in which his father had sung the role of Farlaf), catching sight of Tchaikovsky, all white-haired at the age of fifty-two.[154] Stravinsky had practically grown up in the Marinsky Theatre. It was only a few yards from his family's apartment on the Kryukov Canal. When they went to see the house where he had lived for the first twenty-four years of his life, Stravinsky displayed no emotion. But, as he explained to Craft, it was only because 'I could not let myself'.[155] Every building was '*chudno*' (magical) or '*krasivo*' (beautiful). The queue for the concert in Stravinsky's honour at the Great Hall of the Philharmonia was a living monument to the role of art in Russia and his own place in that sacred tradition: the queue had begun a year before and had developed as a complex social system, with people taking turns to stand in the line for a large block of seats. An 84-year-old cousin of Stravinsky was forced to watch the concert on the television because her number in the queue was 5001.[156]

'Where is Shostakovich?' Stravinsky kept asking from the moment he arrived. While Stravinsky was in Moscow, Shostakovich was in Leningrad; and just as Stravinsky went to Leningrad, Shostakovich returned to Moscow. 'What is the matter with this Shostakovich?' Stravinsky asked Khachaturian. 'Why does he keep running away from me?'[157] As an artist Shostakovich worshipped Stravinsky. He was his secret muse. Underneath the glass of his working desk Shostakovich kept two photographs: one of himself with the Beethoven Quartet; the other, a large portrait of Stravinsky.[158] Although he never expressed any public sympathy for Stravinsky's music, its influence is clear on many of his works (such as the *Petrushka* motif in the Tenth Symphony, or the adagio of the Seventh Symphony, which is clearly reminiscent of Stravinsky's *Symphony of Psalms*).

The Khrushchev thaw was a huge release for Shostakovich. It enabled him to re-establish links with the classical tradition of St Petersburg where he and Stravinsky had been born. Not that his life was entirely trouble-free. The Thirteenth Symphony (1962), based on Yevgeny Yevtushenko's poem *Babi Yar* (1961), was attacked by the Party (which tried to prevent its first performance) for supposedly belittling the suffering of the Russians in the war by focusing attention on the Nazi massacre of the Jews in Kiev. But otherwise the thaw was a creative spring for Shostakovich. He returned to his teaching post at the Leningrad Conservatory. His music was widely performed. He was honoured with official prizes and allowed to travel abroad extensively. Some of his most sublime music was composed in the last years of his life – the last three string quartets and the Viola Sonata, a personal requiem and artistic summing-up of his own life which was completed a month before his death on 9 August 1975. He even managed to find time to write two film scores – *Hamlet* (1964) and *King Lear* (1971) – commissioned by his old friend, the film director Grigory Kozintsev, for whom Shostakovich had written his first film score in 1929. Much of the music he composed in these years found its inspiration in the European heritage of Petersburg which had been lost in 1917. In his private world Shostakovich lived in literature. His conversation was full of literary allusions and expressions from the classic Russian novels of the nineteenth century. He loved the satires of Gogol and the stories of Chekhov. He felt a particularly close affinity for Dostoevsky which he was careful to conceal – until the final years, when he composed a song cycle based on the 'Four Verses of Captain Lebyadkin' from *The Devils*. Shostakovich once confessed that he had always dreamed of composing work on Dostoevsky's themes, but that he had always been 'too frightened' to do so. 'I love him and admire him as a great artist', Shostakovich wrote. 'I admire his love for the Russian people, for the humiliated and the wretched.'[159]

Shostakovich and Stravinsky met at last in Moscow, at the Metropole Hotel, where a banquet for Stravinsky was being laid on by the Minister of Culture, Ekaterina Furtseva (whom Shostakovich called 'Catherine the Third'). The meeting was neither a reunion nor a reconciliation of the two Russias that had gone their separate ways in 1917. But it was a symbol of a cultural unity which in the end would triumph over politics. The two composers lived in separate worlds but their music kept a single Russian beat. 'It was a very tense meeting', Khachaturian recalls:

They were placed next to each other and sat in complete silence. I sat opposite them. Finally Shostakovich plucked up the courage and opened the conversation:

'What do you think of Puccini?'

'I can't stand him,' Stravinsky replied.

'Oh, and neither can I, neither can I,' said Shostakovich.[160]

That was virtually all the two men said. But at a second banquet at the Metropole, the evening before Stravinsky left, they resumed their conversation and a dialogue of sorts was established. It was a memorable occasion – one of those quintessentially 'Russian' events which are punctuated by a regular succession of increasingly expansive vodka toasts – and soon, as Craft recalled, the room was turned into a 'Finnish bath, in whose vapours everyone, proclaiming and acclaiming each other's Russianness, says almost the same thing ... Again and again, each one abases himself before the mystery of their Russianness, and so, I realize with a shock, does I.S., whose replies are soon overtaking the toasts.' In a perfectly sober speech – he was the least alcoholically elevated of anyone in the room – Stravinsky proclaimed:

'The smell of the Russian earth is different, and such things are impossible to forget ... A man has one birthplace, one fatherland, one country – he *can* have only one country – and the place of his birth is the most important factor in his life. I regret that circumstances separated me from my fatherland, that I did not give birth to my works here and, above all, that I was not here to help the new Soviet Union create its new music. I did not leave Russia of my own will, even though I disliked much in my Russia and in Russia generally. Yet the right to criticize Russia is mine, because Russia is mine and because I love it, and I do not give any foreigner that right.'[161]

He meant every word.

Notes

References to archives in the notes are as follows:

AG   Gorky Archive, Institute of World Literature, Moscow
GARF   State Archive of the Russian Federation, Moscow
IRL RAN   Institute of Russian Literature, Russian Academy of Sciences, St Petersburg
RGASPI   Russian State Archive of Social and Political History
RGIA   Russian State Historical Archives, St Petersburg
SP-PLMD   St Petersburg Public Library, Manuscript Division
TsGADA   Central State Archive of Ancient Acts, Moscow

INTRODUCTION

1. L. Tolstoy, *War and Peace*, trans. L. and A. Maude (Oxford, 1998), p. 546.
2. See, for example, E. Khvoshchinskaia, 'Vospominaniia', *Russkaia starina*, vol. 93 (1898), p. 581. This subject is discussed in chapter 2.
3. L. Tolstoi, *Polnoe sobranie sochinenii*, 91 vols. (Moscow, 1929–64), vol. 16, p. 7.
4. See the brilliant essay by Richard Taruskin, 'N. A. Lvov and the Folk', in his *Defining Russia Musically: Historical and Hermeneutical Essays* (Princeton, 1997), pp. 3–24.
5. A. S. Famintsin, *Domra i rodnye ei muzykal'nye instrumenty russkogo naroda* (St Petersburg, 1891).
6. V. Nabokov, *Speak, Memory* (Harmondsworth, 1969), p. 35.

1 EUROPEAN RUSSIA

1. S. Soloviev, *Istoriia Rossii ot drevneishikh vremen*, 29 vols. (Moscow, 1864–79), vol. 14, p. 1270.

2. 'Peterburg v 1720 g. Zapiski poliaka-ochevidtsa', *Russkaia starina*, 25 (1879), p. 265.

3. *Peterburg petrovskogo vremeni* (Leningrad, 1948), p. 22; 'Opisanie Sanktpeterburga i Kronshlota v 1710-m i 1711-m gg.', in *Russkaia starina*, 25 (1879), p. 37.

4. A. Darinskii, *Istoriia Sankt-Peterburga* (St Petersburg, 1999), p. 26. This gives a figure of 150,000 workers, but excludes soldiers and Swedish prisoners-of-war.

5. A. S. Pushkin, *Polnoe sobranie sochinenii*, 17 vols. (Moscow, 1937–49), vol. 5, p. 436.

6. A. Bulak and N. Abakumova, *Kamennoe ubranstvo tsentra Leningrada* (Leningrad, 1987), pp. 4–11.

7. Ia. Zembnitskii, *Ob upotreblenii granita v Sankt-Peterburge* (St Petersburg, 1834), p. 21.

8. O. Monferran, *Svedeniia o dobyvanii 36-ti granitnykh kolonn, naznachen-nykh dlia portikov Isaakievskogo sobora* (St Petersburg, 1820), pp. 18ff.

9. S. Alopeus, *Kratkoe opisanie mramornykh i drugikh kamennykh lomok, gor i kamennykh porod, nakhodiashchikhsia v rossiiskoi Karelii* (St Petersburg, 1787), pp. 35–6; V. P. Sobolevskii, 'Geognosticheskoe obozrenie staroi Finliandii i opisanie ruskol'skikh mramornykh lomok', *Gornyi zhurnal* (1839), kn. 2–6, pp. 72–3.

10. *Journey for Our Time: The Journals of the Marquis de Custine*, trans. P. Penn Kohler (London, 1953), p. 110.

11. G. Kaganov, *Images of Space: St Petersburg in the Visual and Verbal Arts*, trans. S. Monas (Stanford, 1997), p. 15.

12. 'Peterburg v 1720 g. Zapiski poliaka-ochevidtsa', p. 267.

13. S. Luppov, *Istoriia stroitel'stva Peterburga v pervoi chetverti XVIII veka* (Moscow–Leningrad, 1957), p. 48; *Ocherki istorii Leningrada*, vol. 1, *Period feodalizma* (Moscow–Leningrad, 1955), p. 116.

14. *Letters to Lord Harvey and the Marquis Scipio Maffei, containing the state of the trade, marine, revenues, and forces of the Russian empire: with the history of the late war between the Russians and the Turks* (Glasgow, 1770), p. 76.

15. A. I. Gertsen, 'Moskva i Peterburg', *Polnoe sobranie sochinenii*, 30 vols. (Moscow, 1954), vol. 2, p. 36.

16. A. Benua, 'Zhivopisnyi Peterburg', *Mir iskusstva*, vol. 7, no. 2. (1902), p. 1.

17. F. Dostoevsky, *Notes from Underground. The Double*, trans. J. Coulson (Harmondsworth, 1972), p. 17.

18. L. E. Barry and R. O. Crumney (eds.), *Rude and Barbarous Kingdom: Russia in the Accounts of Sixteenth-century English Voyagers* (Madison, Wisc., 1968), p. 83.

19. L. Hughes, *Russia in the Age of Peter the Great* (New Haven, 1998), p. 317.

20. Benua, 'Zhivopisnyi Peterburg', p. 1.

21. *Journey for Our Time*, p. 97.

22. Cited in N. P. Antsiferov, *Dusha Peterburga* (Petrograd, 1922), p. 98.

23. Hughes, *Russia in the Age of Peter the Great*, p. 222.

24. *Peterburg i drugye novye rossiiskie goroda XVIII-pervoi poloviny XIX vekov* (Moscow, 1995), p. 168.

25. 'Shards' (1952), in *The Complete Poems of Anna Akhmatova*, trans. J. Hemschemeyer (Edinburgh, 1992), p. 701.

26. B. M. Matveev and A. V. Krasko, *Fontanny dom* (St Petersburg, 1996), p. 16.

27. *The Travels of Olearius in Seventeenth-century Russia*, ed. and trans. S. Baron (Stanford, 1967), p. 155.

28. *Yasnaya Polyana. Putevoditel'* (Moscow–Leningrad, 1928), pp. 10–12.

29. *The Travels of Olearius in Seventeenth-century Russia*, p. 131.

30. S. Collins, *The Present State of Russia: In a Letter to a Friend at London* (London, 1671), p. 68.

31. P. Roosevelt, *Life on the Russian Country Estate: A Social and Cultural History* (New Haven, 1995), p. 12.

32. N. Chechulin, *Russkoe provintsial'noe obshchestvo vo vtoroi polovine XVIII veka* (St Petersburg, 1889), p. 35.

33. Ia. Tolmachev, *Voennoe krasnorechie, osnovannoe na obshchikh nachalakh slovesnosti*, chast' 2 (St Petersburg, 1825), p. 120.

34. E. Lavrent'eva, *Svetskii etiket pushkinskoi pory* (Moscow, 1999), pp. 23, 25.

35. Iu. Lotman, *Besedy o russkoi kul'ture; byt i traditsii russkogo dvorianstva XVIII-nachalo XIX veka* (St Petersburg, 1994), p. 31.

36. *Zhizn', anekdoty, voennye i politicheskie deianiia rossiiskogo general-fel'd-marshala grafa Borisa Petrovicha Sheremeteva* (St Petersburg, 1808), p. 182.

37. V. Staniukevich, *Biudzhet sheremetevykh (1798–1910)* (Moscow, 1927), pp. 19–20; G. Mingay, *English Landed Society in the Eighteenth Century* (London, 1963), pp. 10ff.

38. Staniukevich, *Biudzhet sheremetevykh*, p. 17.

39. V. S. Dediukhina, 'K voprosu o roli krepostnykh masterov v istorii stroitelstva dvorianskoi usad'by XVIIIv. (na primere Kuskovo i Ostankino)', *Vestnik moskovskogo gosudarstvennogo universiteta (Istoriia)*, ser. 8, 4 (1981), p. 85.

40. Staniukevich, *Biudzhet sheremetevykh*, p. 10; Matveev and Krasko, *Fontanny Dom*, p. 55; B. and J. Harley, *A Gardener in Chatsworth: Three Years in the Life of Robert Aughtie (1848–1850)* (n.p., 1992).

41. *Memoirs of Louis Philippe Comte de Ségur*, ed. E. Cruickshanks (London, 1960), p. 238.

42. *Zapiski Dmitriia Nikolaevicha Sverbeeva*, 2 vols. (St Petersburg, 1899), vol. 1, p. 48.

43. V. V. Selivanov, *Sochineniia* (Vladimir, 1901), pp. 25, 35.

44. M. D. Priselkov, 'Garderob vel'mozhi kontsa XVIII-nach. XIX v.v.', in *Zapiski istoriko-bytovogo otdela gosudarstvennogo russkogo muzeia*, 1 (Leningrad, 1928), pp. 107–15.

45. N. Sindalovskii, *Peterburgskii fol'klor* (St Petersburg, 1994), pp. 149, 281.

46. L. D. Beliaev, 'Zagranichnye zakupki grafa P. B. Sheremeteva za 1770–1788 gg.', in *Zapiski istoriko-bytovogo otdela gosudarstvennogo russkogo muzeia*, vyp. 1 (Leningrad, 1928), p. 86.

47. Matveev and Krasko, *Fontanny dom*, pp. 27, 29, 35–6.

48. As above, p. 38.

49. A. Chenevière, *Russian Furniture: The Golden Age, 1780–1840* (New York, 1988), pp. 89–93, 122–3; E. Beskin, *Krepostnoi teatr* (Moscow, 1927), p. 12.

50. L. Lepskaia, *Repertuar krepostnogo teatra Sheremetevykh* (Moscow, 1996), pp. 26, 31, 39; N. Elizarova, *Teatry Sheremetevykh* (Moscow, 1944), pp. 30–32.

51. E. Beskin, *Krepostnoi teatr* (Moscow, 1927), pp. 13–14.

52. V. K. Staniukevich, 'Krepostnye khudozhniki Sheremetevykh. K dvukhsotletiiu so dnia rozhdeniia Ivana Argunova', in *Zapiski istoriko-bytovogo otdela*, pp. 133–65.

53. S. D. Sheremetev, *Otgoloski VIII veka*, vyp. 11, *Vremia Imperatora Pavla, 1796–1800* (Moscow, 1905), pp. 15, 142, 293.

54. As above, p. 161.

55. Lepskaia, *Repertuar krepostnogo teatra Sheremetevykh*, p. 24.

56. See the medical reports in Lepskaia, *Repertuar krepostnogo teatra Sheremetevykh*, pp. 21–9.

57. RGIA, f. 1088, op. 1, d.68, l. 3.

58. P. Bessonov, *Praskovia Ivanovna Sheremeteva, ee narodnaia pesnia i rodnoe ee Kuskovo* (Moscow, 1872), pp. 43, 48; K. Bestuzhev, *Krepostnoi teatr* (Moscow, 1913), pp. 62–3.

59. Sheremetev, *Otgoloski VIII veka*, vyp. 11, pp. 102, 116, 270. See also Roosevelt, *Life on the Russian Country Estate*, p. 108.

60. As above, p. 283.

61. S. T. Aksakov, *The Family Chronicle*, trans. M. Beverley (Westport, Conn., 1985), pp. 55–62.

62. See, for example, Selivanov, *Sochineniia*, p. 37; N. D. Bashkirtseva, 'Iz ukrainskoi stariny. Moia rodoslovnaia', *Russkii arkhiv* (1900), vol. 1, no. 3, p. 350.

63. 'Zapiski Ia. M. Neverova', *Russkaia starina* (1883), vol. 11, pp. 429ff. For more on Koshkarov see Roosevelt, *Life on the Russian Country Estate*, pp. 183–7.

64. Lepskaia, *Repertuar krepostnogo teatra Sheremetevykh*, pp. 37–8.

65. Bestuzhev, *Krepostnoi teatr*, pp. 66–70.

66. Lepskaia, *Repertuar krepostnogo teatra Sheremetevykh*, p. 42; Sheremetev, *Otgoloski VIII veka*, vyp. 4 (Moscow, 1897), p. 12.

67. Sheremetev, *Otgoloski VIII veka*, vyp. 4, p. 14.

68. Sheremetev, *Otgoloski VIII veka*, vyp. 11, *Vremia Imperatora Pavla, 1796–1800*, p. 322; Matveev and Krasko, *Fontanny dom*, p. 45.

69. 'Iz bumag i perepiski grafa Nikolaia Petrovicha Sheremeteva', *Russkii arkhiv* (1896), no. 6, p. 189.

70. It can now be found in RGIA, f. 1088, op. 1, d. 65, l. 3.

71. 'Iz bumag i perepiski grafa Nikolaia Petrovicha Sheremeteva', p. 517.

72. RGIA, f. 1088, op. 1, d. 24, l. 4.

73. RGIA, f. 1088, op. 1, d. 24, ll. 6–7.

74. 'Iz bumag i perepiski grafa Nikolaia Petrovicha Sheremeteva', p. 515.

75. S. D. Sheremetev (ed.), *Otgoloski XVIII veka*, vyp. 2 (Moscow, 1896), pp. 10–11; Sheremetev, *Otgoloski XVIII veka*, vyp. 11, pp. 249, 277; RGIA, f. 1088, op. 1, d. 770, l. 27.

76. S. D. Sheremetev, *Strannoprimny dom sheremetevykh, 1810–1910* (Moscow, 1910), p. 22.

77. Sheremetev, *Otgoloski XVIII veka*, vyp. 2, p. 11.

78. 'Iz bumag i perepiski grafa Nikolaia Petrovicha Sheremeteva', p. 511.

79. RGIA, f. 1088, op. 1, d. 76, l. 11.

80. RGIA, f. 1088, op. 1, d. 24, l. 5.

81. RGIA, f. 1088, op. 1, dd. 770, 776, 780.

82. RGIA, f. 1088, op. 1, d. 79, ll. 1–8. I have edited the Russian text and made short cuts to make it comprehensible. It is published here for the first time.

83. D. Blagovo, 'Rasskazy babushki. Iz vospominanii piati pokolenii (Elizaveta Petrovna Iankova, 1768–1861)', in *Rasskazy babushki, zapisannye i sobrannye eio vnukom* (St Petersburg, 1885), p. 207.

84. Lepskaia, *Repertuar krepostnogo teatra Sheremetevykh*, p. 17; *Glinka v vospominaniiakh sovremennikov* (Moscow, 1955), p. 30.

85. Beskin, *Krepostnoi teatr*, p. 13.

86. Lepskaia, *Repertuar krepostnogo teatra Sheremetevykh*, pp. 19, 28–9.

87. As above, p. 23.

88. See Roosevelt, *Life on the Russian Country Estate*, pp. 130–32.

89. A. Pushkin, *Eugene Onegin*, trans. J. Falen (Oxford, 1990), p. 15.

90. *Iunosti chestnoe zertsalo* (St Petersburg, 1717), pp. 73–4.

91. Iu. Lotman, L. Ginsburg, B. Uspenskii, *The Semiotics of Russian Cultural History* (Ithaca, 1985), pp. 67–70.

92. Cited in Lavrent'eva, *Svetskii etiket pushkinskoi pory*, p. 228.

93. L. Tolstoy, *Childhood, Boyhood and Youth*, trans. L. and A. Maude (Oxford, 1969), p. 339.

94. E. Lansere, 'Fontanny dom (postroika i peredelki)', in *Zapiski istoriko-bytovogo otdela gosudarstvennogo russkogo muzeia*, vyp. 1 (Leningrad, 1928), p. 76.

95. Matveev and Krasko, *Fontanny dom*, p. 55.

96. I. A. Bogdanov, *Tri veka peterburgskoi bani* (St Petersburg, 2000), p. 59.

97. *Zapiski Iusta Iulia, datskogo poslannika pri Petre Velikom* (Moscow, 1899), p. 85.

98. See E. Levin, 'Childbirth in Pre-Petrine Russia: Canon Law and Popular Traditions', in B. Clements *et al.* (eds.), *Russia's Women. Accommodation, Resistance, Transformation* (Berkeley, 1991), especially pp. 44–51; and (for evidence of these same customs at a later time) T. Listova, 'Russian Rituals, Customs and Beliefs Associated with the Midwife (1850–1930)', in H. Balzer (ed.), *Russian Traditional Culture* (Armonk, N.Y. 1992), pp. 130–31.

99. Bogdanov, *Tri veka peterburgskoi bani*, p. 16.

100. *Memoirs of Louis Philippe Comte de Ségur*, pp. 236–7.

101. Pushkin, *Eugene Onegin*, p. 196.

102. *A. S. Pushkin v vospominaniiakh sovremennikov*, 2 vols. (Moscow, 1974), vol. 1, p. 63.

103. Cited in S. M. Volkonskii, *Moi vospominaniia*, 2 vols. (Moscow, 1992), vol. 1, p. 130.

104. A. Pushkin, *The Queen of Spades and Other Stories*, trans. R. Edmonds (Harmondsworth, 1962), p. 158.

105. V. V. Sipovskii, *Ocherki iz istorii russkogo romana* (St Petersburg, 1909), kn. 1, vyp. 1, p. 43.

106. See Karamzin's article of 1802, 'Otchego v Rossii malo avtorskikh talantov?', in *Sochineniia*, vol. 3, pp. 526–33.

107. *Pomeshchich'ia Rossiia po zapiskam sovremennikov* (Moscow, 1911), p. 134.

108. V. Vinogradov, *Ocherki po istorii russkogo literaturnogo iazyka XVII–XIX vv.* (Leiden, 1949), p. 239.

109. Pushkin, *Eugene Onegin*, p. 16.

110. Iu. Lotman and B. Uspenskii, ' "Pis'ma russkogo puteshestvennika" Karamzina i ikh mesto v razvitii russkoi kul'tury', in N. M. Karamzin, *Pis'ma russkogo puteshestvennika* (Leningrad, 1984), p. 598; N. Kheraskov, *Izbrannye proizvedeniia* (Moscow–Leningrad, 1961), p. 83.

111. L. Tolstoy, *War and Peace*, trans. L. and A. Maude (Oxford, 1998), p. 3.

112. Vinogradov, *Ocherki po istorii russkogo literaturnogo iazyka XVII–XIX vv.*, p. 239.

113. S. Karlinsky, *Russian Drama from Its Beginnings to the Age of Pushkin* (Berkeley, 1985), pp. 143–4.

114. *Rossiiskii featr*, 43 vols. (St Petersburg, 1786–94), vol. 10 (1786), p. 66.

115. *Rossiiskii featr*, vol. 16 (1787), p. 17; *Russkaia komediia XVIII veka* (Moscow–Leningrad, 1950), pp. 76–7.

116. D. I. Fonvizin, *Sobranie sochinenii*, 2 vols. (Moscow–Leningrad, 1959), vol. 1, pp. 77–8.

117. F. Dostoevsky, *A Writer's Diary*, trans. K. Lantz, 2 vols. (London, 1993), vol. 2, p. 986.

118. L. Tolstoy, *Anna Karenin*, trans. R. Edmonds (Harmondsworth, 1974), p. 34.

119. M. E. Saltykov-Shchedrin, *Polnoe sobranie sochinenii*, 20 vols. (Moscow, 1934–47), vol. 14, p. 111.

120. *Vospominaniia kniagini E. R. Dashkovoi* (Leipzig, n.d.), pp. 11, 32.

121. C. Sutherland, *The Princess of Siberia: The Story of Maria Volkonsky and the Decembrist Exiles* (London, 1984), pp. 172–3. See also Volkonskii, *Moi vospominaniia*, vol. 2, p. 20.

122. Tolstoy, *War and Peace*, p. 3.

123. E. Khvoshchinskaia, 'Vospominaniia', *Russkaia starina*, vol. 89 (1898), p. 518.

124. A. K. Lelong, 'Vospominaniia', *Russkii arkhiv* (1914), kn. 2, nos. 6/7, p. 393.

125. E. I. Raevskaia, 'Vospominaniia', *Russkii arkhiv* (1883), kn. 1, no. 1, p. 201.

126. Tolstoy, *Anna Karenin*, pp. 292–3.

127. V. Nabokov, *Speak, Memory* (Harmondsworth, 1967), p. 57.

128. A. Herzen, *My Past and Thoughts: The Memoirs of Alexander Herzen*, trans. C. Garnett (Berkeley, 1982), p. 242; J. Frank, *Dostoevsky: Seeds of Revolt, 1821–1849* (Princeton, 1977), pp. 42–3.

129. *Four Russian Plays*, trans. J. Cooper (Harmondsworth, 1972), p. 74.

130. 'Derevnia' ('The Village') in P. A. Viazemskii, *Izbrannye stikhotvoreniia* (Moscow–Leningrad, 1935), p. 123.

131. *Satiricheskie zhurnaly N. I. Novikova* (Moscow–Leningrad, 1951), pp. 65–7.

132. 'Neizdannye stikhi N. A. Lvova', *Literaturnoe nasledstvo*, nos. 9–10 (1933), p. 275.

133. A. Radishchev, *A Journey from St Petersburg to Moscow*, trans. L. Wiener (Cambridge, Mass., 1958), p. 131.

134. Pushkin, *Eugene Onegin*, p. 37.

135. Pushkin, *Polnoe sobranie sochinenii*, vol. 11, p. 249.

136. H. M. Hyde, *The Empress Catherine and the Princess Dashkov* (London, 1935), p. 107. Dashkova's *Journey* ('Puteshestvie odnoi rossiiskoi znatnoi gospozhi po nekotorym angliiskim provintsiiam') can be found in *Opyt trudov vol'nogo rossiiskogo sobraniia*, vyp. 2, (1775), pp. 105–45.

137. Lotman and Uspenskii, ' "Pis'ma russkogo puteshestvennika" Karamzina i ikh mesto v razvitii russkoi kul'tury', pp. 531–2.

138. N. M. Karamzin, *Pis'ma russkogo puteshestvennika* (Leningrad, 1984), pp. 12, 66. On French attitudes, see D. von Mohrenschildt, *Russia in the Intellectual Life of Eighteenth-century France* (Columbia, 1936), pp. 56–7.

139. Karamzin, *Pis'ma russkogo puteshestvennika*, p. 338.

140. Fonvizin, *Sobranie sochinenii*, vol. 2, pp. 449, 480.

141. See Mohrenschildt, *Russia in the Intellectual Life of Eighteenth-century France*, pp. 40, 46.

142. Fonvizin, *Sobranie sochinenii*, vol. 2, pp. 420, 439, 460, 476–7, 480–81, 485–6.

143. Karamzin, *Pis'ma russkogo puteshestvennika*, p. 243; A. P. Obolensky, *Food Notes on Gogol* (Machitoba, 1972), p. 109.

144. A. Nikitenko, *The Diary of a Russian Censor*, ed. and trans. H. Jacobson (Amherst, 1975), pp. 213–14.

145. R. Jakobson, 'Der russische Frankreich-Mythus', *Slavische Rundschau*, 3 (1931), pp. 639–40.

146. A. I. Gertsen, 'Dzhon-stiuart Mill' i ego kniga "On Liberty" ', in *Sobranie sochinenii*, 30 vols. (Moscow, 1954–65), vol. 11, p. 66.

147. Herzen, *My Past and Thoughts*, p. 97.

148. *Aglaia*, kn. 2 (1795), p. 68.

149. Karamzin, *Sochineniia*, vol. 3, p. 349.

150. As above, p. 444.

151. V. P. Semennikov (ed.), *Materialy dlia istorii russkoi literatury* (St Petersburg, 1914), p. 34.

152. Cited in H. Rogger, *National Consciousness in Eighteenth-century Russia* (Cambridge, Mass., 1960), p. 247.

153. Karamzin, *Sochineniia*, vol. 7, p. 198.

2 CHILDREN OF 1812

1. S. M. Volkonskii, *Zapiski* (St Petersburg, 1901), p. 193.

2. M. I. Murav'ev-Apostol, *Vospominaniia i pis'ma* (Petrograd, 1922), p. 178.

3. A. Bogdanov, *Skazanie o volkonskikh kniaz'iakh* (Moscow, 1989), pp. 4–5.

4. S. M. Volkonskii, *O dekabristakh: po semeinum vospominaniiam* (Moscow, 1994), p. 77.

5. Volkonskii, *Zapiski*, pp. 136–7. The three other aides-de-camp were Nikita and Nikolai Volkonsky (Sergei's two brothers) and Prince Peter Mikhailovich Volkonsky (his brother-in-law). General Paul Volkonsky was also to be found in the Emperor's intimate circle.

6. C. Sutherland, *The Princess of Siberia: The Story of Maria Volkonsky and the Decembrist Exiles* (London, 1984), p. 111.

7. RGIA, f. 844, op. 2, d. 42.

8. F. Glinka, *Pis'ma russkogo ofitsera* (Moscow, 1815), part 5, pp. 46–7, 199.

9. TsGADA, f. 1278, op. 1, d. 362, l. 183.

10. *Vosstanie dekabristov*, 11 vols. (Moscow, 1925–58), vol. 1, p. 267.

11. Volkonskii, *Zapiski*, p. 387.

12. IRL RAN, f. 57, op. 1, n. 9, ll. 1–9.

13. IRL RAN, f. 57, op. 1, n. 21, ll. 9–10.

14. N. P. Grot, *Iz semeinoi khroniki. Vospominaniia dlia detei i vnukov* (St Petersburg, 1900), pp. 1–8.

15. D. Davydov, *Sochineniia* (Moscow, 1962), p. 320.

16. Volkonskii, *Zapiski*, p. 327.

17. E. Lavrent'eva, *Svetskii etiket pushkinskoi pory* (Moscow, 1999), pp. 198, 290–91.

18. *Zapiski, stat'i, pis'ma dekabrista I. D. Iakushkina* (Moscow, 1951), p. 9.

19. 'To Chaadaev' (1821), in A. S. Pushkin, *Polnoe sobranie sochinenii*, 17 vols. (Moscow, 1937–49), vol. 7, p. 246.

20. A. Herzen, *My Past and Thoughts*, trans. C. Garnett (Berkeley, 1973), p. 68.

21. I. Vinogradov, 'Zapiski P. I. Vinogradova', *Russkaia starina*, vol. 22 (1878), p. 566.

22. F. F. Vigel', *Zapiski*, chast' 1 (Moscow, 1891), p. 159.

23. Lavrent'eva, *Svetskii etiket pushkinskoi pory*, p. 22.

24. N. Rimsky-Korsakov, *My Musical Life* (London, 1989), p. 9.

25. N. Gogol, *Diary of a Madman and Other Stories*, trans. R. Wilks (Harmondsworth, 1972), p. 32; A. Chekhov, 'Uprazdnili!', in *Polnoe sobranie sochinenii*, 30 vols. (Moscow, 1974–83), vol. 3, p. 226.

26. *The Complete Prose Tales of Alexander Sergeyevitch Pushkin*, trans. G. Aitken (London, 1966), p. 73.

27. Volkonskii, *Zapiski*, pp. 130–31.

28. N. A. Belogolovoi, *Vospominaniia i drugie stat'i* (Moscow, 1898), p. 70.

29. See Iu. Lotman, 'Dekabrist v povsednevnoi zhizni', in *Besedy o russkoi kul'ture: byt i traditsii russkogo dvorianstva XVIII-nachalo XIX veka* (St Petersburg, 1994), pp. 360–64.

30. 'To Kaverin', in Pushkin, *Polnoe sobranie sochinenii*, vol. 1, p. 238.

31. Volkonskii, *Zapiski*, p. 4.

32. L. Tolstoy, *War and Peace*, trans. L. and A. Maude (Oxford, 1998), pp. 417–18.

33. Ia. A. Galinkovskii, *Korifei ili kliuch literatury* (St Petersburg, 1802), kn. 2, p. 170.

34. 'The Time Has Come' (19 October 1836), in *The Complete Works of Alexander Pushkin*, 15 vols., ed. I. Sproat *et al.* (Norfolk, 1999), vol. 3, pp. 253–4.

35. Pushkin, *Polnoe sobranie sochinenii*, vol. 2, p. 425.

36. See his Letter No. 8 in 'A Novel in Letters' – written in 1829 but not published (and then with cuts) until 1857 – in Pushkin, *Polnoe sobranie sochinenii*, vol. 8, pp. 52–4.

37. *Vosstanie dekabristov*, vol. 7, p. 222.

38. *Syn otechestva* (1816), chast' 27, p. 161.

39. A. Bestuzhev, 'Pis'mo k N. A. i K. A. Polevym, 1 ianvaria 1832', *Russkii vestnik* (1861), vol. 32, p. 319.

40. Cited in A. Ulam, *Russia's Failed Revolutions: From the Decembrists to the Dissidents* (New York, 1981), p. 21.

41. IRL RAN, f. 57, op. 1, n. 63, l. 57.

42. Pushkin, *Polnoe sobranie sochinenii*, vol. 6, p. 525.

43. *Arkhiv dekabrista S. G. Volkonskogo*, t. 1., *Do sibiri* (Petrograd, 1918), p. 149.

44. Pushkin, *Polnoe sobranie sochinenii*, vol. 12, p. 303.

45. Volkonskii, *Zapiski*, p. 212.

46. As above, p. 402.

47. A. Pushkin, *Eugene Onegin*, trans. J. Falen (Oxford, 1990), p. 19.

48. Pushkin, *Polnoe sobranie sochinenii*, vol. 2, p. 72.

49. On Volkonsky's role in recruiting Pushkin, see S. M. Volkonskii, *O dekabristakh: po semeinum vospominaniiam* (Moscow, 1994), pp. 35–6.

50. Volkonskii, *Zapiski*, p. 434.

51. Ulam, *Russia's Failed Revolutions*, p. 44.

52. Volkonskii, *Zapiski*, p. 421.

53. GARF, f. 48, op. 1, d. 412, l. 19.

54. Ulam, *Russia's Failed Revolutions*, p. 5.

55. RGIA, f. 1405, op. 24, d. 1344, l. 12; GARF, f. 1146, op. 1, d. 2028, l. 6.

56. *Arkhiv dekabrista S. G. Volkonskogo*, pp. xix, xxiii.

57. IRL RAN, f. 57, op. 1, n. 61, l. 65.

58. GARF, f. 1146, op. 1, d. 2028, l. 7.

59. GARF, f. 1146, op. 1, d. 2028, l. 13.

60. 'Neizdannye pis'ma M. N. Volkonskoi', *Trudy gosudarstvennogo istoricheskogo muzeia*, vyp. 2 (Moscow, 1926), p. 16.

61. Cited in K. Bestuzhev, *Zheny dekabristov* (Moscow, 1913), p. 47.

62. Lotman, 'Dekabrist v povsednevnoi zhizni', pp. 352–3.

63. F. F. Vigel', *Zapiski*, chast' 1 (Moscow, 1891), p. 12.

64. K. Batiushkov, *Sochineniia* (Moscow–Leningrad, 1934), p. 373.

65. Lotman, 'Dekabrist v povsednevnoi zhizni', pp. 353–4.

66. K. Ryleev, *Polnoe sobranie stikhotvorenii* (Leningrad, 1971), p. 168.

67. GARF, f. 1146, op. 1, d. 2028, l. 12.

68. IRL RAN, f. 57, op. 5, n. 22, l. 88.

69. *The Complete Works of Alexander Pushkin*, vol. 3, p. 42.

70. GARF, f. 1146, op. 1, d. 2028, l. 28.

71. *Zapiski kniagini M. N. Volkonskoi* (Chita, 1960), p. 66.

72. As above, p. 67.

73. As above, p. 70.

74. *Arkhiv dekabrista S. G. Volkonskogo*, p. xxxi.

75. *Dekabristy. Letopisi gosudarstvennogo literaturnogo muzeia*, kn. 3 (Moscow, 1938), p. 354.

76. *Zapiski kniagini M. N. Volkonskoi* (Chita, 1960), p. 101.

77. Cited in Sutherland, *The Princess of Siberia*, p. 253.

78. M. P. Volkonskii, 'Pis'ma dekabrista S. G. Volkonskogo', *Zapiski otdela rukopisei*, vyp. 24 (Moscow, 1961), p. 399.

79. Volkonskii, *O dekabristakh*, p. 66.

80. *Dekabristy. Letopisi gosudarstvennogo literaturnogo muzeia*, pp. 91, 96, 100; Volkonskii, 'Pis'ma dekabrista S. G. Volkonskogo', pp. 369, 378, 384.

81. N. A. Belogolovoi, *Vospominaniia*, p. 36.

82. IRL RAN, f. 57, op. 1, n. 50, ll. 11–19.

83. IRL RAN, f. 57, op. 1, n. 63, l. 52.

84. IRL RAN, f. 57, op. 1, n. 65, l. 2.

85. IRL RAN, f. 57, op. 1, n. 97, l. 1.

86. Belogolovoi, *Vospominaniia*, p. 37.

87. Volkonskii, 'Pis'ma dekabrista S. G. Volkonskogo', p. 371.

88. As above, p. 372.

89. Volkonskii, *Zapiski*, p. 478.

90. Belogolovoi, *Vospominaniia*, p. 37.

91. Tolstoy, *War and Peace*, p. 582.

92. F. F. Vigel', *Zapiski*, chast' 2 (Moscow, 1892), p. 56.

93. RGIA, f. 1088, op. 1, d. 439.

94. N. S. Ashukin, *Pushkinskaia Moskva* (St Petersburg, 1998), p. 44.

95. S. L. Tolstoi, *Mat' i ded L. N. Tolstogo* (Moscow, 1928), p. 45.

96. Iu. Lotman, 'Zhenskii mir', in *Besedy o russkoi kul'ture*, p. 57.

97. Tolstoy, *War and Peace*, pp. 159, 898.

98. See, for example, RGIA, f. 1035, op. 1, d. 87, ll. 1–2, 14; f. 914, op. 1, d. 34, ll. 3–10 (esp. l. 5).

99. N. A. Reshetov, 'Delo davno minuvshikh dnei', *Russkii arkhiv* (1885), kn. 3, no. 11, pp. 443–5.

100. I. S. Zhirkevich, 'Zapiski', *Russkaia starina*, vol. 9 (1875), p. 237.

101. D. I. Zavaliashin, 'Vospominaniia o grafe A. I. Osterman-Tolstom (1770–1851)', *Istoricheskii vestnik* (1880), vol. 2, no. 5, pp. 94–5.

102. Lavrent'eva, *Svetskii etiket*, p. 321.

103. E. Khvoshchinskaia, 'Vospominaniia', *Russkaia starina* (1898), vol. 93, p. 581.

104. M. N. Khrushchev, 'Petr Stepanovich Kotliarevskii (otryvok iz vospominanii)', *Izvestiia tavricheskoi uchenoi arkhivnoi komissii*, no. 54 (1918), p. 298; K. A. Soloviev, 'V vkuse umnoi stariny'. *Usadebnyi byt rossiiskogo dvorianstva II poloviny VXIII – 1 poloviny XIX vekov* (St Petersburg, 1998), p. 30; V. V. Selivanov, *Sochineniia* (Vladimir, 1901), p. 151; S. M. Zagoskin, 'Vospominaniia', *Istoricheskii vestnik* (1900), vol. 79, no. 1, p. 611; V. N. Kharuzina, *Proshloe. Vospominaniia detskikh i otrocheskikh let* (Moscow, 1999), p. 312; N. P. Grot, *Iz semeinoi khroniki. Vospominaniya dlia detei i vnukov* (St Petersburg, 1900), pp. 58–9.

105. Tolstoy, *War and Peace*, p. 544.

106. Selivanov, *Sochineniia*, p. 78.

107. E. Mengden, 'Iz dnevnika vnuchki', *Russkaia starina*, vol. 153, no. 1, p. 105.

108. See, for example, *Pomeshchich'ia Rossia. Po zapiskam sovremennikov* (Moscow, 1911), pp. 61–2; N. V. Davydov, 'Ocherki byloi pomeshchechei zhizni', *Iz Proshlogo* (Moscow, 1914), p. 425; and the wonderful memoir of S. T. Aksakov, *The Family Chronicle*, trans. M. Beverley (Westport, Conn., 1985), especially p. 199.

109. I. Turgenev, *Sketches from a Hunter's Album*, trans. R. Freeborn (Harmondsworth, 1967), p. 247.

110. *Sharfy i shali russkoi raboty pervoi poloviny XIX v.* (Leningrad, 1981).

111. Sverbeev, *Zapiski, 1799–1826*, vol. 1, p. 415.

112. M. Fairweather, *The Pilgrim Princess: A Life of Princess Zinaida Volkonsky* (London, 1999), p. 36.

113. Iu. Lotman, 'Zhenskii mir', p. 52.

114. As above.

115. Pushkin, *Eugene Onegin*, p. 209.

116. As above, p. 232.

117. As above, p. 65.

118. As above, p. 167.

119. As above, p. 210.

120. W. M. Todd III, '*Eugene Onegin*: "Life's Novel"', in same author (ed.), *Literature and Society in Imperial Russia, 1800–1914* (Stanford, 1978), pp. 228–9.

121. M. Azadovskii, *Literatura i fol'klor* (Leningrad, 1938), pp. 89, 287–9.

122. Letter of 21 August 1831 in *Letters of Nikolai Gogol*, ed. and trans. C. Proffer (Ann Arbor, 1967), p. 38 (I have modified the translation).

123. *Mikhail Lermontov: Major Poetical Works*, trans. A. Liberman (London, 1984), p. 103.

124. See R. Taruskin, *Defining Russia Musically* (Princeton, 1997), pp. 41–7.

125. R. Taruskin, *Musorgsky: Eight Essays and an Epilogue* (Princeton, 1993), pp. 302–8.

126. Cited in Taruskin, *Defining Russia Musically*, p. 33.

127. *Aleksei Gavrilovich Venetsianov* (Leningrad, 1980), p. 13.

128. Selivanov, *Sochineniia*, p. 12. E. I. Stogov (1797–1880) gives a similar account of his upbringing in 'Zapiski E. I. Stogova', *Russkaia starina*, vol. 113 (1898), pp. 137–8.

129. V. A. Sollogub, *Otryvki iz vospominaniia* (St Petersburg, 1881), p. 7.

130. N. I. Shatilov, 'Iz nedavnego proshlogo', *Golos minuvshego* (1916), no. 4, p. 219.

131. See, for example, A. Labzina, *Vospominaniia* (St Petersburg, 1914), p. 9; A. N. Kazina, 'Zhenskaia zhizn', *Otechestvennye zapiski*, 219, no. 3 (1875), p. 211; E. Iunge, *Vospominaniia* (Moscow, 1933), p. 41.

132. L. Tolstoy, *Anna Karenin*, trans. R. Edmonds (Harmondsworth, 1974), p. 650.

133. Herzen, *My Past and Thoughts*, p. 26.

134. As above, pp. 32–3.

135. See, for example, A. K. Lelong, 'Vospominaniia', *Russkii arkhiv* (1913), kn. 2, chast' 6, p. 789.

136. Pushkin, *Eugene Onegin*, p. 115.

137. Lelong, 'Vospominaniia', pp. 794, 808. On village games, see I. I. Shangina, *Russkie deti i ikh igry* (St Petersburg, 2000).

138. Herzen, *My Past and Thoughts*, p. 26.

139. K. Grup, *Rukovodstvo k vospitaniiu, obrazovaniiu i sokhraneniiu zdorov'ia detei*, 3 vols. (St Petersburg, 1843), vol. 1, p. 63.

140. P. Sumarokov, *Stary i novy byt. Maiak sovremennogo prosveshcheniia i obrazovannosti* (St Petersburg, 1841), no. 16, p. 20.

141. Lelong, 'Vospominaniia', chast' 6, p. 788 and chast' 7, p. 99.

142. A. Tyrkova-Williams, *To, chego bol'she ne budet* (Paris, 1954), p. 38.

143. Lelong, 'Vospominaniia', chast' 6, p. 785.

144. A. K. Chertkova, *Iz moego detstva* (Moscow, 1911), p. 175.

145. A. V. Vereshchagin, *Doma i na voine* (St Petersburg, 1885), p. 48.

146. V. A. Tikhonov, 'Byloe (iz semeinoi khroniki)', *Istoricheskii vestnik*, vol. 79, no. 2 (1900), pp. 541–2; no. 3 (1990), pp. 948–9.

147. *Druz'ia Pushkina*, 2 vols. (Moscow, 1984), vol. 2, p. 117.

148. 'To My Nanny' (1826), in *The Complete Poems of Alexander Pushkin* 15 vols. (London, 1999–   ), vol. 3, p. 34.

149. S. Lifar, *Diagilev i s Diagilevym* (Moscow, 1994), pp. 17–19.

150. L. Tolstoy, *Childhood, Boyhood and Youth*, trans. L. and A. Maude (London, 1969), p. 58. On this canon, see A. Wachtel, *The Battle for Childhood: Creation of a Russian Myth* (Stanford, 1990).

151. Herzen, *My Past and Thoughts*, p. 10.

152. Lelong, 'Vospominaniia', chast' 6, pp. 792, 797.

153. *Pis'ma N. M. Karamzina k I. I. Dmitrievu* (St Petersburg, 1866), p. 168.

154. Pushkin, *Polnoe sobranie sochinenii*, vol. 11, p. 57.

155. V. G. Belinskii, *Polnoe sobranie sochinenii*, 13 vols. (Moscow, 1953–9), vol. 10, p. 18.

156. *Sochineniia i pis'ma P. Ia. Chaadaeva*, 2 vols. (Moscow, 1913–14), vol. 1, p. 188.

157. As above, pp. 74–92.

158. R. T. McNally, *Chaadayev and His Friends* (Tallahassee, Fla., 1971), p. 32.

159. Cited in M. Gershenzon, *Chaadaev* (St Petersburg, 1908), p. 64.

160. A. Koryé, *La Philosophie et le problème national en Russie au début du XIX siècle* (Paris, 1929), p. 286.

161. I. Turgenev, *A Nobleman's Nest*, trans. R. Hare (London, 1947), p. 43.

162. I. I. Panaev, *Literaturnye vospominaniia* (Leningrad, 1950), p. 151.

163. *Dekabristy-literatory. Literaturnoe nasledstvo* (Moscow, 1954), vol. 59, p. 582.

164. N. M. Karamzin, *Istoriia gosudarstva rossiiskogo*, 3 vols. (St Petersburg, 1842–3), vol. 1, p. 43.

165. S. S. Volk, *Istoricheskie vzgliady dekabristov* (Moscow–Leningrad, 1958), pp. 331–3, 342.

166. D. V. Venevitanov, *Polnoe sobranie sochinenii* (Leningrad, 1960), p. 86.

167. V. A. Ashik, *Pamiatniki medali v pamiat' boevykh podvigov russkoi armii v voinakh 1812, 1813 i 1814 godov i v pamiat' Imperatora Aleksandra I* (St Petersburg, 1913), p. 182.

168. IRL RAN, f. 57, op. 1, n. 62, l. 31.

169. L. N. Tolstoi, *Polnoe sobranie sochinenii v 90 tomakh* (Moscow, 1949), vol. 60, p. 374.

170. The Tolstoy scholar Boris Eikhenbaum, while acknowledging the debt to Volkonsky, suggests that Bolkonsky was modelled too on another Decembrist, D. I. Zavalishin (*Lev Tolstoi: 60e gody* (Leningrad–Moscow, 1931), pp. 199–208).

171. Cited in V. Shklovsky, *Lev Tolstoy*, trans. O. Shartse (Moscow, 1988), p. 31.

172. S. L. Tol'stoi, *Mat' i ded L. N. Tol'stogo* (Moscow, 1928), p. 9.

173. L. Tolstoy, 'The Devil', trans. A. Maude, in *The Kreutzer Sonata and Other Tales* (Oxford, 1968), p. 236.

174. Volkonskii, *O dekabristakh*, p. 82.

175. IRL RAN, f. 57, op. 3, n. 20, l. 1.

176. Belogolovoi, *Vospominaniia*, p. 37; *Dekabristy. Letopisi gosudarstvennogo literaturnogo muzeia*, p. 119.

177. IRL RAN, f. 57, op. 1, n. 65, l. 79.

178. Volkonskii, *O dekabristakh*, p. 81.

179. As above, pp. 81–2.

180. RGIA, f. 914, op. 1, d. 68, ll. 1–2.

181. IRL RAN, f. 57, op. 1, n. 7, l. 20.

182. IRL RAN, f. 57, op. 1, n. 7, l. 16.

183. *Dekabristy. Letopisi gosudarstvennogo literaturnogo muzeia*, p. 113.

184. IRL RAN, f. 57, op. 1, n. 7, ll. 20–23.

185. RGIA, f. 914, op. 1, d. 68, ll. 1–3.

186. IRL RAN, f. 57, op. 1, n. 80, ll. 58–9.

187. Volkonskii, *O dekabristakh*, p. 3.

3 MOSCOW! MOSCOW!

1. D. Olivier, *The Burning of Moscow*, trans. M. Heron (London, 1966), p. 43.

2. L. Tolstoy, *War and Peace*, trans. L. and A. Maude (Oxford, 1998), p. 935.

3. S. N. Glinka, *Zapiski* (St Petersburg, 1895), p. 263.

4. N. Nicolson, *Napoleon: 1812* (London, 1985), pp. 95–7; Count P. de Ségur, *Napoleon's Russian Campaign*, trans. J. Townsend (London, 1959), p. 114

5. As above, p. 117.

6. *The Memoirs of Catherine the Great*, ed. D. Maroger, trans. M. Budberg (London, 1955), p. 365.

7. *Four Russian Plays*, trans. J. Cooper (Harmondsworth, 1972), p. 155.

8. See A. Schmidt, 'The Restoration of Moscow after 1812', *Slavic Review*, vol. 40, no. 1 (Spring 1981), pp. 37–48.

9. Tolstoy, *War and Peace*, p. 1186.

10. K. N. Batiushkov, *Sochineniia* (Moscow, 1955), pp. 308–9.

11. V. G. Belinskii, *Polnoe sobranie sochinenii*, 13 vols. (Moscow, 1953–9), vol. 8, p. 391.

12. Marquis de Custine, *Empire of the Czar* (New York, 1989), p. 419.

13. A. Brett-James (ed.), *1812: Eyewitness Accounts of Napoleon's Defeat in Russia* (London, 1966), pp. 176–7.

14. K. N. Batiushkov, 'Progulka po Moskve', in *Sochineniia* (Moscow, 1902), p. 208.

15. As above.

16. A. Gaydamuk, *Russian Empire: Architecture, Decorative and Applied Arts, Interior Decoration 1800–1830* (Moscow, 2000), pp. 26–37.

17. S. D. Sheremetev, *Staraia Vozvdvizhenka* (St Petersburg, 1892), pp. 5–7.

18. S. D. Sheremetev, *Moskovskie vospominaniia, 1860 gg.* (Moscow, 1900), p. 8.

19. N. V. Gogol, *Sobranie sochinenii v semi tomakh* (Moscow, 1978), vol. 6, p. 172.

20. M. I. Semevskii, *Slovo i delo! 1700–1725* (St Petersburg, 1884), pp. 87–90.

21. A. D. P. Briggs, *Alexander Pushkin: A Critical Study* (London, 1983), p. 117; W. Lednicki, *Pushkin's Bronze Horseman* (Berkeley, 1955), p. 80.

22. R. D. Timenchuk, '"Medny Vsadnik" v literaturnom soznanii nachala XX veka', *Problemy pushkinovedeniia* (Riga, 1938), p. 83.

23. A. S. Pushkin, *Polnoe sobranie sochinenii*, 17 vols. (Moscow, 1937–49), vol. 5, p. 447.

24. N. Gogol, *Plays and Petersburg Tales*, trans. C. English (Oxford, 1995), pp. 35–6.

25. Cited in W. Rowe, *Through Gogol's Looking Glass* (New York, 1976), p. 113.

26. See D. Fanger, *Dostoevsky and Romantic Realism* (Cambridge, Mass., 1965), p. 132.

27. F. M. Dostoevskii, *Polnoe sobranie sochinenii*, 30 vols. (Leningrad, 1972–88), vol. 19, p. 69.

28. Pushkin, *Polnoe sobranie sochinenii*, vol. 11, p. 246.

29. 'Dnevniki N. Turgeneva', in *Arkhiv brat'ev Turgenevykh*, vol. 3, no. 5 (Petrograd, 1921), p. 259.

30. F. F. Vigel', *Zapiski*, chast' 1 (Moscow, 1891), p. 169.

31. V. Giliarovskii, *Moskva i moskvichi* (Moscow, 1955), pp. 151–2, 304–15.

32. M. I. Pyliaev, *Staroe zhit'e. Ocherki i rasskazy* (St Petersburg, 1892), pp. 5–6, 10.

33. As above, pp. 15–16.

34. S. D. Sheremetev, *Otgoloski XVIII veka*, vyp. 11, *Vremia Imperatora Pavla, 1796–1800* (Moscow, 1905), p. 15. One serf cook was able to lend his master 45,000 roubles when the dues from his estate were late in coming in (see E. Lavrent'eva, *Svetskii etiket pushkinskoi pory* (Moscow, 1999), p. 470).

35. Pyliaev, *Staroe zhit'e*, p. 6.

36. E. Lavrenteva, *Kul'tura zastol'ia XIX veka pushkinskoi pory* (Moscow, 1999), p. 51.

37. As above, p. 2.

38. R. E. F. Smith and D. Christian, *Bread and Salt: A Social and Economic History of Food and Drink in Russia* (Cambridge, 1984), pp. 174–6.

39. S. Tempest, 'Stovelore in Russian Folklife', in M. Glants and J. Toomre (eds.), *Food in Russian History and Culture* (Bloomington, 1997), pp. 1–14.

40. Lavrenteva, *Kul'tura zastol'ia*, pp. 44–5.

41. G. Munro, 'Food in Catherinian St Petersburg', in Glants and Toomre, *Food in Russian History and Culture*, p. 32.

42. A. Chekhov, *Plays*, trans. E. Fen (Harmondsworth, 1972), p. 344.

43. As above, p. 275.

44. *The Complete Tales of Nikolai Gogol*, ed. and trans. L Kent, 2 vols. (Chicago, 1985), vol. 2, p. 24.

45. Smith and Christian, *Bread and Salt*, p. 324.

46. E. I. Stogov, 'Zapiski', *Russkaia starina* (April 1903), p. 135.

47. N. Matveev, *Moskva i zhizn' ee nakanune nashestviia 1812 g.* (Moscow, 1912), p. 35.

48. Iu. Shamurin, *Podmoskov'ia*, in *Kul'turnye sokrovishcha Rossii*, vyp. 3 (Moscow, 1914), pp. 30–31; L. Lepskaia, *Repertuar krepostnogo teatra Sheremetevykh* (Moscow, 1996), p. 39; E. Beskin, *Krepostnoi teatr* (Moscow,

1927), pp. 13–14; K. Bestuzhev, *Krepostnoi teatr* (Moscow, 1913), pp. 58–9.

49. Lavrent'eva, *Svetskii etiket pushkinskoi pory*, pp. 81–2, 84.

50. 'Zametka iz vospominanii kn. P. A. Viazemskogo (o. M. I. Rimskoi Korsakovoi)', *Russkii arkhiv* (1867), no. 7, p. 1069.

51. 'Vospominaniia o Lialichakh', *Istoricheskii vestnik*, vol. 120 (1910), no. 4.

52. *Russkii byt' po vospominaniiam sovremennikov. XVIII vek*, chast' 2, *Ot petra do pavla 1* (Moscow, 1918), p. 66.

53. D. I. Zavalishin, 'Vospominaniya o grafe A. I. Osterman-Tolstom (1770–1851)', *Istoricheskii vestnik*, vol. 2, no. 5 (1880), p. 90; Lavrent'eva, *Svetskii etiket pushkinskoi pory*, p. 376.

54. S. M. Volkonskii, *Moi vospominaniia*, 2 vols. (Moscow, 1992), vol. 2, p. 191.

55. E. V. Dukov, 'Polikhroniia rossiiskikh razvlechenii XIX veka', in *Razvlekatel'naia kul'tura Rossii XVIII–XIX vv.* (Moscow, 2000), p. 507.

56. S. I. Taneev, 'Maskarady v stolitsakh', *Russkii arkhiv* (1885), no. 9, p. 152.

57. C. Emerson, *The Life of Musorgsky* (Cambridge, 1999), pp. 122, 169.

58. N. Sultanov, 'Vozrozhdenie russkogo iskusstva', *Zodchii* (1881), no. 2, p. ii.

59. On Solntsev and the Stroganov School, see E. Kirichenko, *Russian Design and the Fine Arts: 1750–1917* (New York, 1991), pp. 78–86.

60. V. I. Plotnikov, *Fol'klor i russkoe izobratel'noe iskusstvo vtoroi poloviny XIX veka* (Leningrad, 1987), p. 58.

61. V. Stasov, *Izbrannye sochineniia*, 3 vols. (Moscow–Leningrad, 1937), vol. 2, p. 214.

62. Cited in Kirichenko, *Russian Design and the Fine Arts*, p. 109.

63. *The Musorgsky Reader: A Life of Modeste Petrovich Musorgsky in Letters and Documents*, ed. and trans. J. Leyda and S. Bertensson (New York, 1947), pp. 17–18.

64. *M. A. Balakirev: vospominaniia i pis'ma* (Leningrad, 1962), p. 320.

65. V. Stasov, 'Dvadtsat' pisem Turgeneva i moe znakomstvo s nim', in *Sobranie kriticheskikh materialov dlia izucheniia proizvedenii I. C. Turgeneva*, 2 vols. (Moscow, 1915), vol. 2, vyp. 2, p. 291.

66. *V. V. Stasov i russkoe iskusstvo* (St Petersburg, 1998), p. 23.

67. See R. Taruskin's brilliant essay 'How the Acorn Took Root' in his *Defining Russia Musically* (Princeton, 1997), ch. 8.

68. V. V. Stasov, *Izbrannye sochineniia*, 2 vols. (Moscow, 1937), vol. 2, p. 536.

69. As above, p. 557.

70. See R. Taruskin, *Defining Russia Musically*, pp. xiii ff.

71. N. A. Rimsky-Korsakov, *My Musical Life*, trans. J. Joffe (London, 1924),

p. 331; V. V. Yastrebtsev, *Reminiscences of Rimsky-Korsakov*, trans. F. Jonas (New York, 1985), p. 38.

72. *The Musorgsky Reader*, p. 120.

73. N. M. Karamzin, *Istoriia gosudarstva rossiiskogo*, 12 vols. (St Petersburg, 1892), vol. 11, p. 57.

74. R. Taruskin, '"The Present in the Past": Russian Opera and Russian Historiography, *c.* 1870', in M. H. Brown (ed.), *Russian and Soviet Music: Essays for Boris Schwarz* (Ann Arbor, 1984), pp. 128–9.

75. As above, pp. 124–5.

76. N. I. Kostomarov, *Sobranie sochineniia*, 8 vols. (St Petersburg, 1903–6), vol. 2, p. 43.

77. M. P. Musorgskii, *Pis'ma* (Moscow, 1981), p. 138.

78. *The Musorgsky Reader*, pp. 17–18.

79. *Modeste Petrovich Musorgsky. Literaturnoe nasledie*, 2 vols. (Moscow, 1971–2), vol. 1, p. 132.

80. *The Musorgsky Reader*, p. 244.

81. M. A. Voloshin, 'Surikov (materialy dlia biografii)', *Apollon* (1916), nos. 6–7, p. 65.

82. S. Glagol', 'V. I. Surikov', *Nasha starina* (1917), no. 2, p. 69; Voloshin, 'Suritov', p. 56.

83. *Vasilii Ivanovich Surikov. Pis'ma, vospominaniia o khudozhnike* (Leningrad, 1977), p. 185; V. S. Kemenov, *V. I. Surikov. Istoricheskaia zhivopis'*, *1870–1890* (Moscow, 1987), p. 385.

84. Kemenov, *V. I. Surikov*, p. 402.

85. J. Bradley, 'Moscow: From Big Village to Metropolis', in M. Hamm (ed.), *The City in Late Imperial Russia* (Bloomington, 1986), p. 13.

86. V. G. Belinskii, *Sochineniia*, 4 vols. (St Petersburg, 1900), vol. 4, p. 198.

87. M. M. Dostoevskii, '"Groza" A. N. Ostrovskogo', *Svetoch*, vol. 2 (March 1860), pp. 7–8.

88. J. Patouillet, *Ostrovski et son théâtre de moeurs russes* (Paris, 1912), p. 334.

89. V. Nemirovitch-Dantchenko, *My Life in the Russian Theatre*, trans. J. Cournos (London, 1968), pp. 131–2.

90. Cited in S. Grover, 'Savva Mamontov and the Mamontov Circle, 1870–1905. Artistic Patronage and the Rise of Nationalism in Russian Art', Ph.D. diss. (University of Wisconsin, 1971), p. 18.

91. C. Stanislavski, *My Life in Art* (London, 1948), p. 296; Nemirovitch-Dantchenko, *My Life*, p. 117.

92. *Pis'ma khudozhnikov Pavlu Mikhailovichu Tret'iakovu 1856–1869* (Moscow, 1960), p. 302.

93. Ia. Minchenkov, *Vospominaniia o peredvizhnikakh* (Leningrad, 1963), p. 118.

94. A. Benois, *Vozniknoveniia mira iskusstva* (Leningrad, 1928), p. 23.

95. Cited in J. Ruckman, *The Moscow Business Elite: A Social and Cultural Portrait of Two Generations, 1840–1905* (DeKalb, Ill., 1984), p. 98.

96. V. I. Konashevich, 'O sebe i svoem dele', *Novyi mir*, no. 10 (1965), p. 10.

97. A. Chekhov, 'Poprygun'ia', *Polnoe sobranie sochinenii*, 30 vols. (Moscow, 1974–83), vol. 7, p. 9.

98. RGIA, f. 528, op. 1, d. 960, ll. 9–10; f. 1340, op. 1, d. 545, l. 10; f. 472, op. 43, d. 19, l. 179.

99. *Viktor Mikhailovich Vasnetsov: zhizn' i tvorchestvo* (Moscow, 1960), p. 148.

100. Plotnikov, *Fol'klor i russkoe izobratel'noe iskusstvo vtoroi poloviny XIX veka*, p. 156.

101. *Vrubel: perepiska, vospominaniia o khudozhnike* (Moscow, 1963), p. 79.

102. Stanislavski, *My Life in Art*, pp. 141–2.

103. SP-PLMD, f. 640, op. 1, d. 1003, ll. 25–32.

104. Cited in V. V. Iastrebtsev, *Nikolai Andreevich Rimskii-Korsakov: vospominaniia, 1886–1908*, 2 vols. (Leningrad, 1959–60), vol. 1, p. 434.

105. RGIA, f. 799, 'Cherez 10 let posle protsessa po neizdannym dokumentam' (1910).

106. Stanislavski, *My Life in Art*, pp. 12, 22–3.

107. Nemirovitch-Dantchenko, *My Life in the Russian Theatre*, pp. 80–81, 159–60.

108. As above, p. 108.

109. As above, p. 188.

110. A. Chekhov, *Sredi milykh moskvichei* (Moscow, 1988), p. 3.

111. Chekhov, *Polnoe sobranie sochinenii*, vol. 11, p. 311.

112. O. Mandel'shtam, 'O p'ese A. Chekhova "Diadia Vania"', *Sobranie sochinenii*, 4 vols. (Paris, 1981), vol. 4, p. 107.

113. A. Chekhov, *Plays*, trans. E. Fen (Harmondsworth, 1954), p. 306.

114. Cited in D. Rayfield, *Understanding Chekhov* (London, 1999), p. 117.

115. A. P. Chekhov, *Polnoe sobranie sochinenii i pisem*, 18 vols. (Moscow, 1973–83), vol. 17, p. 17.

116. Chekhov, *Plays*, pp. 244–5.

117. P. S. Sheremetev, *O russkikh khudozhestvennykh promyslakh* (Moscow, 1915), p. 469.

118. Nemirovitch-Dantchenko, *My Life in the Russian Theatre*, p. 209.

119. A. P. Chekhov, *Polnoe sobranie sochinenii i pisem*, 20 vols. (Moscow, 1944–51), vol. 20, p. 160.

120. E. Clowes, 'Social Discourse in the Moscow Art Theatre', in E. Clowes, S. Kassow and J. West (eds.), *Between Tsar and People: Educated Society and the Quest for Public Identity in Late Imperial Russia* (Princeton, 1991), p. 279.

121. V. Meyerhold, 'The Naturalistic Theatre and the Theatre of Mood', in

Meyerhold on Theatre, trans. and ed. Edward Braun (London, 1969), p. 29.

122. Cited in S. Grover, 'The World of Art Movement in Russia', *Russian Review*, vol. 32, no. 1 (1973), p. 34.

123. A. Belyi, *Mezhdu dvukh revoliutsii* (Leningrad, 1934), p. 244.

124. As above, pp. 219, 224-5.

125. A. Lentulov, 'Avtobiografiia', in *Sovetskie khudozhniki*, 3 vols. (Moscow, 1937), vol. 1, p. 162.

126. F. Bowers, *Scriabin*, 2 vols. (London, 1969), vol. 2, p. 248.

127. 'From Street into Street' (1913), in V. Maiakovskii, *Polnoe sobranie sochinenii*, 13 vols. (Moscow, 1955-61), vol. 1, pp. 38-9.

128. Cited in N. Khardzhiev and V. Trenin, *Poeticheskaia kul'tura Mayakovskogo* (Moscow, 1970), p. 44. On the close links between Mayakovsky and Malevich, see J. Stapanian, *Mayakovsky's Cubo-Futurist Vision* (Houston, Texas. 1986), especially ch. 4.

129. M. Tsvetaeva, *A Captive Spirit: Selected Prose*, trans. and ed. J. King (London, 1983), p. 168. The verse is from the cycle 'Poems to Akhmatova', in *Sochineniia v dvukh tomakh* (Moscow, 1980), vol. 1, p. 85.

130. N. Mandelstam, *Hope Abandoned*, trans. M. Hayward (London, 1989), p. 467.

131. M. Bulgakov, *The Master and Margarita*, trans. M. Glenny (London, 1984), p. 397.

132. 'Spring' (1944), in C. Barnes, *Boris Pasternak: A Literary Biography*, 2 vols. (Cambridge, 1989-98), vol. 2, p. 202.

4 THE PEASANT MARRIAGE

1. O. V. Aptekhman, *Obshchestvo 'Zemlia i Volia' 70-kh godov* (Petrograd, 1924), p. 168.

2. Cited in T. Szamuely, *The Russian Tradition* (London, 1974), p. 201.

3. F. M. Dostoevskii, *Polnoe sobranie sochinenii*, 30 vols. (Leningrad, 1972-88), vol. 18, p. 57.

4. G. I. Uspenskii, *Polnoe sobranie sochinenii*, 15 vols. (Moscow–Leningrad, 1940-54), vol. 14, pp. 576-7.

5. I. S. Turgenev, *Polnoe sobranie sochineniia i pisem*, 28 vols. (Moscow–Leningrad, 1960-68), vol. 2, p. 160.

6. 'Silence' (1857), in N. A. Nekrasov, *Sochineniia*, 3 vols. (Moscow, 1959), vol. 1, p. 201.

7. F. Buslaev, 'Etnograficheskie vymysly nashikh predkov', *Sbornik antropologicheskikh i etnograficheskikh statei o Rossii i stranakh ei prilezhashchikh* (Moscow, 1868), p. 95.

8. I. D. Beliaev, 'Po povodu etnograficheskoi vystavki imeiushchei otkryt'sia vesnoi 1867 goda', *Den'* (1865), no. 41, p. 983.

9. See C. Frierson, *Peasant Icons: Representations of Rural People in Late Nineteenth-century Russia* (Oxford, 1993), p. 128.

10. B. Sokolov, 'Muzhik v izobrazhenii Turgeneva', in I. N. Rozanov and Iu. M. Sokolov (eds.), *Tvorchestvo Turgeneva: sbornik statei* (Moscow, 1920), p. 203.

11. S. Birkenmayer, *Nikolaj Nekrasov: His Life and Poetic Work* (The Hague, 1968), p. 76. The charge of an 'assault on poetry' was made by A. Grigor'ev, 'Stikhotvoreniia N. Nekrasova', *Vremia*, vol. 12 (1862), p. 38.

12. Dostoevskii, *Polnoe sobranie sochinenii*, vol. 22, p. 44.

13. K. S. Aksakov, *Polnoe sobranie sochinenii*, 2 vols. (St Petersburg, 1861), vol. 1, p. 292.

14. F. Dostoevsky, *A Writer's Diary*, trans. K. Lantz (Illinois, 1993), p. 160 and elsewhere.

15. V. G. Belinskii, *Izbrannye filosofskie sochineniia*, 2 vols. (Moscow, 1948), vol. 2, p. 443.

16. See, for example, I. S. Aksakov, 'Moskva, 24 marta', in *Den'* (24 March 1862), pp. 2–3.

17. A. Blok, 'The People and the Intelligentsia', in M. Raeff, *Russian Intellectual History: An Anthology* (New Jersey, 1978), p. 359.

18. Szamuely, *The Russian Tradition*, p. 383.

19. For a perceptive view of Turgenev's profound ambivalence on this, see A. Kelly, 'The Nihilism of Ivan Turgenev', in *Toward Another Shore: Russian Thinkers between Necessity and Chance* (New Haven, 1998).

20. F. Seeley, *Turgenev: A Reading of His Fiction* (Cambridge, 1991), p. 339.

21. V. S. Pritchett, *The Gentle Barbarian: The Life and Work of Turgenev* (London, 1977), p. 216.

22. GARF, f. 112, op. 1, d. 395, l. 96.

23. Aptekhman, *Obshchestvo 'Zemlia i Volia' 70-kh godov*, p. 145.

24. GARF, f. 112, op. 1, d. 282, l. 151.

25. I. Repin, *Dalekoe i blizkoe*, 5th edn (Moscow, 1960), p. 238.

26. As above, p. 247.

27. As above, p. 272.

28. As above, pp. 251–2, 272–3.

29. V. V. Stasov, *Izbrannye sochineniia*, 2 vols. (Moscow, 1937), vol. 1, p. 94.

30. E. Valkenier, *Ilya Repin and the World of Russian Art* (New York, 1990), p. 32.

31. See his letters to Antokolsky in IRL LAN, f. 294, op. 1, d. 22.

32. *I. Repin. Izbrannye pis'ma v dvukh tomakh* (Moscow, 1969), vol. 1, pp. 184–5.

33. R. Taruskin, *Musorgsky: Eight Essays and an Epilogue* (Princeton, 1993), p. 9.

34. *The Musorgsky Reader: A Life of Modeste Petrovich Musorgsky in Letters and Documents*, trans. and ed. J. Leyda and S. Bertensson (New York, 1947), p. 244.

35. *M. P. Musorgskii. Pis'ma i dokumenty* (Moscow–Leningrad, 1932), p. 251.

36. For a pioneering critique of the Populist version, see R. Taruskin, *Musorgsky*, especially 'Who Speaks for Musorgsky?', pp. 3–37.

37. M. P. Musorgskii, *Literaturnoe nasledie*, 2 vols. (Moscow, 1971–2), vol. 1, p. 270.

38. N. Gogol, *Village Evenings near Dikanka and Mirgorod*, trans. C. English (Oxford, 1994), p. 12.

39. *M. P. Musorgskii. Pis'ma i dokumenty*, p. 250.

40. V. V. Stasov. *Pis'ma k deiateliam russkoi kul'tury*, 2 vols. (Moscow, 1962), vol. 1, p. 19.

41. *I. Repin. Izbrannye pis'ma*, vol. 1, p. 143.

42. Repin, *Dalekoe i blizkoe*, p. 382.

43. *Tolstoy's Diaries*, ed. and trans. R. F. Christian (London, 1994), p. 100.

44. V. Shklovsky, *Lev Tolstoy*, trans. O. Shartse (Moscow, 1988), p. 33.

45. A. Fodor, *Tolstoy and the Russians: Reflections on a Relationship* (Ann Arbor, 1984), p. 27.

46. A. N. Wilson, *Tolstoy* (London, 1988), pp. 219–20.

47. *Reminiscences of Lev Tolstoi by His Contemporaries* (Moscow, 1965), pp. 148–9.

48. Cited in K. Feuer, *Tolstoy and the Genesis of War and Peace* (Cornell, 1996), p. 29.

49. L. Tolstoy, *Anna Karenin*, trans. R. Edmonds (Harmondsworth, 1974), pp. 272–3.

50. *Tolstoy's Diaries*, p. 134.

51. As above.

52. As above, p. 140.

53. *Pis'ma k A. B. Druzhininu. Gosudarstvennyi literaturnyi muzei* (Moscow, 1948), p. 328.

54. See V. S. Pritchett, *The Gentle Barbarian: The Life and Work of Turgenev* (London, 1977), p. 71.

55. L. N. Tolstoi, *Polnoe sobranie sochinenii*, 90 vols. (Moscow–Leningrad, 1928–58), vol. 57, p. 218.

56. Tolstoi, *Polnoe sobranie sochinenii*, vol. 7, p. 58.

57. Cited in A. Tolstoi, 'Tolstoy and the Peasants', *Russian Review*, vol. 19, no. 2 (April 1960), p. 151.

58. *I. E. Repin i L. N. Tolstoi*, 2 vols. (Moscow–Leningrad, 1949), vol. 2, p. 36.

59. Repin, *Dalekoe i blizkoe*, p. 370.

60. L. Tolstoy, *War and Peace*, trans. L. and A. Maude (Oxford, 1998), p. 1040.

61. I. Tolstoy, *Tolstoy, My Father: Reminiscences*, trans. A. Dunnigan (London, 1972), p. 174.

62. L. Tolstoy, *Anna Karenin*, trans. R. Edmonds (Harmondsworth, 1974), p. 467.

63. A. Pushkin, *Eugene Onegin*, trans. J. Falen (Oxford, 1990), pp. 65–6.

64. Tolstoy, *Anna Karenin*, pp. 481–2.

65. See J. Hajnal, 'European Marriage Patterns in Perspective', in D. Glass and D. Eversley (eds.), *Population in History: Essays in Historical Demography* (London, 1965), pp. 101–43.

66. P. Laslett, 'Characteristics of the Western Family Considered over Time', in *Family Life and Illicit Love in Earlier Generations* (Cambridge, 1977), p. 29.

67. D. A. Sverbeev, *Zapiski, 1799–1826*, 2 vols. (Moscow, 1899), vol. 2, p. 43.

68. E. I. Raevskaya, 'Vospominaniia', *Russkii arkhiv* (1883), kn. 2, ch. 3, p. 72.

69. On peasant customs and wedding rituals, see C. Worobec, *Peasant Russia: Family and Community in the Post-emancipation Period* (Princeton, 1991), chs. 4 and 5.

70. V. Dal', *Tolkovyi slovar' zhivogo velikorusskogo iazyka*, 4 vols. (St Petersburg, 1882), vol. 3, p. 119.

71. W. R. Shedden-Ralston, *The Songs of the Russian People, as Illustrative of Slavonic Mythology and Russian Social Life* (London, 1872), p. 289.

72. S. T. Aksakov, *The Family Chronicle*, trans. M. Beverley (Westport, Conn., 1985), p. 108.

73. N. Chechulin, *Russkoe provintsial'noe obshchestvo vo vtoroi polovine XVIII veka* (St Petersburg, 1889), pp. 43–4.

74. Aksakov, *The Family Chronicle*, p. 109.

75. *Russkii byt' po vospominaniiam sovremennikov. XVIII vek*, chast' 2, Ot petra do pavla 1 (Moscow, 1918), p. 275.

76. Pushkin, *Eugene Onegin*, p. 168.

77. F. F. Vigel', *Zapiski*, chast' 1 (Moscow 1891), p. 174.

78. Tolstoy, *Anna Karenin*, pp. 483–4.

79. Chechulin, *Russkoe provintsial'noe obshchestvo vo vtoroi polovine XVIII veka*, p. 44.

80. W. Wagner, *Marriage, Property, and Law in Late Imperial Russia* (Oxford, 1994), p. 63.

81. As above, p. 134.

82. See further Wagner, *Marriage, Property and Law in Late Imperial Russia*, p. 66.

83. V. Dal', *Poslovitsy russkogo naroda*, 2 vols. (Moscow, 1984), vol. 1, p. 291.

84. Dostoevskii, *Polnoe sobranie sochinenii*, vol. 21, p. 21.

85. A. Labzina, *Vospominaniia* (St Petersburg, 1914), pp. 16-109.

86. M. Adam, 'Iz semeinoi khroniki', *Istoricheskii vestnik*, vol. 94, no. 12 (1903), pp. 816-21.

87. Wagner, *Marriage, Property and Law in Late Imperial Russia*, p. 70.

88. Tolstoy, *Anna Karenin*, p. 483.

89. Tolstoi, *Polnoe sobranie sochinenii*, vol. 52, p. 143.

90. A. Chekhov, 'Peasants', in *The Kiss and Other Stories*, trans. R. Wilks (Harmondsworth, 1982), pp. 79-80.

91. *L. N. Tolstoi i A. P. Chekhov: Rasskazyvaiut sovremenniki, arkhivy, muzei* (Moscow, 1998), p. 233.

92. A. P. Chekhov, *Polnoe sobranie sochinenii*, 30 vols. (Moscow, 1974-83), vol. 9, pp. 519-23; D. Rayfield, *Anton Chekhov: A Life* (London, 1997), p. 431.

93. D. Rayfield, *Chekhov: The Evolution of His Art* (London, 1975), p. 177.

94. Chekhov, *Polnoe sobranie sochinenii*, vol. 9, p. 400.

95. A. Chekhov, *Letters of Anton Chekhov*, selected by S. Karlinsky (London, 1973), p. 237.

96. Rayfield, *Chekhov: The Evolution of His Art*, p. 171.

97. P. Gatrell, *The Tsarist Economy 1850-1917* (London, 1986), pp. 50-51; G. T. Robinson, *Rural Russia under the Old Régime* (Berkeley, 1932), pp. 94-7; T. Shanin, *The Awkward Class* (Oxford, 1972), p. 48.

98. J. Brooks, *When Russia Learned to Read: Literacy and Popular Literature, 1861-1917* (Princeton, 1985), pp. 13, 55-6.

99. S. T. Semenov, *Dvadtsat' piat' let v derevne* (Petrograd, 1915), pp. 5-6.

100. T. Lindstrom, 'From Chapbooks to Classics: The Story of the Intermediary', *The American Slavic and East European Review*, vol. 15 (1957), p. 193.

101. As above, p. 195.

102. *Landmarks: A Collection of Essays of the Russian Intelligentsia*, trans. M. Schwartz (New York, 1977), pp. 80-81.

103. A. M. Gor'kii v epokhu revoliutsii, 1905-1907 gg. Materialy, vospominaniia, issledovaniia* (Moscow, 1957), p. 52.

104. T. Marullo, *Ivan Bunin: Russian Requiem, 1885-1920* (Chicago, 1993), pp. 112-13.

105. I. Bunin, *Stories and Poems*, trans. O. Shartse (Moscow, 1979), p. 179.

106. Cited in R. Pipes, *The Russian Revolution, 1899-1919* (London, 1990), p. 113.

107. M. Gorky, *Letters* (Moscow, 1964), p. 54.

108. M. Gorky, *My Childhood* (Harmondsworth, 1966), p. 9.

109. M. Gorky, *My Universities* (Harmondsworth, 1966), pp. 140–50.

110. M. Gorky, 'On the Russian Peasantry', in R. E. F. Smith (ed.), *The Russian Peasant 1920 and 1984* (London, 1977), pp. 18–19.

111. Cited in R. Buckle, *Diaghilev* (New York, 1979), p. 300.

112. *V. D. Polenov. E. D. Polenova. Khronika sem'i khudozhnikov* (Moscow, 1964), p. 363.

113. N. V. Polenova, *Ambramtsevo: vospominaniia* (Moscow, 1922), p. 44.

114. *V. D. Polenov. E. D. Polenova. Khronika sem'i khudozhnikov*, p. 507.

115. M. Tenisheva, *Vpechatleniia moei zhizni* (Paris, 1933), p. 337.

116. W. Salmond, *Arts and Crafts in Late Imperial Russia: Reviving the Kustar Art Industries, 1870–1917* (Cambridge, 1996), p. 86.

117. S. Diaghilev, 'Neskol'ko slov o S. V. Maliutine', *Mir iskusstva*, no. 4 (1903), pp. 159–60.

118. Tenisheva, *Vpechatleniia moei zhizni*, p. 263.

119. S. Diaghilev, 'Slozhnye voprosy. Nash mnimyi upadok', *Mir iskusstva*, no. 1 (1898–9), pp. 10–11.

120. A. Benua, *Moi vospominaniia*, 2 vols. (Moscow, 1980), vol. 1, p. 500.

121. A. Haskell, *Diaghileff. His Artistic and Private Life* (London, 1935), p. 160.

122. S. Diaghilev, 'Evropeiskie vystavki i russkie khudozhniki', *Novosti i birzhevaia gazeta* (26 August 1896).

123. M. Normand, 'La Russie à l'Exposition', *L'Illustration* (5 May 1900), pp. 282, 283.

124. See Salmond, *Arts and Crafts in Late Imperial Russia*, pp. 102–3, 161–3.

125. Tenisheva, *Vpechatleniia moei zhizni*, p. 426.

126. Quoted in *Sergei Diaghilev i russkoe iskusstvo* (Moscow, 1982), pp. 109–10.

127. Prince P. Lieven, *The Birth of the Ballets-Russes* (London, 1936), p. 56.

128. R. Taruskin, *Stravinsky and the Russian Traditions: A Biography of the Works through Mavra*, 2 vols. (Oxford, 1996), vol. 1, p. 536.

129. N. A. Rimsky-Korsakov, *Polnoe sobranie sochinenii: literaturnye proizvedeniia i perepiska*, 8 vols. (Moscow, 1955–82), vol. 8b, p. 105.

130. P. Chaikovskii, *Polnoe sobranie sochinenii: literaturnye proizvedeniia i perepiska* (Moscow, 1953–81), vol. 15b, p. 293.

131. A. Benois, *Reminiscences of the Russian Ballet* (London, 1941), p. 124.

132. As above, p. 266.

133. A. Benois, 'Russkie spektakli v Parizhe', *Rech'* (25 July 1909), p. 2.

134. A Benois, 'Khudozhestvennye pis'ma: russkie spektakli v Parizhe: "Zhar ptitsa"', *Rech'* (18 July 1910).

135. For a brilliant analysis of the music and scenario, see Taruskin, *Stravinsky and the Russian Traditions*, vol. 1, ch. 9.

136. E. Lineva, *Velikorusskie pesni v narodnoi garmonizatsii*, 2 vols. (St Petersburg, 1904–9). There is an English version: *The Peasant Songs of Great Russia as They Are in the Folk's Harmonization: Collected and Transcribed from Phonograms by Eugenie Lineff* (St Petersburg, 1905–12).

137. Lineva, *Velikorusskie pesni v narodnoi garmonizatsii*, vol. 2, pp. xxv–xxvi.

138. L. Bakst, 'Puti klassitsizma v iskusstve', *Apollon*, no. 2 (1909), p. 77.

139. For a detailed analysis, see Taruskin, *Stravinsky and the Russian Traditions*, vol. 1, pp. 695–717.

140. N. Rerikh, 'Na Kurgane', in *Pervaia kniga* (Moscow, 1914).

141. Taruskin, *Stravinsky and the Russian Traditions*, vol. 1, pp. 881–6.

142. For a brilliant analysis of these folklore sources, see Taruskin, *Stravinsky and the Russian Traditions*, vol. 1, pp. 891–965.

143. Cited in M. Oliver, *Stravinsky* (London, 1995), p. 88.

144. R. Rolland, *Journal des années de guerre, 1914–1919* (Paris, 1952), p. 59.

145. E. White, *Stravinsky: The Composer and His Works* (London, 1979), p. 151.

146. The notes for the songs are unpublished. They can be found in the Paul Sacher Archive in Basel (Igor Stravinsky Sketchbook A). On the emotional effort invested in the songs, see Taruskin, *Stravinsky and the Russian Traditions*, vol. 2, p. 1192.

147. I. Stravinsky and R. Craft, *Expositions and Developments* (Berkeley, 1980), p. 138. Stravinsky made the observation for the first time in *Chronique de ma vie*, 2 vols. (Paris, 1935–6).

148. C.-F. Ramuz, *Souvenirs sur Igor Strawinsky*, in *Oeuvres complètes*, 20 vols. (Lausanne, 1941), vol. 14, p. 68.

149. Stravinsky and Craft, *Expositions and Developments*, p. 118.

150. B. Nijinska, 'Creation of *Les Noces*', *Dance Magazine* (December 1974), p. 59.

5 IN SEARCH OF THE RUSSIAN SOUL

1. L. Stanton, *The Optina Pustyn Monastery in the Russian Literary Imagination: Iconic Vision in Works by Dostoevsky, Gogol, Tolstoy, and Others* (New York, 1995), pp. 63–4.

2. S. Chetverikov, *Optina Pustyn* (Paris, 1951), p. 26.

3. As above, p. 40; Stanton, *The Optina Pustyn Monastery in the Russian Literary Imagination*, p. 46.

4. See further V. Lossky, *The Mystical Theology of the Eastern Church* (London, 1957), especially ch. 1.

5. R. Ware, *The Orthodox Church* (Harmondsworth, 1997), pp. 264–5.

6. A. Chekhov, *Polnoe sobranie sochinenii*, 30 vols. (Moscow, 1974–83), vol. 5, pp. 100–101 (translation by Rosamund Bartlett).

7. A. Gertsen, *Byloe i dumy*, 2 vols. (Moscow, 1962), vol. 1, p. 467.

8. L. Ouspensky, 'The Meaning and Language of Icons', in *The Meaning of Icons* (New York, 1982), p. 42.

9. See M. Cherniavsky, *Tsar and People: Studies in Russian Myths* (New Haven, 1961), pp. 44–71.

10. A. K. Lelong, 'Vospominaniia', *Russkii arkhiv* (1913), kn. 2, no. 7, p. 65.

11. N. M. Zernov (ed.), *Na perelome: tri pokoleniia odnoi moskovskoi sem'i* (Paris, 1970), p. 228.

12. As above, p. 230.

13. M. Nikoleva, 'Cherty starinnogo dvorianskogo byta', *Russkii arkhiv* (1893), kn. 3, chast' 10, pp. 130–31.

14. V. N. Kharuzina, *Proshloe. Vospominaniia detskikh i otrocheskikh let* (Moscow, 1999), pp. 363–4.

15. V. D. Bonch-Bruevich, 'O religii, religioznom sektanstve i tserkvi', *Izbrannye sochineniia*, 3 vols. (Moscow, 1959–63), vol. 1, pp. 174–5.

16. V. S. Solov'ev, *O khristianskom edinstve* (Moscow, 1994), p. 171.

17. F. Dostoevsky, *A Writer's Diary*, trans. K. Lantz, 2 vols. (London, 1994), vol. 2, p. 1351.

18. A. Tereshchenko, *Byt russkogo naroda* (St Petersburg, 1848), chast' 3, p. 254.

19. K. V. Chistov, *Russkie narodnye sotsial'no-utopicheskie legendy XVII–XIX vv.* (Moscow, 1967), pp. 290–91; N. K. Rerikh, 'Serdtse Azii', in *Izbrannoe* (Moscow, 1979), p. 177.

20. Z. Gippius, 'Svetloe ozero. Dnevnik', *Novyi put'* (1904), no. 1, pp. 168–9.

21. Chistov, *Russkie narodnye sotsial'no-utopicheskie legendy XVII–XIX vv*, pp. 239–40, 248–9.

22. As above, pp. 261–70.

23. Stanton, *The Optina Pustyn Monastery in the Russian Literary Imagination*, p. 51.

24. V. Setchkarev, *Gogol: His Life and Works* (New York, 1965), p. 5.

25. V. Veresaev, *Gogol v zhizni: sistemacheskii svod podlinnikh svidetel'stv sovremennikov* (Moscow, 1990), p. 43.

26. See Gogol's letter to S. P. Shevyrev ('I came to Christ by the Protestant path') in *Letters of Nikolai Gogol*, ed. and trans. C. Proffer (Ann Arbor, 1967), pp. 171–2.

27. G. Florovsky, *Puti russkogo bogosloviya* (Paris, 1937), p. 262.

28. See J. Schillinger, 'Gogol's "The Overcoat" as a Travesty of Hagiography', *Slavic and East European Journal*, 16 (1972), pp. 36–41; V. E. Vetlovskaia, 'Zhitiinye istochniki gogolevskoi "Shinel"', *Russkaia literatura*, 1 (1999), pp. 18–35.

29. L. Knapp, 'Gogol and the Ascent of Jacob's Ladder: Realization of Biblical Metaphor', *Christianity and the Eastern Slavs, Californian Slavic Studies* vol. 3, no. 18 (1995), p. 8.

30. Florovsky, *Puti russkogo bogosloviya*, p. 278.

31. K. Aksakov, *Polnoe sobranie sochinenii*, 3 vols. (Moscow, 1861–80), vol. 1, p. 630.

32. F. Odoevsky, *Russian Nights*, trans. O. Koshansky-Olienikov and R. E. Matlaw (New York, 1965), pp. 37–8.

33. 'Nechto o vrozhdennom svoistve dush rossiiskikh', *Zritel'* (1792), no. 3, p. 173.

34. N. Gogol, 'Taras Bulba', in *Village Evenings near Dikanka and Mirgorod*, trans. C. English (Oxford, 1994), pp. 327–8.

35. N. Gogol, *Dead Souls*, trans. D. Magarshack (Harmondsworth, 1961), p. 258.

36. M. Malia, *Alexander Herzen and the Birth of Russian Socialism* (Cambridge, 1961), p. 223.

37. *Letters of Nikolai Gogol*, p. 162.

38. V. A. Kotel'nikov, 'Optina pustyn' i russkaia literatura', *Russkaia literatura*, no. 1 (1989), p. 69.

39. N. Gogol', *Polnoe sobranie sochinenii*, 14 vols. (Moscow–Leningrad, 1937–52), vol. 6, p. 200; vol. 10, p. 181. See further E. A. Smirnova, *Poema Gogolia 'Mertvye dushi'* (Leningrad, 1987), pp. 70–74.

40. Smirnova, *Poema Gogolia 'Mertvye dushi'*, p. 143.

41. Gogol', *Polnoe sobranie sochinenii*, vol. 14, p. 191.

42. N. V. Gogol, *Pis'ma*, 4 vols. (St Petersburg, n.d.), vol. 2, p. 508.

43. V. G. Belinskii, *Polnoe sobranie sochinenii*, 13 vols. (Moscow, 1953–9), vol. 10, p. 212.

44. S. T. Aksakov, *Istoriia moego zhakomstva s gogolem* (Moscow, 1960), p. 170.

45. Cited in D. P. Bogdanov, 'Optina Pustyn' i polomnichestvo v nee russkikh pisatelei', *Istoricheskii vestnik*, 112 (October 1910), pp. 332–4.

46. Cited in J. M. Holquist, 'The Burden of Prophecy: Gogol's Conception of Russia', *Review of National Literatures*, vol. 3. no. 1 (1973), p. 39.

47. 'Pis'mo k N. V. Gogoliu', in Belinskii, *Polnoe sobranie sochinenii*, vol. 4, p. 215.

48. I. S. Belliutsin, *Description of the Clergy in Rural Russia*, trans. G. Freeze (Cornell, 1985), p. 35.

49. M. Gorky, *My Universities* (Harmondsworth, 1966), p. 122.

50. G. Fedotov, *The Russian Religious Mind*, 2 vols. (Cambridge Mass., 1966), vol. 1, pp. 12–14, 358–62; J. Hubbs, *Mother Russia: The Feminine Myth in Russian Culture* (Bloomington, 1988), pp. 19–20.

51. V. G. Vlasov, 'The Christianization of the Russian Peasants', in M. Balzer (ed.), *Russian Traditional Culture: Religion, Gender and Customary Law* (London, 1992), p. 25.

52. J. Billington, *The Face of Russia* (New York, 1999), p. 52.

53. E. A. Boriak, 'Traditsionnye znaniia, obriady i verovaniia ukraintsev sviazannye s tkachestvom (seredina XIX v – nachalo XX v)', Kand. diss. (Kiev University, 1989), p. 157.

54. P. P. Chubinskii, *Trudy etnografichesko-statisticheskoi ekspeditsii v zapadno-russkii krai* (St Petersburg, 1877), vol. 4, p. 4.

55. I. V. Kostolovskii, 'K pover'iam o poiase krest'ian' iaroslavskoi gubernii', *Etnograficheskoe obozrenie* (1909), no. 1, pp. 48–9; I. A. Kremleva, 'Ob evoliutsii nekotorykh arkhaichnykh obychaev russkikh', in *Russkie: semeiny i obshchestvennyi byt* (Moscow, 1989), p. 252.

56. A. Pushkin, *Eugene Onegin*, trans. J. Falen (Oxford, 1990), p. 52.

57. N. Chechulin, *Russkoe provintsial'noe obshchestvo vo vtoroi polovine XVIII veka* (St Petersburg, 1889), p. 36; Lelong, 'Vospominaniia', *Russkii arkhiv*, kn. 2, no. 6, p. 807.

58. Lelong, 'Vospominaniia', *Russkii arkhiv*, pp. 52–3.

59. C. Beaumont, *Serge Diaghilev* (London, 1933), p. 26.

60. See the comments made on this by P. A. Vyazemskii in *Pushkin v vospominaniiakh sovremennikov* (Moscow, 1985), p. 194.

61. A. P. Mogilianskii, *Lichnost' Pushkina* (St Petersburg, 1995), p. 38; *Druz'ia Pushkina*, 2 vols. (Moscow, 1985), vol. 2, p. 318.

62. V. V. Gippius, *Gogol* (Ann Arbor, 1981), p. 176. On Tolstoy, see K. Parthe, 'Death-masks in Tolstoi', *Slavic Review*, vol. 41, no. 2 (1982), pp. 297–305; and same author, 'The Metamorphosis of Death in L. N. Tolstoi', *Language and Style*, vol. 18, no. 2 (1985), pp. 205–14.

63. *Vospominaniia o Chaikovskom* (Moscow, 1962), p. 29.

64. See Dostoevsky's letter to V. V. Mikhailov (16 March 1878) in F. Dostoevsky, *Complete Letters*, ed. and trans. D. Lowe and R. Meyer, 5 vols. (Ann Arbor, 1988–91), vol. 5, p. 18.

65. Stanton, *The Optina Pustyn Monastery in the Russian Literary Imagination*, pp. 174–5.

66. V. A. Kotel'nikov, 'Optina Pustyn' i russkaia literatura', *Russkaia literatura*, no. 1 (1989), pp. 20, 22.

67. F. Dostoevsky, *The Brothers Karamazov*, trans. D. Magarshack (Harmondsworth, 1988), pp. 51–3.

68. As above, p. 287.

69. Dostoevsky, *Complete Letters*, vol. 5, p. 83.

70. J. Frank, *Dostoevsky: The Seeds of Revolt* (Princeton, 1977), pp. 43ff.

71. Dostoevsky, *A Writer's Diary*, vol. 1, p. 129.

72. Dostoevsky, *Complete Letters*, vol. 1, p. 190 (I have modified the translation).

73. F. Dostoevsky, *The House of the Dead*, trans. D. McDuff (London, 1985), pp. 35–6.

74. Dostoevsky, *A Writer's Diary*, vol. 2, pp. 351–5.

75. As above, vol. 2, p. 354.

76. As above, vol. 2, p. 355.

77. As above, vol. 2, pp. 347–8.

78. Dostoevsky, *Complete Letters*, vol. 3, p. 114.

79. F. M. Dostoevskii, *Pis'ma*, 4 vols. (Moscow, 1928–59), vol. 1, p. 141.

80. F. Dostoevsky, *The Devils*, trans. D. Magarshack (Harmondsworth, 1971), p. 259 (my italics).

81. For an excellent discussion of Dostoevsky on these lines, see A. Kelly, 'Dostoevsky and the Divided Conscience,' in *Toward Another Shore: Russian Thinkers between Necessity and Chance* (New Haven, 1998), pp. 55–79. A similar argument is made by T. Masaryk, *The Spirit of Russia*, 3 vols. (London, 1967), vol. 3, pp. 54–63.

82. Dostoevsky, *Complete Letters*, vol. 1, p. 95.

83. Dostoevsky, *The Brothers Karamazov*, p. 152.

84. F. Dostoevsky, *Crime and Punishment*, trans. D. McDuff (Harmondsworth, 1991), p. 629.

85. Iu. Mann, *V poiskakh zhivoi dushi. 'Mertvye dushi': pisatel' – kritika – chitatel'* (Moscow, 1984), pp. 321–2; Gogol', *Polnoe sobranie sochinenii*, vol. 14, pp. 264–5.

86. S. G. Volkonskii, *Zapiski* (St Petersburg, 1901), p. 499.

87. Dostoevsky, *A Writer's Diary*, vol. 1, p. 130 (my italics).

88. As above, vol. 1, p. 135.

89. As above, vol. 1, p. 162.

90. Dostoevsky, *The Brothers Karamazov*, pp. 190, 339, 356.

91. As above, p. 350.

92. As above, pp. 596–7.

93. As above, p. 667.

94. As above, p. 694.

95. On the views of the Archimandrite Bukharev, which may have had an influence on Dostoevsky, see G. Freeze, 'Die Laisierung des Archimandriten Feodor (Bucharev) und ihre kirchenpolitische Hintergründe. Theologie und Politik im Russland der Mitte des 19. Jahrhunderts', *Kirche im Osten*, 28

(1985), pp. 26–52. Also K. Onasch, 'En quête d'une orthodoxie "alternative". Le Christ et l'église dans l'œuvre de F. M. Dostoïevski', *Mille ans de christianisme russe 988–1988. Actes du Colloque International de L'Université de Paris X–Nanterre 20–23 Janvier 1988* (Paris, 1989), pp. 247–52.

96. Dostoevsky, *The Brothers Karamazov*, pp. 65–75 (quotation on page 73). For the political context, see O. Khakhordin, 'Civil Society and Orthodox Christianity', *Europe–Asia Studies*, vol. 50, no. 6 (1998), pp. 949–68.

97. Dostoevsky, *The Brothers Karamazov*, pp. 73–4. On the link with Optina, see Stanton, *The Optina Pustyn Monastery in the Russian Literary Imagination*, pp. 174–5.

98. V. S. Solov'ev, *Sobranie sochinenii*, 6 vols. (St Petersburg, 1901–7), vol. 3, p. 182.

99. Dostoevsky, *The Brothers Karamazov*, p. 612.

100. As above, p. 32.

101. V. Lebedev, 'Otryvok iz romana "Brat'ia Karamazovy" pered sudom tsenzury', *Russkaia literatura*, no. 2 (1970), pp. 123–5.

102. Dostoevsky, *A Writer's Diary*, vol. 2, p. 1351.

103. See R. Gustafson, *Leo Tolstoy, Resident and Stranger: A Study in Fiction and Theology* (Princeton, 1986).

104. As above, pp. 334–5.

105. See, for example, N. Berdiaev, 'Vetkhii i novyi zavet v religioznom soznanii L. Tolstogo', in *O religii L'va Tolstogo* (Moscow, 1912). For further details of these views, see D. Matual, *Tolstoy's Translation of the Gospels: A Critical Study* (Lewiston, 1992), p. 14. Literary scholars have found traces of Buddhism in Tolstoy's works, especially the death scene of Prince Andrei in *War and Peace*. See A. N. Strizhev (ed.), *Dukhovnaia tragediia L'va Tolstogo* (Moscow, 1995), pp. 17–18.

106. A. S. Suvorin, *Diary* (Moscow–Petrograd, 1923), p. 263.

107. S. Pozoiskii, *K istorii otluchenii L. Tolstogo ot tserkvi* (Moscow, 1979), pp. 65–71.

108. A. N. Wilson, *Tolstoy* (London, 1988), p. 458.

109. *Lev Tolstoi i V. V. Stasov. Perepiska 1878–1906* (Leningrad, 1929), pp. 227, 235.

110. A. Donskov (ed.), *Sergei Tolstoy and the Doukhobors: A Journey to Canada (Diary and Correspondence)* (Ottawa, 1998), pp. 151–2. Pozoiskii, *K istorii otluchenii L. Tolstogo ot tserkvi*, pp. 113–17.

111. See Donskov, above.

112. A. Etkind, *Khlyst: Sekty, literatura i revoliutsiia* (Moscow, 1998), pp. 128–9. For Tolstoy's correspondence with other sects, see A. Donskov (ed.), *L. N. Tolstoi i T. M. Bondarev: perepiska* (Munich, 1996); A. Donskov (ed.), *L. N. Tolstoi i M. P. Novikov: perepiska* (Munich, 1996); V. Bonch-

Bruevich, *Materialy k istorii i izucheniu russkgo sektanstva i raskola*, vyp. 1 (St Petersburg, 1908). For a critical appraisal of Tolstoyism as a sect, see T. V. Butkevich and V. M. Skvortsov, 'Tolstovstvo kak sekta', *Missionerskoe obozrenie* (1897), no. 1, pp. 807–31.

113. A. Heard, *The Russian Church and Russian Dissent, Comprising Ortho-doxy, Dissent and Errant Sects* (London, 1887), pp. 37–8.

114. L. Tolstoi, *Polnoe sobranie sochinenii*, 91 vols. (Moscow, 1929–64), vol. 26, p. 401.

115. See M. Aucouturier and M. Sémon, *Tolstoï et la mort*, Cahiers Léon Tolstoi, no. 4 (Paris, 1986).

116. A. P. Chekhov, *Polnoe sobranie sochinenii i pisem*, 20 vols. (Moscow, 1944–51), vol. 18, p. 386.

117. As above, vol. 17, p. 64.

118. *Dnevnik A. S. Suvorina* (Moscow–Petrograd, 1923), p. 165.

119. G. McVay, 'Religioznaia tema v pis'makh A. P. Chekhova', in V. Kataev *et al.* (eds.), *Anton P. Cechov – Philosophische und religiose Dimensionen im Leben und im Werk* (Munich, 1997), pp. 251–64; A. Izmailov, *Chekhov, 1860–1904, biograficheskii ocherk* (Moscow, 1916), p. 536.

120. A. V. Chanilo, 'Ikony i kresty A. P. Chekhova i ego blizkikh v yaltinskom muzee', in Kataev *et al.* (eds.), *Anton P. Cechov*, pp. 385–9.

121. A. P. Kuzicheva, 'Ob istokakh rasskaza "Arkhierei"', in Kataev *et al.* (eds.), *Anton P. Cechov*, pp. 437–9.

122. McVay, 'Religioznaia tema v pis'makh A. P. Chekhova', pp. 253–9, 262.

123. Izmailov, *Chekhov*, p. 552.

124. Letter of December 1895 in McVay, 'Religioznaia tema v pis'makh A. P. Chekhova', p. 258.

125. A. Chekhov, *Three Sisters*, trans. M. Frayn (London, 1983), p. 35.

126. A. Chekhov, *Polnoe sobranie sochinenii i pisem*, 30 vols. (Moscow, 1974–83), vol. 2, pp. 280–81.

127. Izmailov, *Chekhov*, p. 546.

128. Chekhov, *Polnoe sobranie sochinenii*, vol. 5, p. 468.

129. A. Chekhov, *Plays*, trans. E. Fen (Harmondsworth, 1972), pp. 244–5.

130. *Perepiska A. P. Chekhova v trekh tomakh* (Moscow, 1996), vol. 3, p. 536.

131. V. Feider, *A. P. Chekhov. Literaturnyi byt i tvorchestvo po memuarnym materialam* (Leningrad, 1927), p. 453.

132. As above, p. 456.

133. See J. Metzele, *The Presentation of Death in Tolstoy's Prose* (Frankfurt, 1996).

134. L. Tolstoy, *The Death of Ivan Ilich and Other Stories*, trans. R. Edmonds (Harmondsworth, 1960), pp. 140, 143.

135. Aucouturier and Sémon, *Tolstoï et la mort*, pp. 77–8.

136. D. I. Pisarev, *Sochineniia*, 4 vols. (Moscow 1955), vol. 1, p. 36.

137. I. Turgenev, *Sketches from a Hunter's Album*, trans. R. Freeborn (Harmondsworth, 1990), p. 222.

138. As above, p. 225.

139. A. Solzhenitsyn, *Cancer Ward*, trans. N. Bethell and D. Burg (London, 2000), pp. 110–11.

140. For memoir sources, see E. Fevralev, *Russkii doreformenny byt i khristianskie idealy* (Kiev, 1907); N. V. Davydov, 'Ocherki byloi pomeshchechei zhizni', *Iz Proshlogo* (Moscow, 1914), pp. 384–5; D. I. Nikiforov, *Vospominaniia iz vremen imp. Nik. I* (Moscow, 1903), pp. 116–25. For ethnographic studies, see V. Nalimov, 'Zagrobnyi mir po verovaniiam zyrian', *Etnograficheskoe obozrenie* (1907), nos. 1–2, pp. 1–23; and P. V. Ivanov, 'Ocherk vozzrenii krest'ianskogo naseleniia kupianskogo uezda na dushi i na zagrobnuiu zhizni', *Sbornik khar'kovskogo istoriko-filologicheskogo obshchestva* (1909), no. 18, pp. 244–55. See further C. Worobec, 'Death Ritual among Ukrainian Peasants: Linkages between the Living and the Dead', in S. Frank and M. Steinberg (eds.), *Cultures in Flux: Lower-class Values, Practices and Resistance in Late Imperial Russia* (Princeton, 1994), pp. 11–33.

141. Fevralev, *Russkii doreformenny byt i khristianskie idealy*, p. 161.

142. D. Ransel, 'Infant-care Cultures in the Russian Empire', in *Russia's Women: Accommodation, Resistance, Transformation*, ed. B. Clements, B. Engel, C. Worobec (Berkeley, 1991), p. 120.

143. T. Ivanovskaia, 'Deti v poslovitsakh i pogovorkakh russkogo naroda', *Vestnik vospitaniia* (1908), no. 19, p. 124.

144. Ransel, 'Infant-care Cultures in the Russian Empire', p. 121; same author, *Mothers of Misery: Child Abandonment in Russia* (Princeton, 1988).

145. 'Smert' i dusha v pover'iakh i v razskazakh krest'ian' i meshchan' riazanskogo, ranenburgskogo, i dankovskogo uezdov riazanskoi gubernii', *Zhivaia starina* (St Petersburg, 1898), vyp. 1, p. 231.

146. For a good account of this process from the memoir literature, see Nikiforov, *Vospominaniia iz vremen imp. Nik. I*, pp. 120–25. See also Nalimov, 'Zagrobnyi mir po verovaniiam zyrian', p. 10; Ivanov, 'Ocherk', pp. 248–9; also Worobec, 'Death Ritual among Ukrainian Peasants', pp. 16–18.

147. Worobec, 'Death Ritual among Ukrainian Peasants', p. 30.

148. Ivanov, 'Ocherk', pp. 250–53; A. Tereshchenko, *Byt russkogo naroda* (St Petersburg, 1848), p. 84; Nalimov, 'Zagrobnyi mir po verovaniiam zyrian', pp. 5–7.

149. Tereshchenko, *Byt russkogo naroda*, pp. 95, 121–4; 'Smert' i dusha', pp. 231–2.

150. Dostoevsky, *The Brothers Karamazov*, p. 906.

151. Strizhev, *Dukhovnaia tragediia L'va Tolstogo*, p. 67.

152. L. Tolstoi, *Polnoe sobranie sochinenii*, vol. 54, p. 133.

153. Pozoiskii, *K istorii otluchenii L. Tolstogo ot tserkvi*, pp. 128–34.

154. Wilson, *Tolstoy*, p. 517.

6 DESCENDANTS OF GENGHIZ KHAN

1. N. A. Dobrotvorskii, 'Permiaki', *Vestnik evropy*, no. 3 (1833), p. 261.

2. See P. Weiss, *Kandinsky and Old Russia. The Artist as Ethnographer and Shaman* (New Haven, 1995).

3. V. V. Kandinskii, 'Stupeni', in *Tekst khudozhnika* (Moscow, 1918), p. 27.

4. V. V. Kandinskii, 'Iz materialov po etnografii sysol'skikh i vychegodskikh zyrian', *Etnograficheskoe obozrenie*, no. 3 (1889), pp. 105–8.

5. L. N. Zherebtsov, *Istoriko-kul'turnye vzaimootnosheniia komi s sosednimi narodami* (Moscow, 1982), p. 19; Kandinsky's unpublished diary of the trip is in Fonds Kandinsky, Centre Georges Pompidou, Musée National d'Art Moderne, Paris.

6. M. A. Castren, *Nordische Reisen* (St Petersburg, 1853–6).

7. See F. Oinas, 'Shamanic Components in the *Kalevala*', in J. Fernandez-Vest (ed.), *Kalevale et traditions orales du monde* (Paris, 1987), pp. 39–52.

8. N. Findeizin, *Ocherki po istorii muzyki v Rossii*, 2 vols. (Moscow–Leningrad, 1929), vol. 2, pp. 219–21.

9. On Kandinsky's ancestry, see V. V. Baraev, *Drevo dekabristy i semeistvo kandinskikh* (Moscow, 1991).

10. N. A. Baskakov, *Russkie familii tiurkskogo proiskhozhdeniia* (Moscow 1979), pp. 11, 58, 83, 100, 155–6, 169, 201–3, 223.

11. As above, p. 142; V. Nabokov, *Strong Opinions* (New York, 1973), p. 119.

12. For an appraisal of the work, see B. Farmakovskii, *N. I. Veselovskii – Arkheolog* (St Petersburg, 1919).

13. E. V. Anichkov *et al.*, *Istoriia russkoi literatury* (Moscow, 1908), vol. 1, p. 99; P. Bogaevskii, 'Religioznye predstavleniia votiakov', *Etnograficheskoe obozrenie* (1890), no. 2.

14. V. G. Tan-Bogoraz, 'K psikhologii shamanstva narodov severno-vostochnoi Azii', *Etnograficheskoe obozrenie*, nos. 1–2 (1910).

15. D. Zelenin, *Le Culte des idoles en Siberie* (Paris, n.d.), pp. 13–59, 118–20, 153.

16. See J. Fennell, *The Crisis of Medieval Russia* (London, 1983), pp. 78–9, 87–9.

17. D. Likhachev, *Russkaia kul'tura* (Moscow, 2000), p. 21.

18. N. M. Karamzin, *Istoriia gosudarstva rossiiskogo* (St Petersburg, 1817), vol. 5, pp. 358, 359–60, 373–4.

19. Letter (in French) to Chaadaev, 19 October 1836, in *Sochineniia Pushkina. Perepiska*, 3 vols. (St Petersburg, 1906–11), vol. 3, p. 388.

20. A. Pushkin, *Eugene Onegin*, trans. J. Falen (Oxford, 1990), p. 26.

21. V. O. Kliuchevskii, *Kurs russkoi istorii*, 5 vols. (Moscow, 1937), vol. 4, p. 352.

22. M. Cherniavsky, 'Khan or Basileus: An Aspect of Russian Medieval Political Theory', *Journal of the History of Ideas*, 20 (1959), pp. 459–76; C. Halperin, *Russia and the Golden Horde: The Mongol Impact on Medieval Russian History* (Bloomington, 1985), p. 98.

23. B. Ischboldin, *Essays on Tartar History* (New Delhi, 1973), pp. 96–109.

24. V. V. Stasov, 'Kritika moikh kritikov', *Sobranie sochinenii V. V. Stasova, 1847–1886*, 3 vols. (St Petersburg, 1894), vol. 3, pp. 1336, 1350.

25. Cited in G. Vernadsky, *The Mongols and Russia* (New Haven, 1953), p. 383.

26. N. I. Veselovskii, 'Perezhitki nekotorykh Tatarskikh obychaev u russkikh', *Zhivaia starina*, vol. 21, no. 1 (1912), pp. 27–38.

27. V. Nabokov, *Speak, Memory* (Harmondsworth, 1969), pp. 26–7.

28. D. Mackenzie Wallace, *Russia*, 2 vols. (London, 1905), vol. 1, pp. 331–2.

29. L. Tolstoy, *Childhood, Boyhood, Youth*, trans. R. Edmonds (London, 1964), pp. 43–4.

30. See P. Longworth, 'The Subversive Legend of Stenka Razin', in V. Strada (ed.), *Russia*, 2 vols. (Turin, 1975), vol. 2, p. 29.

31. *Russkii traditsionnyi kostium. Illiustrirovannia entsiklopedia* (St Petersburg, 1999), pp. 21–2, 91–2, 107, 282–6, 334–5.

32. R. Wortman, *Scenarios of Power: Myth and Ceremony in Russian Monarchy*, 2 vols. (Princeton, 1995), vol. 1, p. 26.

33. E. Edwards, *Horses: Their Role in the History of Man* (London, 1987), p. 213; F. Simmons, *Eat Not This Flesh: Food Avoidance from Prehistory to the Present* (London, 1994), p. 183.

34. M. Khodarkovsky, *Where Two Worlds Met: The Russian State and the Kalmyk Nomads 1600–1771* (Ithaca, 1992), pp. 5–28.

35. M. Bassin, 'Inventing Siberia: Visions of the Russian East in the Early Nineteenth Century', *American Historical Review*, vol. 96, no. 3 (1991), p. 767.

36. M. Khodarkovsky, '"Ignoble Savages and Unfaithful Subjects": Constructing Non-Christian Identities in Early Modern Russia', in D. Brower and E. Lazzerini (eds.), *Russia's Orient: Imperial Borderlands and Peoples, 1700–1917* (Bloomington, 1997), p. 10.

37. Bassin, 'Inventing Siberia', pp. 768–70.

38. Cited in A. I. Stepanchenko, *Gordost' nasha Sibir': molodym o zavetnom krae* (Irkutsk, 1964), p. 5.

39. Bassin, 'Inventing Siberia', p. 772. There was in fact a folk legend that the Siberian steppe was originally a sea. See F. F. Vigel', *Zapiski*, chast' 2 (Moscow, 1892), p. 154.

40. V. Dal', *Tolkovyi slovar' zhivago velikoruskago iazyka*, 4 vols. (St Petersburg, 1882), vol. 4, p. 180.

41. K. Ryleev, 'Voinarovskii' (1825), in *Polnoe sobranie sochinenii* (Leningrad, 1971), p. 192.

42. Iu. Lotman, L. Ginsburg, B. Uspenskii, *The Semiotics of Russian Cultural History* (Ithaca, 1985), p. 111; A. Herzen, *My Past and Thoughts*, trans. C. Garnett (Berkeley, 1999), pp. 170ff.; Vigel', *Zapiski*, p. 144; E. Lavrent'eva, *Svetskii etiket pushkinskoi pory* (Moscow, 1999), p. 346.

43. Marquis de Custine, *Empire of the Czar: A Journey through Eternal Russia* (New York, 1989), p. 211.

44. S. T. Aksakov, *The Family Chronicle*, trans. M. Beverley (Westport, Conn., 1985), pp. 208–11.

45. E. I. Stogov, 'Zapiski', *Russkaia starina* (1903), vol. 114, p. 123.

46. S. M. Volkonskii, *O dekabristakh: po semeinum vospominaniiam* (Moscow, 1994), p. 72.

47. S. Sebag Montefiore, *Prince of Princes: The Life of Potemkin* (London, 2000), p. 293.

48. See D. Shvidkovsky, *The Empress and the Architect: British Architecture and Gardens at the Court of Catherine the Great* (New Haven, 1996), ch. 4.

49. F. I. Lobysevich, *Gorod Orenburg: Istoricheskii-statisticheskii ocherk* (St Petersburg, 1878), p. 7; A. Alektorov, *Istoriia orenburgskoi gubernii* (Orenburg, 1883), p. 4.

50. S. M. Volkonskii, *Arkhiv dekabrista S. G. Volkonskogo*, t. 1, *Do sibiri* (Petrograd, 1918), pp. 79–80, 276.

51. As above, pp. 45–51.

52. As above, pp. 116–18.

53. P. I. Rychkov, *Istoriia orenburgskaia* (Orenburg, 1896), p. 13

54. Volkonskii, *Arkhiv dekabrista S. G. Volkonskogo*, p. 261.

55. IRL RAN, f. 57, op. 2, n. 20, ll. 95, 130, 154; op. 4, n. 96, l. 17.

56. IRL RAN, f. 57, op. 4, n. 144, ll. 17–18.

57. IRL RAN, f. 57, op. 4, n. 95, l. 14.

58. IRL RAN, f. 57, op. 4, n. 95, l. 29.

59. IRL RAN, f. 57, op. 2, n. 20, ll. 7, 9 and elsewhere.

60. IRL RAN, f. 57, op. 4, n. 95, ll. 12, 16.

61. IRL RAN, f. 57, op. 4, n. 96, l. 6.

62. Cited in G. Semin, *Sevastopol': istoricheskii ocherk* (Moscow, 1954), p. 24.

63. S. Dianin, *Borodin* (Oxford, 1963), p. 307.

64. S. Layton, *Russian Literature and Empire: The Conquest of the Caucasus from Pushkin to Tolstoy* (Cambridge, 1994), p. 54.

65. As above, p. 110.

66. V. K. Kiukhel'beker, *Sochineniia* (Leningrad, 1989), p. 442.

67. L. Grossman, 'Lermontov i kul'tura vostoka'. *Literaturnoe nasledstvo*, nos. 43–4 (1941), p. 736.

68. N. Gogol', *Polnoe sobranie sochinenii*, 14 vols. (Moscow–Leningrad, 1937–52), vol. 8, p. 49.

69. As above, pp. 56–8.

70. Pushkin, *Polonoe sobranie sochinenii*, vol. 8, p. 463.

71. *Izmail Bey* (1832), in M. Lermontov, *Polnoe sobranie sochinenii*, 10 vols. (Moscow, 1999), vol. 3, p. 189.

72. As above, pp. 275–6.

73. See, for example, the photographic insets in *M. A. Balakirev: vospominaniia i pis'ma* (Leningrad, 1962) and *Balakirev: Issledovaniia i stat'i* (Leningrad, 1961).

74. E. Brown, *Balakirev: A Critical Study of his Life and Music* (London, 1967), pp. 48–50.

75. N. Rimsky-Korsakov, *My Musical Life*, trans. J. Joffe (London, 1924), p. 33; I. Stravinsky and R. Craft, *Conversations with Igor Stravinsky* (London, 1959), p. 45.

76. *M. A. Balakirev i V. V. Stasov. Perepiska*, 2 vols. (Moscow, 1970–71), vol. 1, p. 188.

77. 'Tamara' (1841), in M. Lermontov, *Polnoe sobranie sochinenii*, 5 vols. (St Petersburg, 1910–13), vol. 2, p. 342.

78. A. N. Rimskii-Korsakov, *N. A. Rimskii-Korsakov: zhizn' i tvorchestvo*, vyp. 2 (Moscow, 1935), p. 31.

79. V. Stasov, *Izbrannye sochineniia v trekh tomakh* (Moscow, 1952), vol. 2, p. 528.

80. Cited in V. Karenin, *Vladimir Stasov. Ocherk ego zhizni i deiatel'nosti*, 2 vols. (Leningrad, 1927), vol. 1, p. 306.

81. V. Stasov, *Russkii narodnyi ornament* (St Petersburg, 1872). The book took several years to publish and hence appeared later than Stasov's work on the *byliny* (published in 1868) – see note 83 below.

82. As above, p. 76.

83. V. Stasov, *Proiskhozhdenie russkikh bylin'*, 3 vols. (St Petersburg, 1868), vol. 1, pp. 225–62.

84. As above, vol. 2, pp. 651–75; vol. 3, p. 617.

85. Stasov, 'Kritika moikh kritikov', pp. 1317–18. The main philologist

concerned was Wilhelm Schott, *Uber das Altaische oder finnische-tatarische Sprachgeschlecht* (Berlin, 1849).

86. Stasov, *Proiskhozhdenie russkikh bylin'*, vol. 3, pp. 334–6.

87. G. Gilferding, 'Proiskhozhdenie russkikh bylin V. V. Stasova', *Vestnik evropy* (1868), vols. 1–4, p. 687; Stasov, 'Kritika moikh kritikov', pp. 1324, 1350; A. A. Shifner, 'Otzyv o sochinenii V. Stasova: "O proiskhozhdenii russkikh bylin"' (St Petersburg, 1870), p. 2.

88. V. Miller, 'O sravnitel'nom metode avtora "Proiskhozhdeniia russkikh bylin"', n.d., Petersburg Public Library, cat. no. 18.116.2.292.

89. K. Aksakov, 'Bogatyri vremen velikogo kniazia Vladimira', *Sochineniia*, 2 vols. (St Petersburg, 1861), vol. 1, p. 342.

90. F. Buslaev, 'Russkii bogatyrskii epos', *Russkii vestnik* (1862), vol. 5, p. 543.

91. N. Rimskii-Korsakov, *Literaturnye proizvedeniia i perepiska* (Moscow, 1963), p. 417.

92. See, for example, R. Zguta, *Russian Minstrels: A History of the Skomorokhi* (Pennsylvania, 1978).

93. A. S. Famintsyn, *Skomorokhi na Rusi. Izsledovanie* (St Petersburg, 1889), pp. 161–7.

94. SP-PLMD, f. 738, op. 1, d. 17; Rimskii-Korsakov, *Literaturnye proizvedeniia*, p. 420.

95. Rimsky-Korsakov, *My Musical Life*, p. 79.

96. Stasov, *Russkii narodnyi ornament*, pp. xiii–xiv, xviii–xix.

97. A. Chekhov, *Polnoe sobranie sochinenii*, 30 vols. (Moscow, 1974–83), vol. 4, p. 31.

98. Chekhov, *Polnoe sobranie sochinenii*, vol. 16, pp. 236–7.

99. As above, vol. 4, p. 19.

100. As above, vol. 4, pp. 31–2.

101. A. Chekhov, *The Island of Sakhalin*, trans. L. and M. Terpak (London, 1989), p. 208. B. Reeve's translation of this passage can be found on pp. 329–30 of A. Chekhov, *A Journey to Sakhalin* (Cambridge, 1993).

102. See N. Frieden, *Russian Physicians in the Era of Reform and Revolution, 1856–1905* (Princeton, 1985), pp. 189–90.

103. Chekhov, *A Journey to Sakhalin*, p. 59.

104. As above, p. 72.

105. As above, p. 338.

106. As above, p. 145.

107. R. Hingley, *A Life of Chekhov* (Oxford, 1976), pp. 63–4.

108. V. S. Pritchett, *Chekhov: A Spirit Set Free* (London, 1988), pp. 111, 148, 155–6.

109. A. Fedorov-Davydov, *Isaak Il'ich Levitan: Pis'ma, dokumenty, vospominaniia* (Moscow, 1956), p. 37.

110. Chekhov, *Polnoe sobranie sochinenii*, vol. 6, p. 210.

111. A. Chekhov, 'Three Years', in *The Princess and Other Stories*, trans. R. Hingley (Oxford, 1990), pp. 128-9.

112. S. Lafitte, 'Deux amis: Cechov et Levitan', *Revue des Etudes Slaves*, 41 (1962), p. 147.

113. Fedorov-Davydov, *Isaak Il'ich Levitan*, p. 136.

114. A. Chekhov, 'The Steppe', trans. C. Garnett and D. Rayfield, in *The Chekhov Omnibus: Selected Stories* (London, 1994), pp. 5-6.

115. Fedorov-Davydov, *Isaak Il'ich Levitan*, pp. 8, 133.

116. Chekhov, *Polnoe sobranie sochinenii*, vol. 15, p. 368.

117. S. P. Kuvshinnikova, 'Iz vospominanii khudozhnitsy', in A. Fedorov-Davydov, *Isaak Il'ich Levitan*, p. 58.

118. Chekhov, 'The Steppe', pp. 3, 13.

119. See, for example, N. Berdyaev, *The Russian Idea* (London, 1947), pp. 2-3.

120. Chekhov, 'The Steppe', p. 34.

121. O. Mandelstam, *The Collected Critical Prose and Letters*, trans. J. Harris and C. Link (London, 1991), p. 352; *M. P. Musorgskii. Pis'ma i dokumenty* (Moscow, 1932), p. 250 (letter to the painter Repin, 1873).

122. Cited in T. Shanin (ed.), *Peasants and Peasant Societies* (Oxford, 1987), pp. 382-3.

123. M. Saltykov-Shchedrin, *The Golovlyov Family*, trans. R. Wilks (Harmondsworth, 1988), p. 113.

124. N. A. Dobroliubov, *Sobranie sochinenii*, 9 vols (Moscow, 1962), vol. 4, p. 336.

125. I. Goncharov, *Oblomov*, trans. D. Magarshack (Harmondsworth, 1954), p. 14.

126. V. I. Lenin, *Polnoe sobranie sochinenii*, 56 vols. (Moscow, 1958-65), vol. 45, p. 13.

127. SP-PLMD, f. 708, op. 1, d. 1315, l. 20.

128. F. I. Bulgakov, *V. V. Vereshchagin i ego proizvedeniia* (St Petersburg, 1905), p. 9.

129. SP-PLMD, f. 708, op. 1, d. 1315, l. 6.

130. *Perepiska V. V. Vereshchagina i V. V. Stasova. I: 1874-1878* (Moscow, 1950), p. 15.

131. SP-PLMD, f. 708, op. 1, d. 1315, l. 22.

132. SP-PLMD, f. 708, op. 1, d. 1315, l. 24.

133. *Russkii mir* (1875), no. 65, p. 27.

134. Bulgakov, *V. V. Vereshchagin i ego proizvedeniia*, p. 17.

135. As above, p. 44.

136. SP-PLMD, f. 708, op. 1, d. 1315, l. 23.

137. As above, l. 30.

138. As above, l. 31.

139. As above, l. 27.

140. V. Grigor'ev, *Ob otnoshenii Rossii k vostoku* (Odessa, 1840), pp. 8–9, 11.

141. M. I. Veniukov, 'Postupatel'noe dvizhenie Rossii v Srednei Azii', *Sbornik gosudarstvennykh znanii* (1877), no. 3, p. 164.

142. A. Malozemoff, *Russian Far Eastern Policy 1881–1904* (Berkeley, 1958), pp. 43–4.

143. F. Dostoevsky, *A Writer's Diary*, trans. K. Lantz, 2 vols. (London, 1994), vol. 2, pp. 1369–74.

144. Cited in J. Frank, *Dostoevsky: The Years of Ordeal, 1850–1859* (London, 1983), p. 182.

145. Pushkin, *Polnoe sobranie sochinenii*, vol. 3, p. 390.

146. A. I. Gertsen, *Sobranie sochinenii v tridtsati tomakh* (Moscow, 1954–65), vol. 23, p. 175.

147. G. S. Lebedev, *Istoriia otechestvennoi arkheologii 1700–1917 gg.* (St Petersburg, 1992), p. 238.

148. *N. K. Rerikh. Pism'a k V. V. Stasovu. Pis'ma V. V. Stasova k N. K. Rerikhu* (St Petersburg, 1993), p. 27.

149. As above, pp. 28–9.

150. E. Iakovleva, *Teatral'no-dekoratsionnoe iskusstvo N. K. Rerikha* (n.p., 1996), pp. 56–7, 134–40.

151. A. Blok, *Sobranie sochinenii v vos'mi tomakh* (Moscow–Leningrad, 1961–3), vol. 3, pp. 360–61.

152. A. Blok, *Polnoe sobranie sochinenii i pisem v dvadtsati tomakh* (Moscow, 1997–), vol. 5, pp. 77–80.

153. Cited in *Istoricheskii vestnik*, no. 1 (1881), p. 137.

154. Cited in N. P. Antsiferov, *Dusha Peterburga* (St Petersburg, 1922), p. 100.

155. 'Na pole Kulikovom' (1908), in Blok, *Polnoe sobranie sochinenii i pisem*, vol. 3, p. 172.

156. A. Bely, *Petersburg*, trans. R. Maguire and J. Malmstad (Harmondsworth, 1983), pp. 52–3.

157. As above, p. 167.

158. N. S. Trubetskoi, *K probleme russkogo samopoznaniia* (Paris, 1927), pp. 41–2, 48–51. A similar idea was advanced by the philosopher Lev Karsavin in *Vostok, zapad i russkaia ideia* (Petrograd, 1922).

159. See R. Taruskin, *Stravinsky and the Russian Traditions: A Biography of the Works through Mavra*, 2 vols. (Oxford, 1996), vol. 2, pp. 1319–1440; and same author, *Defining Russia Musically* (Princeton, 1997), pp. 389–467.

160. Kandinskii, 'Stupeni', p. 27.

161. Cited in C. Gray, *The Russian Experiment in Art, 1863–1922* (London, 1986), p. 138.

162. A. Shevchenko, 'Neoprimitivism: Its Theory, Its Potentials, Its Achievements', in J. Bowlt (ed.), *Russian Art of the Avant-garde: Theory and Criticism, 1902–34* (New York, 1976), p. 49.

163. *Kandinsky: Complete Writings on Art*, ed. K. Lindsay and P Vergo, 2. vols. (Boston, 1982), vol. 1, p. 74.

164. Weiss, *Kandinsky and Old Russia*, pp. 49–52.

165. As above, pp. 56–60.

166. As above, pp. 153–70.

167. Oinas, 'Shamanic Components in the *Kalevala*', pp. 47–8.

168. A. Pushkin, *Collected Narrative and Lyrical Poetry*, trans. W. Arndt (Ann Arbor, 1984), p. 437.

7 RUSSIA THROUGH THE SOVIET LENS

1. N. Drizen, 'Iz stat'i "Teatr vo vremia revoliutsii"', in R. D. Timenchik and V. Ia. Morderer (eds.), *Poema bez geroia* (Moscow, 1989), p. 147.

2. *The Complete Poems of Anna Akhmatova*, trans. J. Hemschemeyer, ed. R. Reeder (Edinburgh, 1992), p. 417.

3. A. Naiman, 'Introduction', in *The Complete Poems of Anna Akhmatova*, p. 24.

4. *The Complete Poems of Anna Akhmatova*, pp. 210–11.

5. N. I. Popova and O. E. Rubinchuk, *Anna Akhmatova i fontanny dom* (St Petersburg, 2000), p. 18.

6. O. Figes, *A People's Tragedy: The Russian Revolution, 1891–1924* (London, 1996), pp. 603–5.

7. 'Petrograd, 1919', from *Anno Domini MCMXXI* in *The Complete Poems of Anna Akhmatova*, p. 259.

8. Figes, *A People's Tragedy*, p. 727.

9. N. Mandelstam, *Hope Abandoned*, trans. M. Hayward (London, 1989), p. 64.

10. '15 September, 1921', from *Anno Domini MCMXXI* in *The Complete Poems of Anna Akhmatova*, p. 297.

11. 'July 1922', from *Anno Domini MCMXXI*, as above, p. 263.

12. The title of chapter 3 in *Anno Domini MCMXXI*, as above.

13. K. Chukovskii, 'Akhmatova i Maiakovskii', *Dom iskusstv*, no. 1 (1921), p. 42.

14. 'Prayer, May 1915, Pentecost', from *White Flock* in *The Complete Poems of Anna Akhmatova*, p. 203.

15. See, for example, her poem 'The Way of All the Earth' (1940), as above, pp. 530–34.

16. *Zapisnye knizhki Anny Akhmatovy (1958–1966)* (Moscow, 1996), p. 32.

17. *Poem without a Hero* (1940–63), in *The Complete Poems of Anna Akhmatova*, p. 583.

18. The articles ('Vneoktiabr'skaia literatura') were published in *Pravda* on 17 and 22 October 1922.

19. N. N. Punin, 'Revoliutsia bez literatury', *Minuvshee*, no. 8 (1989), p. 346.

20. Popova and Rubinchuk, *Anna Akhmatova i fontanny dom*, p. 68.

21. As above, p. 67.

22. L. Chukovskaya, *The Akhmatova Diaries: Volume 1. 1938–41*, trans. M. Michalski and S. Rubashova (New York, 1994), p. 10.

23. L. Anninskii and E. L. Tseitlin, *Vekhi pamiati: o knigakh N. A. Ostrovskogo 'Kak zakalialas stal' i Vs. Ivanova 'Bronepoezd 14–69'* (Moscow, 1987), p. 23. See further, V. S. Panaeva, *Nikolai Ostrovskii* (Moscow, 1987).

24. S. M. Volkonskii, *Moi vospominaniia v dvukh tomakh* (Moscow, 1992), vol. 2, pp. 326–7.

25. O. Matich, 'Utopia in Daily Life', in J. Bowlt and O. Matich (eds.), *Laboratory of Dreams: The Russian Avant-garde and Cultural Experiment* (Stanford, 1996), pp. 65–6; V. Buchli, *An Archaeology of Socialism* (Oxford, 1999), p. 29.

26. Buchli, *An Archaeology of Socialism*, pp. 65–8.

27. R. Stites, *Revolutionary Dreams: Utopian Vision and Experimental Life in the Russian Revolution* (Oxford, 1989), pp. 190–99; M. Bliznakov, 'Soviet Housing during the Experimental Years, 1918 to 1933', in W. Brumfield and B. Ruble (eds.), *Russian Housing in the Modern Age: Design and Social History* (Cambridge, 1993), pp. 89–90, 99; F. Starr, 'Visionary Town Planning during the Cultural Revolution', in S. Fitzpatrick (ed.), *Cultural Revolution in Russia, 1928–1931* (Bloomington, 1978), pp. 207–11.

28. V. I. Lenin, *Polnoe sobranie sochinenii*, 56 vols. (Moscow, 1958–65), vol. 42, p. 262.

29. L. Trotskii, *Sochineniia* (Moscow, 1925–7), vol. 21, pp. 110–12.

30. On the Ideology of the Constructivists, see C. Lodder, *Russian Constructivism* (New Haven, 1983).

31. See C. Kaier, 'The Russian Constructivist "Object" and the Revolutionizing of Everyday Life, 1921–1929', Ph.D. diss. (Univ. of California, 1995), pp. 66–8.

32. Lodder, *Russian Constructivism*, p. 159; Matich, 'Utopia in Daily Life', p. 60.

33. Pavel Lebedev-Polianskii cited in L. Mally, *Culture of the Future: The Proletkult Movement in Revolutionary Russia* (Berkeley, 1990), p. 160.

34. Mally, *Culture of the Future*, p. xix; RGASPI, f. 17, op. 60, d. 43, l. 19; C. Read, *Culture and Power in Revolutionary Russia: The Intelligentsia and the Transition from Tsarism to Communism* (London, 1990), pp. 113–14.

35. V. Kirillov, 'My' (1917), in *Stikhotvoreniia i poemy* (Moscow, 1970), p. 35.

36. K. Zetkin, *Reminiscences of Lenin* (London, 1929), p. 14.

37. M. Bliznakov, 'Soviet Housing during the Experimental Years, 1918 to 1933', p. 117.

38. T. Colton, *Moscow: Governing the Socialist Metropolis* (Cambridge, Mass., 1995), p. 223.

39. M. Chagall, *My Life* (London, 1965), p. 137.

40. J. Brooks, 'Studies of the Reader in the 1920s', *Russian History*, vol. 9, nos. 2–3 (1982), pp. 187–202; V. Volkov, 'Limits to Propaganda: Soviet Power and the Peasant Reader in the 1920s', in J. Raven, *Free Print and Non-commercial Publishing since 1700* (Aldershot, 2000), p. 179.

41. R. Fülöp-Miller, *Geist und Gesicht des Bolschewismus* (Zurich, 1926), p. 245.

42. *Samoe vazhnoe iz vsekh iskusstv. Lenin o kino* (Moscow, 1963), p. 124.

43. P. Kenez, *The Birth of the Propaganda State: Soviet Methods of Mass Mobilization* (Cambridge, 1985), p. 73.

44. L. Trotsky, 'Vodka, tservkov i kinematograf', *Pravda* (12 July 1923), cited in translation in L. Trotsky, *Problems of Everyday Life and Other Writings on Culture and Science* (New York, 1973), pp. 31–5.

45. On Soviet audience figures, see D. Youngblood, *Movies for the Masses: Popular Cinema and Soviet Society in the 1920s* (Cambridge, 1992), pp. 25–8.

46. K. Samarin, 'Kino ne teatr', *Sovetskoe kino*, no. 2 (1927), p. 8.

47. G. M. Boltianskii, 'Iskusstvo budushchego', *Kino*, nos. 1/2 (1922), p. 6.

48. D. Vertov, *Stat'i, dnevniki, zamysli* (Moscow, 1966), p. 90.

49. R. Taylor, *The Politics of the Soviet Cinema, 1917–1929* (Cambridge, 1979), p. 129. For Vertov's theoretical writings in translation, see D. Vertov, *Kino-Eye*, ed. A. Michelson, trans. K. O'Brien (Berkeley, 1984).

50. V. Pudovkin, *Film Technique and Film Acting*, trans. I. Montagu (New York, 1970), pp. 168–9.

51. For a good general survey of this subject, see I. Christie, 'Making Sense of Early Soviet Sound', in R. Taylor and I. Christie (eds.), *Inside the Film Factory: New Approaches to Russian and Soviet Cinema* (London, 1991), pp. 176–92. The statement about the contrapuntal use of sound (made in 1928 by Eisenstein and Pudovkin) is in R. Taylor and I. Christie (eds.), *The Film Factory: Russian and Soviet Cinema Documents, 1896–1939* (London, 1994), pp. 234–5.

52. S. M. Volkonskii, *Moi vospominaniia v dvukh tomakh* (Moscow, 1992), vol. 1, p. 19.

53. S. M. Volkonskii, *Vyrazitel'nyi chelovek: stsenicheskoe vospitanie zhesta (po Del'sartu)* (St Petersburg, 1913), p. 132.

54. M. Yampolsky, 'Kuleshov's Experiments and the New Anthropology of the Actor', in Taylor and Christie, *Inside the Film Factory*, pp. 42-50.

55. S. Eisenstein, *Selected Works*, 4 vols. (London, 1988-95), vol. 4, p. 67.

56. As above, vol. 4, p. 527.

57. Cited in R. Bergan, *Eisenstein: A Life in Conflict* (London, 1997), p. 28.

58. Eisenstein, *Selected Works*, vol. 4, p. 27.

59. Cited in Bergan, *Eisenstein*, p. 50.

60. For Eisenstein's own comments on this sequence, see his essay 'A Dialectic Approach to Film Form', in *Film Form: Essays in Film Theory*, ed. and trans. J. Leyda (New York, 1949), p. 62.

61. Eisenstein, *Selected Works*, vol. 1, p. 131.

62. K. Rudnitsky, *Russian and Soviet Theatre: Tradition and Avant-garde*, trans. R. Permar (London, 1988), p. 63.

63. V. Maiakovskii, *Polnoe sobranie sochinenii*, 13 vols. (Moscow, 1955-61), vol. 2, p. 248.

64. E. Braun, *The Theatre of Meyerhold: Revolution and the Modern Stage* (London, 1986), pp. 169-73, 180-82.

65. See A. Fevralskii, *Puti k sintezu: Meierhol'd i kino* (Moscow, 1978).

66. Braun, *The Theatre of Meyerhold*, pp. 196, 211, 218.

67. For an eyewitness account of one of Meyerhold's biomechanics classes in the early 1930s, see A. van Gyseghem, *Theatre in Soviet Russia* (London, 1943), pp. 27-9.

68. A. Law and M. Gordon, *Meyerhold, Eisenstein and Biomechanics: Actor Training in Revolutionary Russia* (Jefferson, N.C., 1996), pp. 30-31.

69. As above, pp. 40-41.

70. *Deiateli soiuza sovetskikh sotsialisticheskikh respublik i oktiabr'skoi revloiutsii. Entsiklopedicheskii slovar*, 7th edn (Moscow, 1989), vol. 41, pt 2, pp. 101-2.

71. Stites, *Revolutionary Dreams*, pp. 146-57; E. Toller, *Which World? Which Way?* (London, 1931), p. 114.

72. On Orwell's debt to Zamyatin, see E. Brown, *Brave New World, 1984, and We: An Essay on Anti-Utopia* (Ann Arbor, 1976), especially pp. 221-6. For Orwell's writings on Zamyatin, see S. Orwell and I. Angus (eds.), *The Collected Essays, Journalism and Letters of George Orwell*, 4 vols. (London, 1968), vol. 4, pp. 72-5, 485.

73. E. Wilson, *Shostakovich: A Life Remembered* (London, 1994), p. 61.

74. D. Flanning, *Shostakovich Studies* (Cambridge, 1995), p. 426.

75. For a good introduction to this subject, see T. Egorovna, *Soviet Film Music: An Historical Survey* (Amsterdam, 1997).

76. Flanning, *Shostakovich Studies*, p. 426.

77. G. Kozintsev, *Sobranie sochinenii v piati tomakh* (Leningrad, 1984), vol. 4, p. 254.

78. V. Maiakovskii, 'Teatr i kino', in *Polnoe sobranie sochinenii*, vol. 1, p. 322.

79. As above, vol. 11, p. 339.

80. For a fascinating discourse on this cultural history, see S. Boym, *Common Places: Mythologies of Everyday Life in Russia* (Cambridge, Mass., 1994).

81. Maiakovskii, *Polnoe sobranie sochinenii*, vol. 2, pp. 74–5.

82. As above, vol. 4, p. 436.

83. As above, vol. 4, p. 184.

84. 'Presdsmertnoe pis'mo maiakovskogo', in *Literaturnoe nasledstvo*, vol. 65 (Moscow, 1958), p. 199.

85. A. Charters and S. Charters, *I Love: The Story of Vladimir Mayakovsky and Lily Brik* (London, 1979), p. 362.

86. V. Skoriatin, 'Taina gibeli Vladimira Maiakovskogo: novaia versiia tragicheskikh sobytii, osnovannaia na poslednikh nakhodkakh v sekretnykh arkhivakh', *XX vek: liki, litsa, lichiny* (Moscow, 1998), pp. 112–14, 125, 139, 233 (quote by Eisenstein on p. 112).

87. K. Rudnitsky, *Meyerhold the Director* (Ann Arbor, 1981), p. 445.

88. *Izvestiia* (26 February 1929).

89. O. Berggoltz, 'Prodolzhenie zhizni', in B. Kornilov, *Stikhotvoreniia i poemy* (Leningrad, 1957), p. 10.

90. Maiakovskii, *Polnoe sobranie sochinenii*, vol. 12, p. 423.

91. Cited in H. Borland, *Soviet Literary Theory and Practice during the First Five-year Plan, 1928–1932* (New York, 1950), p. 24.

92. W. Woroszylski, *The Life of Mayakovsky*, trans. B. Taborski (New York, 1970), p. 516.

93. Borland, *Soviet Literary Theory and Practice during the First Five-year Plan*, pp. 57–8.

94. *Soviet Writers' Congress, 1934. The Debate of Socialist Realism and Modernism* (London, 1977), p. 157.

95. On Socialist Realism as a form of panegyric art, see A. Tertz, *On Socialist Realism* (New York, 1960), p. 24.

96. See the brilliant argument of K. Clark, *The Soviet Novel: History as Ritual* (Chicago, 1981), upon which the first part of this paragraph is based.

97. L. Feuchtwanger, *Moskva, 1937* (Tallinn, 1990), p. 33.

98. I. Berlin, 'Meetings with Russian Writers in 1945 and 1956', in *Personal Impressions* (Oxford, 1982), p. 162.

99. P. Kenez, *Cinema and Soviet Society, 1917–1953* (Cambridge, 1992), pp. 91–2; Taylor, *The Politics of the Soviet Cinema*, pp. 95–6.

100. *Puti kino: pervoe vsesoiuznoe soveshchanie po kinematografii* (Moscow, 1929), p. 37.

101. Youngblood, *Movies for the Masses*, pp. 93–4; Taylor, *The Politics of the Soviet Cinema*, p. 141.

102. Cited in M. Turovskaya, 'The 1930s and 1940s: Cinema in Context', in R. Taylor and D. Spring (eds.), *Stalinism and Soviet Cinema* (London, 1993), p. 43.

103. See D. Youngblood, *Soviet Cinema in the Silent Era, 1917–1935* (Ann Arbor, 1985), pp. 230–2.

104. 'O fil'me "Bezhin lug" ', *Pravda* (19 March 1939), p. 3.

105. Bergan, *Eisenstein*, pp. 283–6.

106. *Pervyi vsesoiuznyi s'ezd sovetskikh pisatelei* (Moscow, 1934), p. 316.

107. R. Taruskin, 'Shostakovich and Us', in R. Bartlett (ed.), *Shostakovich in Context* (Oxford, 2000), pp. 16–17.

108. 'Sumbur vmesto muzyki', *Pravda* (28 January 1936).

109. On his torture and confession, see V. Shentalinsky, *The KGB's Literary Archive: The Discovery and Ultimate Fate of Russia's Suppressed Writers*, trans. J. Crowfoot (London, 1995), pp. 25–6.

110. Cited in M. Brown, *Art under Stalin* (New York, 1991), p. 92.

111. Iu. Molok, *Pushkin v 1937 godu* (Moscow, 2000), p. 31.

112. M. Levitt, *Russian Literary Politics and the Pushkin Celebration of 1880* (Cornell, 1989), p. 164.

113. A. Platonov, *Thoughts of a Reader* (Moscow, 1980), pp. 24, 41.

114. Cited in Levitt, *Russian Literary Politics*, p. 165.

115. N. Mandelstam, *Hope Against Hope*, trans. M. Hayward (London, 1989), p. 159.

116. R. Conquest, *Tyrants and Typewriters: Communiqués from the Struggle for Truth* (Lexington, 1989), p. 61.

117. Mandelstam, *Hope Against Hope*, p. 26.

118. R. Reeder, *Anna Akhmatova: Poet and Prophet* (London, 1995), p. 197.

119. Mandelstam, *Hope Against Hope*, p. 161.

120. As above, p. 13. This is the first version of the poem which came into the hands of the NKVD.

121. A. Akhmatova, *My Half Century: Selected Prose*, ed. R. Meyer (Ann Arbor, 1992), p. 101.

122. E. Polyanovskii, *Gibel' Osipa Mandelstama* (St Petersburg, 1993), p. 104.

123. Shentalinsky, *The KGB's Literary Archive*, p. 183.

124. On Pasternak's behaviour in this famous incident, where he has been

accused of betraying Mandelstam, it is best to consult the account by Nadezhda Mandelstam, who claims that her husband was 'entirely happy with the way Pasternak had handled things' (*Hope Against Hope*, p. 148).

125. 'A Little Geography, O.M.' (1937), in *The Complete Poems of Anna Akhmatova*, p. 664.

126. Akhmatova, *My Half Century*, p. 108.

127. O. Kalugin, 'Delo KGB na Annu Akhmatovu', in *Gosbezopasnost' i literatura na opyte Rossii i Germanii* (Moscow, 1994), p. 32.

128. Popova and Rubinchuk, *Anna Akhmatova i fontanny dom*, p. 70.

129. *The Complete Poems of Anna Akhmatova*, p. 384.

130. As above, p. 393.

131. As above, p. 386.

132. Epigraph to *Requiem* (1961), as above, p. 384.

133. Mandelstam, *Hope Abandoned*, p. 252.

134. B. Pasternak, *Doctor Zhivago*, trans. M. Hayward and M. Hari (London, 1988), p. 453.

135. Cited in O. Ivinskaia, *V plenu vremeni: gody s B. Pasternakom* (Moscow, 1972), p. 96.

136. *On Early Trains* (1943), in B. Pasternak, *Sobranie sochinenii v piati tomakh* (Moscow, 1989), vol. 2, pp. 35–6.

137. *Pravda* (23 June 1941).

138. *Krasnaia zvezda* (24 June 1941).

139. See F. Corley, *Religion in the Soviet Union: An Archival Reader* (Basingstoke, 1996), pp. 142–4.

140. Berlin, 'Meetings with Russian Writers', pp. 160–61.

141. *Mikhail Zoshchenko: materialy k tvorcheskoi biografii*, ed. N. Groznova (St Petersburg, 1997), pp. 173, 193.

142. Popova and Rubinchuk, *Anna Akhmatova i fontanny dom*, pp. 91–2.

143. 'Courage' (1942), in *The Complete Poems of Anna Akhmatova*, p. 428.

144. Cited in A. I. Pavlovskii, *Anna Akhmatova* (Leningrad, 1982), p. 99.

145. A. Haight, *Anna Akhmatova: poeticheskoe stranstvie: dnevniki, vospominaniia, pis'ma* (Moscow, 1991), p. 122.

146. G. P. Makogonenko, 'Iz tret'ei epokhi vospominanii', in *Ob Anne Akhmatovoi* (Leningrad, 1990), pp. 263–4.

147. D. Oistrakh, 'Velikii khudozhnik nashego vremeni', in *Shostakovich: stat'i i materialy* (Moscow, 1976), p. 26.

148. I. MacDonald, *The New Shostakovich* (Oxford, 1991), pp. 153–5.

149. Wilson, *Shostakovich*, p. 134.

150. On the Mahlerian sources of the symphony's finale, see I. Barsova, 'Between "Social Demands" and the "Music of Grand Passions": The Years

1934–1937 in the Life of Dmitry Shostakovich', in R. Bartlett (ed.), *Shostakovich in Context* (Oxford, 2000), pp. 85–6.

151. A. Rozen, 'Razgovor s drugom', *Zvezda*, vol. 2, no. 1 (1973), p. 81.

152. Cited in H. Robinson, 'Composing for Victory: Classical Music', in R. Stites (ed.), *Culture and Entertainment in War-time Russia* (Indiana, 1995), p. 62.

153. *Sergei Prokofiev: materialy, dokumenty, vospominaniia* (Moscow, 1960), p. 457.

154. See H. Robinson, *Sergei Prokofiev* (London, 1987), ch. 22.

155. S. Eisenstein, 'From Lectures on Music and Colour in *Ivan the Terrible*', in *Selected Works*, vol. 3, pp. 153, 168–9, 317–19, 326–7.

156. See *Sergei Prokofiev: materialy, dokumenty, vospominaniia*, pp. 481–92.

157. Ivinskaia, *V plenu vremeni*, p. 96.

158. L. Kozlov, 'The Artist and the Shadow of Ivan', pp. 114–15.

159. A clear statement of Eisenstein's intention can be found in Io. Iuzovskii, *Eizenshtein v vospominaniiakh sovremennikov* (Moscow, 1974), p. 402. On the influence of Pushkin and his drama on the director at this time, see Kozlov, 'The Artist and the Shadow of Ivan', pp. 115, 123.

160. For the latest evidence on Stalin's mental condition, see R. Brackman, *The Secret File of Joseph Stalin: A Hidden Life* (London, 2001), pp. 195–7, 219–21, 416–17.

161. Kozlov, 'The Artist and the Shadow of Ivan', p. 127.

162. *Moscow News* (1988), no. 32, p. 8.

163. Kozlov, 'The Artist and the Shadow of Ivan', p. 148.

164. J. Goodwin, *Eisenstein, Cinema and History* (Urbana, 1993), p. 191.

165. Cited in Kozlov, 'The Artist and the Shadow of Ivan', p. 123.

166. Iuzovskii, *Eizenshtein v vospominaniiakh sovremennikov*, pp. 412–13.

167. Berlin, 'Meetings with Russian Writers', p. 198.

168. Iu. Budyko, 'Istoriia odnogo posviashcheniia', *Russkaia literatura*, no. 1 (1984), p. 236.

169. Berlin, 'Meetings with Russian Writers', p. 189.

170. As above, p. 190.

171. '20 December 1945', in *The Complete Poems of Anna Akhmatova*, p. 454.

172. Mandelstam, *Hope Abandoned*, pp. 368–72.

173. 'Doklad t. Zhdanova o zhurnalakh *Zvezda* i *Leningrad*', *Znamiia*, vol. 10 (1946), pp. 7–22.

174. Mandelstam, *Hope Abandoned*, pp. 350–57.

175. E. Gershtein, *Memuary* (St Petersburg, 1998), p. 345.

176. Berlin, 'Meetings with Russian Writers', p. 202.

177. See G. Dalos, *The Guest from the Future: Anna Akhmatova and Isaiah Berlin* (London, 1998), p. 85.

178. Mandelstam, *Hope Abandoned*, p. 375.

179. G. Carleton, *The Politics of Reception: Critical Constructions of Mikhail Zoshchenko* (Evanston, Ill., 1998), pp. 231–2.

180. B. Schwarz, *Music and Musical Life in Soviet Russia, 1917–1970* (London, 1972), pp. 208, 218.

181. *Pravda* (9 January 1949).

182. A. Tarkhanov and S. Kavtaradze, *Architecture of the Stalin Era* (New York, 1992), p. 144; A. V. Ikonnikov, *Istorizm v arkhitekturu* (Moscow, 1997), pp. 462–84; A. Ryabushin and N. Smolina, *Landmarks of Soviet Architecture, 1917–1991* (New York, 1992), p. 122.

183. See M. Slobin (ed.), *Returning Culture: Musical Changes in Central and Eastern Europe* (Durham, N.C., 1996).

184. M. Frolova-Walker, ' "National in Form, Socialist in Content": Musical Nation-building in the Soviet Republics', *Journal of the American Musicological Society*, vol. 51, no. 2 (1998), p. 334.

185. Frolova-Walker, ' "National in Form, Socialist in Content" ', pp. 331–8, 349–50; T. C. Levin, 'Music in Modern Uzbekistan: The Convergence of Marxist Aesthetics and Central Asian Tradition', *Asian Music*, vol. 12 (1979), no. 1, pp. 149–58.

186. Brackman, *The Secret File of Joseph Stalin*, p. 373.

187. On Stalin's hatred of the Jews, see the illuminating comments of his daughter, Svetlana Allilueva, *Dvadtsat' pisem k drugu* (New York, 1967), p. 150.

188. A. Vaisberg, 'Evreiskii antifashistskii komitet u M. A. Suslov', *Zveniia-istoricheskii almanakh* (Moscow, 1991), pp. 535–54.

189. Brackman, *The Secret File of Joseph Stalin*, p. 380.

190. J. Garrard and C. Garrard, *The Bones of Berdichev: The Life and Fate of Vasily Grossman* (London, 1996), p. 298.

191. I. Ehrenburg, *Men, Years – Life*, 6 vols. (London, 1961–6), vol. 6, p. 55.

192. As above, vol. 6, p. 55.

193. Berlin, 'Meetings with Russian Writers', p. 183.

194. C. Barnes, *Boris Pasternak: A Literary Biography*, 2 vols. (Cambridge, 1998), vol. 2, pp. 233–4.

195. Egorovna, *Soviet Film Music*, p. 122.

196. Cited in Wilson, *Shostakovich*, p. 242.

197. V. Raznikov, *Kirill Kondrashin rasskazyvaet o muzyke i zhizni* (Moscow, 1989), p. 201.

198. Wilson, *Shostakovich*, p. 235.

199. *Shostakovich 1906–75* (London, 1998), p. 62.

200. H. G. Wells, 'The Dreamer in the Kremlin', in *Russia in the Shadows* (London, 1920).

201. Cited in R. Marsh, *Soviet Science-fiction since Stalin: Science, Politics and Literature* (London, 1986), p. 216.

202. A. Tarkovsky, *Sculpting in Time: Reflections on the Cinema*, trans. K. Hunter-Blair (Austin, 1986), p. 42.

203. As above, p. 192.

204. As above, p. 89.

205. A. Tarkovskii, *Time Within Time: The Diaries, 1970–1986*, trans. K. Hunter-Blair (Calcutta, 1991), p. 159.

206. Tarkovsky, *Sculpting in Time*, p. 42.

207. Y. Brudny, *Reinventing Russia: Russian Nationalism and the Soviet State, 1953–1991* (Cambridge, Mass., 1998), pp. 61–73; John B. Dunlop, *The Faces of Contemporary Russian Nationalism* (Princeton, 1983), pp. 226–7.

208. *Veche*, no. 1 (January 1971), p. 2.

209. Cited in B. Eisenschitz, 'A Fickle Man, or Portrait of Boris Barnet as a Soviet Director', in Taylor and Christie, *Inside the Film Factory*, p. 163.

210. 'Leningrad, 1959', in *The Complete Poems of Anna Akhmatova*, p. 716.

211. Berlin, 'Meetings with Russian Writers', p. 194.

212. *The Complete Poems of Anna Akhmatova*, p. 545.

213. O. Mandel'shtam, *Selected Poems*, trans. D. McDuff (London, 1983), p. 69.

8 RUSSIA ABROAD

1. M. Tsvetaeva, 'Homesickness' (1934), in *Twentieth-century Russian Poetry*, ed. Y. Yevtushenko (London, 1993), pp. 234–5. Translation by Elaine Feinstein.

2. Cited in Inna Broude, *Ot Khodasevicha do Nabokova: nostal'gicheskaia tema v poezii pervoi russkoi emigratsii* (Tenafly, N. J., 1990), p. 49.

3. N. Mandelstam, *Hope Abandoned*, trans. M. Hayward (London, 1989), p. 468.

4. M. Tsvetaeva, *Neizdannye pis'ma*, ed. G. and N. Struve (New York, 1972), p. 415; I. Kudrova, *Posle Rossii. Marina Tsvetaeva: gody chuzhbiny* (Moscow, 1997), p. 203.

5. Kudrova, *Posle Rossii*, p. 203.

6. V. Khodasevich, *Stikhotvoreniia* (Leningrad, 1989), p. 295.

7. O. Friedrich, *Before the Deluge* (New York, 1972), p. 86; B. Boyd, *Nabokov. The Russian Years* (London, 1990), p. 376.

8. Boyd, *Nabokov: The Russian Years*, p. 197.

9. 'To the Tsar at Easter, 21 May 1917', in M. Tsvetaeva, *Stikhotvoreniia i*

poemy v piati tomakh, ed. A. Sumerkin and V. Schweitzer (New York, 1980–90), vol. 2, p. 63.

10. R. Taruskin, *Stravinsky and the Russian Traditions: A Biography of the Works through Mavra*, 2 vols. (Oxford, 1996), vol. 2, p. 965.

11. Tsvetaeva, *Stikhotvoreniia i poemy*, vol. 3, pp. 168–9.

12. From 'Otplytie na ostrov Tsiteru' (1937), in G. Ivanov, *Izbrannye stikhi* (Paris, 1980), p. 35.

13. See Broude, *Ot Khodasevicha do Nabokova*, p. 66.

14. A. Saakiants, *Marina Tsvetaeva: zhizn' i tvorchestvo* (Moscow, 1997), p. 725.

15. 'White Guards' (27 July 1918), from *The Camp of Swans* (1917–21) in M. Tsvetaeva, *Selected Poems*, trans. D. McDuff (Newcastle, 1987), p. 62.

16. Cited in V. Schweitzer, *Tsvetaeva*, trans. H. Willetts (London, 1992), pp. 182–3.

17. Unpublished letter cited in Schweitzer, *Tsvetaeva*, p. 168.

18. Cited in L. Feiler, *Marina Tsvetaeva* (London, 1994), p. 203.

19. 'Russkoi rzhi ot menia poklon' (7 May 1925), in Tsvetaeva, *Stikhotvoreniia i poemy*, vol. 3, p. 126.

20. Tsvetaeva, *Stikhotvoreniia i poemy*, vol. 3, p. 164.

21. Tsvetaeva, *Neizdannye pis'ma*, p. 411. Many of these pieces are available in English in M. Tsvetaeva, *A Captive Spirit: Selected Prose*, trans. J. King (London, 1983).

22. Tsvetaeva, 'Homesickness', in *Twentieth-century Russian Poetry*, p. 234.

23. S. M. Volkonskii, *O dekabristakh: po semeinum vospominaniiam* (Moscow, 1994), p. 214. Zinaida Volkonsky's ideas for a Museum of Fine Arts were published in the journal *Teleskop* in 1831. See further M. Fairweather, *Pilgrim Princess: A Life of Princess Zinaida Volkonsky* (London, 1999), pp. 226–7.

24. Saakiants, *Marina Tsvetaeva*, p. 249.

25. Tsvetaeva, *Stikhotvoreniia i poemy*, vol. 3, p. 187.

26. S. M. Volkonskii, *Moi vospominaniia v dvukh tomakh* (Moscow, 1992), p. 32.

27. As above, pp. 234–5.

28. V. Nabokov, *Speak, Memory: An Autobiography Revisited* (Harmondsworth, 1969), p. 216.

29. As above, p. 216.

30. As above, pp. 213–14.

31. B. Boyd, *Nabokov: The Russian Years* (London, 1990), p. 161.

32. See M. Raeff, *Russia Abroad: A Cultural History of the Russian Emigration, 1919–1939* (New York, 1990), ch. 4.

33. A. Pushkin, *Evgenii Onegin*, trans. V. Nabokov, 4 vols. (London, 1964).

34. F. Stepun, 'Literaturnye zametki', *Sovremennye zapiski*, vol. 27 (Paris, 1926), p. 327; N. Berberova, *The Italics Are Mine*, trans. P. Radley (London, 1991), p. 180.

35. *Ivan Bunin: From the Other Shore, 1920–1933: A Portrait from Letters, Diaries and Fiction*, ed. T. Marullo (Chicago, 1995), p. 5.

36. J. Woodward, *Ivan Bunin: A Study of His Fiction* (Chapel Hill, 1980), p. 164.

37. Cited in J. Haylock, *Rachmaninov* (London, 1996), p. 82.

38. S. Rakhmaninov, *Literaturnoe nasledie v 3-x tomakh* (Moscow, 1978), vol. 3, pp. 144–8.

39. As above, p. 52.

40. As above, p. 53.

41. Haylock, *Rachmaninov*, p. 58.

42. Rakhmaninov, *Literaturnoe nasledie*, pp. 128–31.

43. A. Swan and K. Swan, 'Rachmaninoff: Personal Reminiscences', *The Musical Quarterly*, vol. 30 (1944), p. 4.

44. B. Martin, *Rachmaninov: Composer, Pianist, Conductor* (London, 1990), p. 312.

45. Berberova, *The Italics Are Mine*, p. 347.

46. As above, p. 268.

47. Tsvetaeva, *Stikhotvoreniia i poemy*, vol. 1, p. 140.

48. Berberova, *The Italics Are Mine*, p. 348.

49. As above, p. 321.

50. As above, p. 319.

51. Nabokov, unpublished manuscript cited in Boyd, *Nabokov: The Russian Years*, p. 51.

52. Nabokov, *Speak, Memory*, p. 63.

53. V. Nabokov, *Strong Opinions* (London, 1973), p. 178.

54. Nabokov, *Speak, Memory*, p. 201.

55. As above, p. 61.

56. As above, p. 59.

57. Cited in Boyd, *Nabokov: The Russian Years*, p. 177.

58. Nabokov, *Speak, Memory*, p. 214.

59. Cited in B. Boyd, *Nabokov: The American Years* (London, 1992), pp. 463–4.

60. Cited in A. Milbauer, *Transcending Exile: Conrad, Nabokov, I. B. Singer* (Miami, 1985), p. 41.

61. *The Garland Companion to Vladimir Nabokov* (New York, 1995), p. 64.

62. V. Nabokov, 'On a Book Entitled *Lolita*', in *Lolita* (Harmondsworth, 1995), pp. 316–17.

63. S. Schiff, *Vera (Mrs Vladimir Nabokov)* (New York, 1999), pp. 97–8.

64. Nabokov, *Speak, Memory*, p. 215.

65. M. Tsvetaeva, 'An Otherworldly Evening', in *A Captive Spirit*, p. 166.

66. Interview with Alvin Toffler in Nabokov, *Strong Opinions*, p. 37.

67. Cited in V. S. Yanovsky, *Elysian Fields* (De Kalb, Ill., 1987), p. 12.

68. Boyd, *Nabokov: The American Years*, p. 13.

69. As above, p. 22; Nabokov, *Strong Opinions*, p. 26.

70. Schiff, *Vera*, p. 246.

71. V. Nabokov, *Look at the Harlequins!* (Harmondsworth, 1980), p. 105.

72. Cited in Schiff, *Vera*, p. 338.

73. Boyd, *Nabokov: The American Years*, pp. 84–5.

74. See, for example, V. Nabokov, *Selected Letters* (New York, 1989), pp. 47–8.

75. Boyd, *Nabokov: The American Years*, pp. 371, 648.

76. Cited in the above, p. 490.

77. Berberova, *The Italics Are Mine*, pp. 240–41.

78. M. Oliver, *Igor Stravinsky* (London, 1995), p. 96.

79. A. Bruneau, *Musiques de Russie et musiciens de France* (Paris, 1903), p. 28.

80. Cited in Taruskin, *Stravinsky and the Russian Traditions*, vol. 2, pp. 1529, 1532.

81. A. Benois, *Reminiscences of the Russian Ballet* (London, 1941), p. 130.

82. R. Craft, *Stravinsky: Chronicle of a Friendship* (New York, 1994), p. 31; Nabokov, *Speak, Memory*, p. 212.

83. S. Volkov, *St Petersburg: A Cultural History* (London, 1996), p. 315.

84. Cited in H. Sachs, *Music in Fascist Italy* (London, 1987), p. 168.

85. Oliver, *Igor Stravinsky*, p. 139.

86. Cited in the above, p. 143.

87. *Twentieth-century Russian Poetry*, pp. 379–80. Translation by the poet.

88. Cited in F. Lesure (ed.), *Stravinsky: Etudes et témoignages* (Paris, 1982), p. 243.

89. Taruskin, *Stravinsky and the Russian Traditions*, vol. 1, p. 891.

90. I. Stravinsky, *Chronique de ma vie* (1935); quoted from the English translation: *An Autobiography* (New York, 1962), p. 53.

91. N. Nabokov, *Old Friends and New Music* (London, 1951), p. 143.

92. T. Stravinsky, *Catherine and Igor Stravinsky: A Family Album* (London, 1973), p. 4.

93. S. Walsh, *Igor Stravinsky: A Creative Spring. Russia and France 1882–1934* (London, 2000), p. 531.

94. I. Stravinsky and R. Craft, *Expositions and Developments* (London, 1962), p. 33.

95. Craft, *Stravinsky*, p. 120.

96. As above, p. 320.

97. Cited in Walsh, *Igor Stravinsky*, p. 500.

98. Stravinsky and Craft, *Expositions and Developments*, p. 76.

99. V. Stravinsky and R. Craft, *Stravinsky in Pictures and Documents* (New York, 1978), p. 76.

100. Craft, *Stravinsky*, p. 329.

101. S. Alexander, *Marc Chagall: A Biography* (London, 1979), p. 52.

102. O. Figes, *A People's Tragedy: The Russian Revolution, 1891–1924* (London, 1996), pp. 749–50.

103. Alexander, *Marc Chagall*, p. 312.

104. *The New York Times* (15 February 1944).

105. Alexander, *Marc Chagall*, pp. 255, 434.

106. On this aspect of Mandelstam's persona, see C. Cavanagh, 'Synthetic Nationality: Mandel'shtam and Chaadaev', *Slavic Review*, vol. 49, no. 4 (1990), pp. 597–610.

107. Nabokov, *Speak, Memory*, p. 217.

108. Kudrova, *Posle Rossii*, p. 201.

109. M. Tsvetaeva, *Pis'ma k A. Teskovoi* (Prague, 1969), pp. 96–7.

110. Berberova, *The Italics Are Mine*, p. 202.

111. Feiler, *Marina Tsvetaeva*, p. 189.

112. Tsvetaeva, *Stikhotvoreniia i poemy*, vol. 3, p. 176.

113. Tsvetaeva, *Pis'ma k A. Teskovoi*, p. 112.

114. Schweitzer, *Tsvetaeva*, p. 345.

115. Cited in Broude, *Ot Khodasevicha do Nabokova*, pp. 19–20.

116. Berberova, *The Italics Are Mine*, p. 352.

117. Tsvetaeva, *Pis'ma k A. Teskovoi*, p. 147.

118. Tsvetaeva, *Stikhotvoreniia i poemy*, vol. 2, p. 292.

119. AG, Pg-In.

120. Berberova, *The Italics Are Mine*, p. 189.

121. See V. Shentalinsky, *The KGB's Literary Archive: The Discovery and Ultimate Fate of Russia's Suppressed Writers*, trans. J. Crowfoot (London, 1995), pp. 252–4.

122. L. Spiridonova, 'Gorky and Stalin (According to New Materials from A. M. Gorky's Archive)', *Russian Review*, vol. 54, no. 3 (1995), pp. 418–23.

123. Shentalinsky, *The KGB's Literary Archive*, p. 262.

124. See further R. Conquest, *The Great Terror: A Reassessment* (London, 1990), pp. 387–9; V. V. Ivanov, 'Pochemu Stalin ubil Gor'kogo?', *Voprosy literatury* (1993), no. 1.

125. *Sergei Prokofiev: materialy, dokumenty, vospominaniia* (Moscow, 1960), p. 166.

126. Berberova, *The Italics Are Mine*, p. 352.

127. *Sergei Prokofiev*, p. 150.

128. S. S. Prokofiev, *Soviet Diary 1927 and Other Writings* (London, 1991), p. 69.

129. *Sergei Prokofiev*, pp. 161–2.

130. See S. Moreux, 'Prokofiev: An Intimate Portrait', *Tempo*, 11 (Spring 1949), p. 9.

131. *Sergei Prokofiev*, p. 453.

132. N. Mandelstam, *Hope Abandoned* (London, 1973), p. 464.

133. Tsvetaeva, *Stikhotvoreniia i poemy*, vol. 3, p. 212.

134. As above, vol. 3, p. 213.

135. Cited in Feiler, *Marina Tsvetaeva*, p. 263.

136. I. Stravinsky and R. Craft, *Memories and Commentaries* (London, 1960), p. 26.

137. Craft, *Stravinsky*, p. 171.

138. Cited in B. Schwarz, *Music and Musical Life in Soviet Russia* (Bloomington, 1982), p. 355.

139. As above, p. 354.

140. Craft, *Stravinsky*, p. 461.

141. Schwarz, *Music and Musical Life in Soviet Russia*, p. 355.

142. Craft, *Stravinsky*, p. 313.

143. As above, p. 317.

144. N. Slominsky, *Music Since 1900* (New York, 1971), p. 1367.

145. Craft, *Stravinsky*, p. 316.

146. As above, pp. 316–17.

147. As above, p. 315.

148. As above, p. 318.

149. As above, p. 319.

150. See further Taruskin, *Stravinsky and the Russian Traditions*, vol. 2, pp. 1605–75.

151. *Komsomol'skaia pravda* (27 September 1962).

152. Stravinsky and Craft, *Stravinsky in Pictures and Documents*, p. 470.

153. Craft, *Stravinsky*, p. 331.

154. Stravinsky and Craft, *Expositions and Developments*, p. 86.

155. As above, p. 335.

156. As above, p. 332.

157. E. Wilson, *Shostakovich: A Life Remembered* (London, 1994).

158. As above, p. 466.

159. As above, pp. 460–61.

160. As above, p. 375.

161. Craft, *Stravinsky*, p. 328.

Glossary

artel a labour collective

balalaika a type of Russian guitar, probably derived from the *dombra* of Central Asia

banya Russian steam bath heated usually by burning wood

bogatyr knight or hero of folklore; features in *byliny* (see below)

bogoroditsa Mother of God

boyar an order of the Russian aristocracy (phased out by Peter the Great in the early eighteenth century)

bylina an old epic folk song or history with mythological elements. The *byliny* (pl.) are thought by most folklorists to date from Kievan Rus' in the tenth century. Originally sung by the singers of the princes' retinues, they were taken over by the *skomorokhi* (see below) or wandering minstrels of the lower classes. Folklorists began to collect them from the eighteenth century. Ilia Muromets is a prominent hero of the Kievan cycle of *byliny*. *Sadko* is the prototype of the Novgorod cycle, which is close in spirit to the European ballad of medieval times

byt way of life (from the verb *byvat'*: to happen or take place); from the nineteenth century the term was increasingly associated with the 'old' Russian way of life by the intelligentsia, who contrasted *byt* with *bytie* (see below)

bytie meaningful existence – the transcendence of *byt* – in the sense defined by the intelligentsia

chastushka simple, often bawdy, rhyming song

dacha small country or suburban house; often a summer house for urbanites

devichnik a pre-nuptial ritual accompanied by songs: the bride is washed and her maiden's braid is unplaited and then replaited as two braids to symbolize her entry into married life

gusli an ancient type of Russian zither or psaltery associated with the *skomorokhi* (see below)

Holy Fool (*yurodivyi*) a clairvoyant or sorcerer, the 'fool for the sake of

Christ', or Holy Fool for short, wandered like a hermit round the countryside. The Holy Fool was held in high esteem by the common people, and he was often given hospitality by noble families. Rather like a shaman, the Holy Fool performed ritual dances with shrieks and cries; he dressed in bizarre ways, with an iron cap or harness on his head; and he used a drum or bells in his magic rituals

izba peasant house

kaftan a long tunic with waist band

khalat a type of dressing gown

khan Mongol prince

khorovod a group ceremonial dance

kokoshnik traditional female head-dress – its shape was used as an ornament in the neo-Russian architectural style

koumis fermented mare's milk

kuchka literally the 'little heap' – a phrase coined by Vladimir Stasov in 1867 to describe the young Russian nationalist composers (*kuchkists*) grouped around Balakirev and generally known as the 'New Russian School'. Also sometimes referred to as 'The Mighty Five' or 'Mighty Handful': Balakirev, Rimsky Korsakov, Borodin, Cui and Musorgsky

kulak capitalist peasant

kvas a mild type of Russian beer usually made with fermented rye, water and sugar

LEF Left Front of Art (1922–5); revived as New LEF between 1927 and 1929

lubok a coloured woodcut or broadside print with images and texts on subjects from folklore

matrioshka Russian nesting doll

muzhik peasant

narod the labouring people

NEP New Economic Policy (1921–9)

nepodvizhnost' the quality of immobility or non-developmental stasis ascribed by musicologists to Russian folk music

NKVD People's Commissariat of Internal Affairs; became the political police in the 1930s

Oblomovshchina a term for 'Russian' inertia or laziness – from the character Oblomov in Goncharov's novel of that name

oprichnina personal militia of Ivan the Terrible

pliaska a Russian dance

pochvennichestvo, pochvenniki the 'native soil' movement: a group of intellectuals in the 1860s who espoused a synthesis of Slavophile and Westernizing principles

Proletkult Proletarian Culture organization

RAPP Russian Association of Proletarian Writers (1928–32)

raznochintsy people of mixed social background (usually with one parent of noble birth and one from the clergy or the merchantry); particularly common among the radical intelligentsia of the nineteenth century

samizdat unofficial or underground publication; usually associated with the dissidents in the Brezhnev era

samovar large metallic urn with tap for heated water used in making tea

sarafan a type of tunic

skomorokhi wandering minstrels, *gusli*-players (see above) and singers of folk stories or *byliny* (see above), they were probably descendants of the ancient Slav shamans. Banned by Tsar Alexei in 1648

smotrinie the customary inspection of the bride by the bridegroom's family prior to the agreement of a wedding contract

sobornost' Slavophile conception of the Russian Church as a true community of Christian love and brotherhood

streltsy musketeers who rose up in a series of revolts to defend the Moscow *boyars* and the Old Belief against the reforms of Peter the Great at the end of the seventeenth century

troika a three-horse carriage or sleigh

veche republican assembly of Novgorod and other city states before their subjugation to Moscow in the late fifteenth century

zakuski hors-d'oeuvres

zemstvo gentry-dominated assembly of district and provincial government between 1864 and 1917

Zhdanovshchina literally 'the Zhdanov reign': the regime of Andrei Zhdanov, Stalin's chief of ideology and cultural policy, after 1945

Table of Chronology

HISTORICAL EVENTS	CULTURAL LANDMARKS
862– Kievan Great Princes	
911 Slavs raid Constantinople	
960s raids by Khazars and Pechenegs	
988 Prince Vladimir converts to Byzantine Christianity	*c.* 1017 *Primary Chronicle*
	c. 1040 first chronicles of Kievan Rus'
	1041 St Sophia, Kiev
	1050 St Sophia, Novgorod
1054 split between Byzantine and Roman Churches	
1094 Polovtsians occupy Kiev	
	1103 Annunciation Church, Novgorod
1136 Novgorod breaks away from Kiev	1158 Uspensky Cathedral, Vladimir
1185 Prince Igor's campaign against Polovtsians	
	c. 1187 *Tale of Igor's Campaign*
	1216–25 cathedrals in Yaroslav, Vladimir-Suzdal
c. 1230– Mongol invasion	
1236–63 Alexander Nevsky rules in Novgorod	
1240–42 Nevsky defeats Swedes and Teutonic knights	
1270 Novgorod joins Hanseatic League	

1326 Metropolitanate moves to Moscow

1359–89 Dmitry Donskoi rules in Moscow

1380 Dmitry defeats Mongols at Kulikovo Field

1389–95 Tamerlane attacks Golden Horde

1326 Cathedral of the Assumption, Moscow Kremlin

1333 Archangel Cathedral, Moscow Kremlin

c. 1400 Uspensky Cathedral, Zvenigorod

1405 Rublev icon of Nativity

1410–22 Rublev icon of Holy Trinity

1433 b. Nil Sorskii

1439 Council of Florence

1453 fall of Constantinople

1462–1505 reign of IVAN III

1471 Moscow annexes Novgorod

1480s break-up of the Golden Horde

1485 Moscow annexes Tver

1487 Kremlin armoury

1505–33 reign of VASILY III

1510 Moscow annexes Pskov

1533–84 reign of IVAN IV ('THE TERRIBLE')

1552–6 conquest of khanates of Kazan and Astrakhan

1560 St Basil's Cathedral, Moscow

1564 first Russian book printed

1565 establishment of *oprichnina*

1582 Ermak conquers khanate of Siberia

1584–98 reign of FEDOR I; Boris Godunov regent

1589 creation of Moscow patri-archate

1598–1605 reign of BORIS GODUNOV

1598 Trinity Church, Moscow

1605–13 'Time of Troubles'

1610 Polish troops occupy Moscow

1612 Minin and Pozharsky's militia expels Poles

1613–45 reign of MIKHAIL ROMANOV

1639 Cossacks reach Pacific coast
1645–76 reign of ALEXEI
1653 Patriarch Nikon's reforms
1654 Old Believers divide Church
1670–71 Stenka Razin rebellion
1676–82 reign of FEDOR ALEXEIVICH
1682–1725 reign of PETER I ('THE GREAT')
1697–8 Peter visits Europe
1698 suppression of *streltsy* rebellions
1703 foundation of St Petersburg

1709 defeat of Swedes at battle of Poltava
1711 establishment of Senate
1712 Imperial court moves to St Petersburg

1721 Patriarchate replaced by Holy Synod
1722 Table of Ranks
1725–7 reign of CATHERINE I
1727–30 reign of PETER II
1730–40 reign of ANNA I

1614 Moscow printing house
1632 Kiev Academy
1636 Kremlin Terem Palace

1648 ban on *skomorokhi*

1678 Ushakov: *Saviour Not Done by Hands*
1685 Slav–Greek–Latin Academy, Moscow

1700 adoption of Julian calendar
1703 first Russian newspaper
Peter and Paul Fortress

1710 new civil alphabet

1714 Summer Palace, St Petersburg
Kunstkamera
1717 *Honourable Mirror to Youth*

1725 Academy of Sciences

1731 first opera performance in Russia
1733 Trezzini: Peter and Paul Cathedral
1734 Winter Palace Theatre
1737 Commission for the Orderly Development of St Petersburg
1739 Tatishchev: Urals as boundary of Europe
1740– rebuilding of Fountain House (Sheremetev palace)

1741–61 reign of ELIZABETH	**1741–** Rastrelli's Summer Palace, St Petersburg
	1750 Sumarokov: *The Monsters*
	1754– Rastrelli's Winter Palace
	1755 establishment of Moscow University
	1757 Academy of Arts, St Petersburg
	1757 Lomonosov's *Russian Grammar*
1762–96 reign of CATHERINE II ('THE GREAT')	
1762 emancipation of nobility from compulsory state service	
1764 state seizure of Church lands Smolny Convent for noblewomen	**1766** Trediakovsky: *Tilemakhida*
1768–74 war with Turkey	**1768–** Falconet's *Bronze Horseman*
	1769 Fonvizin: *The Brigadier*
	1772 Fomin: *Anyuta*
1773–4 Pugachev rebellion	
1775 reform of provincial administration	**1777–** Sheremetev Theatre at Kuskovo
	1779 début of Praskovya in Sheremetev opera Kniazhnin: *Misfortune from a Carriage*
	1780– Cameron's ensemble at Pavlovsk
	1782 Fonvizin: *The Minor*
1783 annexation of Crimea	**1783** establishment of Russian Academy
	1784 Shcherbatov: *Journey to the Land of Ophir*
1788–91 war with Turkey	
1789 French Revolution	
	1790– building of Ostankino (Sheremetev palace)
	1790 Lvov–Prach: *Collection of Russian Folk Songs*
	1790 Radishchev: *Journey from St Petersburg to Moscow*

1840 Lermontov: *A Hero of Our Times*

1842– building of first railway

1842 Gogol: first part of *Dead Souls*

1844 Odoevsky: *Russian Nights*

1846 Gogol: *Selected Passages from Correspondence with Friends*

1846– Solntsev: *Antiquities of the Russian State*

1847 Belinsky: *Letter to Gogol*

1849 Petrashevsky circle arrested (Dostoevsky)

1852 Turgenev: *Sketches from a Hunter's Album*

1852– Herzen: *My Past and Thoughts*

1853–6 Crimean War
1855–81 reign of ALEXANDER II
1858 conquest of Amur region
1859 conquest of Caucasus

1859 Goncharov: *Oblomov*

1860 Ostrovsky: *The Storm*
Stroganov Art School, Moscow

1861 Emancipation of the Serfs

1861 revolt of artists ('Wanderers') from Academy
establishment of Conservatory in St Petersburg

1862 Dostoevsky: *House of the Dead*
Turgenev: *Fathers and Children*
Chernyshevsky: *What Is to Be Done?*

1863– Nekrasov: *Who Is Happy in Russia?*

1864 establishment of *zemstvos*
judicial reforms
new provisions for primary education

1865 relaxation of censorship
1865–76 conquest of Samarkand, Khiva, Bukhara

1865 Tolstoy: *War and Peace*

1866– Balakirev: *Tamara*
Dostoevsky: *Crime and Punishment*
Afanasiev: *Slavs' Poetic View of Nature*

1870– Przhevalsky's exploration of
Central Asia

1877–8 Russo-Turkish War

1881 assassination of Alexander II
1881–94 reign of ALEXANDER III
1881 establishment of political
police (Okhrana)
1882 anti-Jewish laws

1890 restrictions on *zemstvos*

1891–3 famine crisis

1868 Stasov: *Origins of the Russian
Byliny*
Dostoevsky: *The Idiot*
1868–74 Musorgsky: *Boris Godunov*
1871– Abramtsevo artists' colony
1872 Dostoevsky: *The Devils*
1873 Repin: *The Volga Barge
Haulers*
Rimsky-Korsakov: *The Maid
of Pskov*
1873– Tolstoy: *Anna Karenina*
1874– 'going to the people'
movement
1874 Musorgsky: *Khovanshchina*;
Pictures at an Exhibition
Vereshchagin exhibition in
St Petersburg
1877 Balakirev's transcriptions of
peasant songs
1879– Tolstoy: *A Confession*
1880 Dostoevsky: *Brothers
Karamazov*

1883 Cathedral of Christ the
Saviour, Moscow
1884 Surikov: *Boyar's Wife
Morozova*
1885 Mamontov's Private Opera
1886 Tolstoy: *Death of Ivan Ilich*
1887 Chekhov: 'The Steppe'
Levitan: *Evenings on the Volga*
1890 Borodin: *Prince Igor*
Tchaikovsky: *The Queen of
Spades*; *The Sleeping Beauty*
1891 Rachmaninov: First Piano
Concerto
1892 Levitan: *The Vladimirka*
Tretiakov Museum established

1893–4 Chekhov: *The Island of Sakhalin*

1894–1917 reign of NICHOLAS II

1894– Russian Symbolists

1895 Tchaikovsky: *Swan Lake*
Surikov: *Ermak's Conquest of Siberia*
Ethnographic Museum, St Petersburg

1896 Chekhov: *The Seagull; Uncle Vanya*

1897 first national census

1897 Rimsky-Korsakov: *Sadko*
Chekhov: 'Peasants'

1898 formation of Social Democratic Workers' Party

1898 Moscow Arts Theatre

1898– 'World of Art'
Talashkino artists' colony

1899 Tolstoy: *Resurrection*

1900 Russian occupation of Manchuria

1901 formation of Socialist Revolutionary Party

1901 Roerich: *The Idols*
Chekhov: *Three Sisters*

1903 Trans-Siberian Railway completed
Social Democrats split: Bolsheviks formed

1904–5 Russo-Japanese War

1904 Chekhov: *The Cherry Orchard*
Blok: *Verses on a Beautiful Lady*

1904– Linyova's transcriptions of peasant songs

1905 revolutionary protests
October Manifesto

1905– Scriabin: *Poem of Ecstasy*

1906 First Duma

1906 Gorky: *Mother*
Church of the Spilt Blood

1906– Stolypin Prime Minister

1907 Second Duma; Third Duma

1907 Kandinsky: *Motley Life*
Rimsky-Korsakov: *The Legend of the Invisible City of Kitezh*

1909 *Vekhi* publication
Rachmaninov: Third Piano Concerto

1910 Bunin: *The Village*
Stravinsky/Ballets Russes: *The Firebird*
Goncharova: *Haycutting*

1910– 'Jack of Diamonds' exhibition

1911 assassination of Stolypin

1911 Stravinsky/Ballets Russes: *Petrushka*
Kandinsky: *All Saints II*

1912 Fourth Duma

1913 Romanov Tercentenary

1913 Stravinsky/Ballets Russes: *The Rite of Spring*
Malevich: *Black Square*
Mandelstam: *Stone*
Tsvetaeva: *From Two Books*

1913–14 Bely: *Petersburg*

1914– First World War
Petersburg renamed Petrograd

1914 Akhmatova: *Rosary*

1916 assassination of Rasputin

1915 Rachmaninov: *Vespers*

1917 February Revolution
abdication of Tsar
Provisional Government
Bolsheviks seize power
LENIN Chairman of Soviet government

1917– Proletkult
Tsvetaeva: *The Camp Of Swans* (Soviet pub. 1957)

1918 closure of Constituent Assembly
Treaty of Brest Litovsk

1918–21 civil war

1918 Blok: *The Twelve; Scythians*
Mayakovsky/Meyerhold: *Mystery Bouffe*

1920 Tatlin Tower for III International
Zamyatin: *We* (Soviet pub. 1988)

1921– New Economic Policy (NEP)

1921–2 famine crisis

1922 STALIN appointed General Secretary of the Party
formation of USSR

1921 execution of Gumilev
Tsvetaeva: *Mileposts*

1922 Trotsky's attack on Akhmatova and Tsvetaeva
Akhmatova: *Anno Domini MCMXXI*
Mandelstam: *Tristia*
Meyerhold's production of *Magnanimous Cuckold*
formation of Left Front (LEF)

1940– Akhmatova: *Poem without a Hero*

1941 German invasion of Soviet Union

1941 Nabokov: *The Real Life of Sebastian Knight*

1941–4 siege of Leningrad

1941– Prokofiev: *War and Peace*

1942 battle of Stalingrad

1942 Shostakovich: Seventh Symphony ('Leningrad')

1943 Stalin allows Church Council

1945 Soviet troops in Berlin

1945 Eisenstein/Prokofiev: *Ivan the Terrible* (Part 7)

1946 Party attack on Akhmatova and Zoshchenko

1947 beginning of Cold War

1948 anti-Jewish campaign; murder of Mikhoels
attacks on 'formalists'

1951 Nabokov: *Speak, Memory*

1953 Doctors' Plot
death of Stalin
KHRUSHCHEV confirmed as General Secretary

1955 Nabokov: *Lolita*

1956 anti-Stalin campaign: 'The Thaw'

1957 launch of first Sputnik

1957 Pasternak: *Doctor Zhivago* (first pub. in Italy)

1958 Pasternak awarded Nobel Prize

1961 Gagarin space flight

1962 Cuban missile crisis

1962 Solzhenitsyn: *One Day in the Life of Ivan Denisovich*

1964 fall of Khrushchev
BREZHNEV appointed General Secretary

1966 Tarkovsky: *Andrei Rublev*

1970 Solzhenitsyn awarded Nobel Prize

1972 Tarkovsky: *Solaris*

Acknowledgements

This book has taken a long time to write and it could not have been written without the assistance of many institutions and people.

I owe a great debt of gratitude to the British Academy and the Leverhulme Trust for awarding me a Senior Research Fellowship during the final year of the project. It liberated me from most of my teaching duties at Birkbeck College, London, where Laurence Cole, who replaced me in my teaching, was a generous colleague. I was also very fortunate to receive a two-year Institutional Research Grant from the Leverhulme Trust, which allowed Birkbeck College to employ three part-time researchers on my project. I am deeply grateful to the Trust, and in particular to Barry Supple, Director of the Trust, for his generous attention and support.

I was blessed with a superb research team. Mariana Haseldine provided expert guidance on musical matters, and much else besides. I am particularly grateful to her for leaving her young children in her husband Richard's care and accompanying me on a month-long trip to Russia, where Mariana's charm opened many doors for me. Rosamund Bartlett was my main adviser on literature, and a valuable assistant on many other topics of research. She tracked down and sifted through a huge number of sources, looking for materials to test out my ideas, and checked through my typescripts for mistakes. Any errors that remain are mine. Halfway through the project we were joined by Daniel Beer, then just finishing his Ph.D. on Russian history. Daniel's enthusiastic industry was a huge booot to the project at a crucial time. Hannah Whitley, Mandy Lehto, Timofei Logvinenko and Masha Kapitsa have also worked for me as research assistants at various times, and I am deeply grateful to them all.

In Russia I was fortunate to gain access to a wider range of archives and museums than is normally accessible to scholars from the West. The people who helped me are too numerous to be mentioned all by name, but some should be singled out for thanks. At the Russian Museum in St Petersburg, Tatiana Vilinbakhova, Deputy Director, helped with issues of access; Irina

Lapina gave expert guidance to the manuscripts; and Lena Basner gave sound advice on the collections. I am extremely grateful to Liuba Faenson, Senior Researcher at the Hermitage in St Petersburg, who gave up her free time to show me round the museum and helped me with many questions of research. At the Institute of Russian Literature (Pushkin House) in St Petersburg I owe a debt of gratitude to Tatiana Ivanova, Director of the Manuscripts Division, for granting special access to the archives; to Natalia Khokhlova for her expert help on the Volkonsky papers; and to Galina Galagan for her advice about Tolstoy. I should also like to thank Lia Lepskaia at the Ostankino Museum for her help on the Sheremetev opera; Serafima Igorovna (as she will always be) for helping to locate the Sheremetev papers and a great deal more besides at the Russian State Historical Archive in St Petersburg; Vladimir Zaitsev, Director of the Manuscripts Division of the Public Library in St Petersburg, for his help on Stasov and Rimsky-Korsakov; and Galia Kuznetsova at the State Archive of the Russian Federation in Moscow, for helping to track down the Mamontov papers. I owe a huge debt of gratitude to the staffs of the Public Library in St Petersburg and the Lenin Library in Moscow, where most of my research was done; and to the staffs of the Nekrasov Museum in St Petersburg, the Pushkin Museum (in the old Volkonsky house at Moika 12) in St Petersburg, the Sheremetev Palace (Fountain House) and Akhmatova Museum, and the Tolstoy Museum at Yasnaya Polyana, who all helped in my research.

I am deeply grateful to my agent Deborah Rogers, who, as usual, has been enormously supportive at all times.

I also owe a great debt to my editors: Simon Winder at Penguin and Sara Bershtel at Metropolitan. Simon urged me on with inspirational enthusiasm – his comments always tempered by a passion for my theme. Sara read the draft chapters with a sensitivity and attention to detail which are seldom to be found in an editor these days. I am also grateful to Neil Belton, my first editor at Granta Books, who read the early drafts.

Two other people read the whole typescript: my mother, Eva Figes, whose literary judgement is the litmus test of everything I write; and Richard Yarlott, whose intellect is as brilliant today as I remember it from our student days in Cambridge over twenty years ago.

I would also like to thank Jonathan Hourigan for his deeply learned commentaries on Soviet cinema and the cinematic art – a far cry indeed from our usual electronic banter about Chelsea Football Club.

Finally, at Penguin Books I should like to thank Cecilia Mackay, who tracked down all the pictures for this book, and Andrew Barker, who designed it.

Lots of people helped me with points of detail and directed me to sources that I did not know. I am particularly indebted to Irina Kirillova for putting me right on matters of the Orthodox liturgy; to Stephen Unwin for giving me some ideas on the Stanislavsky method and on Meyerhold; to Professor William Clarence-Smith of the School of Oriental and African Studies for information about Mongol eating habits and rituals of food; and to Edmund Herzig and Raj Chandavarkar for helping me shape my thesis about Russian attitudes towards the Orient. I also learned a lot from conversations with Mark Bassin, Geoffrey Hosking, Gerard McBurney, Michael Holquist, Boris Kolonitskii, Laura Engelstein, Alex McKay, Helen Rappoport and Simon Sebag Montefiore.

Above all, I should like to thank Stephanie Palmer, my beloved wife and friend, who has lived with this monster from the start. Stephanie has been the audience for the less-than-dressed rehearsals of my arguments. She has accompanied me to more performances of obscure Russian plays than perhaps even she would care to know. And despite her busy schedule, she has always found the time to read and comment on my working drafts. This book is dedicated to our daughters, whose loveliness in no small part inspired it. It was written in the hope that one day they might understand their father's other love.

London
November 2001

Permissions

The author would like to thank the following for permission to quote extracts from copyright sources:

The British Film Institute for Richard Taylor's edition of Eisenstein's *Selected Works*.

Cambridge University Press for quotations in Christopher Barnes' *Boris Pasternak: A Literary Biography*.

Carcanet Press for Elaine Feinstein's translations of Marina Tsvetaeva.

Harvill Press/Random House and Atheneum/Simon & Schuster for Max Hayward's tanslation of *Hope Against Hope*.

Northwestern University Press for Kenneth Lantz's translation of Dostoevsky's *A Writer's Diary*.

Oxford University Press for L. and A. Maude's translation of *War and Peace*; for James E. Falen's translation of *Eugene Onegin*; for C. English's translation of *Village Evenings near Dikanka* and for Robert Hingley's translation of *The Princess and Other Stories*.

Penguin Books for Rosemary Edmonds' translations of *Anna Karenina*, *The Death of Ivan Ilyich* and *Childhood, Boyhood, Youth*; for David Magarshack's translations of *Dead Souls* and *The Brothers Karamazov*; for Charles Johnston's translation of *Eugene Onegin*; for Ronald Wilk's translations from *The Kiss and Other Stories*, *My Childhood* and *My Universities*; for David McDuff's translation of *The House of the Dead*; for Elisaveta Fen's translation of Chekhov's *Plays* and for Richard Freeborn's translation of *Sketches from a Hunter's Album*.

Pocket Books/Simon & Schuster for Luba and Michael Terpak's translation of *Sakhalin Island*

Zephyr Press for Judith Henschmeyer's translations of Anna Akhmatova and for the extract from Anatoly Naiman's introduction to *The Complete Poems of Anna Akhmatova*

Extracts from the works of Vladimir Nabokov are reprinted by arrangement with the Estate of Vladimir Nabokov.

A Guide to Further Reading

The research for this book involved too many sources to be listed in a bibliography. On any subject there is an enormous Russian literature. In the Notes I have included only those sources from which I have cited or borrowed heavily. The purpose of this section is to guide the English reader to texts which I enjoyed or found helpful as an introduction to their subject. With one or two exceptions, I have not listed sources in French, German or Russian.

INTRODUCTION

For a general history of Russia I recommend Geoffrey Hosking's *Russia and the Russians: A History from Rus to the Russian Federation* (London, 2001), though two other books are also very good: Nicholas Riasanovsky's *A History of Russia*, 6th edition (New York, 2000); and Paul Dukes, *A History of Russia: Medieval, Modern, Contemporary, c. 882–1996*, 3rd edition (Basingstoke, 1998).

There are two first-rate chronological surveys of the Russian arts since medieval times: James Billington's *The Icon and the Axe: An Interpretive History of Russian Culture* (New York, 1966); and W. Bruce Lincoln's *Between Heaven and Hell: The Story of a Thousand Years of Artistic Life in Russia* (New York, 1998). James Billington's *The Face of Russia* (New York, 1998) bears all the hallmarks of a TV tie-in book but it has some interesting things to say. Three older books deserve mention: Pavel Miliukov, *Outlines of Russian Culture*, 3 vols. (New York, 1972) (originally published 1896–1903); Tomas Masaryk, *The Spirit of Russia* (New York, 1961); and Nikolai Berdyaev, *The Russian Idea* (London, 1947).

Robin Milner-Gulland's *The Russians* (Oxford, 1997) is a perceptive and concise analysis of some of the major themes in Russian cultural history. It is particularly good on belief systems and iconic forms of art. There are some useful essays in Nicholas Rzhevsky (ed.), *The Cambridge Companion to*

Modern Russian Culture (Cambridge, 1998), and in Catriona Kelly *et al.* (eds.), *Constructing Russian Culture in the Age of Revolution, 1881–1940* (Oxford, 1998).

On belief systems, myths and symbols I also recommend: Michael Cherniavsky, *Tsar and People: Studies in Russian Myths* (New York, 1969); J. Hubbs, *Mother Russia: The Feminine Myth in Russian Culture* (Bloomington, 1988); and Elena Hellberg-Hirn, *Soil and Soul: The Symbolic World of Russianness* (Aldershot, 1997).

The most detailed history of Russian art in English is George Hamilton's *Art and Architecture of Russia*, 3rd edition (Harmondsworth, 1983), though *The Cambridge Companion to Russian Studies*, vol. 3, *An Introduction to Russian Art and Architecture*, by Robin Milner-Gulland and John Bowlt (Cambridge, 1980) is also very good. For a more detailed study of architecture, start with William Brumfield, *A History of Russian Architecture* (Cambridge, 1993).

The Handbook of Russian Literature, edited by Victor Terras (New Haven, 1985) is an indispensable resource. I can also recommend: Charles Moser (ed.), *The Cambridge History of Russian Literature*, revised edition (Cambridge, 1992); Victor Terras, *A History of Russian Literature* (New York, 1991); Richard Freeborn, *Russian Literary Attitudes from Pushkin to Solzhenitsyn* (London, 1976); and *The Cambridge Companion to the Classic Russian Novel*, eds. Malcolm Jones and Robin Feuer Miller (Cambridge, 1998). The doyen of Russian music history in the West is Richard Taruskin: his collection of essays in *Defining Russia Musically* (Princeton, 1997) is as good as any place to start. For travellers to Russia, I strongly recommend they pack a copy of *Literary Russia: A Guide* (London, 1997) by Anna Benn and Rosamund Bartlett.

1 EUROPEAN RUSSIA

On eighteenth-century Russia and its place in Europe, start with Simon Dixon's *The Modernization of Russia, 1676–1825* (Cambridge, 1999), which is full of thoughtful insights on Russian culture and society. A good general history of Peter's reign is Lindsey Hughes, *Russia in the Age of Peter the Great* (New Haven, 1998) and of Catherine's reign: Isabel de Madariaga, *Russia in the Age of Catherine the Great* (London, 1991). Marc Raeff has written a wide range of influential essays on the intellectual history of the Petrine state: twenty of the best can be found in his *Political Ideas and Institutions in Imperial Russia* (Boulder, 1994). For a fascinating study of the state's mythic representation, see Richard Wortman's *Scenarios of Power: Myth and Ceremony in the Russian Monarchy*, vol 1: *From Peter the Great to the Death of Nicholas I* (Princeton, 1995). Simon Sebag Montefiore's *Prince of Princes: The Life of Potemkin* (London, 2000) gives a splendid vantage point on the eighteenth-century state – and is hugely enjoyable.

The best writing on the cultural history of St Petersburg is in Russian. However, English readers could begin with Solomon Volkov, *St Petersburg: A Cultural History* (London, 1996), a slightly rambling and eccentric work. For the avant-garde culture of the revolutionary period, see Katerina Clark, *Petersburg: Crucible of Cultural Revolution* (Cambridge, Mass., 1995). The city's architectural history is explored by James Cracraft in *The Petrine Revolution in Russian Architecture* (London, 1988), which recounts the story of the city's foundation; and more generally by Kathleen Murrell in *St Petersburg: History, Art and Architecture* (London, 1995). Iurii Egorov's *The Architectural Planning of St Petersburg* (Athens, Ohio, 1969) is a useful monograph translated from Russian.

Palace-building in St Petersburg is a cultural history in itself. A good place to start is Priscilla Roosevelt, *Life on the Russian Country Estate: A Social and Cultural History* (New Haven, 1995). Elements of style are dealt with by Dimitri Shvidkovsky in his splendid book, *The Empress and the Architect: British Architecture and Gardens at the Court of Catherine the Great* (New Haven, 1996). On the Winter Palace and the Hermitage start with Geraldine Norman's *The Hermitage: The Biography of a Great Museum* (London, 1997).

On St Petersburg as a literary theme, see Sidney Monas, 'Unreal City: St Petersburg and Russian Culture', in Kenneth Brostrom (ed.), *Russian Literature and American Critics* (Ann Arbor, 1984), pp. 381–91; and the same author's 'St Petersburg and Moscow as Cultural Symbols', in Theofanis Stavrou (ed.), *Art and Culture in Nineteenth-century Russia* (Bloomington, 1983), pp. 26–39. Two other essays are also very good: Yury Lotman, 'The Symbolism of St Petersburg', in his *Universe of the Mind: A Semiotic Theory of Culture*, trans. Ann Shukman (London, 1990), pp. 191–216; and Aileen Kelly, 'The Chaotic City', in her *Towards Another Shore: Russian Thinkers between Necessity and Chance* (New Haven, 1998), pp. 101–20. On Pushkin and St Petersburg, see Veronica Shapovalov, 'A. S. Pushkin and the St Petersburg Text', in Peter Barta and Ulrich Goebel (eds.), *The Contexts of Aleksandr Sergeevich Pushkin* (Lewiston, N.Y., 1988), pp. 43–54. On Dostoevsky and St Petersburg, see Sidney Monas, 'Across the Threshold: *The Idiot* as a Petersburg Tale', in Malcolm Jones (ed.), *New Essays on Dostoevsky* (Cambridge, 1983), pp. 67–93. The apocalyptic theme is discussed in the thoughtful monograph by David Bethea, *The Shape of Apocalypse in Modern*

Russian Fiction (Princeton, 1989). On Akhmatova, see Sharon Leiter, *Akhmatova's Petersburg* (Cambridge, 1983). More generally I can also recommend Grigorii Kaganov's *Images of Space: St Petersburg in the Visual and Verbal Arts*, trans. Sidney Monas (Stanford, 1997), a brilliant book on the city's place in the Russian imagination. This, too, is the theme of Joseph Brodsky's lyrical essay, 'A Guide to a Renamed City', in his *Less Than One: Selected Essays* (London, 1986), pp. 69–94.

The intellectual history of the eighteenth-century Russian aristocracy is a vast and complex subject. Readers may begin with Marc Raeff's *Origins of the Russian Intelligentsia* (New York, 1966) and, for a comparative study which draws heavily on Russian evidence, Dominic Lieven's *The Aristocracy in Europe, 1815–1914* (London, 1992). There are some useful essays by Isabel De Madariaga in her *Politics and Culture in Eighteenth-century Russia* (London, 1998). Iurii Lotman's semiotic studies of Russian literature and cultural history are essential reading on this theme. For a sample of his writing, including the important essay 'The Decembrists in Everyday Life', see Iu. Lotman, L. Ginsburg, B. Uspenskii, *The Semiotics of Russian Cultural History* (Ithaca, 1985). There are a number of illuminating essays about various aspects of Russian noble culture and society in John Garrard (ed.), *The Eighteenth Century in Russia* (Oxford, 1973). On the development of the salon and other literary institutions, see William Mills Todd, *Fiction and Society in the Age of Pushkin: Ideology, Institutions and Narrative* (Cambridge, Mass., 1986). There is very little in English on the musical life of eighteenth-century Russia; but on the theatre (including comic opera) readers should refer to Simon Karlinsky, *Russian Drama from Its Beginnings to the Age of Pushkin* (Berkeley, 1985). For more on Fonvizin, consult Charles Moser, *Denis Fonvizin* (Boston, 1979); and for more on Karamzin, see Anthony Cross, *N. M. Karamzin: A Study of His Literary Career* (London, 1971), and Joseph Black, *Nicholas Karamzin and Russian Society in the Nineteenth Century: A Study in Russian Political and Historical Thought* (Toronto, 1975). The best general study of Russian nationalism in the eighteenth century is still Hans Rogger's *National Consciousness in Eighteenth-century Russia* (Cambridge, Mass., 1960). But there are some interesting ideas in Liah Greenfeld, *Nationalism: Five Roads to Modernity* (Cambridge, Mass., 1992).

2 CHILDREN OF 1812

On Napoleon in Russia, start with Nigel Nicolson, *Napoleon: 1812* (London, 1985), or Alan Palmer, *Napoleon in Russia* (London, 1967). On the Moscow fire, see D. Olivier, *The Burning of Moscow* (London, 1966). There are also some useful extracts in A. Brett-James (ed.), *1812: Eyewitness Accounts of Napoleon's Defeat in Russia* (London, 1966). But the best first-hand accounts are the *Memoirs of General de Caulaincourt Duke of Vicenza*, 2 vols. (London, 1935); and Philippe-Paul de Ségur, *Napoleon's Russian Campaign* (London, 1959). On the impact of the invasion on the Russian countryside, see Janet Hartley, 'Russia in 1812: Part I: The French Presence in the Gubernii of Smolensk and Mogilev', *Jahrbücher für Geschichte Osteuropas*, vol. 38, no. 2 (1990), pp. 178–98; and 'Part II: The Russian Administration of Kaluga Gubernia', *Jahrbücher für Geschichte Osteuropas*, vol. 38, no. 3 (1990), pp. 399–416.

Tolstoy's *War and Peace* is itself a sort of history of the 'men of 1812'. For a brilliant discussion of its evolution and historical conception, see Kathryn Feuer's *Tolstoy and the Genesis of War and Peace* (Cornell, 1996). See also R. F. Christian, *Tolstoy's 'War and Peace'* (Oxford, 1962).

On the Decembrists, start with Marc Raeff (ed.), *The Decembrist Movement* (Englewood Cliffs, N.J., 1966). For the intellectual context, see Iurii Lotman's essay 'The Decembrists in Everyday Life', in Iu. Lotman, L. Ginsburg, B. Uspenskii, *The Semiotics of Russian Cultural History* (Ithaca, 1985); Marc Raeff, 'Russian Youth on the Eve of Romanticism: Andrei I. Turgenev and His Circle', in his *Political Ideas and Institutions in Imperial Russia* (Boulder, 1994); and Franklin Walker, 'Christianity, the Service Ethic and Decembrist Thought', in Geoffrey Hosking (ed.), *Church, Nation and State in Russia and Ukraine* (Basingstoke, 1991), pp. 79–95. I can also recommend Patrick O'Meara, *K. F. Ryleev: A Political Biography of the Decembrist Poet* (Princeton, 1984).

On the Volkonskys there are just two books in English: Christine Sutherland, *The Princess of Siberia: The Story of Maria Volkonsky and the Decembrist Exiles* (London, 1984); and Maria Fairweather, *Pilgrim Princess: A Life of Princess Zinaida Volkonsky* (London, 1999).

The literature on Pushkin is voluminous. Elaine Feinstein's *Pushkin* (London, 1998) is a good introduction to the poet's life, as is Robin Edmond's *Pushkin: The Man and His Age* (London, 1994). On the poetry, begin with A. D. P. Briggs, *Pushkin: A Critical Study* (London, 1983), and John Bayley's *Pushkin: A Comparative Commentary* (Cambridge, 1971). On *Eugene Onegin* I learned a great deal from two studies: Douglas Clayton's *Ice and*

Flame: Alexander Pushkin's Eugene Onegin (Toronto, 1985); and William Mills Todd III, '*Eugene Onegin*: "Life's Novel"', in same author (ed.), *Literature and Society in Imperial Russia, 1800–1914* (Stanford, 1978), pp. 203–35. The 'social reading' of *Eugene Onegin* goes back to the work of Vissarion Belinsky in the 1840s. Belinsky's most important article has been published in English as 'Tatiana: A Russian Heroine', trans. S. Hoisington, *Canadian–American Slavic Studies*, vol. 29, nos. 3–4 (1995), pp. 371–95. For the intellectual context of *Eugene Onegin*, read the notes of Vladimir Nabokov's *Eugene Onegin*, 4 vols. (Princeton, 1975), though readers may be put off by Nabokov's literal translation of the text. As an alternative I recommend the lively (rhyming) translation by James Falen (Oxford, 1990). For other Pushkin verse, see *The Bronze Horseman and Other Poems*, translated with an introduction by D. M. Thomas (Harmondsworth, 1982).

There are few specific studies on the influence of folklore on Russian literature. Some idea of the subject can be obtained from Faith Wigzell's article 'Folk Stylization in Leskov's *Ledi Makbet of Mtsensk*', *Slavonic and East European Review*, vol. 67, no. 2 (1986). On Gogol the best place to start is Donald Fanger, *The Creation of Nikolai Gogol* (Cambridge, Mass., 1979). On the Ukrainian influence, by the way, there is a splendid book by David Saunders, *The Ukrainian Impact on Russian Culture, 1750–1850* (Edmonton, 1985). On Lermontov, see Jessie Davies, *The Fey Hussar: The Life of the Russian Poet Mikhail Yur'evich Lermontov, 1814–41* (Liverpool, 1989). On the literary aesthetics of the period, see Victor Terras, *Belinsky and Russian Literary Criticism: The Heritage of Organic Esthetics* (Madison, 1974); and the extracts from Belinsky's criticism in V. Belinsky, 'Thoughts and Notes on Russian Literature', in Ralph Matlaw (ed.), *Belinsky, Chernyshevsky and Dobrolyubov: Selected Criticism* (Bloomington, 1962), pp. 3–32.

On folklore and music I owe a great debt to Richard Taruskin, *Defining Russia Musically* (Princeton, 1997), especially the articles 'N. A. Lvov and the Folk', (pp. 3–24), 'M. I. Gliunka and the State' (pp. 25–47) and 'How the Acorn Took Root' (pp. 113–51). I also recommend Alfred Swan, *Russian Music and Its Sources in Chant and Folk Song* (New York, 1973). On folk themes in Russian art, see S. Frederick Starr, 'Russian Art and Society, 1800–1850', in Theofanis Stavrou (ed.), *Art and Culture in Nineteenth-century Russia* (Bloomington, 1983), pp. 87–112. On Venetsianov there is an excellent article by Rosalind Gray, 'The Real and the Ideal in the Work of Aleksei Venetsianov', *Russian Review*, vol. 4 (1999), pp. 655–75. Alison Hilton's *Russian Folk Art* (Bloomington, 1995) is a fascinating study which touches on some aspects of this theme.

Russian literary attitudes towards childhood are discussed in Andrew Wachtel, *The Battle for Childhood: Creation of a Russian Myth* (Stanford,

1990), a superb book which taught me a great deal. Catriona Kelly also touches on childhood in her fascinating study of Russian manners, *Refining Russia: Advice Literature, Polite Culture, and Gender from Catherine to Yeltsin* (Oxford, 2001).

The best introduction to Alexander Herzen is to read his winning memoirs, *My Past and Thoughts* (Berkeley, 1999). Isaiah Berlin is Herzen's most eloquent exponent in the West. See his essays: 'Herzen and His Memoirs', in *The Proper Study of Mankind: An Anthology of Essays*, ed. H. Hardy and R. Hausheer (London, 1997) (this essay is also in the edition of *My Past and Thoughts* cited above); 'Alexander Herzen' and 'Herzen and Bakunin on Individual Liberty' in *Russian Thinkers* (Harmondsworth, 1978). Aileen Kelly has perceptive things to say about Herzen's philosophy in *Toward Another Shore: Russian Thinkers between Necessity and Chance* (New Haven, 1998) (especially chapters 6, 15 and 16); and *Views from the Other Shore: Essays on Herzen, Chekhov and Bakhtin* (New Haven, 1999). There are two excellent political biographies: Martin Malia, *Alexander Herzen and the Birth of Russian Socialism* (Cambridge, Mass., 1961); and Edward Acton, *Alexander Herzen and the Role of the Intellectual Revolutionary* (Cambridge, 1979).

Chaadaev's Philosophical Letters are available in English in *Philosophical Works of Peter Chaadaev*, ed. Raymond McNally and Richard Tempest (Boston, 1991). For more on Chaadaev, see Raymond T. McNally, *Chaadayev and His Friends: An Intellectual History of Peter Chaadayev and His Russian Contemporaries* (Tallahassee, 1971).

On the Slavophiles, readers should begin with the superb study by Andrzej Walicki, *The Slavophile Controversy: History of a Conservative Utopia in Nineteenth-century Russian Thought* (Oxford 1975). There is also a fascinating study of Ivan Kireevsky by Abbott Gleason, *European and Muscovite: Ivan Kireevsky and the Origins of Slavophilism* (Cambridge, Mass., 1972). Some of the Slavophiles' writings can be found in English: Ivan Kireevsky, 'On the Nature of European Culture and Its Relation to the Culture of Russia', in Marc Raeff (ed.), *Russian Intellectual History: An Anthology* (New York, 1966), pp. 174–207; and Konstantin Aksakov, 'On the Internal State of Russia', in the same book, pp. 230–51. More generally, on the intellectual history of the early nineteenth century I can also recommend Nicholas Riasanovsky, *A Parting of the Ways: Government and the Educated Public in Russia 1801–1855* (Oxford, 1976); Peter Christoff, *The Third Heart: Some Intellectual–Ideological Currents and Cross-currents, 1800–1830* (The Hague, 1970); and the lively memoirs of the nineteenth-century writer Pavel Annenkov, *The Extraordinary Decade*, trans. I. Titunik (Ann Arbor, 1968). Isaiah Berlin is essential reading – especially the essays, 'The Birth of the Russian Intelligentsia', 'Vissarion Belinsky' and 'German Romanticism in

Petersburg and Moscow', in *Russian Thinkers* (Harmondsworth, 1978), and his superb essay on Belinsky, 'Artistic Commitment: A Russian Legacy', in *The Sense of Reality: Studies in Ideas and Their History*, ed. Henry Hardy (London, 1996), pp. 194–231.

Karamzin's historical writing is explored by S. Mark Lewis, *Modes of Historical Discourse in J. G. Herder and N. M. Karamzin* (New York, 1995). See also the introduction by Richard Pipes in N. M. Karamzin, *A Memoir on Ancient and Modern Russia: The Russian Text*, ed. R. Pipes (Cambridge, Mass., 1959). For the debate on Russia's origins, see Nicholas Riasanovsky, 'The Norman Theory of the Origin of the Russian State', *The Russian Review*, vol. 7, no. 1 (1947), pp. 96–110; and for the debate about the monarchy, Frank Mocha, 'The Karamzin–Lelewel Controversy', *Slavic Review*, vol. 31, no. 3 (1972), pp. 592–610.

The 'spirit of 1855' – the intellectual liberation following the death of Nicholas I – is captured very well by Aileen Kelly in 'Carnival of the Intellectuals', in *Toward Another Shore: Russian Thinkers between Necessity and Chance* (New Haven, 1998), pp. 37–54. On Alexander II, see W. E. Mosse, *Alexander II and the Modernization of Russia* (London, 1992) (originally published in 1958); or Norman Pereira, *Tsar Liberator: Alexander II of Russia* (Newtonville, 1983). For more information on the emancipation of the serfs, see Terence Emmons, *The Russian Landed Gentry and the Peasant Emancipation of 1861* (Cambridge, 1967).

3 MOSCOW! MOSCOW!

The reconstruction of Moscow after 1812 is discussed in A. Schmidt, 'The Restoration of Moscow After 1812', *Slavic Review*, vol. 40, no. 1 (1981), pp. 37–48; and in Kathleen Berton's useful general survey, *Moscow: An Architectural History* (London, 1990). For the Empire style, see A. Gaydamuk, *Russian Empire: Architecture, Decorative and Applied Arts, Interior Decoration 1800–1830* (Moscow, 2000). Laurence Kelly (ed.), *Moscow: A Traveller's Companion* (London, 1983) includes memoirs which evoke the atmosphere of Moscow in the early nineteenth century. *Moscow: Treasures and Traditions* (Washington, 1990) contains useful essays on the Moscow style in various arts. I owe a debt to the work of Evgenia Kirichenko, *Russian Design and the Fine Arts: 1750–1917* (New York, 1991), which also traces the emergence of the Moscow style.

On food and drink it is worth consulting R. E. F. Smith and David Christian, *Bread and Salt: A Social and Economic History of Food and Drink in Russia* (Cambridge, 1984), and M. Glants and J. Toomre (eds.), *Food in Russian*

History and Culture (Bloomington, 1997). R. D. LeBlanc, 'Food, Orality, and Nostalgia for Childhood: Gastronomic Slavophilism in Mid Nineteenth-century Russian Fiction', *Russian Review*, vol. 58, no. 2 (1999) is a specialized but fascinating article. The literature on vodka is appropriately large but the best introductory sources are David Christian, *'Living Water'. Vodka and Russian Society on the Eve of Emancipation* (Oxford, 1990), and V. V. Pokhlebin, *A History of Vodka* (London, 1992).

Our understanding of Musorgsky has been dramatically revised by the work of two outstanding American scholars who have sought to rescue the composer from the populist and nationalist ideology of Soviet music history and to highlight the complexity of his intellectual development: Richard Taruskin, *Musorgsky: Eight Essays and an Epilogue*, 2nd edition (Princeton, 1997), and Caryl Emerson, *The Life of Musorgsky* (Cambridge, 1999). On Musorgsky's friendship with Gartman, see Michael Russ, *Musorgsky, Pictures at an Exhibition* (Cambridge, 1992); and Alfred Frankenstein, 'Victor Hart-mann and Modeste Musorgsky', *Musical Quarterly*, 25 (1939), pp. 268–91 (which also contains illustrations of Gartman's work). For the intellectual history of *Boris Godunov*, see Caryl Emerson and Robert Oldani, *Modest Musorgsky and Boris Godunov: Myths, Realities, Reconsiderations* (Cambridge, 1994). Richard Taruskin has done more than anyone to revise our views of Musorgsky's operas. See his ' "The Present in the Past": Russian Opera and Russian Historiography, *c.* 1870', in Malcolm Brown (ed.), *Russian and Soviet Music: Essays for Boris Schwarz* (Ann Arbor, 1984), pp. 77–146. On *Khovanshchina*, see the useful essays in Jennifer Batchelor and Nicholas John (eds.), *Khovanshchina* (London, 1994). For more on Musorgsky's life, see Alexandra Orlova, *Musorgsky Remembered* (Bloomington, 1991); *Musorgsky: In Memoriam 1881–1981*, ed. Malcolm Brown (Ann Arbor, 1982); *The Musorgsky Reader: A Life of Modest Petrovich Musorgsky in Letters and Documents*, ed. and trans. J. Leyda and S. Bertens-son (New York, 1947).

The best introduction to Stasov is Yuri Olkhovsky, *Vladimir Stasov and Russian National Culture* (Ann Arbor, 1983). Some of his musical writings are available in English: V. V. Stasov, *Selected Essays on Music*, trans. Florence Jonas (New York, 1968). The story of the founding of the Russian music school is told by Robert Ridenour, *Nationalism, Modernism, and Personal Rivalry in Nineteenth-century Russian Music* (Ann Arbor, 1981). Balakirev is explored in Edward Garden, *Balakirev: A Critical Study of His Life and Music* (London, 1967). For the music of the *kuchkists*, start with David Brown *et al.*, *The New Grove Russian Masters 1: Glinka, Borodin, Balakirev, Musorgsky, Tchaikovsky* (London, 1986). More specifically on Rimsky Korsakov, see V. V. Yastrebtsev, *Reminiscences of Rimsky-Korsakov*, ed. and trans. Florence Jonas (New York, 1985); Gerald Abraham, *Rimsky Korsakov: A Short Biography* (London, 1945); and Gerald Seaman, *Nikolai Andreevich Rimsky-Korsakov: A Guide to Research* (New York, 1988).

There is a large literature on the merchants of Moscow. On their social and cultural life I found the most useful: Jo Ann Ruckman, *The Moscow Business Elite: A Social and Cultural Portrait of Two Generations, 1840–1905* (DeKalb, Ill., 1984); T. Owen, *Capitalism and Politics in Russia: A Social History of the Moscow Merchants, 1855–1905* (Cambridge, 1981); E. Clowes, S. Kassow, J. West (eds.), *Between Tsar and People: Educated Society and the Quest for Public Identity in Late Imperial Russia* (Princeton, 1991); R. W. Thurston, *Liberal City, Conservative State: Moscow and Russia's Urban Crisis, 1906–1914* (Oxford, 1987); J. L. West, 'The Riabushinkii Circle: Russian Industrialists in Search of a Bourgeoisie 1909–1914', *Jahrbücher für Geschichte Osteuropas*, vol. 32, no. 3 (1984), pp. 358–77; W. Blackwell, 'The Old Believers and the Rise of Private Industrial Enterprise in Early Nineteenth-century Moscow', *Slavic Review*, vol. 24, no. 3 (1965), pp. 407–24. For a description of the Zamoskvoreche district there is no better source than the nineteenth-century writer Apollon Grigor'ev, *My Literary and Moral Wanderings*, trans. Ralph Matlaw (New York, 1962). See also Robert Whittaker, ' "My Literary and Moral Wanderings": Apollon Grigor'ev and the Changing Cultural Topography of Moscow', *Slavic Review*, vol. 42, no. 3 (1983), pp. 390–407. On Tretiakov, see John Norman, 'Pavel Tretiakov and Merchant Art Patronage, 1850–1900', in E. Clowes, S. Kassow, J. West (eds.), *Between Tsar and People: Educated Society and the Quest for Public Identity in Late Imperial Russia* (Princeton, 1991), pp. 93–107. On Mamontov there is a first-rate study by S. R. Grover, *Savva Mamontov and the Mamontov Circle, 1870–1905: Art Patronage and the Rise of Nationalism in Russian Art* (Ann Arbor, 1971). On merchant patronage in general, see Beverly Kean, *All the Empty Palaces: The Merchant Patrons of Modern Art in Pre-revolutionary Russia* (London, 1983). For more on Ostrovsky, see Marjorie Hoover, *Alexander Ostrovsky* (Boston, 1981); and the more recent study by Kate Rahman, *Ostrovsky: Reality and Illusion* (Birmingham, 1999). For my account of the *pochvenniki* I drew a great deal from Wayne Dowler, *Dostoevsky, Grigor'ev and Native Soil Conservatism* (Toronto, 1982).

The Abramtsevo, Solomenko and Talashkino colonies are explored by Wendy Salmond in *Arts and Crafts in Late Imperial Russia: Reviving the Kustar Art Industries, 1870–1917* (Cambridge, 1996). I learned a huge amount from Salmond's pioneering book. Abramtsevo and Talashkino also feature in John Bowlt's superb study, *The Silver Age: Russian Art of the Early Twentieth Century and the 'World of Art' Group* (Newtonville, Mass., 1979). On Moscow's *style moderne*, see William Brumfield, *Origins of Modernism in Russian Architecture* (Berkeley, 1993). And on Shekhtel and the Riabushin-sky mansion in particular: Catherine Cook, 'Fedor Osipovich Shekhtel: An Architect and His Clients in Turn-of-century Moscow', *Architectural Association Files*, nos. 5–6 (1984), pp. 5–31; William Brumfield, 'The Decorative Arts in Russian Architecture: 1900–1907', *Journal of Decorative and Propaganda Arts*, no. 5 (1987), pp. 23–6. The literature on Fabergé is voluminous but there is relatively little on the Moscow workshops of the firm. The best place to start is: Gerard Hill (ed.), *Fabergé and the Russian Master Goldsmiths* (New York, 1989) and Kenneth Snowman, *Fabergé* (New York, 1993). Evgenia Kirichenko's *Russian Design and the Fine Arts: 1750–1917* (New York, 1991) discusses Fabergé and the other Moscow silver craftsmen, including Vashkov and Ovchinnikov. Viktor Vasnetsov has yet to find a Western scholar of his work but Vrubel is the subject of a fine study by Aline Isdebsky-Prichard, *The Art of Mikhail Vrubel (1856–1910)* (Ann Arbor, 1982).

The obvious place to start on Stanislavsky is David Magarshack, *Stanislavsky: A Life* (London, 1986). There are endless books on Stanislavsky's system of rehearsal but I found the director's own explanations the most illuminating: *Stanislavsky on the Art of the Stage*, trans. David Magarshack (London, 1967). The story of the founding of the Moscow Arts Theatre is likewise told best by the founders themselves: C. Stanislavski, *My Life in Art* (London, 1948); V. Nemirovitch-Dantchenko, *My Life in the Russian Theatre* (London, 1968). For my account I also borrowed from E. Clowes, 'Social Discourse in the Moscow Art Theatre', in E. Clowes, S. Kassow, J. West (eds.), *Between Tsar and People: Educated Society and the Quest for Public Identity in Late Imperial Russia* (Princeton, 1991), pp. 271–87.

Chekhov is a vast and complex subject. I learned most from Donald Rayfield, *Understanding Chekhov* (London, 1999), and the same author's *Anton Chekhov: A Life* (London, 1997) and *Chekhov: The Evolution of His Art* (New York, 1975). V. S. Pritchett, *Chekhov: A Biography* (Harmondsworth, 1988) and Ronald Hingley, *A Life of Anton Chekhov* (Oxford, 1976) are older but still worth a read. I learned a great deal about Chekhov's roots in the popular culture of Moscow from Vera Gottlieb's *Chekhov and the Vaudeville: A Study of Chekhov's One-act Plays* (Cambridge, 1982). On Chekhov's major plays I recommend: Richard Pearce, *Chekhov: A Study of the Four Major Plays* (New Haven, 1983); Gordon McVay, *Chekhov's Three Sisters* (London, 1995); Laurence Senelick, *The Chekhov Theatre: A Century of the Plays in Performance* (Cambridge, 1997). *The Cambridge Companion to Chekhov*, ed. Vera Gottlieb and Paul Allain (Cambridge, 2000) is full of useful insights. On the complex subject of Chekhov's religion (a subject discussed in chapter 5) see (for lack of any major English work) Vladimir Kataev *et al.* (eds.), *Anton P. Cechov – Philosophische und religiose*

Dimensionen im Leben und im Werk (Munich, 1997). Julie de Sherbinin's *Chekhov and Russian Religious Culture: The Poetics of the Marian Paradigm* (Evanston, 1997) is highly specialized. Chekhov's attitudes to death are explored by Jerome E. Katsell, 'Mortality: Theme and Structure of Chekhov's Later Prose', in Paul Debreczeny and Thomas Eekman (eds.), *Chekhov's Art of Writing: A Collection of Critical Essays* (Columbus, 1977), pp. 54–67. Chekhov's enigmatic personality is revealed in his correspondence. I recommend: *Letters of Anton Chekhov*, ed. Simon Karlinsky (London, 1973); *Chekhov: A Life in Letters*, ed. Gordon McVay (London, 1994); *Anton Chekhov's Life and Thought: Selected Letters and Commentary*, trans. Michael Heim, commentary by Simon Karlinsky (Evanston, Ill., 1997); and *Dear Writer – Dear Actress: The Love Letters of Olga Knipper and Anton Chekhov*, trans. and ed. Jean Benedetti (London, 1996).

On the Moscow avant-garde (a subject taken up again in chapter 7) I recommend as an introduction: Camilla Gray, *The Russian Experiment in Art, 1863–1922*, revised edition (London, 1986); John Bowlt, *The Silver Age: Russian Art of the Early Twentieth Century and the 'World of Art' Group* (Newtonville, Mass., 1979); and same author (ed.), *Russian Art of the Avant Garde: Theory and Criticism, 1902–1934* (New York, 1988). On Riabushinsky and the *Golden Fleece* circle, see William Richardson, *Zolotoe Runo and Russian Modernism, 1905–1910* (Ann Arbor, 1986). I also learned a great deal from John Bowlt, 'The Moscow Art Market', in E. Clowes, S. Kassow, J. West (eds.), *Between Tsar and People: Educated Society and the Quest for Public Identity in Late Imperial Russia* (Princeton, 1991), pp. 108–28.

On Goncharova it is worth consulting Mary Chamot, *Goncharova: Stage Designs and Paintings* (London, 1979). The spirit of Goncharova's art is beautifully evoked by Marina Tsvetaeva in the long prose work (translated only into French), *Nathalie Goncharova* (Paris, 1990). More generally on the women artists of the avant-garde, see Myuda Yablonskaya, *Women Artists of Russia's New Age, 1900–1935* (London, 1990); and John Bowlt and Matthew Drutt (eds.), *Amazons of the Avant-garde*, exhibition catalogue, Royal Academy of Arts (London, 1999).

On Scriabin I recommend: Faubion Bowers, *Scriabin: A Biography*, 2 vols. (London, 1969); James Baker, *The Music of Alexander Scriabin* (New Haven, 1986); and on the composer's mystical ideas, Boris de Schloezer, *Scriabin: Artist and Mystic*, trans. Nicolas Slonimsky (Oxford, 1987). For works on Pasternak, Mayakovsky, Tsvetaeva and Bulgakov, see chapters 7 and 8 below.

4 THE PEASANT MARRIAGE

The classic account of the Populist movement is Franco Venturi, *Roots of Revolution: A History of the Populist and Socialist Movements in Nineteenth-century Russia*, trans. Francis Haskell (New York, 1960). I also borrowed from the brilliant (and polemical) essay by Tibor Szamuely, *The Russian Tradition* (London, 1988); and from the more sensitive psychological study by Richard Wortman, *The Crisis of Russian Populism* (Cambridge, 1967). I also recommend, on the 'going to the people', Daniel Field, 'Peasants and Propagandists in the Russian Movement to the People of 1874', *Journal of Modern History*, no. 59 (1987), pp. 415–38; and on the intellectual background to the Populist movement, Abbott Gleason, *Young Russia: The Genesis of Russian Radicalism in the 1860s* (New York, 1980). Cathy Frierson's *Peasant Icons: Representations of Rural People in Late Nineteenth-century Russia* (Oxford, 1993) is an excellent account of the changing image of the peasantry in the late nineteenth century.

For more on Repin and the Wanderers, readers should begin with the excellent account by Elizabeth Valkenier, *Russian Realist Art: The State and Society: The Peredvizhniki and Their Tradition* (Ann Arbor, 1977), followed by her equally superb *Ilya Repin and the World of Russian Art* (New York, 1990). I learned a great deal from both works. Alternatively readers may consult Fan and Stephen Parker's *Russia on Canvas: Ilya Repin* (London, 1980) or *Ilya Repin* by Grigory Sternin and Yelena Kirillina (Bournemouth, 1996).

On Turgenev and his complex attitudes towards the student revolutionaries I owe a debt to three brilliant essays: Isaiah Berlin, 'Fathers and Children: Turgenev and the Liberal Predicament', in *Russian Thinkers* (Harmondsworth, 1978), pp. 261–305; Leonard Schapiro, 'Turgenev and Herzen: Two Modes of Russian Political Thought', in his *Russian Studies* (London, 1986), pp. 321–37; and Aileen Kelly, 'The Nihilism of Ivan Turgenev', in *Toward Another Shore: Russian Thinkers between Necessity and Chance* (New Haven, 1998), pp. 91–118. On Turgenev in general I recommend three further works: Leonard Schapiro, *Turgenev: His Life and Times* (Oxford, 1978); F. Seeley, *Turgenev: A Reading of His Fiction* (Cambridge, 1991); and V. S. Pritchett, *The Gentle Barbarian: The Life and Work of Turgenev* (London, 1977). Much less is written about Nekrasov, but there is one decent general work: Sigmund Birkenmayer, *Nikolaj Nekrasov: His Life and Poetic Work* (The Hague, 1968). I learned a great deal from two important works on the literary aesthetics of the 1860s and the revolutionary movement: Rufus Matthewson, *The Positive Hero in Russian Literature* (Stanford, 1975); and Irina Paperno,

Chernyshevsky and the Age of Realism (Stanford, 1988). There is a fine essay by Donald Fanger, 'The Peasant in Literature', in Wayne Vucinich (ed.), *The Peasant in Nineteenth-century Russia* (Stanford, 1968). I owe a debt to this work.

The literature on Tolstoy is large enough to fill a library on its own. As a general biography I highly recommend: A. N. Wilson, *Tolstoy* (London, 1988), although I still love the book that inspired me as a schoolboy: Henri Troyat, *Tolstoy*, trans. Nancy Amphoux (Harmondsworth, 1970). Much of my argument about Tolstoy in this chapter, but more especially in chapter 5, was inspired by Richard Gustafson, *Leo Tolstoy, Resident and Stranger: A Study in Fiction and Theology* (Princeton, 1986). Other works on Tolstoy's religion which I found useful include: E. B. Greenwood, 'Tolstoy and Religion', in M. Jones (ed.) *New Essays on Tolstoy* (Cambridge, 1978), pp. 149–74; David Matual, *Tolstoy's Translation of the Gospels: A Critical Study* (Lewiston, 1992); and Josef Metzele, *The Presentation of Death in Tolstoy's Prose* (Frankfurt, 1996). Tolstoy's letters and diaries are essential reading for an understanding of the man: *Tolstoy's Letters*, ed. R. F. Christian (London, 1978); *Tolstoy's Diaries*, ed. R. F. Christian (London, 1985). For more on Tolstoy's life and work I recommend: Viktor Shklovsky, *Lev Tolstoy*, trans. Olga Shartse (Moscow, 1988); Boris Eikhenbaum, *Tolstoy in the Sixties*, trans. D. White (Ann Arbor, 1979), and *Tolstoy in the Seventies*, trans. Albert Kaspin (Ann Arbor, 1972); Donna Orwin, *Tolstoy's Art and Thought, 1847– 1880* (Princeton, 1993); Malcolm Jones (ed.), *New Essays on Tolstoy* (Cambridge, 1978); A. Donskov, 'The Peasant in Tolstoy's Thought and Writing', *Canadian Slavonic Papers*, no. 21 (1979), pp. 183–96; Alexander Fodor, *Tolstoy and the Russians: Reflections on a Relationship* (Ann Arbor, 1984); Alexander Fodor, *A Quest for a Non-violent Russia – the Partnership of Leo Tolstoy and Vladimir Chertkov* (London, 1989); Andrew Donskov and John Wordsworth (eds.), *Tolstoy and the Concept of Brotherhood* (New York, 1996).

On Russian marriage customs I am particularly indebted to the work of Christine Worobec: *Peasant Russia: Family and Community in the Post-emancipation Period* (Princeton, 1991); and *Russia's Women: Accommodation, Resistance, Transformation*, ed. Barbara Clements, Barbara Engel and Christine Worobec (Berkeley, 1991). I also owe a debt to William Wagner, *Marriage, Property, and Law in Late Imperial Russia* (Oxford, 1994); David Ransel (ed.), *The Family in Imperial Russia: New Lines of Research* (Urbana, 1978); and Laura Engelstein, *The Keys to Happiness: Sex and the Search for Modernity in Fin-de-siècle Russia* (Cornell, 1992).

The impact of Chekhov's 'Peasants' is discussed at length by Lee J. Williams, *Chekhov the Iconoclast* (Scranton, 1989); and in an older but still useful book by Walter Bruford, *Chekhov and His Russia: A Sociological Study*, 2nd edition (London, 1948). For more on Bunin I recommend James Woodward, *Ivan Bunin: A Study of His Fiction* (Chapel Hill, 1980), and Thomas Gaiton Marullo, *Ivan Bunin: Russian Requiem, 1885–1920* (Chicago, 1993).

On urban popular culture at the turn of the century I recommend Richard Stites, *Russian Popular Culture: Entertainment and Society since 1900* (Cambridge, 1992). For the impact on the rural population, see the splendid book by Jeffrey Brooks, *When Russia Learned to Read: Literacy and Popular Literature, 1861–1917* (Princeton, 1985). There are also some interesting essays in Stephen Frank and Mark Steinberg (eds.), *Cultures in Flux: Lower-class Values, Practices and Resistance in Late Imperial Russia* (Princeton, 1994).

For more on *Vekhi* and the intelligentsia reaction to the 1905 Revolution, consult Leonard Schapiro, 'The Vekhi Group and the Mystique of Revolution', *Slavonic and East European Review*, no. 44 (1955), pp. 6–76. On the philosophical aspects of the movement there is a perceptive essay by Aileen Kelly, 'Which Signposts?' in *Toward Another Shore: Russian Thinkers between Necessity and Chance* (New Haven, 1998), pp. 155–200.

There is an ever-growing bibliography on Diaghilev and the Ballets Russes, mostly in English, although several valuable new Russian books have appeared in recent years. Lynn Garafola's *Diaghilev's Ballets Russes* (Oxford, 1989) is the most detailed study of the company. See, too, Lynn Garafola and Nancy Van Norman Baer (eds.), *The Ballet Russes and Its World* (New Haven, 1999). Alternatively, for an all-round survey of the Ballets Russes I recommend Ann Kodicek (ed.), *Diaghilev: Creator of the Ballets Russes: Art, Music, Dance*, exhibition catalogue, Barbican Art Gallery (London, 1996). John Drummond's unique book, *Speaking of Diaghilev* (London, 1997), provides eyewitness accounts of the Ballets Russes phenomenon from members of the company. I also recommend the classic book by Peter Lieven, *The Birth of the Ballets Russes* (London, 1936). On Diaghilev, the best book is still Richard Buckle, *Diaghilev* (London, 1979). But there is also much of interest in Serge Lifar, *Serge Diaghilev: His Work, His Legend. An Intimate Biography* (New York, 1976) (originally published 1940). Benois' memoirs, though incomplete in English, are a splendid read: Alexander Benois, *Memoirs*, 2 vols., trans. Moura Budberg (London, 1964). See, too, his *Reminiscences of the Russian Ballet*, trans. Mary Britnieva (London, 1941). On the artistic aspects of the Ballets Russes I recommend Alexander Schouvaloff, *The Art of the Ballets Russes: The Serge Lifar Collection of Theater Designs, Costumes and Paintings at the Wadsworth Atheneum, Hartford, Connecticut* (New Haven, 1997), and John Bowlt, *Russian Stage Design: Scenic Innovation, 1900–1930*

(Jackson, Miss., 1982). On the choreographic tradition: Tim Scholl, *From Petipa to Balanchine: Classical Revival and the Modernization of Ballet* (London, 1993); and (a fascinating read in its own right) Michel Fokine, *Memoirs of a Russian Ballet Master*, trans. Vitale Fokine (Boston, 1961). Richard Buckle's *Nijinsky* (London, 1980) remains the best introduction to the life of the dancer. There is only one study of Roerich in English: Jacqueline Decter, *Nicholas Roerich: The Life and Art of a Russian Master* (Rochester, Vt., 1989).

On Stravinsky and the Ballets Russes there is nothing to compare with Richard Taruskin's, *Stravinsky and the Russian Traditions: A Biography of the Works through Mavra*, 2 vols. (Berkeley, 1996). I owe a great debt to this awesome masterpiece. It is not an easy work (I needed help from a musicologist to follow much of it). Readers who are put off by its massive size (1,756 pages) or by the density of musical quotation may prefer to consult Stephen Walsh, *The Music of Stravinsky* (Cambridge, 1993), or the same author's detailed biography, *Igor Stravinsky: A Creative Spring. Russia and France, 1882–1934* (London, 2000). For more on the famous première of *The Rite of Spring*, see Thomas Kelly, 'The Rite of Spring', in *First Nights: Five Musical Premières* (New Haven, 2000), pp. 258–99. Igor Stravinsky, *The Rite of Spring: Sketches* (London, 1969) contains Stravinsky's letters to Roerich and the composer's own self-serving account of the 'Stravinsky–Nijinsky Choreography'. On other versions of the history of *The Rite*, see Richard Taruskin, 'Stravinsky and the Subhuman: A Myth of the Twentieth Century: *The Rite of Spring*, the Tradition of the New, and "The Music Itself"'', in *Defining Russia Musically* (Princeton, 1997), pp. 368–88. On *Les Noces* I learned a great deal from the fascinating essay by Richard Taruskin, 'Stravinsky and the Subhuman: Notes on *Svadebka*' (in *Defining Russia Musically*, pp. 389–467), though I have my doubts about its argument about the ballet as a Eurasian work.

5 IN SEARCH OF THE RUSSIAN SOUL

As a general guide to the Orthodox religion I recommend: Timothy Ware, *The Orthodox Church* (Harmondsworth, 1997). On the Russian Church the most detailed and wide-ranging study is by Georges Florovsky, *Ways of Russian Theology*, 2 vols. (Belmont, Mass., 1979–87), although it is not an easy book. Readers may find Jane Ellis, *The Russian Orthodox Church: A Contemporary History* (Bloomington, 1986) rather more digestible. Georgii Fedotov, *The Russian Religious Mind*, 2 vols. (Cambridge, Mass., 1946) has interesting things to say about the Russian religious consciousness in a broad context of cultural history. For a concise overview of the role of religion in Russian culture I recommend Dmitry Likhachev, 'Religion: Russian Orthodoxy', in Nicholas Rzhevsky (ed.), *The Cambridge Companion to Modern Russian Culture* (Cambridge, 1998). Gregory Freeze has done important work on the institutions of the Church. For a discussion of its relationship with the Imperial state, see his 'Handmaiden of the State? The Church in Imperial Russia Reconsidered', *Journal of Ecclesiastical History*, vol. 36 (1985). On the hermitic tradition I learned a great deal from V. N. Lossky, *The Mystical Theology of the Eastern Church* (London, 1957). A good account of the Church's role in Muscovite society is Paul Bushkovitch, *Religion and Society in Russia: The Sixteenth and Seventeenth Centuries* (New York, 1992). For more on Optina and its cultural influence, see Leonard Stanton, *The Optina Pustyn Monastery in the Russian Literary Imagination: Iconic Vision in Works by Dostoevsky, Gogol, Tolstoy and Others* (New York, 1995).

On the cultural role of icons, readers should begin with the seminal work of Leonid Ouspensky: 'The Meaning and Language of Icons', in L. Ouspensky and V. Lossky, *The Meaning of Icons* (New York, 1989), pp. 23–50. Boris Uspensky, *The Semiotics of the Russian Icon* (Lisse, 1976) is an important work. For a fascinating exploration of the icon's influence on the Russian artistic tradition, see Robin Milner-Gulland, 'Iconic Russia', in *The Russians* (Oxford, 1997), pp. 171–226. Some of the same themes are taken up by John Bowlt in 'Orthodoxy and the Avant-garde: Sacred Images in the Work of Goncharova, Malevich and Their Contemporaries', in William Brumfield and Milos Velimirovic (eds.), *Christianity and the Arts in Russia* (Cambridge, 1991).

Robert Crumney is the leading Western scholar on the Old Belief. His study of the Vyg community, *The Old Believers and the World of the Antichrist: The Vyg Community and the Russian State, 1694–1855* (Madison, 1970), is a fascinating read. I also owe a debt to his article, 'Old Belief as Popular Religion: New Approaches', *Slavic Review*, vol. 52, no. 4 (1993), pp. 700–712; Michael Cherniavsky, 'The Old Believers and the New Religion', *Slavic Review*, vol. 25, no. 1 (1966), pp. 1–39; and Roy R. Robson, 'Liturgy and Community among Old Believers, 1905–1917', *Slavic Review*, vol. 52, no. 4 (1993), pp. 713–724. For more about the sects, consult: A. I. Klibanov, *History of Religious Sectarianism in Russia, 1860s–1917*, trans. Ethel Dunn (Oxford, 1982), and Laura Engelstein, *Castration and the Heavenly Kingdom* (Ithaca, 1999).

The religious beliefs of the Russian peasantry are a fascinating subject which still awaits an authoritative book. Aspects are explored in several interesting articles: Eve Levin, '*Dvoeverie* and Popular Religion', in S. K.

Batalden (ed.), *Seeking God: The Recovery of Religious Identity in Orthodox Russia, Ukraine, and Georgia* (De Kalb, Ill., 1993), pp. 31–52; Chris Chulos, 'Myths of the Pious or Pagan Peasant in Post-emancipation Central Russia (Voronezh Province)', *Russian History*, vol. 22, no. 2 (1995), pp. 181–216; Simon Dixon, 'How Holy was Holy Russia? Rediscovering Russian Religion', in G. Hosking and R. Service (eds.), *Reinterpreting Russia* (London, 1999), pp. 21–39; V. Shevzov, 'Chapels and the Ecclesial World of Prerevolutionary Russian Peasants', *Slavic Review*, vol. 52, no. 3 (1996), pp. 593–607. Linda Ivanits, *Russian Folk Belief* (New York, 1989) is a useful summary of popular religious beliefs and rituals. On the Church's efforts to Christianize the peasants, see: Gregory Freeze, 'The Rechristianization of Russia: The Church and Popular Religion, 1750–1850', *Studia Slavica Finlandensia*, no. 7 (1990), pp. 101–36; and V. G. Vlasov, 'The Christianization of the Russian Peasants', in M. Balzer (ed.), *Russian Traditional Culture: Religion, Gender and Customary Law* (London, 1992). On peasant attitudes to death I owe a debt to Christine Worobec, 'Death Ritual among Russian and Ukrainian Peasants: Linkages between the Living and the Dead', in S. Frank and M. Steinberg (eds.), *Cultures in Flux: Lower-class Values, Practices and Resistance in Late Imperial Russia* (Princeton, 1994), pp. 11–33.

On the theology of the Slavophiles I recommend as an introduction Peter K. Christoff's *An Introduction to Nineteenth-century Russian Slavophilism: A. S. Xomjakov* (The Hague, 1961) and the same author's *An Introduction to Nineteenth-century Russian Slavophiles: F. Samarin* (Westview, 1991); and *An Introduction to Nineteenth-century Russian Slavophiles: I. V. Kirevskii* (The Hague, 1972). On the idea of *sobornost'* which underpinned the notion of the 'Russian soul': Georges Florovsky, '*Sobornost'*: The Catholicity of the Church', in E. Mascall (ed.), *The Church of God* (London, 1934), pp. 53–74; N. Riasanovsky, 'Khomiakov on sobornost'', in E. J. Simmons (ed.), *Continuity and Change in Russian and Soviet Thought* (Cambridge, Mass., 1955), pp. 183–196; P. Tulaev, '*Sobor* and *Sobornost'*: The Russian Orthodox Church and Spiritual Unity of the Russian People', *Russian Studies in Philosophy*, vol. 31, no. 4 (1993), pp. 25–53.

On Gogol as a religious writer there is a good deal in Vsevolod Setchkarev, *Gogol. His Life and Works* (New York, 1965); and Robert Maguire, *Exploring Gogol* (Stanford, 1994). Religious aspects of his writings are explored in: Dmitry Merezhkovsky, 'Gogol and the Devil', in Robert Maguire (ed.), *Gogol from the Twentieth Century* (Princeton, 1974); A. Ebbinghaus, 'Confusions and Allusions to the Devil in Gogol's *Revizor*', *Russian Literature*, vol. 34, no. 3 (1993), pp. 291–310; J. Schillinger, 'Gogol's "The Overcoat" as a Travesty of Hagiography', *Slavic and East European Journal*, no. 16 (1972), pp. 36–41; and L. Knapp, 'Gogol and the Ascent of Jacob's Ladder: Realization of Biblical Metaphor', in *Christianity and the Eastern Slavs, Californian Slavic Studies* vol. 3, no. 18 (1995). The *Letters of Nikolai Gogol* (ed. and trans. C. Proffer (Ann Arbor, 1967)) are illuminating on the writer's struggle to complete *Dead Souls*. On this subject I also learned a lot from James Woodward, *Gogol's 'Dead Souls'* (Princeton, 1978); Susanne Fusso, *Designing Dead Souls: An Anatomy of Disorder in Gogol* (Stanford, 1993); and J. M. Holquist, 'The Burden of Prophecy: Gogol's Conception of Russia', *Review of National Literatures*, vol. 3, no. 1 (1973), p. 39.

On Dostoevsky the work of Joseph Frank is seminal: *Dostoevsky: The Seeds of Revolt, 1821–1849* (Princeton, 1979); *Dostoevsky: The Years of Ordeal, 1850–1859* (Princeton, 1983); *Dostoevsky: The Stir of Liberation, 1860–1865* (Princeton, 1988); and *Dostoevsky: The Miraculous Years, 1865–1871* (Princeton, 1995). My ideas about the writer's struggle over faith were inspired by the brilliant article by Aileen Kelly, 'Dostoevsky and the Divided Conscience', in *Toward Another Shore: Russian Thinkers between Necessity and Chance* (New Haven, 1998), pp. 55–79. On this subject I learned a great deal from: V. Zenkovsky, 'Dostoevsky's Religious and Philosophical Views', in Rene Wellek (ed.), *Dostoevsky: A Collection of Critical Essays* (Englewood Cliffs, 1962); Gein Kjetsaa, *Dostoevsky and His New Testament* (Oslo, 1984); Robert L. Jackson, *The Art of Dostoevsky* (Princeton, 1981); Sergei Hackel, 'The Religious Dimension: Vision or Evasion? Zosima's Discourse in *The Brothers Karamazov*' in M. V. Jones and G. M. Terry (eds.), *New Essays on Dostoevsky* (Cambridge, 1983), pp. 139–68; Sven Linnér, *Starets Zosima in* The Brothers Karamazov: *A Study in the Mimesis of Virtue* (Stockholm, 1975); Frank Seeley, 'Ivan Karamazov', in *Old and New Essays on Tolstoy and Dostoevsky* (Nottingham, 1999), pp. 127–44; and Ellis Sandoz, *Political Apocalypse: A Study of Dostoevsky's Grand Inquisitor* (Baton Rouge, Lou., 1971). On *Crime and Punishment* I recommend: Victor Terras, 'The Art of *Crime and Punishment*', in *Reading Dostoevsky* (Madison, Wis., 1998), pp. 51–72; Robert L. Jackson (ed.), *Twentieth-century Interpretations of* Crime and Punishment (Englewood Cliffs, 1974); Joseph Brodsky, 'The Power of the Elements', in *Less Than One* (London, 1986), pp. 157–63. On *The Idiot* and the theme of the Holy Fool, see: S. Lesser, 'Saint & Sinner: Dostoevsky's *Idiot*', *Modern Fiction Studies*, vol. 4 (1958); Frank Seeley, 'The Enigma of Prince Myshkin', in *Old and New Essays on Tolstoy & Dostoevsky*, pp. 111–18. On the *Writer's Diary* and the complex problem of Dostoevsky's nationalist messianism, see Gary Morson, *The Boundaries of Genre: Dostoevsky's Diary of a Writer and the Traditions of Literary Utopia* (Austin, 1981); and Hans Kohn, 'Dostoevsky and Danielevsky: Nationalist Messianism', in E. J. Simmons (ed.), *Continuity and Change in Russian and Soviet Thought* (Cambridge, Mass., 1955), pp. 500–15.

On the religious attitudes of Chekhov and Tolstoy, see my recommendations for chapters 3 and 4 respectively.

6 DESCENDANTS OF GENGHIZ KHAN

On Kandinsky I owe a great debt to the splendid book by Peg Weiss, *Kandinsky and Old Russia. The Artist as Ethnographer and Shaman* (New Haven, 1995). I also learned a lot from Ulrik Becks-Malorney, *Wassily Kandinsky, 1866–1944: The Journey to Abstraction* (London, 1999); and Rose-Carol Washton Long, *Kandinsky: The Development of an Abstract Style* (Oxford, 1980). For more on Kandinsky's Russian connections I recommend: John Bowlt and Rose-Carol Washton Long (eds.), *The Life of Vasilii Kandinsky in Russian Art: A Study of 'On the Spiritual in Art'* (Newtonville, Mass., 1980). Some of Kandinsky's own writings are in translation: Kenneth Lindsay and Peter Vergo (eds.), *Kandinsky: Complete Writings on Art*, 2 vols. (London, 1982) (his account of the trip to the Komi region is in vol. 1, pp. 886–98).

On shamanism in Eurasia I recommend Ronald Hutton, *Shamans: Siberian Spirituality and the Western Imagination* (London, 2001). Hutton discusses, among other things, the study of the shamans in the eighteenth and nineteenth centuries. For more on this, see Gloria Flaherty, *Shamanism and the Eighteenth Century* (Princeton, 1992).

More generally on the Russian encounter with the pagan tribes of Siberia, see the superb study by Yuri Slezkine, *Arctic Mirrors: Russia and the Small Peoples of the North* (Cornell, 1994). See also: Galya Diment and Yuri Slezkine (eds.), *Between Heaven and Hell: The Myth of Siberia in Russian Culture* (New York, 1993); James Forsyth, *A History of the Peoples of Siberia: Russia's North Asian Colony, 1581–1990* (Cambridge, 1994); and Michael Khodarkovsky, ' "Ignoble Savages and Unfaithful Subjects": Constructing Non-Christian Identities in Early Modern Russia', in D. Brower and E. Lazzerini (eds.), *Russia's Orient: Imperial Borderlands and Peoples, 1700–1917* (Bloomington, 1997). I also owe a debt to the work of Mark Bassin: 'Expansion and Colonialism on the Eastern Frontier: Views of Siberia and the Far East in Pre-Petrine Russia', *Journal of Historical Geography*, no. 14 (1988), pp. 3–21; 'Inventing Siberia: Visions of the Russian East in the Early Nineteenth Century', *American Historical Review*, vol. 96, no. 3 (1991); and 'Asia' in Nicholas Rzhevsky (ed.), *The Cambridge Companion to Modern Russian Culture* (Cambridge, 1998).

The Mongol impact on Russia is emphasized by the Eurasianist historian George Vernadsky, *The Mongols and Russia* (New Haven, 1953). See too his article 'The Eurasian Nomads and Their Impact on Medieval Europe', *Studii*

Medievali, series 3, vol. 4 (1963). For a more sober view consult Charles Halperin, *Russia and the Golden Horde* (Bloomington, 1985). On Holy Fools and minstrels, see Eva Thompson, *Understanding Russia: The Holy Fool in Russian Culture* (Lanham, Mad., 1987) and Russell Zguta, *Russian Minstrels: A History of the Skomorokhi* (Pennsylvania, 1978). The history of the Kalmyk tribes is told by Michael Khodarkovsky, *Where Two Worlds Met: The Russian State and the Kalmyk Nomads 1600–1771* (Ithaca, 1992). Other aspects of the Russian encounter with Central Asia are discussed in Emmanuel Sarkisyanz, 'Russian Conquest in Central Asia: Transformation and Acculturation', in Wayne Vucinich (ed.), *Russia and Asia* (Stanford, 1972); Seymour Becker, 'The Muslim East in Nineteenth-century Russian Popular Historiography', in *Central Asian Survey*, vol. 5 (1986), pp. 25–47; Peter Weisensel, 'Russian Self-identification and Travelers' Descriptions of the Ottoman Empire in the First Half of the Nineteenth Century', in *Central Asian Survey*, vol. 10 (1991).

On Russian perceptions of the Orient I also owe a debt to: Daniel Brower and Edward Lazzerini (eds.), *Russia's Orient: Imperial Borderlands and Peoples, 1700–1917* (Bloomington, 1997); Milan Hauner, *What is Asia to Us?* (London, 1990); and Nicholas Riasanovsky, 'Asia through Russian Eyes', in Wayne Vucinich (ed.), *Russia and Asia* (Stanford, 1972). On the Orient in the Russian literary imagination I highly recommend Susan Layton, *Russian Literature and Empire: The Conquest of the Caucasus from Pushkin to Tolstoy* (Cambridge, 1994). See, too, Robert Stacy, *India in Russian Literature* (Delhi, 1985). The Cossack question is discussed by Judith Kornblatt, *The Cossack Hero in Russian Literature: A Study in Cultural Mythology* (Madison, Wisc., 1992).

Excerpts from Stasov's work on Russian ornament are available in translation: Vladimir Stasov, *Russian Peasant Design Motifs for Needleworkers and Craftsmen* (New York, 1976). The Benfey theory (on the movement of folk tales) is discussed by William Clouston, *Popular Tales and Fictions: Their Migrations and Transformations*, 2 vols. (London, 1887). For more on the folk epics, see Alex Alexander, *Bylina and Fairy Tale: The Origins of Russian Heroic Poetry* (The Hague, 1973); and Felix Oinas and Stephen Soudakoff (eds.), *The Study of Russian Folklore* (The Hague, 1975).

There is no English work on Levitan. But for more on Vereshchagin readers may refer to Vahan Barooshian, *V. V. Vereshchagin: Artist at War* (Gainesville, Flo., 1993).

On Blok and the Symbolists I am indebted to the magisterial work of Avril Pyman, *The Life of Aleksandr Blok*, 2 vols. (Oxford, 1979–80), and the same author's *A History of Russian Symbolism* (Cambridge, 1994). I also owe a debt to Stefani Hoffman, 'Scythianism: A Cultural Vision in Revolutionary Russia', Ph.D. diss. (Columbia University, N.Y., 1975). For more on Bely I recommend: Samuel Cioran, *The Apocalyptic Symbolism of Andrej Belyj*

(The Hague, 1973); John Elsworth, *Andrey Bely: A Critical Study of His Novels* (Cambridge, 1983); Vladimir Alexandrov, *Andrei Bely: The Major Symbolist Fiction* (Cambridge, Mass., 1985); and John Malmstad and Gerald Smith (eds.), *Andrey Bely: Spirit of Symbolism* (Cornell, 1987). On *Petersburg*, see Magnus Ljunggren, *The Dream of Rebirth: A Study of Andrej Belyj's Novel* Peterburg, *Acta Universitatis Stockholmiensis, Stockholm Studies in Russian Literature*, no. 15 (Stockholm, 1982); and Robert Mann, *Andrei Bely's Petersburg and the Cult of Dionysus* (Lawrence, Kan., 1986). I also recommend the translators' notes in Andrei Bely, *Petersburg*, trans. Robert A. Maguire and John E. Malmstad (Harmondsworth, 1983). On Soloviev there is a decent book by Eugenia Gourvitch, *Soloviev: The Man and the Prophet*, trans. J. Deverill (Sussex, 1992).

The Eurasian movement is discussed by Nicholas Riasanovsky, 'The Emergence of Eurasianism', *Californian Slavic Studies*, no. 4 (1967), pp. 39–72; Charles Halperin, 'Russia and the Steppe: George Vernadsky and Eurasianism', *Forschungen zur osteuropäischen Geschichte*, no. 36 (1985), pp. 55–194. A selection of the writings of Nikolai Trubetskoi is available in translation: *The Legacy of Genghiz Khan and Other Essays on Russia's Identity*, trans. Anatoly Liberman (Ann Arbor, 1991).

7 RUSSIA THROUGH THE SOVIET LENS

Akhmatova is the subject of several fine biographies: Roberta Reeder, *Anna Akhmatova: Poet and Prophet* (London, 1995); Amanda Haight, *Anna Akhmatova: A Poetic Pilgrimage* (Oxford, 1979); and Jessie Davies, *Anna of All the Russias: The Life of Anna Akhmatova (1889–1966)* (Liverpool, 1988). Much of the best writing about her is in the form of reminiscences: Lydia Chukovskaya, *The Akhmatova Journals* (New York, 1994); Anatoly Nayman, *Remembering Anna Akhmatova*, trans. Wendy Rosslyn (London, 1991). She also features prominently in Nadezhda Mandelstam, *Hope Abandoned*, trans. M. Hayward (London, 1989). The friendship with Isaiah Berlin is discussed by György Dalos, *The Guest from the Future: Anna Akhmatova and Isaiah Berlin* (London, 1999). Aspects of Akhmatova's poetry are explored by David Wells, *Anna Akhmatova: Her Poetry* (Oxford, 1996); Susan Amert, *In a Shattered Mirror: The Later Poetry of Anna Akhmatova* (Stanford, 1992); Wendy Rosslyn, *The Prince, the Fool and the Nunnery: The Religious Theme in the Early Poetry of Anna Akhmatova* (Amersham, 1984); and Sharon Leiter, *Akhmatova's Petersburg* (Cambridge, 1983). There are valuable materials and notes in *The Complete Poems of Anna Akhmatova*, trans. J. Hemschemeyer, ed. R. Reeder (Edinburgh, 1992).

There is an enormous literature on the Soviet utopian avant-garde. As a general introduction I highly recommend the lively book by Richard Stites, *Revolutionary Dreams: Utopian Vision and Experimental Life in the Russian Revolution* (Oxford, 1989). See, too, Victor Arwas, *The Great Russian Utopia* (London, 1993). There are useful essays in John Bowlt and Olga Matich (eds.), *Laboratory of Dreams: The Russian Avant-garde and Cultural Experiment* (Stanford, 1996); and Abbott Gleason, Peter Kenez and Richard Stites (eds.), *Bolshevik Culture: Experiment and Order in the Russian Revolution* (Bloomington, 1985).

On communal housing projects I recommend a rather brilliant book by Viktor Buchli, *An Archaeology of Socialism* (Oxford, 1999). See also Milka Bliznakov, 'Soviet Housing during the Experimental Years, 1918 to 1933' and Vladimir Paperny, 'Men, Women, and Living Space', in William Brumfield and Blair A. Ruble (eds.), *Russian Housing in the Modern Age: Design and Social History* (Cambridge, 1993), pp. 85–148 and 149–70 respectively. More generally on early Soviet architecture, readers should consult: William Brumfield (ed.), *Reshaping Russian Architecture: Western Technology, Utopian Dreams* (Cambridge, 1990); Catherine Cooke, *Russian Avant-garde: Theories of Art, Architecture and the City* (London, 1995); same author, 'Beauty as a Route to "the Radiant Future": Responses of Soviet Architecture,' *Journal of Design History*, vol. 10, no. 2 (1997), pp. 137–60; Frederick Starr, 'Visionary Town Planning during the Cultural Revolution', in Sheila Fitzpatrick (ed.), *Cultural Revolution in Russia, 1928–1931* (Bloomington and London, 1978), pp. 207–40; Sima Ingberman, *ABC: International Constructivist Architecture, 1922–1939* (Cambridge, Mass., 1994); and Hugh Hudson, *Blueprints and Blood: The Stalinization of Soviet Architecture, 1917–1937* (Princeton, 1994).

On visions of the new Soviet man, see Lynne Attwood and Catriona Kelly, 'Programmes for Identity: The "New Man" and the "New Woman"', in Catriona Kelly and David Shepherd (eds.), *Constructing Russian Culture in the Age of Revolution* (Oxford, 1998), pp. 256–90. Trotsky's writings on this subject can be found in *Problems of Everyday Life and Other Writings on Culture and Science* (New York, 1973). The Bolsheviks were fascinated by psychoanalysis. For more on this topic, see Martin Miller, *Freud and the Bolsheviks: Psychoanalysis in Imperial Russia and the Soviet Union* (New Haven, 1998), and David Joravsky, *Russian Psychology: A Critical History* (Oxford, 1989). Svetlana Boym's *Common Places: Mythologies of Everyday Life in Russia* (Cambridge, Mass., 1994) is a brilliant work with much to say on, among other things, the Russian and the Soviet urge to transcend the culture of the everyday.

The role of the artistic avant-garde in the cultural revolution of the 1920s and 1930s is a complex and controversial subject. Some recent historians have stressed the contribution of the avant-garde to the development of Socialist Realism: Boris Groys, *The Total Art of Stalinism, Avant-garde, Aesthetic Dictatorship and Beyond*, trans. Charles Rougle (Princeton, 1992); Igor Golomshtock, *Totalitarian Art*, trans. Robert Chandler (London, 1990). Others have portrayed the avant-garde as an ally of the libertarian vision contained in the Revolution and the New Economic Policy: David Elliot, *New Worlds: Russian Art and Society, 1900–1937* (London, 1986); John Bowlt, *The Russian Avant-garde: Theory and Criticism, 1902–34* (New York, 1976).

On the Constructivists, readers should begin with the marvellous book by Christine Lodder, *Russian Constructivism* (New Haven, 1983). See, too, George Rickey, *Constructivism: Origins and Evolution* (New York, 1995); Richard Andrews *et al.* (eds.), *Art into Life: Russian Constructivism, 1914– 1932* (New York, 1990); Alexander Lavrent'ev and John Bowlt, *Varvara Stepanova: A Constructivist Life* (London, 1988); John Milner, *Vladimir Tatlin and the Russian Avant-garde* (New Haven, 1983); Peter Noever (ed.), *Aleksandr M. Rodchenko, Varvara F. Stepanova: The Future is Our Only Goal* (New York, 1991). I also learned a great deal from the brilliant dissertation by Christine Kaier, 'The Russian Constructivist "Object" and the Revolutionizing of Everyday Life, 1921–1929', Ph.D. diss. (Univ. of California, 1995). The best guide to the Proletkult is Lynn Mally, *Culture of the Future: The Proletkult Movement in Revolutionary Russia* (Berkeley, 1990).

On Soviet cinema I recommend: Peter Kenez, *Cinema and Soviet Society, 1917–1953* (Cambridge, 1992); Dmitry and Vladimir Shlapentokh, *Soviet Cinematography, 1918–1991: Ideological Conflict and Social Reality* (New York, 1993); Richard Taylor and Ian Christie (eds.), *Inside the Film Factory: New Approaches to Russian and Soviet Cinema* (London, 1991); same editors, *The Film Factory: Russian and Soviet Cinema in Documents, 1896–1939*, trans. R. Taylor (Cambridge, Mass., 1988); Richard Taylor, *The Politics of the Soviet Cinema 1917–1929* (Cambridge, 1979); Denise Youngblood, *Movies for the Masses: Popular Cinema and Soviet Society in the 1920s* (Cambridge, 1992); same author, *Soviet Cinema in the Silent Era, 1917–1935* (Ann Arbor, 1985); Richard Taylor and Derek Spring (eds.), *Stalinism and Soviet Cinema* (London, 1993). For more on the *kinoki* I suggest reading *Kino-Eye: The Writings of Dziga Vertov*, ed. Annette Michelson, trans. Kenneth O'Brien (Berkeley, 1984). The same goes for Kuleshov and Pudovkin: *Lev Kuleshov on Film: Writings of Lev Kuleshov*, trans. and ed. Ronald Levaco (Berkeley, 1974); Vsevolod Pudovkin, *Film Technique and Film Acting*, trans. I. Montagu (New York, 1970). On Eisenstein there is a fairly decent life by Ronald Bergan, *Eisenstein: A Life in Conflict* (London, 1997), and an excellent account of his history films by Jason Goodwin, *Eisenstein, Cinema and History* (Urbana,

1993). Otherwise I recommend: David Bordwell, *The Cinema of Eisenstein* (Cambridge, Mass., 1993); Ian Christie and Richard Taylor (eds.), *Eisenstein Rediscovered* (London, 1993); and the older but still very interesting book by Jay Leyda and Zina Voynow, *Eisenstein at Work* (New York, 1982).

The best general English-language source on Meyerhold is Edward Braun, *The Theatre of Meyerhold: Revolution and the Modern Stage* (London, 1986); see, too, the same author (ed.), *Meyerhold on Theatre* (London, 1969); Robert Leach's study, *Vsevolod Meyerhold* (Cambridge, 1989), is also useful. On the narrower topic of biomechanics, Alma Law and Mel Gordon's book, *Meyerhold, Eisenstein, and Biomechanics: Actor Training in Revolutionary Russia* (Jefferson, N.C., 1996), is essential reading. For more on the Soviet avant-garde theatre I recommend the work of the distinguished Soviet scholar Konstantin Rudnitsky, *Russian and Soviet Theatre: Tradition and Avant-garde*, trans. R. Permar (London, 1988). Also: Lars Kleberg, *Theatre as Action: Soviet Russian Avant-garde Aesthetics*, trans. Charles Rougle (London, 1993); Nancy Van Norman Baer, *Theatre in Revolution: Russian Avant-garde Stage Design 1913–1935* (London, 1991). On street art and theatre, see Vladimir Tolstoi *et al.* (eds.), *Street Art of the Revolution: Festivals and Celebrations in Russia 1918–33* (London, 1990), and James von Geldern, *Bolshevik Festivals, 1917–1920* (Berkeley, 1993).

Shostakovich is the subject of a growing literature. For the most recent and accurate biography, see Laurel Fay, *Shostakovich: A Life* (Oxford, 2000). It is also worth consulting Ian MacDonald, *The New Shostakovich* (London, 1990), though one may question its presentation of Shostakovich as a dissident. There are important essays in David Fanning (ed.), *Shostakovich Studies* (Cambridge, 1995); Allan Ho and Dmitry Feofanov (eds.), *Shostakovich Reconsidered* (London, 1998); and Rosamund Bartlett (ed.), *Shostakovich in Context* (Oxford, 2000), especially the nuanced reading of his life and art by Richard Taruskin in 'Shostakovich and Us'. I also recommend the specialist study by Esti Sheinberg, *Irony, Satire, Parody and the Grotesque in the Music of Shostakovich* (Ashgate, 2000). Elizabeth Wilson, *Shostakovich: A Life Remembered* (London, 1994) contains valuable memoirs about the composer. In this category I learned a lot from Dmitri Sollertinsky and Ludmilla Sollertinsky, *Pages from the Life of Dmitri Shostakovich*, trans. G. Hobbs and C. Midgley (New York, 1980), and *Story of a Friendship: The Letters of Dmitry Shostakovich to Isaak Glickman, 1941–1975* (Cornell, 1997). Solomon Volkov's *Testimony: The Memoirs of Dmitri Shostakovich* (New York, 1979) is a controversial work, which may or may not represent what Shostakovich said to its author. On Shostakovich and the cinema I drew mainly from Tatiana Egorova, *Soviet Film Music: An Historical Survey* (Amsterdam, 1997).

The literature on Mayakovsky is older, though recent research on his death is yet to be reflected in the English-language literature. Among the works I would recommend are: Victor Terras, *Vladimir Mayakovsky* (Boston, 1983); Edward Brown, *Mayakovsky: A Poet in the Revolution* (Princeton, 1973); A. D. P. Briggs, *Vladimir Mayakovsky: A Tragedy* (Oxford, 1979); Wiktor Woroszylski and Bolesaw Taborski, *The Life of Mayakovsky* (London, 1972). More specifically on Mayakovsky's complex relations with the Briks, see Vahan Barooshian, *Brik and Mayakovsky* (New York, 1978), and Ann Charters and Samuel Charters, *I Love: The Story of Vladimir Mayakovsky and Lili Brik* (London, 1979).

There is no really satisfactory work in English on Soviet satire. For more on Zoshchenko I would recommend: Gregory Carleton, *The Politics of Reception: Critical Constructions of Mikhail Zoshchenko* (Evanston, Ill., 1998); Linda Scatton, *Mikhail Zoshchenko: Evolution of a Writer* (Cambridge, 1993); and A. B. Murphy, *Mikhail Zoshchenko: A Literary Profile* (Oxford, 1981). On Bulgakov, consult Leslie Milne, *Mikhail Bulgakov: A Critical Biography* (Cambridge, 1990); Edythe Haber, *Mikhail Bulgakov: The Early Years* (Cambridge, 1998); and Julie Curtiss, *Bulgakov's Last Decade: The Writer as Hero* (Cambridge, 1987). On Platonov, see Thomas Seifrid, *Andrei Platonov: Uncertainties of Spirit* (Cambridge, 1992); and the appreciation of Platonov by Joseph Brodsky, 'Catastrophes in the Air', in *Less Than One* (Harmondsworth, 1986). For more on Zamyatin and his influence on Orwell's *1984*, I suggest that readers should begin with Gary Kern (ed.), *Zamyatin's We: A Collection of Critical Essays* (Ann Arbor, 1988); and Robert Russell, *Zamiatin's We* (Bristol, 2000).

The idea of the Five-year Plan as 'cultural revolution' is advanced by Sheila Fitzpatrick (ed.), *Cultural Revolution in Russia, 1928–1931* (Bloomington, 1978), and the same author's *The Cultural Front: Power and Culture in Revolutionary Russia* (Cornell, 1992). For the literary politics of the period, begin with the old but not outdated work by Harriet Borland, *Soviet Literary Theory and Practice during the First Five-year Plan, 1928–1932* (New York, 1950). And more generally on the 1920s and 1930s, begin with Victor Erlich, *Modernism and Revolution: Russian Literature in Transition* (Cambridge, Mass., 1994). Katerina Clark's *The Soviet Novel: History as Ritual* (Chicago, 1981) is a brilliant study of the Socialist Realist novel as a literary form. Other good books on this theme include: Abram Tertz, *On Socialist Realism* (New York, 1960); Nina Kolesnikoff and Walter Smyrniw (eds.), *Socialist Realism Revisited* (Hamilton, 1994); Thomas Lahusen, *How Life Writes the Book: Real Socialism and Socialist Realism in Stalin's Russia* (Cornell, 1997); and Piotr Fast, *Ideology, Aesthetics, Literary History: Socialist Realism and Its Others* (New York, 1999). On Soviet reading habits and mass culture I also owe a debt to Jeffery Brooks, *Thank You, Comrade Stalin! Soviet Public Culture from Revolution to Cold War* (Princeton, 2000); and Stephen Lovell, *The Russian Reading Revolution: Print Culture in the Soviet and Post-Soviet Eras* (London, 2000). On the Sovietization of Russian literature there is a good book by Maurice Friedberg, *Russian Classics in Soviet Jackets* (New York, 1962). For more on the cult of Pushkin, see Marcus Levitt, *Russian Literary Politics and the Pushkin Celebration of 1880* (Cornell, 1989). I also recommend the insightful argument of Vera Dunham, *In Stalin's Time: Middle-class Values in Soviet Fiction* (Cambridge, 1976).

There is no better description of living through the Terror than the memoirs of Nadezhda Mandelstam, *Hope Against Hope*, trans. M. Hayward (London, 1989). For more on Mandelstam, see: Clarence Brown, *Mandelstam* (Cambridge, 1973). Vitaly Shentalinsky, *The KGB's Literary Archive*, trans. John Crowfoot (London, 1995) contains useful information from the KGB archives. On this theme there is also a good book by the pre-eminent historian of the Terror, Robert Conquest, *Tyrants and Typewriters: Communiqués in the Struggle for Truth* (Lexington, Mass., 1989).

On the war years there is a useful collection of essays edited by Richard Stites, *Culture and Entertainment in Wartime Russia* (Bloomington, 1995). On Prokofiev it is best to start with Daniel Jaffe, *Sergey Prokofiev* (London 1998); or Harlow Robinson, *Sergei Prokofiev* (London 1987). I also learned a lot from Izrael Nestyev, *Prokofiev* (Stanford, 1960); David Gutman, *Prokofiev* (London 1990); and Neil Minturn, *The Music of Sergei Prokofiev* (New Haven, 1997).

On the post-war export of Russian culture to the Soviet empire I recommend the memoirs of Iurii Elagin, *Taming of the Arts* (Tenafly, N.J., 1988). On the Russification of native music cultures there are useful articles in M. Slobin (ed.), *Returning Culture: Musical Changes in Central and Eastern Europe* (Durham, N.C., 1996); Maria Frolova-Walker, ' "National in Form, Socialist in Content": Musical Nation-building in the Soviet Republics', *Journal of the American Musicological Society*, vol. 51, no. 2 (1998), pp. 331–50; T. C. Levin, 'Music in Modern Uzbekistan: The Convergence of Marxist Aesthetics and Central Asian Tradition', *Asian Music*, vol 12, no. 1 (1979), pp. 149–58.

For more on Grossman it is worth consulting John Garrard and Carol Garrard, *The Bones of Berdichev: The Life and Fate of Vasily Grossman* (New York, 1996); and Frank Ellis, *Vasiliy Grossman: The Genesis and Evolution of a Russian Heretic* (Oxford, 1994).

On Pasternak the place to start is Christopher Barnes, *Boris Pasternak: A Literary Biography*, 2 vols. (Cambridge, 1989–98), though there is also much to learn from Lazar Fleishman, *Boris Pasternak: The Poet and His Politics*,

(Cambridge, Mass., 1990), and Larissa Rudova, *Understanding Boris Paster-nak* (Columbia, S.C., 1997). Peter Levi (*Boris Pasternak*, London, 1991) is good on the poetry. Two memoirs are also worth a read: one by his son, Evgeny Pasternak, *Boris Pasternak: The Tragic Years 1930–60*, trans. Michael Duncan (London, 1991); the other by his long-time mistress (and the inspi-ration for Lara in *Doctor Zhivago*), Olga Ivinskaya, *A Captive of Time: My Years with Pasternak: The Memoirs of Olga Ivinskaya*, trans. Max Hayward (London, 1979).

On the subject of science fiction there is a decent book by Rosalind Marsh, *Soviet Science Fiction since Stalin: Science, Politics and Literature* (London, 1986). See, too, David Suvin, 'The Utopian Tradition of Russian Science Fiction', *Modern Language Review*, no. 66 (1971), pp. 138–51. On the post-Stalin cinema I owe a debt to Josephine Woll, *Reel Images: Soviet Cinema and the Thaw* (London, 2000). For more on Tarkovsky I recommend Maya Turovskaya, *Tarkovsky: Cinema as Poetry* (London, 1989); Vida Johnson and Graham Petrie, *The Films of Andrei Tarkovsky: A Visual Fugue* (Bloomington, 1994); Mark Le Fanu, *The Cinema of Andrei Tarkovsky* (London, 1987); and Tarkovsky's own interpretation of the cinematic art, *Sculpting in Time: Reflections on the Cinema*, trans. K. Hunter-Blair (Austin, 1986).

8 RUSSIA ABROAD

The most authoritative work on the émigré communities is Marc Raeff, *Russia Abroad: A Cultural History of the Russian Emigration, 1919–1939* (New York, 1990). On Paris there is a good book by Robert Johnston, *New Mecca, New Babylon: Paris and the Russian Exiles, 1920–1945* (Montreal, 1988). And on the Russians in Berlin, Robert Williams, *Culture in Exile: Russian Emigrés in Germany, 1881–1941* (Ithaca, 1972). Nina Berberova's splendid memoirs, *The Italics Are Mine*, trans. Philippe Radley (London, 1991) are essential reading on the émigrés. *Ivan Bunin: From the Other Shore, 1920–1933: A Portrait from Letters, Diaries and Fiction*, ed. T. Marullo (Chicago, 1995) is less evocative but still worth mentioning. Michael Glenny and Nor-man Stone (eds.), *The Other Russia: The Experience of Exile* (London, 1990) is a useful collection of reminiscences.

On Tsvetaeva, begin with the biography by Maria Razumovsky, *Marina Tsvetaeva: A Critical Biography*, trans. A. Gibson (Newcastle, 1994); or Lily Feiler, *Marina Tsvetaeva: The Double Beat of Heaven and Hell* (Durham, N.C., 1994). Three other lives are worth a read: Viktoria Schweitzer, *Tsvet-aeva*, trans. Robert Chandler and H. T. Willetts (London, 1992); Elaine Feinstein, *Marina Tsvetayeva* (London, 1989); and Simon Karlinsky, *Marina*

Tsvetaeva: The Woman, Her World and Her Poetry (Cambridge, 1985). Joseph Brodsky gives a special insight to her poetry in 'Footnote to a Poem', in *Less Than One: Selected Essays* (London, 1986), pp. 195–261. For a more detailed study of her verse, see Michael Makin, *Marina Tsvetaeva: Poetics of Appropriation* (Oxford, 1993).

On Rachmaninov I recommend: Geoffrey Norris, *Rachmaninoff* (Oxford, 2000); Barrie Martyn, *Rachmaninov: Composer, Pianist, Conductor* (London, 1990); Julian Haylock, *Sergei Rakhmaninov: An Essential Guide to His Life and Works* (London, 1996); Sergei Bertensson and Jay Leyda, *Sergei Rachmaninoff* (London, 1965); and the classic Soviet account by Nikolai Bazhanov, *Rachmaninov*, trans. A. Bromfield (Moscow, 1983).

There is a fine biography of Nabokov by Brian Boyd, *Nabokov: The Russian Years* (London, 1990); and *Nabokov: The American Years* (London, 1992). There is also Neil Cornwell's *Vladimir Nabokov* (Plymouth, 1999). Vladimir Alexandrov's compendium of essays, *The Garland Companion to Vladimir Nabokov* (New York, 1995), is a valuable and wide-ranging source. *The Nabokov–Wilson Letters: 1940–71*, ed. Simon Karlinsky (New York, 1980) is well worth a read. I also owe a debt to the immensely enjoyable *Vera (Mrs Vladimir Nabokov)* by Stacy Schiff (New York, 1999). But no book on Nabokov can supplant his own memoirs, *Speak, Memory: An Autobiography Revisited* (Harmondsworth, 1969).

Index

i indicates an illustration within the text
figures in bold indicate a colour illustration in either the first (1) or second (2)
  section of plates
n indicates footnote

balls: children's 119; conduct at 18–19, 42; Decembrists and 77; merchants excluded 194; in Moscow 154, 162, 168, 169, 171, 204, 249; national costume at 108; peasant dances at 105; polonaises at 274; Peter the Great and 43; Sheremetev family 21, 22, 25, 28

Balmont, Konstantin (poet, 1867–1942) 580

banquets, Moscow 163–4

banyas 46–7, 46i

Barnet, Boris (film director) 454, 455

Barthe, Gérard de la, *A Cure Bath in Moscow* (painting) 46i

Bashilov, Arkady (senator), as cook 169

Bashkirs 365; revolts, Grigory Volkonsky and, 382–3

bath houses 46–7, 46i

Batiushkov, Konstantin (poet), on Moscow 154–5, 156

Bazhenov, Vasily (architect) 153

Bazykina, Aksinia (peasant), Tolstoy and 241–2

beards, and Europeanization 43

Beethoven, Ludwig van, use of Russian folk songs 115

Beethoven Quartet, The 580

Bekbulatovich, Simeon 369–70

Beliaev, Ivan (ethnographer) 222

Belinsky, Vissarion (critic, 1811–48): and Gogol 317, 318; on *Eugene Onegin* 110; on European Russia 132; on peasant issue 224–5; on socialism and religion 328–9; on Zamoskvoreche district 192

bells, in music 179

Belogolovoy, N. A., on Sergei Volkonsky 98, 99

Belovode (promised land) 309

Bely, Andrei (poet, 1880–1934) 416–7; in Berlin 530; *Petersburg* 6, 262, 420–23, 459; on Society of Free Aesthetics 212

Benckendorff, Count Alexander (Chief of Police) 90

Benfey, Theodor (philologist), on cultural borrowing 393–4

Benois, Alexander (artist, 1870–1960) 41n, 560; and ballet 130, 268, 273–4, 275; Diaghilev and 268; on Filosofov family, 269; on *Firebird* 275; illustrations for *The Bronze Horseman* 421; *Le Pavillon d'Armide* 275; on Mamontov 198; in Paris 532, 557; on Petersburg 9, 13; Petersburg lithographs 269; and *Petrushka* (ballet) 130; and Tchaikovsky 275

Benois, Camille (Cavos) 41n

Berberova, Nina (writer): in Berlin 529, 532; on Nabokov 546–7; in Paris 532; on literary style 545

Berdyaev, Nikolai (philosopher, 1874–1948) 261, 361

Berezovsky, Maxim (composer) 40–41, 41n, 62, 557

Berggolts, Olga, on Mayakovsky 470

Berlin: as art centre 211; Berberova in 532; emigration to 528, 529–30, 538, 546; Gorky in 541, 571; Jews and Russians in 538; Khodasevich and 528, 532; as 'Little Russia' 538; Nabokov and 539, 547, 549, 550, 552–3; Tsvetaeva and 535

PENGUIN CLASSICS

WAR AND PEACE   LEO TOLSTOY

'[A] momentous panorama of human activity' John Updike

'Magnificent . . . *War and Peace* reaches a simplicity and gravitas unknown in Western literature outside the pages of *The Iliad*' A. N. Wilson

Translated and with an introduction by Rosemary Edmonds.

ANNA KARENINA   LEO TOLSTOY

'The new and brilliantly witty translation by Richard Pevear and Larissa Volokhonsky is a must' Lisa Appignanesi, *Independent*, Books of the Year

'Pevear and Volokhonsky are at once scrupulous translators and vivid stylists of English, and their superb rendering allows us, as perhaps never before, to grasp the palpability of Tolstoy's "characters, acts, situations"' James Wood, *New Yorker*

Translated and edited by Richard Pevear and Larissa Volokhonsky.

THE DEATH OF IVAN ILYICH AND OTHER STORIES
LEO TOLSTOY

Three of Tolstoy's most powerful and moving shorter works are brought together in this volume. *The Death of Ivan Ilyich* is a masterly meditation on life and death, recounting the physical decline and spiritual awakening of a worldly man faced with his own mortality. *The Cossacks*, the tale of a disenchanted young nobleman who seeks fulfilment amid the wild beauty of the Caucasus, was hailed by Turgenev as the 'finest and most perfect production of Russian literature.'

Translated and with an introduction by Rosemary Edmonds.

CHILDHOOD, BOYHOOD, YOUTH   LEO TOLSTOY

Tolstoy's first published sketches are an expressive self-portrait, in which we can discern the man and writer Tolstoy was to become, the moralist, the aristocrat in sympathy with the people, the meticulous observer of men and of nature, the immortal author of *War and Peace*, and even the tragic fugitive of his last unhappy days.

Translated and with an introduction by Rosemary Edmonds.

MORE PENGUIN

CRIME AND PUNISHMENT   FYODOR DOSTOYEVSKY

This vivid translation by David McDuff has been acclaimed as the most
accessible version of Dostoyevsky's great novel, rendering its dialogue with a
unique force and naturalism.

'McDuff's language is rich and alive' *The New York Times Book Review*

Translated and with an introduction by David McDuff.

THE BROTHERS KARAMAZOV   FYODOR DOSTOYEVSKY

The murder of brutal landowner Fyodor Karamazov changes the lives of his sons
irrevocably: Mitya, the sensualist, whose bitter rivalry with his father
immediately places him under suspicion for parricide; Ivan, the intellectual,
whose mental tortures drive him to breakdown; the spiritual Alyosha, who tries
to heal the family's rifts; and the shadowy figure of their bastard half-brother,
Smerdyakov. As the ensuing investigation and trial reveal the true identity of the
murderer, Dostoyevsky's dark masterwork evokes a world where the lines
between innocence and corruption, good and evil blur, and everyone's humanity
is tested.

Translated and with an introduction by David McDuff.

THE HOUSE OF THE DEAD   FYODOR DOSTOYEVSKY

In January 1850 Dostoyevsky was sent to a remote Siberian prison camp for his
part in a political conspiracy. The four years he spent there were the most
agonizing of his life. In this fictionalized account he recounts his soul-destroying
incarceration through the cool, detached tones of his narrator, Aleksandr
Petrovich Goryanchikov. *The House of the Dead* is far more than a work of
documentary realism: it is a powerful novel of redemption, describing one man's
spiritual and moral death and the miracle of his gradual reawakening.

Edited with an introduction and notes by David McDuff.

MORE PENGUIN

DEAD SOULS   NIKOLAI GOGOL

Chichikov, a mysterious stranger, arrives in the provincial town of 'N', visiting a succession of landowners and making each a strange offer. He proposes to buy the names of dead serfs still registered on the census, saving their owners from paying tax on them, and to use these 'souls' as collateral to re-invent himself as a gentleman. In this ebullient masterpiece, Gogol created a grotesque gallery of human types, from the bear-like Sobakevich to the insubstantial fool Manilov, and, above all, the devilish con man Chichikov. *Dead Souls*, Russia's first major novel, is one of the most unusual works of nineteenth-century fiction and a devastating satire on social hypocrisy.

Translated with an introduction by David Magarshack.

EUGENE ONEGIN   ALEXANDER PUSHKIN

'More than a translation, it is a re-creation. One day a young English poet will write a sonnet to it' *Observer*

'This *Onegin* is a landmark' *Washington Post*

Translated by Charles Johnston. Revised and with a new introduction by Michael Basker.

A HERO OF OUR TIME   MIKHAIL LERMONTOV

'Vigorous and audacious . . . it retains its power as a psychological study' Julian Barnes

Proud, wilful and intensely charismatic, Pechorin is bored by the stifling world that envelops him. With a predatory energy for any activity that will relieve his ennui, he embarks on a series of adventures, leaving a trail of broken hearts behind him. With its immoral hero, Lermontov's novel outraged many critics when it was published in 1840. Yet it was also a literary landmark: an acutely observed psychological novel, narrated from a number of different perspectives, through which the true and complex nature of Pechorin slowly emerges.

Translated and with an introduction by Paul Foote.

MORE PENGUIN

FATHERS AND SONS   IVAN TURGENEV

'[Turgenev] was, all his life, profoundly and painfully concerned with his country's condition and destiny . . . incomparable sharpness of vision, poetry and truth' Isaiah Berlin

Rosemary Edmonds' superb translation of Turgenev's masterpiece is accompanied by Isaiah Berlin's 1970 Romanes Lecture, *Fathers and Children*, which has been acclaimed by scholars as a classic in itself.

PLAYS   ANTON CHEKHOV

Contains *Ivanov*, *The Seagull*, *Uncle Vanya*, *Three Sisters*, and *The Cherry Orchard*.

Realistic and sensitive, Chekhov's plays revolve around a society which is on the brink of a tremendous upheaval. The dramatic works of Chekhov present the actions of ordinary people – in his own words, 'as complex and yet just as simple as they are in life'.

Translated by Peter Carson and with an introduction by Richard Gilman.

LOLITA   VLADIMIR NABOKOV

'Lolita is comedy, subversive yet divine . . . You read Lolita sprawling limply in your chair, ravished, overcome, nodding scandalized assent' Martin Amis, *Observer*

'This high-souled genius . . . communicates in every sentence his own playful and godlike bliss' *Sunday Times*

With an afterword by Craig Raine.

PNIN   VLADIMIR NABOKOV

'Pnin is not more human or more important than other people, he is what humanity looks like when it is faltering and foolish, and trying to rescue a few shreds of dignity and privacy' Michael Wood

'Nabokov can move you to laughter in the way the masters can – to laughter that is near to tears' *Guardian*

With an afterword by Michael Wood.

MORE PENGUIN

THE GIFT   VLADIMIR NABOKOV

'It was Nabokov's gift to bring Paradise wherever he alighted' John Updike

The Gift is the phantasmal autobiography of Fyodor Godunov-Cherdyntsev, a writer living in the closed world of Russian *émigré* intellectuals in Berlin shortly after the First World War. In this his last, and to many his greatest, Russian novel, Nabokov unfolds the story of a writer's pursuit; a gorgeous tapestry of literature and Lepidoptera whose true hero is not Fyodor's elusive beloved Zina, but Russian prose and poetry itself.

Translated by Michael Scammell and Dmitri Nabokov, in collaboration with the author.

THE REAL LIFE OF SEBASTIAN KNIGHT
VLADIMIR NABOKOV

'One of the most subtle, delicately profound novels in the language'
Nicholas Lezard, *Guardian*

Spurred on by admiration for his novelist half-brother and irritation at the biography written about him by Mr Goodman, the narrator, V, sets out to record Sebastian Knight's life as he understands it. But buried amid the extensive quoting, digressions, seeming explanations and meaningful digs at Mr Goodman, Sebastian's erratic and troubled persona remains as elusive as ever. In the unresolved confusion between the real and unreal there are no answers, for this is a book that defies summing up in its quest for human truth.

With an afterword by John Lanchester.

THE MASTER AND MARGARITA   MIKHAIL BULGAKOV

'Magnificent . . . a gloriously ironic gothic masterpiece . . . had me rapt with bliss' Patrick McGrath, *Guardian*

One spring afternoon the Devil, trailing fire and chaos in his wake, weaves himself out of the shadows and into Moscow in Bulgakov's fantastical, funny and frightening satire of Soviet life.

Translated by Richard Pevear and Larissa Volokhonsky with an introduction by Richard Pevear.